Tunisia

Mediterranean Sea

Bizerte
Menzel Bourguiba
Kalaât el Andalous
El Haouaria
Mateur
Sidi Daoud
Kerkouane
Tabarka
Carthage
Gulf of Tunis
Kélibia
Aïn Draham
TUNIS
Korbous
Hammam Bourguiba
Béja
Bulla Regia
Médjez-el-Bab
Nabeul
El Feidja NP
Jendouba
Dougga
Zaghouan
Hammamet
Thuburbo Majus
Gulf of Hammamet

Makthar
Port el Kantaoui
Sousse
Monastir
Kairouan
Sebkha Sidi el Hani
Mahdia
Haïdra
Sbeïtla
El Djem
Chaâmbi NP

Sfax
El Kantara
Bou Hedma NP
Moularès
Gafsa
Metlaoui
Gulf of Gabès
Chott el Rharsa
Houmt Souk
Isle of Djerba
Tozeur
Nefta
Chott el Fedjaj
Gabès
Chott el Djerid (Salt Lake)
Kebili
Zarat
Djorf
Matmata
Zarzis
Douz
Medenine
Ras Ajdir

Ksar Ghilane
Tataouine

ALGERIA
Remada
LIBYA
Dehiba

Lorzot
Borj Jenein
Bir Zhar

M'Chiguig

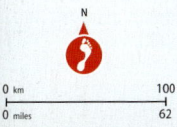

N

0 km ____ 100
0 miles ____ 62

Tunisia Handbook

Published by Footprint Handbooks
6 Riverside Court
Lower Bristol Road
Bath BA2 3DZ. England
T +44 (0)1225 469141
F +44 (0)1225 469461
Email discover@footprintbooks.com
Web www.footprintbooks.com

ISBN 1 900949 34 2
ISSN 1363-7487
CIP DATA: A catalogue record for this
book is available from the British Library

In USA, published by
Passport Books, a division of
NTC/Contemporary Publishing Group
4255 West Touhy Avenue, Lincolnwood
(Chicago), Illinois 60712-1975, USA
T 847 679 5500 F 847 679 24941
Email NTCPUB2@AOL.COM

ISBN 0-8442-2192-9
Library of Congress Catalog Card
Number: 99-74055

© Footprint Handbooks Ltd 1999
Second edition

Credits

Series editors
Patrick Dawson
Rachel Fielding
Editorial
Senior editor: Sarah Thorowgood
Maps: Sarah Sorensen
Production
Pre-press Manager: Jo Morgan
Typesetting: Richard Ponsford and
Emma Bryers
Maps: Kevin Feeney, Robert Lunn,
Claire Benison, Alasdair Dawson and Map
Creation Ltd
Proof reading: Tim Heybyrne and
John Work

Design
Mytton Williams

Photography & drawings
Front cover: Tony Stone Images
Back cover: Robert Harding Picture
Library
Inside colour section: Art Directors and
TRIP Photo Library; Impact Photos; Justin
McGuinness; Pictor International; Pictures
Colour Library; Robert Harding Picture
Library; Tony Stone Images
Illustrations: Justin McGuinness

Printed and bound
in Italy by LEGOPRINT

Tunisia

Footprint

Handbook with western Libya

Justin McGuinness

Ô minarets, si beaux au-dessus des boutiques,
Cris de pierre jaillis du coeur de l'Orient,
Blanches tours qui guettez, sentinelles mystiques,
Les frissons de l'espoir au fond du ciel riant.

Minarets, so beautiful above the souks,
Cries in stone soaring from heart of Orient,
Mystic sentinels against the smiling sky,
White towers lying in wait for shivers of hope.

Mario Scalesi, *Poèmes d'Orient*
(Tunis, Ed. Saliba, 1935)

Contents

Left: wrought iron arabesques protect the last resting place of Habib Bourguiba, father of Tunisian independence and a modernizing leader in the tradition of Kamal Ataturk.

Inside front cover

Map symbols
Hotel and restaurant
price guide
Telephone dialling
codes

Inside back cover

Arabic alphabet and
useful words and
phrases

Right: carving on the door to the main prayer hall, Mosque of Okba ibn Nafi', Kairouan.

A foot in the door

Highlights

Tunisia is a country where the shores of exotica begin. Mediterranean whitewashed villages, beaches of fine sand and palm trees meet souks bright with carpets, caftans and copper trays, deserts and Roman ruins fit for a sword-and-sandal epic. But this is also arguably the Arab world's most forward-looking state, 'a Mediterranean tiger' economy. This blend of old and new is both a product of tourism and a reason for it - the country's great classical set-peices are as much of a pull as its coastline or its spectacular sand dunes at Douz.

Imperial Africa   Tunisia is the land that saw despairing Queen Dido throw herself on a pyre, Jugurtha fight his wars and Hannibal set out with his elephants, heading for dramatic victories over Rome. But after years of conflict, Rome won over Carthage, and a new province, *Africa*, was created. It was to become one of the richest in the empire, exporting wheat, olive oil, wine and wild beasts. Carthage was also a centre of early Christianity, conquered by the Vandals, reoccupied by the vainglorious Byzantines and then in the 7th century, taken by invading Arab-Muslim armies, and renamed *Ifrikiya* in the process.

Of all these empires, much has survived: Punic Kerkouane, hilltop Dougga, contemplating a valley of gentle farmland, the dramatic temples of Sbeïtla, remote Haïdra with its Byzantine fortress, and the great coliseum of El Djem, once a place of spectacular carnage, now the setting for an occasional summer concert.

Arab Ifrikiya   Rather like its northern neighbour Sicily, Tunisia has a strategic location, right at the heart of the Mediterranean. The northernmost point of Africa is in Tunisia, a fact not lost on the area's frequent invaders. The area had a distinctly tumultuous history from the eighth century onwards, with first the various Arab dynasties and the Normans, and later the Ottomans and Habsburgs, competing for power. Kairouan was the first Muslim power centre in North Africa, and its great ochre mosque is one of the finest in all Islam. From the late 15th century, Tunis and Tripoli were Ottoman provincial capitals and the Turks left a heritage of mosques (such as the pointy towered Hanefite mosques in Tunis) and fortifications.

Colonial heritage   In the 19th century, North Africa was the object of European colonial designs. Tunisia was to come under French rule in 1881, and Libya was conquered by Italy in 1911. They built pleasant, spacious cities, filled with buildings from the neo-Moorish, Art Deco, Functionalist and Modern Movements. Much of this architecture still survives today, especially in Tunis, Bizerte and Sfax.

Coasts, hills and deserts   The potential of the new protectorates in terms of their natural assets was also exploited by their colonial rulers: tourism soon developed and has grown steadily since the late 19th century. A couple of hours' flight from Europe are hills covered in evergreen forest, open steppe lands and great salt lakes. There is a remote and rocky northern coast and a gentle east-facing coast of sandy beaches, which provides swimming, suntans and thalassotherapy. Finally, down in the far southwest corner of Tunisia, is the desert. Here you can contemplate the landscapes only glimpsed at in sci-fi movies. While most of Tunisia's southern regions are stony waste, the sand dunes of Douz and Zaâfrane are among the most popular places on the tourist itinerary – with good reason. In the remote southern regions you can also find ecologically adapted forms of architecture that survived well into the mid-20th century: the fortified granaries or *ksour* of Tataouine, the stone-built citadel villages, and the Djerba farmstead or *menzil*. And you don't need to be Lawrence of Arabia to get to them: hotels have sprung up across the south and new roads have put these previously inaccessible places within easy reach for the traveller.

Left: the Roman ruins of Dougga, one of the finest ancient sites in Tunisia. **Below**: the olive harvest, a time of hard work for the rural communities of the Sahel region.

Centre: souk scene in the médina of Tunis. **Left**: Chébika, once a Roman outpost, today a stop on the four-wheel drive trail, looks out over the desert towards Algeria.

Right: at night in the silent labyrinths of the médina in Tunis. *Below*: marketplace at Houmt Souk, capital of the island of Djerba.

Centre: charming a snake in Hammamet, the heart of Tunisian tourism. *Right*: neo-traditional Mediterranean style buildings and pleasure craft at Port el Kantaoui, Sousse.

For some Tunisia compares well with say, Greece or Portugal in the 1970s, rather than **Modern Tunisia** certain Middle Eastern states. The closeness to Europe is reflected in social attitudes: with advanced legislation on women's status and a strong middle class, Tunisians consider themselves the most advanced people in the Arab World. If the present rate of development can be maintained, this will be one of the most interesting Arab countries to watch over the next ten years. Will it eventually apply for membership of the European Union, as both Morocco and Turkey have? Close economic ties with Europe may eventually imply political ties as well.

For the moment, Tunisia is busy with a major structural reform programme, privatizing **Reform and** industry and developing business-friendly institutions. The difficulty lies in keeping **development** the right balance between economic growth and social stability, ensuring that local businesses do not go under as international competition arrives. State policy has a reassuring old-style social-democrat feel: everyone is to get a slice of the increasingly prosperous national cake. Remote rural communities, where life is structured still by the rains and the Muslim year, now have phones, electricity and drinking water. Relatives settled abroad, mainly in France and Italy, are an important source of income. (The élite is French speaking – but likes to feel it has tradition.) Women work in all sectors of the economy, the business community has mobile phones and the Internet – but Ramadhan, the Muslim month of fasting, is taken very seriously. Tunisians are very much family people, with a deep love of children, immediately noticeable when travelling with kids.

Perhaps the word 'youth' best sums up late-1990s Tunisia. This is a young – and **A young** surprising country. None of the clichés about Arab lands seem to fit. The woman aren't **country** veiled, there is an upbeat air of prosperity. Visitors generally start in one of the east coast resorts, pleasant, clean, where beaches are beautiful and sunshine reliable. Street crime is extremely rare, getting around on public transport is easy. But if you take time to get away from the hotel complex, you may explore teeming cities. Look out for small souk restaurants, markets fragrant with fresh produce. Listen out for music – the cassette stalls are piled high with sounds unfamiliar. In summer, you might get to an open-air concert by an Algerian *raï* singer or a gaudy Lebanese starlet, packed with an enthusiastic, vocal crowd. Or you might find yourself embroiled in a wedding, a big family affair with bride and groom perched on gilded thrones, the women decked out in Oriental splendour and a noisy six-piece traditional orchestra. Such weddings are time for noisy family reunions; the relatives are back from Europe and conversations race along in Franco-Arabe. On a more cultural level, Tunisia is home to the Arab world's most interesting cinema and avant-garde theatre.

But perhaps Tunisia is at its best in the density of close detail. There are the great set **Glassy seas &** piece sights – the amphitheatre of El Djem, magnificent Dougga, the dunes of Douz – **birds of prey** it is true, but you need to be attentive to the fine grain: dusty-red skeins of peppers drying against a white-washed wall; alleys of olive trees and the wind shifting the silvery leaves in a vast landscape; birds of prey riding the air currents off Jugurtha's Citadel; sunlight through latticework patterning tiles and marble; the honey-tobacco gurgling of a water pipe; warm smells of tabouna bread or fish frying; the glass-clear sea at Kélibia … For some, Tunisia is the most typical corner of the Mediterranean – more Mediterranean than even a Greek island or the Iberian coast. Happily, even in the face of the development of its tourist industry, it manages to maintain a homely feel, at ease with its contradictions like a sprawling old family. People still have time for you, and no doubt you will be made welcome in a way no longer possible in hectic, career-driven Europe.

The deep south

Right: at the local store in Nefta, a Bedouin version of Paris, Texas in southern Tunisia. *Below*: some of the best examples of stone Ghorfas (used to store the grain) at Ksar Soltane, dating from the 15th and 19th centuries.

Centre: crossing the desert. Seasonal nomad migrations are a thing of the past but tourists can trek off to seek the white dunes of the Nefzaoua. *Right*: Zaâfrane, palm trees in the desert bear witness to a lost village.

Architecture

Left: the minaret of the Great Mosque in Tunis displays a late 19th century version of medieval lozenge motif.

Below: Mosque of Sidi Sahbi (also known as the Barber's Mosque) in Kairouan, spiritual and religious 'capital' of Tunisia.

Centre: the splendidly preserved colosseum of El Djem, once site of cruelty and carnage, today the most impressive Roman monument in Tunisia.

Left: typical marabout's (holy man) burial place near Tozeur, in southern Tunisia.

Right: men walk down an alley in Tripoli, old city.
Below: the Jabal Akakus, Fezzan, southwestern Libya. The Fezzan has some of the finest desert scenery in Africa.

Above: Imperial Leptis Magna, pet city of African-born emperor Septimus Severus and rival to Carthage in the 2nd and 3rd centuries BC.
Right: children playing in the streets of old Tripoli. *Page 16*: shopping in the market at Sousse.

Excursions to western Libya

Until the late 1990s, Tunisia's southeastern neighbour, Libya, was off the tourist map. But the one-time maverick state of the Arab world, demonized by Reagan's America, has come back into the international fold – and fortunately so, for it is a land with great Roman sites and some of the finest prehistoric rock art in the world. Although the hotels often leave much to be desired, the easing of visa restrictions and the growth in specialized tourist agencies in Libya means that the country is attracting visitors again.

On the Mediterranean coast, are two truly spectacular Roman sites. East of Tripoli lies **A tale of** Leptis Magna, limestone-white city transformed on an imperial whim. Leptis-born **three cities** Septimus Severus gave his home town splendour: marble facings and columns, statuary, an ornate four-way triumphal arch and the most elegant market in the Roman world. In its heyday, in the early third century AD, Leptis was second only to Carthage in the African provinces. A monument to conspicuous consumption – and the thoroughness of Roman civil engineers – the city marks a high point in ancient city planning. After the fall of Rome, it was saved for posterity: no other settlement grew up near by and the sands and saltbush covered its forums and colonnades. Sabrata, the other great Roman site, west of Tripoli, is truly stagey. The theatre and its façades of slender colonnades await a tragedy of toga-draped actors. At both Leptis and Sabrata, the Italian archaeologists of the 1930s reconstructed the ruins in a way unthinkable in the more authentic-minded late 20th century, but the result is very fine, even without the statuary, much of which is now in Tripoli Museum.

Little, bar the triumphal arch of Marcus Aurelius, remains of Oea, the third city of Roman Tripolitania. On its ruins, Tripoli grew up: today effectively capital of Libya. It has a médina of narrow streets and souks, and a modern town where the Italians left a heritage of 20th century architecture. Today, the city has a cosmopolitan mix of Arabs and Africans, skyscrapers and ring-roads and great panels of public art.

Inland from Tripoli rises the Jabal Nafusa. Here are fortified granaries like Kasr Bir Niran **Jabal Nafusa** and Kasr el Haj, or the impressively ruined citadel village of Nalut, once known as the Potala Palace of Libya. Further inland, towards the western frontier, oasis town Ghadamès tells of caravan links with distant African lands. (Imagine Tuareg-led camel trains padding up from the deep Sahara). The cool tunnel-like streets and adobe buildings are now silent – but only recently abandoned. Across a plateau of roof terraces, the women would go about domestic tasks, living in a different world and socializing without ever venturing into the streets below.

The Fezzan is Libya's southwestern province, home to the ancient Garamantian **Fezzan** civilization – charioteers of the desert – and surprisingly modern agricultural projects using underground water to make the arid lands bloom. The Ghat region has a great ancient art gallery, discovered barely fifty years ago. In the canyon labyrinth of the Jabal Akakus and in the Wadi Mathendush, the rock paintings and carvings show a savannah bestiary in a time before the desert took over: giraffes and mouflons, hippotami and elephants, along with obscure peoples – mysterious round-head hunters, herders with their livestock and shamans. The prehistoric artists, working more than 8000 years ago, mixed their paints from natural materials and used feathers for brushes. The survival of their frescoes is practically a miracle.

With such sights, much maligned Libya is a fine destination which the committed traveller (visas having been obtained) can combine with more comfortable Tunisia. The distances are great – but the sights spectacular and unique.

Essentials

2

Essentials

Planning your trip

Where to go

Tunisia is a small country, with short distances between the main tourist areas and sights, so the traveller can see a lot in a 2 week trip. To make the most of your time, some careful planning is not a bad thing. What can you expect to see, without pushing yourself too hard, within the time you have for your trip? Rather than try to take in a maximum of towns and places, perhaps it is better to try to get to know a couple of places really well. Off the beaten track, Tunisia has some surprises – and for those with time, and a visa, an excursion into neighbouring western Libya is now becoming a real possibility.

Traditionally, Tunisia was one of the more unusual cheap package destinations. Its selling point was beaches, sun and 'a touch of the exotic'. Well-run 3 star hotels catered for the needs of the mass market, resort towns Hammamet, close to Tunis, and Sousse-Monastir were the destinations. In the late 1980s, the Tunisian authorities woke up to the fact that the typical tourist was spending little in the country and tour operators were making all the profits, and since then there has been a bid to develop more upmarket tourism and certain niche areas like golf, thalassotherapy and 'desert safaris'. In fact, the country really does have a lot to offer beyond the resort towns. Travelling by hire car or by *louage* (the ubiquitous inter-city shared taxis) will enable you to see a lot in a short space of time.

Tunisia's cities are concentrated on its eastern coastline. If you have bought a package, you will fly into Tunis-Carthage airport (for **Hammamet**) or Skanès-Monastir (for **Sousse**, **Mahdia** and **Monastir**). There are clean, safe, sandy beaches at these resorts and the shallow waters are perfect for kids. Both Tunis and Sousse have well preserved *médinas*, as the old walled towns are known, and the striking old city of **Kairouan** as well as the **Cap Bon** region are within easy distance of both cities. In the interior, there are some of the most spectacular Roman sites, which can be taken in as organized day excursions from the resorts.

To explore the **Roman sites**, you would be best to hire a car, however. Inland from Tunis is **Dougga**, perhaps the most beautiful site, **Bulla Regia** and its underground villas and marble quarry town of **Chemtou**, which has the best museum in the country, (after the Bardo in Tunis with its enormous collection of mosaics). Although these sites can be covered by public transport, the advantage of three days' car hire is that it allows you to take in lots of minor places. Close to Hammamet is **Zaghouan** and its mountain, and the **hill crest villages** of Jeradou, Takrouna and Zriba. Heading west for Dougga, is Andalusian Testour. If you opted to overnight in **Le Kef**, you could cover places on the western border, including the remote plateau of **Kalaât Senan**, and Roman cities **Haïdra** and **Sbeïtla**. South of Sousse is the spectacular amphitheatre of **El Djem**.

Tunisia's other big selling point is the **desert**. Although there are organized trips, which can work out cheap for a group, there is no problem getting to the southern areas by public transport. Basically, there are 4 areas to visit: the **Djerid** and the **Nefzaoua**, the **Matmatas** and the **Tataouine region**. The Djerid centres on the oasis town of Tozeur; close by is Nefta and the hill villages of Chebika, Midès and Tamerza. The Nefzaoua, south of the Djerid across a great salt flat, has the best dunes, near Douz and Zaâfrane. A new road links Douz to the Matmata region, famed for its underground houses. Tatouine, a couple of hours south of Djerba, has rock desert and a set of Berber villages perched up in the hills, Chenini, Douiret and Guermessa.

In its effort to diversify its tourist industry, Tunisia has invested heavily in the southern island of **Djerba**, and on a more modest scale in **Tabarka**, a tiny harbour town up in the northwest near the Algerian frontier. Djerba is said to be where Odysseus stopped off for a spot of lotus-eating. The island, flat, planted with palms and olives, ringed with splendid beaches, is great for anyone with a desperate need to slow

Essentials

down and relax. (The energetic could bicycle round the interior, looking at mosques and villages.) Tabarka, once a winter haunt of wild-boar hunters, now has a golf course and beach hotels. Further east, all along the north coast, are beautiful unspoiled beaches at places like Sidi Mechrig and Cap Serrat, and, moving closer to Bizerte, Ras Angela and Aïn Dammous.

Tunisia has a lot of more quirky things to interest the visitor too: birdwatching at Haouaria during the annual migrations, the old city centres with their heritage of 19th and 20th century architecture, *hammams* (Turkish baths) and cafés with hubbly-bubbly pipes, tonnes of kitsch in the tourist bazaars, fashion horrors at the *friperie*, the big second-hand clothes souks. Although vegetarians will have a hard time, meat eaters will be spoiled at roadside *mechoui* (barbecue) restaurants. In summer, you might find your way into a Tunisian wedding. Tunisians are a sociable and interesting lot and generally at ease in European languages.

So how should you go to Tunisia? Apart from doing flight only and arranging accommodation yourself, the cheap package is one of the best options. A sufficiently cheap package will give you a base in a resort from which you can travel out to other areas, spending nights away in places of interest. Note that Tunisia, while very reasonable in price terms when compared with Western Europe, is not a cheap destination.

For people who want interesting sites to visit – and whose kids want a beach, Tunisia is a good compromise destination. Late adolescents and 20-somethings looking for clubs will find it a little tame, however. Out of season, reasonable prices make Tunisian resorts a good destination for senior travellers seeking to escape the winter grey of northern Europe. Backpackers on a very tight budget will need to plan their money carefully. While upscale travellers will not (as yet) find chic hotels with very high standards of service, for the independent traveller prepared to make an effort, Tunisia has a lot of cultural interest.

When to go

Though Tunisia is a good destination all year round, spring, early summer and autumn are undoubtedly the best times to go if you are aiming to explore the more out of the way places, médinas and Roman sites. At these times of year, you have the advantages of pleasant weather, longer days, and cheaper resort-hotel rates. July and August can be extremely hot, making urban tourism a painful sweaty experience. The main coastal resorts are extremely crowded at these times of year. If you travel in winter, you have the disadvantage of shorter days, often rainy in the north. Nevertheless, Djerba (and Hammamet to a lesser extent) have superb micro-climates which produce balmy winter days. Note that for the beach, Tabarka is really a summer only sort of place, there being rough sea and wind at other times. The desert is not a summer destination, especially if you are going to bivouac.

What to take

Travellers always tend to take too much. Most 3 star Tunisian hotels, and even some of the cheaper ones, will have a laundry service of some kind, and T-shirts and jeans are cheap anyway. A travel-pack will survive the holds of rural buses and sitting on the roof-rack of a louage. If you acquire a carpet, there is plenty of cheap luggage on sale – some Tunisians frequently travel down to Libya to bring cheap merchandise back.

Regarding clothing, outside summer you will need woollens or a fleece for evenings. Longish cotton skirts are a good idea for women travelling in rural areas. Women visiting cities alone should have an item of smartish clothing. Tunisians like to dress well, and smartness is appreciated. (A generation ago, in many areas there was a lot of poverty.)

If you are hoping to travel out into the desert, you will need a warm sleeping bag. The penetrating cold of the desert at night is a well-known phenomenon, so bring your warm undergarments. The coastal towns can have a special damp cold in winter, so long johns are a good idea. Wear layers of clothing at these times. The following checklist might help you plan your packing:

Air-cushions for hard seating; cagoule (for wet Tunisian winter days); insect repellant/cream (essential); anti-mosquito plug-in device (very useful); neck pillow; driving licence; padlocks for luggage; photocopies of essential documents; plastic bags; short-wave radio; spare passport photographs, sun hat, sun protection cream, Swiss army knife; torch; umbrella; wet wipes; zip-lock bags. **Health kit**: Anti-acid tablets; anti-diarrhoea tablets; anti-septic cream; condoms; contraceptive tablets; mini-first aid kit; sachets of rehydration salts; tampons; travel sickness pills; water sterilization tablets for desert travel.

Tours and tour operators

Martin Randall Travel 10 Barley Mow Passage, Chiswick, London W4 4PH, T0181-9946477 (Roman and Islamic Cities). *Branta Holidays* 7 Wingfield St, London SE15 4LN, T0171-6344812 (birdwatching winter visitors on Lake Ichkeul and Tozeur). *Andante Travel* Grange Cottage, Winterbourne Dauntsey, Salisbury, Wilts, SP4 6ER, T01980-610555 (Art and Archaeology). *Explore Worldwide* 1 Frederick St, Aldershot, Hants, T01252-319448 (offer interesting excursions to the ancient sites and into the mountains). *Prospect Music and Art Tours* 454 Chiswick High Rd, London W4 5TT, T0181-9952151 (accompanied tours with experts in art and art history, archaeology and architecture). *Discovery Cruises* 47 St Johns Wood High St, London NW8 7NJ, T0171-5867191 (sailing from Athens). *Medward Travel* 304 Old Brompton Rd, London, SW5 9JF, T0171-3734411, F0171-2448174 (for individual requirements). *Regency Cruises* 2 Telfords Yard, 6 The Highway, London E1 9BQ, T01473-292222 (sailing from Nice). *Wigmore Holidays* 122 Wigmore St, London W1H 9FE, T0171-4864425, F0171-4863559 (specialize in Fly-Drive and Tailor-Made travel as well as breaks in Tunis and beach resorts, not cheap).

Before you travel

Getting in

No visas are required for full passport holders of EU, USA, and Canada. Visitors from Australia and New Zealand/Aotearoa need visas which are best obtained in advance, but can, in principle, be given on arrival. On the aeroplane or boat, or at the border, travellers will be required to fill a form with standard personal and passport details, an exercise to be repeated in almost all hotels throughout the country. From the point of entry, European Union travellers can stay in Tunisia for 3 months, while US visitors have 4 months. Travelling outside main tourist areas in Tunisia, have a photocopy of the key pages of your passport on you at all times. **Visas**

Visa Extensions are complicated to arrange, and will require a visit to the local police station near your hotel in a larger town, as well as patience. An easier option is to leave Tunisia for a few days, either to Malta or Italy, both short flights away. Given the large number of foreigners resident in the upmarket Tunis suburbs of La Marsa and Carthage, it may be easiest to arrange visa extensions in these cities. The operation will probably entail a visit to the Ministry of the Interior on the Av Bourguiba in Tunis. It should be stressed, however, that the least time consuming procedure is to leave the country.

☞ **Tunisian tourist boards overseas**

Austria 1010 Wien Opernring 1, Stiege R. Tür 109, Vienna
T1-5853480
F1-5853418
Email: tunesien@magnet.at

Belgium Office National du Tourisme Tunisien, Galerie Ravenstein 60, 1000 Bruxelles
T2-5111142/2893/5145642
F2-5113600
Email : tourismetunisien@skynet.be

Canada Tunisian Tourist Office, 1253 McGill College, Bureau # 655 Montreal, Quebec H3 B2 Y5
T514-3971182/0403
F514-3971647
Email : tunisinfo@qc.aira.com

Czech Republic Sokolska 39, 12000 Praha 2
T2-4941824/2424/2425
F2-4941825
Email : onttpraha@mbox.vol.cz

France Office National du Tourisme Tunisien, 32 Avenue de l'Opéra, 75002 Paris
T1-47427267
F1-47425268
Email : ontt@wanadoo.fr

Germany Fremdenverkehrsamt Tunesien, Kurfuerstendamm 171, 10707 Berlin
T30-8850457
F30-8852198

Greece Tunisian National Tourism Office, Tunisian Embassy. Anthen 2, Palais Psychico 15452, Athens
T1-6717590/47791
F1-6713432

Italy Ente Nazionale Tunisino Per il Turismo, Via Calabria 25, 00187 Roma
T6-42010149
F6-42010151

Japan Embassy of Tunisia, Tourism Office 29-2 Ichibancho 0 Chiyoda-Ku, Tokyo 102
T3-2627716

Netherlands Tunesisch National Verkeersbureau, Muntplein 2111, 1012 WR Amsterdam
T20-622 4971/ 625 0286
F2-638 3579
Email : info@worldonline.nl

Poland Al.Jerosolimskie 42m.68, 00-024 Warszawa
T2-8264019/4424/2425
F2-8271825
Email : onttvar@zigzag.pl

Russia Embassy of Tunisia, 28/1, Katchalova, Moscow
T095-2029504
F 095-7378815
Email : tunisia@orc.ru

Spain Oficina Nacional del Turismo Tunesino, Plaza de Espana 18, Torre de Madrid 28008, Planta 4 Oficina 1, Madrid
T1-5481435/1843/2136
F1-5483705
Email: tunezturismo@mad.servicom.es

Sweden Tunisiska Statens Turistbyra, Stureplan 15, 11145 Stockholm
T8-6780645/3366
F8-6781905
Email : tst@swipnet.se

Switzerland Tunesisches Fremdenverkehrsburo, 69 Bahnhofstrasse, 8001 Zurich
T1-2114830/4831
F1-2121353
Email : fmami@tunisie.ch

UK Tunisian National Tourist Office 77-A Wigmore Street, London W1 H9 LJ
T0171-2245598/6201
F0171-2244053
Email: tntolondon@aol.com

USA C/O Embassy of Tunisia, 1515 Massachussets, Avenue Washington DC 20005
T202-86218 50
F202-8621858
Email : ezzedine@ix.netcom.com

Tunisian embassies abroad

Australia *See UK.*

Algeria *Rue Ammar Rahmani, El Biar, 16000 Algiers, T2-6920857*

Austria *3-4 Ghaegastrasse, 1030 Vienna, T1-5815281/2*

Belgium *278 Av de Tervueren, 1150 Brussels, T2-7717395*

Canada *515 O'Connor St, Ottawa, Ontario, K1S 3P8, T613-2370330/2*

Egypt *26 Rue el Jazirah, Zamalek, 11211 Cairo, T2-3404940*

France *17-19 Rue de Lubeck, 75016 Paris, T1-45535094*

Germany *110 Esplanade 12, 1100 Berlin, T30-4722064/7*

Italy *Via Asmara 5, 00199 Rome, T6-8604282*

Libya *Av Jehara, Sharia Bin Ashur, 3160 Tripoli, T21-607161*

Morocco *6 Rue de Fès, Rabat, T7-730576*

Netherlands *Gentestraat 98, 2587 HX, The Hague, T70-3512251*

Norway *Haakon VII'sgt 5B, 0161 Oslo, T22-831917*

South Africa *850 Church St, Arcadia, 0007 Pretoria, T12-3426283*

Sweden *Drottningatan 73C, 11136 Stockholm, T8-6635370*

Switzerland *Kirchenfeldstrasse 63, 3005 Bern, T31-3528226*

UK *29 Prince's Gate, London, SW7 1QG, T0171-5848117*

USA *1515 Massachusetts Av NW, Washington DC 20005, T202-8621850*

For a list of foreign embassies and consulates in Tunis, see the Tunis directory page 108

Essentials

Residence permits

If you have come to Tunisia for work or to study Arabic, you will be able to obtain a residence permit (*carte de séjour*). You have to constitute a file (*dossier*) with all the necessary documents, photocopied and certified (*copie conforme*). Expect to waste much time going back and forth to your local police station because you have not been told the full list of documents necessary. The completed dossier goes to the Ministry of the Interior, and a carte de séjour may eventually be granted. Students of Arabic should note that there has been an unwillingness to grant residence permits in recent years.

Passport loss

Report immediately to police giving number and date and place of issue. The last hotel at which you stayed will have this information on the registration form but it ought to be carried separately. Getting fresh documents will probably entail a trip to Tunis to your embassy.

Customs

Visitors may take in, free of duty, 400 grams of tobacco, 200 cigarettes or 50 cigars and such personal items as a camera, binoculars, a portable radio receiver, computer or typewriter. You may also take your pet to Tunisia. It will need a health certificate and an anti-rabies certificate less than 6 months old.

Prohibited items

Narcotics Tunisia is not the Netherlands, and there are **extremely severe penalties** for possession of, or trade in, narcotic drugs: 1 to 5 years' imprisonment and/or fines. You do not want to be involved in a Tunisian remake of Midnight Express. Cannabis (*takrouri*) was part of everyday life in Tunisia until independence, after which it became illegal. The plant is still cultivated (in secret) in certain rural areas. If you want to have a quiet smoke, do not share with Tunisian friends, unless you know them really well. If caught, they will be in very serious trouble. Possession gives you a 2 year prison term.

Wildlife

Be aware that wild animal skin and some other items openly on sale in Tunisia cannot be legally imported into the UK and EU. This includes products made from tortoise shell, snake skin, lizards and many fur products. It is too late to save these creatures but buying such products puts the death sentence on others. Visitors should certainly not purchase live animals for export from Tunisia and import into EU and USA as it is in most cases illegal and punishable by large fines and confiscation.

👉 *Exchange rates (9 November, 1999)*

	US$	£	Ffr	DM	Ptas
Tunisian Dinar *(1Dt)*	0.83	0.51	5.23	1.56	132.93

Vaccinations None required unless travelling from a country where yellow fever and/or cholera frequently occurs. You should be up to date with polio, tetanus, and typhoid protection. If you are going to be travelling in rural areas where hygiene is often a bit rough and ready, then having a hepatitis B shot is a good thing. You could also have a cholera shot, although there is no agreement among medics on how effective this is. There is no malaria in Tunisia.

Money

Currency
A list of banks can be found in each town's individual directory

The major unit of currency in Tunisia is the **dinar** (in this Handbook: Dt). 1 **dinar**=1,000 **millimes**. There are coins for 5 millimes (the aluminium *douro*), 50 and 100 millimes (yellow metal, confusingly similar), cupronickel 500 millimes, and the larger 1 dinar cupronickel coin. There are notes for 5, 10, 20, and 30 **dinars**. Note that Tunisia uses international figures, not Arabic ones, so there is no confusion, although coins are labelled in Arabic only. Banknotes are labelled in Arabic and French. Most transactions are in cash.

The banknotes can be a little confusing, as there are 2 models in circulation for the lower denomination notes, as follows: for 5Dt, there is the older reddish-pink note and the newer, smaller green Hannibal model; for 10Dt, there is the older brown and green note and the newer blue Ibn Khaldun. The 20Dt is pink and purple, the brightly coloured 30Dt green and yellow.

In late 1999, £1 bought 1.930Dt, the $US bought 900 millimes. £100 bought close on 190Dt, a very favourable rate indeed. The rates of course fluctuate, and the dinar was held to be overvalued in some quarters in 1999. You can on occasion buy Tunisian dinars at bureaux de change at Gatwick and Heathrow airports. Dinars may not be taken out of Tunisia. If you have bought too many dinars, you can exchange them back into French francs at a bank on production of exchange receipts. However, as European cash and Visa cards function in Tunisian cash points (*guichets automatiques* or *DAB, distributeur automatique de billets*), in major towns it is possible to withdraw more or less exactly the amount one needs on a daily basis.

Arriving at Tunis-Carthage Airport, there are exchange facilities in the main concourse and several cash points. Note, however, that at weekends cashpoints at both airport and in the cities can be temperamental, so have cash and travellers' cheques to exchange. The most reliable cashpoints are those of the *BIAT* (Banque internationale arabe de Tunisie) identified by its green and white colours. The *Banque de l'Habitat* cashpoints are also generally reliable. Tunisia has a plethora of banks, and not all have kept up with the technological investments necessary for cashpoints.

Note that Tunisians among themselves will count in older currency units. To the complete confusion of travellers, most Tunisians refer to **francs**, a franc being equal to 1 millime, although this is a unit existing only in speech. *Alf franc* (1,000 francs) is one dinar, *alfayn* is 2 dinars, *khams alaf* is 5 dinars, etc. Unless you are good at calculations, it's probably easiest to stick to dinars.

Banking facilities Hours are 0830-1130 and 1500-1630. In the summer and during the fasting month of Ramadan they are 0830-1400. The separate *bureaux de change* in the major cities, mainly BIAT, STB and Banque de l'Habitat often open for longer hours (0800-1700), which in theory give the same rates of exchange but charge different amounts of commission. There are numerous banks in Tunisia, with *BIAT*, *Société tunisienne de banque* (STB – blue and white livery), *Banque de Tunisie* (blue and yellow) all widespread. Banking in Tunisia can be a slow process, with several different desks for different purposes. The easiest way to get hold of cash is to use your Visa or cash card at a cash dispenser – provided that this is in service.

There is a fixed exchange rate for changing notes and no commission ought to be charged for this. A small commission will be charged for changing travellers' cheques.

These are widely accepted at banks, top hotels, restaurants and shops, but it is wise to check first. *American Express* are represented by *Voyages Schwartz* in Tunisia, with limited services. Remember to keep all credit card receipts – and before you sign, check where the decimal marker (a comma in Tunisia, as in Europe, rather than a dot), has been placed and that there isn't a zero too many. You don't want to be paying thousands rather than tens of dinars.

Foreign currency may be imported freely. **Eurocheques** These are accepted in Tunisia, and can be a good way to make sure one will not run out of money. Try at banks with the *Eurocheque* sticker. **Travellers' cheques** These are usable in Tunisia, although the traveller may be sent from bank to bank before the appropriate one is found. Use travellers' cheques from a well known bank or company, and preferably with UK, US, French or German currency, although this is not an absolute rule. Some hotels and shops will exchange travellers' cheques.

As a **budget traveller**, it is possible to get by in Tunisia for US$25-30 a day. Accommodation, food and transport are all cheap, and there is a lot of atmosphere to take in for free. Cheap accommodation will cost around 8 to 12Dt a night. Anything less will be pretty rough, and probably unadvisable for women travelling alone. If your budget can stand it, then you can find nice rooms around the 20Dt price mark. Out of season, there may be some latitude to negotiate in smaller hotels.

Prices for food and drink are non-negotiable, of course. In ordinary cafés, sample prices include: bottled water 700 mills, tea/coffee 300 to 500 mills, branded fizzy drink 400 mills. (A top tourist zone café will charge you considerably more.) You can have a very filling meal for 5Dt, a big, fat sandwich will cost you around 1.200Dt, seasonal fruit will be around 1Dt per kilo. Concerning transport, as a guideline, by shared taxi (*louage*), the 9 hour trip from Tunis to Zarzis, in the far southeast of the country, costs 27Dt. Museum/site entrance tickets will be 2Dt (you have all the sites of Carthage for just 5Dt 100).

If you start buying imported goods, notably cosmetics, books and electrical goods, things can get expensive. The least central tourist areas (Djerba in particular, also Tabarka) are easily the most expensive places. If you are looking for small, kitsch presents, there are plenty of things to buy in Tunisia, and the prices, if you bargain, can be quite reasonable. Souk-sellers will often start with absurdly high prices for tourists, as the gullible (or those unfamiliar with the local currency) can be persuaded to part with large sums of money after much blarney. For 250Dt or more, you could go home with a nice bit of textile or carpet.

It you want to travel in a **moderate** degree of comfort, in summer you could expect to find a room for 40Dt in a simple resort hotel with a small pool. At this price, you would probably also have air-conditioning. Outside the high season (July and August), prices can be very reasonable indeed in some of the 3 star hotels in Sousse and Hammamet. You could be eating out in the evening very well for 20Dt a head. Car hire might be your major expense, at around 200Dt a week for a small car, unlimited mileage.

Essentials

Bamboozling the visitor: whys and wherefores

At the weekly traditional market in Sousse, a man waves a crudely carved wooden camel under your nose: ' Only sixty dinars', but you move on, pressed forward by the crowd. There are at least another thousand people coming through, one of whom might be convinced into paying $60 (£30) for the small wooden dromedary in question. Getting off the tour bus at Nabeul, a man thrusts a reed pipe into your hand. 'C'est un cadeau', he declares warmly. Seconds later, this is followed by 'Give me dinars'. The tourist bubble has been pierced, we have malfunction in the brochure world of sky-blue swimming pools, palm trees and colourful bazaars.

As in any tourist destination, Tunisia's resorts have salesmen ready to benefit from visitors' unfamiliarity with local prices. The myth that bargaining is the basis for transactions in Tunisia, carefully maintained in the holiday literature, keeps the tourist souks going. Thus a pair of silverish metal bracelets can start out at 35Dt , only to descend, after 15 minutes' discussion, to 8Dt. (The profit margin will still be at least 50 percent.)

The truth of the matter is that for the character selling the souvenir beast, 60Dt is a real killing. Compare with this sum local salaries. A factory worker on a short term contract will be getting around 180Dt a month; someone more skilled, say in garment manufacture, will be on 250Dt. Neither have any job security. A tour rep will earn 450Dt, plus lots of good commissions for tours sold – though this is seasonal work. An experienced university lecturer might earn 800Dt. Tunisia's new rich BMW-wielding classes, in managerial positions in the private sector or banking could be on 1500Dt or more a month, with an extra month's pay and access to various loans at preferential rates. Although many basic food products are subsidized, life for those at the bottom of the salary scale has got more difficult over the last five years. A visit to the doctor costs 12Dt and medicines have become expensive. Rents in the capital start at around 120Dt. A single minimum salary is clearly inadequate for even a small family. Thus those with the gift of the gab are tempted to make a fast buck in the tourist resorts. They are few in number – but can create a very unfavourable impression. Beware the bearers of free wooden flutes and other trinkets. Smile blandly and ignore – easier said than done.

The **upscale traveller** will find that in top quality hotels and nightclubs prices are similar to Europe. Hotel service may not always be what you are used to in this price bracket. Restaurants, however, are substantially cheaper than in Europe. A fine meal, without wine, can cost around 60Dt a head but upmarket restaurants bump their profits up by charging heavily for wine.

Getting there

Air

Most travellers fly to Tunisia, either from Europe, the Middle East or certain adjacent African countries. (There are no direct flights from North America or Australasia.) *Tunisair* is the national flag carrier, and there are two main airports, Tunis-Carthage and Skanès-Monastir. Djerba is an important airport, and there are smaller airports at Sfax, Tabarka and Tozeur. With the air embargo now lifted, Tunisair will be offering flights to Tunis from Tripoli. While Tunisair has flights from most European capitals and numerous French and German cities, from the UK it only flies out of Heathrow (terminal 2), where *Air France* deals with check-in. Flight time from London to Tunis-Carthage is around 2 hours 30 minutes. **British Airways** has four scheduled flights a week from London Gatwick to Tunis-Carthage, while regional UK airports have numerous charter flights to Tunis-Carthage, Skanès-Monastir and Djerba. Flight time from Cairo is 4 hours 30 minutes, from Paris 2 hours. *Tunisair* operates scheduled services from the French provinces to Tunisian regional airports, depending on the time of year. Demand is much greater in the summer, when French Tunisians return for the holidays. For the moment, *Tunisair* seems unlikely to break the charter airlines, hold on flights from the UK. *Tunisair* flights to and from London are often late.

If you buy your flight in Tunisia, note that most travel agents and airline offices apply 2 rates, *tarif résident* and *tarif non-résident*. If you are not resident in Tunisia, you will find yourself paying the latter rate, generally anything up to 50 percent more. Not all travel agents ask or apply this rate, however, and you should shop around. The same rules apply for ferry tickets bought by non-resident foreigners in Tunisia.

On flights to Tunisia, the usual general airline restrictions apply with regard to luggage weight allowances before surcharge (*excédent de bagage*), normally 30 kg for first class and 20 kg for business and economy class. Understanding of the term 'limited' with regard to amount of hand luggage has been known to vary greatly.

Discounts It is possible to obtain significantly cheaper tickets by avoiding school holiday times, by flying at night, by shopping around and by booking early to obtain one of the quota of discounted fares.

Sea

Ferries Numerous ferries operate across the Mediterranean carrying both vehicles and foot passengers. Prices vary according to the season. Main points of departure are Marseille, Genoa, and Palermo, arrival is at Tunis port, La Goulette. In summer, certain ferries run from Toulon and Naples, and there is a hydrofoil from Trapani to Kelibia.

Ferry routes & international airports

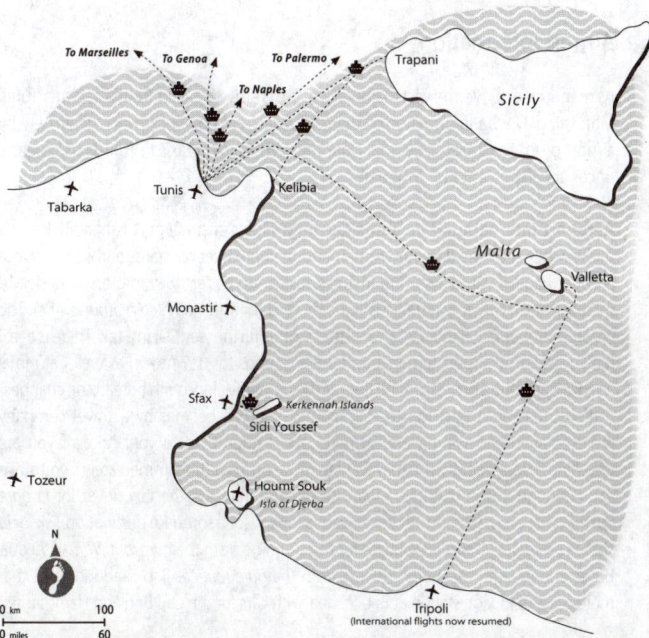

To Marseilles   To Genoa   To Palermo   Trapani

To Naples

Sicily

Tabarka   Tunis   Kelibia

Malta

Valletta

Monastir

Sfax   *Kerkennah Islands*
Sidi Youssef

Tozeur

Houmt Souk
Isla of Djerba

N

0 km   100
0 miles   60

Tripoli
(International flights now resumed)

Ferry is a far less convenient way to travel than aeroplane. Prices are not cheaper, and even as a foot passenger, you will have long waits at passport control and customs in the port at La Goulette. Expect to have considerable difficulty buying a ferry ticket at short notice in Tunis in the summer. The CTN has an office for this purpose on the rue de Yougoslavie, behind the French Embassy.

The following companies do the Marseille/Genoa to La Goulette run: *CTN* (Compagnie tunisienne de navigation) and *SNCM* (Société nationale maritime Corse-Méditerranée (61 Blvd des Dames, 13002 Marseille, T04-91563030, 12 rue Godot-de-Mauroy, Paris T08-36679500; c/o Tirrenia, Ponte Colombo, Genoa 010 258041; c/o Southern Ferries, 179 Piccadilly, London, W1V 9DB, T0171-4914968).

In summer, *Linee Lauro* does 1 sailing a week from Naples to Tunis (Piazza Municipio 88, Naples, Italy, T0039-081-5513352), in Tunis *Ag Carthage Tour*, 59 Av Habib Bourguiba, Tunis, Tunisia, T00216-01-1347015, Ag Viamare, 2 Sumatra Rd, London, UK, T0044-0171-4315456, Ag Neptunia, Schmiedwergel, 1 Munich, T0049-89-89607320, Germany). *Tirrenia Navigazione* operates the hydrofoil service (Corso Italia 52/56 Trapani, T0923-27480, c/o Tourafric 53 Av Habib Bourguiba, Tunis, T01-341488). The hydrofoil – which calls in at Pantelleria on the way – is subject to the vagaries of the weather, and crossings may be cancelled early and late in the season. Note that if buying tickets in Tunis, CTN has a more expensive non-resident rate whereas Linee Lauro charges the same rate for all.

Road and rail

It is not possible to travel to Tunisia from Algeria at the present time, although since the election of President Bouteflika in 1999, there seems to be a real chance of the situation improving. Access from Libya by land is by shared service taxi, details given in the western Libya section of the book.

Touching down

Airport information

As mentioned above, the vast majority of tourists arrive by air in Tunisia at either Tunis, Monastir, or Djerba. Information on onward travel from point of arrival is given here by airport or, for La Goulette, by port. Note that yellow town taxis in Tunisia use meters, prices are 50 percent higher at night.

Aéroport international de Tunis-Carthage Tunis' main airport is handily located midway between the downtown Tunis and the upmarket coastal suburbs of La Marsa and Carthage. If you are staying in Tunis, taxi is the easiest way into town, under 10 minutes' ride away if the traffic is light, more during the day (cost around 4Dt). The coastal hotel strip at Raoued/Gammarth is slightly further, say 5Dt in a taxi. There is a taxi rank outside the airport terminal, and there is a bus for downtown as well. Car rental agencies are found on the ground floor of the terminus, along with bureaux de change.

If you are on a package to Hammamet, you will be met by a travel company representative, and will have a 50 minute bus ride down to your hotel. If you are travelling independently, you may want to move on from Tunis immediately, if you arrive early enough in the day. If you want to get the train, ask the taxi driver for *la gare, Barshelona* (see map page 38). If you want a louage for a southern destination, ask for *la station de louage, Moncef Bey*. Buses for the south go from the *gare routière*, Bab 'Alioua, buses and louages for the northwest, from the *gare routière*, Bab Saâdoun. Note that there is a 2nd louage station at Bab 'Alioua, with cars for the Cap Bon and Hammamet.

Touching down

Business hours **Banks**: 0830-1130 and 1500-1630. In the summer and during the fasting month of Ramadan they are 0830-1400. The separate bureaux de change in the major cities, mainly BIAT, STB and Banque de l'Habitat often open for longer hours (0800-1700). **Post office**: 0800-1230 and 1500-1800 and **shops** generally: 0800-1300 and 1500 to 1745, Monday to Thursday, with Friday-Saturday 0800-1300, except in summer, when hours are 0730-1300. Hours during Ramadhan are 0800-1400. **Emergency services** Police: 197, Fire: 198 (Protection civile), Ambulance: (SAMU): 190 **Directory enquiries**: (les renseignements), 120 for business, 121 for personal calls. **Official time**: GMT +1 all year round. **Weights and measures**: metric.

If you want to travel on to Libya, you need the Libyan taxi rank in the médina, about 200m south of *Porte de France*, on your right as you go down rue Jazira. There are Algerian service taxis on the first section of rue Jazira. After a line of apartment buildings, there is a small shaded square with shoe repair stands. Turn right. The Libyan service taxis park up here waiting for custom. (Tunis to Tripoli single fare 35Dt/75LD, 12 hour journey.) Another taxi departure point for Libya is the Hotel Ayachi, Bab Souika, in the northern part of the médina (old part) of Tunis.

Aéroport international de Skanès-Monastir This is the main airport for the Sahel region, ie Sousse, Monastir and Mahdia. Just outside the terminus building, you have a stop on the Sahel metro line, a train service which runs from Sousse to Mahdia. Buses for Sousse and Monastir are also available. Taxi drivers are well aware that tourists arriving are unfamiliar with the currency. A taxi into Monastir will be around 4Dt, into Sousse 7Dt 500. Shared taxis for Sousse and Monastir will stop on the main road beyond the rail line. There are car rental agencies on the main concourse.

Aéroport international de Djerba The airport on Djerba is near Mellita, in the northwest of the island, a short taxi ride (say 3Dt) from Houmt Souk, where most independent travellers stay. The main hotel strip (Sidi Mahares) starts some 12 km from the airport, and your taxi fare to your hotel will start at around 6Dt, depending on the distance. There are yellow and white service taxis for Libya outside the terminal building.

Port de La Goulette (Tunis) The boats from France and Italy and cruiseships come in to La Goulette. Formalities are often slow, especially in summer, when Tunisians resident abroad are returning with cars loaded to the gunnels with household items. There will be taxis waiting to do the 15 minute run from port to town centre (say 3Dt), across the causeway which crosses the Lac de Tunis. Otherwise, take the TGM (Tunis-Goulette-Marsa) light railway. Outside the port, you will see a big stone citadel. Leaving the fort on your left, go straight ahead, towards the petrol station (to the right of the road). Turn right after the petrol station and you will come to a TGM stop. Going into Tunis, you need to be on the far side of the line from the port.

Tourist information

In Tunisia, many of the main towns have *syndicats d'initiative* (town information offices) and branches of the national tourist office, the ONTT. On the whole, they are not much help, restricting their activities to giving out brochures about the different regions of the country. Hours are generally Monday-Thursday 0830 to 1300 and 1500 to 1745, Friday and Saturday, 0830 to 1330.

For local tourist offices, see under the directory for individual towns

👉 *Islamic Fundamentalism*

Islam has been marked over the course of history by the emergence of rigorous revivalist movements. Most have sought a return of the faithful to the fundamentals of Islam – the basic doctrines of the Prophet Mohammed – uncluttered by the interpretations of later Islamic jurists and commentators. Behind the movements was generally the idea that Muslim people should go back to the simple basics of their religion. Some, like the Wahhabi movement in Saudi Arabia were puritan in concept, demanding plain lives and an adherence to the tenets of Islam in all daily aspects of life. Others, imposed a rigorous schedule of ritual in prayer and avoidance of the 'unclean' in public life. A good example of this type of reformist tendency was the Senusi Movement in North Africa which in the period from the close of the 19th century to 1969 created an educational, commercial and religious society.

Until recent times the fundamentalist movements inside Islam arose from a desire to cleanse the religion of unnecessary ideology and to make all the Islamic community observe the basic pillars of the Islamic religion – prayer, belief and righteous actions on a consistent and demonstrable basis. In the last 100 years there has been a growing tendency in the Islamic world for revivalist movements to be reactions to political, military and cultural setbacks. The aim of the reformers has been to make good the disadvantage and backwardness of the Muslim states in contrast with the powerful countries of Europe, America and the Far East. The matter is varied and complex, depending on the particular cases involved but the clear linkage between an increasingly dominant Western culture and economy and the growth of reactive Islamic movements is inescapable. The Muslim Brotherhood was an early form of revivalist movement of this kind. Founded by an Egyptian school teacher, Hassan al-Banna in 1928, it initially tried to take Islam back to its

Maps In Tunisia, the visitor will find maps of the country on sale in kiosks and bookshops. The better maps include the GeoCenter 1:800,000 map to Tunisia, with plans of Kairouan, Sousse and Tunis. Travellers will find certain inaccuaracies, especially in showing minor roads in rural areas. In the UK, try *Stanfords*, 12-14 Long Acre, WC2E 9LP, T0171-7301314, near Covent Garden for maps. One of the best maps, not always available in Tunisia, is the Michelin sheet 958, Algérie Tunisie, 1:1,000,000. The tourist offices may provide free maps which are perfectly adequate for navigating between main towns, but not much more.

Student travellers Prices in Tunisia are very reasonable when compared with Europe but there is no system of student discounts in operation.

Disabled travellers Tunisia cannot be said to be a very easy country to get around for those with disabilities. Nevertheless, there seems to be a growing awareness of disability issues, and the newer hotels have wheelchair ramps. Trains can be difficult to get onto – you have to climb up into the train. Tunis-Carthage airport now has satellite buildings, so you get off the plane directly into the airport and can go by wheelchair from plane to customs. (Not all planes use the satellites, however.) Other airports are more tricky, using buses to take passengers to and from the planes.

Gay and lesbian travellers In Tunisia, men may wear jasmine bouquets lodged jauntily behind the ear, or walk hand in hand down the street. (Some of the women in country areas are tatooed and tough.) However, such signs must be seen in context.

Though there is no public perception of what a Tunisian lesbian might look like, gay visitors have long been a feature of the Tunisian tourist scene, although at a discrete

roots and therefore to its perceived strengths. The movement was later taken over by extremists who used its organization for political ends. The development of the Muslim Brotherhood in Egypt as a clandestine political group and the harnessing of religious fervour to political objectives, including the assassination of political enemies, set the pattern for most later movements of the kind. For a short time in the 1980s there were Islamist emulators in Tunisia.

Tunisia is unique in that secularization of the laws affecting official and private life has gone further here than anywhere else in the Middle East and North Africa, largely thanks to the liberalizing activities of the former President, Habib Bouguiba. The Personal Status Code has given women in particular immense freedom of economic opportunity and, with the 1992 legislation on family rights, enables women to have custody of children, protection against violence in the home, and guaranteed rights to a passport. The scale of female emancipation is such that any real threat to it from Islamist forces is resisted strongly by an increasingly urban, educated and economically active female population, whose position is in great contrast to its sisters in Algeria and Libya, for example. It is estimated that women now occupy a quarter of all employment, 35 percent of industrial jobs and 22 percent of serviced activities in addition to managing 1 in 10 farms. Their role is crucial to economic success in national and family budgets. What is more, Tunisian women are well aware of their new-found economic importance.

The Islamist parties such as El Nahda have no real power base, thanks to continued economic growth and social reform. Short of a major change of regime favouring the Algerian Islamists, the Ben Ali administration has drawn most of the sting of the local Islamist movement and has enough of a popular mandate in its secular social and political programmes to survive any fundamentalist challenges.

level. (French and Italian A-gays have tasteful homes in Hammamet and Sidi Bou Saïd.) There are no gay areas or bars (although your average bloke-filled city bar might look like one) and no 'scene' as such. In city centres, Tunisians tend to stare a lot. This does not necessarily mean anything more than curiosity. The 'hard stare' quickly gives way to a smile. If initial contact in a shop or small restaurant is a bit cold, on the second visit it will be friendly, signifying you have been 'adopted' by the assistants or waiters. Tunisian men (and women) are friendly and love to chat and pass the time of day in a way unusual in northern Europe. Ready familiarity does not mean a gay interest, however.

In Tunisian Arabic, the screaming queen is a *karioka* (pl. *krik*), while the pejorative term, roughly equivalent to the English 'queer' is *miboun* (pl. *mwebna*). The moustachioed, macho male is a *taffar*. The French term *pédé* for queer is also used. Talk-shows on French TV mean that educated gay Tunisians are well aware of gay life elsewhere, and may define themselves as *gai* or *homo*. In such circles, discretion is the rule: many men who might adopt a gay lifestyle in Europe will get married in middle life. There are no gay associations.

But Tunisia is not a homophobic place, provided a 'decent' façade is preserved. Single men may find themselves propositioned. In city centres and beach resorts, the *bezness* operate, gigolos keen to extract dinars for services rendered. They will be well known faces in downtown cafés and avenues. (If an unwelcome *bezness* joins you at your café table, just be polite and distant.) If a friendship forms with a chance acquaintance, gifts of clothing may be much appreciated. Some Tunisian young men may play the field, in part out of boredom or lack of contact with women, but close relationships between young men and women, outside the family circle, are more easily formed now than in the past.

Regarding Aids (*le Sida*), Tunisia has very low incidence. People are on the whole well informed thanks to French television. The country also has several associations working to inform the public about Aids.

For more information on the North African gay communcity in France, contact the NGO Kelma (lit: 'word', as in 'word of hohour') on their website at www.kelma.org.

Rules, customs and etiquette

Appearance Tunisians pay great attention to cleanliness and neatness. People are as smart as they can afford to be, and if you have to go to the police station or some other official building, shorts are not acceptable. Do not wander round towns and the souks in your skimpy top and brief shorts, unless you want to attract the full-on comments and the attention of the lads who work there. In a hot climate, it is probably better to cover up when away from the beach, anyway. Having said that, in the hottest weather, at home in their neighbourhood, Tunisian men will sit around in cafés playing cards with their shirts off. And many young Tunisian women keep up with the latest fashions – tight trousers and navel-revealing tops were *de rigueur* in many quarters in summer 1999.

Bargaining Bargaining is expected in the tourist bazaars. Start lower than you would expect to pay, be polite and good humoured, enjoy the experience and if the final price doesn't suit walk away. The experience can be highly entertaining, and sometimes a little traumatic for the seller, who in extreme cases may resort to comments like 'you don't want to buy from me because you're a racist' (sic). In the end, the price you pay must be the price the item is worth to you. (How much would the same thing cost at home?) And then, think, 'do I really need this terracotta bowl/glittery scarf/furry camel?'. The answer to the question is generally NO. If you're a shopaholic, treat it all as a form of therapy: in Tunisia, shopping for inessentials is difficult because you have to bargain. As few shops take credit cards, you can give your plastic money a rest.

Beggars Tunisia does not have the intense poverty of, say, Egypt and Morocco, and there are few beggars. It is unlikely that they will be too persistent. Have a few small coins ready. Arabic has polite phrases to refuse making a donation, namely *rebbi yenoub*, 'may God act for you', or *rebbi/Allah yusahel*, 'may God make things easier'.

Confidence tricksters The most common 'threat' to tourists is found where people are on the move, at ports and railway and bus stations. Strangers may offer extremely favourable currency exchange rates or spin 'hard luck' stories. Confidence tricksters are, by definition, extremely convincing and persuasive. Be warned if the offer seems too good to be true – that is probably what it is. Be distant, even a little bored by the whole thing. (Some of the methods are quite inventive: a few years ago, there was a young guy who would befriend attractive Nordic tourists in Houmt Souk, reading their palms with amazing accuracy – thanks to a briefing from his friend who worked at the frontier police post at the airport.)

Courtesy A certain amount of formality makes life run smoothly in Tunisia. You will see that there is much handshaking and kissing on the cheek. Entering an office or a meeting, or joining a group of friends, you should be sure to shake everyone's hand. With people you have come to know well, you kiss once on each cheek on meeting them, and probably on leaving them too. Even if there are ten people or more in a room, greet everyone with a handshake.

Going into a shop or at a bank or PTT counter, say *bonjour* or *sabah el khir*. When leaving someone who is at work, say *Allah 'ayanek*, 'may God help you'. It may not be appropriate for men to shake hands with older headscarf-wearing 'religious' women. Use your common sense.

Saying thank you, you have a barrage of terms at your disposal in Tunisian, including *merci alayk*, *inshallah merci*, *barakallaw fik*, and the more formal *shokran*. To a young person serving in a shop or restaurant, you might say *inshallah farhatik*, 'may you have a joyful wedding'.

Timekeeping

Tunisians in both private and public sectors are generally punctual, give or take 5 or 10 minutes. Meetings are best held Monday to Thursday. During Ramadhan, especially the last 2 weeks, timekeeping tends to fall apart as Tunisians strive to combine work, fasting, big family meals and late night socializing. The latter 2 categories tend to win.

Two final points: 1, when it comes to getting onto public transport, politeness tends to go out of the window, and you have to be ready to push; 2, be very careful never to criticize the régime because officials, waiters and taxi drivers may understand more English than you think.

Mosques

Visitors to mosques (where permitted) and other religious buildings will normally be expected to remove their shoes and cover-all garments will be available for hire to enable the required standard of dress to be met. Only a few mosques are visitable in Tunisia, including the Great Mosque and the Barber's Mosque in Kairouan, and the colonnade of the Zitouna Mosque in Tunis. On no account go into a mosque uninvited. You will be ejected unceremoniously.

Prohibitions

Ignore all offers of drugs. Narcotics traffic is a very serious offence in Tunisia, and you will be in real trouble if caught. A quiet joint should only be smoked with friends you know very, very well. Firearms may not be taken into Tunisia without prior permission.

Tipping

Tipping in Tunisia is important for waiters and others on low service sector wages. (A waiter might expect to take home 250Dt a month (see box page 26), and will be working extremely long hours.) Tips are thus very important. In hotels and restaurants the service has probably been included so a tip to the waiter is an optional extra. It does no harm to round up the taxi fare or the café bill. 500 mills is a generous tip in a café. If this is a café you go to frequently, being 'a tipper' definitely improves the service.

Safety

Personal security

Travellers in Tunisia are unlikely to experience threats to personal security. Muslims are expected to honour the stranger in their midst. However basic common sense is needed for the protection of personal property, money and papers. Use hotel safes for valuable items as hotel rooms cannot be regarded as secure and when travelling, carry valuables as close to the body as possible, and where convenient, in more than one place. External pockets on bags and clothing should never be used for carrying valuables. Bag snatching and pick pocketing is more common in crowded tourist areas. It is obviously unwise to lay temptation in the way of a man whose annual income is less than the cost of your return airfare. It is wise to keep photocopies of important documents, a record of your passport number, Travellers' cheque numbers and air ticket number somewhere separate from the actual items.

Police

Report any incident which involves you or your possessions. An insurance claim for theft of any size will require the backing of a police report – which will be typed out for you (in Arabic) at the police station in whose area the incident took place. If involvement with the police is more serious, for instance a driving accident, remain calm, and contact the nearest consular office without delay.

The Tunisian police comes in 4 types: the city police (grey blue uniforms), who do traffic duty and urban checkpoints; the Garde Nationale (Arabic: *el haras*), green and khaki uniforms, for rural areas; the *unités d'intervention*, black 'ninja' uniforms, help in crowd control at sporting events, and, of course, plain clothes police. As hire cars are easily identifiable by their blue licence plates, police will often flag them down for spot checks, as they do for cars with foreign licence plates. Show your papers and smile.

In the rural areas, the Garde Nationale has check points on main routes and as you arrive in certain small towns. Drivers travelling frequently in these areas know when to slow down for these checkpoints. The Garde Nationale are polite and professional, and can be helpful on the state of roads, particularly after heavy rain. In remote country areas, they seem to get bored manning their checkpoints, and like to have a chat. They are especially hot on speeding offences: drive at 50kph or less through small settlements.

Women travelling alone

Women face greater difficulties than men or couples. Though young Tunisian women travel between towns for work or study without any problems, in more traditional country areas, young Muslim women rarely travel without a male relative or older female. Thanks to satellite TV, Tunisians are more aware of Western mores than before, and the generation in its early 20s seems more emancipated.

Some women get pestered, others don't, and pestering seems to be more related to how you hold yourself, than your clothes. Main pestering areas will be souks and town centres. Dress modestly, the less bare flesh the better (although young Tunisian women seem to follow the tightest fashions). Certain nationalities seem to cope better with ridiculous macho egos – Italians, for example. Steadfastly ignore rude and suggestive comments directed at you but aimed at boosting the caller's ego, avoid any behaviour which would aggravate the situation, and keep a sense of humour. Shout only *in extremis* (they can always shout louder). Remember that Tunisian towns are small places, and everyone who works in the souk knows everyone else, at least by sight. Single young men often attract greater attention from customs officials and are more liable to receive propositions of various kinds.

One way of preventing hassle in towns is to dress smartly, look confident, busy, and as though you know where you are going. Depending on your age, this may make pesterers think twice – is this person with an official delegation, do they have a Tunisian husband? Observe what smart Tunisian women wear. Women from fairly traditional families may wear longish skirts, others opt for expensive sunglasses.

Obviously, you will want to strike up some acquaintances. Women students waiting (say) at a louage stop or in your train compartment will probably be delighted to have a chance to practise their English on a native speaker – as long as you don't look too outlandish by their dress standards. Remember, a lot of importance is given to looking clean and presentable in Tunisia. Many Tunisians of limited means have to make great efforts to do this, and an unkempt European is a bit like an extra-terrestrial to them, the object of all kinds of prejudices, and not worthy of a great deal of respect.

One way to deal with the pestering male is to develop a schoolmarmish manner. Modestly dressed, you are interested in ancient ruins, architecture, birds, women's issues, economics, you are very serious person. This may put your pesterer off – or lead to some interesting conversation. Then you can lighten up if you get on with the person. And then they might show you areas of their town which you would otherwise miss.

Role playing can be tedious, however. In the final analysis, the twin concepts of *hishma* (shame) and *ihtiram* (respect) go a long way. You may get rid of a consistent pesterer by saying *haram alayk* ('shame on you') or *ma tehshemsh* ('have you no shame'). A Tunisian woman might have to give you lessons in saying these phrases with appropriate disdain.

Where to stay

There is a very wide range of accommodation in Tunisia. In the major cities and the popular tourist resorts, the top quality hotel chains are represented. The best offer top class accommodation with the full range of personal and business facilities while the cheapest are spartan and on occasion, somewhat sordid. While the Tunisian hotel industry is well organized, travellers in Libya will experience greater problems in finding a place to lay their head.

Accommodation is represented on the town maps with a symbol: ■

Essentials

Hotels

Tunisia has a good spread of hotels. At the top end of the range, prices are on a par with Europe, though the service is often poor. There are no really classy hotels, though many of the new hotels in the 5 star category are truly glitzy. There are a lot of standard 3 star and 4 star beachside hotels, all offering more or less the same facilities. In comparison with Europe, prices for these medium range hotels are very reasonable if bought as part of a package. In almost every case, the advertised room price, that charged to the individual traveller, is higher than that paid by the package tourist and it may be worth bargaining. Out of season, prices in this category are very reasonable indeed. The disadvantage for the budget traveller is that they are often in *zones touristiques*, a long way from bus and louage stations.

At the cheaper end of the scale, standards are variable. For around 30Dt a night, you can find a very reasonable room indeed, with en suite bath in a city centre. At the 20Dt a night mark, accommodation will be of a perfectly reasonable standard too. Around 10Dt a night, there will be variations in standards.

The Tunisian hotel industry looks set to undergo some major changes. The big German tour operators are now actually building hotels (whereas before they would buy a certain percentage of beds for a season). At the moment, the vast majority of beach hotels, though efficient, are large and impersonal, and facilities (gym, pool, etc) are often on the small side. Service is not very accommodating, on the whole. Changes in legislation will allow small up-market hotels and family-run guesthouses to open, satisfying a definite demand in the market.

Many resort tourists spend very little time outside the hotel. To compensate selling-off vast numbers of bed nights at cheap rates, hotels tend to charge heavily for drinks and extras. Don't forget your bottle of duty-free gin.

Camping

Campsites are not widespread in Tunisia. At the remoter beaches, poorer Tunisians from inland areas will set up small tents to camp for a few days in summer. Hygiene in such places is rudimentary, however. On main beaches, there will be a Garde Nationale or Police post who will move campers on. Camping is only really an option in remote locations – and you will have to watch your documents, which may be stolen from under your sleeping head. Basically, you are better to go for the security of staying in a cheap hotel. If you do opt to camp, assess the security of any site you choose and where possible ask permission from the local farm to avoid any unpleasantness.

Out of summer, it may be possible to set up a camping trip with a nomad and a couple of camels into the desert from Douz or Zaâfrane. Ask around at travel agents in Douz or at the all-purpose grocers in Zaâfrane. Bring a good warm sleeping bag, if possible, although trip organizers will probably have plenty of blankets.

Youth hostels (Auberges de Jeunesse)

These are found in Tunisia as part of the International Youth Hostel Federation. They differ according to location and size, provide a common room, sleeping provision in dormitories, a self-catering kitchen and often budget meals. There is no maximum age limit, persons under 15 should be accompanied by an adult and in some hostels only male guests are accepted. Permission is necessary to stay more than 3 days in one hostel. Most hostels are open 1000-1200 and 1700-2200. Note that only a handful of

☞ **Hotel ratings**

For a quick-reference hotel price guide, see the inside front cover of the book

The 6 categories used here are graded as accurately as possible by cost converted to American dollars. Our hotel price range is based on a double room with bath/shower in high season and includes any relevant taxes and service charges but no meals. Normally the following facilities will be available and are therefore not repeated in the descriptions.

AL US$90+ This is an international class luxury hotel as found in the capital, large cities and major tourist centres. Good management ensures that all facilities for business and leisure travellers are of the highest international standard. In Tunis, hotels in this category include the Abou Nawas.

A US$70 to $90. A hotel with choice of restaurants, coffee shop, shops, bank, travel agent, swimming pool, some business facilities, some sports facilities, air conditioned rooms with WC, bath/shower, TV, phone, mini-bar, daily clean linen.

B US$50 to $69. Offers most of the facilities in **A** but without the luxury,
reduced number of restaurants, smaller rooms, limited range of shops and sport. Offers pool and air conditioned rooms with WC, shower/bath.

C US$30 to $49. These are the best medium range hotels found in the smaller towns and less popular areas of larger cities. Usually comfortable, bank, shop, pool. Best rooms have air conditioning, own bath/shower and WC.

D US$20 to $29. Might be the best you can find in a small town. Best rooms may have own WC and bath/shower. Depending on management will have room service and choice of cuisine in restaurant.

E US$10 to $19. Simple provision. Perhaps fan cooler. May not have restaurant. Shared WC and showers with hot water (when available).

F under US$10. Very basic, shared toilet facilities, variable in cleanliness, noise, often in dubious locations.

Ungraded hotels – too primitive to reach the standard of **F** – but may be cleaner and more interesting than **F**.

hostels are actually run by the Tunisian Youth Hostels Association (médina of Tunis hostel on rue Saïda Ajoula, Houmt Souk, Rmel south of Bizerte). The catch is of course that the hostels are closed during the day, and in summer you may very well want to siesta in the afternoon. Thus a cheap hotel may be a better option for part of your trip. Many of the hostels are often not any cheaper than hotels.

Getting around

Details of local transport are listed in the 'Essentials, Transport' sections of individual towns. Information about getting to and around a town is given in the 'Ins and outs' sections at the beginning of a town's listing

Tunisia is a small country, well served by public transport. Links between all major towns are good, and the longest distance, Tunis to Djerba, can be done by air as well as by road. Roads are being steadily improved. For those without a hire car, visiting remote archaeological sites can be time consuming, with much time waiting for appropriate connecting transport.

Air

Tuninter flights link Tunis with Djerba, Sfax, and Tozeur, and run to published but infinitely variable schedules. Late 1999 sample flight prices: Tunis to Djerba 55Dt 1-way, 90Dt return.

Road

Conditions vary from excellent dual carriageways to rural roads (unnervingly one-vehicle wide) and far-flung rough, unsurfaced *piste*. Problems can include very occasional blockage by snow in winter in the northwest, flash floods in spring, especially in the central regions, and sand at any time in the far south.

Bus

Buses, the main and cheapest means of transport, link nearly all the towns. Air-conditioned coaches connect the biggest cities and keep more strictly to the timetable. Smaller private vehicles require greater patience and often work on the 'leave when full' principle. Book in advance wherever possible. Orderly queues become a jostling mass when the bus arrives. Town buses are usually crowded and getting off can be more difficult than getting on. Sorting out the routes and the fares makes taking a louage taxi a better option between towns. Tunis is the only town of any real size where you will need to get between sightseeing areas – use the metro or a taxi for getting out to the Bardo Museum rather than the bus.

There are overnight buses from Tunis – Bab Alioua station for distant southern destinations, information on T01-399255. (**NB** Bab Alioua is also referred to as Bab El Fella.) The schedule can also be found on the general information page at the back of *La Presse* newspaper. Look for the box marked *SNTRI – lignes nocturnes*.

Louage (inter-city taxis)

The larger, long distance taxis are good value, sometimes following routes not covered by service buses and almost always more frequent. They run on the 'leave when full' principle and for more space or a quicker departure the unoccupied seats can be purchased. In general, these taxis are 25 percent more expensive than the bus.

	Zarzis	Zaghouan	Tunis	Tabarka	Sousse	Siliana	Sidi Bou Saïd	Sfax	Remada	Nefta	Nabeul	Medenine	Mahdia	Le Kef	Kasserine	Kairouan	Jendouba	Houmt Souk	Gafsa	Gabès	Tataouine	Douz	Bizerte	Ben Gardane
Zaghouan	490																							
Tunis	544	57																						
Tabarka	631	188	175																					
Sousse	401	89	143	261																				
Siliana	417	70	127	160	196																			
Sidi Bou Saïd	382	237	283	301	187	172																		
Sfax	274	216	270	387	127	275	121																	
Remada	189	552	609	727	466	614	422	339																
Nefta	400	434	459	463	372	383	214	306	465															
Nabeul	497	66	67	242	96	192	244	223	562	429														
Medenine	62	428	482	569	339	355	218	212	127	338	435													
Mahdia	378	151	205	223	62	258	249	104	443	410	158	316												
Le Kef	585	154	171	121	232	106	173	278	650	342	238	523	294											
Kasserine	390	264	198	241	202	167	87	192	455	222	259	328	264	120										
Kairouan	410	119	153	251	57	139	130	136	258	315	114	348	119	175	114									
Jendouba	613	166	154	65	260	134	236	339	678	398	221	551	322	56	176	203								
Houmt Souk	52	497	506	623	363	511	344	236	196	362	459	69	340	547	352	372	575							
Gafsa	284	318	343	347	256	267	98	190	324	116	313	222	294	226	106	199	282	667						
Gabès	138	352	406	493	263	411	244	136	203	241	359	76	240	447	252	272	428	521	146					
Tataouine	111	474	531	649	388	536	369	261	78	387	484	49	450	572	377	397	600	396	271	125				
Douz	287	463	488	492	401	412	243	285	352	146	458	225	439	371	397	344	427	670	145	149	274			
Bizerte	609	122	65	136	208	192	348	335	674	524	132	547	270	212	332	218	156	992	408	471	596	553		
Ben Gardane	46	505	559	646	416	432	397	435	169	415	512	77	539	600	405	571	581	487	299	153	91	302	624	
Béja	591	117	105	71	190	183	285	317	656	447	172	529	252	105	225	180	49	974	246	453	578	391	107	606

Tunisia - Road distances in km

Louages leave from special stations, often near the main bus stations. These range from the organized (the big Moncef Bey converted warehouse station in Tunis) to just a stretch of open ground near a village centre. Inter-city louages are white with a red stripe, while local louages are white with blue stripe. The range of vehicles is wide, including large Peugeots and Renaults and various forms of mini-van. In the country areas, the louage vans are referred to as *el nakl el rifi*, 'rural transport'.

The disadvantage of louages is their suicidal speed. Drivers obviously try to fit in as many runs a day as possible, and drive like the clappers to do this. You may prefer to travel more sedately by train or bus. Always try to find a safety belt as you take your seat. Inner city taxis are bilious yellow in colour and always have a working meter. They cannot be shared. Seat belts are compulsory for front-seat passengers

Car hire & driving conditions A number of car hire companies have offices at the main airports, and cars can generally be picked up on arrival. They are not cheap and the condition of the vehicles often leaves much to be desired. Cheapest vehicles are Fiat Uno, Opel Corsa or Peugeot 205. When you take a car, make sure that you check the tyres – the front tyres must not be too worn. Check also that there is a spare tyre. This should be kept preferably in the boot, or padlocked under the car, as it may well be stolen if left unpadlocked. Seat belts are compulsory in the front.

Driving conditions Drivers from northern Europe generally take a while to get used to the driving style and road conditions in Tunisia. Bearing the following points in mind will help avoid potential accidents (UK drivers note that driving is on the right).

Tunis transport

Not to scale

Essentials

Tolls for the Tunis-M'saken Autoroute

	Toll site	(Dt)
Tolls are charged for vehicles using the autoroute at Mornag, Hergla and Sousse and at the exits for Bouficha (Km 65), Enfidha (Km 90) and Hergla (Km 101). Toll rates in 1999 were set at:	Mornag	1.000
	Hergla exit	1.400
	Sousse exit	.400
	Travellers can buy magnetic pre-payment cards from Tunisie autoroutes.	

Autoroute There is 1 stretch of motorway (tolls payable) from Tunis to M'saken, just south of Sousse. The northern section is dual carriageway, the southern section 3 lane. (Works on the Tunis to Bizerte autoroute are set to start soon.) Driving on the autoroute is dangerous due to the mix of vehicles. Problems arise when overpowered saloon car driven at high speed by some wide boy meets slow moving pick-up truck. Look out for louage taxis coming up behind you, flashing their headlights at high speed as well. Particularly dangerous times are Sunday evening when Tunis residents head back northwards after their weekend in Sousse or elsewhere. The Hammamet to Tunis stretch gets very crowded at the start of the weekend as well. Keep your temper at all costs.

Country roads Across Tunisia, country roads have been improved enormously since 1990. Nevertheless, many roads are narrow, and in places, you may be forced onto the hard shoulder (such as it is) by a speeding oncoming lorry. There may well be a tyre-splitting drop from tarmac to hard shoulder. Moped riders are also dangerous in country areas, and may swerve, brake or take unexpected turns without warning. Overtake or keep your distance. Driving in the early evening is also fraught with danger. Slow-moving agricultural vehicles, tractors with loaded trailers – and no lights – pull out onto the narrow roads without warning. Mopeds and bicycles generally seem to have no lights. Have your front seat passenger keep an eye out as well.

Urban driving This is problematic, too, even though speeds are not high. Traffic jostles for position at the lights (always respected), and procedure on roundabouts, if there are no lights, is different from the UK. You drive straight onto the roundabout, and then slow, allowing traffic coming from the right to come on. When all is clear, you move on round.

In urban areas the speed limit is 50kph and is to be observed. There are speed patrols at key points. You may well be able to talk your way out of a fine. Stop signs are also to be respected. When at a stop sign, make sure you stop, or the police officer waiting behind a nearby eucalyptus tree will have reason to ask for your papers.

In practice, pedestrians in most urban areas have a calming effect on traffic. People walk in the road, pavement or no pavement, and mothers seem to use their prams to test oncoming traffic's willingness to slow down. (One Tunis wag proposed that pedestrians pay road tax, too.) For the foreign driver, drive more carefully than you would normally, paying great attention to bicycles, mopeds and pedestrians.

This is really only a consideration in outlying places not served by the very cheap public transport. Here, eventually, a place on a truck or lorry will be available, for which a charge is made.

Hitchhiking

Train

The *SNCFT* (Société Nationale des Chemins de Fer Tunisiens) is the national rail company. The information line at Tunis' main station is T01-345511, then press 13 after the recorded message in French and Arabic. There is an information window in Tunis main station. Trains have 3 classes: *confort*, 1st and 2nd. *Confort* has air-conditioning

Timetable of Sahel Metro

Sousse Bab Djedid	0605	0655	0745	0825	0900	1000	1125		1220
Sousse Sud	0613	0703	0753	0833	0908	1008	1133		1228
Sahline Sebkha	0622	0712	0802	0842	0917	1017	1142		1237
The Hotels	0625	0715	0805	0845	0920	1020	1145		1240
Airport	0617	0717	0817	0901	0932	1036	1147		1242
Monastir	0641	0727	0817	0901	0932	1036	1157	1220	1252
Moknine	0710			0930		1105		1248	
Bekalta	0721			0938		1113			
Mahdia Tourist Zone	0728			0945					
Mahdia	0740			0957		1132			

Mahdia		0500	0550	0625		0700	0750		1020
Mahdia Tourist Zone			0602	0639		0712			1032
Bekalta		0520	0610	0647		0720	0810		1040
Moknine		0528	0618	0657		0728	0818		1048
Monastir		0600	0650	0734	0740	0806	0850	1000	1120
Airport		0610	0700		0750	0816	0900	1010	1130
The Hotels		0612	0702		0752	0818	0902	1012	1132
Sahline Sebkha		0615	0705		0755	0821	0905	1015	1135
Sousse Sud	1545	0625	1715		0805	0834	0915	1025	1145
Sousse Bab Djedid	0552	0632	0722		0812	0841	0922	1032	1152

and big armchairs. Cheaper carriages can be crowded and dirty. The trains have a buffet trolley selling drinks, biscuits and sandwiches. For air-conditioned trains, try to get your ticket in advance. Extra trains are laid on for Ramadhan and public holidays.

Local rail transport includes the TGM (Tunis-Goulette-La Marsa) light railway (see map in Tunis transport section), the Tunis to Borj Cedria suburban line (*ligne de banlieue*) via Hammam Lif, and the Sahel light railway running from Sousse to Mahdia via Monastir. For long distance travel, there are 2 lines with plenty of passenger trains, the Tunis to Bizerte line, via Mateur, and the Tunis to Metlaoui line, via Sousse, Sfax and Gabès. Sadly, the line to Tabarka has been pulled up. There is a Tunis to Nabeul service, via Bir Bou Regba and Hammamet. For those wishing to head west, there is 1 passenger train a day to Kalaâ Khasba at 0600, and a Tunis to Ghardimaou service 5 times a day via Béja. Rail travel to Algeria is not an option at the moment.

Sample single fares in summer 1999 were as follows: Tunis to Bizerte, 2nd class 2Dt 500; Tunis to Sousse, 5Dt 2nd class, 6Dt 800 *confort*; Tunis to Metlaoui, 2nd class 12Dt 250, *confort* 16Dt 500; Tunis to Ghardimaou, 6Dt 700 2nd class; Tunis to Kalaâ Khasba 6Dt 700. Sample journey times are as follows: Tunis to Bizerte, 1 hour 40 minutes; Tunis to Ghardimaou, 2 hours 50 minutes. Tunis to Sousse, 2 hours 20 minutes, Tunis to El Jem, 3 hours, Tunis to Gabès 4 hours 50 minutes, Tunis to Kalaâ Khasba 5 hours. The night train from Tunis to Metlaoui takes 8 hours 20 minutes.

In summer 1999, the SNCFT had a special 'rail and museums' pass on sale. The rail pass, 2nd class 28Dt, *confort* 38Dt, gives you a week's unlimited rail travel and free access to museums and sites managed by the ANEP, Tunisia's national heritage agency.

A word of warning regarding the main southern line. The names of the smaller stations are only given on the actual station building, and not on the platform. To be quite sure you know when you reach your destination, keep an eye out and sit near the front of the train – or ask. The public address system is only used for major stations, Arabic announcement first, French following.

1315	1400	1500	1615		1720		1825	1910	2015
1323	1408	1508	1623		1728		1833	1918	2021
1332	1417	1517	1632		1737		1842	1927	
1335	1420	1520	1623		1740		1845	1930	
1337	1422	1522	1637		1742		1847	1932	
1351	1432	1536	1651	1720	1752	1815	1901	1946	
1420		1605	1720	1752		1844	1930	2015	
1428		1613	1731	1802		1852	1938	2023	
1435				1809		1859			
1447		1632	1750	1823		1911	1957	2042	

trains run every day except Sundays and holidays

connects with trains on Tunis-Gabès line

			1315		1515		1710	1830	
							1722		
			1335		1537		1730	1853	
		1315	1343		1545		1738	1901	
1215	1310	1343	1415	1520	1617	1715	1810	1933	
1225	1320		1425	1530	1627	1725	1820	1943	
1227	1322		1427	1532	1629	1727	1822	1945	
1230	1325		1430	1535	1632	1730	1825	1948	
1240	1335		1440	1545	1642	1740	1835	1958	
1247	1342		1447	1552	1649	1747	1842	2005	

Essentials

Keeping in touch

Arabic is the official language in Tunisia. The language has a formal, written form derived from the Arabic of the religious texts, and a spoken form. The two differ almost as much as medieval English and modern English. French is widely spoken in Tunisia, especially in the north and the eastern coastal towns. The spread of education and in particular access to satellite television mean that the language is widely understood at a basic level, even if it is not spoken. Older people will know very little French. Many Tunisians understand some Italian, a legacy of the days when the only foreign TV channel available was RAI Uno, and English and German are widely understood as well, in particular in tourist areas. Germany generally provides Tunisia with the largest foreign visitor contingent. Hotel staff are generally proficient in English, French and German. Do not expect too much, however, and be prepared to communicate in a mixture of broken French and English. Tunisians have no problems with this – Franco-Arabe, a sort of mixed language where educated speakers happily switch back and forth between French and Arabic, is the local answer to language needs in many situations. Throwing in the odd word you've picked up in Tunisian can help communication along, too.

Language

For a list of useful Arabic words, see the inside back cover and the Footnotes section page 541

Among the main newspapers are *Le Temps*, *Le Renouveau* and *La Presse*, all of which have sister papers in Arabic. *Le Renouveau* is the official organ of the ruling RCD, and thus can, on occasion, be quite critical in tone. *La Presse* carries a lot of advertising, a reflection of Tunisia's current consumer boom. It is good for sports coverage, and has back pages which carry lots of useful information (plane arrival and departure times for Tunis-Carthage airport, late night bus times, ads for Tunis restaurants). On Mondays, *La Presse* has a *page littéraire*, occasionally quite interesting. The arts coverage is hopeless, there are rarely previews of concerts and exhibitions, and no listings to speak of. In English, there is the weekly newspaper *Tunisia News*, a dull publication which does, however, have some good arts coverage. For those who read Arabic, *Ech Chorouk* will keep you up to date with the doings of Tunisia's footballers and singers.

Media

If they haven't got a satellite dish, Tunisians have the choice of the main Tunis Channel 7 (in Arabic), which broadcasts news, Egyptian films and soap operas, sporting events and documentaries dubbed into Arabic. Locally produced material is limited to a Saturday night variety show, *Mindhar* (a current affairs programme), and the Ramadhan soap opera. Tunisians also have Rai Uno, the main Italian channel, and France 2, much watched for news and current affairs, which is rebroadcast in Tunisia. For a couple of hours in the early evening, France 2 broadcasts are replaced by the local youth channel, which does worthy quiz shows and a pop programme. There is a French-language pay channel, Canal Horizons, an off-shoot of Canal Plus, popular for sport in cafés.

Tunisians' desire for entertainment has meant that satellite TV is considered essential by most households. Even in poor neighbourhoods, satellite dishes can be seen everywhere. Popular channels include the Egyptian and French channels along with *Al Jazeera*, a Qatari-based news and current affairs channel which started up when the BBC Arabic TV-service closed. *Arte*, the Franco-German arts channel has a loyal following.

There is a daily hour of English-language radio on RTCI, Radio Tunis Chaine Internationale, the local FM station, which also broadcasts in French, German, Italian and Spanish. There are no independent radio stations.

Post

Local post offices are listed in the directory under individual towns

Stamps are available from post offices (PTT) and from certain news stands and hotel shops. A letter to the Arab states costs 250 millimes, Europe 500 millimes, and to the USA 600 millimes. There is no printed paper rate.

There is a Rapide Poste service, with offices at the airport, the central PTT and El Manar neighbourhood of Tunis. Rapide Poste has links with DHL and other international express mail services. Unfortunately, it is not much quicker than ordinary mail, and not always terribly reliable. The El Manar office stays open late.

Telephones

For a quick guide to local area codes, see the inside front cover of the book

The international dialling code for Tunisia is 216. Tunisie Télécom is the national service provider. Telephone numbers in Tunisia are 6 figures, and are expressed as whole numbers either in 2 blocks of 3, or 3 blocks of 2. Say 0 as *zéro*. Regional dialling codes are 0 plus figure, ie 01, *zéro un*, for Tunis region. For international access, dial 00 plus country code. Directory enquiries is *les renseignements*, dial 120 for business numbers, 121 for personal numbers. The telephone directory is *l'annuaire*, yellow pages, *les pages jaunes*.

The best way to make an international call is from one of the ubiquitous *taxiphones*, as the public call centres are called. Calling from your hotel will be expensive. Taxiphones can be found in the centre of all major towns. Take plenty of 1Dt coins if it is an international call. There may be certain cabins or phones reserved for international calls, *appels internationaux*. The international operator is available on 17, the *service des dérangements* is 11. If you want to reverse the charges, this is *un appel en PCV*, currently not possible with the USA.

Phoning a business, you will probably start by getting through to their switchboard (*le standard*). If you want a given extension number, you ask (for example) for *poste numéro xx*. Make sure you can say the numbers in French.

If you want to send a fax, many taxiphones have fax machines where you can receive and send faxes. Note that they are obliged to make a note of your passport/identity card details before they send your fax.

Internet

For the time being, internet access is extremely limited in Tunisia. Compared with Morocco, for example, there are few cybercafés. In the greater Tunis area, there are 4 *publinets* where you can get on line (in the Ariana, El Manar, Sidi Daoud and Carthage). In downtown Tunis, the easiest solution is to go to the British Council library at Porte de France (old town end of Av Bourguiba), where you can get on line for 3Dt an hour. Certain freemails, notably Hotmail, do not work in Tunisia.

Ariana Publinet next to the Tunisie Telecom building on the main street in Ariana. **NB** Greater Tunis cybercafés 'publinet'
you cannot download files from floppy disk here. **El Manar** Take a taxi for the Centre
Makni, El Manar, a large mall development in north Tunis. 100m before the Centre Makni,
you have a small down-at-heel shopping centre on your right. Go into the central
courtyard. The cybercentre is in small ground floor premises. **Sidi Daoud** Take the Tunis
to La Marsa highway, turn right at the Sidi Daoud turn-off which takes you to Carthage.
The cybercentre is on your left, after 200m, in a converted garage in an undistinguished
line of one storey houses and shops. **Carthage** Cybernet Jean Jaurès, in the centre of
Carthage near the République metro station.

Food and drink

Outside the hotels, Tunisian restaurant food is generally good, quite varied and by
Western European standards, very reasonable in price. (Meals in the 3 star hotels tend
to have a canteen-like quality.) Most local products are fresh and good quality. Food is
cooked with spices but is rarely *piquant*.

In most main towns you will find some very good restaurants indeed, offering a mixed Types of restaurant
Tuniso-Franco-Italian cuisine. Among the top restaurants in this category you have
L'Astragale in the Cité Jardin, Tunis, and *Le Golfe*, at La Marsa. Somewhat cheaper, but
very good value, is *Le Tchevap* at Carthage and *Le Bon Vieux Temps* in Sidi Bou Saïd. A
fairly recent trend in the Tunisian restaurant industry is the 'old Tunis' style restaurant,
of which the best example is *Dar Jeld*, at the Kasbah, Tunis. You might also try a cabaret
restaurant – for example *El Mawel*, in Cité Jardin, Tunis – where there will be a loud
oriental band and a dancer. Be warned, these places, on account of the *spectacle*, are
not cheap.

Along the coast and on the islands, there are some good fish restaurants. Fish in
these eateries is generally sold by the 100 gram. The fish is weighed for you – there is
no embarrassment about asking how much it will cost. If it's too pricey, then have
complet poisson, a fish steak or small fish with chips and a fried vegetable and egg
tastira. Among the better restaurants with fish on the menu are *Les Ombrelles* in
Gammarth and *Le Daurade* at Haouaria.

The small restaurants without alcohol are cheaper. Restaurants with alcohol are
more expensive, even though the quality of the food and service is not necessarily
better. You will also find some reasonably priced restaurants with alcohol (*Le Cosmos*
and *Tantonville* in downtown Tunis or *El Farik* at Monastir). Prices are almost always
indicated on the menu. As anywhere, be sure to check before you order. Few but the
most upmarket restaurants take international credit cards. Few restaurants cater for
vegetarians. Quality of service varies enormously, verging on the pompous in the
'heritage restaurants', unpredictable elsewhere. The best service is often in the small
places, and can improve if you become a regular.

If you want a quick meal, Tunisia's cities have plenty of snack-restaurants where you
can get a sandwich (*cassecroute*), a slice of pizza or a savoury doughnut (*ftira*).
Sandwiches may be made in half a baguette or in *khubz tabouna*, round flat bread.
Tuna and cheese is a popular combination, and *escalope de dinde* (turkey escalope) or
salami de dinde are often on offer. Sandwiches are garnished with spoonfuls of various
salads, and olives – mind your teeth on the stones.

If you are a vegetarian, you will probably be eating lots from this section. Without meat Tunisian starters
is *sans viande/bilesh leham*. *Chorba* (highly flavoured soup, tomato and oil base.) *Brik*
(deep-fried pastry containing egg and generally tuna, possibly potato and parsley, or
even cheese. If you want your brik without tuna, say *sans thon/bilesh tun*.) *Salade
d'aubergines/Salata bitenjal* (grilled aubergines, finely chopped to a near paste-like

Golden oil

In the second and third centuries AD, while under Roman rule, the cultivation of the olive tree (oleo europeae sylvestris) spread through North Africa from Morocco to Libya. Oil 'factories' and stone olive presses can still be seen at certain Roman sites – for instance Sbeïtla.

In fact the method of harvesting and production has not essentially changed. Hitting the trees with sticks to make the fruit fall is harmful, and reminders are given on television at the harvest season. Tree-abuse harms the olives, letting in the air; the resultant oxidization reduces quality. The harvested berries are washed in tepid water then crushed. The oil is separated from the water by centrifuge, filtered, kept at a regulated temperature in airtight steel vats, then bottled. The older method incorporates rotating stone grinders, the resulting paste being fashioned into rings on esparto grass mats which are then squeezed by an animal turning the screw tighter and tighter. The resulting oils, dark and thick, are then purified.

In modern olive cultivation on the plains the trees are planted 10 metres x 10 metres apart, leaving room for machinery and yields reach 50 kilograms per tree. Traditional methods produce 15-20 kilograms per tree.

Around 90 percent of olive trees are in the Mediterranean Basin, leading oil-producers being Spain, Italy, Greece and Tunisia. Some of the finest table olives come from the Meknès region of Morocco. Tuscany considers itself to produce the best oil, Greece prides itself on Kalamat oil from the southern Peloponnese. Some oil is a clear yellow, some is thick and golden like honey. In some countries, they prefer to produce a more bitter oil.

In the 1980s, northern Europe woke up to the fact that olive oil, with its low cholesterol content, is good for the health, and bottles of the precious liquid marked 'extra-virgin' appeared on supermarket shelves. (Since when was anything, or anyone, been 'extra-virgin'?) It may be, however, that long, slow Mediterreanean lunches and siestas are indispensable to an olive oil-based diet, too.

---

consistency, served chilled with olive oil, lemon juice, and capers. Rare in restaurants.) *Salade méchouia* (finely chopped, mixed grilled vegetables, decorated with tuna and egg, can be very *piquant*, served cold.) *Salade tunisienne* (a variant of the *salade niçoise* with tomatoes, onions, green peppers, sometimes cucumber, and the usual tuna and egg garnish.) *Ummek Houriya* (carrots boiled with some peeled garlic, mashed to a paste and seasoned with olive oil, a little vinegar, *harissa* and black pepper, served chilled and garnished with capers. Rare in restaurants.)

Snack foods These are generally found in working men's eateries or in souk areas. *Hergma* (a strong soup made from sheep or goats feet, chopped and boiled at great length.) *Lablabi* (a hearty soup of chick peas, served at any time of the day. Originally a dish of the poor, it is especially popular in winter.)

Typical main dishes **Egg dishes** *Chakchouka* (ratatouille with tomatoes, peppers, garlic and onions, egg is added at the end of the process.) *Keftaji* (fried onions, pumpkin, tomatoes, peppers and eggs, served all chopped up either with meat balls (*ka'abir*) or maybe fried liver.) *Tajine* (a form of quiche, with meat and vegetables, cooked in the oven. Varieties include *tajine ma'kouda*, which contains broad-leaved parsley, potato, and peas, and is sometimes flavoured with smoked herring (*renga*), and *tajine malsouka*, which is egg and chicken between layers of filo pastry.) **Meat dishes** *Couscous* (steamed coarse semolina or millet served with vegetables and meat or fish. Typical dish eaten throughout the Maghreb. The Tunisian version has a tomato sauce, unlike the Algerian and Moroccan versions, where the sauce is served separately. The buttermilk, now sold in cartons which accompanies a good couscous is called *leben*.) *Kamounia* (a slowly cooked meat stew, strongly flavoured with cumin, a delight to find on the menu.) *Koucha* (roast lamb with potatoes and peppers cooked in the oven, excellent.) *Loubiya* (stewed mutton with white beans.) *Marcassin* (meat of the wild boar piglet, the only pork you are likely to find in this Muslim country, very strong flavour and served with a rich gravy. Pork is called *hallouf*, which is also slang for a 'tricky' person.) *Mechoui* (grilled meat (usually lamb), served with a small dish of harissa and olive oil.) *Merguez* (small spicy mutton or beef sausages, generally grilled, the red colour gives an indication of the amount of chilli used in their preparation, and is a guide to how fiery they will be.)

Fish

The best are the *rouget* (red mullet), *mulet* (mullet), *mérou* (cod), *loup de mer* (perch) and sole. You can have your fish *grillé* (barbecued) or *frit* (fried). *Crevettes royales* and *homard* (lobster) are also very good, especially at Tabarka off the rocky northern coast. *Kabkabou* is oven-baked fish with saffron, preserved lemons and vegetables.

Ingredients

The cooks of Tunisia have a wonderful selection of field-fresh ingredients to choose from. Vegetables and fruit are of a quality rarely equalled in northern Europe and North America. There are a number of typical pickles and ingredients used in Tunisian dishes: *akhchef* (preserved quince slices); *bnadak* (meat balls, spiced with dried mint, boiled in oil to preserve them); *filfil barr l'abid* (tiny red peppers used to decorate food amd eaten to stimulate the appetite); *filfil m'sayer* (large green peppers, pickled whole); *harissa* (a thick piquant paste, used to give flavour to all sorts of dishes, and given as a dip at restaurants before the starters arrive, best *harissa 'arbi* ('home-made harissa') comes from Nabeul, too much is best countered by eating bread rather than drinking water); *harous* (similar to salade méchouia, but contains green pepper only); *imalah* (crinkle-cut carrots, cauliflower and turnips preserved in brine, also given as a salty opener to a meal along with harissa); *limoun* (preserved lemons, used in fish dishes and occasionally salads); *turshi* (thin slices of pickled turnip, given as an appetizer).

Desserts

Like all Mediterranean countries, Tunisia has many varieties of dessert, all very sweet and sticky. The Ottoman influence is clear. If you go to a Tunisian wedding, then you will almost certainly get the chance to try some of the many varieties of *helw*, small sweet cakes: *baklawa* (puff pastry with lots of honey and nuts); *bjaouia* (sort of cake combining almonds, pistachio nuts and puffed); *loukoum* (Turkish delight); *makroudh* (semolina cake with crushed dates, baked in oil and dipped in honey); *masfouf* (a dessert made from fine semolina flour served with dates, raisins, pistachio nuts and pine nuts, a meal in itself and particularly appreciated for the *suhour*, the early morning Ramadhan meal taken before fasting begins); *m'lebbes* or *calissons de Sfax* (round sweets made of sweetened ground almonds covered in white icing sugar).

Fruit

Dates (Arabic: *degla*)– the season for fresh dates is October. There are over 100 types but the best, the deglet nur, come from the desert oases, particularly Tozeur and Nefta. *Pastèque* – watermelon, particularly refreshing in summer. *Grenade* (Arabic: *rumène*) – pomegranates, served with sugar and sprinkled with jasmine flavoured water.

Drink

The national drink is **tea**, which comes as *tay akhdhar/thé vert* (green tea) and *tay ahmar/thé rouge*, a dark sugar-saturated brew. **Coffee** is also widely drunk, and is as cheap as tea, between 300 and 800 millimes, for an *express*, depending on the type of café. The most common and cheapest **beer** is Celtia (a Tunisian make) but Tunisian-made Tuborg and Stella, as well as imported beers, can be found. Celtia *pression* (keg) can be found in some bars.

Wine

The Tunisians have been making wine for over 2,000 years. Wines sold under certificate are under the strict control of the state. The **red wines** are more acidic than

Essentials

👉 Tunisian desserts

Stuffed dates

Split the date across the top and remove the stone. Fill the space with ground almond paste or pistachio nut paste. Dip each stuffed date in a thick sugar syrup and roll in granulated sugar. Allow these to dry (overnight) before serving.

Samsa

For these you require sheets of malsouqua *cut in half.*
For the filling:
500g finely crushed almonds (hazelnuts will do)
1 tablespoon dried grated orange peel
250g of granulated sugar
lemon juice/rose water
Form small triangles round a spoonful of filling and fry in very hot oil until golden

brown. Soak in thick sugar syrup and sprinkle with roasted sesame seeds.

Date maqroudh

For the base, mix a thick semolina dough using medium grain flour, baking soda, warm water and a pinch of salt. While it rises make the purée filling using pitted dates, ground cinnamon, olive oil and fresh grated orange rind. Roll and cut the dough into strips 7-8 centimetres wide and 1-2 centimetres thick, place the purée filling down the centre of each strip from end to end, fold the sides across the middle and press flat. Remove ragged edges and cut into maqroudh *diamond shapes. Bake for 25 minutes in a hot oven and when cool soak for 2-3 minutes in a thick sugar syrup.*

Western palates are used to and vary in quality. It is difficult to recommend any particular wine: *Vieux Magon* is the expensive wine, but quality varies greatly. Rosés include: *Haut Mornag, Sidi Rais* and *Château Mornag*. The **white wines** are generally dry – try *Sidi Rais* or *Ugni Blanc*. Also worth a try are *Blanc de Blanc* and *Muscat sec de Kelibia*. Tunisian *vins gris* (light rosé) include *Gris de Tunisie* and *Gris de Bizerte*.

Other alcohol Tunisia also produces 3 types of very strong alcohol. *Boukha* is made from distilled figs, while *Thibarine* is a strong, sweet liqueur dreamed up by the White Fathers at their model farm at Thibar, near Dougga (hence the name). Both are available in special packaging at the airport duty-free. *Laghmi* is palm tree sap left to ferment for a while immediately after it is collected. Most imported alcohols are available generally in hotel bars, more rarely in city bars, and they are very expensive.

Bars & buying alcohol Outside restaurants, stores in the Monoprix, Touta and Magasin Général supermarket chains all have alcohol sections, often separated off from the main part of the supermarket. Older neighbourhoods may also have *débits d'alcohol* (off licences), which tend to be unmarked hole-in-the-wall type affairs. Bars tend to be very crowded and blokey. More upmarket bars are in very short supply, although there are one or two, including a pub with wooden panelling in a Sousse shopping mall (the *Rose and Crown* near the Maracana discothèque and the Hotel Taj Marhaba) and a German *brauhaus* in Hammamet on the main square. There is generally no pool or *flipper* (pinball) in bars. These can be found in *salles de jeux*, a separate affair altogether.

Soft drinks Both local and international soft drinks (*gazouz*) are widely available. Bottled water is very good and is offered, but not free, with all meals. The larger 1½ litre bottle costs about .700Dt. The smaller, resealable plastic bottles are just right for taking on short journeys. If you want fizzy (*gazeuse*) bottled water, the brand is *Garci*. *Boga* is the local lemonade, although *7-Up* is also available. *Boga Cidra* is a black fizzy drink made from carob beans. *Apla* and *Fruité* are fizzy fruit drinks, and in summer you could try *citronade*, freshly made from the huge lemons that Tunisia produces. (Note that citronade is not to be taken on hot bus journeys, as it goes off very quickly.)

Ancient foodies and the unswept room

From looking at the mosaics in museums across Tunisia, it is clear that inhabitants of Roman Africa liked a good meal. Food was a very popular theme, and the Greek term xenia *is used to designate food mosaics, veritable illustrated menus on the floor. The* xenia, *one of the ancestors of the painted still life, was developed by African mosaic artists to decorate the floors of the* triclinium *(the dining room) in private homes. Vitruvius describes* xenia *as being just like food, ready to be eaten. Dating mainly from the late second/early third century, these mosaics show us that Roman Africa was a place of plenty. Its people enjoyed eating goat, antelope, gazelle, wild boar, hare, and various farmyard birds. Animals are portrayed alive, sometimes tied-up, and also as dead game, straight from the larder. There are mosaics showing seafood – fish, crustaceans and shellfish, as well as fruit and vegetables, baskets of flowers, bowls and flasks. One of the famous El Djem* xenia *mosaics shows a wine bottle in a basketwork container and an elegant stemmed glass. No doubt these mosaics were the essential finishing touch for an upper-crust home, clear proof of the wealth and generosity of their proud owners.*

An unusual variation on the xenia *theme was the* asaroton, *'the unswept room'. In these mosaics, crumbs and bits of leftovers from a meal are portrayed scattered on the floor. So why have pictures of half-eaten food on your* triclinium *floor? Was there an obscure aesthetic taste for 'disorder', or did these mosaics have a magic force, ensuring continuity in the daily life of a home? We cannot know for certain. In the* triclinium *of the House of the Months at Thysdrus (El Jecu), there was an 'unswept' mosaic strip surrounding a central panel. Remains of chicken and fish, shellfish and crustaceans, eggshells, fruit peelings and wilted flowers are clearly visible.*

Cafés are an interesting experience. They are generally packed with men (no women) and intensely smokey and noisy. A good way to make contact with the locals is to try a *chicha* (waterpipe), the tobacco is slightly different from cigarette tobacco, and flavoured with honey or sometimes apples. Stronger than cigarettes (but not the local Crystal cigarettes) the chicha is nevertheless a good way to start up a conversation.

Shopping

Tunisia has some interesting craftwork, although not of the variety and quality to be found in somewhere like Morocco. (Your stay in Tunisia could be the time you give your plastic cards a rest.) Unfortunately, a lot of the more interesting, good value items are difficult to transport, (ie rush mats, wrought iron) or are very expensive – silk traditional garments, for example. There is lots of pottery to be bought, and the same items, mostly made in Nabeul, can be found in resorts right across the country. If you are looking for cheap presents, then there is a wealth of things to choose from. The tourist souks are now full of junk from as far afield as Egypt, India, Pakistan and West Africa – just take your pick. For more quality items, you need to go to more specialized shops such as the *Espace Driba* in La Marsa, *El Hanout* in Carthage or the *Ateliers Kène* near Bouficha, south of Hammamet.

Recommended local shops and bargains are listed under 'Shopping' in each town's Essentials section

There is a good variety of high quality Tunisian handmade carpets and a traditional handmade rug makes a fine memento of a visit to Tunisia. A better choice can be made with a little knowledge and by taking your time in choosing. Above all, if you do buy, make sure that you pick a rug that you like and can live with. Acquiring carpets as an investment is only for the experts.

Carpets

Buying carpets

You will need a fair amount of patience and humour when buying a carpet. First of all, before entering the bargaining process make sure that you know what you are looking for – be it rug, tapestry or carpet – and what size of carpet your rooms can accommodate (and you can comfortably carry with you out of Tunisia). Impulse buy if you want, but if you have a specific size and colour range in mind, make sure that the carpet dealer understands this. (If you read this before leaving home, a photo of the room to receive the precious carpet would be useful.) It might also be a good idea to take a local friend along, for an independent viewpoint, although don't expect all Tunisians to know about carpets and traditional textiles. They might be useful for language problems, although most carpet dealers are rarely lost for words when it comes to selling. Remember, however, that tourist guides will lead you to carpet shops which give them commission on your purchase.

Above all, take your time by shopping around and calling more than once at a shop before purchase. There is no need to be rushed, whatever the inducement. Note that in Tunisia carpets ought to carry a lead government seal indicating their date of manufacture, material, area and quality. In official handicraft shops such as the main one at the Palmarium (Avenue Bourguiba/Avenue de Carthage), fixed prices are generally the rule, though this might not make them cheaper than the souq for the avid bargainer. Remember that you must pay for your purchase in Tunisian dinars – exchanging currency through a shopkeeper can be very expensive – and that posting a carpet home from Tunisia is technically possible but best avoided. Remember that VAT and customs duties may be levied at the point of entry/receipt to the customer's home country.

Although Tunisian carpet dealers have seen hordes of tourists through their emporia, they do not on the whole seem aware of the huge quantities of carpets, from a variety of countries, now available in Western countries. Tourists are less likely to be bowled over by the idea of exotic rug bargains than they would have been 20 years ago – tastes have become sophisticated. The colours and designs of Tunisian carpets, however, have not.

In Tunisia as in other North African countries there are 2 main types of handmade carpet – the **kilims** (flat-weave carpets)**, knotted carpets** usually made of wool on a cotton base, and **mergoums**. The **classic knotted carpets** come from the vertical looms of Kairouan's homes and workshops, and are in a variety of weaves. The patterns are geometrical, usually based on a central medallion in the form of single and double diamond shapes, with the linework reflected in similarly geometrical serpentine borders. Most of the original patterns were developed from prayer rugs, perhaps with roots in the Anatolian carpet. Colours are at their best in blues, though Kairouan carpets can also come in very pleasant pastel and deep reds. Their weave is of hand knots of the *ghordes* type, with long tufts looped around the warp. **Mergoum**, the other popular weave, is different, having short tufts emerging on the underside of the warps. Flat weave tapestries are produced in Gabès, Matmata, Kebili and Gafsa and **kilims** in Djerba and Sbeïtla.

Good buys   Finding something really original to take home will take time. **Basketwork** is a good, cheap find, and you might see some fine **rush matwork** in Nabeul. Some of the finer *nattes* with geometric designs make good wall-hangings. Old-fashioned **kitchen articles** in hammered copper are also a good buy – try Souk Ennahas in Tunis or Kairouan. Sometimes these items are covered in silver-nickel (*maillechort*) – and very attractive they are too. Then there is simple rural **hand-shaped pottery** from the north, sometimes painted up with geometric designs. Or you could forget things traditional and benefit from the fact that Tunisia is a major centre for garment manufacture, and pick up a nice pair of jeans or a shirt in a modern shopping mall.

On the whole, however, the best things to buy in Tunisia are **foodstuffs**. The markets are full of spices, dried herbs and various condiments which cost a small fortune in European supermarkets. Try for olive oil, olives, capers, real harissa, bayleaves, garlic, dried mint and various spices. Dates are also a splendid present, and can be bought on the branch in kilo-size boxes. And you have various flower waters, especially orange and geranium, much used in traditional pâtisserie, and almond syrup (*sirop d'orgeat*) which makes a refreshing summer drink. Then there is green henna powder – best bought in Gabès. All in all, the 'consumables' side of souk shopping makes up for the lack of high quality handicrafts.

Holidays and festivals

Religious holidays are scheduled according to the Hejira calendar, a lunar based calendar. (Given the clear night skies of Arabia, it is easily comprehensible that the Muslims should have adopted a year based upon the cycles of the moon.) The lunar year is shorter than the solar year, so the Muslim year moves forward by eleven days every Christian year. Thus in 10 years' time, Ramadhan, currently in the winter, will be at the height of summer. Note that the start of Ramadhan can vary by a day, depending on the *ru'ya*, whether the crescent moon has been observed or not by the religious authorities whose job it is to declare Ramadhan. The main religious holidays are as follows:

Muharram   1st day of the Muslim year
Mouloud   Celebration of the Prophet Mohamed's birthday
Ramadhan   A month of fasting and sexual abstinence during daylight hours
Aïd es Seghir (the Lesser Aïd)   A 2 day holiday ending the month of Ramadhan
Aïd el Kebir (the Great Aïd)   1 day holiday which comes 70 days after Aïd es Seghir. Commemorates how God rewarded Ibrahim's faith by sending down a lamb for him to sacrifice instead of his son. When possible, every family sacrifices a sheep on this day.

Religious holidays
For details of local festivals, see the Essentials sections of individual towns

Main religious holidays (approximate corresponding AD dates)

	1999	2000	2001
Start of Ramadhan	16 November	9 December	28 November
Aïd es Seghir (end of Ramadhan)	28 December	19 January	7 January
Aïd el Kebir	28 March	16 March	4 March
1 Muharram	17 April	5 April	24 March
Mouloud (Prophet Mohamed's birthday)	2 June	26 June	14 June

During Ramadhan, the whole country switches to a different rhythm. Public offices go onto half time, and the general pace slows down during the daytime. Tunisians in general do not eat in public during the day, and the vast majority of cafés and restaurants, except those frequented by resident Europeans and tourists, are closed. The cities are quite lively at night however, with shops opening, especially in the second half of the month. Ramadhan is an interesting time to visit Tunisia as a tourist, but probably to be avoided if possible when you need to do business.

Weekends & public holidays Friday is the Muslim holy day and services in the mosques on this day are better attended as there is a *khutba* or sermon in addition to prayers. On Friday mornings office hours are as usual, with the afternoon off for the civil service. The private sector works Friday afternoons, but takes Saturday mornings off. The public sector works Saturday mornings. The 'day of rest' is Sunday. Major football matches are on Sunday afternoons, and most shops, except those in tourist areas, are closed on that day.

The main public holidays in Tunisia are as follows:

1 January New Year's Day in the Gregorian calendar.
20 March Anniversary of independence.
21 March Youth Day (*Fête de la Jeunesse*)
9 April Anniversary of the 1938 Tunis riots during which a number of demonstrators died when French troops fired on the crowd.
1 May International labour day (*Fête du Travail*)
25 July Anniversary of the declaration of the Tunisian Republic in 1957.
13 August Women's Day (*Fête de la Femme*)
15 October Anniversary of the departure of French troops from Bizerte.
7 November Anniversary of President Ben Ali's coming to power in 1987. Start of 'the era of the Change'.

Sport

Local sports facilities and events are listed in each town's Essentials section

With its pleasant Mediterranean weather conditions, Tunisia offers a variety of sports. Some of the hotel complexes have good tennis facilities, the number of golf courses (8 in 1999) is being expanded. And there are 1 or 2 more off-beat sports on offer, such as hot air ballooning over the desert and oases at Tozeur and sand yachting on the Chott El Djerid.

Cycling Cycling is becoming increasingly popular and the standard of cycles for hire has improved. Quiet places like Kerkennah and Djerba can easily be explored in this way but main roads are to be avoided. Serious cyclists may consider bringing in their own machine. Repairs are no problem, every small town has moped/cycle repair shops.

Hunting & shooting Hunting and shooting of various game birds and wild boar. It is necessary to be part of an organized party for firearm permits during official hunting seasons. Expeditions for wild boar hunting (*sanglier*) can be organized by *Cilium Hotel* in Kasserine; *Sicca Veneria* in Le Kef; *Hotel Morjane* in Tabarka and *Les Chênes* in Aïn Draham. Contact **Club de Chasse** in Radès, T01-297011 for details.

Falconry Enthusiasts will find El Haouaria on Cap Bon the place to be in May and June. Contact the **Club to Fauconniers** at Haouaria.

Fishing **Inland fishing** There is no river fishing but there are some lakes on the Cap Bon where fishing is possible, although a permit must be obtained from the Ministry of Agriculture in Nabeul on Av Mongi Bali.

Sea fishing Tunisia offers lots of sea fishing with no permit required. The Kerkennah Islands are particularly suitable. *Abou Nawas Marine* arranges sea fishing for shark, tuna and swordfish, and provides all equipment, contact T01-780450, F01-780827 or *Tunisie Sailing*, T01-761522, F01-761866.

Undersea fishing Any person wishing to undertake undersea fishing must file a request to the Director of Fisheries. The formula is the following: "I, the undersigned, family name, first name, date and place of birth, profession, address of residence, declare that I intend to take part in undersea fishing during this present year on the coastline of Tunisia. I certify that I am aware of the current regulations concerning this activity and I agree to exercise this activity in accordance with their provisions. Date and signature". This request should be accompanied by a medical certificate stating aptitude for undersea diving, by personal insurance and insurance for bodily injury to third parties.

Football

This is the national sport and Sunday afternoon is the time to watch.

Golf

Golf is an established sport in Tunisia albeit principally for foreign residents and visitors. There are 8 first class golf courses across the country at Tabarka, Carthage, El Kantaoui and Djerba and 2 at both Hammamet and Monastir. All have coastal locations and all are set in fine countryside. Given Tunisia's excellent climate, with only a slight rainfall in the average winter/spring and southern Mediterranean temperatures, these are genuine all-year courses, with sunshine at its best in the southern resorts of Hammamet, Monastir and Djerba. For moderate temperatures go in the period September to June.

There are excellent and easy arrangements for a golfing break in Tunisia either by booking directly with the club or taking golf and accommodation as a package. *Panorama Golf*, for example (UK) T01273-746877, F01273-205338, offer golf resort holidays at Hammamet and Port El Kantaoui. Most courses offer facilities for experienced players and for beginners on a long weekend or weekly plus basis. When pre-booking golf course starting times and discount rates can be negotiated. It is important that golfers take with them their *Handicap Certificates* since clubs in Tunisia demand sight of them before play is permitted. Tariffs for an 18-hole round run at approximately 33Dt in high season and 30Dt in low season, depending on the course and 190Dt (high season) to 170Dt (low season) for a (6-day) week.

Tunisian golf courses

Tabarka course is set in more than 100 ha of pine and oak forest between the sea and the coastal hills. The course was designed by the Ronald Fream Group of the USA and comprises an 18 par golf course of 6,306m in length for 6,030m standard men's competitions and 5,190m for ladies' competitions. There is a 9-hole golf school course of 1,400m. The course is adjacent to the new Tabarka Montazah Tourist complex with good hotels and shopping facilities. The course is managed by *Golf Montazah Tabarka*, Route Touristique, El Morjane, 8110 Tabarka, T644028-38, F644026.

Carthage (La Soukra) Course is situated close to the Tunis international airport at La Soukra on the well wooded plain just above the salt lake, Sebkhat El Ariana. The course is 18-hole at par 66 with an overall length of 4,432m but a variety of course length selections offered down to 3,682m. There is a practice course and club house. The club runs amateur competitions throughout the year. Carthage golf course is only 10 km from Tunis centre and so there is easy access to first class hotel, shopping and entertainments. The ruins of ancient Carthage lie on the shore close by to the east. Contact *Golf de Carthage*, Chotrana 2, 2036 La Soukra, T765919, F765915.

El Kantaoui Golf Course is another Ronald Fream course, which was opened in 1979. It is the main feature of the town and is set in 100 ha of slightly undulating olive groves which drop right down to the sea front at El Kantaoui on the edge of the Sahel Plain. The course has 27 holes ranged in three 9-hole constellations with a further 9 holes planned. The men's championship course of 27 holes is 9,576m in length. There are practice and driving range areas attached to the club, whose club house is modern and well equipped. There is a club competition every Wednesday. The course is within easy reach of some of Tunisia's best hotels and the nightlife in nearby Sousse to the south. Contact *Golf El Kantaoui*, Station Touristique d'El Kantaoui, 4089 Kantaoui, Hammam Sousse, T241500, F241755.

Djerba Golf Club is set by the sea shore as an 18-hole links championship complex, designed by Martin Hawtree of the UK. It works in combination with an adjacent 9-hole intermediate course. The main course is 6,310m in length, 73 par (nine 4-par, six 3-par and five 5-par), beginning in a 9-hole loop through palms close to the sea, in which the 500m par-5 7th hole runs through dunes. A second loop, with three par-5 holes passes through a desert environment of palms and rocky outcrops. Djerba clubhouse has a restaurant, bar and golf shop. The club is in Zone Touristique 4116 Midoun, Djerba, T659055, F659051.

Golf Citrus at Hammamet on the northwest of the town is large at 160 ha in flat country covered in olive and citrus groves and with six small lakes. Built in the early 1990s, it comprises two Fream designed 18-hole courses, *The Forest*, with 18 holes (par 72) at a length of 6,175m, which is regarded as fairly difficult, and *The Oliviers* of 6,178m (par 72), classified as moderately testing. A 9-hole *Executive* course runs over 1,220m with 8x3 par and 1x4 par to give in conjunction with the two other courses a total of 45 holes. There is a practice area, driving range and a clubhouse featuring a pro-shop, restaurant and bar. The handicap requirement is 36. The course has a group of hotel shareholders – *Abou Nawas, Aziza, Manar, Méditerranée, Phénida* and *Sindbad*, though golfers can arrange accommodation at other hotels in Hammamet. Management at *Citrus Golf*, BP 132, 8050 Hammamet, T226500, F226400.

Yasmine Golf Course, Hammamet, is located just to the north of the Citrus course. It was designed by Ronald Fream on a lightly wooded 80 ha site with 2 lakes in its southern section. It has a full 18-hole course and 9 training holes tucked into the centre of the complex together with a practice tee. The course has 5 separate teeing areas provided to give a good variety of challenge. For the 18-hole championship course par is 72 on a 6,115m length. Of noted difficulty are the 540m 10th hole with its adjacent lake and bunkers and the long angled 490m 15th, both with par 5. A good quality clubhouse and a training school complete the facilities, all of which are within easy reach of the Hammamet resort. Contact *Golf Yasmine* Course, BP 61, Hammamet 8050, T227665, F226722.

Palm Links Monastir are located on the dunes between Sousse and Monastir. The course is less well-known than its neighbours to the north and south. It is nonetheless worth a visit at its coastal location in the dunes half an hour's drive south of Port El Kantaoui. Of 6,140m length the course has 18 holes with a par of 72. There is a golf school on a 9-hole course and a 360 degree driving range and practice area are available. The *Hotel Marhaba Palace* in El Kantaoui has a free daily shuttle to the links, T466910/2, F466913.

Monastir Golf Course is set in a magnificent site among scattered olive groves on the coast outside Monastir in slightly broken country which gives a great variety of topography between the various holes. The course itself is designed by Ronald Fream and is rated highly for its test of skills, 18 holes and par 72. The course is 6,140m in length with a choice of 5 tees per hole. There is a 3-hole training course, practice area and driving range. The course is a popular venue for golf holidays with a number of beginners and advanced courses running for 3-6 days. The golf course itself is convenient for hotels at Port El Kantaoui, Sousse and Monastir. Contact *Golf de Monastir*, Route de Ouardanine, BP 168 – 5000 Monastir, T461095, F461145.

Activities used to be based at Jebel Ressas, southeast of Tunis. Following an accident, the club was abandoned. Hang-gliders continue to fly off the mountain, however.

Hang-gliding

There are plenty of horses for hire in the tourist areas. Better to hire from your hotel or a stable with a good reputation. Both Club Hippique in Ksar Saïd and Club Hippique La Soukra in the vicinity of Tunis are recommended. The riding offered by the resorts is not very exciting, however, and tends to be expensive.

Horse racing takes place at Ksar Saïd, in the northwest Tunis suburbs, and at Monastir.

Horse riding

At *Aeroasis Club* in Tozeur, who offer floating trips in a balloon every day of the week, weather permitting. See Tozeur section for details.

Hot air ballooning

On the dunes and on Chott el Djerid organized in Tozeur. Best season November-May. Ask at hotels in Tozeur for details.

Sand yachting/ land yachting

Large tourist complexes will have courts. The quality of provision varies. Some complexes have a large number of courts. *Cap Carthage* in Tunis has 30, *Club Mediterranée* on Djerba has 20, while *El Hambra*, Les Maisons de Mer in Port el Kantaoui have 12 each. The Tourist Office publishes a booklet specifically for tennis enthusiasts.

Tennis

Information on watersports including sailing, skiing, windsurfing, snorkelling, scuba diving, fishing and underwater fishing, can be obtained from *Centre Nautique International de Tunisie*, 22 rue de Medine, Tunis, T01-282209.

Watersports

There are 30 ports and anchorages varying from 5 to 380 berths. The main pleasure ports are Port el Kantaoui, Monastir, Sidi Bou Saïd and Tabarka. See map on next page.

Yachting

Entry regulations and information Except in cases of *force majeure* which must be proved, any pleasure craft arriving by sea from a foreign point of departure may only berth in a harbour where there is a customs station and a police station.

Upon arrival at the port all persons on board must show their passports and complete individual registration cards. Moreover, with regard to personal safety of the persons on board, the harbour police may request that a list of equipment be completed and deposited at the harbour police office, on each occasion that a pleasure craft puts to sea.

On entering any Tunisian port, any foreign vessel should be flying its national flag and the flag of Tunisia on the rear mast and at the brow, so that they are easily visible. Immediately upon entry the owner/user of the vessel must present himself at the customs office with all necessary registration and identity papers. The other occupants must remain on board until entry formalities are complete and a certificate of free circulation has been granted. This certificate allows use of Tunisian territorial waters without further formalities until departure for another country at which time the certificate will be surrendered.

Yacht anchorages

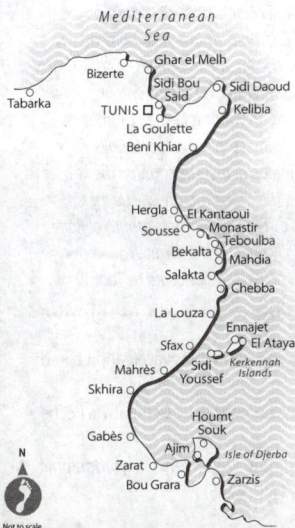

Mediterranean Sea

Ghar el Melh
Bizerte
Sidi Bou Saïd
Sidi Daoud
Tabarka
TUNIS
Kelibia
La Goulette
Beni Khiar

Hergla
El Kantaoui
Sousse
Monastir
Teboulba
Bekalta
Mahdia
Salakta
Chebba
La Louza
Ennajet
El Ataya
Sfax
Kerkennah Islands
Mahrès
Sidi Youssef
Skhira
Houmt Souk
Gabès
Ajim
Isle of Djerba
Zarat
Zarzis
Bou Grara

N

Not to scale

Essentials

☞ *Sporting Tunisians*

The young male Tunisian's leisure time is devoted to cards and the chicha pipe at the café, raising canaries, and above all, to endless discussions about koura (football). Summer is the time for a takwira (a kick around) on the beach, while on winter Sunday afternoons the streets are empty as the men go off to the stadium. Two Tunis-Medina based teams dominate the football scene: the Club Africain (red and white strip) of Bab Jedid, and the EST (Espérance Sportive de Tunisie) or Taraji in Arabic (red and gold strip) of Bab Souika. The passions aroused are as intense as for the racing factions of ancient Rome, the exploits of the young players like Ayyadi Hamrouni on everyone's lips.

Modern Tunisian football's finest hour was the 1978 Argentina World Cup when a team led by Abdel Magid Chettali (The Magician) and Sadok Sassi Attouga won a 3-1 victory over Mexico and held West Germany to a 0-0 draw. Other past heroes of Tunisia's number one sport include Club Africain's Tahar 'Boy' Chaïbi and Tarak Dhieb (The Strategist).

More recently, the 1995 African Football Confederation Cup was won by the Sousse club Etoile Sportive du Sahel. In 1994, Tunisia hosted the Coupe d'Afrique des Nations (only to be ignominiously knocked out by Mali). However, January 1996 saw Tunisia in the finals of the same cup, beaten 2-0 by South Africa.

In 1995, at national level, the Etoile won both the championship and cup (2-1 against Olympique de Béja). The regional clubs are prospering – particularly Taraji Zarzia and Gafsa, while the EST has had a run of poor seasons. The other main Tunis team, Stade Tunisien (red and green strip) are on the way up. Hundreds upon thousands fill the streets after a major

victory and politicians and others squabble furiously to preside over a top football club.

In other team sports, Tunisia is strong in basketball, volleyball and handball. The men's volleyball team went to the Atlanta Olympics and the women's team El Hilal does well in volleyball and handball. Tunisian women regularly win African and Arab swimming titles with top swimmers like Faten Ghattas and Senda el Gharbi.

But Tunisia's greatest sporting legend is undoubtedly runner Mohammed Gammoudi, who struck gold in the 5,000 metres (14'05") in Mexico in 1968. He also won silver in Tokyo (1964) in the 10,000 metres and at Munich (1972) in the 5,000 metres.

However, apart from koura the most popular sports are really Oriental martial arts, bodybuilding (beauté de corps!) and boxing. Every town has its share of private karaté and taekwando clubs and salles de culture physique. In international boxing, two legends have been forged: the Kairouan-born (1958) Kamel Bouali, who took the WBO super featherweight title (59 kilograms) in December 1989 against the Puerto Rican Rivera and light heavyweight Taoufik Balbouli (born La Soukra 1959), Arab champion in Iraq 1980, and holder of a total of 26 victories out of 27 professional fights. French-based Balbouli's finest hour was on 25 March 1989 when he won the World Championship in Casablanca against the American Daniels.

The present government, with its emphasis on youth, is keen to promote sport – witness the new sports halls springing up across the country. The key piece of this infrastructure will be the Cité Sportive in the South Tunis suburb of Radés, especially built for the Mediterranean Games of 2001 to be hosted by Tunisia.

Cats and dogs must have a certificate of health and anti-rabies vaccination dated within the last 6 months.

Fishing is authorized by the regional offices of the Commissariat General à la Pêche located at all coastal ports.

Documents and charts which are highly recommended: French Hydrographic Service maps no 7014, 5017, 4314, 4315, 4316, 4244 and 4245.

Forecasts may be obtained from the marine weather centres at La Goulette, Sfax, Mahdia and Bizerte and from the harbour master's office at Sidi Bou Saïd, El Kantaoui and Monastir where marine weather reports, wind strength warnings, special weather reports (gale warnings) and daily marine weather forecasts are available. In addition all Tunisian national radio stations broadcast daily weather reports.

Weather notes for sailors During winter the Tunisian coast is in the depression track between the Azores and Siberian anticyclones. In summer the Azores high stretches east bringing good weather with steady breezes to an otherwise sheltered coast. In particular: the northeast coast as far as Bizerte commonly experiences winds from the northwest to west and occasionally from northeast to east. On all coasts the winds become very variable nearer to land. In summer the prevailing wind alternates from west to north with sea breezes blowing east to northeast.

On the eastern coast winds from the east prevail during the summer and are almost always moderate (forces 2 to 4). The occasional winds from the southeast can reach force 5 and cause heavy seas. Sirocco winds from the south may affect all sectors of the Tunisia coast. They are usually short-lived but can be strong and unpredictable. The southeast coastline is affected by major tides, with a difference between high and low water of approximately 1.8m at Gabès and 1.4m at Sfax.

Health

There are many well qualified doctors in Tunisia, all of whom speak French. The majority will understand basic English, and often speak it quite well. The availability of medical care does however diminish somewhat away from big cities. However, at least you can be reasonably sure that local practitioners have a lot of experience with the particular diseases of their region. A pharmacy or a large hotel should be able to provide you with names of recommended doctors (*médecins généralistes*). Hopefully, you will not need any more medical care than this. In cases of emergency, a large town will have an *SOS Médecins* or *SAMU* emergency service (call outs cost around 25Dt a call out). Note that the private *polycliniques* generally offer far better (and more expensive) service than the public hospitals, which can be terribly overcrowded.

If you are a long way from medical help, a certain amount of self medication may be necessary and you will find that many of the drugs that are available have familiar names. However, always check the date stamping and buy from reputable pharmacists because the shelf life of some items, especially vaccines and antibiotics is markedly reduced in hot conditions.

With the following precautions and advice you should keep as healthy as usual. Make local enquiries about health risks if you are apprehensive. For completeness sake, the present section includes health risks for Libya.

Before you go

Take out medical insurance. You should have a dental check up, get spare glasses and, if you suffer from a longstanding condition such as diabetes, high blood pressure, heart/lung disease or a nervous disorder, arrange for a check up with your doctor who can at the same time provide you with a letter explaining details of your disability (in English and French). Check the current practice for malaria prevention.

Smallpox vaccination is no longer required. Neither is cholera vaccination, and there have been no outbreaks of the disease for years in Tunisia. Yellow fever vaccination is not required for either Tunisia or Libya. Cholera vaccine is not effective which is the main reason for not recommending it.

Inoculations

Essentials

The following vaccinations are recommended:

Typhoid (monovalent): one dose followed by a booster in 1 month's time. Immunity from this course lasts 2-3 years. Other injectable types are now becoming available as are oral preparations marketed in some countries.

Poliomyelitis: this is a live vaccine, generally given orally and the full course consists of 3 doses with a booster in tropical regions every 3-5 years.

Tetanus: 1 dose should be given with a booster at 6 weeks and another at 6 months and 10 yearly boosters thereafter are recommended.

Children: should, in addition, be properly protected against diphtheria, whooping cough, mumps and measles. Teenage girls, if they have not yet had the disease, should be given rubella (German measles) vaccination. Consult your doctor for advice on BCG inoculation against tuberculosis. The disease is still common in the region. North Africa lies mainly outside the meningitis belt and the disease is probably no more common than at home so vaccination is not indicated except during an epidemic.

On the road

Infectious hepatitis (jaundice) This is common throughout North Africa, though less so in Tunisia and Libya. It seems to be frequently caught by travellers probably because, coming from countries with higher standards of hygiene, they have not contracted the disease in childhood and are therefore not immune like the majority of adults in developing countries. The main symptoms are stomach pains, lack of appetite, nausea, lassitude and yellowness of the eyes and skin. Medically speaking there are 2 types: the less serious, but more common, is hepatitis A for which the best protection is careful preparation of food, the avoidance of contaminated drinking water and scrupulous attention to toilet hygiene. Human normal immunoglobulin (gammaglobulin) confers considerable protection against the disease and is particularly useful in epidemics. It should be obtained from a reputable source and is certainly recommended for travellers who intend to live rough. The injection should be given as close as possible to your departure and, as the dose depends on the likely time you are to spend in potentially infected areas, the manufacturer's instructions should be followed. A new vaccination against hepatitis A is now generally available and probably provides much better immunity for 10 years but is more expensive, being 3 separate injections.

The other more serious version is hepatitis B which is acquired as a sexually transmitted disease, from a blood transfusion or injection with an unclean needle or possibly by insect bites. The symptoms are the same as hepatitis A but the incubation period is much longer.

You may have had jaundice before or you may have had hepatitis of either type before without becoming jaundiced, in which case it is possible that you could be immune to either hepatitis A or B. This immunity can be tested for before you travel. If you are not immune to hepatitis B already, a vaccine is available (3 shots over 6 months) and if you are not immune to hepatitis A already then you should consider vaccination (or gamma globulin if you are not going to be exposed for long).

Meningitis This is not a significant risk in Tunisia. Protection against meningococcal meningitis A and C is conferred by a vaccine which is freely available.

AIDS (Sida) In North Africa AIDS is probably less common than in most of Europe and North America but is presumably increasing in its incidence, though not as rapidly as in Sub-Saharan Africa, South America or Southeast Asia. Having said that, the spread of the disease has not been well documented in the North African region; the real picture is unclear. The disease is possibly still mainly confined to the well known high risk sections of the population i.e. gay men, intravenous drug abusers, prostitutes and children of infected mothers. Whether heterosexual transmission outside these

Essentials

groups is common or not, the main risk to travellers is from casual sex. The same precautions should be taken as when encountering any sexually transmitted disease.

The AIDS virus (HIV) can be passed via unsterile needles which have been previously used to inject an HIV positive patient but the risk of this is very small indeed. It would, however, be sensible to check that needles have been properly sterilized or disposable needles used. A private clinic in Tunisia will probably be using disposable needles anyway – but check. The chance of picking up hepatitis B in this way is much more of a danger. Be wary of carrying disposable needles yourself. Custom officials may find them suspicious. The risk of receiving a blood transfusion with blood infected with the HIV virus is greater than from dirty needles because of the amount of fluid exchanged. Supplies of blood for transfusion are now largely screened for HIV in all reputable hospitals so the risk must be very small indeed. Catching the AIDS virus does not necessarily produce an illness in itself; the only way to be sure if you feel you have been put at risk is to have a blood test for HIV antibodies on your return home.

Desert heat & cold

Full acclimatization to high temperatures takes about 2 weeks and during this period it is normal to feel a degree of apathy, especially if the relative humidity is high. Drink plenty of water (up to 15 litres a day are required when working physically hard in hot, dry conditions), use salt on your food and avoid extreme exertion. Tepid showers are more cooling than hot or cold ones. Large hats do not cool you down but prevent sunburn. Remember that, especially in the mountains, there can be a large and sudden drop in temperature between sun and shade and between night and day so dress accordingly. Clear desert nights can prove astoundingly cold with a rapid drop in temperature as the sun goes down. Loose fitting cotton clothes are still the best for hot weather; warm jackets and woollens are essential after dark in some desert areas, and especially at high altitude.

Insects

These can be a great nuisance. (In other parts of Africa, some are carriers of serious diseases such as malaria and yellow fever.) When camping out, the best way of keeping insects away at night is to sleep off the ground with a mosquito net and to burn mosquito coils containing Pyrethrum. Aerosol sprays or a 'flit' gun may be effective as are those little plug-in anti-mosquito devices. (Check that you have enough 'mats' for your stay, and note that Tunisia uses twin rounded pin plugs like those in France. Do you have an adaptor?)

You can use personal insect repellent, the best of which contain a high concentration of Diethyltoluamide. Liquid is best for arms and face (take care around eyes and make sure you do not dissolve the plastic of your spectacles). Aerosol spray on clothes and ankles deters mites and ticks. Liquid DET suspended in water can be used to impregnate cotton clothes and mosquito nets. Wide mesh mosquito nets are now available impregnated with an insecticide called Permethrin and are generally more effective, lighter to carry and more comfortable to sleep in. If you are bitten, itching may be relieved by cool baths and anti-histamine tablets (care with alcohol or driving) corticosteroid creams (great care – never use if any hint of sepsis) or by judicious scratching. Calamine lotion and cream have limited effectiveness and anti-histamine creams have a tendency to cause skin allergies and are therefore not generally recommended. Bites which become infected (commonly in dirty and dusty places) should be treated with a local antiseptic or antibiotic cream such as Cetrimide as should infected scratches. Skin infestations with body lice, crabs and scabies are unfortunately easy to pick up. Use Gamma benzene hexachloride for lice and Benzyl benzoate for scabies. Crotamiton cream (Eurax) alleviates itching and also kills a number of skin parasites. Malathion lotion 5% is good for lice but avoid the highly toxic full strength Malathion used as an agricultural insecticide.

Intestinal upsets Practically nobody escapes this one so be prepared for it. Some of these countries lead the world in their prevalence of diarrhoea. Most of the time intestinal upsets are due to the insanitary preparation of food. Do not eat uncooked fish or vegetables or meat (especially pork), fruit with the skin on (always peel your fruit yourself) or food that is exposed to flies. Eating large quantities of summer fruit such as grapes is not a good idea. Tap water is generally safe in large towns in Tunisia. Prefer bottled water, however – it is cheap and can save much misery. If your hotel has a central hot water supply this is safe to drink after cooling. Ice for drinks should be made from boiled water but rarely is, so stand your glass on the ice cubes, instead of putting them in the drink. Dirty water should first be strained through a filter bag (available from camping shops) and then boiled or treated. Bringing the water to a rolling boil at sea level is sufficient but at high altitude you have to boil the water for longer to ensure that all the microbes are killed. Various sterilising methods can be used and there are proprietary preparations containing chlorine or iodine compounds. Pasteurized or heat treated milk is now widely available as is icecream and yoghurt produced by the same methods. Unpasteurized milk products including cheese and yoghurt are sources of tuberculosis, brucellosis, listeria and food poisoning germs. You can render fresh milk safe by heating it to 62°C for 30 mins followed by rapid cooling or by boiling it. Matured or processed cheeses are safer than fresh varieties.

Diarrhoea is usually the result of food poisoning, occasionally from contaminated water (including seawater when swimming near sewage outfalls). There are various causes – viruses, bacteria, protozoa (like amoeba) salmonella and cholera organisms. It may take one of several forms coming on suddenly, or rather slowly. It may be accompanied by vomiting or by severe abdominal pain and the passage of blood or mucus when it is called dysentery. Although your intestinal flora will adapt as you travel in Tunisia, you are at risk of getting diarrhoea when you eat poorly cooked food.

Diagnosis and treatment All kinds of diarrhoea, whether or not accompanied by vomiting, respond favourably to the replacement of water and salts taken as frequent small sips of some kind of rehydration solution. There are proprietary preparations consisting of sachets of powder which you dissolve in water or you can make your own by adding half a teaspoonful of salt (3.5 grams) and 4 tablespoonfuls of sugar (40 grams) to a litre of boiled water. If you can time the onset of diarrhoea to the minute, then it is probably viral or bacterial and/or the onset of dysentery. The treatment, in addition to rehydration, is Ciprofloxacin (widely available) 500 mgs every 12 hours.

If the diarrhoea has come on slowly or intermittently, then it is more likely to be protozoal i.e. caused by amoeba or giardia and antibiotics will have no effect. These cases are best treated by a doctor, as is any outbreak of diarrhoea continuing for more than 3 days. If there are severe stomach cramps, the following drugs may help: Loperamide (Imodium, Arret) and Diphenoxylate with Atropine (Lomotil).

Diarrhoea should be treated with lots of rest, fluid and salt replacement, antibiotics such as Ciprofloxacin for the bacterial types and special diagnostic tests and medical treatment for amoeba and giardia infections. Salmonella infections and cholera can be devastating diseases and it would be wise to get to a hospital as soon as possible if these were suspected. Note that fasting, peculiar diets and the consumption of large quantities of yoghurt have not been found useful in calming travellers' diarrhoea or in rehabilitating inflamed bowels. You should, however, avoid spicy foods and go for very plain couscous and/or rice.

Note that giving plenty of mineral water to drink plus rehydration salts has, especially in children, been a lifesaving technique. As there is some evidence that alcohol and milk might prolong diarrhoea, they should probably be avoided during and immediately after an attack. There are ways of preventing travellers' diarrhoea for short periods of time when visiting these countries by taking antibiotics but these are ineffective against viruses and, to some extent, against protozoa, so this technique should not be used other than in exceptional circumstances. Some preventives such as Enterovioform can have serious side effects if taken for long periods.

Diarrhoea can lead to you having a very sore and fragile-feeling stomach. In this case, powders taken mixed with mineral water ('stomach liners' or *pansement gastrique* in French) may be helpful. A pharmacy may sell you Actapulgite powder (Laboratoires Beaufour), which is effective in calming gastric pains and diarrhoea 'avec météorisme'.

Avoiding diarrhoea Always be careful what you drink – go for mineral water and fizzy drinks. Beware unwashed fruit. If you are going to be travelling in remote areas, carry Lomotil and Imodium, something for stomach pains (Actapulgite or equivalent) and an anti-bacterial drug like Intétrix, available at pharmacies throughout Tunisia. Self-medication is not a good thing, but sometimes needs must. If symptoms persist, see a doctor as quickly as possible when you get to a town.

First time exposure to countries where sections of the population live in extreme poverty or squalor and may even be starving can cause odd psychological reactions in visitors. So can the incessant pestering, especially of women. You just have to be prepared for this and try not to over react. It is also oppressive for women to travel in towns where other women have such a limited public presence. Travelling for a long period of time in a place where your first language is not spoken can also be a strain. Remember, they're not trying to be unhelpful, it may just be too difficult for them to make sense of your limited approximate French or Arabic.
Mental pressures

If you are unlucky enough to be bitten by a venomous snake, spider, scorpion, lizard, centipede or sea creature try (within limits) to catch the animal for identification. The reactions to be expected are fright, swelling, pain and bruising around the bite, soreness of the regional lymph glands, nausea, vomiting and fever. If in addition any of the following symptoms supervene, get the victim to a doctor without delay: numbness, tingling of the face, muscular spasms, convulsions, shortness of breath or haemorrhage. Commercial snake bite or scorpion sting kits may be available but are only useful for the specific type of snake or scorpion for which they are designed. The serum has to be given intravenously, so is not much good unless you have had some practice in making injections into veins. If the bite is on a limb, immobilize it and apply a tight bandage between the bite and body, releasing it for 90 seconds every 15 minutes. Reassurance of the bitten person is very important because death by snake bite is in fact very rare. Do not slash the bite area and try to suck out the poison because this kind of heroism does more harm than good. Hospitals usually hold stocks of snake bite serum. Best precaution: do not walk in snake territory with bare feet, sandals or shorts and watch where you sit. Snakes on the whole are more frightened of large galumphing animals like humans, and will tend to disappear as they approach.
Snake bites & other stings

Avoid spiders and scorpions by keeping your bed away from the wall and look under lavatory seats and inside your shoes in the morning. In the rare event of being bitten, consult a doctor.

If swimming in an area where there are poisonous fish such as stone or scorpion fish (also called by a variety of local names) or sea urchins (*retzi/oursins*) on rocky coasts, tread carefully or wear plimsolls or jellyshoes. The sting of such fish is intensely painful but can be helped by immersing the stung part in water as hot as you can bear for as long as it remains painful. This is not always very practical and you must take care not to scald yourself but it does work. Otherwise head for a GP to get a painkilling shot. In areas such as Hammamet where the weaver fish (*bilum* in Arabic, *vive* in French) hides in the sand in shallow water, with just its spine protruding for you to step on, local pharmacies stock the relevant painkillers.
Beach nasties

Sunburn & heat stroke

The burning power of the sun in Tunisia and Libya is phenomenal, especially in the desert. Strong sunlight may damage exposed skin. In the short term, burning can be severe, and even dangerous to children and some adults. There may also be a long term risk of skin cancer and certain individuals, if exposure is prolonged or repeated, are potentially at risk. Those with very fair skin, especially with blonde or red hair and those who hardly tan should be particularly careful about protecting themselves. Babies under 6 months should be kept out of the sun as much as possible. Try to avoid the beach between 2300 and 1500 when the burning power of the sun is at its height.

Normal temperate zone suntan lotions (protection factor up to 7) are not much good. You need to use the types designed specifically for the tropics or for mountaineers or skiers with an SPF, sun protection factor (against UVA) of between 7 and 15. Certain creams also protect against UVB and you should use these if you have a skin prone to burning. Glare from the sun can cause conjunctivitis so wear sunglasses, especially on the beach.

Protective clothing including a lightweight hat is a useful precaution and essential for children. The closely knitted fabric made from 80 percent polymide and 20 percent elastane will help protect a child's skin from damage. Be sure to apply sun lotion every 1 to 2 hours especially after swimming and towel drying. Sprays and roll-on sun screen products make putting lotion on more fun and are easier for children to use.

There are several varieties of heat stroke. The most common cause is severe dehydration. Avoid this by drinking lots of non-alcoholic fluid and adding some salt if you wish.

Other afflictions

Athletes foot and other fungal infections are best treated by exposure to sunshine and a proprietary preparation such as Tolnaftate. **Filariasis** causing such diseases as elephantiasis occurs in Mauritania and again is transmitted by mosquito. **Intestinal worms** do occur in insanitary areas and the more serious ones, such as hook-worm, can be contracted by walking bare foot on infested earth or beaches. **Leishmaniasis** causing a skin ulcer which will not heal is also present in most of the North African countries. It is transmitted by sand flies. **Prickly heat** is a common itchy rash avoided by frequent washing and by wearing loose clothing. It can be helped by the regular use of talcum powder to allow the skin to dry thoroughly after washing. **Rabies** is endemic throughout Tunisia. Remote rural communities invariably seem to have savage dogs in their vicinity. Their main role is to guard sheep and goats, however, they can go beserk as an outsider goes by on a bike. If you are bitten by a domestic animal, try to see a doctor at once. Treatment with human diploid vaccine is now extremely effective and worth seeking out if the likelihood of having contracted rabies is high. A course of anti-rabies vaccine might be a good idea before you go. In any case, steer clear of rough looking dogs.

When you get home

If you have had attacks of diarrhoea, it is worth having a stool specimen tested in case you have picked up amoebic dysentery. If you have been living rough, a blood test may be worthwhile to detect worms and other parasites.

Essentials

Further reading

There is a severe shortage of reading material on Tunisia in English but if you read French, you will be spoiled for choice. Among the bookshops which carry a good selection are *Millefeuilles*, right on the main roundabout by the train station at La Marsa – Plage, *Clairefontaine* on rue d'Alger in downtown Tunis, and *Le Diwan* on rue Sidi Ben Arous in the médina of Tunis. Publishers Alif have a small bookshop next to the Carthage Museum, and do some nice pop-up books on aspects of Tunisian culture as well as some expensive art books.

Ancient history

At a very general – and rather chatty level – look out for David Soren et al's *Carthage, uncovering the mysteries and splendours of ancient Tunisia* (New York: Simon and Schuster, 1990). An excellent background account of Roman Africa is Susan Raven's *Rome in Africa* (London: Routledge, 1993 third ed). Also look out for Colin Wells' readable *The Roman Empire* (London: Fontana, 1992 second ed). In Tunis itself, you will find expensive coffee table books on the ancient mosaics published by Cérès Productions and Alif. The ANPE, Tunisia's national heritage board, has a range of publications on sale at the main archaeological sites. You might take a translation of Virgil's *Aeneid* with you, to have a read of Book IV (Dido and Aeneas in Carthage), Sallust's *Jugurthine War*, or a heavier read in the form of Flaubert's *Salammbô*. All are available in the Penguin Classics.

History

The best generalist history of Islamic North Africa, taking the reader right up to the early 1960s, is Jamil M Abun-Nasr's *A history of the Maghrib in the Islamic period* (Cambridge University Press, 1987). Other scholarly works include Annabi, H (ed) *Itinéraire du savoir en Tunisie* (Paris: CNRS/IMA, 1995), an interesting and beautifully illustrated collection of articles on Tunisian history; Brett, M (ed), *Northern Africa, Islam and Modernisation* (London: Frank Cass, 1973); Brown, LC, *The Tunisia of Ahmed Bey* (Princeton University Press, 1974). A truly scholarly account of the modernizing work undertaken by an early 19th century ruler; Knapp, W, *Tunisia* (London: Thames & Hudson, 1970); Latham, JD, *Towards a study of Andalusian immigration and its place in Tunisian history* (Tunis: Cahiers de Tunisie, 1957); Lloyd, C, *English Corsairs on the Barbary Coast* (London, 1981); Messenger, Charles, *The Tunisian Campaign* (London: Ian Allen); Woodford, JS, *The City of Tunis* (Wisbech: Menas Press Ltd, 1990).

Contemporary Tunisia

There is very little available in English for the generalist reader. On the first president, try Hopwood, D, *Habib Bourguiba of Tunisia – The tragedy of Longevity* (London: Macmillan). Also look out for a forthcoming socio-economic and political survey of modern Tunisia authored by Emma Murphy of Durham University.

Crafts

Here again, as compared with Morocco, very little has been published. On textiles you have: Maurières, Arnaud et al's *Au fil du désert, tentes et tissages des pasteurs nomades de Méditerranée* (Aix-en-Provence: Edisud, 1996).

Contemporary writing

Tunisia has produced few contemporary novelists of any standing – cinema and theatre have been the country's strongpoints. Out-of-print titles worth looking out for include Albert Memmi's *La Statue de sel* and André Gide's *Amyntas*, both readily available in French in the Gallimard Folio collection.

Desert

Louis, André *Nomades d'hier et d'aujourd'hui dans le Sud tunisien* (Aix-en-Provence: Edisud, 1979). A good account of a way of life which has largely disappeared. A little confusing at times, as the book was put together after the author's death. Good bibliography if you are interested in the ways of the desert. Melville, KEM *Stay Alive in the Desert* (London: Roger Lascelles).

Photography Tunisia has adopted the French tradition of the expensive photography book. Recent publications include publication of early 20th century photographers Lehnert and Landrock's studies of black and white nudes (amongst other things) in Charles-Henri Favrod and André Rouvinez' *Lehnert et Landrock Orient 1904-1930*; Jellel Gastelli's *En Tunisie* (Paris: Editions Eric Koehler, 1997) beautiful black and white photography of the Tunisian interior and desert; Z. Mouhli's *Médinances, huit visages de la Médina de Tunis*, (Tunis: Alif, 1998) photographic essay by 5 photographers on old Tunis, texts in English and French; on food, there is Rafik Tlatli's *Saveurs de Tunisie* (Boulogne: Geste Editions, 1998).

Maps The best map by far is Michelin 972, scale 1:million. Map of Tunisia by Kümmerly and Frey, scale 1:million gives geomorphological details and a pictorial view worth studying before the visit. World Map, Geo Centre International, Reise & Verkehrsverlag, Stuttgart, 1:800,000 gives clear information. The Tourist Office will give you a free map which is good enough to pinpoint the main places but lacks detail. There are no ordinance survey-type maps (French: cartes d'état-major) ordinarily available, which makes planning walks in rural places difficult.

Tunis and around

3

Tunis and around

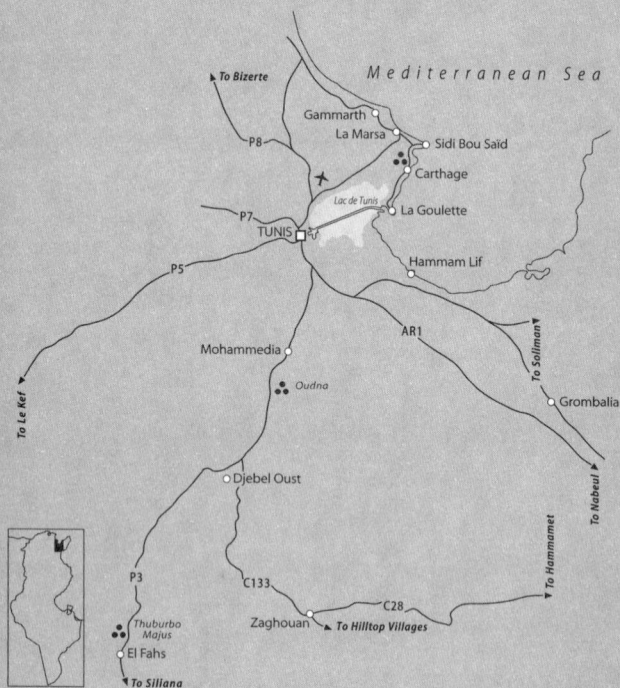

Tunis is the heart of modern Tunisia, the political capital and centre of economic life. Today's visitor comes to a Mediterranean city with sprawling suburbs – and some notable places to visit. Central Tunis has a dual centre: the old town or **médina** is the original Muslim settlement, while next to it, on reclaimed land, is a fine city of boulevards and modern buildings. The **Bardo Museum** houses the world's finest collection of Roman mosaics. To the northeast of Tunis lies a string of beachside suburbs, including **Carthage** (also with a fine museum with objects from Punic and Roman times), and the whitewashed houses of **Sidi Bou Saïd**, everybody's favourite Mediterranean village. Going southwest from Tunis, the visitor keen on all things ancient may also want to visit the Roman sites of **Uthina** and **Thuburbo Majus** and view the grandiose remains of **Hadrian's Aqueduct**. Walkers and birdwatchers can climb twin-peaked **Boukornine** or the brooding **Djebel Ressas**. There are plenty of easy day excursions to small towns of Andalusian ancestry like **Zaghouan**, or one-time Berber villages like **Takrouna, Jeradou, and abandoned Zriba**, also easily visited as day excursions from **Hammamet**.

Tunis تونس

Population: 1,200,000
Phone code: 01
Colour map 1, grid A4

Tunis is a major Mediterranean city. It is often visited by tourists on daytrips up from one of the resort towns. However, to cover the city and its main sites comfortably, you really need a couple of days: a morning could be spent at the Bardo Museum, with an afternoon strolling in the médina, including a visit to the Dar Ben Abdallah Museum; a second day, with lots of walking, would allow you to take in the numerous scattered sites of ancient Carthage, along with a visit to the bijou clifftop village of Sidi Bou Saïd.

Ins and outs

Getting there Arriving by air, you will come into the busy Aéroport de Tunis-Carthage, situated 7 km outside the city. (There are currency exchange facilities in the baggage hall and in the main concourse. **NB** Late night arrivals will find these closed.) To reach the *centre ville* (*wust el-bled*), where most hotels are located, take bus No 35 that stops on Av Habib Bourguiba by Tunis Air. The airport bus normally runs every 30 minutes day and night, but from 2400 to 0600 there is only one every hour. Otherwise take a taxi, which should not cost more than 3Dt, although the driver may want more 'for baggage'. Beware of the unofficial taxis without meters.

Coming in by train, there is only one main station, located on the Place Barcelone, where there are numerous cheap hotels. By bus, you will come in at one of two stations: the Gare Routière Sud at Bab Alioua (for all destinations south) is 15 minutes walk from the city centre; to reach the city centre from the Gare Routière Nord (for Bizerte and the North West), you need to take either a green tram (for Station République), taxi or bus No 3. Arriving by louage (shared taxi) from the South you will come in at the Moncef Bey louage station, 10 minutes walk from the central avenue. Louages from the Cap Bon bring you into another station at Bab Alioua, again only 10 to 15 minutes from the main areas of low-cost hotels at Bab Jedid and the city centre. Coming in from the North, you arrive at the northern bus station at Bab Saâdoun.

Getting around In terms of transport there are three options: overcrowded buses, the efficient light metro network, and yellow taxis. The Ville Nouvelle and the médina can be easily covered on foot. The Avenue Bourguiba is the main street, leading up to the médina at its western end. It is crossed at right angles by the Avenue de Carthage/Avenue de Paris which leads up to République metro station. You will need to make use of public transport or taxi to get to the Bardo Museum and the northern coastal suburbs. The Bardo is easily reached by taxi (say 2.5Dt) or by green metro (line 4 from République station). Carthage and the coast are easily reached by the TGM (Tunis-Goulette-Marsa) light railway, whose terminus is situated at the eastern end of the Avenue Bourguiba. The train takes just over 30 minutes to get to Carthage.

The yellow and white SNT buses are often crowded, but run to most destinations. There are private bus lines (green and white TGV and blue and yellow TUT) serving the more upmarket destinations like La Marsa, the Menzahs and El Manar.

Best time to visit Tunis is best visited in spring, autumn and early winter. The summer is oppressively hot and humid, and the city centre and its traffic best avoided at this time. January and February can be cold and damp.

History and background

The history of Tunis, so close to Carthage, goes back to Punic times. In all likeliood there were Punic and later Roman settlements on the site of present-day Tunis. Roman and later architectural detailing recycled in the old town's buildings is just one indication of this. However, in ancient times, Tunis was a small settlement in the shadow of neighbouring Carthage, centre of the maritime Punic Empire in the western Mediterranean and later capital of the Roman province of Africa. For the whole of the 850 year period of Roman rule, Tunis was an unimportant satellite settlement, and the Latin sources make no mention of its having being made a *municipium*, a Roman town with some degree of self-rule.

However, the hinterland of Carthage, including the rich farmland of the **Roman** Mornag plain to the south, was settled by Roman colonists, square blocks of **settlement** land being allocated on the basis of careful surveying. Smaller settlements, like Tunis, were fitted into this grid, and some recent research sees that there is a correspondence between the street lines of the central médina of Tunis and those of a Roman *colonia*. Around the Zitouna Mosque, street intersections every 240 Roman feet can be identified.

Thus the Muslim Arab invaders of the late seventh century took on a settle- **A defensive site** ment which was already many hundreds of years old. They were no doubt seeking to establish a strong point in the central Mediterranean, but rather than settle in coastal Carthage, they opted for Tunis. The location, a low hill, several kilometres away from the Mediterranean, gave better protection from any marauding Byzantine fleets; from the western, land side, the site has protection in the form of a scarp slope overlooking a *sebkha* or salt lake, fed by winter rainfall. In addition, at Tunis the water table had the advantage of beng close to the surface, making the construction of wells easy.

Subsequently, the médina was to grow in importance under a series of Islamic dynasties. As of the mid-19th century, the modern town of Tunis was laid out between the médina and the shallow Lac de Tunis, beginning the changes which were to lead to the central areas of the old town becoming a focus for the leisure and tourism industries. The Great Mosque Ezzitouna at the heart of the médina retained its role as the city's, and indeed the country's, religious centre.

The history of early Muslim dynasties and their struggles for power and influ- **The Aghlabids** ence – like that of Mediaeval dynasties in Europe, for that matter – is not easy to follow. In the eighth and ninth centuries, Islam had not yet assumed the definitive form it was to acquire under the Abbasids in 10th century Baghdad. Fragile, warring Islamic dynasties in North Africa, though they had the advantages of the power vacuum left by the declining Byzantines and the fact that the Berber tribes were organized on an extremely localized basis, faced problems of communicating over huge distances and an eventual resurgence of Byzantine power. It was important for the new religion to stamp its presence on the region – hence the development of impressive mosques like the Ezzitouna in Tunis under the Aghlabids (794-905). The anarchy which had characterized the late eighth century was ended by the dynasty's founder, Ibrahim Ibn Al-Aghlab, and his successors were able to maintain the peace. There began a period of considerable artistic and architectural development, and it was under Abu Ibrahim Ahmad (856-863 AD) that the Ezzitouna Mosque in Tunis was restored.

Tunis and around

Hafsid Tunis   It was under the rule of the Hafsid Dynasty (1230-1574) that Tunis blossomed,
(1230-1574)   with more than 100,000 inhabitants within its walls. The geographer and philosopher Ibn Khaldoun (1232-1406) was born during this period in Tunis.
During the 13th and 14th centuries, the central part of the old city reached its
present size. The town grew important through trade with southern Europe,
and as a centre of Malikite learning. The Hafsid sultans, originally vassals of the
Almohads, had to establish their legitimacy to rule, and one way to do this was
through the strengthening of Islamic orthodoxy. They founded a number of
medresas or colleges where students of religion and law at the Zitouna Mosque
were housed. By building a power base among a scholar class, the Hafsids thus
hoped to counter the potentially dangerous leadership of soufi saints based in
the countryside.

The 16th   Between 1534 and 1574 the town went through a period of turbulence. The
century,   Mediterranean was the theatre of fierce conflicts between the expansionist
Ottoman &   European powers and the Ottoman Turks, defenders of Islam. The city was
Habsburg   first attacked by Kherredine Pasha, better known as the pirate Barbarossa,
conflict   then captured by the Algerians and subsequently by Don Juan of Austria. It
was only with the Turkish invasion, in 1574, that a period of calm returned.
The influx of 80,000 Muslim refugees from Andalusia at the start of the 17th
century gave a renewed vitality to the city and its surroundings. The
Andalusians were skilled farmers, and gave a new impetus to the *chéchia*
industry (the manufacture of the felt headgear that was exported throughout
the Mediterranean for over three centuries).

Tunis was thus the capital of a minor Ottoman province. Links with Istanbul were always weak, however, and in the course of the 17th century, a local
dynasty emerged in the form of the descendants of a corsair adventurer. By the
early 18th century, the citizens of Tunis had had enough of dynastic infighting,
and they called upon one Hussein Ben Ali to restore peace and order. By the
end of the 18th century, his descendants had established dynastic rule.

Cosmopolitan   In the early 19th century, the beys (as the rulers of Tunisia were called) did
Tunis: their best to keep up with the changes taking place on the northern side of the
1800-1950   Mediterranean. The dangers facing the country became all the more apparent
after the occupation of Algiers by France in 1830 and the increasing competition between the colonial powers. Despite the reforms initiated by Ahmed Bey
(1837-55), and the efforts of reforming minister Kheïredine Pacha in the second half of the 19th century, pressure from the newly industrialiszing powers
to the North grew. The city was to grow out of all recognition.

Epidemics in the early 19th century took a heavy toll among the local Muslim and Jewish populations. Even before the French declared their protectorate over Tunisia in 1881, there was an influx of Europeans. The Tunisian
government granted concessions to Europeans in exchange for loans, and
professional people moved in to manage the modern businesses. Poor Sicilian
and Maltese immigrants provided the semi-skilled labour. A new neighbourhood began to take shape on reclaimed land to the east of the médina, the
future *ville basse* or lower town. France built a fine new consulate (1860), and
the foundations of the Cathedral of St Vincent de Paul were laid. A British
company financed the construction of a railway to La Marsa between 1874-76.

In the 1880s, the French hesitated as to whether they should continue to
extend the new town to the east of the médina. After all, it had a reputation as
an unsalubrious place, despite the sewage lines which had been put in by the
Municipality founded in 1857. A new coastal location was felt to be suitable.
Carthage was out of the question, given the proximity of a beylical palace.

Radès, on the coast south of Tunis, would have been ideal. The strength of the Italian community made such a move impossible, however. The Italians had interests in a railway line linking Tunis to La Marsa and the La Goulette port. Italian interests, namely one Mme Fasciotti, also held the concession for rubble removal and dumping, an important operation given the amount of crumbling ramparts to be demolished and the value of the new infill land. Above all, the French had to placate Italian interests wherever possible, given the fact that the newly unified Kingdom of Italy had colonial designs too. Italian commercial interests had to be respected.

Thus the city centre of Tunis as we know it today was built on reclaimed land to the east of the old médina. Growth was rapid and one source mentions more than 800 new buildings going up between 1881 and 1894. As of 1860, the French had asserted economic authority in Tunisia. Between 1881 and 1900, they made their presence felt in physical terms. The old world of the médina, its people's lives codified by Muslim and Jewish law, was marginalized. The Europeans who had lived in the old town in the 1880s gradually moved out, eventually to be followed by the wealthier Muslim notables and the increasingly Europeanized Jews.

The main symbols of the new French protectorate were in place by the end of the 1890s: a new barracks at the Kasbah, completed 1898 (and today demolished), the cathedral, completely rebuilt by 1897, and, most importantly, the modern port, completed 1892.

In the first half of the 20th century, Tunis became a dual city. At its centre was the old town with its mosques and narrow streets. Around this old core spread the new town. Business was concentrated in the *ville basse*, new residential areas were created – leafy Montfleury, south-west of the médina, Lafayette, second home to the Jewish community with the large Art Déco Synagogue Daniel Osiris, the Cité Jardin and Mutuelleville.

Tunis was occupied by the Germans for six months during the Second World War. For both Axis and Allies, the city functioned as a staging post for supplies and troops. The port and parts of the city, notably Petite Sicile and the Kherba in the eastern médina, were bombarded. After the war, which wrought considerable damage in the Tunisian countryside, immigration from the rural areas increased dramatically. The population of the médina rose from 120,000 in 1936 to 230,000 in 1946. The Muslim bourgeoisie, increasingly westernized, sought homes in the new residential areas.

It was in the early 1950s that Tunis became a focus for an increasingly vocal nationalist movement. Happily, however, there was never any widespread violence. The independence movement was more of a pressure group formed by educated urban Tunisians, many of them from the Sahel. Independence was quickly conceded by France in 1956.

Since the mid-1950s, the population has risen from 400,000 to 1,200,000, resulting in vast expansion into the surrounding countryside, often at the expense of good farming land.

After independence in 1956, the population of Tunis has increased sharply from 400,000 to 1,200,000 by the 1990s. The Italian, Tunisian Jewish and French populations departed, and the city's Muslim population acquired the property left behind at knock down prices or by squatting. The movement of the old Tunisoise families out of the médina accelerated, and an influx of poor rural migrants brought about a huge change in the make-up of the oldest neighbourhoods. The great city residences were divided up as rooming houses or *oukalas*, in local parlance.

After Independence: demolition & expansion

Tunis and around

In the eyes of President Bourguiba, and indeed of many of the leading figures of the newly independent Tunisian Republic, the médina was a symbol of past oppressions, and as such was to be swept away. In the early 1960s, there were great schemes for opening up an avenue to extend the main Avenue Bourguiba as far as the Ezzitouna Mosque. In the event, nothing was done – the médina had far too many poor and potentially rebellious inhabitants, too costly to rehouse in one go. Numerous demolitions took place on the southern and western sides of the médina, however. The Kasbah barracks, most of the Sidi Abdallah gate and the walls from Bab el Assal at the northern end to the southern Bab el Fella were demolished. Presidential architect Clément Cacoub designed the modernist Maison du Parti on the new Kasbah esplanade, while excavations of the site revealed traces of the original Hafsid fortress. (The finds were later replaced with a vast underground car park.)

The city centre also saw its share of new building. The 1950s saw the construction of the imposing Ministry of the Interior on the main avenue. Three large new hotels went up in the 1960s: the blue tower of the Hotel Africa, the distinctive inverted pyramid of the Hotel du Lac, and the bulky Hotel International, at the junction of the Avenue de Paris and the Avenue Bourguiba. The vast majority of old style apartment buildings survived, however. Meanwhile, vast new suburbs, often unplanned, were taking shape on the edge of the city.

Late 20th century Tunis: expanding suburbs & preserving the centre
Tunis in the late 20th century continued to grow. New residential areas appeared almost overnight. The most spectacular of the new neighbourhoods is the Berges du Lac, a new mixed residential and business area built on land reclaimed from the lagoon which separates Tunis from its coastal suburbs. Tunis' first major shopping mall, the Lac Palace, is located here, and the business traveller may have call to visit clients in what is a rapidly expanding neighbourhood. The Berges du Lac will more than double in size when the second phase of building is complete, linking the Berges du Lac with Le Kram Ouest, home to the Foire Internationale de Tunis, the main trade fair complex. Despite its location on the main flightpath into Tunis Carthage Airport, the Berges du Lac has attracted a large number of private developers, and the area seems set to become the main business district, with banks remaining on the Avenue Mohamed V running from the old downtown area northwards towards the upmarket residential areas.

Like any other Mediterranean town, Tunis is increasingly segregated in socio-economic terms. The poorest social groups tend to opt for self-built housing west of the city centre. Beyond the Bardo area and the Cité Ibn Khaldoun lies the sprawling Tadhamen neighbourhood. An area of farmland until the early 1970s, land for housing was sub-divided and put on the market illegally. The result is a vast, semi-planned low-income neighbourhood. To avoid social unrest, State agencies brought in the main utilities. Other areas of low-income unplanned housing include La Cagna and Ouardia south of the centre. There are other pockets elsewhere, too. It should be stressed, however, that Tunis does not have housing problems on anything like the scale of Casablanca's bidonvilles or the multi-occupancy of old cities like Fès.

Further major new neighbourhoods are under way, or on the planners' drawing boards, and the late 1990s buoyancy of the construction industry is probably a sign of the health of the Tunisian economy as a whole. North of the 1980s suburbs of El Manar, the new Cité Ennasr neighbourhood was taking shape. In the southern suburb of Radès, a new stadium and sports complex was under construction in 1999 to host the Mediterranean Games for the year 2000. Plans were also well ahead for cleaning up the south Tunis industrial zone and creating new mixed-use neighbourhoods along the south side of the lagoon, a sort of mirror development to the Berges du Lac on the north side. Gammarth and the hotel strip at Raoued seemed set to expand as well. Some new developments are of high quality (Les Jardins de Carthage), others are of unmitigated tackiness (Le Palace).

The development of new neighbourhoods has been accompanied by renewed interest in the oldest parts of the city centre, the historic médina and ville nou- velle areas, centring respectively on the souks and the Avenue Bourguiba. Upmarket restaurants have been successfully installed in the palatial sur- roundings of restored private residences in the least degraded part of the médina, and since the Municipal Theatre became a listed building, an aware- ness of the value of city centre buildings seems to have taken root. Major new exhibition space the Musée de la Ville de Tunis was created in a restored 19th century building, the Palais Kheireddine, right at the heart of the old town. Heritage tourism, with buildings and galleries as a focus point, seems set to take off in old Tunis.

Preserving the médina

The successful redevelopment of older property in central Tunis will be dependent on all sorts of factors, not the least of them being access. Heavy vehicle traffic, on-street parking, narrow pavements and the general lack of places to sit and relax make Tunis in summer a difficult place for both visitor and locals. Tunis residents prefer the private car to public transport, and the result is growing vehicle pollution, although nothing as compared with Cairo and Istanbul. It remains to be seen whether downtown Tunis can become once more the pleasant Mediterranean destination which it really should be, given its location and climate.

Sights

Tunis, while being an easy city to visit in terms of transport, does not have many obvious sites, apart from the two great museums at the Bardo and Carthage. It is more a matter of atmosphere. Lacking the density and human pressure of Fès or Marrakech, the médina or old town is a gentle introduction to the traditional Arab city: there are a number of restored buildings open to the visitor, and new museums are planned. Despite some recent redevelop- ment, the narrow streets and tree-lined avenues of the central areas of Tunis are still redolent of the mid-20th century, and the stroller will feel the presence of a recent cosmopolitan past – and indeed for a short time Tunis was a fash- ionable resort. The imaginative visitor may enjoy flashback moments to scenes from *Pépé le Moko* or *Casablanca*. The period 1850 to 1950 left behind it numerous handsome buildings, and the historic building enthusiast will enjoy the architectural set pieces (the Art Nouveau Théâtre Municipal, the Art Deco Synagogue Daniel Osiris) and the numerous stylish apartment buildings which make the town such a catalogue of architectural styles.

The town is situated on the shores of a lake linked to the sea at La Goulette. The new city, with **Avenue Habib Bourguiba** as its centre, is laid out on a grid-iron plan. The médina, in contrast, is full of small, initially confusing, winding streets. The médina is no longer walled, as the French replaced the old walls with large boulevards all around the old city. However, cars cannot pene- trate all the streets of the médina, making a welcome change from the over- crowded and noisy streets of the new town.

Downtown Tunis: the médina & the Ville Nouvelle

Tunis and around

Tunis médina

Maison du
Parti (former)

Rue 2 Mars 1934

Municipality

KASBA

Collège
Sadiki

Kasbah
Mosque

Place de
Kasbah

Rue Bou Khriss

Rue de la Rivière

Tourbet
Laz

Place du
Gouvernemi

Sidi Bou
Khrissan
Mausoleum

Yossef Dey
Mosque

Dar El Bey

BABJEDID

Mosque
el Ksar

Souk Sekkajine

Rue Marr

Blvd Bab Menara

Rue Abri

Dar Hussein
(National Heritage
Institute)

Mosque of
Hammouda
Pacha

Zaouia
Sidi Ben
Arous

Bab
Djedid

Rue Ben Rejeb

Hammam

Jamaâ
Ezzitouna
(Great
Mosque)

Chama
Meders

Tourbet
Aziza
Othana

Rue Abba

Rue du Riche

Rue des Andalous

Rue des Juges

M'sid el
Koubba

Rue Tourbet El Bey

Three Medressa
Complex

Rue Jamaâ Ezzitouna

Souk el Ou

Sour El Blat

Tourbet
El Bey

Rue Sidi Essourdou

Rue Sidi Ali Azouz

Rue Ben Ayed

Jamaâ el
Jedid

Dar Ben
Abdallah

Dar
Othman

LA KHERBA

Chapel
Holy Cre

Blvd Bab Jedid

Rue des Teinturiers

Rue de la Commission

Louage
to Alge

Rue Sidi Bou Mendil

Rue El Jazira

N

| 0 metres | 100 |
| 0 yards | 109 |

■ **Sleeping**
1 Des Amis
2 Médina
3 Sfax
4 Youth Hostel

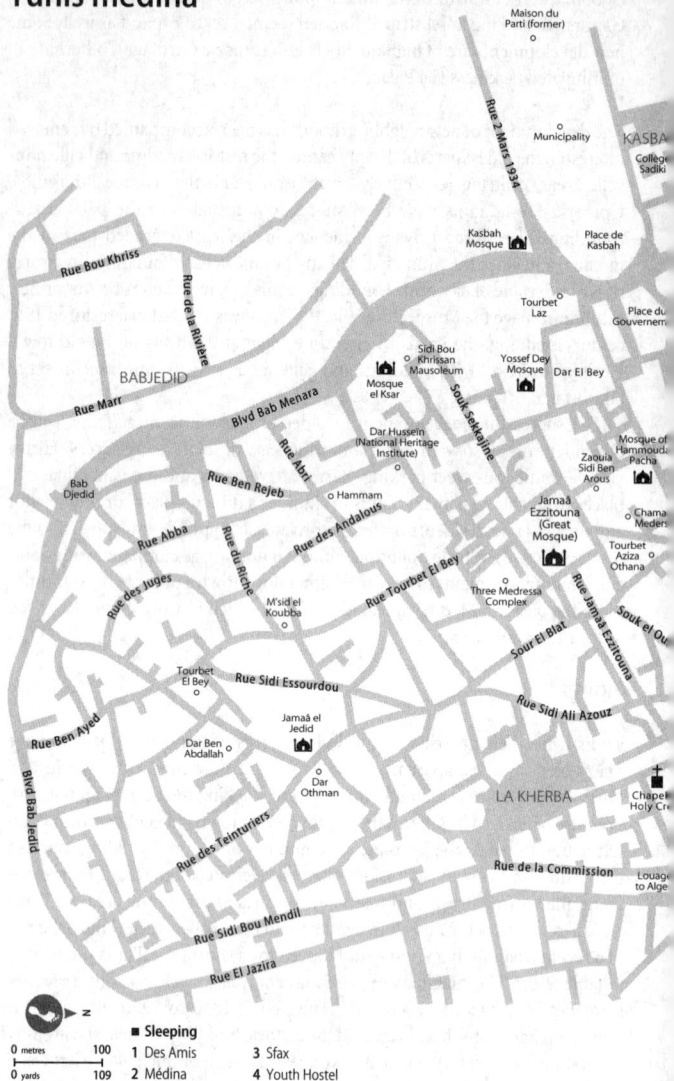

Children will like visiting the médina because many activities & trades take place partly in the street. Care should be taken, however. Mopeds can come hurtling down narrow streets at great speed

Visiting the médina can be a confusing business, especially if you are being rushed in and out on a whistlestop visit to the souks between the Bardo and Carthage. Old Tunis repays a more leisurely visit. Although the monuments are not spectacular, there is much of interest in the streets and boulevards of the central parts of the city. After some general background on the médina, there follows four short walking tours to help you get to know the town. The first two take in the most obvious sights, walks three and four are more for enthusiasts. The médina walks are followed by a fifth route to show you some of the better buildings in the Ville Nouvelle.

Law Courts

Blvd Bab Benat

Rue Gharnouïa

Rue du Sabre

Rue Bab Souïka

Rue Bir Lahjar

Dar Ben Achoor Library

Hammam

Rue du Pacha

Rue Sidi Brahim

Rue Sidi Ali Ben Diat

Medersa Bis Lahjan

Hammam

Dar Lasram

Rue el Cahia

Rue el Kahti

Sidi Mehrez Mosque

Place Bab Souïka

Rue El Jeld

City Museum (exhibition space)

Medersa Achouriya

Rue el Garmattou

Rue Sidi Mehrez

3

Zaouia Sidi Mehrez

Rue Sidi Ben Arous

Rue de la Hafsia

Rue Achour

Rue el Monastiri

1

BAB SOUÏKA

Rue Saïda Ajoula

Rue de Jagna

4

Hammam

Louages to Libya

Av Ali Belhaouane

Rue du Divan

Hammam

AZZAFINE

Rue Sidi Baïan

Rue des Jerbiens

HAFSIA

Souk El Grana

Rue el Mechmaka

Souk du Cuivre

Hammam

Rue de la Verrerie

Rue de la Kasbah

Rue Zarkoun

Anglican Church of St George

Rue el Kramed

Rue el Abbassi

Rue Sidi Kadous

LA TRONJA

Hammam

Rue de l'Ancienne Douane

Rue Bab El Khadra

ce de la ictoire

2

Rue des Glacières

Bab B'har (Porte de France)

British Embassy

Av de France

Rue Mongi Slim

The médina of Tunis was founded some 13 centuries ago on a narrow strip of land lying between the Sebkhat Essedjoumi and the lagoon, separating the site of the future city from the sea. With a steep scarp slope falling down to the saltflats, and a number of outcrops, subsequently fortified, the site had good defensive potential. The water table being near the surface, every house was able to have its own well, an important factor in a land where the rain is often irregular. The Arab conquerors of the seventh and eighth centuries no doubt also chose this site for their settlement because of the availability of abundant building material in the declining city of Carthage. They preferred not to settle at Carthage to be out of reach of Byzantine naval raids. A nomad people, the Arabs had yet to gain mastery of the Mediterranean.

The médina: background & history

Architectural historians and specialists consider the médina of Tunis as an outstanding example of Arab-Muslim urban development. The dense web of narrow streets surrounding the main mosque is little changed since the Hafsid Dynasty (late Middle Ages). Much demolition and rebuilding has taken place since then, however, and there is little genuinely mediaeval building still left. There is, however, a huge variety of architectural styles, from the vernacular to modern-movement, to be seen in the streets of the médina and adjoining parts of the Ville Nouvelle.

The médina divides into three main areas: the central médina, the oldest core of the city; the faubourg nord or Bab Souika neighbourhood, and the faubourg sud or Bab Jazira neighbourhood; perhaps the least obvious of the three for the visitor. Note that as elsewhere in Tunisia, mosques and monuments used as offices are not open to the public. Admission times of those which are accessible are given in the text. Note that ticket policy seems to vary. Some years, one purchases a ticket giving access to several monuments at the Dar Ben Abdallah (Museum of Traditional Arts). Other years, tickets are bought individually at the various monuments. This was the system in 1999.

When visiting Tunis, do not appear in beachwear. You can walk around in brief shorts, shoulders uncovered if you wish, but expect to attract unwelcome attention and comments. Do not expect to be allowed up onto the porch of the Ezzitouna Mosque in skimpy attire.

Walk 1
Faith & Trade:
the Zitouna
Mosque & the
souks

This walk takes you past the finest mosques of old Tunis, through the covered souks which were the commercial nerve centre of the city for centuries. The starting point is **Bab Bhar**, the old sea gate on Place de la Victoire, east side of the médina. The finishing point is the Kasbah esplanade on the west side of the médina. This is a short walk, where you will view buildings mainly from the outside. Still, allow at least one hour 45 minutes.

Bab Bhar ('the Sea Gate') restored in the 1980s, stands in isolation in front of the médina. Behind it stand the three-storey buildings of a neighbourhood once inhabited mainly by European merchants. With Bab Bhar behind you, the **British Embassy**, a whitewashed building in the Neo-Moorish style, is to your right. (On an insalubrious side street behind the Embassy is the old French merchants hostel, the **Fondouk des Francais**, currently being restored.) Ahead of you are the balconies of the **Palazzo Gneccho**, now a restaurant.

Walk 1: faith & trade

Rue du Pacha

Place Romdhane Bey ■ YHA

Fondouk des Français o

British Embassy o

START Bab Bhar/ Porte de France

Rue Jamaâ Ezzitouna

Blvd Bab Benat

Rue Jeld

Rue Sidi Ben Arous

Galerie de la Médina ●

Collège Sadiki o

Dar el Jeld ●

Rue de la Kasbah

Hammouda Pacha Mosque

Eglise Sainte Croix

Zaouia Sidi Ali Azouz

National Library o

o Dar Bayram Turki

Souk Echaouachia o

Souk el Attarine

KASBAH ESPLANADE

Dar el Bey o

● Lunchtime Places

Café Mrabet

Great Mosque

● Lunchtime Places

Sidi Ali Azouz Barracks

o Municipality

Maison du Parti

Aziza Othmana Hospital

Youssef Dey Mosque

● Hammam el Kachachine

Kasbah Mosque

Souk el Berka

3 Medresas Complex o

To Souk El Blat

Cinema Museum

Blvd Bab Menara

N

See Tunis médina map for orientation

Not to scale

▭▭ Walking Route

Head up the street to the left of the palazzo. This is Rue Jamaâ Ezzitouna, ex-Rue de l'Eglise, the main souk street in the médina and home to small shops selling all sorts of junk for the tourist. A few metres inside the médina on the left is the **Eglise de la Sainte Croix**, also currently being restored and scheduled to be turned into some sort of performance/gallery space.

Some 100 metres up the Rue Jamaâ Ezzitouna, you could go left down Rue Sidi Ali Azouz for a few metres. With a little luck, you might be able to take a look into the **Zaouia of Sidi Ali Azouz** (on your right), and, on your left, down a narrow alley, at **Dar Bayram Turki**. This 17th century building has a fine courtyard faced with stone. Now used as workshop space, it is a good example of the fate which has befallen many fine old homes in the old town. A few metres further on, the large building straight ahead of you was once a barracks. Double back to the Rue Jamaâ Ezzitouna. The street leads up past carpet and trinket sellers to a small open square in front of the Great or Zitouna Mosque, **Souk el Fekkia**, the former dried fruit market. To your left, there is a small neighbourhood plan in ceramic tiles on the wall. In front of you is the skifa or main portico of the Great Mosque. Before midday it is possible to go up onto the skifa to view the great courtyard.

Jamaâ Ezzitouna is by far the most venerable mosque in Tunis, attributed to an early Arab conqueror, one Hassan Ibn Nu'man. Some reports date it back to the foundation of the Islamic city in 698. It was completely rebuilt by the Aghlabid Emir Ibrahim Ibn Ahmed in 856-63. The minaret was remodelled on a number of occasions, and the present version, with the interlinked lozenge design on the façades, dates from 1896. The same design is to be found on the nearby Kasbah Mosque. The courtyard gallery dates largely from the 17th century. The prayer hall dates back to the original foundation, and has columns 'quarried' from nearby Roman sites. It is spectacular but unfortunately, unless you are Muslim, off limits. This mosque has extensive cisterns under the main courtyard, which slopes so that a maximum of rainwater could be collected.

Plan of Great Mosque Ez-Zitouna

(Only area 5 can be visited, before midday, by the non-muslim)

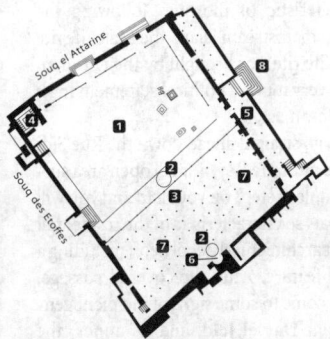

Souq el Attarine

Souq des Etoffes

N

0 metres 10
0 yards 11

1 Courtyard
2 Cupola
3 Main Door to Prayer Room
4 Minaret
5 External Gallery
6 Mihrab
7 Prayer Room
8 Main Entrance from
   rue Jamaâ Zitouna

As you view Jamaâ Ezzitouna, note how it is surrounded on all sides by the souks. (There were originally stalls for rent under the skifa esplanade.) The Renaissance ideology of 'man as the measure of all things' never touched old Tunis. The médina lived closed in on itself, and there was never any need to create open spaces for fountains and statuary, as per the cities of Italy and Spain, post-Renaissance. Next go left in front of the mosque, to visit (if possible) the three **medresas** or colleges next to the mosque. These are on your right, and are the **Medresa Ennakhla**, **Medresa el Bachiya** and **Medresa Slimaniya**. Why are these important? The medresa was basically an institution providing accommodation for students following courses at a major mosque. The latter two were both established by 18th century beys, and bear witness to the piety of their founders. The Slimaniya, built by Ali Pacha in memory of a favourite

Tunis and around

son, Suleiman, who died poisoned in a dynastic feud, is particularly fine (and is today occupied by medical NGOs). There are numerous other medresas in Tunis, and you can imagine the courtyards with students sitting against the columns, hard at work on some weighty religious text.

After the three medresas, double back to the square in front of Jamaâ Ezzitouna. You need to go left at the other end of Souk el Fekkia, up **Souk el Attarine**, the Perfumers' Souk. Here Tunis brides come to buy all their wedding paraphernalia: perfumes, candles, henna and silky cat baskets to put all the wedding presents in. There are things for tourists too, delicate gilt bottles and felt fishes covered in sequins to ward off the evil eye. Note that the souks closest to the Great Mosque are clean or noble trades that is perfumers, sellers of once expensive dried fruit, booksellers and tailors.

Up Souk el Attarine you come to a junction, just below the minaret of the Ezzitouna, in fact. Here you can go straight ahead up **Souk Ettrouk**, once upon a time the street of the Turkish taylors. Half-way along is the **Café Mrabet**, an old saint's shrine now functioning as an attractive café, and probably one of the first cafés in the city. There is a slightly scruffy garden at the back with a good view of the minaret of the Ezzitouna. At the top of Souk Ettrouk, turn left into Souk el Berka, once upon a time the main slave market, now the centre of a flourishing jewellery arcade.

If you go right at the top of Souk Ettrouk, go straight ahead along a narrow street between the high walls of the **Dar el Bey**, today the Prime Minister's offices, on your left, and the outside wall of the chechia makers souk, **Souk Echaouachia**, on your right. You should be able to cut through the souk and observe the chaouachis hard at work, felting and shaping the red felt caps or chechias once so characteristic of Tunis. Back in the 19th century, the cap makers were easily the wealthiest and most influential corporation in the city, masters of a pre-industrial manufacturing process. Your coffee stop could be here at the café in the souk, or, if you cut right through, at the street café on the Rue Sidi Ben Arous. Here you have a magnificent view of the Ezzitouna minaret. The same street also has a small well-stocked bookshop, Le Diwan, and an expensive craftshop, Eddar.

Going up this street, leaving the minaret behind you, you come to the Hammouda Pacha mosque on your right, a splendid 17th century construction. The octagonal minaret is characteristic of mosques following the Hanefite rite. (There are four main rites in mainstream Islam, the Malekite rite dominating in North Africa.) The Hanefite rite was brought by the Ottoman Turks, and the minaret would have been very much a political statement in its day, declaring the supremacy of Tunis' new masters.

At the junction at the top of the street, go straight ahead down the Rue Sidi Ben Arous. You will come to the **Place Romdhane Bey**, a small open area surrounded by small workshops. Go up a couple of steps on your left, and you will come to one of the covered streets or sabats so characteristic of the residential areas of Tunis. There is some magnificent architectural detail here, including a kitsch Tuniso-Roccoco double window feature. After the covered passage, turn left up the Rue El Jeld. Here you will come to some signs of incipient gentrification, including upmarket restaurant **Dar el Jeld**, and its annex, the Diwan Dar el Jeld. The **Galerie de la Médina** holds occasional exhibitions of contemporary Tunisian painters.

Rue el Jeld leads you to **Place du Gouvernement**, with its ficus trees, water feature and shiney granite paving. The Ministry of Finance, with its arcades, is a fine 19th century building in a simple version of the Neo-Moorish style. At the top of Place du Gouvernement, you come to an area generally referred to as the **Kasbah**, after the long-vanished mediaeval fortifications. Cross the busy road and go up the steps, and from the main esplanade you will have a splendid view of some of the key historic buildings of Tunis. Be careful should you wish to take photographs. (No men in uniforms on your photos).

Straight ahead of you are key government buildings, the Finance Ministry with its domes and crenellations and the Dar el Bey, entirely remodelled in the 19th century. This was the guest palace under the Husseinid beys. Moving clockwise, you come to the Aziz Othmana hospital complex, named after the mediaeval princess who was the hospital's original founder. The minaret to your right is that of the **Kasbah Mosque**, built 1231-35. The *darj wa ktef* lozenge motif on the façade recalls that this was a monument to the Almohad brand of Islam, a puritan movement that arose among the Masmouda Berbers of the High Atlas and spread eastwards across the Maghreb in the 12th century. The same motif, symbolizing loyalty to the Almohad cause, can be found on numerous minarets in North Africa. The galleries on the outside of the mosque are late 20th century, and the building should be imagined in context as the central point of a palace complex outside the médina. Still moving clockwise, there is the new Ministry of Culture and some remnant walls of the bastion of Sidi Abdallah. A large chunk of the remaining walls and a late 19th century barracks were demolished after independence.

The largest building in the area, however, is the **Municipality of Tunis**, a vast construction facing directly onto the arcade, behind which is situated the **Maison du Parti**, a modernist building by Olivier Clément Cacoub, favourite architect of former president Habib Bourguiba. The Municipality, completed 1999, features the *darj wa ktef* lozenge motif; the Almohad overtones have long since been forgotten. Try to get a look inside the Municipality: the overwrought decoration combines tiles, carved plasterwork and painted wood ceilings, all elements of 18th century domestic decoration schemes, on a vast scale. The result is somewhat overwhelming.

The next key building is the mid-19th century **Collège Sadiki**. Founded by Kheireddine Pacha, under Sadok Bey (hence the name, Sadiki), the college was the first institution in Tunisia to dispense a modern secondary education. Architecturally, it is a typical Neo-Moorish building, with traditional features such as minaret and domes being used to 'dress' what is otherwise a typical school building, rather in the same way that Gothic features were used for 19th century British public schools.

Finally, a number of other major buildings can be seen from the Kasbah esplanade. In the far distance, above a wooded hill, the mass of the Arab League headquarters can be seen, with next to it the box-like Hilton Hotel. Rather nearer, in the médina, and surrounded by houses, are the white egg-shell domes of **Sidi Mehrez**, a 17th century mosque of Ottoman inspiration. Unlike the great mosques of Istanbul, it was never to have soaring, pointy topped minarets.

On this route through the médina you will discover some of the finest examples of Tunisoise domestic architecture, and you will be given an idea about life in one of the more residential areas of the city. The high point is Dar Ben Abdallah, palace home to the Museum of Traditional Life. Starting point: the Kasbah. Finish: Porte de France. Allow a good one hour and 45 minutes.

Walk 2 Beldis, beys & a pirate adventurer's home

From the Kasbah, make your way along the Boulevard Bab Menara. On your right are the Kasbah Mosque and then the late 19th century block of the Ministry of Defence. Past a café, down a few steps, and you come to an open area where a small tomb marks the presence of a medieval saint from Majorca, commemorated because he converted to Islam. Go right of the tombs into the covered souk. In the middle of the street is another tomb, in the form of a red and green box, the last resting place of one **Sidi Bou Abdallah** who died here

Tunis and around

defending Tunis against the Spanish foe. Legend has it that Monty Python-like, he continued fighting even when his head had been chopped off.

At the first intersection, turn right into the Rue Ben Mahmoud. On your right, the first door is that of the **Musée Lapidaire Sidi Bou Khrissan**, a small museum of elaborate carved tombstones. Knock on the door, and a member of the family living inside will let you in (no tickets, make a donation). Ninth century Khorassanid emirs were one buried here. Today, the museum with its olive tree and ruined *koubba* is off the tourist circuit.

After the museum, continue along the Rue Ben Mahmoud. You will pass the **Restaurant Essaraya**, a costly and kitsch 'restoration' of an old home (note plexi-glass dome). Turning right after Essaraya, the street widens. On your right, down a narrow alley, Impasse Ettobjiya, is the recently restored **Dar Haddad**, which may eventually house some of the displays currently in Dar Ben Abdallah. At the end of this street, turn right, and the narrow covered passageway will bring you out onto Place du Château, a square currently used as a car park. On your right is one of Tunis' oldest mosques, **Jamaâ el Ksar**. The prayer hall, as usual closed to visitors, is below street level. The huge, irregular stone blocks of the lower walls suggest the mosque was built on a much older building. The minaret is 17th century.

The main building on this square (which could be quite pleasant, given a few trees) is **Dar Hussein**, currently home to the INP, the Tunisian National Heritage Institute. The building is 18th century, much added to in the 19th century, before being taken over by the French military authorities. The grumpy concierge may let you have a peek in at the rather fine main courtyard.

From Place du Château, head down the covered cobbled street to the right of the main door of Dar Hussein. This brings you to a small open space where there is a hammam or Turkish bath with the characteristic red and green door. Go left down the Rue Abri, and then right down the narrow **Rue des Andalous**, with its studded doors and vaulted sections, one of the finest streets in the médina. At the end, turn left down Rue du Riche. At the first junction, you come to the Rue Tourbet el Bey. (Going left here will allow you to have a look at the **Msid el Koubba**, a small domed structure where mediaeval sociologist Ibn Khaldoun is said to have prayed.) Turn right, and after about 75 metres you will come to **Tourbet el Bey**, a mausoleum complex and last

Walk 2: beldis, beys & a pirate adventurer

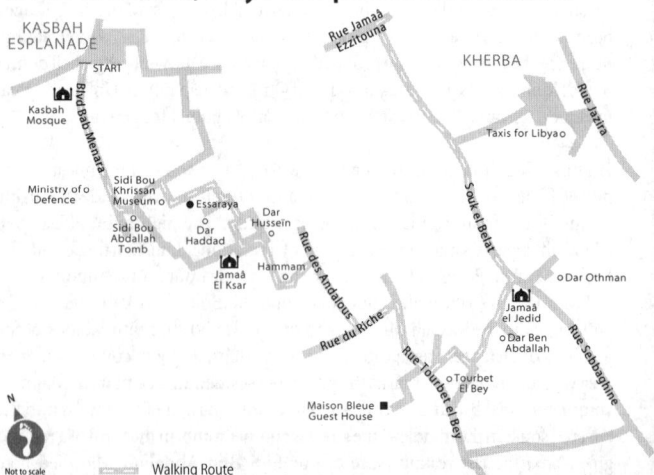

See Tunis médina map for orientation

Not to scale

Walking Route

resting place of the Husseinid princes and princesses. Built by Ali Pasha II (1758-82), this monument is something of a curiosity. Most Islamic dynasties went in for splendid necropolises. It is somehow strange that the beys, who lived isolated from their subjects in palaces well outside the city, should have chosen to be buried in their midst. The first members of the dynasty had been buried in the Tourbet Sidi Kassem, rue Sidi Kassem.

Abandoned to its fate after Tunisian independence, the Tourbet was recently restored. The term *tourbet* derives from the Turkish for tomb, and most of the great Tunisois families had family mausolea near their homes. The building is an odd stylistic mix. The outside features carved stonework with floral motifs, plus domes covered in the green, scale shaped tiles which mean 'burial place' or 'holy person's tomb' in the Tunis streetscape. Inside, the decoration is flamboyant. There are the characteristic 18th century tiled panels (shiny replacement panels stand out a mile) and carved stucco work. In the Hall of the Reigning Princes, the lower walls have elaborate marble marquetry panels, a style imported from nearby Sicily. The princes' tombs are topped with their headgear, turbans and later fezzes of various sizes. ■ *The building can normally be visited 0930-1600 except Sunday, entrance 3Dt. If it seems closed, knock hard, and someone may emerge to let you in (for an unofficial tip).*

After Tourbet el Bey, you may want to see a traditional Tunis family home. The restored **Dar Ben Abdallah**, today home to the **Museum of Traditional Arts**, is close by. Leaving the main door of Tourbet el Bey, go right, and right twice more, following the main outside wall of the Tourbet. On your left, you will come to the Rue Sidi Kassem. A few metres down this street, go right under an arch and you will come to the Dar Ben Abdallah, an 18th century palace restored in the early 19th century by an officer of the Beylical army. He opted for the Italian touch (galleries, marble fountain with dolphin) very much in favour at the time. The museum divides into two parts. Off the main courtyard, are rooms with scenes from Tunisois family life in a fairly recent but idealized past. This is the world of the *beldia*, the old Muslim families of Tunis, proud of their traditions. Little did they know that their world was to be irrevocably destroyed by the changes of the 20th century. The museum also houses a small display of craft implements in a neighbouring stables area.

In the courtyard, the first room on your right deals with childhood. There are cases of small boys' embroidered circumcision costumes, and a scene with small girls learning embroidery from a *maâlema*. There are tiny couscous pots for small girls to play at cooking.

The next two rooms are devoted to women. There is a room showing a scene from upper-class daily life in the 19th century. Note the large, elaborate beds in the alcoves. In the next room along is the bride getting ready for her wedding. The scene is perhaps just before the bride's pre-wedding party. The *hannana* is there, no doubt ready to execute some henna designs on hands and feet, and the bride's friends in their best gear. The styles suggest the 1920s, maybe later. The display cabinets contain a range of silver and mother-of-pearl items. In a room to the left is a display devoted to the *hammam* in Tunis. (**NB**. Between these two rooms, through a small door, is an old fashioned Tunis kitchen.)

The final courtyard room is devoted to men. The scene shows the fiancé, accompanied by a religious scholar, asking for the hand of the daughter of the house. To the right of the main alcove is a room set up as an old-fashioned Tunis study. All the items necessary to a Tunis scholar, before the arrival of the printing press, are on display: inkwells, pencases, Koran-holders, and rosaries. There are some fine costumes as well.

After Dar Ben Abdallah, turn right out onto the Rue Sidi Kassem. The street leads you to onto the Rue des Teinturiers, and a large mosque, the early 18th century **Jamaâ el Jedid**, will be on your right. Go down a covered street opposite the mosque, the Rue el Mbazaâ, which will take you to **Dar Othman**, 17th century home of a corsair leader. The door has a strikingly modern black and white marble surround. The entrance hall or driba has impressive (mainly new) tile panels. Here, no doubt, Othman Dey, pirateer and governor of Tunis, would hold court. If you are allowed into the main courtyard, you will find a pleasant space planted with hibiscus, pomegranate and cypress trees. The building once housed the Department of Traditional Arts, managed by craft expert Jacques Revault. Trained in Morocco, Revault no doubt had a traditional Moroccan garden courtyard or *riyad* in mind when he had the courtyard at Dar Othman planted. Otherwise, Dar Othman follows the usual pattern for a Tunisois house, with narrow sleeping/reception rooms placed around a central courtyard. Today the building houses the offices of the Conservation de la Médina, one of two bodies working to preserve the old town and its monuments.

After viewing Dar Othman, double back up Rue Mbazaâ and turn right into Rue des Teinturiers. Going straight ahead, you will come to **Souk el Belat** and its numerous herborists stalls. (Traditional plant remedies for everything here.) The name of the souk derives from the Greek *palation*, doubtless after some former splendid palace in the area. Continue straight ahead, and you will come to the Rue Jamaâ Ezzitouna, the main tourist drag. Turn right, and head down towards the Porte de France, some five minutes walk away, depending on the human traffic jams.

**Walk 3
From the Hafsia
to Halfaouine:
urban
redevelopment
& 19th century
palaces**

This route is more for médina enthusiasts. Although there are few monuments to visit, it takes you through areas of the old city with a vivid past. The Halfaouine area, in particular, is a lively part of the médina. You will see neighbourhoods which have been remodelled, two major mosques, and 19th century palaces. Starting point is Porte de France, finishing point is the metro at Bab el Khadhra. Allow at least two hours. Café stops are at Bab Souika or on Place Halfaouine.

Walk 3: from the Hafsia to Halfaouine

See Tunis médina map for orientation

Walking Route   Not to scale

Sidi Mehrez, patron saint of Tunis

Abou Mohamed Mahrez Ibn el Khalaf (d.1022), referred to as Sidi Mehrez, lived in the early 10th century, a turbulent and dangerous time for the inhabitants of Tunis. The northeastern Maghreb was ruled by a dynasty which owed allegiance to the Shi'ite Fatimids, based in Cairo. The population was taxed heavily to finance wars the Fatimids intended to fight against the Sunni caliph based in Baghdad. Eventually, in 943, an uprising led by one Abu Yazid developed into a general rebellion against Fatimid rule. Although Abu Yazid was eventually defeated by the Fatimids, it was only after Tunis had been looted by his forces in 944. It was Sidi Mehrez who got the inhabitants of Tunis to work together to reconstruct their town. He reorganized the souks, and got permission for the Jews to settle within the walls. He was also involved in the theological debates pitting the Sunni Malikite scholars of Tunis against the Shi'ites. In the 10th century, Tunis was home to a number of defenders of Sunnni orthodoxy. Sidi Mehrez was cousin of one of the region's most famous scholars, Ibn Abi Zayid el Kayrawani (d.996), author of a synopsis of Malikite law which became famous far beyond the Maghreb.

With Porte de France behind you, go right down the Rue des Glacières, the street leading off between the two cafés. Here you will discover lots of boutiques, bright with trendy clothes and footwear imported from Italy, France, Morocco and Turkey. Go straight ahead at the junction with the Rue Zarkoun. (If you want local music, there is a large cassette emporium here.) You are at the heart of the old **Quartier Franc**, home to the *fondouks* or foreign merchants' hostels. Most of the present buildings were built in the late 19th century, before the new Tunis, outside the médina walls, took shape. Walking along Rue des Glacières, between the crumbling walls, the Italian influence is clearly visible. Note that there is a good deal of demolition/rebuilding in the neighbourhood at present, which will no doubt alter its character.

At the end of Rue des Glacières, you come to a small open area, the entrance to the Hafsia neighbourhood. Until the mid-20th century, this was the Hara or Jewish quarter, an area of narrow streets and tiny courtyard houses. As of the mid-1970s, the neighbourhood was entirely rebuilt in a style that recalls the old médina. Along the main street through the neighbourhood, the Rue de la Hafsia, are two- and three-storey apartment buildings. Behind are small, modern courtyard houses.

Turn left up the Rue de la Hafsia. The garment trade is important in the area today. On your right, the fish souk is now home to the *friperie* (second-hand clothes stalls). There are several clothes wholesalers in the streets off to the left.

On your right, you will come across three large low-rise 1930s apartment buildings, the **immeubles du Dr Cassar**, named for a leading figure in the Tunis Jewish community. (Behind them a former synagogue can be identified by the menara candlestick motif on the metal doors.) The Jews of Tunis were quick to wake up to the possibilities of modern education, and soon adapted to the French protectorate. By the 1930s, a large part of the community had moved out to new residential areas like Lafayette, where they built a splendid Art Déco synagogue. The Hara was crumbling, and the poorest members of the community were rehoused in the Dr Cassar flats.

With the flats on your left, you have a splendid view to the white domes of **Sidi Mehrez**, today considered to be the patron saint of Tunis. Back in the 10th century, it was Sidi Mehrez who allowed the Jews to settle within the walls of Tunis. The story goes that he had a fine earring. He asked a Jewish jeweller to make him a copy, which the craftsman did. Sidi Mehrez granted the Jew's wish

Tunis and around

to live protected within the city walls. Criticized for his decision, Sidi Mehrez is said to have declared, "Why make such a fuss for a handful (*hara*) of Jews?" And so the Jewish neighbourhood came to be referred to as the Hara. Or so the story goes.

Continue up along Rue de la Hafsia, and turn right onto Rue du Tribunal. On this narrow street, the building on your right with the horseshoe arches is the early 20th century Ecole Israelite. Rue du Tribunal opens up after 50 metres into a pleasant square set with poplar trees. The fine white façades on your right belong to the new **Musée de la Ville de Tunis**, housed in the former **Palais Kheireddine**. Look out for temporary exhibitions here until such time as the museum is established.

Proceeding across the Place du Tribunal, the street narrows and turns sharp right and then left. On your left you will find the entrance to the **Club culturel Tahar Haddad**, housed in the undercroft of an early 19th century palace, the Dar Lasram. Once a hotbed of the Tunis feminist movement, the club is a polite, artistic sort of place today. There is a small library. The club is closed at lunchtimes. Look out for evening concerts during Ramadhan. Round the corner on your left is the entrance to **Dar Lasram**, restored in the early 1970s and today home to the Association de Sauvegarde de la Médina de Tunis (ASM). The palace today functions as design offices and meeting space for the ASM, which plays an important role in managing restoration and housing projects in the old neighbourhoods of Tunis. Ask nicely, express an interest in historic Tunis, and you will probably be allowed in to have a look around (no charge). The main patio is splendid, and there is a small display of the ASM's main projects.

After Dar Lasram, continue along the Rue du Tribunal. At the T-junction, go right. At the end, go left onto Rue el Mestiri, and follow the street until you

Zaouia of Sidi Abdelkader at Bab Souika

(Association Sanvegarde de la Médina de Tunis)

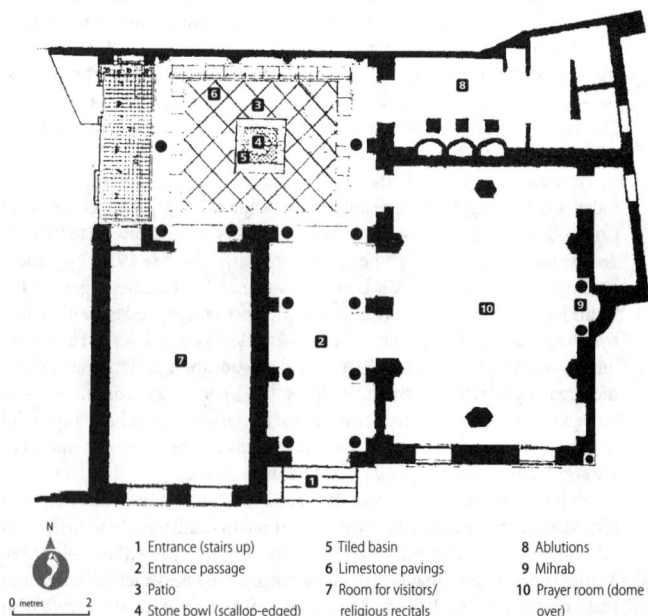

N

0 metres 2

1 Entrance (stairs up)
2 Entrance passage
3 Patio
4 Stone bowl (scallop-edged)
5 Tiled basin
6 Limestone pavings
7 Room for visitors/ religious recitals
8 Ablutions
9 Mihrab
10 Prayer room (dome over)

reach the main souk. If you go right, you can view the entrance to the Zaouia or **shrine of Sidi Mehrez** (rebuilt 1862-63), opposite the mosque with the white domes which you saw from the Hafsia. The shrine is much frequented by women seeking the saint's blessing, and you will find many small stalls selling pilgrims' requisites (candles, little green and red flags, incenses). Going left, you will head up the crowded souk and come out though an arched gateway at **Bab Souika**. Go right to the fountain roundabout, and you will be able to view the results of the second urban redevelopment project on this walk.

The médina of Tunis sits at the heart of the Greater Tunis urban area. By the 1970s, there were severe traffic problems at Bab Souika, transit point for most of the east-west traffic. It was decided to redevelop the area. To resolve the traffic problem, tunnels were put under a new square. New building was to be 'in keeping' with the architecture of the médina. The result is a series of inoffensive, post-modern buildings with vaguely traditional detailing. (The apartment block facing you as you leave the souk has a distinct René Macintosh feel.) One of the more interesting buildings is the **Zaouia of Sidi Abdelkader** (the small domed building on your right, as you stand with the main square behind you), a shrine entirely rebuilt in a simple reworking of the 18th century style.

Note that Bab Souika is something of a Tunis legend. It was home to the nationalist movement – and to bawdy night-time entertainments during Ramadhan, the famous cafés-chantants. The area is also HQ for the Espérance sportive de Tunis, one of Tunis' two big football teams. Flags and banners in the clubs colours, red and yellow, will be draped round the square on big match days.

From Bab Souika, head down the **Rue Halfaouine**, the neighbourhood's main shopping street. (The only pedestrian street leading off the fountain roundabout, between a patisserie and an arcaded building.) There are piles of fresh fruit and vegetables, butchers and wholesale merchants of various kinds.

At the end of Rue Halfaouine, you come to the Place Halfaouine, a tree-shaded square overlooked by the elegant arcades and octagonal minaret of the **Jamaâ Sahib Ettabaâ** (**The Lord of the Seal's Mosque**). The mosque was completed in 1812, and is the focal point of a *kulliye*, a complex comprising medersa, souk, foundouk and hammam. (The imposing Zaouia of Sidi Chiha, behind the mosque, is a mid-19th century foundation.) This complex was the first planned redevelopment of its kind in the médina, a clear reflection of the prestige of Youssef Sahib Ettabaâ, the super-minister under Hammouda Bey (1782-1814). The period was a prosperous one for Husseinid Tunisia, Europe being embroiled in the Napoleonic wars. Youssef Sahib Ettabaâ was to meet a violent end, leaving the minaret unfinished – and a legend grew up suggesting a similar fate for whomsoever attempted to complete it. It was only in 1970 that the legend was actually put to the test.

Standing with the main façade of the mosque behind you, you have Youssef Sahib Ettabaâ's palace to your left, just to the right of the arched entrance of the covered Souk el Jedid. (On the street to the right of the mosque you also have the fine Hammam Sahib Ettabaâ, well worth a visit. Fans of Tunisian cinema will recognize it from scenes in the early 1990s 'coming of age in old Tunis' film, *Halfaouine, l'enfant des terrasses*.) Facing the trees, you have a pleasant covered café to your right, while on the lefthand side of the square is the **Palais du Théâtre**, yet another 19th century palace, built by one Mustapha Khaznadar, state treasurer under Ahmed Bey (1837-55). Today the palace is used as rehearsal space by the Tunisian National Theatre. The building, a sort of Palladian villa behind high walls, is unique in the médina, and reflects the growing taste for all things Italian in 19th century Tunis.

After a coffee stop, head down the **Rue Souki Bil Khir** which leads off the end of the square. This is a street of carpenters' shops and private homes. There is a lot of new building, with workshops at street level and flats above. The simple whitewashed facades of the original vernacaual architecture are disappearing, new homes have street-facing windows and tiled door surrounds. Eventually, after some 10 minutes walking, you reach **Bab el Khadra**, formerly one of the most important gates into the northern part of the city. The twin gates are much restored, but there is a short stretch of 18th century rampart. From outside Bab el Khadra, take the metro (or walk down Avenue de Madrid) back to République station (also referred to as Le Passage).

Walk 4
three gates &
a tile-making
saint

This walk will take you through the southern part of the médina of Tunis. You will discover the atmosphere of a residential part of the old town. Architecture buffs will come across a generous mix of styles, from a mediaeval gate to fine early 20th century apartment buildings. Towards the end of the walk, you visit the National Ceramics Museum at Sidi Museum at Sidi Kacem Ezziligï. Starting point: Porte de France. Finish: the Kasbah esplanade. Allow around two hours, as there is a lot of walking to do.

With the Porte de France behind you, you have the two main entrances to the souk ahead of you: to your right, Rue de la Kasbah; on the left, Rue Jamaâ Ezzitouna. Don't take either of these. Instead, go sharp left down the **Rue de la Commission**, home to Tunis stationery and office supplies wholesalers. The street is lined with building which would not look out of place in Palermo or Naples, witness to the strong Italian presence in the city in the 19th century. Some 50 metres down the street, on the right, is the pedimented façade of the **Maison Evangelisti**, home to one of the oldest Tuniso-Italian families. A marble wall plaque records that Italian liberation hero Garibaldi spent time here. Further along the street, the office supplies give way to cheap goods from the Far East. There are also great aromatic skeins of dried red chilli peppers, *filfil ahmar*, used to make the harissa paste which is an essential part of Tunisian cooking.

Walk 4: three gates & a tile-making saint

START — Porte de France

Maison Evangelisti

Rue de la Commission

La Kherba

Souk el Blat

Rue Sabbaghine (Rue des Teinturiers)

Dâr Ben Ayyed

Place Bab Jazira

Bab Jazira/ Sidi el Bechir Mosque

Hammam

Hammam

Rue de la Rivière

Rue Sidi Bou Khrissan

Rue Morr

Bab Jedid

Blvd Bab Jedid

Jamaâ el Hawa

Institut de Belles Lettres Arabes

Souk Esslah

Junk Market

Hammam Sidi Belghith

To Zaouia Sidi Kassem Ezzilïj, Bastion of Sidi Abdallah & Kasbah

N

See Tunis médina map for orientation

Not to scale

Walking Route

At the end of Rue de la Commission, turn right and you will come into a dusty car park which gives you a fine view of the minaret of the Great Mosque. This area, **La Kherba** (lit: the ruin), as it is called, resulted from Second World War bombardment. Today it provides essential loading space for vans and trucks bringing raw materials to the workshops of the médina, and taking out finished goods. This is also the place to catch shared taxis to Libya and Algeria. (Tunis to Tripoli, 35Dt). Head up the narrow Rue Kuttab Louzir (keeping the Modern Movement primary school on your right), and you will come to **Souk el Blat**, an everyday covered shopping souk with lots of interesting-looking herborist stalls. Buy yourself a dried chameleon or some amber. From here you want to head straight down the **Rue des Teinturiers** to Bab Jazira. Be warned, as you come to the fresh fish and butchers stalls, the street gets crowded with shoppers. But then this is local atmosphere.

Rue des Teinturiers ends on the **Place Bab Jazira**. There is a roundabout with a large marble fountain, and a mosque right on the roundabout. The **Bab Jazira Mosque** was founded in mediaeval times and would have been the main mosque of the southern part of the city. The minaret, with its interlinked lozenge design, was remodelled in the late 19th century. There are some fine tiles at the base of the minaret. Beyond the minaret, there are apartment blocks dating from an extensive redevelopment of the neighbourhood in the 1960s. This was a time when the rural poor were migrating to Tunis, and the insensitive handling of the redevelopment operation led to urban rioting – and the creation of an association to study and preserve the médina (see Dar Lasram, walk 3).

Next, you want to head up the wide (but often traffic-choked) **Boulevard Bab Jedid**. The boulevard is lined with fine early 20th century apartment buildings in a range of styles. Some have a very Haussman feel, others have plaster detailing with a hint of Rococco fantasy. The boulevard was laid out in place of the old ramparts, which were gradually dismantled in the late 19th century, the rubble being used for infill to create building land for the new Tunis growing up east of the médina.

Bab Jedid is home to the supporters of the Club Africain, one of the city centre's two big football teams. The club's red and white colours can be found adorning café awnings. Five minutes brisk walk from Bab Jazira, you come to the actual **Bab Jedid**, the **New Gate**, the only fragment of mediaeval building surviving on this stretch of boulevard. Today home to the Restaurant Granada, this venerable gate dating from 1276 was built by the second Hafsid

Rue de Bab Jedid, Tunis

(sidebar, vertical text) Tunis and around

Tunis and around

👉 *Ibn Khaldoun, early sociologist and national symbol*

Beturbanned Ibn Khaldoun, swathed in a great cloak, gazes down the Avenue Bourguiba, a large tome, no doubt his Muqadimma or Prolegomena under his arm. A man of extensive learning, whose merits as a thinker were only really recognized in the 20th century, Ibn Khaldoun (1322-1406) served various courts in North Africa and Andalusia. He wrote accounts of his travels, but is more widely known for his theory of North African society.

Ibn Khaldoun was the first thinker to have recognized that the Islamic ideal of the State had to be adapted to the political situation prevailing in tribal societies. His theory contends that new dynastic régimes emerge through the conquest of the lands of a decadent state by a rural warrior group, held together by traditional tribal solidarity or 'asabiya'. But after the hardy warriors had settled in the towns, their solidarity would weaken, destroyed by the easy living of the city.

Hence they would resort to mercenaries to maintain their authority, the costs of which implied heavy taxation. Thus the régime in turn was ripe for conquest by a tougher tribal group from the steppes or mountains. And so the cycle was repeated, unless the city-based rulers could replace tribal 'asabiya' with a stronger social glue, namely a government based on the prescriptions of Islamic law and practice.

Ibn Khaldoun's theory fitted nicely with the history of his day: the rise and fall of the Almoravid, Almohad, Merinid and Hafsid dynasties. Although it appears somewhat simplistic today, it is certainly based on the author's direct experience of political life in the Maghreb. More importantly, Ibn Khaldoun now appears as a national symbol, even figuring on the blue 10Dt banknote. For a small country with few intellectual figures, it is no doubt reassuring that a figure now considered as one of the leading mediaeval Muslim

sovereign El Mustansir (1249-77), son of Abu Zakariya el Hafsi (1228-49), who consolidated the dynasty's hold of the eastern Maghreb. Behind the gate is a street where you can see blacksmiths hard at work, making the wrought iron for which Tunis is famous.

Opposite Bab Jedid is an open area still called Souk Esslah, Place des Armes, no doubt after some long-since vanished weaponry market. Today the area is home to eateries such as that of Ould Abba, famous for his *leblebi* (which may roughly be described as chickpea broth). Tunis night owls come here for a feed after the bars close.

From Place des Armes, turn right up a street which will lead you to Jamaâ el Hlak, its simple square minaret typical of the sobre mosques of the Malikite rite. After the mosque, head along a lively shopping street busy in the morning with numerous pavement stalls and students spilling out from the schools. This is the **Rue Marr** (lit: the Street of the Passage), along which the sultan would pass on high days and holidays on his way to the *mesalla*, the great open space on the Gorjani Heights, where he would lead the special prayers for the major festivals of the Muslim year, 'Id Esseghir' and 'Id el Adha'. About 150 metres along the Rue Marr, almost opposite the red, white and green painted door of a hammam, turn left up **Rue de la Rivière** (Nahaj el Oued). This street will take you up through a quiet residential neighbourhood. (Halfway up, at a junction, you may want to go left to look at the fine, early-20th century town-houses on the **Rue Sidi Bou Khrissan**.) At the end of this street, turn right, and you will come to a large well-shaded square, Place de Leader. Up at the top, on your left, you have another Hafsid mosque, **Jamaâ el Hawa** (lit: Mosque of the Air), so named for its position at one of the highest points of the city, overlook-ing the brackish Lac Sejoumi. On the other side of the square, you have the new buildings of the University of Tunis theology school. And next to them, at the topmost point of the square, you have the final stop on this walk, the tomb of a pious tilemaker, the Zaouia of Sidi Kassem Ezzliji.

The shrine or **Zaouia Sidi Kassem Ezzliji** is the last resting place of a pious Andalusian craftsman who came to Tunis at the end of the 15th century. He won popularity for his good works and, more importantly, like the other Andalusian Muslim immigrants of the early 17th century, for bringing an important skill to the city: the Hispano-Moorish art of glazed tile-making. Sidi Kassem's tomb soon became an object of veneration and he had such prestige that some of the last Hafsid princes asked to be buried near it. In liturgical terms, Islam is not a complex religion. Thus the cult of saintly women and men, especially in the fringe areas of the Muslim world, served to relieve the austerity of everyday religious practice, providing a focus for people's need to identify with pious individuals, functioning as interecessors with the Divine. (Note that this is most definitely not part of mainstream Islamic practice.)

The neighbourhood and its *zaouia* became a focus for Moors expelled from Spain in 1607. One Abd el Ghayth el Qachach repaired the damage suffered by the *zaouia* during the 16th century Hispano-Turkish wars, adding the current courtyard and the rooms around it. The inscription inside the actual burial chamber marking the location of Sidi Kassem's tomb and recount his virtues dates from this time. In the 18th century, the building was completely renovated by Hussein Ben Ali, a mosque was built in the south-east of the site and the tomb was covered externally and internally with the decoration still visible today.

In the 20th century, the *zaouia* gradually fell into disrepair, the decoration deteriorated. In the early 1970s, a campaign sponsored by UNESCO and the Tunisian Ministry of Culture was launched to save the built heritage of the médina of Tunis. The Cultural Relations Department of the Spanish Ministry of Foreign Affairs put up the money to restore the *zaouia*. Restoration experts were sent over, and works were completed in 1979. The building today is much as it must have been in the 19th century.

Today, the rooms round the courtyard house a fine collection of Tunisian ceramics. On display are pieces ranging from modern rural ceramics, as well as mediaeval pieces. Greens, yellows and blues are the dominant colours. As elsewhere in the Mediterranean, red was not part of the ceramicists' palette, with the exception of 17th century Iznik ware. The display is worthy homage to Sidi Kassem Ezzliji. Should you be interested, the potter's craft is maintained through evening courses held on the premises. And in the garden, there is a fine collection of Islamic tombstones, from various periods.

After visiting Sidi Kassem, head along the ring road, the Boulevard du 9 avril. On your right, you will come to the **Bastion of Sidi Abdallah**, the only section still surviving of the western walls of the city. Go down the street between bastion and some large recent buildings (the white concrete Maison du Parti and the new Municipalité de Tunis). **The Kasbah**, end point of this walk, is ahead of you on the left. You may go into the souks in search of a café, or take a taxi for your next stop.

Of the modern neighbourhoods of Tunis, the *ville basse* or lower town, centring on the Avenue Bourguiba, goes back to the mid-19th century. (There is another area with some important colonial building up on Boulevard Bab Benat, leading north from the Kasbah.) This walk explores an interesting period of architectural and urban history, roughly 1850 to 1950. Starting point: the Statue of Ibn Khaldoun, Avenue Bourguiba. Finish: Le Passage. Allow a couple of hours, especially if you are going to take pictures. Never photograph any building with a uniformed presence outside.

**Walk 5
Architectures
1850-1950,
visiting the Ville
Nouvelle**

Next to the statue of **Ibn Khaldoun** (1979), you are at the epicentre of modern Tunis. Around you is a variety of buildings bearing witness to the huge changes that Tunis has seen since the 19th century. Facing the statue, on your left, you have the **French embassy**, recently restored, a simple neo-classical mid-19th century building (1856-60) and the first significant construction outside the walls of the old city. In its day it must have been very significant, marking the supremacy of the French consuls over their counterparts. Opposite the embassy are the twin belltowers of the **Cathedral of St Vincent de Paul and St Olive** (1897, a pro-cathedral until 1964, when the Primatial Cathedral of St Louis at Carthage was downgraded). The cavernous, austere interior can be visited. (St Vincent de Paul, a saintly figure of the 17th century was once thought to have worked among the Christians held as slaves in Tunis). Behind Ibn Khaldoun, to the left, built above the arcades at the start of the Avenue de France, is the **Immeuble National** (1950s?), in its day one of the most luxurious apartment buildings in the city.

The Avenue Bourguiba started life as the **Avenue de la Marine**, back in the 1850s, linking the médina to the customs building. On the site of the present cathedral, there would have been the small 17th century Chapelle Saint-Antoine, no doubt built on or next to the ruined remains of the **Nova Arx**, a Spanish fort built in 1573. Later, under the French, this central street was renamed **Avenue Jules Ferry**, for one of the great figures of 19th century French politics, the instigator of universal free primary education. After independence, the avenue, like so many other main streets in Tunisia's towns, was to take the name of the new Tunisian republic's first president, Habib Bourguiba.

Leaving Ibn Khaldoun behind you, head up the street towards the **Porte de France** or **Bab Bhar** (Sea Gate), once upon a time the main eastern gate into the city. (The Avenue Bourguiba here becomes Avenue de France.) The old city walls have disappeared; the gate, dating from the late 18th century when the walls were rebuilt under the supervision of a Dutch engineer, stands in isolation.

Here, on the eastern edge of the médina, you are looking at the buildings of the **Quartier Franc**, the Frankish or first European quarter. There is no real perceptible difference between the médina and the building on reclaimed land. Whereas in Algeria the French had often demolished large areas of building in the old Arab towns, in Tunisia they built alongside the old médinas. In Morocco, where the French presence started much later (1912), policy was to build new towns separate from the old cities. This was partly as a health measure. In the case of Tunis, the building of the new town next to the médina can be explained by a number of reasons. One of the main ones must have been the fact that it was impossible to expropriate Muslim-owned farmland and olive groves around the city. The only solution was to continue building on land reclaimed from the lagoon by the Italian Fasciotti family.

Leaving the Porte de France behind you, head down the **Rue M'barek** (to your right, at 10 past the hour). The buildings on this street have some nice Neo-Moorish touches in the shape of covered balconies with wooden fretwork, and some Art Nouveau mouldings. Next turn left onto Rue d'Allemagne, and right into the fish halls of the **Marché Central** (1891). The main fruit and vegetable area is housed under a fine wooden structure, and in its day must have represented an absolute revelation in Tunis. On the far side of the market is the Rue de Espagne. Go left. On your right, on Rue Charles de Gaulle, is the imposing mass of the central **Post Office** (1893), a Neo-Classical building in the 19th century Beaux Arts tradition. It is surprising that such a significant building, symbolizing a communications revolution, should be so hemmed in.

Continue down the Rue Charles de Gaulle, and you come to a small tree-shaded square, once a place of considerable symbolic importance in colonial Tunis. Dominating the square, once known as Place Philippe Thomas, is the **Italian Embassy**, as impressive as the French Embassy on the main avenue. Until independence, the square had a statue to the memory of **Philippe Thomas**, a French army vet and amateur geologist who discovered phosphates in Tunisia in 1896 in the Metlaoui region. Soon after Tunisia was exporting phosphates to France via a new railway built from Metlaoui to Sfax. Labour conditions in the phosphate mines were tough, and for obvious reasons the statue was removed after independence. On the far side of the square is the Place Barcelone and the **Gare de Tunis** or main railway station. The first railway terminus was built in 1878, the present building dates from 1979. The rail line to Le Kef was opened in 1876, and to Ghardimao on the Algerian frontier by 1880. Cross the Place Barcelone. On the far side, you will come to the main north-south axis of the city, here called the **Avenue de Carthage**, laid out in 1878. Fans of Art Nouveau architecture will want to head a few blocks south to photograph one of the few really Art Nouveau apartment buildings in Tunis. On the east side of the Avenue de Carthage, behind large trees, you can see the former **Municipality of Tunis**, a rather pompous, squat building. The Municipality has now moved to grandiose new premises up at the Kasbah. There are more fine apartment buildings behind the Municipality.

Head northwards up the Avenue de Carthage to the Avenue Bourguiba. At the intersection with the Rue de Yougoslave is the once elegant **Hotel Transatlantique**. Next along is the new **Palmarium** mall, a 1998 construction replacing a 1950s complex. This is now a popular place for young Tunisians to come and hang out, riding up and down the escalators. Back on the main drag, have a look at the white wedding cake of the **Théâtre Municipal**, the work of townhall architect Resplandy. Plaster sea-nymphs ride across the façade, inside all is gilt and cream woodwork and red velvet.

Cross the avenue Bourguiba, following the metro line, and turn left up Rue Mokhtar Attia (ex-Rue Nahhas Pacha). This brings you out on Rue de Rome, at a junction with an interesting selection of buildings including: the recently restored former **Banque d'Algérie**, now the Tunis Governorate (Beaux Arts style); the **Greek Orthodox Cathedral of St Andrew**, now based in Alexandria; and an eclectic apartment building with some fine mosaic detailing. Head right, following the metro line, down the main Avenue Habib Thameur (ex-Avenue Roustan). On your right is the former **Lycée Carnot**, a vast 1930s construction, now one of Tunisia's top State lycées. On your left, you have the **Trésorerie Générale**, designed by Resplandy, with Neo-Moorish decoration.

At this point, you may opt to head back to the Avenue Bourguiba for a citronade and a rest. Real architectural enthusiasts will want to continue up the Av Thameur to Le Passage, where there are some nice examples of Tunisian Art Déco, the angular **Hotel Ritza** for example. After Le Passage intersection, the Av de Paris becomes Avenue de la Liberté, and 10 minutes walk further on you have the amazing Art Déco **Synagogue Daniel Osiris**, meeting point for the Jewish community in the Lafayette neighbourhood.

This walk gives an idea of the architecture to be found in Tunis late 19th/early 20th century neighbourhoods. Enthusiasts will find much to please them in areas both north and south of the central avenue. The area round the **Place Jeanne d'Arc** at the upper end of the Rue de Palestine also merits exploration, and close by on the **Place Pasteur** are a couple of interesting examples of the Neo-Moorish style. Above all, Tunis is interesting for the mix of architecture. Under the French, the médina was left untouched, and a building boom took place. The result is a city with a catalogue of architectural styles dating from 1850 to 1950.

Tunis and around

Bardo Museum Founded in the late 19th century under Ali Bey (hence its original name, the Musée Alaouite), the Bardo Museum, perhaps the largest archaeological museum in North Africa, is situated in a residential neighbourhood, some five kilometres west of the town centre. There are plenty of buses for the Bardo from the Parc Habib Thameur bus-station, or take bus number three from the TGM station or Av Habib Bourguiba and Av de Paris. There is also a green tram (metro line four, destination Denden) from the central République station. A taxi from the town centre to the Bardo will cost around 3Dt.

Bardo Museum

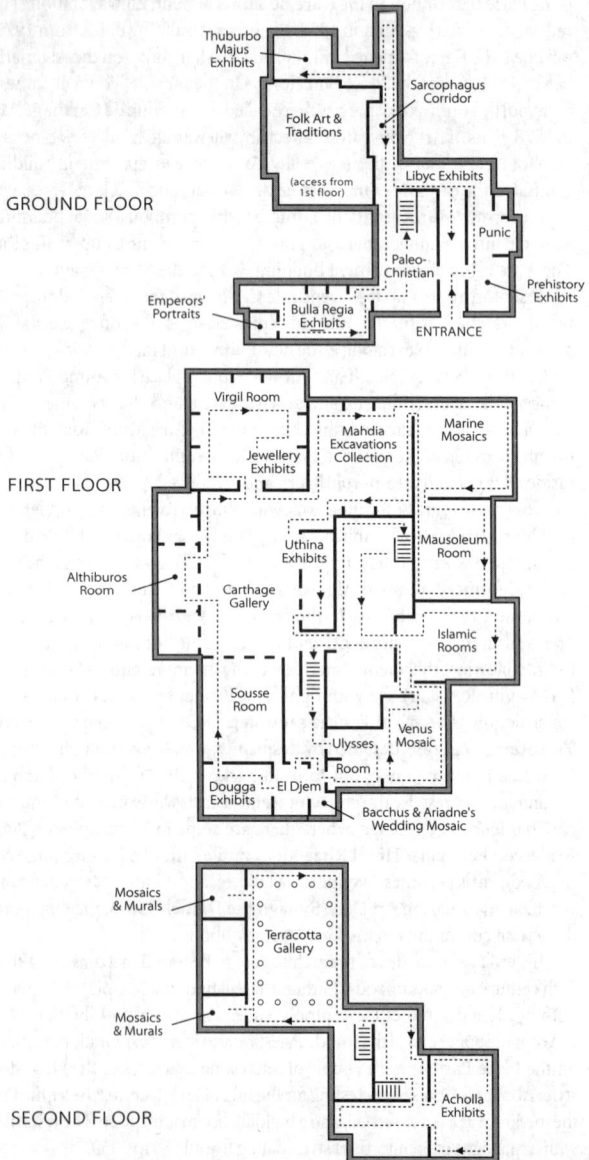

GROUND FLOOR

- Thuburbo Majus Exhibits
- Sarcophagus Corridor
- Folk Art & Traditions
- (access from 1st floor)
- Libyc Exhibits
- Punic
- Paleo-Christian
- Prehistory Exhibits
- Emperors' Portraits
- Bulla Regia Exhibits
- ENTRANCE

FIRST FLOOR

- Virgil Room
- Jewellery Exhibits
- Mahdia Excavations Collection
- Marine Mosaics
- Althiburos Room
- Uthina Exhibits
- Mausoleum Room
- Carthage Gallery
- Islamic Rooms
- Sousse Room
- Ulysses Room
- Venus Mosaic
- Dougga Exhibits
- El Djem
- Bacchus & Ariadne's Wedding Mosaic

SECOND FLOOR

- Mosaics & Murals
- Terracotta Gallery
- Mosaics & Murals
- Acholla Exhibits

Visiting the Bardo in the 1830s

"Under the archway, and forming a rich and animated foreground, are seen groups of splendidly caparisoned horses, awaiting the return of their masters from the audience chamber: on the opposite side of the court, rises a wild flight of steps, almost covered by seated Arabs, wrapped in the graceful and classic folds of their sefsars and burnooses, patiently awaiting their turn to be ushered into the hall of justice. These steps lead to a covered gallery, supported by columns, where are seen walking about or forming little groups, many Moors, soldiers, officers and attendants in their gay attire."

Sir Grenville T. Temple, Excursions in the Mediterranean: Algiers and Tunis (London, 1835)

This museum is one of the largest in North Africa. The great halls on the first floor contain an impressive collection of second and third century Roman mosaics. Walk in past the guarded National Assembly building. The museum is very crowded, especially early morning when it opens, as tour groups 'do' this first before steaming off to Carthage and Sidi Bou Saïd. In the summer, the heat builds up and the upstairs rooms can be a little stuffy. The shop may have some material in English, notably a small, illustrated introduction to Tunisian mosaics published by Cérès Editions. Orientation in the actual building can be a little confusing – as befits a rambling former royal palace. The collection can be easily done in a morning, although you may leave with a distinct feeling of archaeological indigestion.

On display are the material remains of the main civilizations that flourished in what is now Tunisia. The Roman collections take pride of place, and the museum is famed for its vast collection of colourful mosaics picturing the daily life, pastimes and beliefs of the Roman populations in Africa. Unless it is on loan, you will also see a unique collection of Roman bronzes from a wreck discovered off Mahdia, early this century. Some of the material dating from the Muslim mediaeval dynasties has gone to the Raqqada Museum, near Kairouan.

■ *Purchase tickets to right of main door of car park, entrance 3Dt and photography 1Dt. Open summer 0830-1730 and winter 0930-1630. Monday is closing day. Extra charge for photography.* The museum is clearly signed once in the Bardo area of town. If driving from the town centre, you will come to a large and slightly confusing roundabout with fountains and columns. Basically, keeping the fountain on the left, drive straight ahead. The Bardo complex (which also houses the National Assembly) is on your right. Take the first right, and the museum entrance is on your right.

History of the palace Almost as impressive as the mosaics are the actual display rooms themselves. The first floor is composed of a series of great reception rooms and courts, some galleried, others with spectacular gilding – an indication of the style favoured by the 19th century Husseinite princes. The Bardo Palace in fact dates back to the Middle Ages, when the Hafsid rulers built themselves pleasure palaces in the countryside and orchards around Tunis. The palace was extended under 17th and 18th century rulers, becoming the ideal setting for dynastic intrigue and the power-centre of the Husseinid Dynasty, suitably remote from the city of Tunis. By the mid-1800s, the Bardo had become a huge palace complex surrounded by walls and bastions. Parts of it were decaying. The French, keen to prove the 'Latinity' of North Africa, and in need of a place to display the impressive finds that their archaeologists kept discovering, converted part of the building into the Musée Alaouite (opened 1888), named for Ali Bey. Renamed the Musée national du Bardo, this is the museum you can visit today. The constant new discoveries meant that a further, second floor of mosaic display rooms had to be developed.

The plan shows the recommended route, with the main rooms and important features worth noting. It may be best just to wander, however, letting the museum draw you in, marvelling at skilled craftwork from 18 centuries ago, produced in one of the great centres of ancient Romanity.

Visiting the Bardo   **Ground floor**   When in the **Entrance hall** and ticket office, you have a room of early Christian remains to your left. To the right, if open, is a room with the **Prehistory** exhibits – a collection of flint blades, bones, costume ornaments and engraved stones from the Acheulean, Mousterian, Ibero-Moorish, Capsian and Neolithic eras. This then leads into Punic and Libyic exhibits.

Punic rooms   The Punic rooms have a first century, small terracotta statue of the god Baal-Hammon (Thinissut, Cap Bon); a fourth century group of three divinities, Pluto, Demeter and Kore (carrying a piglet); and a fourth century stele of Priest and Child (Carthage). (Is the child being carried ready for sacrifice?) In the second room is a collection of masks made of glass paste or pottery generally placed in tombs with expressions designed to frighten evil spirits; personal decorations, necklaces et cetera; and a Punic tomb reconstruction in a smaller adjoining room with an arrangement of funeral objects (Cap Bon).

Libyic exhibits include bas-reliefs showing gods; funeral monuments with bilingual inscriptions in Libyic/Punic or Libyic/Latin. The **Sarcophagus corridor** has two second century marble sarcophagi, one representing the nine Muses (Porto Farina), the other the four seasons; a third century Roman funeral effigy of a Romano/African citizen (Borj el Amri) and the Boglio stele, also third century Roman, from a series dedicated to Saturn.

The **Thuburbo Majus** corridor and room have inscriptions, statues, marble wall panels, geometric and floral mosaics; a small bas-relief representing Maenads from first century – while the **Palaeo-Christian** corridor and room display a collection of tomb mosaics and church pavements. See particularly the fourth century 'Ecclesia Mater' tomb mosaic (Tabarka) showing the section of a church with candles on the altar; tomb mosaic with two figures and seven crowns inscribed with the names of the seven martyrs; limestone font (Gightis) in centre of room; and tiles showing Biblical scenes.

Bulla Regia room   Bulla Regia was one of the most important Roman settlements in Africa, a wealthy town at the heart of the wheat-growing region on the upper Medjerda. The Bulla Regia room (which follows on from the Palaeo-Christian room) displays items from northwest Tunisia's one time grain capital, close to present day Jendouba. From the Temple of Apollo, second century BC, comes a very languid god. A gallery of portraits of Roman emperors completes the ground floor rooms.

On a staircase leading to the first floor is a series of mosaics, (fourth-sixth centuries), from funeral monuments of the Christian era (Tabarka),

masque d'homme barbu
début IVe siècle av. J.C.
Bardo

some giving age and occupation of the deceased. There is also a statue of Apollo (Carthage).

First floor It is on the first floor that the Bardo is at its most impressive. Looking at the vast mosaics and the somewhat chipped statuary, you begin to feel the wealth and power of the Roman lords of ancient Africa, and how they sought to impress with displays of luxurious imagery, often mythological, sometimes mundane. Though the Romans had huge estates, slavery and repression was the basis of the system. As an indication of just how the wealth was concentrated, the elder Pliny (writing in the first century AD) says that six men alone owned half the province of Africa. Senators came to own vast estates – and the Lord Julius mosaic in the Sousse room shows us a very pleasant country estate.

Marine mosaics The **Ulysses** room is named after the famous Ulysses mosaic (Dougga) on display here. He is depicted bound to the ship's mast to prevent him following the sirens, on the right, playing musical instruments. Ulysses' companions have stopped their ears with wax (not visible) and are looking in the opposite direction to avoid the same fate.

Other mosaics of a marine bent include the very large late third/early fourth century (Utica) Neptune and Amphitrite in a chariot drawn by sea horses with two nereids seated on sea tigers, with three boats each with a bejewelled lady surrounded by cupids – the self crowning of a semi nude/bejewelled Venus, (fourth century, Carthage). There is also a mosaic of Marsyas the satyr and Apollo making music while Minerva looks on (judges?); the surrounds depict the four seasons (third century, El Djem). At one end of the room is a fountain (Thuburbo Majus), no doubt from the largest room of some sumptuous villa, with the head of Oceanus portrayed on the exterior and the interior decorated with nereids (sea nymphs) and sea monsters.

In the corridor is **Bacchus and Ariadne's** wedding mosaic from the fourth century (Thuburbo Majus).

The El Djem room El Djem is a Roman site north of Sfax in the Sahel region of modern Tunisia, chiefly famed for its vast amphitheatre, the third largest to have survived and the setting for large scale games and entertainments. El Jem was evidently a fun sort of place, as the surviving mosaics indicate. On display here are intricate *xenia* (still life) and other mosaics related to food and good times. There are men playing dice, animals (fish, duck) and musical instruments, all themes popular for decorating the dining rooms of wealthy villa owners in the third century. From the same period comes a hunting mosaic, complete with horses, hounds and a hiding hare. On the floor Bacchus rides his triumphal chariot drawn by tigers led by Pan.

The Dougga room Dougga, a couple of hours drive west of Tunis, is for many the country's most beautiful Roman site, set on a hillside looking out over fertile cornlands. In the Dougga room (don't miss the magnificent painted ceiling) are two ancient models of the city, one of the Square of the Capital and the other of the theatre. On the walls and floor are mosaics (La Chebba, Carthage and Thuburbo Majus). Neptune, placed centrally, is magnificent in his chariot with hunting and seasonal agricultural scenes around (second century, La Chebba, Sfax). Opposite are three dark skinned giants working the forge of Vulcan, found in the Cyclops' baths (fourth century, Dougga); also Cup bearers serving guests (Dougga).

Tunis and around

The Sousse room The huge Sousse room houses a large collection of mosaics from Sousse, Carthage and Tabarka; the head and feet of a colossal statue of Jupiter (Thuburbo Majus); Punic, Greek and Roman lamps, ceramics (El Aouja near Kairouan); on the floor a third century mosaic of Neptune surrounded by sea creatures (Sousse); the Lord Julius mosaic (early fifth century, Carthage) – depicting a central imposing villa and pictures of the cycle of the seasons and rural life; three big pavings from apses from private villas (Tabarka), probably of the same age as the Carthage mosaic; and mosaics illustrating a circus (third century, Carthage) and chariot races (sixth century, Gafsa).

The Sculpture Hall A great hall, complete with colonnade, gallery and high ornamented ceiling, houses sculpture, mainly from **Carthage**. In the centre is an altar dedicated to the 'Gens Augusta' with bas-reliefs on all four sides dated between the first century AD and first century BC; on the floor are two famous third century mosaic pavements (Uthina/Oudna), the first of Bacchus surrounded by cupids among the vines and a second showing agricultural activities and hunting scenes. There are statues of Roman gods and an imposing statue of the Emperor Hadrian, creator of the great aqueduct which linked the springs of Mount Zaghouan to Carthage.

The Althiburos room To the side in the Althiburos room are mosaics (Althiburos and Carthage); on the floor a fourth century mosaic of Roman boats, all correctly titled; also a fourth century banqueting scene with guests seated on benches rather than reclining on couches; and a mosaic of hunting scenes, a temple containing Apollo and Diana and a crane being sacrificed (5th-7th centuries AD, Carthage-Salammbo) indicating a survival of pagan practices into the Christian era. For the record, Althiburos, today an obscure site south of Le Kef close to the village of Medeina, was once a major stop on the Carthage to Tebessa road.

Virgil, epic poet The Virgil room is octagonal with a magnificent dome of carved plaster work. The third century mosaic, showing a seated Virgil in meditation between the muses of history and tragedy (Sousse), is the only portrait of the poet. Whether Virgil ever visited Carthage is a matter of debate. Whatever, Aeneas, the hero of his epic, *The Aeneid*, fell in love with Carthage's Queen Dido, only to leave her heartbroken as he travelled on to Italy to found Rome. Dido committed suicide, and later in The Aeneid reappears to reproach her former love when he visits the Underworld. It is a serene epic poet, scroll in hand, who gazes at the visitor today. He is flanked by thoughtful muses, a wistful Melpomene (Tragedy), carrying a mask, and Clio (History), bearing another scroll.

In the centre of the floor the third century mosaic has medallions with the signs of the zodiac surrounding godheads of the days of the week (Bir Chana near Zaghouan).

Hachette-rasoir
du IIIᵉ siècle av. J.C.
Kerkouane

The Jewellery room The ornamentation in the Jewellery room is mainly Punic, some from as long ago as the seventh century BC, mainly from Carthage but also Utica and Kerkouane. There are matching necklaces and earrings of tiny ceramic/ivory figures/objects, rings, seals et cetera, solid gold jewellery and gold plate on bronze.

The Mahdia room The contents of a Roman ship was discovered off Mahdia by sponge divers early this century. The display (if not on loan) includes Helle-nistic bronze and marble, furniture, pieces of the wrecked ship, and marble stat-ues of Aphrodite (second-first century BC) which look only a little worse for wear after their immersion. The bronzes reflect the Romans taste for all things Greek. (A similarly fine selection, discovered at the Roman site of Volubilis near Meknès, is on display in the Musée archaeologique in Rabat, Morocco.)

Marine mosaics At the back of the Mahdia room is room of mosaics on marine themes. On display are sections of a huge mosaic of a seascape includ-ing dolphins, nereids and sea monsters (Carthage).

The Mausoleum Room The Mausoleum room takes its name from a large Roman tomb displayed here. All four sides feature bas-reliefs with a strong symbolic charge: there is a proconsul's legate on horseback, fasces and funeral putti. On the walls are some important fourth century mosaics from Thuburbo Majus, including a hunting scene, Venus doing her hair assisted by two putti, and Bacchus and Ariane, accompanied by a satyr and a bacchante.

The Uthina room The Uthina (Oudna) room has many mosaics of hunting or mythology. Of particular interest is the fine mosaic showing the remains of a meal. There is also a large pavement portraying Orpheus (unfortunately head-less), with his lyre charming the wild beasts.

Tunisian folk art At this point it is necessary to go downstairs to see the **Folk art and traditions room** before ascending to view the **Islamic rooms** situated in the smaller, older (1831) building set around a patio. (With luck the displays will be open.) The hall displays artifacts from the 9th-13th centuries, including musical instruments, weapons, household objects; jewellery, in particular gold necklaces, bracelets and earrings; traditional costumes, furniture; parchments, manuscripts, verses of the Koran, most of the documents from the great mosque of Kairouan, in particular pages from the Blue Koran; *tiraz* fabrics with Koranic inscriptions; astralobes, sundials and compasses; and ceramics.

The last room on this floor has a number of fourth century mosaics, including one called Hunting the Wild Boar, showing three stages of the hunt; Venus being crowned by two female centaurs; and a splendid peacock with a spread tail.

Second floor The main staircase leads to the second floor, where the **gallery** overlooking the Carthage room contains terracotta statuettes of protective gods such as Venus and Mercury from temples and tombs. Here also are objects from necropoli of the 1st-3rd centuries, glasses, bowls, dishes from tombs, funeral urns and statuettes. Don't miss the surgeons kit with lancets, scalpels and forceps.

The corridors and rooms around the top of the stairs have yet more mosaics (fourth century), depicting Theseus slaying the Minotaur in a large maze of brown on cream, while the border depicts the walls and gates of a city (Thuburbo Majus); two mosaics on the theme of animal sports with a haloed Bacchus (El Djem) and a fourth century example from Thelepte/Feriana; and a

Tunis and around

Tunis and around

second century paving (Thuburbo Majus), depicting a meditating poet seated on a column shaft, a mosaic in praise of intellect. In a separate room is a third century Diana the Huntress on a deer, the medallions portraying animals of the hunt, boars, gazelle, et cetera (Thuburbo Majus); and Venus on a rock (third century, Utica).

The Acholla room The items in the Acholla room (a site north of Sfax) were collected from private houses. There is a splendid mosaic of Dionysus riding a tiger, guiding his mount with a thyrsus. The main piece in this room is the Triumph of Dionysus, showing the god standing in a chariot drawn by two sea-centaurs. Also shown are allegorical figures of Spring and Winter. Still on a marine theme, look out for the fountain mosaic portraying the head of the God Ocean, with two oversized lobster claws sticking out of his head.

Another fine mosaic in this room depicts the Labours of Hercules. Each of 13 boxes shows a human, animal or monster symbolizing one of Hercules' labours.

Leaving the Bardo If you are now looking for somewhere nearby to have a coffee or a meal while you digest what you have seen, there is not too much choice. There is a small pizzeria, almost opposite the entrance, crowded to the doors at lunchtime. Going left out of the entrance, across the main road junction, are two sandwich places. If you are on a short trip, it is probably best to head back to town (a taxi to the Kasbah, if rushed), to have lunch in the médina and take in something of the old city in the afternoon (if it is not too hot). To complete your dose of Tunisian heritage, you could aim for the **Dar Ben Abdallah Museum** in the Tourbet El Bey neighbourhood. ■ *Open until 1630, closed Monday*. (See Médina Walk 2, page 77.)

Other museums in Tunis The **Numismatic Museum** has an exhibition of Tunisian coins dating back to Carthaginian times. This is located in the entrance hall of the Central Bank, rue Hedi Nouira, T254000, entrance free. **Postal Museum** Here exhibitions relate to the history of the Tunisian postal system. There are many displays of old postage stamps and some interesting collections on view. Located on the corner of rue Gamel Abdel Nasser and rue d'Angleterre, entrance free.

Military Museum, Palais de la Rose, Manouba, T520220. Set in a fine 19th century palace, a short taxi ride from the Bardo, this museum has displays of Tunisian military history from the earliest times to the present. Little visited, but worth a look if you are in Tunis for some time. Even closer to the Bardo there is the projected **Museum of Husseinid Tunisia**. (Turn right out of Bardo gate, cross road and 20 metres on you will find the road leading to the entrance). This museum, set in a beylical palace used as a hospital until recently, will house portraits and memorabilia of the Husseinid beys.

Parks & the zoo Tunis does not have a large amount of green space. In the city centre, the **Jardin Habib Thameur** is chiefly interesting for being on the site of the main Jewish cemetery. This was deconsecrated at the orders of ex-president Habib Bourguiba, leading to a massive loss of confidence in his government by members of the once numerous and influential Jewish community. The park does however provide a modicum of green in an otherwise noisy and traffic saturated city centre.

Almost outside the urban area, north of Ariana on the Bizerte road, is the **Parc Ennahli**, a recent creation which provides somewhere for people to let their kids off the leash at weekends. In the new Berges du Lac neighbourhood is the **Dahdah** entertainment complex, with a full range of fairground rides, including a big wheel and dodgems. Not a cheap treat, but will certainly please most children. There is another funfair behind the swimming pool at the Bardo.

The city's green lung is the **Parc du Belvédère**, which occupies a large stretch of hillside separating upmarket residential neighbourhoods Mutuelleville and Notre Dame from El Omrane and quarters north of the médina. To get there, take the bus number five from Place de l'Indépendence and get off at Place Pasteur or Metro line number two from Place de Barcelona to Palestine station. It is then a short walk to the park.

The lower areas near the main gates have some sizeable trees. From the upper reaches of the park, there are some splendid views over Tunis, the most interesting being to the southeast towards Korbous and Cap Bon and to Djebel Bou Kornine and Djebel Ressas. In the summer, the vegetation tends to dry out, leaving arid expanses between wilting trees. Two roads through the park are open to traffic and there are numerous narrow paths for pedestrians. The area is patrolled by mounted police, presumably on the look out for winos and courting couples. On the northern side of the park is a signposted jogging circuit, the *Parcours de santé*. (There is another, shorter circuit, in a small pine-planted enclosure at the Cité Olympique, Menzah I, just behind the Coupole (Sports' Dome).)

Venturing into the park, women should probably be accompanied. It takes about a half an hour walk to get to the top of the Belvédère hill, so you might take a taxi to the top and walk down calling in at the Koubba an orientalist domed pavilion, on the way. This is in an enclosed area with grass and trees, but a call might bring out the caretaker who, for a tip, will show you round. The view from the terrace is well worth the tip. The story goes that the building was constructed in Turkish style by the Bey of Tunis in 1789, as a retreat from his daughter. It consists of a large room surmounted by a magnificent dome decorated with exquisitely carved plaster work. In recent years, the Koubba has been used for filming Tunisian TV's Sunday morning breakfast show.

At the foot of the hill, within the park, off Av Taieb Mehiri (ex-Albert I), is the entrance to the **Zoological Garden**. By the entrance is a café. Adjacent is a small lake complete with water fowl and three fountains. There are toilets just 50 metres to the left after entering the zoo. This is a well established zoo, perhaps only one recommendable in Tunisia. The zoo covers a large area and houses a full range of birds and animals but no indoor displays. (Aquaria enthusiasts will be off to the Musée Océanographique, Dar el Hout, in Salammbô near Carthage in the Banlieue Nord.) The information is given in Arabic and French. ■ *3Dt, children under nine 1Dt, photographs 1Dt, open 0900-1800 (ticket office closes 1700), closed Monday. There is nothing to prevent anyone standing in close proximity to the cages. Keep an eye on children to avoid anyone being accidentally fed to the beasts.*

Essentials

Few of the cheaper hotels in the centre of Tunis have any character and many of the cheapest hotels in the médina cater mainly for male Algerian visitors on shopping trips. Should you need to stay overnight in Tunis, there are several reasonable hotels close to the Place Barcelone in the neighbourhood of the Rue de Grèce (hotels Salammbô and Maison Dorée in particular). Business travellers will find several acceptable hotels in the Belvédère district (Les Ambassadeurs, El Mechtel, Le Belvédère). These are generally better placed for meeting clients than the more pleasant (and expensive) coastal hotels in the Gammarth section of the Banlieue Nord (see below). The 5 star hotels are nothing special, and service can be just as effective in some of the smaller 4 and 3 stars. The best hotel today is probably Résidence out at Raoued (see below page 124).

Sleeping
■ *on maps*
Price codes:
see inside front cover

Tunis and around

Tunis centre

To Parc du Belvédère

Rue du Royaume

d'Arabie Saoudite

Rue d'Irak

Rue des Syrie

Rue d'Iran

Av Hedi Chaker

14

24

Rue du Koweit

Mohamed V Ⓜ

12

Rue de Cologne

Market

Rue de Palestine

Rue de l'Inde

Av Mohammed V

Parc des Sports

Av Chedly Kallala

21

Institut Bourgiba

Synagogue Daniel Osiris

Former Fair Ground

Liaison Nord Sud

To Menzal, La Marsa & Airport

Av de la Liberté

Rue du Train

Av de Lyon

Av de Madrid

Rue Cyrus le Grand

Lac de Tunis

Nelson Mandela Ⓜ

Mosque el Fatah

Kennedy Park

1

République Ⓜ

Place de la République

Av Jean Jaurès

Av de Ghana

Palais du Congrès

Av de Londres

Jardin Thameur

19

Av de Paris

Rue Kamel Ataturk

Car Park

16

Rue Ghandi

17

Rue Lénine

Av Habib Thameur

Rue d'Athens

Ibn Rachid (southbound)

Habib Thameur (northbound) Ⓜ

Rue de Marseille

Rue du Caire

Av Jean Jaurès

Rue Garibaldi

BAB B'HAR

Av Mohammed V

Rue Makhtar Attia

Ⓢ

Rue d'Alger

✉ Ⓢ

Cathedral

To Medina

Place de l'Indépendence

Av de France

French Embassy

Supermarket

13

3

2

4

Av H Bourguiba

Av 7 Novembre

22

11

18

Rue de Yougoslavie

ℹ 9

Place d'Afrique

Tunis Marine Ⓜ Ⓣ

Rue Farès El Khoury

Av de la République

A

Rue de Turquie

7

5

Rue d'Allemagne

Rue Charles de Gaulle

8

15

6

20 23

10

Rue de Grèce

Rue de Holland

Market

Rue d'Espagne

Place de Barcelone

✉ Barcelone Ⓜ

Train Station

🚌

Rue Ibn Kozman

To Southern Bus Station

Av de Carthage

Rue Ibn Khaldoun

Rue 18 Janvier 1952

Rue Houssine Bouzaiene

Rue Abderrazak Cheraibi

Av Farhat Hached

Farhat Hached Ⓜ

Rue Om Kaltoum

Rue Ali Darghouth

■ Sleeping

1 Abou Nawas	7 De France	13 International	19 Ritza
2 Africa (Méridien)	8 De Suisse	14 Le Belvédère	20 Salammbo
3 Capitole	9 Du Lac	15 Maison Dorée	21 St Georges
4 Carlton	10 El Omrane	16 Majestic	22 Tej
5 Commodore	11 Golf Royal	17 Oriental Palace	23 Transatlantique
6 De Bretagne	12 Ibn Khaldoun	18 Rex	24 Tunis Park

Related maps
A Tunis transport,
page 38

N

Not to scale

Tunis and around

A *Africa Méridien Hotel*, 50 Av Habib Bourguiba, T347477, F347432. Large blue tower block in the middle of Tunis, in need of refurbishement. 170 rooms, a/c, 3 restaurants, 3 bars, cinema, pool, hairdresser, car rental, conference facilities, automatic cash dispensers for Visa and Mastercard holders at street level. **A** *Abou Nawas*, Park Kennedy, Av Mohammed V, T350355, F352882. Large hotel with all facilities close to the main banks. Well located for both city centre and Lafayette (where bodies like the FIPA, Foreign Investment Promotion Agency, are located), and a short taxi ride to the Berges du Lac and airport. **A** *El Hana International*, 49 Av Habib Bourguiba, T331144. Informally known as the 'hôtel des deux avenues'. Large block at meeting point of Avenue Bourguiba and Avenue de Paris. Pleasant rooftop bar open to all-comers with view over the city. **A** *Hilton*, Av de la Ligue Arabe, T782800, F782208. Set high on a hill outside the city centre, next to unfinished carcass of the Arab League building. Best placed hotel for the Menzah and Manar districts, handy for Mutuelleville and Lafayette as well. Managed by the Marhaba Group today. Has had mixed reports of late. **A** *Oriental Palace*, Av Jean Jaurès, T348846. Centrally located and often used for conferences. Characterized by large over-tiled lobby smelling of cheap disinfectant. Restaurant said to have a good floorshow with spectacular *danseuse orientale*. Popular with Libyan visitors.

B *Hotel des Ambassadeurs*, rue Hedi Chaker, T288011. Rooms facing the Belvédère Park, a/c, restaurant. Pleasant. **B** *Hotel Mechtel*, T783200, Av Taieb Mehiri, Belvédère Park. 450 rooms, minute pool, light sleepers should beware of taking rooms on the upper floors on the nightclub side of the hotel. A basic business hotel often used for conferences. Well situated for getting to both city centre and Menzah and Manar districts. **B** *Hotel Golf Royal*, Rue de la Yougoslavie, T342422. Centrally located hotel in a street parallel to the Avenue Bourguiba. Expensive, poor value for money. **B** *Hotel Ibn Khaldoun*, rue de Palestine, by the Marché Lafayette, T783211. A/c, restaurant, recently refurbished. **B** *Hotel Le Belvédère*, Av des Etats-Unis, T783133. Quiet, close to the Belvédère Park, a/c, restaurant, easily the nicest of the business hotels, willing service, pleasant.

C *Hotel Carlton*, 31 Av Habib Bourguiba, T258167. Clean, 40 rooms with bath, a/c, slightly noisy position on main avenue. Popular, so reservations a good idea. **C** *Hotel Excel*, 35 Av Habib Bourguiba, T355088, F341929. Central position, TV, no breakfast. **C** *Hotel du Lac*, Av Habib Bourguiba, central, T258322. Restaurant, 208 rooms all a/c. The 'upside-down pyramid' hotel near the city centre. Has seen better days. **C** *Hotel El Omrane*, 65 Av Farhat Hached. One of the better hotels in this price bracket. **C** *Hotel El Oumara*, 42 bis rue Ali Darghouth. Another adequate business hotel. Recommended. **C** *Hotel Tej*, 14 rue Lt. Aziz Tej, T344899. Clean, overpriced, a/c. **C** *Hotel de Russie*, 18 rue de Russie, T328883, F321685. 23 rooms, single at 35Dt, some triple rooms, best room No 102. Clean, centrally located on a quiet street off rue Jazira, very handy for southern bus and louage stations. Recommended.

D *Hotel Dar Masmoudi*, 18 rue du Maroc, off rue d'Algerie, T342428. Very close to médina, very quiet, most rooms with bath. **D** *Hotel de Suisse*, 5 rue de Suisse, T243821. 23 rooms, most with bath, clean, quiet, parking. **D** *Hotel Maison Dorée*, 6 rue de Hollande, just off Av de la Yougoslavie behind the French Embassy, T240632. Must have been very swish in its day, good condition, spotlessly clean, good service, quite quiet, 54 rooms with bath, breakfast included, restaurant Les Margaritas on Rue de Hollande has a good lunchtime menu at only 6Dt. **D** *Hotel Majestic*, Av de Paris, T242848. Old-fashioned, 100 rooms, 40 with a/c, large terrace, central, restaurant. **D** *Hotel Ritza*, 35 Av Thameur, T245428, close to the Thameur park, 30 rooms, communal shower. Overlooks noisy junction (Place République). **D** *Hotel Transatlantique*, 106 Av de Yougoslavie, T240680. Relatively quiet for a central hotel, most rooms with bath, breakfast included. A good central option. **D** *Tunis Park Hotel*, 7 rue de Damas off Av Taieb Mehiri by the Belvédère Park, T286696. 28 rooms, quiet and in need of refurbishment, restaurant.

E *Hotel de France*, 8 rue Mustapha M'Barek, T245876. Very close to the *Hotel Commodore* and the médina, clean, 49 rooms with bath, good value. **E** *Hotel Médina*, 1 Place de la Victoire, T255056. Close to Bab Bhar and the British Embassy, 12Dt double rooms with shower, 25 rooms, clean, tidy and basic, shared toilets, the café/restaurant forms the front lower part of the hotel facing the square. **E** *Hotel St Georges*, 16 rue de Cologne, behind Av de la Liberté, T781029. 36 rooms, 26 with bath, a/c, restaurant, parking available. Has seen better days. The location, remote from both centre and sights, has little to recommend it. **E** *Hotel Salammbo*, 6 rue de Grèce, off Av Habib Bourguiba, T337498. Clean hotel, 52 rooms, most with bath. Good reputation with travellers. Recommended.

F *Gare Hotel*, rue de la Gare. **F** *Hotel Cirta*, 42 Av Charles de Gaulle, T241582. Communal pay showers, very cheap. **F** *Hotel Commodore*, 17 rue d'Allemagne opposite the central market, T244941. Clean, quiet hotel just by the entrance to the médina, 48 rooms, most have bath, no breakfast, recently refurbished. **F** *Hotel Continental*, 5 rue de Marseille, T259834. Very quiet and cheap, communal shower. **F** *Hotel Crystal*, Av de Carthage, quiet, clean, communal shower. **F** *Hotel de Bretagne*, 7 Rue de Grèce, T242146. 25 rooms, quite clean and quiet. Has had mixed reports, so in this area prefer the Salammbô or the Transatlantique. **F** *Hotel de l'Agriculture*, 25 Av Charles de Gaulle, T246394. Opposite *Hotel Cirta*, very quiet situation, clean. **F** *Hotel de la Victoire*, 7 Bab el Menara, T26. 20 rooms (those on front are noisy), communal shower, clean, best of this category. **F** *Hotel des Amis*, 7 rue Monastir, T565653. A short walk down Souq Sidi Mehrez, leading from Bab Souika, only 6Dt for a double room with no breakfast, 24 rooms, shared bath and toilet, beds on iron frames, clean, basic, this and *Hotel Sfax* are in the médina, and are for the adventurous seeking authenticity – or those wanting very cheap accommodation. **F** *Hotel Rex*, 65 rue de Yougoslavie, T257397. 29 rooms, communal pay shower, rather depressing. **F** *Hotel Sfax*, 5 rue de l'Or, T260275. A short way down Souq Sidi Mehrez, leading from Bab Souika, 5Dt, 4 double rooms, no breakfast, 12 rooms, communal toilet, no bathroom, use nearby *hammam*, iron bed frames, very basic. **F** *Nouvel Hotel*, T243379, 3 Place Mongi Bali. Next to the station, could be cleaner, communal showers, noisy.

Youth hostels *Tunisian Youth Hostel Association*, 10 rue Ali Bach Hamba, 1000 Tunis, T353227. 1) Radès, 10 km southwest of Tunis, T483631. 120 beds, meals provided, take the train from the main station, a 10-minute walk from Radès station. 2) In the médina, 25 rue Saida Ajoula, T567850. 70 beds, 500m from Place du Gouvernement (La Kasbah), 1.5 km from central station. 3) *Centre d'hébergement Jelili ez Zahra*, Oued Meliane Ezzahara, BP1140, T481547. 72 beds, kitchen, meals provided, take bus No 26A from Place Barcelone. 4) Possibility of staying in the Bardo University campus in the summer, contact T784241, rue du Mali, Tunis.

Eating Tunis has quite a range of restaurants, although exotic cuisine is more or less unrepresented. When Tunisians want something special, they go for a fish restaurant. Very basic French and Italian cooking is represented, although nothing very exciting, which is surprising given the proximity of both these countries.

In the city centre, there is a good concentration of long-established places in the streets off the Avenue Bourguiba. The Lafayette district also has one or two good places. Several upmarket 'old Tunis' type restaurants can be found in the Kasbah district of the médina. There are some no-alcohol lunchtime haunts for business people in the Menzah area. The offspring of the middle class hang out at the pizzerias and cafés-glacier at the Arcades in El Manar. In summer, people tend to head out of the city to eat of an evening, to the Banlieue Nord (see below).

Downtown Tunis Expensive: *Bagdad*, Av Habib Bourguiba. Tunisian food accompanied by an '*awwada*' (small local band), belting out Arab and Tunisian favourite tunes. *Chez Gaston*, 73 rue de Yougoslavie, T340417. Adequate, seafood specialities. *Chez Nous*, rue de Marseille. French cooking with some Tunisian specialities, alcohol. Staff play party tricks. Has declined in recent years. Black and white photographs of stars of the 1960s and 1970s recall a once glorious clientele. *Chez Slah*, 14 rue Pierre de Coubertin, T258588. Perhaps the best restaurant in central Tunis, highly recommended but the bill will be large, good idea to book. Good fish.

Phone code: 01

Mid-range: *Le Boléro*, small restaurant hidden away in a side street off the rue de Yougoslavie, almost opposite Gaston's. Alcohol and reasonable food. Has a slightly maverick air to it. Clients are Tunisian men seeking a low-key boozy lunch. *Le Cosmos*, rue Ibn Khaldoun, very good food, especially the fish, service sometimes but endearingly eccentric service. Has a cast of regulars, and is especially popular during the Carthage Film Festival. *L'Etable*, Av Habib Bourguiba, near Place d'Afrique, Tunisian specialities, alcohol. *Le Poisson Doré*, rue Ibn Khaldoun, specializes in seafood. *La Mama*, rue de Marseille, mixture of French, Italian and traditional Tunisian cooking, alcohol. Occasional live music. *Les Margaritas*, Rue de Hollande. This is the restaurant for the Maison Dorée. A very reasonably priced menu, and, in season, tender *marcassin* (wild boar piglet). *Le Regent*, 16 rue de Lieutenant Abdel Aziz Tej, behind the Africa Hotel, T341723. Popular with business people. On the unimaginative side, but more than adequate. At the top end of the mid-range price bracket. *La Trattoria*, 44 Av Habib Bourguiba, between the Africa Hotel and the Ministry of the Interior. Adequate. The *Restaurant Bouchoucha* and *Chez Noureddine* are 2 fine eateries down on the rue Farhat Hached, just by the metro stop (and before rue de Turquie, on your right) as you head away from Place Barcelone. Go at lunchtime, prefer Bouchoucha, which does excellent pasta (big portions) and specials like rabbit with mushrooms. Ambience: splendidly boozy, loud and cheerful. The clientele: dockworkers, traders from the central market, the occasional Italian tourist, etc. The boss and Abdessatar keep their cast of regulars in order. Also a feature are the street pedlars, who will sell you nuts, chickpeas, a fan or a mosque-shaped clock, or even a *sifsari* (traditional woman's cream wrap) – if you're feeling guilty about having lunch with lots of wine and the wife's at home.

Cheap: *Restaurant Abid*, 98 Rue de Yougoslavie, near the intersection with Rue Ibn Khaldoun. Well cooked filling food. Very reasonable prices. *Abdelaziz Elleuch*, 6 rue de Caire, T257701. Couscous and fish. *Le Capitole*, 60 Av Bourguiba. Cheap restaurant on 1st floor, almost above the Café de Paris. A well-established place with a very reasonably priced menu. *Le Carcassonne*, Av de Carthage, fine for a cheap fill-up. *Pizza Sprint*, small pizzeria next to the Café de Paris on the Av Bourguiba, T343131. Generally perfectly acceptable, apart from the pasta with pesto. Good grilled green pepper salad. Alcohol. (The same people run Pizza Sprint-Arthé at La Marsa-Plage.) *Le Prince*, Place de Barcelone, opposite the main train station, self-service, clean, cheap, some typical Tunisian food and the usual slices of pizza.

Suburban Tunis (Lafayette, Cité Jardin, etc) Expensive: *L'Astragale*, 17 Av Charles Nicolle, Cité Jardin, T890455. A very fine restaurant, one of the most elegant in Tunisia with prices to match. Would not look out of place in Marrakech.

Mid-range: *Circolo Italiano* 102 Av de la Liberté, entrance opposite the French Cultural Centre, T288037. One of the best Italian addresses in Tunis, popular at both lunchtime (with business people and bank and embassy staff) and in the evenings (reservations a good idea). Officially, a private club for Tunis' Italian community. *La Romanesca*, 29 Av Ahmed Tlili, Menzah V, T753241. Excellent Italian food. No alcohol, as unfortunately the Ariana governorate has a dry policy. Otherwise a good address.

Médina Expensive: *Dar el Jeld*, 5 rue Dar el Jeld in the médina, off Place du Gouvernement, T260916. Very good traditional Tunisian cooking provided in a home restored and converted to restaurant use by the Abdelkafi family. Upmarket dining to the tinkling sound of the lute. Try the *kabkabou* (fish with preserved lemons). Large portions, so go carefully if you want to have room for one of their really rather tempting desserts. Service excruciatingly formal. Closed Sunday, booking recommended. Just down the street, the *Diwan Dar el Jeld*, in a similarly restored house, has banqueting and reception facilities and a giftshop with Dar el Jeld merchandise (Jasmine soap makes a good present). *Essaraya*, 6 rue Ben Mahmoud, T560310. Also in a restored property, a 3 forks de luxe restaurant. The interior is (disappointingly?) kitsch. Unctuous welcome. You can eat Tunisian far more cheaply than this. Closed Sunday. *Le Mrabet*, Souk Ettrouk, T563681. The original 'traditional cuisine' restaurant in the médina. On the first floor above the Café Mrabet. Floor show.

Mid-range: *Dar Bel Hadj*, 17 rue des Tamis, T336910 (just 5 minutes from the Place du Gouvernement, turn right onto Rue des Tamis as you go down Rue de la Kasbah). Private house, unauthentic restoration. No booze. If you think you might get lost, they have a noddy train to bring clients from the Kasbah esplanade. Go for Dar el Jeld or one of the cheap lunchtime places in the central médina for Tunisian food.

Cheap: as elsewhere in Tunisia, the cheap eateries are generally the best, even if the seating conditions often leave a little to be desired. In this category, there are 2 sorts of restaurant in the médina, the lunchtime haunts of civil servants and students, mostly situated close to the Ezzitouna Mosque, and late-night places at Bab Jedid. Try *Mehdaoui*, under the covered passageway in front of the Great Mosque. Good nosh sitting at tables in the street. Fills up quickly at 1300, specials run out quickly. Lunch only. *Grill Soltane* (chez Sidki), Blvd Bab Jedid, a few doors right of the old gate. For grilled fish and crevettes. Clean. *Ould Abba*. Late night eatery on Place des Armes at Bab Jedid. Stand at the zinc counter with the wide boys and assorted seedy characters and lap up a bowl of lablabi chick-pea soup. The mural décor changes regularly, but look out for the spangly Hand of Fatima set in the wall behind glass. (Is there a real hand in there?) Ould Abba himself presides the proceedings. *Restaurant Granada*, Blvd Bab Jedid. Large dining room with TV actually in the former arms room of the old gate. Can work out expensive, but you can eat cheaply nevertheless.

Bars & cafés　For a Mediterranean city, central Tunis has disappointingly few pleasant cafés with terraces (and clean loos). Forget sipping an elegant campari, as the bars are spit and sawdust affairs, not for the fainthearted. Try the following. **Café Africa**, by the *Africa Hotel*, for an opportunity to watch the crowds. Unpleasant service but serves alcohol. **Café de l'Hotel El Hana International**, indoor air-conditioned café in a small building on the Avenue Bourguiba mainly used by courting couples. Tour buses pull up in front of the neighbouring hotel, which also has a fine rooftop bar-café. **Café de Paris**, corner of Av Habib Bourguiba and Av de Carthage, the only decent-sized pavement café on Av Habib Bourguiba, has inner seating area with bar and a few tables on the pavement for surveying the scene. Attracts an odd but occasionally interesting mix of mainly male people. Not really recommended for unaccompanied women. Unaccompanied men seem to like it. Serves alcohol.

Chicha cafés The chicha or waterpipe café is a relatively recent feature on the Tunis street scene, compensating for the lack of brasseries and comfortable cafés. The most atmospheric chicha cafés are in the médina, with 1 or 2 good ones in Lafayette. Chichas can only be smoked inside the café. Try the following. *Café Ezzitouna*, on Rue Jamaâ Ezzitouna, on your left just before you get to the Great Mosque. Tiled walls, tiled benches, and a few seats in the street to watch the tourists come lumbering up through the souk. Good value on Ramadhan evenings. *Café Mnouchi*, obscure doorway at the meeting of Souk el Leffa and Souk Kebabjia. Dark passageway set with ancient tile panels leads you into a courtyard full of cardplayers at lunchtimes, the souk sellers, apprentices and workmen of the médina letting off steam. *Chez Kamel*, Rue Sidi Ben Arous, central médina, just below the minaret of the Ezzitouna Mosque. Tiny café where you sit cosily wedged in smoking your chicha. Good in winter. Late on summer nights it may be possible to smoke outside. Two more chicha cafés are on the small open area next to the entrance to Souk Essakagine, near Bab Menara, opposite the Hotel de la Victoire.

Entertainment

For nightlife of any kind, you will have to head out to the Banlieue Nord. There are a few other attractions in the form of art galleries and some good local theatre, in Tunisian Arabic. The French and Italian cultural centres occasionally bring over theatre, music and even the odd opera. Of the cinemas, the Colisée dating from the 1930s, is the largest. Avoid the Africa cinema – the sound is appalling. Most of the other cinemas cater to macho tastes (kung-fu, Schwarzenegger and soft porn).

Art Galleries *Club Tahar Haddad*, 20 rue du Tribunal, in the médina, T561275, occasional exhibitions; *Galerie Alyssa*, 3 Av Casablanca, Bardo, T223107; *Galerie Blel*, 70 Av d'Afrique, El Menzah, T231044.

Hammams Turkish baths are an institution in Tunisia. Many people go at least once a week. A visit to the hammam is a revitalizing experience and well worth while. Some hammams operate for men only, others for women only. Another pattern of opening reserves the morning for men and the afternoon (until 1800 after which the men can return) for women. The oldest hammams are in the médina. Try any of the following: Hammam Sahib Ettabaâ, Halfaouine; Hammam Hafhouf, rue de la Rivière, near place du Leader (reopening soon); Hammam Sidi Belghayth, rue Hajjamine, Bab Jedid neighbourhood (men only).

Music The *Hotel Mechtel* has a nightclub on the top floor. There are occasional jazz evenings in the winter at *El Teatro*, a mini-theatre housed in the same complex. There are occasional concerts by foreign orchestras and ensembles at the Théâtre Municipal. For Tunisian music, you will be best served during Ramadhan, when there are concerts in restored buildings in the médina. At the conservative end of the range, you may find concerts of traditional choral music, *malouf*, by groups like the Rachidia. The crowd will be altogether more spontaneous at the café in the Souk Echaouachia off the rue Sidi Ben Arous, where a small Tunisian band belts out favourites to an appreciative and sometimes rowdy crowd. If karaoke is your thing, you might try *La Brasserie*, the up-market bar of the Hotel La Maison Blanche close to the intersection of the Av Mohamed V and Av Kheireddine Pacha.

Theatre *Municipal Theatre*, Av Habib Bourguiba, T860888. Tunis' main theatre is a fine Art Nouveau wedding cake of a building on the city's main drag. Back before the Second World War, it must have seen opera and theatre productions with all the leading stars of the day. You could also look out for productions *at Le Quatrième Art* on Av de Paris, the city centre home to the Théâtre national tunisien directed by the energetic Mohamed Driss. Almost opposite Le Quatrième Art is the *Maison de Culture Ibn Rachik*, which also occasionally hosts theatre and the odd art-house movie.

Shopping **Bookshops** Tunisians are not great readers, and there are correspondingly few bookshops and libraries. There are a number of papeteries/bookshops on the Avenue de France, but most books are in Arabic or French. Paperbacks in English can be found in the souvenir shops in the larger hotels. If you read Arabic or French go to the *Librairie Clairefontaine*, 4 rue d'Alger. The *Librairie Alif*, which used to be on the Rue de Hollande, is currently in search of new premises. Other bookshops in downtown Tunis which can occasionally turn up surprises include *El Kitab* next to the Colisée cinema arcade on Avenue Bourguiba and *Le Gai Savoir*, rather more academic, on Place Barcelone. The bookshop in the Carlton shopping arcade, off ave Bourguiba, has a good range of local books in French too. In El Menzah I, try the bookshop close to the mosque, opposite the Touta Supermarket on the Rue Moez.

Hairdressers Men looking for a short-back-and-sides will have no problem in Tunis, a haircut costing around 3Dt. You can also be shaved with an old-fashioned cut-throat razor at the same time. Women seeking an unstructured natural look may have a little trouble finding a suitable hairdresser. Tunisian women like perms, blonde streaks and big hair. *Chantal* at Carthage (T275676), in the Touta supermarket complex, chic and expensive; *Donna* in La Soukra is the leading beauticians. Pay through the nose and then some. *Sofiène*, 22 rue des Narcisses, Menzah V, T766362, is a reliable address in Carnoy/El Menzah V residential area. In Sidi Bou Saïd, *Enzo Martelli*, T747973, and *Crystal*, T741862, have a good name.

Handicrafts Tunisian craftsmanship can be excellent and it is possible (after a bit of bargaining) to get good deals, although ultimately the price you pay really depends on what the article is actually worth to you. Leather goods and brass objects are plentiful and of reasonable quality. There are some quite nice cheap ceramics, too. On the whole, however, the craftwork lacks the imagination and verve that characterizes the best Moroccan goods, without having the fine quality of European handmade items.

To get an idea of prices and the craft items produced, visit the *Office National de l'Artisanat*, (the ONAT), now housed in splendid premises at the intersection of Avenue Bourguiba and the Avenue de Carthage. Their showroom displays crafts from around Tunisia. Prices are generally higher than elsewhere, but at least you can get an idea of what is available. The ONAT also has a list of the official prices for carpets according to the quality. You will find many of these, among lots of less interesting goods, in the médina in rue Jemaa Zitouna. Be selective – there is an awful lot of imported junk in the souks these days. If you are looking for kitsch presents for people back at work, you will be spoilt for choice.

Up-market gifts: In the Lafayette district, on Av de la Liberté, try *Nakcha*, a small craft shop opposite the Centre culturel français. Good range of Tunisian and Moroccan craft items. Well-off the tourist track is the *Galerie Morjana*, boutique No 219, on the 2nd floor of the Lac Palace mall, Berges du Lac. Expensive, but well worthwhile for its jewellery, frames, painted woodwork and various bits.

In the souks By the Great Mosque, the *Souq el Attarine* originally specialized in perfumes. The goods are more mixed these days, with modern perfumes and imitations outdistancing the traditionally made perfume essences. *Jewellery* can be found in the *Souq des Orfèvres*, and *Souq el Berka*. For *carpets and blankets* go to *Souq el Leffa*, but carpets are generally cheaper in Kairouan. If you get a carpet be sure you have the receipt and that there is a quality stamp on the back. *Leather* can be found in numerous touristy shops, including those on *Souq el Trouk*, an extension of Souk el Attarine. Quality is often mediocre, the styles on offer out-of-date. On *Souk el Belghadjia*, just off Souk el Attarine, you can find old style Tunis footwear among the modern styles.

If you are looking for cheap imported goods or household electrical goods, you could do worse than go to the covered market on the Rue Moncef Bey, visited by

Perfume

The art of distilling perfume essences has all but disappeared (Announ has a small distillation unit off Souq en-Nahhas) and many of the essences on sale today are imported. Unromantically, they come in metal cans (stamped and sealed). The advantage is that the salesmen in Souq el-Attarine can make up your favourite eau de toilette to the strength you require and at half the price. Maher in Souq el-Attarine (opposite the steps leading up to the 15th century ablutions building Midhat es-Soltane) does a fine imitation Kenzo for Men. More traditionally, various flower waters are on sale very cheaply (orange flower or geranium), and are excellent for perfuming fruit salads and Turkish coffee.

buses Nos 2 and 100 and next door to the main louage station for destinations south. If you are not looking for souvenirs, the best place to go is Av Charles de Gaulle in the new city where you will find supermarkets (*Monoprix*), chemists and camera shops. (Note that both the Monoprix and the Magasin Général on the Av de France sell alcohol.) There are many smart shops and boutiques in Tunis, especially in the area of Av Habib Bourguiba, Av Habib Thameur and Av de France.

Mall shopping A sign of Tunisia's growing prosperity are the new shopping malls which sprung up in the second half of the 1990s. In downtown Tunis, you have the Palmarium, with plenty of shops selling expensive sports and leisure gear. Up in El Manar, you have the Centre Makni, complete with a Levi's boutique, and opposite it, the Centre X. Out on the La Marsa highway, the focal point of Les Berges du Lac is the Lac Palace mall. Fully a/c, it has 3 levels of shops around a central atrium where metal birds 'fly' and the retailers wait for the consumers. The setting may be wholly unecological, the concept is the same as the souks of the old médina.

Sports

Diving Contact the Fédération des activités subaquatiques de Tunisie, Piscine olympique d'El Menzah, BP 486, 1082 Cité El Mahrajène, T234041, they have a small office which can provide information on diving events – most notably, underwater photography competitions are held in Tabarka, where most diving activity takes place. Tunisian kids, equipped with goggles, spend many happy hours fishing for sea-urchins (poor man's oysters) on the rockier sections of coastline. **Gliding and flying** The *Gliding Club* at Djebel Rassas south of Tunis was closed a few years ago after a particularly appalling accident. However, like the numerous birds of prey using the currents eddying round this strange mountain, hang-gliders continue to fly at weekends. **Golf** There is an 18-hole course at La Soukra (close to the airport), T765919, F765915, 4,432m, par 66. **Gymnasia** If you are looking for a gym, there are any number in central Tunis. The bigger hotels often have tiny 'fitness centres', which, given the high charges and limited equipment, have few takers. Of the gyms, the biggest is easily the *Panda Club*, on Rue du Train, close to Le Passage. Monday/Wednesday/Friday for women, Tuesday/Thursday/Saturday for men. Open early morning to 2100. There is a smaller Panda Club in a basement close to the Rue Jean Jaurès, with the opposite timetable. Otherwise there are a number of gyms up in Menzah VI (Gold's Gym and others). Serious weightlifters might want to try the *Power Club* in the Ariana. **Riding** Some of the hotels at Raoued can organize riding. Try also the *Club Hippique de la Soukra*, 15 km north of Tunis, T203054 and Ksar Saïd, 10 km from Tunis. Race meetings every Sunday at Ksar Saïd, T223252. **Swimming pools** At El Menzah (Cité Olympique) you take out a monthly membership card, and times are limited to early morning and lunchtimes. Try also the pool at Menzah VI near the Cité Jamil, open to the public at lunchtimes and in the evening. In summer, there is the piscine municipale on Place Pasteur, although this is more for swimming lessons for local kids. The Gorjani Pool near the Faculté des Sciences Humaines is presently closed. The Bardo neighbourhood has a brand new pool, open all day to those taking out membership cards. (Take first right after main entrance to Bardo Museum). Wealthy Tunisians and residents take out summer memberships for the pools in the big hotels. **Tennis** Try the Tennis Club on Rue Alain Savary, Cité Jardin. Out on the coast, the *Hotel Cap Carthage* has a large number of courts.

Transport

Note that you often have to change metro trains at République if you are heading for the main station at Place Barcelone. The distance between the two is 15-20 mins on foot

Local Bus: you will probably not need to use more than a few routes during your stay in Tunis. For more information go to the bus station in front of the train station on Place de Barcelone. Bus No 3 leaves from Av Habib Bourguiba in front of Tunis Air, or from Av de Paris in front of the *Hotel Majestic* and goes to the Bardo Museum and south bus station. Bus No 5 leaves from Place de l'Indépendence and goes to Place Pasteur by Belvédère Park. Bus No 35 leaves from Av Habib Bourguiba for a half an hour ride to the airport. **Car hire**: many firms have an agent at airport. *Avis*, Av Habib Bourguiba, in the *Africa Hotel* lobby, Av Habib Bourguiba, T341249; *Ben Jemaa*, Excelsior Garage, 53 Av de Paris, T240060; *Budget*, 14 Av de Carthage, T256806; *Carthage Tours*, 59 Av Habib Bourguiba, T254605; *Chartago Rent*, 3 Av Habib Bourguiba, T349168; *Europacar*, 17 Av Habib Bourguiba, T340303; *Garage selection*, 65 Av Hedi Chaker, T284698; *Hertz*, 29 Av Habib Bourguiba, T248559; *Topcar*, 23 Av Habib Bourguiba, T344121; *National Automobile Club of Tunisia (NACT)*, 29 Av Habib Bourguiba, T349837; *SOS Car recovery*, 6 rue Ahmed Amine, T891000. **Car parking, central Tunis**: Parking in central Tunis is a nightmare during the day. You could try parking at the *Hotel Abou Nawas*. This is a convenient and safe place to park with a barrier and gate keeper. Convenient for the metro, a short taxi ride or a 10-minute walk to Place de la République. Open every day, charges 0600-1300 0.35Dt, 1300-2100 0.35Dt, 2000-0600 2Dt. There is an underground car park at the Palmarium mall, behind the Municipal Theatre, and a small carpark on Rue Kamal Ataturk. Note that Denver shoes are in use for illegal parking. **Metro**: Tunis has a 5 line network of small green trams. All lines run into the city centre, severely adding to congestion as they are all above ground. Visitors may want to take the tram to get out to the Bardo Museum (take line 4, destination Den Den, at République, get off at Bardo). The central tram station is at the Place Barcelone, along with the mainline train station and another large station is on Place de la République. There is a ticket kiosk at each stop. Simply buy a ticket to the desired destination and board the next tram. The place names are clearly marked at each stop.

Louages (inter-city taxis): Tunisia has a system of inter-city shared taxis. For destinations in the north of the country, you need the Bab Saâdoun bus station, for main southern destinations, the Moncef Bey louage station, and for the Cap Bon, the Bab Alioua louage station. The latter 2 are only 5 minutes walk from each other. Note that quite often destinations are indicated in Arabic only. **Taxis**: Tunis bilious yellow taxis are quite cheap but generally difficult to find, particularly at rush hour. The maximum you should have to pay is about 4-5Dt and that is for a long trip to La Marsa. All taxis have meters and use them, so make sure they have switched it on Try; also *Allo Taxi*, T282211; *Telephone Taxi*, T492422.

Air To get to the airport either take a taxi or bus No 35 from Av Habib Bourguiba, opposite *Africa Hotel*, 30 minutes. **Airline information** *Aeroflot*, 24 Av Thameur, T340845; *Air Algérie*, 28 Av de Paris, T341590; *Air France*, 1 rue d'Athènes, T341577; *British Airways*, 17 Av Habib Bourguiba, T330046; *Egypt Air*, 49 Av Habib Bourguiba, T341182 in the *International Hotel*; *KLM*, 50 rue Lucy Faure, T341309; Lufthansa, Av Ouled Haffouz, close to the Belvédère Park, in the *Mechtel Hotel*; *Tunis Air*, 48 Av Habib Bourguiba, T259189, central office 133 Av de la Liberté, T288100. Reservations T700700, F700008. Prepaid tickets, T337169/330100. Fright office T754000, 755000, p3078. **Internal flights**: *Tunisair* operates a number of internal flights. Sample prices are as follows: Tunis-Sfax 75.6Dt – daily; Tunis-Djerba 90.6Dt daily; Tunis-Tozeur 86Dt – daily except Tuesday and Wednesday (this may vary).

Train TGM: the TGM (Tunis-La Goulette-La Marsa) is the train linking Tunis to the coastal resorts and suburbs. The station is at the end of Av Habib Bourguiba, T244696, beyond Place de l'Afrique. It is open 24 hours a day with trains every 10-15 minutes during the day and every hour at night. The service goes to La Goulette, Carthage, Sidi Bou Saïd and La Marsa. The main train station is in the centre of the new city on Place de Barcelone. Information: SNCFT, Av Farhat Hached, T244440/252225. **National departures** (times subject to seasonal variations): **Bizerte** 0550, 1130, 1600, 1830; **Bir Bou Regba** and **Sousse** 0710 (on to El Djem, Sfax, Mahares and Gabès); 0900, 1840 (on to Monastir); 1205, 1535 (on to Monastir and Mahdia); 1305, 1410, 1730 (on to El Djem and Sfax); 2120 (on to El Djem, Sfax, Gabès, Gafsa and Metlaoui); Nabeul 1420, 1805 to Hammamet and Nabeul. To **Algeria**: only 1 train goes on to Algiers, all others stop at the border. **Algiers** 1255; **Ghardimaou** (border with Algeria) 0635, 1200, 1425, 1620, 1750. All trains go via Béja and Jendouba (except the 1425). Sample fare: Tunis to Sfax 2nd class 8Dt, bicycle 6.5Dt; to Sousse 5Dt, to Gabès 12Dt, to Metlaoui 12Dt, to Gafsa 11Dt.

Road Bus: there are two bus stations in Tunis. The *North bus station* is situated at Bab Saâdoun. To get there take the bus No 3 from Av Habib Bourguiba by *Hotel Africa Méridien*. Get off just after Bab Saadoun, the bus station is on the right. Buses from here go to the northern areas of the country. For information about buses to the North, T562299/562532. Departures from here to Bizerte; Raf Raf and Ras el Djebel; Medjez el Bab and Béja, change here for Aïn Draham, Jendouba and Tabarka; Mateur and Tabarka; Medjez el Bab, Teboursouk and Le Kef, change here for Thala. For southern destinations, the bus station (Gare routière Sud) is at Bab El Fella and has buses to all other places including Algeria and Libya. To reach the station walk from the main

Tunis and around

Tunis Metro & TGM

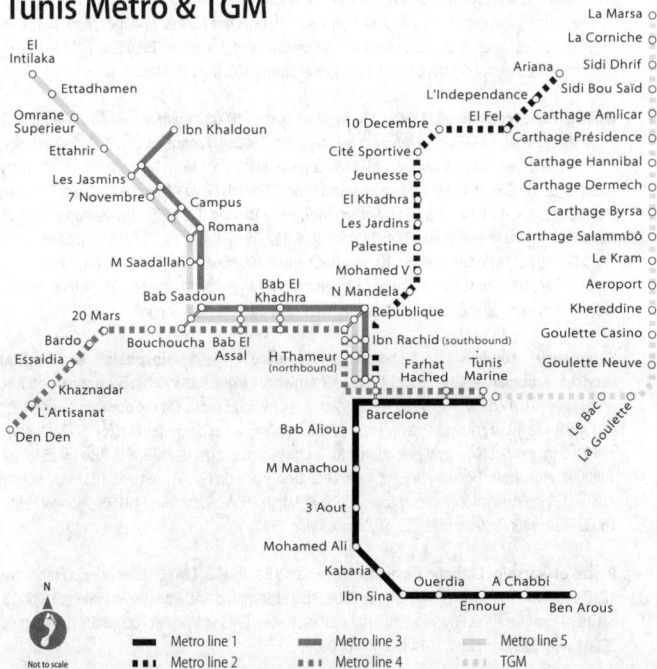

train station, a distance of 800m. Take the rue de La Gare on the right of the station, at the end of the street, go over a small road bridge, and you will see the station over on your right. For information about buses to the South, T495255/490440. Departures from here to Hammamet and Nabeul; to Kairouan via Enfida or El Fahs and on to Gafsa (change here for Tozeur and Nefta) or Kasserine; Sousse (change here for El Djem), Sfax and Gabès, change for Tataouine, Medenine, Ben Gardane, Zarzis and Matmata. **Buses to Algeria and Libya: Algeria** (Annaba) daily at 0700; **Libya** (Tripoli) Monday, Wednesday, Friday and Sunday at 1700, cost 25Dt plus 2Dt/piece of luggage, takes 8-10 hours. **NB** During the summer it can be difficult to get a seat on a bus. You may have to put up a bit of a fight at the ticket office. The best thing is to book. This service is available for most lines, but it is best to check.

Sea Ferry: T255239 for information, see page , Compagnie Tunisienne de Navigation, 5 Av Dag Hammarskjoeld, T242999. The CTN also has a major office on Rue de Yougoslavie, close to the intersection with Rue Jamel Abdel Nasser (ex-rue Sadikia).

Directory

Banks *American Express*, c/o Carthage Tour, 59 Av Habib Bourguiba, T254820. Open 0800-1900, Sun 0900-1200. *BIAT*, Av Habib Bourguiba (American Express). *BT*; *STB*, Av Habib Bourguiba, by the *Africa Hotel*, open daily 0700-1900, has automatic cash dispenser for Visa and Mastercard holders. *UBCI*, Av Habib Bourguiba. Other banks with cash dispensers on the main avenue include the BIAT and the Banque de l'Habitat.

Communications Area code: 01. **Post Office:** main PTT rue Charles de Gaulle, open Mon-Thur 0730-1230 and 1700-1900, Fri-Sat 0730-1330, Sun 0900-1100. A 24-hour telephone centre is off rue Gamal Abdul Nasser. The city also has numerous taxiphones (public call centres), some of which stay open late. **Cybercafés:** Unfortunately, not yet a widespread feature in Tunisian towns and cities. However, all is not lost. The *British Council* at 5 Place de la Victoire (the big white building behind the big stone gate at the city centre entrance to the médina) can provide visitors with internet access. They have 7 computers permanently on line. Open all week 1000 to 1700, Sat 0900 to 1200, closed Mon. The other option is to trek out to the northern suburbs. There is a small cybercentre in a converted garage on the Sidi Daoud Rd. Coming from Tunis, turn right for Carthage. The cybercentre is some 200m on your left. **Internet access:** *Publinet Jean Jaurès*, 70 Av Jean Jaurès, near République/Le Passage central metro station, T350626, F253541. Very handily located in city centre, open 7 days a week from 0800, later on Sun.

Embassies and consulates *Algeria*, 136 Av de la Liberté, T280082; *Canada* (and Australian affairs), 3 rue de Sénégal, T796557; *Egypt*, 16 rue Essayouti, T230004; *France*, Place de l'Indépendence, T245700; *Germany*, 18 Av Challaye, T281246; Italy, rue de Russie, T361811 (open 0930-1130); *Ivory Coast*, 6 rue Ibn Charaf, T283878; Jordan, 4 rue Didon, T288401; *Libya*, 48 bis rue du 1 juin, T283936; *Morocco*, 39 rue du 1 Juin, T288063; *Netherlands*, 6 rue Meycen, T287455; *New Zealand* (see UK); *Norway*, 7 Av Habib Bourguiba, T245933; *Senegal*, 122 Av de la Liberté, T282393; *Sweden*, 87 Av Taïeb Mehri, T283433; *Switzerland*, 10 rue ech-Chenkiti, 1002 Belvédère, T795957; *UK*, 5 Place de la Victoire, T245100, consulate on Av de la Liberté; *USA*, 144 Av de la Liberté, T282566 (a move is projected to a site off the Tunis-La Marsa highway near the American School).

Emergency services Fire station and Police: T197. **Hospitals & medical services** Ambulance: T3412350, T491286. **Chemists:** all night, 43 Av Habib Bourguiba, opposite *Africa Hotel*; 20 Av de la Liberté, by Av de Madrid; 44 Av Bab Djedid. On the door of any chemists you will find a list of chemists staying open at night (*pharmacies de garde*). **Doctor:** *SOS Médecins*, T341250 (to call out a general practitioner for a simple illness, cost of call 20Dt). Also try T346767, T780000. **Hospitals:** *Hôpital Principal Aziza Othmana*, Place du Gouvernement, T633655. *Hôpital Ariana*, T713266. *Hôpital Charles Nicolle*, T663000. *Hôpital Habib Thameur*, T491600. *Hôpital Rabta*, T662276. *Institut Pasteur*, T680539. *SOS Ambulance*, T341250.

Places of worship Catholic: Cathedral on Av Habib Bourguiba, T247290. Services in French Sat 1830 and Sun 1100 and in Italian Sun at 0900. Also St Jeanne d'Arc, 1 rue de Jerusalem, T287213, Sat 1830 and Sun 1000. Foyer Familial, rue du Parc, Radès, T245444. Sun at 1000. 1 rue des Vergers, 2000 Le Bardo, Khaznadar, T514850. Sun at 0900.

Tour companies & travel agents *Abou Nawas Travel*, 8 rue Ibn Jazzar, 1002 Tunis, T781351, F782113. *Ariana Voyages*, 80 Av Habib Bourguiba, 2080 Ariana, T71516. *Atlas Voyages*, 6 rue Saha Ibn Abbah, T286299. *Carthage Tours*, 59 Av Habib Bourguiba, T347015, F352740. *Cyrine Tours*, 3 rue Abou Dhabi, T338063, F243670. *Forum Travel*, 3 rue Houcine Bouzaine, T225193. *Key Tours*, 15 rue d'Angleterre, T351122. *Loisitours*, 6 rue Tetouan, T783653, F788868. *La Maison du Voyage*, Av Gamal Abdul Nasser, beside the Post Office. *Sedec* Tour, rue de Marseille. *Tourafrica*, Av Habib Bourguiba, next to *Africa Hotel*. *Tunisian Travel Service*, 19 Av Habib Bourguiba, T348100 and 28 rue Hassan Ibn Nomene, 1002 Tunis, T785855, F780682. *Ulysse Tours*, 31 Av de Paris, T344727 and 20 rue 18 Janvier, T255082. *Voyages 2000*, 2 Av de France, T248554. **Tourist offices** The tourist information offices are: *Tunisian National Tourist Office*, 1 Av Mohammed V (Place de l'Afrique), T341077, F350997. Open 0730-1330 in summer, 0830-1200 and 1500-1800 in winter, closed Sun and public holidays. Not very helpful, but they may have a few illustrated brochures to hand out.

Carthage and the Banlieue Nord

Northeast of Tunis is the Banlieue Nord, the northern suburbs, a coastal strip including the remains of Carthage, the most expensive residential areas and the nearest beaches. This growing suburban area extends for over 20 kilometres along the coast, a succession of small settlements described as 'pearls on a neck-lace'. La Goulette is the first port of Tunis, very popular and very lively at night with the many restaurants along the bay. Carthage is most definitely a smart sub-urb and is famous for its Phoenician and Roman remains. Sidi Bou Saïd is the well known blue and white 'bird cage' village perched on the cliff top. Once elegant La Marsa has a beach which is pleasant out of season, while Gammarth has been rebranded as the Côtes de Carthage to fit its new role as an area of large expensive hotels. There are wide open sands, windsurfing and horseriding at Raoued.

Ins and outs

The Banlieue Nord is easily accessible on public transport, either by the TGM (Tunis-Goulette-Marsa) light railway or on the road that runs alongside it on the causeway. The train has frequent stops. For those in search of Carthaginian remains, get off at Salammbô. For the amphitheatre and the museum up on the hill, get off at Carthage-Hannibal. Sidi Bou Saïd is also on the same line. You can also reach La Marsa by one of the green and white private line buses (TGV), downtown stop by the Hotel Africa in Tunis.

Getting there

If you are travelling by car, there is a very practical, free ferry service between La Goulette and Radès, which enables travellers going south to bypass downtown Tunis. (A bridge is said to be planned for the near future.) The service runs 24 hours a day.

For short hops between the different areas of the northern suburbs, the visitor will find plenty of taxis available. Note that La Marsa Plage is the last stop on the light railway. For those without a car, taxi is the only real option for getting up to the hotels at Gammarth and Raoued. For visiting the ruins of Carthage, you may opt for a *calèche* (horse-drawn carriage) to drive round the leafy streets from sight to sight. Otherwise, be prepared for lots of pleasant walking. From the Tophet to the Carthage Museum on the hill is a half an hour walk at the most.

Getting around

La Goulette حلق الوادى

La Goulette (The Gullet, Halk el Oued in Arabic) is at the narrow entrance to the Lac de Tunis and is the main port of Tunisia. Ferries leave here for Europe. It is dominated by a fortress built by Charles V of Spain in 1535, when he assisted the Hafsids in their fight against Barbarossa. It functions as a harbour,

Phone code: 01
Colour map 1, grid A5

Tunis and around

an important naval base, and a dormitory for Tunis. In summer evenings, the main street of La Goulette, with restaurants and bars everywhere, comes to life.

Since the 19th century, La Goulette has been a summer resort. Gaston Loth, writing in the early 1900s, wrote that "There are five thousand people in La Goulette within the walls; in summer fifteen thousand are jammed into villas which neighbour the little town." Thanks to the railway line, it quickly developed as the centre of a cosmopolitan sort of coastal strip, where the families of French administrators and Italian entrepreneurs could enjoy the sea and sand alongside local Jewish residents. They were joined by such Muslim notables who did not have a *borj* at La Marsa or a summer residence at Sidi Bou Saïd. Court dignitaries built palaces further up the coast at Kheireddine. La Goulette remains popular as a summer resort even today, although the capital's wealthy have long since deserted it in favour of Hammamet and more remote elsewheres.

Sights La Goulette has few sights. You might be able to have a look around the **Karraka** and enjoy a splendid view over the harbour and the Gulf of Tunis. The fortress, which was built by the Habsburg forces in the 16th century, was a prison and no doubt has an appropriately gruesome history. In summer, concerts are held in the main courtyard. The Karraka is also, on occasion, the setting for ram fights (*béliomachie* in French), a 'sport' which has a small if devoted following. ■ *Entrance 1Dt, photography 3Dt.*

On your left as you come into La Goulette by car you may see an area dominated by the tall square tower of a church. This is **La Petite Sicile**, now largely demolished, once home to a considerable Italian, Tunisian Jewish and Maltese community. The one time multi-culturalism of the area is celebrated in Férid Boughedir's feel-good-movie, *Un été à la Goulette*. The film, set just before the outbreak of the Six Day War of 1967, tells the tale of adolescent loves in a community where three religions, Judaism, Islam and Catholicism, still managed to co-exist.

Tunis region

La Goulette now has the equestrian statue of former President Habib Bourguiba which originally stood in Place d'Afrique in Tunis. Astride a proud stallion, Tunisia's befezzed first president strikes the pose of a 19th century South American liberation leader. Although he has no crowd to wave to, the reforms he pushed through in the late 1950s were in no small way the ground-work for the country's present prosperity.

Travelling over the causeway from Tunis, you may note fishermen in small boats out on the lagoon, the **Lac de Tunis** (El Bahira). In many cases, they are not netting fish but dredging for shell fish. These are sent to Korbous, where they are suspended in sacks in the clean sea water there until the grime of their original surroundings has been washed from their systems. Each case sold from Korbous has a government controlled certificate. In the winter months, you can spot cormorants and flocks of flamingoes out on the lagoon.

Once upon a time, La Goulette was the place for a summer night out. Sadly, its restaurants, famed for their fresh fish, have declined in quality, and the charm of al fresco eating on the Avenue Franklin Roosevelt is marred by the quantity of traffic. The newer restaurants are gaudy (*Le Lucullus*) or bottom of the range *gargottes*, which can be fun in their way. Note that fish is sold by weight, with prices given per 100g. Get the waiter to tell you what you will be paying, as the bill can be severe. Otherwise go for the fixed price *poisson complet* (grilled fish with chips and tastira, an egg and fried vegetable sauce). On the seaside promenade are lots of cafés, and you might find a stand making old-style *brik à l'oeuf* or barbecuing spicy merguez sausages. The following restaurants might be worth a try.

Eating

Expensive *Le Café Vert*, 68 Rue Franklin Roosevelt, T736156. Expect to pay at least 30Dt a head with wine. Generally considered the most reliable address in La Goulette, business entertains its clients here. However, the food does not compensate for being wedged in on plastic chairs at tables right next to the exhaust fumes. In this price bracket, better go the whole hog and eat at a really upmarket place on the coast at Gammarth.

Mid-range Expect to pay around 25Dt a head in the following. *Le Chalet*, 42 Av Franklin Roosevelt, T735138. The one with the pleasant open courtyard with a palm tree. Choose your crustacean from the vivarium. Recommended. *Club Les Jasmins*, 6 Rue Bach Hamba, La Goulette, T736016. Discreet entrance to the left of the Restaurant Vénus on the main roundabout as you come into La Goulette from Tunis. Authentic kosher Jewish cuisine supervised by owner William Sebag. Good *kémia* (appetizers) and a splendid *poisson malin* in spicy tomato sauce. Quiet courtyard away from the traffic. *Mamie Lily*, 14 Av Pasteur, La Goulette-Casino, T737633. Traditional Tunisian Jewish cooking. Mixed reports. *Restaurant Vénus*, 2 Av Habib Bourguiba, La Goulette, T737541. Large restaurant with terraces overlooking the main drag. A bit of a factory. Adequate.

Yachting Club de la Goulette, T276017.

Sports

Tour companies & travel agents *Asfar el Hana*, 64 Av Habib Bourguiba, T736761. **Useful numbers** Port de la Goulette, T735300. Port de Radès, T449300.

Directory

Carthage قرطاج

Phone code: 01
Colour map 1, grid A5

Carthage today is lush green suburb. On the slopes below the old basilica, old Tunis money resides next to ambassadors and assorted foreigners. There is a scattering of schools and municipal buildings and, here and there between the villas, small archaeological sites pop up. A stroll through Salammbô to Carthage can make a very pleasant afternoon. The microclimate is superb: everything seems to grow, and you can see why the Phoenicians chose to put their most important trading post here.

Although the Roman and Punic ruins are not spectacular, they are well worth seeing. Remember that Carthage had a long history, and was one of the most important cities in the Roman Empire. It was also a nerve-centre for early Christianity. The smaller sites are well worth visiting, including in particular the Tophet and the Palaeo-Christian Museum. The main museum on the hill is surprisingly dull for a site with so much history to tell.

History and background

Legendary beginnings
According to Roman epic poet Virgil, Carthage was founded in 814 BC by the Phoenician Princess Dido (Didon), who came there as a refugee after her husband had been killed by her brother, Pygmalion. According to Greek legends, she fled from Tyre in the eastern Mediterranean to North Africa where she bought land from local ruler Iarbas. The story of the sale is that Dido agreed to acquire land no more than could be covered by an ox hide. Cleverly, she cut the hide into narrow strips and so surrounded a much larger area than the locals had bargained on selling. It was certainly enough to build a new city, which the Phoenician settlers named *Kart Hadascht*, meaning New Town.

Other largely apocryphal tales tell of Dido's courtship with Aeneas, the Trojan warrior and future founder of Rome, an affair celebrated in Purcell's 17th century opera *Dido and Aeneas*, based on Book Four of Virgil's classic the *Aeneid*. Dido reputedly died of a broken heart when Aeneas resumed his wanderings. In fact the two were not living at the same period – but why spoil a good yarn?

Another tale goes that local king Iarbas was the son of Jupiter and an African nymph. Iarbas wanted to marry Dido. She, however, was determined to remain faithful to the memory of her late husband. Thus she built a pyre as if preparing an offering to the gods, and then committed suicide by leaping into the flames. A more dramatic method of escaping a suitor's attentions could hardly be imagined.

Carthage, Mediterranean power
Certainly the foundation of Carthage was an enormous success. It soon became a major power and trade centre, with as many as 500,000 residents, making it the third largest city in the empire after Rome and Alexandria. It attempted to rival both the Greeks and the Romans by setting its sights, unsuccessfully, on Sicily. Everybody knows the extraordinary story of Hannibal who crossed the Alps with 40,000 men and 38 elephants to attack Rome. The Romans eventually took revenge and Scipio's armies won a decisive battle in Zama in 202 BC. Carthage was subjected to a siege lasting three years and was eventually seized and razed to the ground in 146 BC to the delight of Cato, who had had this in mind for some time.

Rome in African capital
However, this was not to be the end of Carthage as the Romans, under Caesar Augustus in 44 BC, returned to make it the capital of the Roman Province of Africa, the cultural and intellectual centre. At this time Carthage was known as

Rome's bread basket due to its fertile hinterland. It collapsed as a significant power after the successive invasions of the Vandals, Byzantines and Arabs.

After the Arab invasion of the late seventh century, Carthage was mainly used as a source of building material for Islamic monuments and the expanding city of Tunis. By the 19th century, there was little to see. The myth of ancient

Excavating Carthage

Carthage

To La Marsa

SIDI-BOU-SAÏD

Magasin Général

To Harbour

US War Cemetery

Rue Roosevelt

Basilica St Cyprien

Av Habib Bourguiba

Basilica de Damous el Karita

Odéon

Antiquarium

Roman Villas

Presidential Palace

Malga Cisterns

Rue Mohamed Ali

Theatre

Av Bourguiba

Archaeological Park

Antonine Baths

8

Amphitheatre

Thermes de Bargillus

Av 7 Novembre

Cathedral

National Museum

6

Byrsa Hill

2

MAGON QUARTER

Rue Taha Houssine

Circus

Paleo-Christian Museum

5

Mad'art Theatre

Supermarket

Gulf of Tunis

5

7

Av 2 Mars

6

DOUAR ECH-CHOTT

Old Naval Port

Dar el Hout

PUNIC PORTS

Oceanographic Museum

4

Hannibal

3

Ancient Merchant Harbour

7

Av Farhat Hached

1

SALAMMBO

Tahiti

To La Goulette & Tunis

N

0 metres 250
0 yards 273

■ Sleeping		● Eating	
1 Amilcar	3 La Bagatelle	1 Baâl	
2 Reine Didou	4 Le Gerrys	2 Café Tam Tam	
3 Tophet	5 Le Tchevap		
	6 Le Tie-Break		
	7 Pâtisserie Charlotte		
	8 Phénix de Carthage		

● Eating
1 Baâl
2 Café Tam Tam

🚉 TGM Stations
1 Sidi Bou Saïd
2 Carthage Amilcar
3 Carthage Présidence
4 Carthage Hannibal
5 Carthage Dermech
6 Carthage Byrsa
7 Carthage Salammbo

Tunis and around

☛ The Aeneid, founding myth of empire

Probably written between 29 and 19 BC, and still unfinished when Virgil died, The Aeneid tells the tale of a warrior hero, Aeneas, who was to found Rome. Though son of Venus and a Trojan mortal, Anchises, Aeneas is of very different stuff to the Greek heroes of Iliad and Odyssey. Though watched over by gods and goddesses, Aeneas is a human being, hesitant and weak. A Trojan, he leaves his hometown behind in ruins, and his journey across the Mediterranean to Italy is a hard one. In Book IV, he nearly loses all in Carthage, distracted by his love for a foreign queen.

For Virgil, Aeneas is the vehicle by which, as a writer, he can raise issues about Rome's destiny as an imperial power. The Romans of the first century BC were sought explanations for their city state's rise to Mediterranean dominance. **The Aeneid**, a 12 book epic poem, was one such explanation. Rome, like Aeneas, won through, but only after much lonely struggle. The imperial peace under Augustus was the logical conclusion of the fight which left Rome master in the lands of kingdoms destroyed, not the least of them Carthage.

Carthage remained alive, however, nourished by the classical education dispensed in Europe's schools and universities. British traveller Sir Grenville Temple described his reaction after climbing Byrsa Hill: "... my heart sang within me, when, ascending one of its hills (from whose summit the eye embraces a view of the whole surrounding country to the edge of the sea) I beheld nothing more than a few scattered and shapeless masses of masonry." The beys granted permits to 'quarry' Carthage.

The first, rather amateur excavations were started in 1857 by Beulé. The situation was to improve shortly after the arrival of the French. Under the leadership of Cardinal Lavigerie, the Pères Blancs set to work, excavating Carthage's past with energy and enthusiasm. A major museum was established on Byrsa Hill. In the early 1970s, the Unesco and the Tunisian government sponsored a major campaign to save the ancient sites. Research teams from 14 countries participated, each working on a specific area. The British under Henry Hurst revealed the secrets of the Punic ports, while the French worked on a unique Punic residential quarter up on Byrsa Hill.

Today, the site of ancient Carthage, some 545 hectares, including almost the whole area of the municipalities of Carthage and Sidi Bou Saïd, plus parts of La Marsa and La Goulette, is a national archaeological park. Much still remains to be excavated on this unique site, and every year, teams of archaeologists return to continue the quest.

Visiting the sites of Carthage

A short visit to Carthage only gives an overview. Tours provided by hotels are usually only half-day affairs, hardly adequate to get from one end of Carthage to the other (three kilometres) and visit a few remains on some of the 12 main sites. Enthusiasts of all things ancient will want to allow at least a full day if possible. If you are not a ruins enthusiast, try to take in a selection of sites located close to each other. Starting early, you could start at the southernmost site, the Tophet, view the Punic Ports, the Palaeo-Christian Museum and the main museum on the hill. (You could also do the Oceanographic Museum at the same time.) Real enthusiasts would want to pack in the Antonine Baths and a look at the theatre before lunch. ■ *All sites here open 0800-1900 summer, 0830-1730 winter, closed Sunday. Entrance 200Dt, photography 2Dt covers all sites and the museum, valid only for day of issue.*

Ancient Carthage: main dates

814 BC	Founded by Tyrian princess Dido	44 BC	Carthage refounded as Colonia Julia by Caesar Augustus
260 BC	Beginning of the three Punic wars between Carthage and Rome	14 AD	The city much increased in prosperity
146 BC	Carthage destroyed after a three year siege by the Romans	439 AD	Carthage seized by Vandals for one century
122 BC	Gracchus attempted to refound Carthage	533 AD	Reconquest by Byzantines

Get off at the TGM station at Carthage Salammbo and walk down towards the sea. Take second left turn, and the Tophet, which simplifying broadly can be described as an ancient Punic crematorium, is on your right behind a tangly hedge. Further along the road you come to the Oceanographic Museum (in a large 19th century building to your right) and the Punic Ports. It is then only a short walk up to the TGM station at Carthage Byrsa.

The Tophet, the Oceanographic Museum & the Punic Ports

The **Tophet** houses the remains of the sanctuary of the Carthaginian divinities Tanit and Baal-Hammon, the oldest Punic religious site in Carthage. There is not much left to see. According to legend, for seven centuries the noble Carthaginian families brought their children here to be ritually sacrificed, and urns containing ashes and remains of many children have in fact been found. This site was discovered in 1921 and is considered to be the largest of all known sacrificial compounds. The ashes of the victims, sometimes small children but more often birds and young animals, were placed in a stone-lined trench. Other offerings such as dishes and lucky charms were buried too. When the whole area was filled with covered trenches, a layer of earth was placed across and the whole process began again.

The **Oceanographic Museum** is of most interest to those who are keen on fish and fishing. Children will like the new aquaria in the basement. There is an extensive collection of stuffed birds upstairs, and some nice models of the different types of sailboat no longer found on Tunisia's coasts. You can also learn about the different islands and islets in Tunisian territorial waters.

The main **harbour** used to be the very heart of Carthaginian prosperity. The northern basin functioned as a naval base, boasting safe anchorage for 220 vessels. It was circular in shape and bordered by quays. The southern base, originally rectangular in shape, was for merchant ships. The ports, well protected from attack, must have been the keystone of Punic commerce, situated as they were right in the middle of the Mediterranean.

The Punic Ports & Admiralty Island

The small **island** in the middle of the northern port was the subject of research by a British archaeological mission in the 1970s, which revealed a fascinating Roman docking system. The island was built up as a circular space, with a spine carrying an upper service gantry, below which ships could be winched up into a covered dry dock. A bridge linked the island to the shore. This sophisticated dock was constructed to handle exports of wheat to Rome. Adjacent was the **Commercial Harbour** joined to the sea by a dredged channel. This harbour was a large circular basin surrounded by large warehouses.

The **Antiquarium** situated alongside Avenue Habib Bourguiba has exhibits from excavations of the harbour and the surrounding area. There are numerous coins (over 9,000) and pieces of metal and marble. The best exhibit is the mosaic from the House of the Greek Charioteers.

The Carthage Museum, amphitheatre, theatre & Roman villas

Alight at TGM station Carthage Hannibal. Walk up Avenue de l'Amphithéatre to the summit of **Mount Byrsa** which was the Acropolis of Punic and Roman Carthage, an ideal view point. The Byrsa quarter, recently discovered by French archaeologists, dates from the time of Hannibal and gives an idea of urban life in the early second century BC. We have to be grateful that when the Romans returned to rebuild Carthage they covered over the ruins of the 146 BC destruction on Byrsa Hill with thick layers of rubble and earth – a Roman landfill programme. Hence the whole segment of history was preserved for later examination.

Here there is the large cathedral named in honour of St Louis and seminary (now the museum), constructed by the French during the Protectorate which has been made into a cultural centre. On the southern slope are the remains of the Punic residential quarter (second century BC), built in a regular rectangular grid, houses, water tanks, drains, plastered walls, tiled floors. Down the other side of the hill the amphitheatre is on one side of the road and a collection of cisterns on the other. Returning towards the sea down Avenue 7th Novembre on the left is the theatre behind which lie the Roman Villas. If you visit the Basilicas of Damou and St Cyprien next then backtrack to the Baths of Antoninus, you will have visited all the major sites and be back at the TGM station.

The **Magon Quarter** dating from the fifth century BC is approached down Avenue de la République. It was destroyed in 146 BC and rebuilt under Caesar Augustus. Following the excavations by the German Archaeological Institute, the site was turned into a garden and it is possible to walk along the restored Roman road by the sea front. A small museum displays household items, found during excavations. Models and diagrams illustrate the development of the Punic settlement and the rebuilding a century after its destruction.

In the **amphitheatre**, built during Hadrian's reign and capable of seating 35,000 spectators, early Christians were thrown to the lions and gladiators as entertainment for the audience. Unfortunately there is very little to be seen since only limited excavation work has been carried out. The cisterns at La Maalga, behind Le Phénix de Carthage entertainment complex, were the main reservoirs for the Carthage water supply. Their very size and complexity is a good indication of the population of the ancient city. Today they are in a bad state.

The **Odeon Quarter** is set to the west of the railway and Avenue Habib Bourguiba. The Roman theatre which could hold 10,000 spectators is located in the Odeon area, though most of what can be seen is a restoration. The original pieces exist only in fragmentary form (see diagram), but at least give an idea of what the entire seating area (*cavea*) of the monument was once like. The semicircular *orchestra* with some of its original marble flooring can still be seen too. The building is not very interesting in itself as it is not very true to the original, but the **International Carthage Festival** held here every year receives great praise.

Also on Odeon Hill, north of the theatre, are a series of excavations of fine Roman villas (on the whole badly restored) and similar buildings, reached via the entrance at the *nymphaion* with its water feature. The villas are of classical proportions, built around the peristyle or central pillared courtyard giving access to the main living rooms. This form can be seen clearly in the famous and now restored fifth-sixth century **House of the Aviary**, named after the subject of a mosaic found at the site bearing a well executed polychrome of a fowl and fruit, now in the Bardo Museum. This house has an octagonal garden in the middle of its courtyard. Many of the artefacts on show here in the house, including statues and a bust of Dionysus, are from other sites at Carthage. Other adjacent villas such as the **House of the Horse** and the Odeon itself are worth a visit. The Odeon was an indoor theatre but only its confused ruins remain – most of the material has long gone, used to construct new buildings.

The **Antonine Baths**, once the biggest baths in North Africa and the third largest in the Roman world, were truly enormous. They are in a splendid position between Avenue Habib Bourguiba and the sea and are one of the best preserved sites in Carthage. Even though there are only a few pieces of building still standing, they give, with a little imagination, a good idea of the grandeur that was.

Their construction began under Hadrian and Antonius officiated at the opening ceremony in the middle of the second century. The finance for the project, donated by some rich inhabitant, gives an indication of the wealth at that time. The complex array of rooms in the baths is shown on the plan below. The layout is symmetrical around a central axis of the swimming pool, with the *frigidarium* and *calderium* running from the seashore frontage to the second façade facing west onto the archaeological gardens. The two wings each contained a *palaestra* or open pillared exercise yard, an indoor gymnasium, hot bath, *tepidarium* and *destrictarium* or warmed cleaning room. A *laconicum* or sweating room was included, while the main *frigidarium* was shared by both wings. Many of the minor rooms are hexagonal or octagonal in shape. Water for the baths came from the main city aqueduct. Being at sea level, the heating and service areas had to be built above ground, the boilers immediately below the heated rooms for efficiency and economy.

To the south of the baths lie the present-day **archaeological gardens**, comprising two main northwest-southeast roads (Decumanus III to IV) of the original gridiron layout of roads and their crossroads (Cardo). Originally the road system was aligned along the summit of the acropolis of Byrsa (northwest-southeast) and defined all the blocks of property in the city. The residual area encompassed by the archaeological gardens is mainly in ruins, but the former esplanade of the baths can be identified together with its porticos and annexes, of which the most singular is the latrines, laid out in two great 35 metres semicircles. There is a small basilica in this same corner featuring a main aisle and two side aisles, but the main church in the gardens is to the west – that of the late Byzantine Dermech Basilica (Douimès). Part of the Punic necropolis is the only sign of the older foundation in the gardens. The Schola House on Decumanus III has a peristyle and contained fine mosaics.

So many of the original stones of Carthage have been taken. Many originally here were used in the construction of Tunis. Others travelled much further and make-up parts of a number of monuments including Pisa cathedral.

Antonine Baths

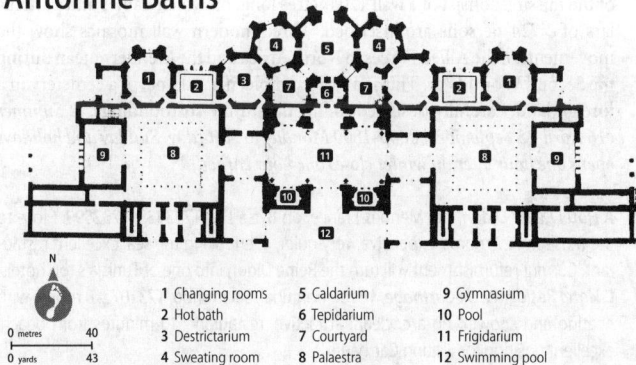

1 Changing rooms	5 Caldarium	9 Gymnasium
2 Hot bath	6 Tepidarium	10 Pool
3 Destrictarium	7 Courtyard	11 Frigidarium
4 Sweating room	8 Palaestra	12 Swimming pool

0 metres 40
0 yards 43

The **Musée de Carthage**, T730036, situated by the former Basilica Saint-Louis at the top of Byrsa Hill, presents some of the finer finds from the Carthage excavations. The approach road winds round the shoulder of the hill with vestiges of ruins protruding from the hillside. The road terminates in a car park in front of the cathedral. Entrance kiosk to the museum and the second century BC Punic ruins is to the right of the Basilica.

It is worth making a short detour to wander among the partly restored walls. Take a walk in the garden which faces the museum entrance. This stands on the site of an ancient basilica and here more examples of pillars and carved stone-work can be examined. The walls of the garden are inlaid with small pieces found in the area.

Follow the path from the entrance kiosk and turn right to the toilets or left to the museum door, where there are some rather plain sarcophagi on display on either side. By contrast, just inside on the right are two fourth century BC sarcophagi with recumbent statues on the lid. This is the room devoted to Punic stelae and sarcophagi. The Paleo-Christian room is on the left as you enter. It contains some important terracotta tiles and two sculptured panels known as *The Adoration of the Kings and The Annunciation*. Opposite the entrance is the room devoted to modern scientific methods relating to excavations and archaeology. Upstairs to the left is an amazing display of oil lamps, while the rest of the room is divided into the main periods of Carthaginian history. Items from Punic Carthage denoted with beige include items from graves: Roman Carthage (blue) has ceramics, glassware and sculpture in marble; Christian and Byzantine Carthage (pink) has figurines, ivory, terracotta tiles and glassware; Arab Carthage, mainly ceramics, is denoted in green. There is no leaflet to explain about the exhibits though most are named in Arabic, English and French. It is a worthwhile stop, but is overshadowed by the magnificent collection in the Bardo museum, and in terms of the display, by the new museum at Chemtou.

The **circus** was on the extreme west of the city. Only the outline can be made out. It would have been used for chariot racing as depicted in the mosaic exhibited in the antiquarium, the four teams wearing distinguishing colours. The site became a cemetery.

The American Military Cemetery

After leaving Carthage and before reaching Sidi Bou Saïd, take a left turn to the American Military Cemetery. There is a car park inside the entrance gates and a visitors' reception and restroom.

On a site covering over 10 hectares are the graves of 2,841 American military men and women (240 unnamed), who died in the fighting which culminated in the liberation of Tunisia. Walk down the steps and along the tree shaded avenue to the immaculate lawn marked with rows of white crosses. The tablets of the missing consist of a wall 120 metres long, on which names and particulars of 3,724 persons are inscribed. Three modern wall mosaics show the movements of the Allied Forces in North Africa and the Mediterranean during the Second World War. This is a fine example, if a sad one, of a cemetery in a foreign land, carefully designed to blend with the surroundings. ■ *Summer (16 April-15 September) 0800-1800 Monday to Saturday, Sunday and holidays opens one hour later, in winter closes one hour earlier.*

Sleeping
Phone code: 01

A *Hotel Reine Didon*, rue Mendès France, on Byrsa Hill, T733433, F732599. Close to the museum, 22 rooms, expensive, very quiet, overlooking the sea, excellent restaurant. Current refurbishment will turn the Reine Didon into one of Tunisia's top hotels. **C** *Hotel Résidence de Carthage*, 16 rue Hannibal, Salammbô, T731072. 8 rooms with heating and shower, no a/c, clean, attractive, restaurant, 10 minutes from beach, excellent position for visiting Carthage.

Carthage, as you would expect of such an upscale area, has a choice of eateries. **Eating**

Expensive *Le Punique*, Hotel-Résidence Carthage, 16 rue Hannibal, Salammbô, T731072. **Mid-range** *Le Gerry's* at Salammbô on the main drag. Good if unimaginative Italian food. Alcohol and reasonable prices make this restaurant popular with young locals. Good service. Recommended. T73008. *Le Neptune*, 2 rue Ibn Chabbat, T731456. Hidden away in the residential streets to the right of the main road as you leave Le Kram and Salammbô behind you. Right on the sea. Pleasant. *Le Tchevap*, on main road, almost opposite Carthage main supermarket, T277089. At the expensive end of the mid-range price bracket, good pasta and filet de sole, very decent service, for once. Recommended. The Italian restaurant of the *Palm Hotel*, Le Kram, right on the beach, has had good reports. (Look for signs at main roundabout in Le Kram.) **Cheap** *Frigolo*, next to the Le Passage supermarket at Carthage-Dermech, T275959. Does good ice-cream, cakes, fruit teas and snacks. The usual sloppy service lets the place down, however. For extremely good cakes, you need the *Pâtisserie Charlotte*, over the road from the supermarket,heading back towards Le Kram. *Le Vagabondo*, Av Habib Bourguiba, Le Kram. A no frills (and no alcohol) sort of place which does very reasonable pizzas and a mean spaghetti fruits de mer. Recommended. There are plenty of cheap sandwich places along the main drag on Le Kram.

Le Comptoir d'Amilcar, about 1 km from Sidi Bou Saïd, on your left on main road as you **Shopping** approach the Lycée de Carthage. Expensive furnishings shop, but also has wrought iron and household linen. *El Hanout* and *El Hanout - enfant*, rue J.F. Kennedy, Carthage-Hannibal (1st left as you go uphill on Av de l'Amphithéâtre from Carthage-Hannibal station). Bijou emporium with lots of expensive itemlets. Nice handmade toys, lamps and fittings for children's rooms at El Hanout - enfant. *Phénicia*, 27 Av Habib Bourguiba (the main road), Carthage-Byrsa, turn right after you leave the station, just before you cross to head for the Punic Ports. Personable little shop with an excellent range of contemporary ceramics, textiles, embroidery and jewellery. One of the few shops to stock really authentic Tunisian crafts. Well worth a visit.

Communications **Internet access:** If you can't get into town, there are 2 internet access places **Directory** in the Carthage area. *Club Informatique de Carthage, CIC*. Close to the Antonine Baths, almost opposite Carthage PTT (post office), and a couple of doors down from Police Station. Look for small plaque next to door. You have to become a member of the club. Access times are very irregular, according to the training sessions they are running. Bureaucratic, rude staff. Best bet between 1600 and 1800. *Cyberespace Sidi Daoud*. As you leave Carthage for Sidi Daoud, about 200m before the junction with the La Marsa highway, on your left in a converted garage. Again, irregular hrs, 6 computers.

Sidi Bou Saïd   سيدي أبو سعيد

Hilltop Sidi Bou Saïd is everyone's favourite Mediterranean village, a jumble of *Phone code: 01* whitewashed houses with blue-painted doors and windows on a hilltop over- *Colour map 1, grid A5* looking the sea. Until a couple of decades ago it was quite an isolated place, a fact hard to remember these days when the village car park is full of tourist buses. Yet the back alleys of the village maintain their charm. Cats snooze on doorsteps, canaries trill behind lattice work windows, and elaborate studded doors pose for photographs. And from the heights of the village, there are some breathtaking views out across the Mediterranean and the Gulf of Tunis.

The original Sidi Bou Saïd was a mystic back in the 13th century. In 1207, **History &** Abou Saïd Khalaf Ben Yahia el Béji, returning to Tunis from a pilgrimage to **background** Mecca, settled on the Djebel el Manar (Lighthouse Hill), all the better to commune with the divine. For some 20 years he resided out on the coast, arousing the admiration of the local fishing community for his ascetic ways. Abou Saïd's fame spread to Tunis, and on his death in 1236 he was practically the patron saint of the village. (The Tunisian Arabic term 'sidi' roughly corresponds to the Christian saint, although there is no practise of canonization in Islam.) The tomb of Sidi Bou Saïd gradually became a place of pilgrimage, and his disciples continued his ascetic ways. Other soufis settled on Djebel Manar.

In the 18th century, the Husseinid beys rebuilt the tomb and extended the mosque. In order to benefit from the saint's *baraka* (blessing), they made the village their summer resort, and despite the distance from Tunis, a number of old Tunisois families followed suit, building themselves pleasant summer residences in the clifftop village with its views over the Mediterranean, the Cap Bon and Carthage. Under Naceur Bey, in 1915, the village was given listed status to protect it from the ravages of potential developers. Sea bathing became fashionable, and the old families built themselves wooden bathing cabins on stilts over the sea down by the discreet village beach.

The musical baron
But it was a French baron who did a lot to put Sidi Bou Saïd on the map. The story goes that Baron Rodolphe d'Erlanger, scion of a Parisian banking house which had lent Tunisia large sums of money, fell in love with the village on a visit in 1908. He acquired a piece of prime land overlooking the Mediterranean, and with his Italian wife, the beautiful Bettina Amidei, had a palace constructed, the Dar Nejma Ezzahra, 'the House of the Star of Venus'. Works lasted from 1912 to 1921, but it was with a heavy heart that the baron completed his dream Tunisian residence, for he lost his son in the First World War.

Dar Nejma Ezzahra is a building unique in Tunisia. Essentially it is an early 20th century British country house dressed up in orientalist garb. As such it is definitely worth a visit (see below).

Artists & gentrification
Something of a backwater, yet close to Tunis, Sidi Bou Saïd once attracted intellectuals and artists. André Gide passed through on one of his North African perambulations, painters Paul Klee and Macke are said to have been dazzled by its shapes and colours. In the late 1960s, philosopher Michel Foucault lived for a couple of years in Dar Patou in the upper village. For his habit of keeping a human skull as a decorative feature in his study, he gained a reputation as a necromancer. In the 1990s, the village began to gentrify, and money was pumped into new property. Some of the seemingly oldest homes are in fact recent creations of top Tunisian traditionalist architect Tarak Ben Miled, one of whose earliest projects was the holiday village in a simple vernacular style down by the port.

Colours, tastes & smells
At Sidi Bou Saïd the walls are white, the woodwork is blue. The doors are set with patterns of black-painted nails, no doubt forming highly traditional patterns. Whitewashing the walls is certainly a long established practice. How traditional the blue of the doors is remains an unanswered question. Guides will tell you that blue is the Arab colour of happiness (that's a good one) or that it keeps the flies off (possibly). The modern lacquer paint must be a long way off the original blue stains which may have been used for woodwork in the past. Note that the Café des Nattes makes extensive use of red and green in its colour scheme, as befits a place that was once the ante-chamber to the tomb of the saint himself.

The character of Sidi Bou lies in tiny details, in tastes and smells as well as colour. At the *Café des Nattes*, up a steep flight of steps leading off the cobbled square in the centre of the village, the drinks are Turkish coffee (*kahwa 'arbi'*), scented with geranium or orange flower water, and mint tea with pine-nuts, or even fresh almonds, when in season. The tea is a rich butter toffee brown, and is pure liquid mint with almost the consistency of a liqueur. If this isn't sweet enough for you, just round the corner below the Café des Nattes is a hole-in-the-wall shop selling *bonbalone*, fried doughnuts dipped in sugar.

The most characteristic smell of Sidi Bou Saïd has to be jasmine. The flower sellers go by, with round baskets of jasmine bouquets balanced on their heads. "Smeen, smeen", they cry. For men, a *mechmoum*, a delicately made bouquet lodged behind the ear, is *de rigueur*. (Wearing it behind the left ear means you're single, and behind the right ear that you're married.) Women wear long necklaces of jasmine flowers. And note that there are two types of jasmine on sale: the strong smelling pinkish *yasmine* and the more delicate waxy cream blossoms of *fell* or *jasmin d'Arabie*.

Another place to have a drink, particularly at sunset, is the *Café Sidi Chabaane*, situated at the end of the village. The view from here over the sea is quite exceptional. There are two routes from the upper village down to the harbour: one following the road which leads to the promontory at the end of the village, the other a steep flight of steps to the right just before the Hotel Dar Saïd. **Backstreets & panoramas**

Being on every tourist's itinerary, Sidi Bou Saïd can get very crowded, especially in summer, but most people tend to congregate in the main streets and it is possible to find some peace in the small back streets. Look out for the lighthouse. At the very top of Sidi Bou Saïd, towards Sidi Dhrif, a presidential palace is being built to accommodate official guests.

The Kharja (from the Arabic *kharaja*, to bring out), marks the high point of the Sidi Bou Saïd summer. This is the annual pilgrimage to the tomb of Sidi Bou Saïd, which generally takes place in August. In days gone by, with the beldi families and at least part of the court in residence for the summer, members of the different religious brotherhoods of Tunis would come to the village to pay homage to the saint. The banners of the saint would be brought out and paraded through the village, accompanied by chanting and a swaying line of members of the Aissaoua brotherhood. There is no way you can miss the Kharja when it's on. The main street is packed, and the unmistakeable thud of drums and tambourines accompanies the procession as it moves slowly up through the crowded village. Non-Muslims will not, however, see the transe-dance ceremonies that take place in the main courtyard of the mosque. **The Kharja**

Sidi Bou Saïd

Tunis and around

Dar Nejma Ezzahra The Baron d'Erlanger's palace was constructed between 1912 and 1922 by Tunisian builders and decorated by Moroccan craftsmen. D'Erlanger had a marked artistic bent, being both a gifted amateur painter and a musician. He was instrumental in bringing together Arab musicians, and it was at his instigation that the First Congress of Arab Music was held in Cairo, under the patronage of the King of Egypt, in 1932. Rodolphe d'Erlanger also sponsored a five volume history of Arab music in French, the first in any European language. It is thus highly appropriate that the palace on which he lavished so much attention, and which was such a magnet for artists and musicians, is now a historic monument, functioning as the *Centre for Arab and Mediterranean Music*. Here is housed the most complete collection of Tunisian musical instruments. ■ *Summer 0900-1200 and 1600-1900, winter 0900-1200 and 1400-1700. Entrance 3Dt*

Sleeping
Phone code: 01

Surprisingly, Sidi Bou Saïd does not have a lot of accommodation. At the time of writing, the holiday village by the beach at the foot of the hill was undergoing major works. As you arrive at the village, there is a *simsar* (informal real estate agent) who hangs out in a small kiosk on your left before you reach the spring. For a longer stay, he may be able to find you something.

B *Hotel Amilcar*, at the foot of Sidi Bou Saïd cliff, T470788. All 250 rooms have a view over the Gulf looking towards the Cap Bon peninsula, private beach, pool. Situated next to a rather jolly beach which gets very crowded in summer, given its handiness for public transport. **B** *Hotel Dar* Saïd, undergoing extensive refurbishment. T740215, F336908. 100-year-old building built round an attractive central courtyard, beautiful tiles, 12 (?) rooms with high ceilings and bath en suite. Jackie Kennedy stayed here. At the time of going to press, restoration works were well underway. The revamped Dar Saïd will surely be a top address. **C** *Sidi Bou Saïd*, on a hill slightly out of the village, T740411. 34 rooms, good standard, pool, view looking out westwards towards Tunis. **E** *Hotel Bou Fares*, central, T740091. 8 rooms centred around a shaded patio in a typical house, very clean and cheap, cold in winter, excellent breakfast, no restaurant, it is vital to book in the summer season. The manager and his mates can be found doing impromptu jam sessions on their lute and guitar in the courtyard. A popular address.

Self-catering Dar Lasram in the upper village, owned by the Turki family, has upmarket accommodation for short lets in the grounds of their palatial dwelling, close to the main car park.

Eating

Expensive *Restaurant le Pirate*, T748266. By the harbour at the bottom of the cliff, specializes in fish and sea-food, expensive but worth it as the food is excellent. *Le Bon Vieux Temps*, T744788, 744733, F728100. Try to reserve. Leaving the central Café des Nattes on your left, head straight ahead, the restaurant is on your left after 200m. An off-shoot of the restaurant of the same name in La Marsa, has had very good reports – although some say portions too small, good view from terrace across Gulf of Tunis. Le Bon Vieux Temps. **Mid-range** *Restaurant La Bagatelle*, at the bottom of the hill before the village, good setting, good, food, very popular. **Cheap** *Restaurant Chergui*, T740987, on the main street, on the right of *Café des Nattes*. Large terrace with a fantastic view, food is good value, if not very exciting. The sort of place to have a brik à l'oeuf and barbecued lamb. *Café Tam Tam*, on your left as you come up from the station. Good (but small) terrace above the street, so you can watch all the trendies coming up to parade round Sidi Bou. Excellent pizzas, but no booze, attentive, pleasant service, bright and cheerful décor. Recommended for an outing with the kids. At the bottom of the village, there are any number of sandwich places which stay open late, plus the *Gelateria di Ricardo*.

Dance classes Want to learn oriental dancing? Try the *Espace forme et beauté* at **Entertainment**
17 Av de la République, Carthage-Amilcar, T741326. Classes by Mme Houda
Maknassi Rouissi.

Galleries Sidi Bou Saïd has a reputation as a painter's paradise, a sort of Tunisian
Montmartre, and a number of contemporary painters have (or have had) their ateliers
here, including Jellal Ben Abdallah the miniaturist, Brahim Dhahhak, and Rachid
Koreïchi, master of the calligraphed sign. In particular, try the *Galerie Chérif Fine Art*,
20 rue de la République and *Galerie Ammar Farhat*, 3 rue Sidi el Ghemrini. The *Musée
de Sidi Bou Saïd*, on your right as you go up the hill, is not in fact a museum, but rather
hosts exhibitions of varying quality.

Hammam Recommended is Hammam Sidi Bou Saïd in the street opposite the
Magasin Général in the lower part of the town. Modern and tiled, it lacks the character
of the older hammams in the médina. Still, if you haven't time to get into town!

Sailing The ancient fishing port has been developed as a marina, with a sailing club **Sports**
and a windsurfing school. There are 360 berths (minimum-maximum draft 2-4
metres) and all the necessary services are now in place including a 26 tonne travel lift.

Banks For changing money, you have the UIB and the Banque du Sud in the new part of town at **Directory**
the bottom of the hill. **Hospitals & medical services** Chemist: all night pharmacy next to the
UIB bank.

La Marsa and Gammarth

At the end of the TGM line is the once royal resort of La Marsa (lit. 'the port'). *Phone code: 01*
The town grew up around a beylical palace, and among the new constructions *Colour map 1, grid A5*
a scattering of early 20th century villas still survives. After independence, the
palace was almost completely demolished by vengeful minister Taïeb Mehiri.
The town retains traces of the enervating atmosphere of an old-fashioned
summer resort. There is a long beach (crowded in summer) and a promenade
with palm trees. There is little to do apart from sit on the beach or contemplate
the world from a café. Merging with La Marsa is upscale Gammarth with its villas and chic restaurants. And beyond the hill is Raoued, a long windy beach
backed by a salt marsh, today lined with tourist hotels.

La Marsa is a quiet sort of place during the day. In the early evening and at **Sights**
weekends, the area around the TGM station comes alive with families out to
enjoy the air and an ice-cream. Enjoy the atmosphere, smoke a chicha at the
Café Safsaf, or maybe take in an exhibition at the Galerie Mille Feuilles.
    If you need some sights, then the remains of the beylical palace can be found
down a side-street near the Café Safsaf. At the end of the street, you come to a
junction where the elegant Municipalité de La Marsa sits opposite the French
ambassador's residence. Cross the road, and a right turn after some 50 metres
will take you into Marsa-Cubes, a small area of villa housing next to the beach.
This is a nice place to swim.

Turning left at the Municipality, you have a long tree-lined avenue which will **The Palais**
take you to La Marsa-Ville and the main bus-station. Cross over to **Abdillia**
Tunisie-Télécom and go right. Beyond a dusty open space popular with
pétanque players in the early evening, you will see the restored 16th century
Hafsid Palais Abdillia. Rumour has it that a future Museum of Modern Art is to
be housed in the premises. The palace, an unusual survival, is well worth a visit

should there be a temporary exhibition on show. The story behind the palace runs that Hafsid ruler Abu Abdullah Mohammed had a sickly daughter for whom fresh sea air was recommended. Not to be found wanting, Abu Abdullah had three palaces constructed at La Marsa, of which only this, the third, remains. It follows the classic design with the main rooms arranged around an open central courtyard complete with fountain. The dominant feature, a high tower, offers superb views. (The palace entrance is in a side-street round the back.)

After a look at the Abdillia, you may want to go back to La Marsa Plage. Retrace your steps, cross opposite the bus-station to the line of shops. Down a side-street to the right of the newsagents, you have a couple of very popular sandwich shops, one Ould el Bey, run by a descendant of the former ruling family, no less. In need of a beer? The options are limited, as the Café-Restaurant el Hafsi, a La Marsa institution, is shortly to be redeveloped. However, up rue du Maroc on the Corniche you have the splendidly kitsch Hotel Plaza, for pizza and a quiet beer.

Sleeping There are 2 main hotel areas. Lower Gammarth has a selection of older establishments. By the beach at Raoued, the hotels are almost all recent, 3-star and above establishments, good value if you've bought your package in Europe. The Raoued stretch of coast is very crowded in July and August, and beach hygiene tends to suffer.

AL *Abou Nawas*, Blvd Taieb Méhiri, Lower Gammarth, T741444, F740400. 45 apartments, 127 rooms with a/c, pool in summer, good beach, 6 restaurants/bars, excellent food. A toney establishment. **A** *The Résidence*, Raoued. Pretentious name for the giant hotel of the Raoued strip. Despite its Leading Hotels of the World label, opinions are divided on this recent (1997) establishment. A serious competitor for the Abou Nawas chain for the business end of the market. Tastefully furnished rooms and equipped with a thalassotherapy centre with traditional hammam. If you have meetings in Tunis, bear in mind that you will have to brave the morning traffic on the La Marsa to Tunis highway. Basically, an OK place if the company's paying. **B** *Mégara*, on Blvd Taieb Méhiri, T740366, F740916. A 1970s hotel with more recent Moorish decor, 77 rooms, large pool, mature gardens. **C** *Acqua Viva*, 110 rooms, T748567, F342411. **C** *Cap Carthage*, 350 rooms, T740064, F741980. **C** *Kahena*, 70 rooms, T748200, F747911. **C** *Karim*, 220 rooms, T740700, F741200. **C** *La Tour Blanche* on the Av Mehiri, Gammarth, T271697. Situated overlooking the beach. Nice pool. **C** *Molka*, 206 rooms, T740242, F741646. **C** *Nova Park*, 70 rooms, T748764, F748611.

Koubet el Haoua
La Marsa

La Marsa and Gammarth have a large number of eateries in the top price bracket, as **Eating** you might expect in a neighbourhood with some of the country's leading fortunes and diplomats' homes. Note however that service is very up and down. Regulars tend to get preferential treatment, for others the service can be indifferent.

Expensive *Au Bon Vieux Temps*, on the roundabout at La Marsa Plage, T774322. Some very good French cooking indeed. Portions on the small side. *Le Golfe*, overlooking the beach at 5 Rue Larbi Zarrouk, near the Hotel Abou Nawas, Gammarth, T748219. Generally held to be the best restaurant in this neck of the woods. Service steady. Try their filet de Saint Pierre or the paella. *Les Dunes*, Lower Gammarth, T743379. Seafood a speciality, good food, smarmy service and pretty tacky décor. *La Falaise*, on your left as you begin the steep climb up to Sidi Bou Saïd coming from La Marsa, T747806/742575. Try their couscous au poisson, expensive but reliable. *Le Grand Bleu*. Up on the clifftop with views looking out over the sea, T746900. Excellent service if you are with an official delegation, variable for occasional visitors. The next door piano-bar is popular. *Les Ombrelles*, T742964/727364. Superb location right on the seafront in Lower Gammarth. Expensive drinks. *Le Sindbad*, T749876, seafront, Lower Gammarth. Pricey and popular with a young set, expensive wine list will bump the cost of a meal up considerably.

Mid-range Easily the best place in this price bracket is *Pizza-Sprint Arthé* at 5 rue Ibn Abi Rabiaâ. Good starters (try the *involtini de crevettes*), pizzas, a good range of pasta and pleasant desserts including mousse au chocolat and fondant au chocolat, served in the pleasant garden of a villa. Children can be let off the leash safe from the traffic. Occasional exhibitions of local crafts in the villa. Easy to find: turn left out of the TGM and right at the end of the road. Downside: no alcohol, but they are working on this. Also try the *Hotel Plaza-La Corniche*, rue du Maroc, T743577. This must be one of the most overdecorated places in Tunisia, despite heavy competition from places in Sousse and Tozeur. On balmy summer nights, disco balls glitter between the palm trees. Have a drink on the poolside terrace. The kids will love the tack of it all. *La Closerie*, near the main regional hospital (CHU Mongi Slim) in La Soukra. T765537, F765790. A trendy place serving mainly Italian food, open everyday except Monday, in summer open everyday, evenings only. Pleasant lawn area round small pool, occasional exhibitions, uncomfortable wrought iron chairs is the main minus point, the bar is lively in summer with a young and *branché* crowd. At the top end of the mid-range category. *Le Pied dans le Plat*, no phone. Small, pleasant restaurant next to Polyclinique La Marsa on the road to Sidi Bou Saïd, run by owners Mado and Dalila, French and Tunisian food, lively on winter weekend evenings, popular, no alcohol as yet.

Cheap Have a drink at the *Café afsaf*, and try some of their pastries or Tunisian cooking. There are numerous casse-crouteries (stand-up sandwich bars) at La Marsa. Try Chez Joseph at La Marsa-Plage, or Ould el Bey at La Marsa-Ville.

Perhaps the best place for dancing in the Banlieue Nord is *Le Boeuf sur le Toit* (lit: 'the **Nightclubs** cow on the roof'), a restaurant with a dancefloor in La Soukra. Franco-Tunisian management and a relaxed atmosphere. The food is ordinary, but there is a good mix of nationalities. The minstrel-type floorshow, performed by black Tunisians, may be offensive to some. To get there, take a taxi to La Soukra, the restaurant is near the Boukhobza distillery and the entrance to the golf course.

The clubs can be depressingly stuck up, but some of the following might be worth a try. *La Plaza*, 22 rue du Maroc, La Marsa, T743577, F742554, has a clientèle eager to display its money; a drink by the pool can be pleasant in the early evening. The nicest of the banlieue nord clubs, *La Barraka*, housed in a converted barn down a track on the La Marsa/Sidi Bou Saïd road, a long established Tunis institution, was demolished in 1999, much to the distress of numerous Tunis clubbers of all ages; the ageing sound system did its best to keep up the required level of decibels, the club was always packed in summer. In Gammarth, *La Tour Blanche* has a club which changes its name every few years – the current appellation is **Cyklone**. The fashionable place for a pre-club drink is at the snooty **Sindbad** piano bar – right on the beach at Gammarth, just along from the *Cyklone* and next to the restaurant *Les Ombrelles*. Of the hotels on the Raoued strip, the best clubs are **Le Queen** at the *Hotel Karim* and Tunis' largest club, **Maxximum**. Really keen clubbers, however, will head for **Hammamet** (*Manhattan* Le Guitoun or the *Ranch Club*) or **La Maracana** in Sousse, just 2 hours down the motorway in the Taj Marhaba complex.

Galleries Look out for exhibitions at *Driba*, 4 rue Omar Ibn Abi Rabia, La Marsa Plage. Attractive contemporary craft work. *Espace d'Art Mille Feuilles*, La Marsa Plage, above the bookshop. Exhibitions of local and foreign artists' work in the spacious gallery.

Hairdressers Try Dalila Mathari, a Tunis legend, at the salon de coiffure of the Hotel Abou Nawas, Gammarth. Held to be a true artist, by some. (Does hair for fashion shows.)

Transport **Car rental** *Hotel Cap Carthage*, T741596, and at *Hotel Molka*, T740118. *Tunisair*, La Marsa-Ville T775222, 740680, F746455.

Directory **Hospitals & medical services** **Chemist:** all night pharmacy next to the UIB bank. **Places of worship** **Catholic:** Station TGM, Sidi Dhrif, T740854. Services Sat at 1930 and Sun at 1000. Also 1 rue Scipion, T734228. Service in French Sat 1700, English Sun 0930.

Tunis, Banlieue Sud (Southern Suburbs)

South of Tunis are the newly sprawling suburbs of Ben Arous, Radès, Ez Zahra, Hammam Lif and Borj Cedria. The energetic will want to climb twin-peaked Bou Kornine. (Birdwatchers may find some rare raptors, although the Bou Kornine has attracted a lot of visitors of late.) There are some pleasant beaches, particularly at Borj Cedria. Colonial architecture buffs will seek out interesting buildings at Hammam Lif, while strollers will enjoy the evening paseo along the pedestrian corniche here.

Hammam Lif A coastal resort, once mainly for the bourgeois of Tunis, situated at the foot of Djebel Bou Kornine whose rocky outcrops slope steeply to the edge of the road. There are a couple of *hammams* here, not terribly well managed but functioning with naturally hot springwater (2.80Dt per session). Real spa enthusiasts will want to head for the better establishments at Korbous, Hammam Zriba and Hammam Jdidi.

Borj Cedria, the last place on the southern suburbs rail line, has a quarry producing reddish marble of moderate quality stone. More importantly for the sun seeker it also has a good beach used by people from Tunis at weekends and in summer. Many of them come out by train. Borj Cedria, with its beach backed by pine and eucalyptus forest, once felt quite remote. The amount of new housing in the area has changed this, and further developments are planned for the future.

Sleeping The Banlieue Sud has two main sorts of hotel. You have the tourist hotels and holiday clubs (*Dar, Médi-Sea, Selwa*) at Borj Cedria, and a large tourist hotel at Ez Zahra. Less ambitiously, there are a few cheap places at Hammam Lif.

B *Médi-Sea*, Route touristique, 2055 Borj Cedria, T430261, F430013. (Expensive, 63Dt single in high season.) **C** *Dar*, 2055 Borj Cedria T290188. 144 beach bungalows. **C** *Salwa*, T290764, 116 rooms, pool. **D** *Hotel du Bon Repos*, rue Bel Hassen Chedli, Hammam Lif, T291458. Short walking distance from the main road on slope of Djebel Bou Kornine, fairly basic hotel, 20Dt for rooms per person, breakfast 2Dt, 18 rooms some with separate bath and toilet, some have shared facilities, some rooms have fine view over bay to Sidi Bou Saïd, no restaurant. **F** *Hotel Majed*, 1 rue Salammbô (the main road through Hammam Lif). 6.5Dt per person, bed only, 10 rooms shared facilities, very basic. *Youth hostel Banlieue Sud*, T483631, 10 km from Tunis, 10 minutes from Radès station. 56 beds, meals available, book as it takes groups and can get full.

Note that the southern suburbs are served by regular (every half-hour) trains from the main Tunis train station on place Barcelone. Radès has a particularly useful feature, the passenger and car ferry to La Goulette, which enables you to avoid driving through Tunis. It operates all day, carries 10 cars, takes 5 minutes and costs nothing. **Transport**

Tour companies & travel agents *Gulf Travel Agency*, 70 Av de la République, Hammam Lif, T292100, F291954. *Romulus Voyages*, Km 12 Ezzahra, T450544, F450582. *Mondial Tours*, Place 9 Avril, Hammam Lif, T293727. **Directory**

Southwest of Tunis: Roman towns and hilltop villages

Southwest of Tunis is an area of fertile rolling countryside, a wealthy region back in Roman times as the large number of Roman settlements demonstrates. An **aquaeduct**, the longest in the Roman world, once transported the spring water from forbidding Mount Zaghouan to Carthage. In a hire car, the energetic visitor can easily take in the Roman sites of **Oudna**, **Thuburbo Maius** and **Zaghouan** in a day, with possibly a stop at **Djebel Oust** (remains of Roman baths) for lunch. Also worth a visit are the once isolated hill villages of the region south of Zaghouan: **Takrouna**, now well on the tourist itineraries, abandoned **Zriba** and **Jeradou**. The Roman remains, although not as spectacular as sites in the interior like Dougga, Sbeïtla and El Jem, are worth a look, and a pleasant day out can be put together by combining them with a trip up **Mount Zaghouan** or to one of the hilltop villages. Such excursions can be done equally well from both Hammamet and Tunis.

Touring the region southwest of Tunis

For a 'south-west of Tunis circuit', exit Tunis along the motorway through Ouardia and Kabaria, suburbs of cheap housing, mixed small scale industry and uncontrolled development. Turn right for Fouchana and Kairouan along the GP3. This will take you past car breaking yards and urban sprawl to Fouchana and Mohamedia, site of the crumbling remains of Ahmed Bey's vast palace complex, once touted as the 'Tunisian Versailles'.

Beyond Mohamedia, farming takes and the wide corn lands open up with views of distant hills. And there is Hadrian's aqueduct which once took water to Carthage. It appears first on the west and then on the east, the road cutting through a breach south of Mohammedia. Where parts of the supporting structure have crumbled away the actual aqueduct has fallen and here it is possible **Hadrian's aqueduct** to view a cross section of the amazing structure. The channel carrying the water was oval, large enough for a man to walk along, lined with cement to prevent leakage and covered to prevent evaporation. The structure was brought back into use in the 19th century, when French engineer Colin restored it to bring water to the growing town of Tunis.

The accuracy of the Roman engineering is awesome considering the equipment available. To maintain the level the aqueduct required varying heights for the supporting pillars. As you follow the aqueduct note that the pillars get wider where the structure gets higher and needs more support to soar above the land. As the contours rise again the structure is less spectacular and runs at about one metre above the ground here, as it did when it cut through the centre of Mohammedia to the north.

South from Oudna At 23 kilometres from Tunis is the left turn to Oudna, Roman Uthina. Here you may branch off for the Roman site on the C133. After visiting Oudna, one possibility is to continue along the GP3/C133 heading south to Zaghouan, which you approach via an attractive avenue of huge eucalyptus trees. Another option is to take the more direct C36 for Zaghouan. (One possible lunchstop is the small restaurant next to the Nymphaeum archaeological site, in the shadow of Mount Zaghouan.)

The other option at the Oudna turn off is to continue along the GP3 in the direction of El Fahs. The other major Roman site in this region, Thuburbo Maius, is some 20 kilometres farther on, just three kilometres before the sleepy agricultural town of El Fahs. From El Fahs, you have a direct run back eastwards into Zaghouan. Also in the region is a semi-forgotten spa-town, Djebel Oust. Specialists looking for excavated provincial Roman bath houses will want to make the detour. Following the P3 south of Oudna, turn left onto the C133. The spa complex is clearly visible on your right after a couple of kilometres.

Southwest of Tunis

The hilltop villages lie south of Zaghouan. For **Zriba**, some 10 kilometres south of Zaghouan, you will turn off the main road at the new village of Zriba, heading for Hammam Zriba. If you have a solid sort of hire car, then you turn off for Upper Zriba (Zriba el 'Ulya') before the cement works. Park the car on the side of the track in the shade of an olive tree when the going gets too rough. There is no-one to pull you out. You will need 30 minutes walk to reach the village which lies hidden in a small col up in the hills.

Takrouna is altogether more obvious, 25 kilometres south of Zaghouan on the Enfida road (and is dealt with in the next chapter as an excursion from Hammamet). For **Jeradou**, perhaps the least spectacular of the three villages, you need to turn off south as you head from Zaghouan to Hammamet.

Uthina

Nestling on the north facing foothills of the Djebel Mekrima, Uthina is famous for the quantity and quality of its mosaics, most of which are now on display in the Bardo Museum along with sculpture and inscriptions from the site. Only certain areas have been excavated and it was from the upper class residential area to the north that many mosaics came. Among the remains discovered are a large public baths, some huge cisterns and a theatre. It is clear that much still remains to be discovered on this site.

The capitol

Perhaps the most spectacular feature is the large vaulted chamber, topped by a French farmer's home, which occupies the site of the former main temple. You will see a large square – the farmyard, which was once the forum. The 'ramp' below the front door to the farmer's house was once the temple steps, and at the bottom, there are some huge stone drums, 140 centimetres across, which means that the main temple here would have had columns around 14.5 metres high! There are piles of marble fragments, an indication of the wealth of the temple. Below, in the large vaulted chamber, there are six stone piers which would have supported the columns' weight. The foundations of the much smaller, flanking temples have been partly excavated. At the back, you can see the semi-circular back wall of the cella, the temple sanctuary, partly masked by later Byzantine masonry.

The baths

As you leave the forum, you can see Uthina's vast cisterns on your right, just behind some farm buildings. Head for the baths, large mounds of rubble clearly visible about 200 metres east. Kids will love this bit. Underground vaulted rooms – for storing fuel? – have been excavated (use your pocket torch). Looking back towards the capitol/farmer's house, you can see the remains of the aqueduct close to the cisterns.

The amphitheatre

The other main area of recent archaeology is the amphitheatre, just next to the car park. It is partly carved out of the hillside, rather than being a free-standing structure as at El Jem. A number of blocks have been replaced. The large blocks all have small 'grip-holes' in them, to enable the Roman cranes to lift and swing them into place. You will also see that the blocks often have rough sides, to enable plaster rendering or mortar to adhere to the surface. There is a lot of work to do, however, if ever the amphitheatre is to be home to entertainments again, like the theatre at Carthage.

Marine mosaics from Uthina

One of the largest houses uncovered at Uthina, known today as the House of the Laberii, was a splendid dwelling with numerous rooms and even more numerous outbuildings. All the rooms and the atrium were paved with rich mosaics. You will have to go to the Bardo (see page 90) to see the fine mosaic of Venus seated on a rock while three cupids play with her veil, or the huge 'oceanic' picture with Neptune, Amphrite, sea-horse drawn chariots around three boats carrying three ladies and a cluster of cupids.

Detour to the spa at Djebel Oust Djebel Oust, 30 kilometres southwest from Tunis, is one of Tunisia's three main health spas (the others being Hammam Bourguiba in the Northwest and Korbous, now privately managed, on the northwest side of the Cap Bon). After a long period of uncertainty about the thermal treatment centre's future, the Ministry of Health has taken the complex over. Considerable investment will be necessary. The spa has the atmosphere of a backwater East European bathing establishment in the 1960s. The concrete carcass of an unfinished swimming pool stands below the hotel, close to the excavated remains of a Roman bathing establishment.

Sleeping C *Les Thermes*, 98 beds, T604477, F640074. Room with breakfast 34Dt. Bungalows available, too. Cheap lunchtime menu. D *Cheylus*, 90 beds, T677240, F677074.

Zaghouan زغوان

Phone code: 02
Colour map 1, grid B4

Zaghouan, Roman Ziqua, was the starting point of the complex system of second century AD cisterns and aqueducts which carried fresh water over 132 km to Carthage. Today's Zaghouan is dominated by the towering 1,300 metre high Djebel Zaghouan. The spring and the beginning of the aqueduct can be visited, about two kilometres out of town. The real interest, however, is the beauty of the site.

Ins & outs Lying 60 kilometres south of Tunis, Zaghouan, has a regular bus service from Tunis and louages from Tunis and Hammamet. It is an interesting journey travelling inland and gaining in altitude.

Sights Zaghouan is built on the lower slopes of Djebel Zaghouan. Close to the centre of the village, opposite the municipal food market, is a second century honorific arch, dating from the time when Zaghouan was Roman Ziqua. Climb up the steps to the arch, noting the bull's head on the keystone. Continue along a street lined with cheap eateries and shops, turn sharp right up-hill, and you come to a small square with a café and the police station. Close to the square is a former church, now used as a private school, and the more recent Jamaâ Errahma, with its octagonal minaret. There is a wall fountain with a decorative tile surround. Take the narrow street uphill, and you will come to the Zaouia of Sidi Ali Azouz, on your right, now a centre for Koran studies. (Take a peek through the door.) After the zaouia, on your right, is a small shop selling honey and the *nisri* rose water (at 18Dt a litre!) for which the town is famous.

The narrow street widens, and you can continue upwards to the Temple des Nymphes some two kilometres distant. The dignity of the ancient site has been impaired by the addition of a new arch and some 'environmental awareness' statuary, including a fat blue water drop and the usual fennec fox (or is it a bat-eared rat?) in a tight blue jumpsuit. There is a small café-restaurant (slow service, basic food) here, with views towards the temple and across the plain. The temple, which dates from the reign of Hadrian (early second century) is built into the hillside with steps leading up to a semi-circular wall. The 12 alcoves in the wall once held life size statues (of nymphs?), but unfortunately all have now gone. The pool in the centre has been restored and again (occasionally) holds water. Contemplate the panoramic view, north and east over the plain towards the sea. The Romans must have done just the same. Rising steeply behind you is Djebel Zaghouan. The temple steps down have been renewed making access much safer. **NB** Small children should not be allowed to roam unattended, as there are some sharp drops into the empty stone basins.

There is no entry charge to the Nymphaeum. New concrete villas have appeared on the wooded hillside between the town and the temple. It is now possible to drive practically the whole way to the top of Djebel Zaghouan.

Andalusian immigrants introduced rose cultivation here in 1795 and from this has developed the rose essence production for which this region is justly famous. The rose essence is very popular in cakes and pastries. A project to increase the area of the already considerable rose gardens has just been finished, and a wild rose nursery is to be developed. The wild rose festival is held here each May.

Rose water production

C *Les Nymphes*, T675094. Zaghouan 1100, PO Box 11, 1.5 km out of town towards Roman aqueduct, 80 beds, situated in quiet wooded surroundings along a track off the road up to the Temple. Youth hostel: *Maison des Jeunes*, Zaghouan, 85 beds, meals available, T675265.

Sleeping

Communications Area code: 02. **Hospitals & medical services** A new regional hospital opened here Apr 1996. **Tour companies & travel agents** *Gulf Travel Agency*, 70 Av de la République, Hammam Lif, T292100, F291954. *Romulus Voyages*, Km 12 Ezzahra, T450544, F450582. *Mondial Tours*, Place 9 Avril, Hammam Lif, T293727.

Directory

The C28 road east from Zaghouan leads to Hammamet. It leads down through the prairie-like cereal fields to the *oued* and the almond and olive groves. The road skirts a small lake with a spectacular rocky ridge as a backdrop and crosses the plain. It comes to the villages of **Hammam Jedidi** and **Sidi Jedidi**, the latter to be avoided at all costs on a Tuesday when coaches deposit their passengers to view an 'authentic market'. Despite the neighbouring quarry, Hamman Jedidi is interesting on account of the hot springs, and Tunis residents rent little houses here to enjoy the waters *en famille*. The intensive cultivation continues to the motorway and the outskirts of Hammamet.

West of Zaghouan to Hammamet

The C133 road south from Zaghouan which leads to **Enfidia** descends steeply to the plain. After five kilometres take the right fork for an interesting ride. It ascends to the old village of **Zriba** (another seven kilometres) where you can sit among the ruins and watch the birds of prey circle overhead. This old Berber village sits in a col below a rocky outcrop. There are views northwards across to **Djebel Zaghouan** (1,295 metres). The village has a fortified granary or *kalaâ*, a small mosque with a much decayed oblong crenelated tower and a *zaouia*, to Sidi Abdelkader el Jilani complete with cupola. Under the French protectorate, the village was an important rural centre, and the main streets paved with blocks of stone. Just below the village proper, the large building on your left, today used as a stables, is a school from the reconstruction period, 1943-48. Designed by architect Kyriacopoulos, model schools, built according to local techniques with stone and brick vaulting, were constructed across Tunisia.

Today, the old village is largely deserted. Modern Zriba is a post-independence settlement, on the C133, 10 km from Zaghouan, established as part of a policy to end local particularities and bring isolated communities into contact with the modernizing Tunisian Republic. No doubt there were financial considerations, it being cheaper to build a new settlement on the plain rather than to take modern services and infrastructure up to the old village.

South of Zaghouan: the hill-crest villages

The Berber village of **Djeradou** can also be reached from this road, though easier access, avoiding a very rough road, is from the C35. The villagers work with esparto, plaiting long bands of this tough grass which is then turned into a variety of bags and baskets, olive mats and panniers. The same technique is much in evidence at the coastal village of **Hergla**. From the ruined fort can be seen the square white mosque and the domed *zaouia*.

Thuburbo Majus

Ins & outs
Colour map 1, grid B4

This is 60 kilometres south along the P3 from Tunis. Access by bus or louage from Tunis. Get off at El Fahs and walk (three kilometres) or get a taxi. If coming from Tunis, ask the driver to stop at Thuburbo Majus (before you get to El Fahs) from which it is a short walk to the site. It is better not to follow the signposts, but to cut across between the two hills, just behind the signpost. There is a car park at the entrance, a small café and a clean toilet. Open 0800-1200 and 1500-1900 in summer and 0930-1630 in winter, closed Monday, entrance 2Dt, photography 1Dt.

History

Thuburbo Majus was originally a Punic city, but when the Romans conquered Carthage they agreed to pay dues to Rome and so survived. In 27 BC the Emperor Augustus founded a colony of veterans in order to control the strategic situation of the city. Thuburbo Majus was placed in a strategic position, encircled by hills except to the west, permitting a close watch on movement of people and trade between the plain and the coast along the route of the Oued el Kebir. The hinterland, a fertile land producing cereals in abundance, provided a further boost to the economy, added to that of toll/tax collection. The Punic heritage mixed well with the Roman presence and it was at this time that most of the major monuments were repaired or reconstructed, such as the Capitol and the Baths. The town declined as the Romans' authority slackened. With the Vandals in power the town reverted to a village.

Exploring the site

Thuburbo Majus is a large site on the hill slopes, overlooking a fertile agricultural plain and the Oued Kebir which provided the water. It was at an important crossing of trade routes which permitted collection of tolls. The production of cereals, olives and wine were important factors in the city's prosperity.

This large city covered over 40 hectares. The **Forum** and the **Capitol** dominate the ruins. The forum is well preserved. It was built between 161-192 AD and restored with some changes in layout around 376 AD. It stands 49 metres square, surrounded by a portico on three sides. The fourth side leads, by means of a broad flight of stairs, to the Capitol built in 168 AD. This is the best place to visit first as it enables one to view the whole site. Great efforts were made to raise the level of this building to give it the height it needed for its imposing position overlooking the town. Six fluted Corinthian columns, each eight and a half metres high, continue to dominate the site. Dedications were made to Emperor Marcus Aurelius and to Commodius. The temple is also dedicated to the triad of Jupiter, Juno and Minerva. The head and foot, all that remains of the statue of Jupiter, once an impossible eight metres high, are in the Bardo Museum.

To the northeast of the Forum are the remains of the **Curia** (town hall/meeting place of the council). The **Temple of Peace** adjacent to/part of Curia has a marble-paved courtyard with a peristyle leading on to a large hall paved with marble. It is thought a statue to Peace stood here.

The **Temple of Mercury** built in 211 AD has an unusual circular courtyard though the outer walls are straight. The eight column bases remain. He was the god of Merchants and overlooked the market area.

The **Agora**, the paved market place, stood opposite the Capitol and beyond the south corner of the Forum. There are two smaller annexes. This was used for retail of produce but also as a gathering place. The arcades on three sides were divided into 21 small shop spaces.

The **Winter Baths** covering 1,600 square metres were completely rebuilt between 395 and 408 AD. They were very luxurious. There were more than 20 rooms here decorated with elegant mosaics, square pools, round pools,

Thuburbo Majus

Entrance

Capitol

Oil Press

Curia

Temple of Peace

Forum

Temple of Mercury

To Temple of Ceres

Agora

House of the Labyrinth

House of the Victorious Charioteer

Winter Baths

Palaestra of the Petronii

Temple of Aesculapius

To Temple of Saturn

Summer Baths

Byzantine Church

To Amphitheatre

Temple of Caelestis

Temple of Baalit

N

0 metres 25
0 yards 27

fountains, latrines and urinals. The entrance from the small square was a four-column portico.

The **Summer Baths** were larger, covering 2,400 square metres. These were restored in 361 AD. Here there were cold, warm and hot rooms, all with lavish decoration – much marble, many mosaics and fountains. These were fed from three large cisterns.

The **Palaestra of the Petronii** was built in 225 AD and named after the family who endowed the construction – Petronius Felix. This, a rectangular area surrounded by a portico (supported by grey/black marble columns which still stand), was for games and gymnastic activities (wrestling, boxing) before bathing. The mosaic from here, depicting these activities, is in the Bardo Museum. In the south corner there are alphabetic signs carved into the pavement, explained as a Roman game rather like Lexicon.

The large, very overgrown, area to the southeast of Palaestra was a shrine to the god of healing, the **Temple of Aesculapius**.

Further east is the **Temple of Caelestis** (Tanit) who required the periodic sacrifice of young children (see Carthage).

On the other side of the track is the Temple of Baalit. She was a Punic goddess who slipped into the Roman mythology. The building has three straight sides while the short northeast side is semicircular and has a door opening on to a small square, smaller than but similar to the square before the Winter baths.

The **Temple of Saturn** (not much left here), to the west of the site and at the highest point in town, later became a church. Again there is evidence of 'building up the land' before constructing the temple.

The ruins of the **Amphitheatre**, hollowed out of the hillside, can be found to the very edge of the site. Nearby is one of the cisterns for water supply. This cistern to the south of the site is huge – large enough to have an inner gallery constructed on the inside rim.

The **oil factories** behind and to the west of the Capitol are a reminder of the activities which helped to make this town so prosperous.

In the residential area around the Forum were homes of wealthy Roman inhabitants. They are named after the mosaics found there – for example Neptune, Theseus. Another residential has been excavated in the southwest area by the summer and winter baths. The **House of the Victorious Charioteer** by the Winter Baths had rich mosaics and painted stucco. The **House of the Labyrinth** is by the market. From here was retrieved the well known fourth century mosaic which covered the floor of the *frigidarium* in the baths of this private house. The mosaic, in the form of a maze (labyrinth) has at the centre Theseus cutting off the head of the Minator. The ground surrounding the two figures is littered with bits of humans, the remains of the monster's victims. The mosaic is bordered with walls and gates, depicting the city. This mosaic is in the Bardo Museum.

The **Temple of Cérès**, to the west of the site, on sloping ground, had a courtyard 30 metres by 30 metres, the centre decorated with mosaics and a portico with three gateways. Later this was turned into a church, using half of the courtyard. A number of tombs were found in the church, one containing jewels.

Sleeping There is no accommodation at or near the site. Thuburbo Majus makes a good day trip from Tunis, returning via Zaghouan. The nearest youth hostel is in Zaghouan, convenient for travellers going southwards to Enfida and Sousse.

El Fahs El Fahs, a busy agricultural centre, larger than Zaghouan, holds an important cattle market each Saturday. Expensive harvesting equipment is for sale. There are several engineering establishments here, more advanced than the casual car/van repair merchants on the outskirts of every town.

Cap Bon Peninsula

4

Cap Bon Peninsula

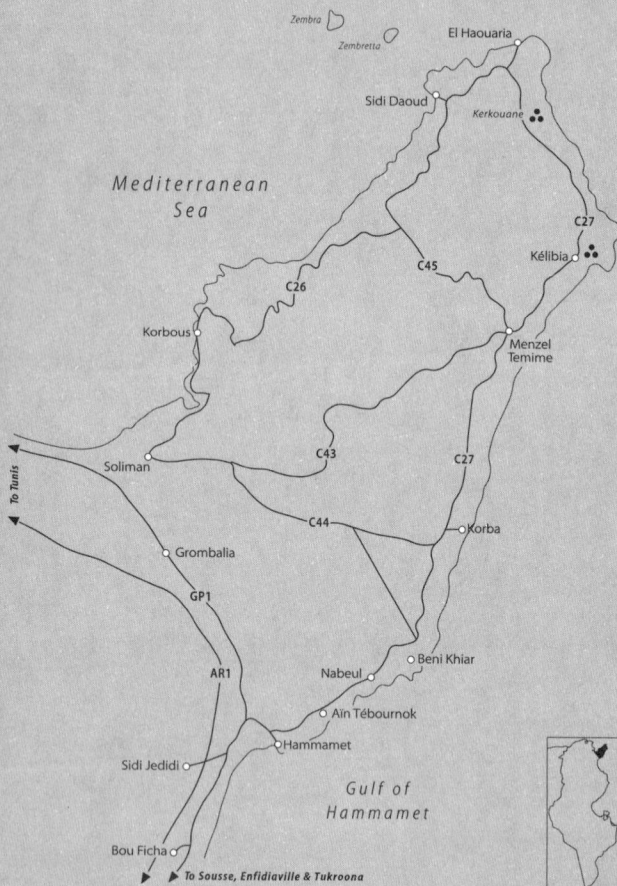

The Cap Bon, protruding like a thumb into the Mediterranean, is one of the most fertile regions in Tunisia. From Tunis, across the sea, the steep and rocky coast of the peninsula's northwest coast is clearly visible. On the sheltered southeast coast, there are fine sand beaches and small towns all the way down to the tourist resort of **Nabeul,** *and half-an-hour's drive from here is the burgeoning resort of* **Hammamet**. *Once a quiet fishing port, the village has become a sprawling town with a vast new beach resort, Hammamet-Sud, also known as Hammamet-Yasmine. There is much of interest in the region, however. Inland lies the hill-crest village of* **Takrouna,** *while at the tip of the Cap Bon lie the remains of a remote Punic settlement,* **Kerkouane,** *and quiet stretches of coast can still be found. Birdwatchers will find much to delight them on* **coastal lagoons** *and above all at* **Haouaria** *during the twice yearly migrations across the Mediterranean.*

Background

With an area of 2,837 square kilometres, much of it fertile agricultural land with abundant water, the Cap Bon has long been an important farming region. Roman writers noted the fertility of the area. Wrote Diodorus of Sicily, describing a fourth century invasion: "Agathocles led his army towards the big city (Carthage ?). All the lands he crossed were set with gardens and orchards watered by numerous springs and canals. Along the route were well-constructed country houses, built with lime, a sign of widespread wealth. The houses were filled with all the things which make life pleasant, stored up by the inhabitants thanks to a long peace. The land was planted with vines, olive trees and a whole host of fruit trees."

Today the south-western part of the Cap Bon is still an important fruit producing region, with the majority of Tunisia's citrus fruit coming from the region around Menzel Bouzelfa and important vineyards around Grombalia. Inland, cultivation turns to dry farming. Running down the centre of the peninsula is a line of hills which culminate in the west at Djebel Sidi Abderrahman (421 metres) and in the east at Djebel Ben Oulid (637 metres), virtually separating the north coast from the southeasterly region.

Along the south-eastern coast market gardening is important. Korba is famed for strawberry production, and Nabeul for its *harissa*, the spicey chilli paste which is such an essential part of Tunisian cooking.

The administrative centre of the region is Nabeul, also important as an industrial town, with pottery, stone-carving and manufacturing important. The other main economic factor in the region is the development of the all year holiday hotels to serve the package-holiday market. Fortunately, the main *zones touristiques* are located in the Hammamet area, accessible from the main motorway by fast link roads. Kélibia, Korba and other towns of the south-eastern Cap Bon have seen considerable expansion too, with new suburbs of Tunisian-owned holiday homes growing up. Today the Cap Bon has a population of over 500,000, concentrated along the southeast coast.

Northwest coast

The northwestern coast of the Cap Bon makes a pleasant excursion from Tunis or Hammamet. Coming from Tunis, the first town of interest is **Soliman**, founded by 17th century Andalusian immigrants. There are sandy beaches nearby. Then, on a rocky stretch of coast, you have the tiny spa of **Korbous**. After the cliffs, you have more beach – **Port aux Princes** is one possible bathing spot, frequented almost exclusively by locals. Then after kilometres of farmland, you are at the tip of the Cap Bon. There is the fishing port of **Sidi Daoud** and **Haouaria**, ancient Aquilaria, famed for its falconry festival and ancient underground quarries. For those looking for unusual if unspectacular ancient remains, **Kerkouane**, a unique Punic site a few kilometres round the Cape, is an essential stop. If you need to stay overnight, there are small hotels in Korbous, Haouaria and Kélibia. If travelling with your own car from Tunis, then driving on to Nabeul or Hammamet is perfectly feasible.

Visiting the towns and beaches of the northwest coast of the Cap Bon with a hire car **Getting there**
from Tunis or Hammamet-Nabeul is no problem at all, although it can make quite a
long day out with children. The country roads are being improved all the time, and
you have small restaurants in the little towns.

By public transport, things are considerably slower. By bus or louage, you can easily
travel up to Haouaria and do the Roman grottoes and Kerkouane in a day. You would
really be pushing it if you wanted to see Soliman and Korbous as well. Soliman plus
beach could make a nice day trip from Tunis, although unless you are Muslim, you
won't see the inside of the mosque. For getting to Kerkouane from Haouaria, there are
buses that can drop you at the top of the minor road leading down to the site.

Soliman سليمان

The market town of Soliman goes back to the 17th century, and like many   *Phone code: 02*
other small towns in Tunisia, takes great pride in its Andalusian heritage. The   *Colour map 1, grid A5*
town is named after its patron, a rich Turkish farmer who came to this area
around 1600 and began the construction of a new town. The subsequent influx
of immigrants from Andalucía left their mark in the form of building style, irrigation methods and even culinary preferences. The town was severly hit by the
plague in the 19th century, and only really recovered in the 20th century.

The town centre with its trees, arcades and cafés is a pleasant sort of place.
Soliman's most outstanding architectural feature is its **Malikite Mosque**,
whose solid square minaret dominates the town centre. Parts of the building
are roofed with Spanish-style rounded tiles recalling that the building was
founded in the early 17th century by Andalusian refugees. (The main mosque
in Testour has a similarly strong Andalusian identity.)

Otherwise, things Andalusian are rather elusive in Soliman today. Taking a
walk though the town, you will be struck by the amount of new buildings. In
many other modern Tunisian towns, this is often very jarring. Here at least the
style is quite harmonious. Old features, stone framed doorways and the like,
are fast disappearing. In a few years' time, the whole character of the town will
have been radically altered, with two- and three-storey building and façades
with large windows taking the place of the original vernacular houses. But such
is the price of progress …

Across the flat marsh land northwest of the town lies the beach area of Soliman   **Soliman Plage**
Plage, where locals and migrant workers have built themselves summer   **and Sidi Raïs**
homes. There is a good stretch of fine sand and two hotels. In summer, there
may be a noddy train doing the four kilometres journey between town and
beach. Note that the beach closest to the vague square which functions as taxi
and bus terminus gets very crowded in summer.

Moving northeast of Soliman, Sidi Raïs is three kilometres from the C26
across flat marshland. There are a few seaside holiday homes built on stilts over
the water's edge on a beach of fine sand. This is where the Tunisian families
from the surrounding areas come each weekend or for their longer holidays.
There is a small jetty where a few local fishing boats tie up and from which they
sell their daily catch of fresh fish.

Solymar, 400 beds, T290105, F290155. Right on beach of fine white sand, 200 rooms   **Sleeping**
with bath and toilet, restaurant, pool, nightly disco entertainment. **E** *El Andalous*, 288
beds, T290199, F290280. Right on beach.

Travel agents *Mek Tours*, 9 bis Av de la République, T290177, F291600. *Soly Holiday*, 8 rue Hedi   **Directory**
Chaker, T291649, F291753.

Cap Bon Peninsula

From Soliman to the southeast coast: cutting across the Cap Bon

The main road from Soliman through the flat marshlands to the west connects with the GP1 near Bordj Cedria. This will take you down to Hammamet. Otherwise, take the C43, direction Menzel Bou Zelfa. No need to go into Menzel Bou Zelfa if you are headed for Korba, the C44 road runs across the Cap Bon.

If you are going from Soliman to Kélibia, then you need to go through Menzel Bouzelfa. The town has a small tree-planted square, the attractive older building is disappearing. Then after Menzel Bouzelfa, the urban sprawl disappears, and the road (C34) will take you up to Menzel Temime across heath and open farmland and finally, 12 kilometres further on, you reach Kélibia.

From Soliman to Bir Meroua

From Soliman, the C26 runs northeastwards up to Haouaria, a distance of some 60 kilometres. The road rises through prosperous agricultural land towards Sidi Aïssa. The Djebel Korbous rises up on the left to cut out any views of the sea. At the small village of Bir Meroua, you can turn off left for the beach at Port aux Princes, some eight kilometres away, about half of which is down a country track. In summer, this gets busy with pick-up trucks packed with extended families heading for a day at the beach.

If you go via **Korbous** north of Sidi Rais, the coast becomes one of rugged, wild, unspoilt splendour. This detour is recommended even if you have no intention of stopping in Korbous. The route is highly scenic, but not for nervous drivers, as the road follows the cliff, with sharp drops down to the sea below. The view towards La Goulette and Sidi Bou Saïd is very impressive.

Korbous   قـربص

Phone code: 02
Colour map 1, grid A5

A small spa resort, said to have seven springs, Korbous would be a splendid setting for an Agatha Christie novel. Poirot should be twirling his moustache, gazing out over the glittering sea as the sun goes down. ('The Crime of the Moorish Baths' would be the title.) Coming up from Soliman, the road hangs onto the cliff. You pass **Aïn Oktor** and its curious concrete wigwam, once a trendy *bar à eau*, and then, round a corner, you are heading down into a tiny narrow valley full of buildings. There is a large hotel, and a villa looking down from a rock. The main spa building has a minaret. The place is not, however, terribly chic any more. There are groups of daytripping Tunisian students, the tour buses stop off and thunder on. Yet, in the evenings, Korbous in its rocky setting has an outpost feel, almost as though it were on the edge of some great ocean.

The Romans, a people in love with bathing establishments if ever there was one, were first in at *Aquae Calidae Carpitanae*. No doubt they had the usual well-appointed pleasure baths, no traces of which have survived, however. In the early 19th century, reforming ruler Ahmed Bey had a pavilion here for enjoying the thermal springs. In the 1950s, Korbous was home to one Charles Carpentier, known as Sidi Karbanti to the locals. His tomb was in the village, but the Main Rouge, the irredentist settler terrorist group, unburied him, refusing to admit that a Frenchman could have been integrated into local society to the point of being considered a holy man by the people of the region.

Tunisia's first president, Habib Bourguiba, had palaces and residences in all the right places, and Korbous was no exception. The villa on the hilltop was one of his summer homes. (His second wife, Wassila Ben Ammar, had her summer pavilion along the coast at Port aux Princes.) Korbous' other claim to fame is the **Zerziha Stone**, accessible from the terrace next to the *Hotel des Thermes*. Adopting the correct position, women in search of a cure for sterility may slide down it.

The waters of Korbous are the real cure here, it has to be said, and are used for **The springs** treating arthritis and rheumatism, obesity, cellulite and hypertension. They are faintly radioactive, contain calcium, sodium and sulphur, and sometimes smell of rotten eggs. They come boiling out of the earth at a hefty 60°C. Moving northeastwards along the coast, the springs have splendid names like Aïn Oktor and Aïn Chifa, Aïn El Atrous and Aïn Kala Sirra.

Aïn Oktor is the first spring you reach, approaching Korbous from the Soliman direction. The isolated hotel complex, overlooking the sea, dates from 1966, and was designed, like so many other public buildings of the period, by President Bourguiba's then favourite architect, Olivier Clément Cacoub. The spring water emerges slowly, its name meaning 'the spring which emerges drop by drop', and contains a high proportion of chlorine and soda used in the treatment of kidney disorders and urinary problems.

Aïn Chifa is the main spring in the village. For those in need of a cure, there is the thermal institute where you can enjoy such delights as *fangiothérapie* (mud baths) and other treatments which will leave you feeling squeaky clean. ■ *0800-1600, every day of the year, T284520.* The main, everyday baths is called the **Arraka** (from the Arabic *arak*, sweat), and in the underground grotto, you really will get a sweat going. A new baths has been built above the old Arraka, and men and women's hours alternate between the two. Disappointingly, there are no great quantities of water in the Arraka. (In terms of water flow, the hotsprings at Hammam Zriba are far better.)

Rather more exciting is **Aïn Atrous** (Billy Goat Spring), one kilometre north of the village on the main road. The spring gushes out of a duct in the hillside at 50°C and runs across the rocks for a few metres before tumbling down about three metres over a few rocks into the sea. The smell of hydrogen sulphide is difficult to avoid. You can sit with your feet in a small concrete basin while wisps of steam and whiffs of rotten eggs rise from the nearly scalding water. Even in winter it is possible though not really pleasant to bathe in the sea here. There is a car park and a few small cafés and restaurants close by. It is a favourite spot for locals, so Saturday and Sunday are very busy.

Beyond Aïn Atrous, the main road swings up right, eventually giving you some superb views across the sea to Tunis. Walking along a narrow path along the hillside above the sea, you can eventually drop down to a small bay with a pebbly beach after a couple of kilometres walk. (Four-wheel drive vehicles could also get some way down, access from the main road much higher up than Aïn Atrous.) This is **Aïn Kala Sirra** (*kala* being an inlet, *sirra* a sort of fish), where there is a tiny grotto with a trickle of water used by local people for mud baths. Off the coast here there is a hot spring bubbling up into the sea, find it if you can. You might do some snorkelling here, and the area is quite popular for underwater fishing.

Most of the hotels are expensive and used by the people undergoing treatment at **Sleeping** the spa.

The hotel **C** *Aïn Oktor* has been privatized and is in new hands. In summer 1999, it was still scruffy, the pool empty. The bar is popular, however, and has a beautiful view. Hopefully it will be returned to its original minimalist splendour. T284553. 4 km along the road to Soliman. Overlooks the sea, no beach. **C** *Chiraz*, route de Korbous, T02-293230. 16 beds, pool, small personal hotel, may no longer be open. **C** *Les*

Cap Bon Peninsula

> ☞ **Festivals on the Cap Bon**
>
> The towns and villages of the Cap Bon all seem to have an annual festival of some kind, some centred on the local agricultural speciality, others with a traditional or cultural content. Sponsored by the local authorities, these are generally occasions which allow otherwise rural backwaters to get a bit of the limelight in the sleepy Tunisian press. So, over the year, in chronological order, there is:
>
> **March /April**
> Orange Flower Festival at Menzel Bou Zelfa
>
> **Late April/early May**
> Spring Festival at Nabeul
> **Late June**
> Falconry Festival at Haouaria
> **July and August**
> International Festival of Hammamet (theatre and music)
> **August** (every other year)
> Amateur Theatre Festival at Korba
> **September**
> Festival of the Vine at Grombalia

Sources, T284540, F284601. Large terrace overlooking the sea, 103 beds, thermal cures, pool, (42Dt full board, high season, 37Dt off-season). The posh address in Korbous. **C** *Résidence des Thermes*, T284664. On main road in town centre, 5 minutes walk from spa baths, clean, tidy rooms with balcony on 2 floors, 18 twin-bedded rooms, all with bath and toilet, heating, meals if required are provided in newly built restaurant across the road (30Dt full-board, 25Dt half-board, no seasonal variation.)

Eating *Chez Korbsi* and *Restaurant Dhrib* in town centre serve good cheap meals. Also try *La Brise* at Sidi Rais, if still operational.

From Bir Meroua to El Haouaria

Bir Meroua is on the C26 and is reached directly from Soliman or recognized as the sharp left turn towards El Haouaria when approached from the coast. After **Sidi Aïssa**, you drive through rolling countryside, with occasional views of the sea glinting in the distance off to the left. Vines, cereals and vegetables (lots of tomatoes) are cultivated.

There are stands of cane and on occasion the road is lined with eucalyptus. After Tozghrane and Zaouiet el Magaïez, the land gets drier and the views open up. **Zaouiet el Mgaïez**, a one horse sort of town whose chief claims to fame are an elaborately tiled modern minaret and the production of baskets and beach parasols from local cane, holds a busy market in the main street each Wednesday. But as in many other localities like it across the Cap Bon, signs of development are everywhere. There are new school buildings and lots of powerlines, and wherever you go, the children look well-dressed and well-fed.

Detour to Sidi Daoud Driving up to Haouaria, you can make a quick detour to Sidi Daoud, a small fishing port just off the coast road to Korbous. On the way to nowhere, with views looking out to the steep cliffs of the islands of Zembra and Zembretta, Sidi Daoud feels a remote place. The strangeness is enhanced by a large fish canning plant. In late May to early June each year, the fishermen of the area take part in the *matanza*, the high point of the fishing season when shoals of large tuna fish (at times weighing more than 200 kilograms), innocently migrating from the Atlantic Ocean via the Straits of Gibraltar, are caught in carefully positioned nets, only to be dragged towards the shore and then harpooned between the boats. The panicking tuna thrash the nets, and the sea foams with blood. Enthusiasts may be able to get permission to go on the *matanza*. The event is more talked about in the tourist brochures than actually viewed by camcorders, however.

Sidi Daoud has factories which deal with the tuna fish and then export it to other Mediterranean countries. Tunisian red-meat tuna, canned with olive oil, is very good, and the top brand is El Manar. Note that the Romans caught on to this: Sidi Daoud occupies the site of ancient Missua, whose shipowners' corporation was represented at Ostia. No doubt salt fish was being shipped to Rome.

There are moorings at Sidi Daoud for pleasure boats with between 1.8 metres and three metres depth – with all the expected facilities, security and comfort. Near here is the tiny beach of **Bir Jeddi**, about two kilometres down a wooded track from the village. The beach is fine sand, but has lots of pebbles too. There are some huts for hire and a cool freshwater spring near the remains of an old cemetery.

Back on the main road, you continue northeastwards the short distance towards El Haouaria, Ghar el Kebir and Cap Bon.

El Haouaria   الهـوارية

Approaching from the Korbous direction, El Haouaria appears in the bare landscape as an expanse of low, flat-roofed houses below the gently rising mass of the djebel. There is the usual tall, onion-domed Cap Bon minaret. The town is a sleepy sort of place. For the tourist, attractions include the bizarre underground Roman quarries, the off-chance of seeing someone flying a falcon, and the low-key beach at Rass Eddreck. The scenery is rugged, and birdwatchers will have much to look at during the annual trans-Mediterranean migrations.

*Phone code: 02
Colour map 1, grid A6*

Ins and outs

El Haouaria is easily accessible by public transport from Tunis, Nabeul and Kélibia. If you are driving from Tunis, allow around 1hr 40mins, as you may be held up in traffic leaving Tunis. The louages and buses come into the station on Av Habib Bourguiba in the town centre.

Getting there

No particular problems here. The Roman quarries and the falconry centre are some 30 mins walk out of the town centre. If you want to get down to the Ras Eddreck beach, then either hitch or, in season, take the local bus from the main square. For Kerkouane, you would need to take a local bus or louage to Kélibia, and get off at Kerdouane, sign-posted some three kilometres after the one-horse settlement of Dar Allouche. Getting back, you might have to hitch or try to flag down the bus.

Getting around

Sights

In Roman times, El Haouaria was referred to as Aquilaria, 'the place of eagles'. The capture and rearing of falcons, still part of local life today, was no doubt an important activity in ancient times. The present day **Falconry Festival** goes back to 1967 when the tourist board decided to do something to cash in on this 'feature' of an out of the way corner of the Cap Bon. The festival rather died a death in the 1980s, but re-emerged as a three-day event in 1995. Modern Haouaria has erected a large concrete hawk as a monument to its birds and their handlers, smack in the town centre.

The festival (Le Festival de l'Epervier) is held each May or June. The country people bring their hawks to put them through their paces in front of other bird handlers. Live prey are used for these flying displays, and the falconers operate their birds with no mean skill.

Two sorts of birds are used at El Haouaria for falconry: the sparrow hawk (*épervier* in French, *essaf* in Tunisian Arabic) and the peregrine falcon (*faucon pélérin* or *el burni*). Sparrow hawk are captured up on the mountain during the April migration from Africa, and after around three weeks training are ready to hunt in time for the festival. Quail is the favourite prey. Generally, after the festival, most of the sparrowhawks are released. Takes of the much rarer peregrine falcons are very closely controlled. Only one or two nestlings may be taken each year, and the young birds are reared in capacity. Permits are issued to bona fide falconers only.

Today El Haouaria has a gleaming white new **falconry centre** (*Nadi el Bayazara*) up on the hill on the road to the Roman quarries (up on your right before you get to the crenellated *Restaurant Les Grottes*). There is a carnival atmosphere about the town during the festival, which coincides with the start of the hunting season.

The Roman quarries (Les Grottes) Three kilometres from the village on the shore near the extremity of the Cap are the **Ghar el Kebir Caves**. It is thought that the rock quarried from here was used to build parts of Carthage. There are said to be 97 caves in total. There is a car park and a restaurant by the car park next to the new entrance building (1Dt). It is a short easy walk to the main caves which are interlinked and have small openings in the roof, originally for the exit of the quarried stone, so daylight can now enter. Caper plants grow in the sandy stone, hanging down through the openings. If you are accompanied by a guide, they will point out the 'camel' of stone in the big hall, a female we are told. The mountains along the coast and behind the villages offer interesting walks. ■ *1Dt, open winter 0830-1730, summer 0800-1200 and 1500-1900.* **NB** Children should not be let too far off the leash in the vicinity of the caves, as not all have had iron bars placed over their 'access hatches'.

Ancient quarrying technique The question is, why did the Romans opt for quarrying on this remote stretch of coast. One major factor must have been the accessibility of such a large amount of easily worked soft sandstone right on the coast. The stone could be easily shipped to Carthage and other settlements across the Bay of Tunis. One wonders whether Aquilaria sandstone was used for the great amphitheatre at El Jem, speculating about the difficulties of transporting stone blocks to an inland site. And then there is the matter of how they worked the stone. As they cut down from above, the quarry workers created pyramid-shaped underground chambers. The operation was a skilled one, especially when it came to hoisting the blocks out through the 'skylights'. No room for cutting the blocks to the wrong size. Getting the blocks on the fragile ancient ships would have been another skilled manoeuvre using simple cranes. Depending on the demand for the stone, there must have been a sizeable population living out at ancient Haouaria.

Just down from the caves, below *Le Daurade* and another café-type place (no beers, hideous piped music), there is a good spot for swimming. Although the rocks are sharp, you can dive straight into several metres of clear water. Bring your mask, there are shoals of small fish. The local kids fish for *retzy* (sea urchins).

Zembra and Zembretta **Zembra and Zembretta** are small, steep-cliffed islands about eight nautical miles northwest from the coast by Sidi Daoud. Zembra is clearly visible from the Roman quarries at Haouaria, and the view at sunset is magnificent. The sea for one and a half nautical miles beyond low tide is designated as a *nature reserve* with no fishing, professional or sports allowed. Grey puffins nest here.

Once upon a time, there was a hotel and a scuba diving centre. For their names alone the islands would be worth visiting, but they are now occupied by the military. Access is only given to authorized research teams, so their unique biotopes look set to go undisturbed for some time yet.

Zembra rises straight out of the sea to its summit of 435 metres. Evidence shows that it was colonized from the time of the Phoenicians. The Romans called the islands the *Aégimures*. Zembra's special feature? A special type of rabbit, thought to descend from animals introduced by Phoenician sailors, perhaps to ensure a source of meat if forced to spend time on the island. Zembretta, the smaller of the two islands as its name suggests, has a lighthouse.

Towards the end of the Cap Bon peninsula there is a beautiful little beach, Ras Eddrak, which is quite secluded and still relatively unknown. A number of holiday homes have gone up, and it is possible to find month-long summer lets, though at a price. (Starting at 800Dt a month in summer, fully furnished.) It is four kilometres from the village along a road leading to the end of the peninsula. The view from the end of Cap Bon is superb. It is said that on a clear night the lights of Sicily, 140 kilometres away, can be seen. Note that this being a peninsula, the sea can be turbulent and dangerous if swimming close to the rocks.

Ras Eddrak

Essentials

D *De l'Epervier*, Av Habib Bourguiba, T297017, F297258. 28 beds in 10 rooms, with bath, very good restaurant. **F** *Dar Toubib*, T297163.

Sleeping

Mid-range *Restaurant de l'Epervier* (English spoken). Recommended. If you can stand the sub-Disney castle décor, then try the **Restaurant les Grottes**, T297296. Grottes Romaines. Rather better and less offensive on the eye, is *La Daurade*, T269080, F269090. Situated next to the carpark for the Roman quarries. Here you can eat fairly cheaply, or even pretty expensively if you go for some clawed sea-beast (*langouste*, *cigale de mer* or whatever), fresh from the depths and beautifully prepared. You might also see the resident falcon being put through its paces, or maybe just pulling a sparrow to pieces for its lunch.

Eating

Falconry *Club des Fauconniers*, Aquilaria, on road to quarries, open 1000-1600 daily. Said to do occasional displays of falconry during the season (June/July).

Sports

Road Bus: there is an irregular bus service, either via the north coast from Tunis (but this takes a while because the bus stops everywhere) or via Kélibia. **Louage**: taking a louage is much faster.

Transport

Banks On Av Habib Bourguiba near the Post Office. **Communications** Post Office: at the start of Av Habib Bourguiba, by the louages and bus station.

Directory

Cap Bon Peninsula

Southeast coast

From Haouaria to Kélibia

Kélibia is just a 20 minute drive from Haouaria, Kerkouane being the main stop-off en route. You pass through some small, strung out settlements, including **Dar Allouche** (two petrol stations). After Kerkouane (a left turn after the long concrete wall of a private estate), you run through a small forest and then the farming villages of Ezzahra and **Hammam el Ghezez** (splendid beaches, no concrete monster hotels) and the sandy spit of Ras Mellah. The beach is accessible across the fields, but don't get the car bogged down in the sandy tracks. The fortress of Kélibia can be seen up on its hill.

Kerkouane كركوان

Phone code: 02
Colour map 1, grid A6

Set in a Brittany-like corner of Tunisia, the ruins of Kerkouane, although as not spectacular as the great inland Numidian and Roman towns, have a charm of their own. Perhaps it is the site's location, on the edge of a low cliff overlooking the Mediterranean, backed by a hinterland of dark, windswept pines and heath. Certainly it must have something to do with the fact that Kerkouane, unlike so many other ancient sites, was never built upon by subsequent peoples. The old Punic town decayed into a jungle of briars, gorse and tamarisk, waiting for some archaeologist prince-charming. Today the visitor has a labyrinth of low intersecting walls and courtyards to contemplate, relieved here and there by a truncated column or two. Kerkouane does not deliver up its secrets readily.

■ *Kerkouane is open from 0800 to 1900 in summer and from 0930 to 1600 in winter. (Entrance 1Dt, photography 1Dt, T294033.)* If you are lucky, the small site museum, inaugurated June 1987, may be open. Here are displayed some of the finest discoveries at Kerkouane, including the sole example of a carved wooden Punic coffin. Enthusiasts of things pre-Roman might want to go in search of the Punic necropolis of Sidi Salem near Menzel Temime, further down the coast.

History Kerkouane is thought to have been built in the sixth century BC and probably abandoned following the fall of Carthage to the Romans in 146. It may, however, have been abandoned earlier. The settlement had a small port, and it is likely that its people made their living both from the sea and the farming. The murex, a shellfish well known in ancient times, was harvested and processed at Kerkouane for its purple-dye, and may have been one of the town's main sources of wealth. The ruins of Kerkouane were discovered in 1952 by Charles Saumagne and Pierre Cintas, and there have been excavations on and off ever since, as funds and enthusiasm permitted. What the actual Punic name of Kerkouane was, we do not know, as surviving Punic written records, mainly inscriptions, are rare to say the least.

The necropolis of Arg el Ghazouani Several decades before the discovery of the actual town of Kerkouane, archaeologists became aware of an ancient presence in the area. Some 500 metres northwest of the ancient town lies a burial area, with vaults carved into a hillside looking out over the sea. This necropolis (lit: 'city of the dead') was discovered completely by chance by a local notable, a *meddeb* or Koran school teacher, in 1929. On discovering that the tombs contained scarabs, jewellery, and black-figure ceramics, he was to mine his discovery for all it was worth,

What did the Punics do for lunch?

The ancient Mediterranean world had neither the tomato nor the potato, and even the vegetation in ancient Tunisia must have been very different to today. There were no eucalyptus trees (a 19th century introduction), no prickly pear hedges nor giant yuccas, both of which were introduced from the New World. What might have been the mainstays of the Punic diet? One thing is certain, the Punic peoples were noted farmers, and the Greeks considered Mago, fourth-century author of a treatise on agriculture, now lost, as the father of farming.

Echoes of what the Punic peoples were eating come down to us in the ancient texts. Another, more visual remnant, are terracotta models discovered in tombs. One such model, from fifth-century Carthage, shows a be-headscarved woman making bread in a round cylindrical pisé oven of the type still used to make flat tabouna bread in rural Tunisia today. Terracotta model fruit of various kinds have also been discovered in tombs.

The Cap Bon was a verdant region where Carthaginian nobles had estates. They grew fruit almonds, grapes, figs and pomegranates, mala punica or 'Punic apples' to the Romans, but not citrus fruits, which did not arrive until modern times.

They were good at bee-keeping, honey being the only available sweetener. The Greek and Latin historians tell us that cabbages and 'Carthage thistles' or artichokes featured in the market gardens. The Carthaginians are also said to have had an inordinate love of garlic, and the chick pea is referred to by one author as the punicum cicer. With bread, chick peas and eggs, plus a few spices, the Carthaginians had all the ingredients to conjure up something very like the modern Tunisian leblebi, a hot broth popular on winter mornings.

To complete the picture, the Carthaginians were also a dab hand at wine-making, and Latin writer Columella quotes Mago's vinification methods at some length. The consumption of wine was severely controlled, however, and Plato describes the measures taken at Carthage at some length. Wine was off limits for soldiers on campaign, ship's pilots, slaves (male and female), magistrates and men and women intending to procreate. The very existence of such a list of proscriptions suggests that things had been getting a little out of hand with a few boozy lunches too many taking their toll of Carthaginian business acumen.

selling off the most valuable finds to treasure hunters. Other funerary objects and pottery were too cumbersome, and were broken up to fill in already ransacked tombs.

The 'official' discovery of the necropolis had to wait until one J. Combre, an officer appointed to conduct a local murder enquiry, met the *meddeb*. He noted that our schoolteacher's wife was wearing a superb pair of gold earrings, obviously of great age. The teacher eventually told the tale of the tomb robberies, but official awareness does not seem to have put an end to the pillage. In the light of the finds at Arg el Ghazouani, archaeologist Cintas began to research tombs elsewhere in the region. Despite all the pillaging, there were tombs which survived unopened into the 1960s and later. In July 1970, a tomb at Arg el Ghazouani was found to contain a wooden sarcophagus, its lid carved with the bas-relief image of a woman, thought by some to be Ashtart, protector goddess of the dead. This piece can be viewed today in the site museum.

Kerkouane was discovered almost by accident. It was the sort of scoop that archaeologists dream of. In fact, the area could all too easily have gone the way of so many other sites, the land subdivided for villa development, with building too far advanced for anything to be done. One version of the story goes that **The discovery of Kerkouane**

(margin) Cap Bon Peninsula

🖐 **Our lady Tanit**

At Carthage, Tanit, goddess of Phoenician origin, was referred to as 'lady'. Mother goddess, symbol of fertility, her name often precedes that of Baal-Hammon on the stelae of Carthage. In all probability, Tanit and Baal-Hammon formed a sort of divine couple.

The Tanit sign is to be found on stelae and is formed by a triangle topped by a horizontal line on which rests a circle. The general theory is that it is a stylized representation of a female figure, shown in long, flowing robes. At Kerkouane, a famous example of the Tanit sign is to be found in a proto-mosaic pavement, picked out in white against a dull-red ground. It has also be found decorating funerary chambers, stamped on the handles of amphorae and on terracotta medallions.

What was the function of the Tanit sign? It may be that the Tanit is derived from the Egyptian ankh, symbol of life. Thus when it is placed on the doorstep of a home, it has a great protective force. In funerary chambers, the Tanit would seem to promote the forces of life over death. It is one of the earliest sacred signs known in North Africa. Today Tunisians use the fish (hout) and the khomsa, the so-called Hand of Fatima. But some see the Tanit still very much present in contemporary Tunisia. Feminist film-maker Nadia El Fani created a dream-like short feature film, Tanitez-moi (1992), emphasizing the Carthaginian side in the identity of today's Tunisian women.

Charles Saumagne was a great amateur fisherman. One afternoon in 1952, sitting on the cliffs of Kerkouane, he noticed some black-glaze pot shards and fragments of stucco in the soil. As an archaeologist, he immediately gave this loose surface material a closer inspection, realizing that it was probably pre-Roman. The Department of Antiquities was informed, and test-trenches were dug. The results were conclusive, for with almost the first shovelful, a Punic mask was brought to light.

A unique survival Looking out across the low expanse of sun-baked ruins, you may find yourself thinking: so why is this place so important? Quite simply, Kerkouane is practically unique. Unless archaeology in the Levant or possibly Sardinia comes up trumps, then Kerkouane is the only example of a Punic settlement to have survived untouched until the present day. Other sites were practically all built upon by later settlers, foremost among which were the Romans. Given that their boats had to be drawn up on the shore at night, the Phoenicians and Punics tended to pick good safe places to establish their settlements. Carthage is a case in point. And the Romans were not likely to miss out on such good places when they took over the Punic lands.

Why the Romans did not establish a settlement at Kerkouane is another question. It may be that they preferred Hammam Ghezaz further down the coast. Or perhaps the quarrying activities up at Haouaria took all their energies.

Dating Kerkouane Hassine Fantar, today the leading authority on Kerkouane, sees the town as being a sort of ethno-cultural melting pot, with Libyic, Punic and Greek influences all present. The rock tombs in the area attest to a strong Libyic presence, while a Greek black figure wine jug from the site can be dated to the sixth century BC. Excavations of the houses have not brought to light any material later than the third century BC, which would suggest that the town was pillaged and abandoned at the time of Roman consul M. Atilius Regulus' invasion of Africa in 256 BC. The town was never to rise again.

Further reading on Kerkouane

Those interested in all things Punic will want to find out more. M'hamed Hassine Fantar is the acknowledged Tunisian expert on Kerkouane, to the point that the site is nicknamed 'Fantarville'. Look out for his scholarly works, or the generalist Kerkouane, a Punic town in *the Berber region of Tamezrat (Alif: Tunis, 1998). Other names to have published on the site include Cintas and Mahjoubi. Just for the record, Cintas is the author of a weighty* Manuel d'archéologie punique *(Paris, 1970 and 1976).*

From an aerial photograph, you get a very clear idea of the town's layout. There were long streets, some open public areas and blocks of building which on closer inspection turn out to be carefully planned town-houses. The main streets are wide, often around four metres, and the houses tend to follow a courtyard plan.

Streets and town-houses

Looking over the ruins of the houses, the untrained eye begins to pick out clues to what was actually here in Punic days. The people of Kerkouane were a clean lot, and you can see stone guttering and some very modern hip-baths, carefully finished in stone-chip rendering. The walls were mainly built with rubble-stone, strengthened here and there by big rectangular upright stones or orthostats (to use the technical term). This building technique is referred to as *opus africanum* (lit: 'African work') by the archeologists. Interior walls might be built using an earth, lime and gravel mix packed down between wooden formwork.

Here and there, you may come across some rough hewn steps, an indication that there was a first floor, perhaps a light wood-built structure. The buildings probably had flat, terrace roofs, and there were stone waterspouts to ensure that water did not accumulate on the roofs. No doubt the roofing technology was not so very different from that used until the mid-20th century in many urban Tunisian homes: the room was covered with a bed of juniper or pine trunks, subsequently covered with rammed earth and gravel; the whole roof was then sealed with lime wash. Sometimes a stone pillar in the middle of a large room would be used to hold the roof up, and Ionic column capitals have been discovered. Another solution was to place a pine trunk in an amphora, and use it as a central pillar, the amphora protecting the wood from any ground damp. Kerkouane does not seem to have had any elaborate arches or vaulting.

The Kerkouanese liked to have their homes well-finished. A form of stucco was in use, and here and there you can see layers of stucco flaking on the clay-and-gravel walls. (So don't go jumping up and down on the walls.) There may well have been wall paintings like the simple elegant designs discovered in certain Punic burial chambers. Floors had the most elegant finish, however. The preferred paving technique, referred to by archaeologists as *opus signinum*, involved setting white marble chips in a hard mix of old pottery and primitive cementing. The resulting overall colour is terra-cotta pink flecked with white.

If it is open, the site museum is definitely worth a look, giving a bit more of an insight into the everyday goings-on in ancient Kerkouane. There are a few items from Carthage and other sites (the column capitals from Gammarth). Under the porticoes are amphorae and bits of masonry, inside are sundry items related to both work and worship. There are weights and obsidian objects, murex shells and basalt grindstones, pottery, both local and imported, stelae and altars. There are amulets, toilet requisites, scarabs and glass-paste decorative items. The jewellery, if on display, has an interesting story to tell.

The site museum

The vast majority was discovered in the burial grounds near Kerkouane. Many of the finest tomb finds, discovered before Punic archaeology really got going in the 1950s, found their way abroad. The Fragonard museum at Grasse, for example, has a fine collection of perfume flasks.

The Lady of Kerkouane The most unusual item in the museum has to be the wooden sarcophagus carved with the image of the goddess Ashtart, protector of the dead. The robed goddess is almost complete, with only the feet missing. The find is unique, no other example of Punic wood-carving has survived. After the discovery, wood-conservation experts were flown in from Switzerland, and in the event, the statue had to be flown off to Zurich for treatment.

The survival of Kerkouane In many ways, the survival of Kerkouane is as miraculous as that of Ashtart on the sarcophagus lid. Once exposed to the elements, however, the sea winds and the mist, the walls are really rather vulnerable. Visiting the site, avoid walking on the walls and roped off areas (a cross warden might well come racing up anyway to warn you off). A photograph in a genuine Punic bathtub is a tempting proposition, but if everyone clambered in and out, the pink rendering would become fragile. Save the ancient heritage photo-call for the headless statues at the Bardo Museum.

Kélibia قليبية

Population: 35,000
Phone code: 02
Colour map 1, grid A6

Kélibia is one of those attractive backwater sort of places. Too far from Hammamet to have attracted the developers' interest, it has neither baleful, calculating souks nor stretches of lumpish hotels (yet). There are some entirely beautiful beaches, a busy fishing port, and a hilltop fort, no doubt home to the odd Ottoman ghost. Kélibia is a working town: farming, furniture making and serving the needs of the local rural communities keep people busy, so tourism is just a side-line. There is nothing swish here, but everything for a siesta-like stay.

Ins and outs

Getting there Kélibia is easily accessed on public transport. There are buses and louages from Bab Alioua (Tunis) and Nabeul. In the summer season, you could also come in on the hydrofoil from Trapani in Italy.

Getting around Buses and louages come into the central avenue Ali Belhaouane. From here, it is a short walk to the Pension Anis. Other hotels are really a taxi ride away. (The Youth Hostel is nearly 2 km away.) To get to the ruins at Kerkouane, you could take the local Haouaria bus, or a louage and ask to be let off at the turn off for the site.

History and background

Kélibia is one of the more pleasant small towns on the southeastern coast of the Cap Bon. Settlement goes back to Punic times. Phoenician traders no doubt appreciated the defensive value of the site: Kélibia holds the key to the straits separating Africa from Sicily. Greek historians referred to the town as Aspis, the Greek for 'shield'. The Romans adopted the same term, and redubbed Aspis as Clipea, 'shield' in Latin. Today, the town is dominated by an impressive fortress, symbol of the 18th/19th century Husseinid Dynasty's authority over the Cap Bon. There has been a fortress on the site since Punic times. From the outside, at the base of one of the recent square towers, the base of a Punic fortification is clearly visible. The remains of a large Punic necropolis has been discovered near the Hotel Mansoura.

Kélibia is home to an important fishing fleet with a commercial fish market on the quayside. The main catch is 'blue' fish. The quiet port was modernized to become the main fishing port of Cap Bon and is at times a haven for the whole Cap Bon fleet which comprises 360 coastal fishing boats, 46 trawlers and seven boats for game fish. The Tunisian fishing fleets suffer from heavy competition from better equipped, more powerful Italian vessels.

There is also a thriving shipbuilding and ship repair section at the port. Kélibia also provides a hydrofoil ferry link to Trapani in Italy. In the late afternoon, the fishing fleet can be seen chugging up the coast for night fishing. (Some lamparo fishing still goes on.) On summer nights, all Kélibia seems to come out for a paseo in the port area. Families, gaggles of local kids, scooters and sundry strollers parade along the quay and up to the Café Sidi el Bahri.

Note also that the best lettuces in Tunisia are grown in the Kélibia region. The town is an important furniture-making centre and many workshops can be seen in and around the town. A pleasant white wine, the *Muscat sec de Kélibia*, is a legacy of early 20th century Italian settlement. Unfortunately, the grape juice is sent up to the main UCCV production unit in Tunis for fermenting, so boringly there will be no jolly *dégustations* in the local winery.

Sights

Kélibia fortress sits on top of a 150 metres high rocky hill. The present structure would seem to go back to the Byzantine sixth century, but has been changed and rebuilt many times since. The crenellated walls, almost complete, are made of huge blocks of stone and are reinforced with square towers at the corners. The fortress surrounds the remains of an much more ancient fort and some deep wells. Inside the fortress there are several vaulted rooms, one of which, with three naves, was probably a chapel. The fortress is accessible up a steep road leading off the road north of the port. Excavations in the vicinity of the fort are of Roman **Clupea**. Alternate years, generally in July, a minor international amateur film festival is held here. ■ *Entrance is 2Dt or free for students, open summer 0800-1900, winter 0830-1700.*

Beaches North of Kélibia, **Mansourah** with its graceful beaches is a pleasant little corner of Tunisia, despite the growing number of large concrete private houses. The water is green-glass clear, the sand fine and white, there is a very 1970s restaurant where the chairs and tables are set on little platforms around the rock pools. Too pleasant to be true in the early summer. Further up the coast, is **Hammam el Ghezaz** and the sandly headland of Ras el Melah.

For many years, rumour went that there would be an 'integrated touristic development' in the Mansourah area, but it seemed that Hammamet had sucked all the investment in – given the easy motorway access, the economies of scale linked to vast infrastructure development and the Hammamet label. Building started spring 1999, and the Kélibia la Blanche development seems set to ruin what was a wonderfully unspoiled stretch of coast.

Cap Bon Peninsula

Essentials

Sleeping Kélibia has limited accommodation, so it is a good idea to try and reserve. Most tourists here are Tunisians in rented villas or houses, or else staying with family or in second homes.

C *Palmarina* (ex-Hotel Ennasim) T274062, F274055. 36 rooms, pool, prices in high season, 32Dt with breakast, 39Dt half-board.

D *Florida* Long established small hotel, by the sea, T296248. Now rather overshadowed by the neighbouring Palmarina. 25 beds, most rooms with sea view, shaded terrace. Neighbouring beach none too clean, but then this is the beach by the port. Choice of rooms or bungalow accommodation (ie room with small veranda). Single with breakfast, 21Dt in high season. **D** *El Mansoura Holiday Village*, a self-catering option which had a long-established clientèle. The low, vaulted bungalows were perfectly integrated into the site, right on the beach without being an overbearing presence. In summer 1999 works were underway, and a large new hotel (called, surprise surprise, the *Kélibia Beach*) will be ready for 2000. **D** *Mamounia Holiday Village*, 208 beds, T296088, F286858. Close to the new sports hall. Accommodation in simple, whitewashed vaulted buildings with verandahs. Small pool. Might suit families. A quiet sort of place which no doubt had its heyday back in the 1970s. **NB** Jungle gel and other mosquito repellants essential.

E *Anis*, T295777, F273128. Clean, no ensuite bathrooms. Single 19Dt, no seasonal variation in prices. *Youth hostel*: T296105, 80 beds, on the road to Mansoura, by the sea.

Eating & The restaurants in both the hotels are adequate, and there is a small selection of res-
drinking taurants, some of which are very pleasant indeed.

Middle range *El Mansoura*, T296321. Right on the sea. A very popular address for a long, slow lunch. Gets very crowded at weekends. *Hotel Palmarina* has a very reasonably priced set menu. *Restaurant Anis*, Av Erriadh, Kélibia's most upmarket place. Not far from the main market.

Cheap *Café Sidi el Bahri* by the port. Kélibia's happening place in the evening. Chairs among the rocks and on the sand. Limited menu. More of a café than a restaurant. *Café el Borj*. Just below the fortress, next to a saint's tomb among the pine trees. with fine views looking northwards over Mansoura towards Kerkouane. Plastic chairs and overamplified music spoil what is really a rather wonderful place. No food but good *café turc*. *Clupea*, T296296. A bar more than a restaurant. *Dina*, on rue Ibn Khaldoun in the town centre. Does the usual pizzas. Fine for a cheap fill-up.

Sports Some watersports are available but the resort is not really set up for this. Harbour has berths for 20 yachts, minimum-maximum draft 2-5m, with all the expected facilities, security and comfort.

Transport **Road** Buses leave every hour in the morning to El Haouaria and there are frequent departures to Nabeul. Bus from Tunis leaves from Bab Alioua. **Sea** An interesting hydrofoil link with Trapani in Sicily is advertised during the summer, taking 4 hours and carrying up to 180 passengers. For information T296276.

Directory **Tour companies & travel agents** *Kerkouane Voyages*, Place Sidi Abdessalem, T295370-410, F296836.

South to Nabeul via Menzel Temime and Korba

Some 12 kilometres south of Kélibia is the busy agricultural town of Menzel Temime with an Ariane rocket of a minaret, no doubt built with donations from prosperous local farmers. Groundnuts (or peanuts) are grown in the area north of the town towards El Haouaria. For those who want to see how salted peanuts start off life, then this is the place to look. The plants actually push the seed pods down into the ground, hence the name. Peppers are another major crop here, and the house fronts are hung with strings of pimentoes, big, bunchy garlands the colour of drying blood.

Menzel Temime
Population: 30,000
Phone code: 02

Human settlement in the Menzel Temime area goes back to at least the fourth century BC. Ruins have been found out in the farmland. There are some ancient caves, perhaps first century BC, badly signposted, dug in the rocks overlooking the beach. As per usual, the various invaders/settlers left their mark, there being Roman cisterns, fortresses, mosques and mausoleums.

D *Temime*, 88 beds, T298262-266, F298291. **Youth hostel**: 40 beds, T298116.

Sleeping

A good straight road lined with eucalyptus runs from Menzel Temime to Korba. Agriculture enthusiasts will note extensive cultivation and some beef-cattle rearing. The level of mechanization ranges from camel and horse-powered ploughs to sophisticated, heavy machinery. Approaching Korba the salt lakes and marshes to the southeast become more extensive. There are fields devoted to tomatoes and pimentoes, processed/concentrated in local factories, and battery chicken farms.

Menzel Temime to Korba

Korba is a small town on the coast road just 20 kilometres north of Nabeul. It stands on the Oued Bou Eddine. Once upon a time, there was a *Club Mediterranée* here. A rough road leads inland up to a barrage on the *oued*. Korba's claim to fame today is strawberry production. Extensive areas next to the sea have been developed with moderately ugly suburbs of holiday homes.

Korba
Phone code: 02

There aren't too many sights in Korba. Almost nothing of the ancient city of *Julia Curubis* remains, although you might seek out the traces of the aqueduct. Curubis is thought to have been the seat of an archbishop associated with the presence of St Cyprien here in 275AD. From the Islamic period there are remains of the mausoleum of Sidi Moaouia and a mini *ribat* to protect the settlement from attacks by pirates. Every other year, in August, there is a week-long national festival of amateur theatre. Market day is Sunday.

Former **Club Mediterranée**, T226400, is currently being renovated but is due to open in 2000. **Youth hostel**, T298116. 100 beds, meals provided, family run.

Sleeping

Cap Bon Peninsula

Nabeul نابل

Population: 50,000
Phone code: 02
Colour map 1, grid B5

One of the first places to attract tourist development on the Cap Bon, Nabeul has long featured in the holiday brochures. It has a long clean beach, with some large hotels, and swathes of new estates of second homes. Nabeul also makes the best harissa (red chilli pepper) paste in Tunisia. It would be nice if the town had some sort of real attraction. While there are few nice bits of early 20th century official architecture, most of the local vernacular and Italian-style building is being altered out of all recognition. Nabeul has a roundabout with a big araucaria tree in a giant ceramic pot, shops of pottery for visitors, and lots of industry on the north-western outskirts. The people are a friendly lot, and tourism is not the mainstay as it is in Hammamet: no-one seems very bothered about history, culture and projecting a tourist image in Nabeul.

Ins and outs

Getting there Easily accessible by public transport, Nabeul is reached by buses and louages from Tunis, Kélibia and Hammamet. The main bus and louage station is on Av Habib Thameur. There is a second bus and louage station for Cap Bon destinations on Av Farhat Hached, near the weekly market. You can also come into Nabeul by train from Tunis, the station being in the middle of town on the Av Bourguiba, just where this turns into the main avenue leading to the sea.

Getting around Nabeul can easily be done on foot. The main concentration of small hotels is in 15 to 20 minutes walking distance south of the town centre (turn left out of bus station). You may, however, want to get out to some of the beaches a way out from the town, at, say, Maâmoura to the north. Here you need to get a local bus from the Av Habib Thameur.

History and background

The modern town of Nabeul, 65 kilometres southeast of Tunis, has become a place of some importance: it is the capital of the Governorate of the Cap Bon, and so there are various regional government buildings and colleges.

The modern name Nabeul is a corruption of the ancient Neapolis ('new town'). A Roman area has been excavated, and can be seen beside the *Hotel Aquarius*, not far from the beach, one kilometre to the southeast of the central area. The original Phoenician town was occupied by Roman troops during the third Punic war in 148 BC.

Sights

Colonia Julia Neapolis Colonia Julia Neapolis was apparently developed by Julius Caesar on an earlier Punic site. Under Caesar Augustus it grew in importance, developing quickly, and by 258 had obtained the status of a full blown Roman city or colonia. Note the Romans had a hierarchy of cities in their provinces: first came the *colonia*, whose inhabitants were Roman citizens; the *municipium* had fewer rights, and elected two representatives a year; at the bottom of the scale were the *civitates* or native towns and villages. Nabeul was thus well up on the Romanity index.

The ruins are rather unspectacular, but you can see the 'House of Nymphs', from which the seven beautiful mosaics now exhibited in the town's museum (closed) were removed. It is also said to be the place where Artemonis, a superb horse, doted on by his Roman master, was buried. Just beside it there is a 'factory' where fish entrails were processed to make the famous highly flavoured *garum* seasoning. This condiment was used in many Roman dishes.

The Roman excavations

The entrance to the site off the Route Touristique is a gate (where there may still be a sign reading 'This is closed'). Continue about 50 metres further east and take the track which leads to the sea. About 200 metres down the track on the left is a small gate, the entrance. The site, which is privately owned, extends to about eight hectares and it is now you wish you had memorized the map from the entrance of the museum in Nabeul. ■ *Daily 0900-1200, entry Dt1, photos Dt1.*

Nabeul's small museum is in a small park at 44 Avenue Habib Bourguiba, just opposite the railway station and the famous ceramic *jarre* roundabout. There are displays, the best of the local remains from nearby Neapolis and a few from the excavations at Kerkouane and Kélibia. It is built round the traditional square courtyard with a gallery to the left exhibiting Punic pottery and statuettes and an extensive display of pottery and oil lamps through to the third century AD.

Opposite the entrance is a fine display of mosaics. The best by far is a life-size mosaic showing the vanquished Priam (?) kneeling before a seated

Museum
At present closed but may re-open (funding permitting). The information given here concerns the museum as it was, and it seems that most of the objects once on display have been moved elsewhere

Cap Bon Peninsula

Nabeul

■ Sleeping
1 Aquarius
2 Fakir
3 Kheops
4 Le Prince
5 Les Hafsides
6 Les Jasmins
7 Les Pyramides
8 Monia Club
9 Nerolli
10 Pension Habib
11 Pension les Roses
12 Pension Mustapha
13 Pension les Oliviers
14 Youth Hostels
15 Camping

● Eating
1 L'Araucaria
2 L'Olivier

🚌 Buses
1 Main Bus & Louage Station
2 Buses & Louages for Cap Bon

N

Not to scale

Agamemnon, with Mercury and Achilles (?) standing behind them, and another showing Mars standing behind a reclining Neptune. There are rather touching terracotta statuettes from the Punic necropolis and shrine of Thinissut, near Bir Bou Regba (Hammamet). One represents the goddess-mother breast feeding her baby, while another is of a sinister lion-headed goddess. The figurines were probably made as grave-furniture.

The museum, unfortunately, does not provide a descriptive leaflet, and while the pottery has labels in Arabic and French, for the mosaics it is necessary to use the services of a guide who will require a tip. There is a map of the site of Neapolis on display at the entrance to the museum. ■ *Former opening times: Winter 0930-1630, summer 0800-1200 and 1500-1900, entrance 1Dt plus 1Dt for photography, closed Monday. The adjacent park provides benches and shade.*

The pottery industry Nabeul's speciality is pottery, its largest industry after tourism. The art of polychrome ceramics was introduced in the 15th century by the Andalusians. All along the Avenue Farhat Hached you will see stalls of pottery: there is blue and white standard Mediterranean tourist ware, and slightly more upmarket stuff with simple floral or fish motifs with a faint Habitat feel. Production covers the whole span, from the simplest earthen water jar to the white and gilded pot pineapple. The quantities of pottery are such that Jean Genet, visiting Tunisia back in the 1970s, worried that Tunisia would be quarried away to nothing for its clay.

Little actual pot making can be observed today, as the potteries are now industrial concerns located on the outskirts. The following factories might be of some interest: *Maison de l'Artisanat* on Avenue Habib Bourguiba, well down towards the beach, T285438, no showroom; *Ceramics Kedidi* on route de Tunis, T287576, about one and a half kilometres from the town centre, extensive showroom, mainly tiles; *Poterie Artistique Gasteli*, Zone Industrielle, route de Tunis, T222247, abut one and a half kilometres from the town centre, employs about 100 people and will allow visitors to view the manufacturing process (no need for individuals to book, parties must contact M Hedi Hichaeri or M Maghrebi). Showroom at 190 Avenue Habib Thameur, shop at 117 Avenue Farhat Hached.

The recent history of pot-making in Nabeul is quite interesting, although there is very little written on the subject. Under the French protectorate, a special department encouraged the revival of different crafts. The Chemla brothers developed the art of tile-making, and their fine tile panels, generally signed, can be seen even today on various façades in Tunis (Restaurant Baghdad on Avenue Bourguiba, base of the mosque at Bab Jazira). Spanish models were copied too, possibly thanks to immigrants fleeing the political turmoil in Spain. Thanks to the ready availability of high quality clay, the pottery industry at Nabeul has never looked back.

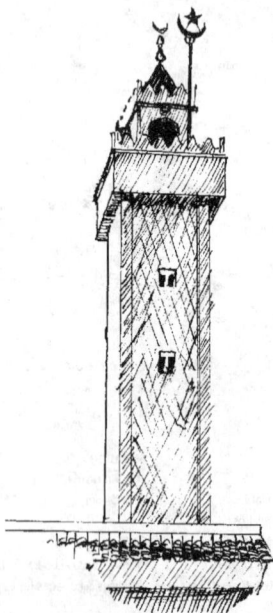

The Minaret of Mosque Salamba

Nabeul is noted for mats woven from rushes and esparto grass, silver and silk embroidery, and the distillation of jasmine, wild orange flowers and roses. These fragrant essences called *zhar* are prized by the locals for their soothing qualities. (Be assured a few drops in the milk will make a fretful baby sleep soundly.)

Other crafts: survivals and revivals

A craft industry which has taken off in a big way since the mid-1980s is the **stone-carving** at the neighbouring town of Dar Chaâbane el Fehri, a few kilometres to the north-east but now effectively part of the greater Nabeul area. The Tunisian construction industry boomed in the 1990s, and new home owners were in need of signs of distinction for their façades. What could be easier than sandstone columns and facing, cut to measure at Dar Chaâbane? These stone features, once limited to the immediate area, can now be found on hotels (generally in the *café maure*) and villas all across Tunisia.

More threatened by technology is the craft of **rush-mat making**. Until the 1970s, no self-respecting mosque would be without its rush mats or *hassira*. The large areas to be covered, plus the need to renew the mats regularly, meant that generations of Nabeulians were kept busy at their horizontal floor looms. After independence, a number of trendy tourist products, including small floor mats, trays, baskets, lampshades and seating were created. Traditionally styled cafés had to have rush mats too, essentially the narrow strips decorated with green and mauve arches to put round the walls behind stone benches. In the 1990s, however, the industry was dealt a severe blow in the form of large, cheap plastic floor mats imported from China via Libya. Now only a few workshops remain. The careful and ecological art of creating expanses of fragrant golden-yellow matting may soon be lost forever.

Essentials

Nabeul does not have a vast range of hotels. Its big plus are the small, family run pensions, situated for the most part down towards the Neapolis excavations and the Hammamet end of town. Some of these places have been going for years, building up a clientele by word of mouth rather than by working with the tour companies.

Sleeping
Phone code: 02

B *Hotel Kheops*, Av Mohamed V, T286555, F286024. Good restaurant, Olympic size pool, indoor pool, 300 rooms, a/c, bath, TV, phone, terrace, watersports, tennis, disco. Sound-proofing in rooms none too good. **B** *Hotel Les Pyramides*, Av Habib Bourguiba, T285444, F287461. Large hotel with accommodation in 350 bungalows, beach, pool, organized activities. Right on beach, an extension of the Kheops complex (you have access to its facilities). **C** *Hotel Les Jasmins*, Av Habib Thameur, T280222, F285073. 188 beds, pool, restaurant, about 1 km in direction of Hammamet, an older hotel, comfortable, not central. Pleasant shaded terrace next to bar. **D** *Pension Les Oliviers*, rue de Havana, off rue Abou el Kacem Echabi, T286865. One of the oldest established family-run hotels. Highly recommended. People come back year after year. **D** *Hotel Fakir*, opposite the Roman remains of Neapolis, T285477. Brand new, small, pleasant rooms, 200m from beach, very welcoming owner prefers individual travellers to groups. **D** *Les Hafsides*, 4 rue Sidi Maaouia, T285823. Just off Av Habib Thameur near the 'orange monument'. 16 beds, toilet in rooms, shared bath, small Tunisian style hotel close to town centre. **E** *Pension Mustapha*, Av Habib el Karma on corner with Av Ali Belhouane, T222262. 5 rooms with wash basin, shared toilet and bath, no restaurant, clean Tunisian style hotel close to the souqs. **F** *Pension el Habib*, Av Habib Thameur, T287190. On the outskirts of Nabeul coming from Hammamet, beach, very clean, communal bath/toilets, all rooms with handbasin, roof terrace, main road is slightly noisy. **F** *Pension Les Roses*, rue Farhat Hached, T285570. Clean, well kept, central, communal bath/toilets.

Cap Bon Peninsula

Camping *Hotel les Jasmins*, T285343. On the road to Hammamet, 1 km out of town, hot/cold water, shop, restaurant, outdoor theatre in an extensive orange grove, 1 ha under shade, prices 1.9Dt per person (under 18 1.3Dt), tent 1.3Dt, caravan 1.5Dt, car 1.1Dt, electricity 1.7Dt, shower 2Dt.

Youth hostels 2 km from town centre at the end of Av Mongi Slim, by the beach, T285547. 56 beds, closed all February. Also *Centre de Séjour et de Vacances 'La Gazelle'*, T221366. 70 beds, meals available. Also *Maison des Jeunes*, Av Taieb Mehiri, T86689. 80 beds, clean, meals available, don't expect hot water.

Eating Nothing very special in the way of restaurants here, apart from the *Slovenia*, T285343, south of the town centre on the main road to Hammamet just before the turn-off to the *Hotel les Jasmins*. Chef Rafik Tlatli is one of Tunisia's most innovative chefs, author of a fine coffee table book of recipes entitled Saveurs de Tunisie (Tunis: Geste Editions, 1998). The hotel behind the restaurant has a pleasant shaded terrace bar where the locals come for a drink.

Expensive *L'Olivier*, T286613. Av Hedi Chaker, decor and food delightful. *Monia*, Av Habib Abdelwaheb. T285713. Fish, crustaceans, shell fish.

Mid-range *Au Bon Kif*, Av Habib Thameur, T222783. *Le Corail*, Av Habib Bourguiba, T223342. *La Rodinella*, 116 Av Habib Bourguiba on corner of Av Farhat Hached, pleasant, central.

Cheap 1 *Les Arcades*, opposite the Galerie Gasteli, on Av Habib Bourguiba, near the main *jarre* roundabout. Slow service, small dry pizzas – avoid. *Er Rachida*, Av Habib Thameur on corner of Av Habib Bourguiba, excellent to sit and watch people going by, an attractive café decorated in traditional Tunisian style, up several steps above street level, tables on covered area overlooking street in town centre. *Karim* snack bar in central square; *Le Malouf*, Av Habib Bourguiba, close to post office. Small Tunisian style café. *La Rotonde*, T285782, Av Taieb Mehiri. Also restaurants down by the beach. Try the *Gelateria Coky*, next to the restaurant *Les Trois Etoiles* on Av Hédi Chaker. Italian-run, nice service. **NB** their *nocciola* (hazelnut ice cream is particularly good.)

Festivals **Nabeul International Fair**, Av Habib Bourguiba (early April each year), details from T285374, F223242.

Shopping You might visit the rather sleepy *ONAT* shop on Av Thameur to see the usual range of Tunisian products and check the prices. No pressure - just wander. The traditional green/yellow pottery is a good buy. There is a modern shopping centre, opposite the hospital on Av Habib Thameur, where you'll find camera film, clothes and sun-creams. There is no médina in Nabeul and the shopping areas along Av Farhat Hached and through to Av Habib el Karma take its place. Good selection of pots at *Céramiqe Slama*, 190 Av Farhat Hached. Look out for the big decorative plates, a bery good buy. Also on Av Farhat Hached, try *Boutique 101*, which has a good selection of traditional slippers and spangly oriental costumes. Recommended. The better quality shops and restaurants are found on Av Habib Bourguiba between Av Farhat Hached and Place du 7 Novembre, where a full grown Norfolk Island pine tree can be seen growing out of a decorative ceramic pot which forms the middle of the roundabout.

Sports Adjacent to Nabeul the port of Béni Khiyar has moorings for 15 pleasure boats, with a depth of 1-3 metres. All facilities are available.

Farming the Cap Bon

For those who like their figures, there are over 180,000 hectares of arable land on the Cap Bon peninsula. The annual rainfall varies between 360 millimetres and 670 millimetres. Irrigation water used to be raised from wells by camels or donkeys, but today the few wells that remain are backed by eight dams and many hill lakes which provide a storage capacity of over 200 million cubic metres. In terms of national fruit and vegetable production, the Cap Bon in the 1990s was a major player, with the Korba region producing 90 percent of strawberries and the triangle formed by Menzel Bou Zelfa, Soliman and Beni Khalled accounting for 70 percent of citrus fruit, including the unique Maltaise juice oranges and the rare leem or bergamote. Grombalia, Bir Bou Regba and Bou Argoub account for 80 percent of table and wine grapes.

The Cap Bon also produces olives, almonds and market garden produce (early potatoes, fennel, carrots and broad beans) in vast quantities, making maximum use of its position between the capital and the tourist centres. Local markets as well as national markets play an important part. Cereals are also grown and there is some pasture for beef rearing.

Local Car hire: *Avis*, Hotel Kheops, T286555; *Hertz*, Av Thameur, T285327; **Transport** *Europacar*, Av Farhat Hached, T287085; *Express Car*, Av Habib Thameur, T287014; *Matei*, Av Habib Bourguiba, T285967; *Méditerranée Car*, Nabeul Centre, T224835, and Av Farhat Hached, T221073; *Next Car*, Av Habib Bourguiba, T285967; *Nova Rent*, Av Habib Bourguiba, T222072; *Rent a Car*, Av Thameur, T286679; *Royal Car*, rue Sidi Maaouia, T287333.

Long distance Train: There is 1 train a day to Tunis 0545, otherwise the nearest trains are at Bir Bou Regba reached by bus or louage. Information T285054. **Bus**: the bus station is on Av Thameur. Information on T285261. The times given here change according to season and demand. There are frequent buses to **Hammamet** starting at 0530, **Tunis** (every half an hour), **Kélibia**, **Zaghouan** 8 each day, **Sousse** starting at 0645, **Mahdia** starting at 0730 and **Kairouan** (direct at 0600, 0800 and 1215). Buses frequent from Nabeul to Kélibia and El Haouaria with final departure from Kélibia at 1830. **Louages**: Av Farhat Hached, T286081. **Taxi**: *Allo Taxi Express*, T222444.

Banks Most banks are on Av Habib Bourguiba and Av Farhat Hached, in the town centre. The STB **Directory** has automatic cash dispenser – for 24-hr service. **Communications Area code**: 02. **Post Office**: main office, Av Habib Bourguiba, open Mon-Sat 0800-1800, also Av Mongi Slim. **Hospitals & medical services** *Regional Hospital*, Av Mohammed Tahar Mâamouri, T285633. *Clinique Les Violettes*, route d'Hammamet, T286668, F286240. *Clinique Ibn Rochd*, rue Mongi Slim, T286668, F286240. **Tour companies & travel agents** *Delta Travel*, 156 Av Habib Bourguiba, T271077, F271177. *Eagle International Travel*, 58 Av Habib Bourguiba, T223355, F223263. *Leader Tours*, Nabeul Centre, T271626, F271166. *Salama Voyages*, 18 Av Habib Bourguiba, T285804, F287043. Sept Voyages, 10 rue de l'Oranger, T286998, F286998. *Tunisian Travel Club*, 76 Av Mongi Slim, T287427, F286977. **Tourist offices** The *Regional Tourism Bureau* stands back from road on Av Taieb Mehiri, T286737. Towards the beach, from town centre. Bus and train times are normally posted outside the office. Closed in winter. The *Nabeul Tourist Office* is at Place 7 Novembre, T223006. **Useful addresses Police**: Av Habib Bourguiba, T285474; Garde National, Av Taieb Mehri, T286153.

Cap Bon Peninsula

A side-trip from Nabeul: Beni Khiar

If you have time on your hands, and enthusiasm for weaving, you might go to Beni Khiar, a small town a few kilometres north of Nabeul.

The Hilalians, a nomadic tribe from Upper Egypt, established a settlement here in the 11th century. A century later, a *ksar* was established, carefully set back from the pirate infested coast. The nomads settled here and supported themselves by weaving, a handicraft for which they are still famous today. The mosque was built later, outside the main *ksar*, and is all that remains of this settlement.

Beni Khiar still specializes in the spinning and weaving of wool, using natural dyes. It produces the traditional stripped blankets, the *kachabia*, a hooded cape and the fine weave and black stitched needlework carpets in small workshops or individual homes. Some of the workshops were built half underground. The finished material is also used in the making of traditional clothing like the *burnous* as well as tents. These, like the reed mats, produced in the same small-scale fashion, are part of the Cap Bon tradition. There are many *kouttab* and *zaouia*, indicating the importance of Beni Khiar as a long established centre of Koranic learning.

Four kilometres from the town is a small attractive lake. It is long and narrow, but the water is clear and deep.

Natural gas has been located in the area of **Es Somaa**, eight kilometres north of Nabeul and at **Belli**, some 20 kilometres west of Nabeul. A gas flare amidst the fields indicates production is underway.

Hammamet الحمامات

Population: 100,000
Phone code: 02
Colour map 1, grid B5

Tourism in Tunisia would not be where it is today without Hammamet. In the first half of the 20th century, visitors discovered a tiny médina, the Mediterranean lapping its honey-coloured walls. Fishermen pulled their boats up on fine white sand, every local family had a shady orchard. The microclimate of Hammamet was discovered by European aesthetes in the 1930s. They indulged themselves with homes of cool vaulted rooms and gardens of cypresses, orange trees and plunge pools. The first tourist hotels were built in this spirit, their silhouettes carefully concealed behind the tree-line. The 1990s saw new construction on an unprecedented scale. Bed capacity will be more than doubled in the new southern hotel zone. Hammamet is now a sprawling town. The microclimate and the beach are still the same, however. In odd corners, traces of the delicate simplicity of old Hammamet have survived the convulsion of mass property development.

Ins and outs

Getting there Hammamet, located 65 km from Tunis, is easily accessible by public transport, there being buses, louages and trains. If you arrive on a package, there will be a fairly quick transfer (say 1 hour 15 minutes maximum) from Tunis-Carthage airport. Buses and louages come into the central bus-station. The train station is a bit of a way out of the centre.

Getting around There are 5 main tourist areas in Hammamet: the M'rezga Zone Touristique Nord, north of the town, the town centre proper centring on the médina (hotels here include the *Alya*, the *Bel Azur*, the *Bellevue*, the *Yasmina* and the *Résidence Hammamet*), another zone touristique southwest of the médina with the oldest hotels (*Les Orangers, Le Miramar*, etc), the Zone Touristique Sud (*Hotel Sheraton*, etc) and finally the new Hammamet-Sud development. Taxis are the way to get from zone to zone. Children will probably like the noddy-train. The tourist information office is at 32 Av Habib Bourguiba, by the new shopping complex in town centre, T280423.

History and background

Hammamet was known as **Pupput** to the Romans. It was a stopping point on the Roman road which linked Carthage to Hadrumetum. The city developed as a result of the expansion of agriculture and maritime trade and also thanks to the generous sponsorship of a wealthy patron, Salvius Julianus. Subsequent 'visitors' included the Sicilians, the Spaniards and the Ottoman Turks.

Today Hammamet is one of the leading tourist resorts in Tunisia, along with Sousse and Djerba. In the 1950s, there was little more than a sleepy village adjoining a beautiful beach. There were two hotels. The locals prospered quietly on agriculture, fishing, crafts including weaving and embroidery and the production of orange flower essence. Elegant Italians and others of taste acquired discreet homes in the ramparts of the médina or in the citrus groves.

Tourism took off in the 1970s. One of Hammamet's first hotels, the *Phoenicia*, was designed by presidential architect Cacoub. A 1st batch of hotels, including *Les Orangers, Le Miramar* and *Le Fourati*, adopted the garden-hotel concept, with the buildings concealed in extensive grounds. In the 1980s, a 2nd major tourist zone was launched at M'rezga, north of Hammamet. The latest phase, Hammamet Sud, constructed on a salt marsh, is on an entirely new scale. A 4-lane boulevard separates the beach from the 1st line of hotels, all 5-star. Glitz is the order of the day, the lobbies are decorated in styles ranging from the Louis-Farouk to an indeterminate marble opulence. The centrepiece of the zone will be an artificial mini-médina. The long term results of this development remain to be seen - notably on the beach. One effect may be to create a demand for the simpler and more central older hotels, which, suitably upgraded, may be tempted to move upmarket.

Hammamet now welcomes tourists in their thousands. On a bedrock of conservative Cap Bon rural life, a Euro-structure of mass tourism has grown up. The days of the peaceful fishing village are long gone. There is a German brewery across the car park from the minaret, and on summer evenings, central Hammamet is as gridlocked as downtown Tunis. The town now stretches over 2 km north inland and some 7 km along the coast.

Porte de hammam (Hammamet)

Sights

Driving through Hammamet, here and there you will see studded doors set in white-washed walls over which the greenery spills, indications that here is an upscale home enshaded by giant eucalyptus and gnarly fig trees. You can, however, visit the former villa of millionaire aesthete **Georges Sebastian**. In 1959, the property was bought by the state and made into an International Cultural Centre (see below). The caretaker will show you round. The lounge is worth seeing with its long table and simple wrought

The Villa Sébastian and the International Culture Centre

Cap Bon Peninsula

iron chairs and the walls hung with some contemporary Tunisian paintings. The novel four-seater sunken bath is the shape of a cross (presumably mixed bathing – all very avant-garde) rather like four hip baths. The caretaker will operate the water system. (A similar style of bath can be seen at Kerkaouane.) The rather small guest bedroom can be viewed. Here Von Arnim, Rommel, Montgomery and Churchill were accommodated as the varying fortunes of the Second World War permitted, no doubt making maximum use of the beach in between bouts of moving counters around on a large map of North Africa. ■ *0830-1800 daily except Monday. Entrance 1Dt, photography 1Dt.*

In summer, you might also try to get to a show at the open-air theatre built in the grounds. The annual **International Festival**, held here in July/August, had ambitions to be a summer showcase for the performing arts, with dance, theatre and music all on view. The theatre was the brainchild of Cecyl Hourani, one of President Bourguiba's advisors, and Ali Ben Ayed, the country's leading actor and descendant of a noble family. Bourguiba, who had enjoyed amateur dramatics in his youth, approved the project, and the theatre, Greek and open-air in design, went up in the 1960s. In its heyday, the festival attracted North African dramatists like Saddiki and Kaki, and productions by Peter

Hammamet overview

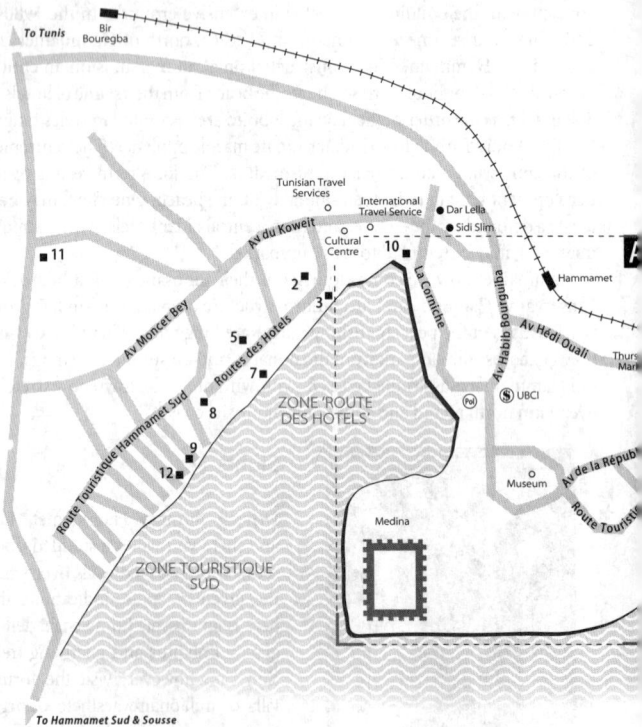

Related maps A Hammamet, page 165

■ Sleeping
1 Abou Nawas   4 Hammamet Club   7 Miramar
2 Bennila   5 Le Hammamet   8 Les Orangers Beach
3 Continental   6 Manar   9 Phénicia

Brook, Littlewood and Béjart. Ali Ben Ayed staged *Othello* there in Arabic, playing the title-role. Unfortunately, Ben Ayed died before his time, and the festival rather lost direction. Today, you might catch summer performances by raï singers like Faudel. Other recent performers have included Césaria Evora, the bare-foot diva of Cap Vert, and the odd jazz band.

The modern town has kept a little of its charm, even though changes are going ahead apace. The most recent victim was the one time Hotel de France, a fine 1920s building with a history. Handily opposite the médina there is a commercial centre (you will find the banks with cashpoints (the BIAT) and a supermarket here). The médina, surrounded by its walls and lying adjacent to the sea, manages to maintain a certain mystique. The **beach** continues to be an attraction; to the east, from the cemetery up towards the hotel region it is of fine white sand, some 30 metres wide with safe bathing. Escape from the tourist shops and walk around the small back streets. On the beach, there might be some fishermen picturesquely mending their nets, but fishing no longer has the importance of earlier days and some of the boats on the beach are more attractive than they are seaworthy.

Central Hammamet

Stepping off the main street, Avenue de la République, for a glimpse of the real Hammamet will reveal a host of small workshops and food shops, selling everything you could need from soap to live chickens. On the main streets, there are eclectically styled low-rise buildings; new villas are set among the older run-down dwellings off the main roads. Black-painted studs are used to make geometric designs on the doors; some of the motifs resemble old-fashioned country women's tattoos and symbols found on flat-weave textiles.

The médina

The small (but perfectly shaped) médina is the main landmark in Hammamet, built right on the beach. Originally constructed in 904, frequently damaged and restored, the walls protect the Great Mosque and narrow, winding streets. Near the kasbah these contain numerous stalls intent on attracting the tourists. The rest of the médina is made up of private dwellings; the impressive doors set into the otherwise blank walls are an attraction in their own right. The most exclusive homes tend to be on the sea-facing side of the médina, the mystique of the waves lapping the walls, gone today now that a walkway has been constructed.

To Nabeul

Av de la Libération

Route Touristique Hammamet

ZONE TOURISTIQUE
NORD, MREZGA

Hammamet Nord

Mediterranean Sea

10 Résidence La Paix
11 Samaris Camping
12 Sheraton

Cap Bon Peninsula

☛ *Thalassotherapy*

One of the most comprehensive ranges of treatment backed up with good organization is the Bio Azur centre in the grounds of Hotel Bel Azur, best known for its heated seawater treatments of rheumatism, arthritis, gout, backache, nicotine dependency, stress and for slimming and post-natal depression. Cost of any four treatments per day is 75Dt.

Individual treatments such as a total marine mud bath 25Dt, general massage 25Dt, local massage 15Dt are only three of the total 25 treatments on offer. A beauty salon forms an integral part of the centre providing facial treatments – from an anti-wrinkle course 220Dt to an evening makeup 20Dt. Contact Centre de Thalassotherapy Bio Azur, Hammamet, T2788500.

Other centres are Abou Nawas Abou Jaâfar in Sousse opened 1993, Gammarth (Résidence) and Djerba (planned). Hammamet-Sud has thalassotherapy in the vast Hotel Amilcar.

The médina contains many reminders of the holy men who spent time in Hammamet. Among them is **Sidi Bou Hadid** (12th century) who may have come from Morocco, perhaps Sakiet el Hamra. It is said that shortly before he died he instructed his family to put his corpse into a coffin and throw it into the sea. He wanted the waves and currents to decide on his final resting place. His tomb was to be built where his coffin was washed ashore. Legend has it that the sea spirits built his tomb by the town walls, from where he can keep watch over the Gulf of Hammamet. For this reason he has become the particular saint of the fishermen who make offerings to him and in times of real danger call on his assistance. He is said to be buried in the médina in the shrine which bears his name, right under the ramparts. Like the former entrance to the shrine of Sidi Bou Saïd up in Tunis, this today functions as a very popular café, the romantic place to watch the sun go down over the sea.

Dar Hammamet
The Dar Hammamet in the médina is a **Museum of Traditional Dress**. Not really a museum, more of a half-converted house. The three rooms have an interesting collection of traditional female clothing and wedding garments. One room is set out as a bedroom. There are additional costumes in the cabinets. ■ *Entry 1.5Dt for adults, 0.5Dt children under 10 years, open 0900-1700 every day of the year, T281206.* Enter from the square by the cemetery or follow the signs by the sea front. This is another place recommended for watching the sunset from the roof.

Great Mosque
The Great Mosque is most easily reached through the gate from the market place from where the minaret can be seen. It is not outstanding, but is obvious by its white square tower where the upper part and just below the crenelations it is covered with yellow tiles patterned in black. At ground level in the white wall there are several light brown wooden doors set in a stone surround. On each is a clear message in four European languages to keep out.

Kasbah
The Kasbah has ancient origins, as you might expect. It was first constructed between the end of the ninth and the beginning of the 10th centuries (between 893 and 904) under the Aghlabite Dynasty. The walls were recently restored, with lots of new pointing. The building you see today, filling the western corner of the médina, dates back to the middle of the 15th century (between 1463 and 1474) and was built while the Hafsids were in power. Its restored walls rise over the surrounding souvenir shops. There are some splendid views to the northwest over the the Gulf of Hammamet, the beach and the garish shopping

centre with its oversized signs and to the southwest over the Mediterranean. The médina's walls practically rise out of the water. To the west you might pick out the Djebel Zaghouan (1,295 metres). These views from the walkway and the battlements are certainly worth the 1Dt entrance fee (photography free). Situated in the north corner of the kasbah is a squat tower on which is a small café (there are many pleasanter places), while the inner courtyard is bare apart from a few trees which provide welcome shade in the summer. There are three cannons and several horse-drawn ploughs on display but no museum.

Next to the car park outside the médina, the tall white modern memorial, sweeping skywards, commemorates the dead of the Second World War. Adjacent to it, on the wall forming the boundary between the market place and the cemetery, is a high relief frieze depicting the horrors of war.

The war memorial

The ancient town of Purput, a staging post on the road from Carthage to Hadrumetum (modern Sousse), has become a small archaeological site next to the Hotel Samira Beach. The remains are slight, but of importance. There are some fine late Roman mosaics here, and a good deal has been written about their hidden symbolism. ■ *Entrance 1Dt, open daily summer 0800-1300 and 1500-1900, winter 0830-1730.*

Ancient Pupput

Cap Bon Peninsula

Hammamet centre

■ Sleeping	7 Khella	● Eating
1 Alya	8 La Residence	1 Angolo Verde
2 Bel Azur	9 Milano	2 Brauhaus
3 Bellevue	10 Olympia	3 Café Sidi Bou Hadid
4 Dar Hayet	11 Sahbi	4 Canari-Tutti Frutti
5 Ideal Camping	12 Yasmina	
6 Kacem Centre	13 Youth Hostel	

N

0 metres 200
0 yards 218

Essentials

Sleeping

Phone code: 02

Hammamet has few independent travellers, and there are few rock-bottom cheap places to stay. Having said that, the package market is fickle, and outside the high-season, it may be possible to pick up some very good deals indeed. It may be that with the doubling of its bed capacity, Hammamet has overreached itself, in which case there should be reasonable rates in some of the older hotels in need of a little refurbishment. Note however that by booking a package, you get a few days on a clean beach and a good base from which to explore Tunisia. Given the huge number of hotels at Hammamet, the following is just a selection.

Town centre **B** *Hotel Bel Azur*, T280544, F280275, Av Assad Ibn el Fourat, about 2½ km north of town centre. 620 beds, located on the water's edge in extensive (10 hectares) landscaped grounds, very high standard, all sports facilities available. **B** *Hotel Kacem Centre*, Av Habib Bourguiba, near train station, T279580, F279588. 67 rooms with 2 ring hob and fridge, crockery and utensils, 2 pools, roof top terrace with BBQ, a/c, 800m to private beach shared with *Yasmina*, restaurant, fitness centre. **B** *Hotel la Résidence*, 72 Av Habib Bourguiba, T280406, F280396. Moorish style, 184 rooms with 2 ring hob, fridge, utensils and crockery, roof top pool heated in winter, full a/c, restaurant, 10 mins from beach, 4 km to golf. **B** *Hotel Yasmina*, Av Bourguiba, T280022, F280593. Attractive early 1970s hotel. Small buildings in pleasant grounds with mature shade trees. Nice pool. Fine view over beach to the old town. Pleasant, slightly faded style. Central but peaceful location. Recommended. **C** *Hotel Khella*, Av de la République, T283900. 10 mins walk from médina, hence quiet, 71 rooms with bath, a/c, heating, good, clean, modern hotel. **C** *Milano*, T280768, rue des Fontaines beds. A small pension type place not too far from the beach west of the centre. **C** *Hotel Olympia*, Av Des Nations Unies, T280622, F283142. 36 rooms with shower and heating, no restaurant but many in vicinity, a clean, tidy hotel. **D** *Hotel Alya*, rue Ali Belhaouane, T280218, F282365. Central, very clean, half the rooms look over the médina, the others over a street, roof terrace, bar, 300m from beach. **D** *Hotel Bellevue*, Blvd Ibn el Fourat, T281121, F283156. Beach, central, clean rooms, most with view. **D** *Hotel Sahbi*, in town centre, T280807. Central, 200m from beach, pleasant large rooms, some with views.

Close to the centre (Hammamet Plage/Rue de Nevers) **A** *Dar Hayet*, 10 mins walk along the beach from Kasbah, T283399. Decor outstanding, comfort superb. Pool small, no garden, but you are right on the beach. Perhaps the only establishment in Hammamet that can justifiably be termed a *hôtel de charme*. **A** *Hotel Miramar*, rue de Nevers, T280344, F280586, 3 km west of Hammamet centre. Gardens lead on to beach, all facilities expected, this is one of the original tourist hotels that has recently been extended, make sure to get a room in the newer part as those in the older part are showing their age (this part only **B** standard) and the a/c is noisy. **B** *Hotel Continental*, T280220, F280409. Right on the beach, a/c, with bath, terrace, restaurant, bar, covered pool, TV, shop, boutiques, sauna, fitness room, tennis, watersports, shares with adjacent *Hotel Parc Plage*, all facilities. Good bargains available out of season. **B** *Hotel Fourati*, rue de Nevers, T280388, F280508, 3 km west of town centre. Enter through gardens to reception, gardens lead down to beach, 772 beds, all facilities, 1 heated indoor pool, 2 outdoor pools. **B** *Hotel Hammamet*, rue de Nevers, T280366, F282105, 3 km west of town centre. Of high standard but does not front the beach which is about 5-mins walk away, 674 rooms, all services include a/c and heating, 1 heated indoor pool, 1 outdoor pool. Too little garden on this overbuilt site. **B** *Hotel Les Orangers/Hotel Les Orangers Beach*, rue de Nevers, T280144, F280157. 766 beds in total, typical, rather overrated tourist hotel providing all facilities which are shared between the 2 establishments, indoor pool, outdoor pool, etc. Again, the site is far too built up, producing a claustrophobic feel. **B** *Bennila*, T280356. Simple pension not far from Centre culturel international. (Coming from Hammamet, turn left after the CCI and bank, Bennila is on your right.) Small, clean, popular place with a swimming pool. Short walk to beach. **B** *Résidence de la Paix*, off the Corniche Road, T283400/283000, F2828710. Self-catering. Apt 2 persons 75Dt a night in summer. Unattractive lawn area at the back, minute first floor pool. Play area for kids. 50 metres from beach. **D** *Les Citronniers*, route des Hotels, by *Hotel Bennila*, T281650, F282601. Modern, very close to beach, no views, barbecue, drinks, food on the beach.

Zone Touristique Nord (M'rezga) **A** *Hotel Abou Nawas*, T281344, F281089. The usual good hotel product from the local Abou Nawas. Indoor pool, gardens, etc. All a bit lacking in soul. On the beach. **A** *Hotel Manar*, route touristique nord, T281333, F280772. 200 rooms, 6 floors, a/c, 2 pools, 5 tennis courts, banks, shops, restaurants. **B** *Hotel Hammamet-Club*, route Touristique, T281882, F281670. 337 rooms on 2 floors, a/c, very good, beach, indoor pool complex, outdoor Olympic size pool, many activities, good food, large rooms facing the sea.

Zone Touristique Sud **A** *Hotel Phénicia*, Av Moncef Bey, T226331, F280337. Designed by former presidential architect Cacoub in the late 1960s, and once somewhat isolated, 7 km west of Hammamet. 14 hectares of garden fronting on to the beach, 370 rooms including suites, all facilities plus indoor heated pool which connects to outside pool, also separate outside pool, luxurious reception lounge, this hotel is very highly recommended in its price range. **A** *Sheraton*, T225555, F227301, Av Moncef Bey. Has a very good name with expatriates. Large, simply furnished rooms in grounds next to the beach. Usual water-based activities on offer.

Hammamet-Sud (Hammamet-Yasmine, a new zone of truly gigantesque proportions) This is the latest addition to Hammamet's hotel zones. And vast it is. Be warned: construction works on the marina and further hotels mean that building will be in progress until at least 2003. The area is too new for the hotels to have mature grounds. To get to the centre you will need to take taxis. If you are booking here for a holiday with children, note that many of the hotels are a considerable way from the beach, and you will have at least 1 main road to cross, if not 2. Prefer the older hotels in Hammamet-Plage. **AL** *Hasdrubal Thalassa*, T248800. A very, very, very big hotel. If you have the money to pay their prices, then you probably rent Caribbean islands for your holidays anyway. Prefer one of the less pretentious places nearer to Hammamet. **A** *Hotel Flora Park*, Hammamet Sud, T227727 F226601, hotel.florapark@planet.tn. Decorated by the same team as the Dar Hayet. Elegant, part of the Spanish Tryp Hotels chain. One of the best if you are going to stay in this part of Hammamet, but you have 2 main roads to cross to get to the beach. **A** *Hotel Mehari*, T249155. Large 5-star hotel on the seafront road which feels like a multi-storey city-centre hotel. Too formal to be a relaxing beach hotel, though might be good for small conferences. All the usual facilities. Tiny indoor pool and small curvy rooftop pool. Kids' play area but not much garden. **A** *Marina Palace*, T248748. And yet another overblown hotel in the concrete expanses of Hammamet-Sud. Small pool hopeless for real swimming, service indifferent, if you are with kids, you will have the main Corniche Road to cross to get to the beach. **B** *Hostellerie L'Ecrin*, T248465, F227375, a/c. Prices around 50Dt per person/night in the high season. Despite being some way from the beach, this is one of the most attractive hotels in Hammamet-Sud. The reception is elegant and if you are on a winter break, you'll find a log fire in the main bar. The rooms are on the small side, but nicely decorated, a/c. Recommended. **B** *Hotel Zakarya*, T248500, F248551, 46 rooms. Pleasant small hotel next to the *Hotel Flora Park*. Disadvantage: 2 main roads to cross to get to the beach.

Next to the autoroute C *Hotel Samaris*, 6 km from town on the P1 road to Tunis, T226353. Family run hotel and campsite to the west of town but convenient after coming off the motorway. Don't be put off by the approach for once inside there is a warm welcome from the owner. The hotel lobby and reception are decorated in traditional style. To the right is the comfortable small restaurant while straight ahead is the terrace where meals can be served. The centrepiece is an ancient olive press, in perfect condition, found on the site. The 20 rooms, situated round the courtyard, near the main building, are simply furnished with twin beds, a/c, heating, shower and wc. There are 3 studios which sleep 4 people and have cooking facilities at 50Dt per day. The thick stone walls make this a rarity: a quiet hotel. **Camping** Adjacent to Samaris in 2 ha enclosed site, electricity, toilets and showers, shares the pool. Fees 3Dt per person; 1.5Dt per car and per tent; 2.5Dt per caravan. The beach is 5 mins by car.

Apartments for rent Try the villa opposite the *Hotel Alya* (see above). Also, look out for signs *appartement/studios à louer* on the Rue de la Corniche.

Camping *Ideal Camping*, 34 Av de la République, T280302. Adequate, restaurant, electric hook-ups, shaded area, book in summer, tent 2.5Dt, car 2.5Dt, person 1.5Dt per night. **Youth hostel** T280440. 100 beds, meals, central location, beside *Hotel Bellevue*.

Eating Hammamet is short on really classy places to eat, the sort where you start with a large gin and tonic on a wonderful terrace overlooking the sea. There are plenty of pizzerias, however, and a reasonable meal with wine can be had at 1 of the places at the Centre Commercial overlooking a busy road, the sea and the médina.

Expensive *Restaurant Achour*, T280140. Central, rue Ali Belhouane, very good reputation, the best fish restaurant in Hammamet, terrace. *Chateau Neuf*, Centre Sunset City, T282976. *La Cupola*, Av du Koweit, T281138. *Dar Lella*, Rue Patrice Lumumba, T280871. Speciality *musli allouche*, oven-baked lamb. A stylish place once upon a time. Small garden area – a little overpriced. *Dar Sidi*, Centre Khayem, T289985. *Fiesta*, Centre Commercial, T280985. *Oasis*, Feten Centre, T227881. *La Pergola*, Centre Commercial. Perhaps the best in this central area, T280993. *Le Pomodoro*, downtown Hammamet, near the palm-tree esplanade. Vastly overrated, small portions.

Mid-range *Angolo Verde*, on Ali Belhaouane, near Hotel Alya, T262641. Good *plats du jour*, excellent pasta, good service. Nice terrace and fine ice cream from the gelateria next door. Recommended. *Aquarium*, Av des Nations Unies, T282449. *Restaurant Barberousse*, in the médina, terrace, pleasant decor, very touristy. *Le Grand Bleu*, downtown Hammamet, tables on beach under parasols. Access off main palm-tree esplanade next to syndicat d'initiative. Lunchtime menu 10Dt. *Jugurtha*, Av des Nations Unies, T280432. *La Médina*, in square near kasbah, T281728. Popular, pleasant Tunisian style café, seating 60 people, get a table on the terrace if possible for a fine view over the médina, beach and esplanade, especially interesting on market day, use the entrance from the seafront, sample price seafood salad 12Dt, royal couscous 7Dt. *La Brise*, Av de la République, close to médina. No alcohol, quantity rather than quality. Next to *Le Palmier Café Bar* (rough and ready). *La Sirene*, Av Assad Ibn el Fourat, right on beach opposite sports stadium, 10-15 mins walk from town so very quiet.

Cheap *Pizzeria*, T80825. Shopping Centre, central. *Restaurant de la Poste*, central square, opposite the médina. Terrace has a great view over the médina and the golf course, good food, quite cheap. *La Rosa*, Av du Koweit, T282864. *Shehrazade*, Av des Nationes Unies, T280436. Several cheap cafés and restaurants overlook the esplanade and the beach.

At some time during your stay in Hammamet, you will wind up sitting on the terrace of the *Tutti Frutti* juice bar, at the junction of Av de la République and Av Ali Belhaouane. Look out for the pâtisserie next door. Try the *m'lebbes*, round mini-almond cakes with white icing. Just below the walls of the kasbah, next to the beach, is the **Café Sidi Bou Hadid**. Facing the square-faced central clock is the blokey **Café Hechiri**, its terrace shaded by mulberry trees. For ice cream, you have **Le Tiramisù**, next to the *Restaurant Angolo Verde* on Av Ali Belhaouane. A very good address.

Cafés & patisseries

Mainly to the south of Hammamet, on the road to Sousse, in the direction of the Route des Hotels. To see the offspring of Tunis bourgeoisie and wannabees, try *Le Ranch Club*, Av Moncef Bey. *Manhattan* also attracts a young crowd. *Le Guitoun*, although grotty, was a happening address in summer 1999 (drag-queen nights, etc). You also have *Le Calypso*, Av Moncef Bey, and **New Mexico** all in Hammamet Sud. Moving downmarket, try the *Garsa* (bar) on the main GP1 (route de Sousse), which attracts a mixed clientele of long-distance lorry drivers and the odd Italian tourist.

Bars & clubs

Apart from the obvious trinket places in the médina, there are not a whole lot of things to buy in Hammamet, so your credit cards can sleep easy. The following may be of some use :

Shopping

In the médina *Fella*. A fashion boutique in a rather 1970s sense of the term. Easily located on the main square in the médina, part of a converted house. Fella (lit: Arabian jasmine) was Madame Couture-Caftan back in the heady days of Hammamet's take-off as a tourist destination. Look out for the black-and-white enlargements of old fashion shows. Pick up something pricey to waft around the hotel in. There are a few bits of local embroidered clothing on display. Shop also has nice cotton beach towels. (**NB** There is a second *Fella* outlet on the Place Pasteur, Tunis-Belvédère.)

Elsewhere *Khamsa*. Small eclectic junk-cum-postcard shop on Av Bourguiba, almost opposite the primary school as you walk towards the Hotel Résidence. Can turn up some interesting things. *Er Rayhane*, on Av des Nations-Unies, T261914. Not far from the Centre culturel international. Essentially specializes in wrought iron (not easy to get on the plane). Also stocks large cotton throws and some ceramics. *Sous le soleil*, also on Av des Nations-Unies, T280297. Tasteful, simple ceramics, lamp-bases and rush-mat items from this small shop located a few metres along from *Er Rayhane*, on the Av des Nations-Unies, leading to the main road south to Sousse.

Miscellaneous Bookshop: there is a reasonable bookshop in the shopping centre, the Librairie Boudhina, opposite the médina, selling informative books in many European languages.

Hairdresser Short back and sides at *Bahles*, near *Hotel Alya* on rue du Stade.

Cinema In shopping centre, performances at 1500 and 2100. Prices 2Dt and 1.5Dt. **Hammam** Turkish bath (Bain Maure) near the Great Mosque in the médina. **Theatre** *Centre culturel International*, T280656, summer only, concerts and very occasionally plays in the open-air theatre.

Entertainment

All watersports are available, also horse (and camel!) riding, golf, tennis, and go-karting. Ask at any hotel. *Yasmin Golf Course*, TF226722, has 18 holes, 6,114m and par 72. *Cytrus Golf Course*, T226500, F226400, 2 18-hole courses of 6,175m at par 72, fees 28-30Dt per day. Hot air ballooning. *Leisure Centre*, T280656, Av Habib Bourguiba.

Sports

Cap Bon Peninsula

Transport **Local Car hire**: *Avis*, route de la Gare, T280164; *Europacar*, Av des Nations Unies, T280146; *Hertz*, Av des Hotels, opposite *Hotel Miramar*, T280187; *Intercar*, Av des Nations Unies, T280423; *Topcar*, Av des Nations Unies, T281247; *Tri Car*, Av Habib Bourguiba, T283580, F283576. **Cycle hire**: 2Dt per hr or 10Dt per day from *Hotel Kacem* Centre. **Taxi**: there is yellow taxi rank in front of the médina.

Long distance Train: there is 1 train daily to Tunis at 0603 and 2 to Nabeul at 1546, 1926, otherwise the nearest trains are at Bir Bou Regba reached by bus or louage. Information: T280174. From **Bir Bou Regba**: to Tunis at 0819, 1020, 1641, 1943 and 2100; to Sousse (Sfax and Gabès) 0700, 0816, 1304, 1500, 1609 and 1850. A Noddy Train provides a shuttle service from the hotels to the town centre on a leave-when-full basis. At slack times it waits by the médina for customers.

Now only 1 train each day operates from Tunis on the branch line to Hammamet. The main train station for both Hammamet and Nabeul is **Bir Bou Regba** where a fine new station building is under construction. The continuation of the journey is by taxi or bus, the fare to Hammamet being 4Dt. The 2nd class train ticket to Tunis is 4.6Dt. Take care at Bir Bou Rebka as the name is marked on the station building but not on the platform – and cannot therefore be seen by passengers on the train.

Bus: the bus and louage station is close to the médina, on Av de la République. Frequent departures for **Tunis**, **Sousse** and **Nabeul**. Hammamet to Nabeul to Hammamet from 0630-1915, every 30 mins; Hammamet to Kélibia at 0830, 1300, 1620 and 1720; Kélibia to Hammamet 0500, 0600, 0630 and 1445; Hammamet to El Haouaria 1720; El Haouaria to Hammamet 0525. All journeys to Korbus are via Soliman; to Monastir via Sousse at 0705; to Kairouan at 0620 with return from Kairouan at 1130; to Mahdia via Sousse at 0735, arriving Sousse at 1035; return from Mahdia at 1400 leaves Sousse at 1530; to Zaghouan (and El Fahs) at 0550, 1120, 1420 and 1720; to Tunis at 0530, 0650, 0715, 0930, 1045, 1246, 1300, 1500 with return buses at 0730, 0915, 0930, 1230, 1430, 1450, 1730, 1815, 1830. The **louage** station is on Av Mongi Slim, off Av de la République.

Directory **Banks** Money can be changed in the big hotels or the banks in the centre of town. *BT*, Av Habib Bourguiba. *STB*, Av du Koweit, has automatic cash dispenser (dinars) for Visa and Mastercard. *UIB*, Av des Nations Unies, an extension of Av du Koweit. There is a bank in the médina, in the square by the kasbah which is open Sun when all other banks are closed. **Communications** Area code: 02. **Post Office**: Av de la République, T250598. Mon-Sat 0730-1230 and 1700-1900 in summer, winter 0800-1200 and 1500-1800. Sun always 0900-1100. **Medical services** Chemist: open nights, two on Av de la République, T280876 or T280257. **Places of worship** Catholic: 13 rue du Lycée, off rue du Stade, adjacent to college, marked Eglise Catholique in ceramic tiles. The church, built in traditional Arab style, is only open for service Sat 1700 and Sun 1100, but the tree shaded garden and bench seats are available at all times. Contact the priest at Grombalia, T255232 (winter) and Hammamet T280865 (summer). Protestant services are also held here. Contact Pastor Dobson at Sousse médina, T03-224073. **Market** Market day – Thur. **Tour companies & travel agents** *Carthage Tours*, rue Dag Hammarskjold, T281926, F281166. *Hammamet Travel Service*, rue Dag Hammarskjold, T280193, F281936. *Royal Travel Club*, rue de Nevers, T281413, F281488. *Tourafrica*, rue Dag Hammarskjold, T280446, F278225. *Tunisia Explorer*, Av des Nations Unies, T283275, F282766. *Tunisian Travel Service*, Av des Nations Unies, T280040. *Visit Tunisia*, 48 Av du Koweit, T287427, F283120. *Voyages Loisirs Tourisme*, Av Habib Bourguiba, T224600-900, F223777. **Useful Addresses** Police: Av Habib Bourguiba, T280079. Toilets: are situated at the gate from the market place towards the mosque, shared entrance but separate inside. Only for an emergency.

Around Hammamet

Inland from Hammamet, to the west and south, are a number of easily reached villages and Roman sites which are definitely worthwhile if you have your own transport. **Zaghouan** (see previous chapter) is a short bus ride away, while you could easily take in the villages of **Hammam Jedidi**, **Jéradou** and **Zriba** (see chapter 3, too), or, more ambitiously, the **Kène** craft village (good textile collection), north of Bou Ficha, the pleasant Roman site of **Phéradi Maius**, and most spectacularly, **Takrouna** on its rocky outcrop. **Enfida** has a museum with a few finds from the region.

The white villages: Bou Ficha, Takrouna, Sidi Khélifa and Sidi Jedidi

For Le Corbusier, whitewash was as old as human buildings. Right from the earliest times, people used lime-wash for their homes, creating a clean environment and a pleasing aesthetic effect. In the villages of the Tunisian coast, lime was used to good effect on the barrel vaults used to roof the little rectangular houses. In villages south of Hammamet, you can see some good examples of Tunisian rural building, not all (as yet) defigured by imported reinforced concrete post and slab technology.

Getting to the 'white villages' of the hinterland of Hammamet is slow without your own transport. Perhaps **Takrouna** is the best, although **Zriba** (see chapter 3) is well worthwhile, and there is a possibility of overnighting at the springs of Hammam Zriba.

If you are driving, take the GP1 south of Hammamet towards **Bou Ficha**. Without going into the town, you will come to the white buildings of the Kène craft village on your right, behind a line of eucalyptus trees. The word *kène* means 'was' in Arabic. Here the reference is *kène min zaman*, 'once upon a time', and the village, the brainchild of civil engineer Slah Smaoui, a man deeply attached to the region, houses craft-workshops, museum displays and a restaurant-café (food nothing special). There is plenty of parking, and it will take you close on 45 minutes to look around thoroughly. On summer evenings, displays of local folklore with dinner under a tent are organized in an open area adjacent to the village. There may even be an authentic local lady under the tent to give you a *harkous* (henna dot) pattern on your hand. ■ *T03-252110, F03-252112, entrance 2Dt, under 15s no charge.*

Along with watching the various craftspeople, including weavers, if they are at work, the best part of the village is probably the textile collection, well-displayed and representative of most regions of Tunisia. Here, without badgering, you can get a feel for what the country's flat-weave or *kelim* carpets are like. There are *mergoums*, too, and a fine collection of women's costumes, including tunics with elaborate silk appliqué work and lace and velvet waistcoats from Hammamet and Sousse. Appliqué sequin designs were another feature, appreciated in more 'modern' urban areas.

The Kène craft village is an almost unique example of private money going into a carefully put together heritage project. The old forms of the region's traditional architecture have been put to new use to good effect.

Kène craft village

Cap Bon Peninsula

Sidi Khélifa &
Phéradi Maius

A 20 minute drive from Kène, and you are at **Sidi Khélifa**, where there are some pleasant Roman ruins and a model village, constructed by the Ministry of Public Works to plans by Smaoui. Start, however, with the Roman site, the former Phéradi Maius, where major excavations were first undertaken back in 1966. In 1972, the baths were brought to light. There is a triumphal arch and up on the hill the ruins of what might have been a temple, later transformed into a small fort. The stone-flagged forum, with what must have been tiny lock-up shops around it, is particularly atmospheric. There is also a nymphaeum, 'a temple of the waters'. Given the quality of the spring water, this is entirely understandable. Bring a plastic bottle so you can fill up at the spring of Aïn Khélifa, close to the site, which you should be able to spot by the concrete well-head and the presence of someone filling up a container of some kind. The spring water has a beautiful, soft feel in the mouth. After the ruins, have a look at the new model village north of the original settlement. The aim was to show what could be done with traditional technology, and you have to admit, the project is rather successful. The proof, however, of such operations, is in the subsequent building. Can people still be persuaded to use the original, local technologies? Or would they really rather have houses with big balconies and individualized decorative features?

Takrouna

After Sidi Khélifa, head back for the GP1 and down to **Enfida** (ex-Enfidaville), famous in the 19th century for various financial scandals surrounding the ownership of the great Enfida estate. In the mid-20th century, Enfida, and the neighbouring hill-crest village of Takrouna, were the scenes of some fierce fighting during the Second World War. You could take a quick look at the town museum, housed in the former French church, which has a collection of stelae and mosaics.

The main aim of being here, however, is to get to **Takrouna**, a village of vaulted houses perched in the region's best defensive position high above the plain. (To get there, take the Zaghouan turn-off ; there may be a *nakl reefee* local mini-bus running up to the village.) Takrouna is now on the tourist trail, as it should be, given its beautiful location. The road climbs steeply up the rocky hill, past olive trees and prickly pears. From the top is a breathtaking view towards Djebel Zaghouan and the surrounding lands. As at Zriba and Jeradou, the main building of the village besides the mosque is the Zaouia of Sidi Abdel Kader, witness to the influence of the Kadiriya *tarika* or brotherhood last century.

The people of Takrouna make a living from agriculture and making the alfa mats used in the oil presses. As in other rural areas, the men may migrate to the building sites of the growing tourist towns, or work as seasonal labour in the hotels. At Takrouna, you may notice a number of blond kids, as is the case in quite a number of Tunisia's remoter hill villages, once peopled almost exclusively by Berber stock.

North from
Takrouna

From Takrouna, head north along the C133 to **Aïn Mdeker**, of which are the extensive remains of ancient Mediccera (for enthusiasts only, to be honest). There are the remains of a Byzantine wall. For yet more unspectacular ruins, you have **Aïn Batria**, site of ancient Biia, 20 kilometres north of Takrouna along the same road. The best plan, however, is to head on up to **Zriba-Village** (**Ezzriba**), described in the previous chapter. (Turn left for **Hammam Zriba**, have a look around, and then have a shot at getting some way to the old village of Zriba (Zriba El Alya, unsignposted), some five kilometres up in the hills along the piste which turns left before the quarry as you come into Hammam Zriba.)

To return to Hammamet, you can continue on to **Zaghouan** (about 40 kilometres in all from Takrouna), and then head back coastwards along the C28 which will take you across farmland via Hammam Jedidi and Sidi Jedidi. (Distance Zaghouan to Hammamet 35 kilometres.) **Hammam Jedidi** is another place which has sprung up thanks to the hot springs. It is popular with Tunisian families, and if you are interested in doing a tour of minor spa towns, it probably should be on your itinerary. Families rent or own small vaulted houses supplied with spring water.

Sidi Jedidi, about 12 kilometres west of Hammamet, is named after a holy man of Moroccan birth called Cheikh Mohammed Jedidi who lived in the region. He was favoured by Mohammed Ben Hassan, a Hafsid prince, who gave him 18,000 hectares on which this hamlet stands. Looking round for something to fill out their day-excursions, tour operators began to offer a visit to 'a typical country market' at Sidi Jedidi. But with the presence of tourism, the nature of the market has changed. But the rural communities are increasingly prosperous, and no longer have to do so much self-provisioning. There is plenty of plastic and ordinary mass-produced clothing on offer.

Sidi Jedidi

Cap Bon Peninsula

Hammamet to Tunis: rolling countryside and Mussolini's villa

Heading northwest to Tunis from Hammamet there are two parallel roads, the A1 autoroute and the P1 trunk road. The A1 is a toll road, and the first *péage* is south of Tunis near Mornag (1Dt to pay here for an ordinary car). At Hammamet, there are two access points for the autoroute, one from the main road south, close to the GP1, the other from the Hammamet Nord zone. The A1 takes you through rolling countryside with views towards the distant mountains. Nearer peaks include **Djebel Bou Kornine** (Two Horns) at 576 metres to the east, part of a national park, and **Djebel Ressas** (Mountain of Lead) at 795 metres, about half way to Tunis. Do not relax your concentration as sheep still graze the verges. The GP1 provides a slower journey through small towns like Grombalia. Another option is to take the train, which runs beside the GP1 most of the way. As the carriages are high up, you have quite a good view of the vineyards near Grombalia.

Should you want to visit a 'natural' local market, then the Wednesday market at **Bou Argoub**, on the GP1, 17 kilometres north of Hammamet, might do. There are no trinkets or souvenirs for tourists here. There are (as yet) no tourists. Many of the dwellings in this region and on towards Grombalia are Italian style, with pitched roofs and clay tiles. The railway station buildings at Fondouk Djedid, Grombalia and Bou Argoub are typical country-town Italian, especially the latter with its two storeys surmounted by a sloping roof and its shuttered windows. The whitewashed walls and blue-painted woodwork give a local touch to a sleepy piece of Italian provincial building.

The unusual feature of this journey back up to Tunis is the presence of the **Villa du Zodiaque**, built for Benito **Mussolini** on a low rise to the west of the GP1, a few kilometres south of Grombalia. (Look out for signs to the Cité Hached, a small self-built housing area left of the GP1 as you go north. Head up the unsurfaced track past the new houses.) The building, with its domed tower, is easily visible across the fields from the A1 as well.

Back in the 1930s, it would seem that some wealthy Italian farmer had the idea of constructing the villa for the Duce. Tunisia with its large Italian population was a theatre for Franco-Italian rivalry in the years leading up to the Second World War. With Mussolini in power, the Italian consul-general began to wield an influence as great as that of the French resident-général. No doubt the

Italian thought the Duce might take up residence there when he conquered Tunisia. The French, in reaction to the growing Italian threat, decided to give French nationality to any non-Muslim born on Tunisian soil.

The villa today survives in a sort of half-life. The structure is intact, although the finishing was extensively damaged when the building was used as a professional training school in the 1970s. Today, a caretaker lives in part of the ground floor, and he'll very kindly show you round for a small tip.

The Villa du Zodiaque is a fine example of the Italian modernist style. It is built to a perfectly round floor plan: the curve is queen here. A splendid circular galleried hall (used for receptions?) is topped by a simple dome set with tiny skylights as in an old-style Turkish bath. Access to the first floor rooms (which have magnificent views over the countryside) is via a staircase housed in a cylinder topped with a green-tiled dome. Inside, the most interesting feature are the mosaics. On the ground floor are animals (a giraffe, a wounded gazelle, an eagle) and people (a Roman soldier, an archer, a dancing woman, a bedouin woman, a Corsican head). Are these symbols of Italy's longed-for African empire? On the first floor are mosaic star signs – hence the name Villa du Zodiaque. Is this a reference to some Roman mosaic – or just a whimsical gesture to the owner's taste for astrology? Whatever, it is a shame that such a unique structure, as fine as Le Corbusier's Villa Savoye or Mallet-Steven's Villa Noailles at Hyères, be abandoned to its fate. A UFO of a building out in the fertile farmland of the Cap Bon, its finely-crafted forms have a simple, plastic elegance, refreshing after the para-Moorish social-housing style of the 1990s hotels.

Grombalia

With around 20,000 inhabitants, Grombalia, the Roman Colombaria is an important route centre and focus point for the surrounding agricultural region. Nothing remains of Roman days, and today the oldest remains here date from the 16th century, the time of the evacuation of Andalucia by the Moors. The oldest mosque here, built by one Mustapha Cardenas, dates from that time. He also found time to have a a public fountain and *hammam* built, as well as a beautiful dwelling for himself. The olive presses found here which date from that time indicate the quick growth in prosperity of the region.

It is in September that Grombalia has its annual moment of glory. A **Festival of the Grape** is held to celebrate the town's central position in wine and table grape production, for since protectoral times the main vineyards in the Cap Bon peninsula have been centred around the town. Until the 1960s, much of the wine was exported to France for blending and the vineyards covered a greater area than they do today. While the vine still plays an important part in the agricultural scene here there is less evidence of future development, few young vines being brought on for

la déco tunisien
Villa Zodiac
Grombalia

Tunisian wines

Tunisia produces a small selection of wines. Until recently, quality was somewhat irregular, given the lack of any deep-rooted savoir-faire. This is changing, however, with new equipment being introduced to control the vinification process and the arrival of new grape varieties.

On your way round a Tunisian supermarket's wine shelves or a restaurant menu, the reds are generally more reliable than the whites. Among the most palatable of wines in hotels and supermarkets are the Tebourba reds (try Vieux Magon) and the reds from Mornag (Haut Mornag). Sidi Saâd is the red in the trendy amphora shaped bottle. Of the many rosé wines few are unpalatable, and the Clairet de Bizerte has a loyal following. Of the cheapies,

Chateau Mornag is an old favourite, real builders' wine, in local parlance. White wines, on the whole, are more problematic, and the choice is generally limited to Ugni Blanc (dry) or the fuller Muscat Sec de Kélibia from the Cap Bon peninsula.

There are not a lot of alcohol outlets in Tunisia's cities, so buying wine can be quite an occasion. The supermarket wine section, especially on a Saturday afternoon, attracts an interesting cross-section of society, some of whom will have come from a long way off to make their weekly purchase. The atmosphere is hearty. The bottles have no need of stylish labelling, customers know the limited selection by heart. Note that wine sales will be off-limits to all but foreigners during the month of Ramadhan.

---

replacement or new vineyards. The vine produces a good crop for up to 50 years and then in reducing quantities for up to 100 years, so although it may look old and gnarled in the winter it will burst forth in the spring. Unlike the terraced fields of France and Germany the vineyards here are planted on flat ground.

Originally, back in the late 19th century, the spread of phylloxera on vines in mainland Europe encouraged grape-growing in Tunisia, though in the inter-war years phylloxera took its toll of Tunisian vineyards too. New grafted stocks were subsequently introduced. Today, wine production runs at between 200,000-400,000 hectolitres per year, two-thirds of which is consumed in Tunisia. The industry looks set to expand in the coming years as domestic demand grows, due to Tunisia's growing prosperity and the tourist industry. New grape varieties have been introduced thanks to some German joint-ventures, and these will be producing wines in the very near future.

As Grombalia is the centre of a vine growing region, there are many roadside stalls in the season and much activity when the grapes are ready for wine production. There is a large market for clothes and shoes each Monday in the street by the railway station. The goods are piled high on trestle tables, a lively affair. Unhindered by visitors, wine-growing Grombalia goes about its business.

Train Trains from Grombalia to **Tunis** (via Hammam Lif) 0634, 0717, 0823, 1451, 1655, 2103; Grombalia to **Nabeul** 1512, 1851; Grombal ia to **Sousse** with onward travel to Mahdia, Sfax, Gabès and Gafsa 0745, 0945, 1245, 1450, 1616, 1922. **Transport**

For a quick dip into the Tunisian hinterland, and if you have a hire-car, you might want to make a side-trip to Aïn Tébournok from Grombalia; take the road from Grombalia towards the Tunis-Sousse motorway, but continue straight across over the motorway bridge heading for Aïn Tebournouk (Tebournoug), a further 5.5 km westwards. The road runs gently upwards, pay great attention, as lorries thunder down from the brick works and quarries up in the hills. (This is where the building materials for Hammamet's new monster hotels are coming from.) About halfway to Aïn Tebournouk, you will see a splendid early 20th century farmer's residence up on your right. Overlooking **A short trip: Grombalia to Aïn Tébournok** vineyards and orchards, it signals the prosperity of the French and their farming methods in the region. Now abandoned, the house is worth a photo as a rare example of a 'neo-Moorish meets early 1900s French suburban' style. The house looks pretty haunted, too.

At Aïn Tebournouk, are the remains of an ancient Roman town, down on your left, just past the café. The site has been partly walled, to prevent further encroachments from new building. Clearly visible are the main temples - three rooms off a small esplanade, and a narrow paved street with a small honorific (?) arch. There are massive foundations of dressed stone, and plenty of rubble, indicating that this was yet another prosperous ancient settlement.

Once at Aïn Tébournok, it is worth continuing south to the **Barrage Masri** which shelters under Djebel el Behelil (556 metres), or on the return take the left turn to a smaller, and rather more attractive barrage (depending on the rainfall) which shelters under Djebel Makki (641 metres).

Northern Tunisia

5

Northern Tunisia

Inland, northern Tunisia has rolling landscapes reminiscent of Andalusia and impressive Roman sites, each with a unique character. **Dougga** stands with imperial confidence on a hillside overlooking a wide valley, while **Bulla Regia** has villas hidden underground to avoid the crushing summer heat. **Chemtou** was the quarry colony which exported fine golden marble to the temples of ancient Rome. Here and there are miscellaneous ancient bridges and Byzantine fortifications.

The coast between Bizerte and the Algerian border offers steep cliffs, small bays and secluded beaches, most well off the main routes. In the lee of the Khroumirie Mountains sits **Tabarka**, its fishing harbour built close to a fine Genoese fort. This is a town half-awaiting a mass tourist influx. Happily the region's short summer season (and infrastructure costs) has kept development to a minimum. In summer the temperature, although high, is far more bearable than in the south, thanks to the thickly wooded hills inland from the coast. Further east, under a couple of hours from Tunis, the **Bizerte** region has coastlines both rocky and sandy and the **Djebel Ichkeul National Park**. There are also some fine east-facing beaches at places with evocative names like **Raf Raf**, **Sounine** and **Cap Zbib**.

Background

The northern regions of Tunisia have a lot to offer the visitor. The distances are not great, the roads constantly being improved, and you can easily include the region on a circular tour of the country. The region has two main port-towns: Bizerte, with tree-lined avenues, petrol refineries, ship-repair and naval base; and Tabarka, important as the only major town in northwest Tunisia and being developed for tourism in a low-key sort of way. The coast divides into two main areas: the east-facing coast south of Bizerte, with several fine beaches; and the longer north-facing seabord, where many of the beaches are accessible only by four-wheel drive. Prevailing winds make the waters of the north-facing shores rougher. The coast here is often rocky, and this, coupled with the hills of the hinterland, has meant little development.

The coast running from Kalaât el Andalus to Bizerte has escaped mainstream tourist development as well. Most summer visitors are Tunisian residents abroad, as the region once exported large numbers of guest workers. Many have built holiday homes in once sleepy villages such as Raf Raf. Agriculture and fishing are still important but various light industries, including garment manufacture at Ras Djebel, have contributed to the massive expansion of Bizerte's satellite towns such as Menzel Jamil.

It remains to be seen whether anything more than standard three-star beach tourism can be developed for northern Tunisia. Diving is gaining popularity, and the Tabarka dive schools maintain a fair standard. In contrast to the mountain regions of Morocco, there is little local initiative to develop hill-walking, and no tradition of cheap local accommodation. There are also no signs of a network of long-distance footpaths being established. Summer 1999 saw a project to develop horse-trekking in the Tabarka area, but for the moment, more independent forms of tourism remain underdeveloped. The subsidy system does not work in their favour. For the local tourism companies, they lack the obvious investment potential of the beach hotel.

Numidian & Roman antiquity The inland areas of northern Tunisia have some fine ancient sites, easily covered with a hire car. The three outstanding sites are Dougga, Bulla Regia and Chemtou, and there are some more obscure destinations like Thuburnica near Ghardimaou, Trajan's bridge south of Béja and Mustis. In the spring, these sites are a botanist's delight, smothered as they are in wild flowers.

If you are travelling by public transport, then Dougga is easily visited from Tunis in a day (bus or louage from Bab Saâdoun, taxi or walk from Téboursouk). Without own transport, Bulla Regia and Chemtou have to be visited from Jendouba, there being *nakl reefee* mini-buses to the latter. With a car, if you got a very early start from Tunis, you could, with plenty of energy and preferably two drivers, do all three main sites. The best place to stay overnight would be in Kef or Aïn Draham. This might be an overdose of ruins, however, and it would be better to take time, and do Testour, Dougga and Le Kef in one day, followed by Bulla Regia, Chemtou and Aïn Draham the next, especially as there is now a very good site museum at Chemtou.

Also in the region is **Béja**, a very pleasant town to wander round with an attractive médina and fine protectoral buildings. **Testour** is a reminder that large numbers of Andalusian Muslims were settled in Tunisia in the 17th century. (The village's Iberian feel has not been totally masked by concrete constructions.) And finally, on the hills above Medjez el Bab, are two obscure villages: Chaouach and Toukabeur, commanding views of the Medjerda plain.

Tunis to Bizerte

South of Bizerte (or north from Tunis) are a number of villages, some like El Alia, founded by Andalusian immigrants in the 17th century. Closest to Tunis is the wide and windy beach of Kalaât El Andalus. Further north, still on the same stretch of coast, is Ghar el Melh, formerly Porto Farina, and the beach of Sidi Ali el Mekki. Round the headland of Cap Farina, and more sheltered, is Raf Raf with its beautiful sand beach, while at nearby Sounine, the coast gets rockier. This is an area increasingly favoured by Tunis families for their summer homes. Finally, after Ras Djebel, comes the rocky headland of Cap Zbib. Some five kilometres south of Bizerte, you have the beach of Rmel, wide sands backed by dunes and forest. With a car, a summer day trip from Tunis or Bizerte could easily take in the Roman site of Utica and one of the beaches. Note that work on the Tunis to Bizerte autoroute was scheduled to start in 2000.

Driving northwards from Tunis up the P8 road, the first major settlement, 28 km out of Tunis, to the right of the road, is **Pont-de-Bizerte** (ex-Protville), where you turn off for **Kalaât el Andalous**. As its name, meaning 'Citadel of the Andalusians', suggests, the village was originally founded by Andalusian refugees. It is situated on what was once a headland before the sea retreated leaving a wide fertile plain, today an agricultural area. Some houses were put up as part of the Medjerda development project sponsored by the World Bank. Market day is Wednesday. Beside the main mosque are post office, bank, petrol and the Haj Ali café. Little remains of the Andalusian past, however. The beach is some five minutes drive across the plain. In summer there are lifeguards and numerous local families enjoying the sands and sea. If you want to escape the crowded beaches around Tunis, and have your own transport, this is probably your best bet.

Kalaât el Andalous

Northern Tunisia

Utica

Aqueduct

To Tunis

N

0 metres 300
0 yards 327

1 Great baths
2 Cisterns
3 Temple (republican period)
4 Palace
5 New forum
6 Great baths
7 Theatre (imperial period)
8 Excavations - house of cascades
9 Reservoir
10 Site of Muslim tombs
11 Great amphitheatre
12 Cisterns
13 Site of Christian tombs
14 Old theatre (republican period)
15 Museum
16 Roman mausoleum
17 Site of Roman tombs
18 Little amphitheatre
19 Circus (republican period)

Utica

At **Zana**, 35 km out of Tunis, you come to the turn-off for the Roman site of Utica, a once-major settlement of which very little remains today.

Colour map 1, grid A4

For those with a car, this is best visited as a short stop on the way to Bizerte or one of the beaches. However, the site, clearly signposted 2½ km east from the new town of Zana, on the main road, is really for enthusiasts only if you are travelling by public transport. The site museum at Utica contains some small items of interest. The museum is on the left, and there is shade for parking and picnics, with the actual ruins another 500 metres down the road.

Getting there & around

Like many ancient cities in Tunisia, Utica was first a Punic city founded in 1101 BC, and later taken over by the Romans. It was the first capital of the Roman province of Africa and, as

History & background

such, rich in public monuments. Utica was a port, exporting agricultural produce from its rich hinterland. The Oued Medjerda has silted up the bay on which Utica stood, leaving it 15 km from the shore. Once upon a time, Utica's superb strategic location was second only to that of Carthage.

With the fall of Carthage in 146 BC, Utica became the capital of the province, and the settlement prospered as a garrison for Roman troops and the residence of many rich and powerful Roman citizens. The reinstatement of Carthage returned Utica to second place. Utica's collapse, like that of other Roman cities, came with the invasions by the Vandals and the Byzantines. The final fall came after the Arab conquest.

The site The Roman site is not extensive and has only been partially excavated. There is evidence of the replacement of smaller buildings by something much larger and grander (due to a more important role as capital perhaps) and in some cases a duplication (two theatres). One of the theatres is centrally placed, the other cut into the hillside. The residential area contains houses, built in the classical style, and often named for the mosaic decorations discovered there, ie House of the Hunt. ■ *Open winter 0830-1730, summer 0800-1900, closed Monday and public holidays. Entrance 2Dt and 1Dt photography charge.*

House of the Cascades, Utica

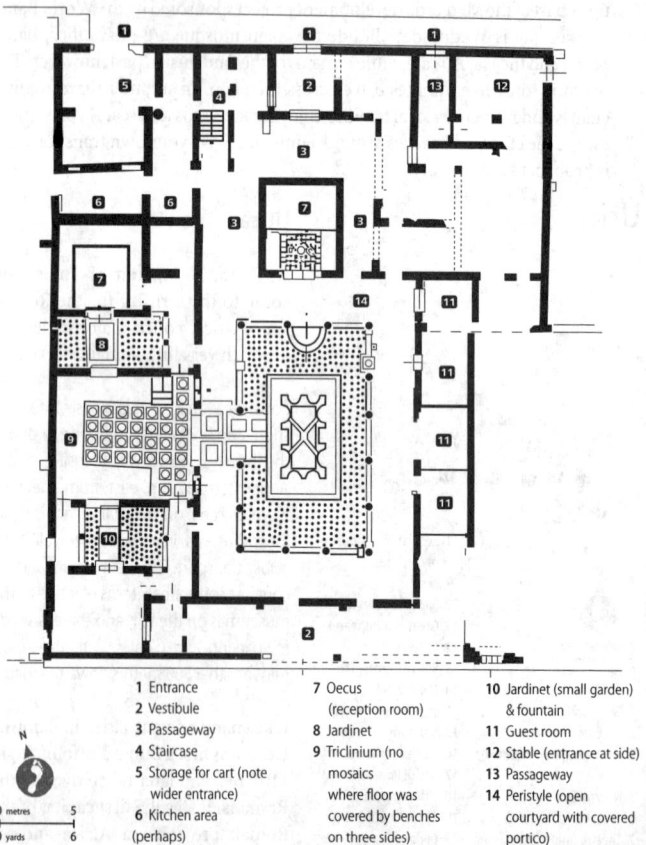

1 Entrance	**7** Oecus	**10** Jardinet (small garden)
2 Vestibule	(reception room)	& fountain
3 Passageway	**8** Jardinet	**11** Guest room
4 Staircase	**9** Triclinium (no	**12** Stable (entrance at side)
5 Storage for cart (note	mosaics	**13** Passageway
wider entrance)	where floor was	**14** Peristyle (open
6 Kitchen area	covered by benches	courtyard with covered
(perhaps)	on three sides)	portico)

0 metres 5
0 yards 6

The **House of the Cascades** is a large dwelling centred round a patio, onto **The houses**
which opened the imposing *triclinium* as well as smaller chambers, many with
basins and fountains. The adjacent **House of the Hunt** had a large garden surrounded by a patio and numerous rooms, one of which contained the famous
mosaic. The **House of the Capitals** had capitals representing human figures.
The **House of the Treasure** produced a hoard of coins. Some mosaics remain,
preserved under wooden covers which the guide will lift for you. The scenes
are mainly fishing. The huge Utica mosaic with Neptune and Aphrodite in a
sea-horse drawn chariot, Nereids on sea tigers and all overlooked by Oceanus,
can be seen in the Ulysses Room at the Bardo Museum. Look out for the use of
yellow Chemtou marble as well as the white and green marble from Greece. At
the foot of the hill are the great baths, great in size, covering over 26,000 square
metres. The cisterns and conduits to service this were fed from an aqueduct
and water tower which came in at the highest point where the remains of the
water tower, sometimes referred to as the citadel, can be found.

The small **Museum** has two main rooms. The Punic room has some gold
brooches and earrings from the fourth to the third century BC, oil lamps from
the seventh to the first century BC, vases from Greece and Italy, indicating
trade and small sarcophagi for the bones and ashes of children who, according
to legend, were sacrificed here. The Roman room has statues, an inscription
from the first to second century AD, a mosaic of a hunting scene and an interesting diagram of the excavations of the House of Cascades. There is no
accommodation at Utica.

Southeast of Bizerte

From Utica, you can either return to the main P8 to travel on to Bizerte, or follow
the narrow country roads to coastal settlements like **Ghar El Melh** (ex-Porto
Farina) and the beaches at **Ras Sidi Ali el Mekki**, **Raf Raf**, **Sounine** and **Cap
Zbib**. There is a beautiful selection of swimming places to choose from, popular
with locals but undiscovered by package tourism – although there were rumours
of a marina development project at Sidi Ali el Mekki in the late 1980s.

Ghar el Melh (Porto Farina)

Until the early 19th century, Ghar el Melh, in its earlier incarnation as Porto *Phone code: 02*
Farina, was quite a happening place as the Beylik of Tunis' main naval base. *Colour map 1, grid A4*
The coast silted up, however, and the same fate befell this port as had already
overcome Utica. Today, Ghar el Melh lives to the rhythm of the farming year
and the large numbers of day-trippers passing through in summer.

If you are using public transport, take buses number 5 and 3A, via Aousdja, from Tunis **Ins & outs**
and Bizerte. There are no buses east to Sidi Ali el-Mekki.

The lagoon at Ghar el Melh emerges from the mists of history in the 16th cen- **History**
tury. In 1535, Charles V's fleet sheltered in the lagoon one night on the way to
besiege La Goulette. Although the Spaniards noted its potential, it wasn't until
1638 that the Kabudan of the Tunis' fleet, Usta Murad Ibn Abdallah, a convert
of Italian origin, decided to develop a port. Round-keeled vessels, and in particular galleons, were of growing importance in his fleet, as opposed to the galleys, and it was essential to have safe anchorage for them and prevent Christian
pirates from taking refuge in the lagoon. Under Usta Murad, a fortified dock
was constructed, complete with stores and slave quarters, and protected by a
fort, today called the Borj el Wustani, the middle fort. In 1653, English admiral

Blake was sent by Oliver Cromwell to punish the Tunis corsairs, and damaged the new fortifications. However, between 1653 and 1665, Mustapha Laz Dey had the port restored and two further forts constructed, the Borj el Loutani to the east and the Borj Tunis to the west. A shipyard was added later in the century, and a full wall in the early 18th century. Porto Farina thus became the main naval port for the Regency of Tunis.

The approaches to the port gradually silted up, however. Ahmed Bey (1837-55) decided to build a modern port, and works were undertaken, at huge cost, with a palace being constructed to house the beylical suite. There was no solution to the silting, however, and Porto Farina became headquarters for a new infantry regiment instead.

Sights Surprisingly perhaps, the building undertaken under Ahmed Bey has largely disappeared, while the three 17th century bastions and the port are still visible. The shipyard and gallery are a mass of ruins. The octagonal corner towers of the Borj el Wustani and the Burj el Loutani are clearly visible. In their day, they represented a considerable innovation, and were no doubt introduced by master builders of Andalusian Muslim origin. The **Borj Tunis**, with its rounded front made up of vaulted chambers, represents the biggest innovation, however. Such a system meant that the fort could absorb more bombardment than a classic rampart, and could have more than one range of cannons.

Today, the lagoon at Ghar el Melh is a peaceful place, its depth of barely one metre making any military activity unlikely. There is a fair amount of fishing, with the main fish caught being red mullet, bream, perch, sole and eel. After the village, the road goes on six km to the splendid beach of **Ras Sidi Ali el Mekki** with a small café/shop and straw cubicles for camping, rented at 5Dt per day. At the end of the peninsula, built partially into the cliff, is the *marabout* of Sidi Ali el Mekki, a place of pilgrimage. Outside the summer season, this is an attractive and secluded spot.

Raf Raf   رفراف

Population 10,000
Phone code: 02
Colour map 1, grid A4

The little town of Raf Raf divides into two parts: the town proper at the top of the hill; and the beach-side suburb where many wealthy Tunisois and migrant workers have pleasant second homes. A steep road dips down from Raf Raf Ville to Raf Raf Plage. The setting is superb, with white sand, clear water, and the fortress-like mass of the Ile Pilau posing strategically for a photograph. Walk along the beach until the crowds thin out. You could also try to walk up the headland, via the track to the watchtower.

Ins & outs Raf Raf can be reached by bus from Ras Djebel and Tunis (No 1B, 2 hour ride, 1 bus a day from Bab Saâdoun).

Sights For the moment, there is little accommodation at Raf Raf. Despite some fairly hideous new building, the place does, however, make a pleasant day excursion from either Tunis or Bizerte, especially at the beginning and the end of the summer season. In July and August, on **Friday market** and especially at weekends, Raf Raf gets very crowded with trippers and the approach roads become jammed with cars. (Raf Raf produces the best table grapes in Tunisia, on sale, in season, all along the road.)

Fishing enthusiasts will want to observe the local beach **fishing** technique. During the seasonal migrations of mackerel, the fisherman attaches a female fish to a line and allows her to swim out parallel to the coast. Then, hawkeyed, he watches the water for the approach of a male fish, and waits for the

Tunisian mosaics

The Romans made a fine art of 'decorating a surface with designs made up of closely set, usually variously coloured, small pieces of material such as stone, pottery, glass, tile or shell': mosaics.

These first mosaics were constructed from pebbles and small stones set in clay, and usually the colours were black or white. The inclusion of other coloured stones, glass, and even broken pottery and shells, was introduced at a later date. The production of small, natural clay and polychrome tiles known as tesserae developed even later as designs for mosaics became more complicated and regular shaped pieces were required.

Although Africa was one of Rome's first overseas provinces, the actual process of Romanization was very slow and there were certainly no major developments before the late second century AD. Despite this late development, the mosaics of North Africa are more numerous and much better preserved than those remaining anywhere else from the empire, due to a combination of climatic conditions and less population pressure. The area we know as Tunisia is richer in mosaics than any other country and provides an enormous number of examples, mainly from the fourth century.

The earliest mosaics in North Africa were very simple, and it is assumed that early examples of more elaborate designs were produced by imported labour or constructed in Italy.

The wealthy Romans decorated both their private and public buildings with mosaics. They were a luxury and though primarily decorative, their size and sophistication would certainly advertise the wealth of the patron. Generally, the finer specimens were in the better, more visited parts of the house, and ornamental/geometric rather than pictorial designs were found in less important areas.

There are clear indications that the central part of the mosaics were constructed by 'master' craftsmen, while the geometric designs and borders were done by workers who were less well trained, and often produced a lower standard of work. Subject matter of the mosaics is frequently repeated and similar examples can be found on many different sites. Examples of the pattern being drawn in the underlying clay have been found but are not common. The workmen must have followed some pattern, especially where the work was more complicated. The recurrence of identical motifs across a wide area shows that designs were probably chosen from a common stock and not drawn for each building.

The common themes to look out for are: hunting scenes and scenes showing rural life; seasons and seasonal activities; scenes from literature; scenes from mythology. The all-important central medallion was set in a circle, square, oval or polygon and the whole mosaic was surrounded with a border usually exhibiting a geometric design. Most common were the three strand rope and Greek key borders.

appropriate moment to cast his net. The technique is clearly one that can only be mastered with patience and observation. (In the spring and early summer, similar techniques are used for trapping male goldfinches which, as the visitor will soon notice, are much appreciated as songbirds for homes and shops.)

Sleeping If you really want to spend time in Raf Raf, there are a fair number of holiday homes which stay empty for much of the year. There may also be cane beach *cabanes* available for rent.

C *Hotel Dalia*, T447668. Small, only 22 rooms, about half have sea view, very clean, close to beach, open all year, expensive due to location.

Eating The restaurant in the *Hotel Dalia* is good, clean and cheap. You can eat outside and watch the sea and the visitors. There are a few other restaurants along the beach, try *Restaurant Andalous*. These eateries tend to be overpriced for what they are.

Transport **Road** **Bus**: departures for Bizerte and Ras Djebel. One daily to Tunis. **Louages**: also available, but in summer towards the end of the day it can be quite crowded as everybody is leaving. Hitching may take time as most cars are already full.

Sounine Further north, Sounine has a rocky beach, some large and not very tasteful weekend homes, a few huts for rent on beach, *Café Budan* on corner, also *Café l'Escale* for snacks. In spring every electricity pylon has a storks' nest. In autumn the fields are full of tall white squills.

Ras Djebel, Metline and Cap Zbib

Phone code: 02
Colour map 1, grid A4

Ras Djebel is a large modern settlement on the coast, east of Bizerte on the road to the beaches of Raf Raf. In recent years, the town has grown quite prosperous thanks to the presence of a large garment factory, working mainly for Lee Cooper and owned by an industrial group headed by Hédi Jilani, president of the Tunisian Federation of Industry or UTICA. The town has a café, a patisserie and the *Hotel Okba* but not much else of interest. By contrast the surrounding area is very beautiful. The beach at Ras Djebel is very crowded in the summer and as most people prefer to camp near the town, anywhere further west is better. To the north-west, **Metline** is a small town built into the hillside, while rocky **Cap Zbib** offers magnificent views and the road from Bizerte to Ras Djebel is very scenic with a panoramic view over the coast by Bizerte. On the beach is a tiny marina with fishing boats. Drive with care as the road stops dead one metre from the cliff edge. Those in the know turn left.

Leaving Ras Djebel, you might head inland towards the P8, and the village of **El Alia**, built at a crossroads. In its day, this would have been a splendid example of the settlements built by immigrants from Andalucía. Thistles were traditionally grown in the region for the felting of *chechias*, the small red fez-like caps on which so much of the wealth of the Andalusian communities of Tunis was built.

Menzel Bourguiba (ex-Ferryville)

Phone code: 02
Colour map 1, grid A4

Situated some 20 km south-west of Bizerte, at the western-most point of the Lac de Bizerte, Ferryville was purpose built in the 1880s at the same time as the car park naval base at Bizerte, and named after Jules Ferry who was then in charge of colonial affairs. Renamed Menzel Bourguiba for independent Tunisia's first president, the town's military installations were to prove useful to Tunisia. In the 1960s, when self-sufficiency was the watchword for the newly independent nation states of Africa, Tunisia had to have a steelworks. Menzel Bourguiba, located close to the shipyards and petrol refineries of Bizerte, was ideally placed for the new installations, named *El Fouladh* (Arabic for steel). In the late 1990s, as the Tunisian State sought to withdraw from industrial activity, El Fouladh was ripe for privatization. Whether this diminutive steel-works can survive remains to be seen. Success or failure will have huge effects on the town. There is now a second industry in the form of garment factories, however. This requires very different sort of skills and labour to the steel mill.

Menzel Bourguiba has some nice pieces of period architecture, including a bandstand and characteristic detached houses with pitched red-tiled roofs, presumably built to house personnel working for the naval yards.

D *Hotel Ichkeul*, a fair way out of Menzel Bourguiba at Guengla, on Lac Bizerte. Owner also runs Tardi vintners. Good reports of the restaurant. **E** *Hotel Moderne*, small and downmarket, in the centre of Menzel Bourguiba, T460551. Bar.

Sleeping

Tour companies & travel agents *Via Bizerte*, rue du 18 Janvier, T460756.

Directory

Lac Ichkeul (Garaet Ichkeul)

Lying west of the Lac de Bizerte and Menzel Bourguiba, **Lac Ichkeul** was a unique biotope, created by the shifting seasonal balance of salt and fresh water in a large and shallow inland lake. The area is dominated by **Djebel Ichkeul**, where a small écomusée is located. Bring your binoculars. Apart from various resident waterfowl and the lead-grey water buffalo out on the water meadows, you may be lucky enough to see large flocks of overwintering migrant grey-lag geese in winter. The best time to visit is November to February.

Phone code: 02
Colour map 1, grid A4

Lac Ichkeul is awkward to get to without your own transport, and your birdwatching will be improved if you can drive round the lake. You could get the Bizerte to Mateur bus or louage, and ask to get off at the turn-off for the Parc National, a few kilometres after Tinja on the main P11. Otherwise, you could get a taxi from Menzel Bourguiba to this point, or maybe into the park to the main gate. From the railway-crossing to the park gate is 5½ km, from main gate to ecomuseum a further 3½ km.

Ins & outs

The Lac Ichkeul area is a conservation area of 12,600 hectares, with a mixed habitat comprising shallow lake (one metre to three metres deep), marshy pasture and maquis-covered mountain. The area was designated by Unesco in 1977 as a biosphere reserve. (The only other such site acknowledged by Unesco is the Everglades in Florida.) The lake was unique in that while it had fresh water in winter, in summer its waters turned saline. In summer, high evaporation levels meant that the water level fell to one and a half metres or less, leading to inflow from the saline Lac de Bizerte via the five kilometres long Oued Tindja. Salinity rose to 20 grams per litre. In winter, with the seasonal rains, the balance shifted, with the rivers supplying fresh water; the depth rose to three metres and salinity fell to five grams per litre. Thanks to the warm winter, large seasonal beds of waterplants could grow, thus providing food for huge flocks of migrant birds.

Background
Note that the Tourist Office in Bizerte can on occasion arrange visits

For birdlilfe, Ichkeul is arguably the most interesting of Tunisia's six National Parks. Water birds and waders are among the thousands of over-wintering migrants (over-wintering grey-lag geese can number 15,000) found here. Among the animal species are water buffalo, wild boar, porcupine, otter and jackal. There are numerous reptiles and amphibians, too.

Birdwatchers may see the purple gallinule (French: *talève sultane*), the retiring marbled teal (*sarcelle marbrée*) and maybe even the white-headed duck. The coot (*foulque macroule*) feeds on water weed. Of the waders, the easiest to spot are the black-and-white avocets and the white storks, which can be seen nesting in various places in northern Tunisia.

Northern Tunisia

🖝 *Buffaloes & Madame Butterfly*

One of the most surprising sights at Ichkeul are the small herds of water buffaloes grazing on the plain below the djebel. The origins of these animals are obscure. One story goes that they descend from a pair given to the bey of Tunis by the king of Sicily in 1729. Another version runs that they were imported by Ahmed Bey (1837-55), a modernizing monarch, who felt they would be the ideal solution to towing his field artillery around. When the buffaloes proved unequal to the task, they were released at Ichkeul. When the French took over in 1881, there were over 1,000 of these beasts at Ichkeul, who presumably found the seasonal marshes like the

rice-paddies of their homeland. The buffaloes were the personal property of HH the Bey, who would grant the occasional buffalo-hunting licence. In the Second World War, American troops stationed in the area nearly wiped the herd out in search of fresh meat.

Finally, still on an Asian theme, in the mid-1990s Lac Ichkeul was considered sufficiently similar to Japan to be used as the setting for a film version of Madame Butterfly. A whole mock-up Japanese village was constructed on the edge of the lake, with Oriental accessories and extras being flown in from Paris' China Town.

The grey-lag goose (*oie cendrée*) was the park's most famous migrant visitor, feeding on club rush. The highest number recorded was 20,500, while 15,000 was a more regular figure. The numbers are down considerably, however, with figures around 4,500 in the late 1990s. The fresh water from the rivers which used to flow into the lake in winter is now being put to other uses. As part of the 'mobilisation of the waters of the North', a large new dam on the Oued Sejnène, west of Ichkeul, was built, sharply reducing fresh-water inflow. The effect of reduced fresh-water input can be seen in the area round the lake. The once extensive reed-beds have receded, and there is far less cane than there used to be. In the local vernacular tradition, houses were roofed with reeds. The preferred option today is plastic sheeting. Given the changes in the ecosystem, the question remains as to whether it will continue to merit its Unesco classification. The authorities are said to be keen to maintain the water balance in the lake by artificial methods.

Ecological museum There is a small ecological museum high above the car park, overlooking the lake. This has information of interest to birdwatchers and ecologists. There is a display of stuffed birds and information on the workings of the lake's special ecosystem. ■ *0700 to 1800. Free.*

The minor road beyond the museum is closed to traffic, but walkers are welcome on the circular route round Djebel Ichkeul. **NB** The minor road marked south of the lake on Michelin 172 to the C51 does not exist.

Bizerte بنزرت

Phone code: 02
Colour map 1, grid A4

Tunisia's fourth largest city, and the biggest town in the north of the country, Bizerte is an atmospheric sort of place. There is a small médina, and a picturesque port area, with angular 18th century bastions and streets of white walls and blue doors and shutters. The town feels quintessentially early 20th century cosmopolitan Mediterranean, even though the population is wholly Muslim today. There are apartment buildings like those in any French provincial town. There are squares, a fine church, plane trees and promenades of palm trees, and a club nautique. When the French departed, jetties, breakwaters and port installations stayed, giving the town a brisk, naval air.

Bizerte's streets have all the usual variety of Tunisian provincial life: shiny new shops with consumer goods, workshops spilling out onto the pavement, repairing motorcycles, varnishing furniture. In the spring, you will see merchants with piles of fragrant geraniums for making flower essence. At the fish-market, you will find the harvest of the local fishing fleet. Bizerte is a pleasant place for a stop-over. And nearby, at Rmel and Ras Angela, are some splendid beaches. Note also that Cap Blanc is the northernmost point of Africa.

Ins and outs

Bizerte is 64 km from Tunis, bus Nos 44 and 62, 1 hour 15 minutes by louage, a pleasant, slightly hilly, journey along the P8 through fertile farmland with large areas of olives and vines. The road crosses the wide flood plain of the Oued Medjerda, Tunisia's only permanently flowing river. Travelling by car, you may want to stop off at the Roman site of Utica, a few kilometres off the road, or you could spend a couple of hours at 1 of the small beach resorts like Ghar el Melh, Raf Raf or Sounine.

Getting there

The main sites of Bizerte can easily be covered on foot. You may want to go to the Corniche and its beaches and to Cap Blanc, a short taxi ride out of the town centre, north of the town. The beaches northwest of Bizerte, notably Ras Angela, require your own transport. The beach at Rmel, south of the town, is easily reached by local bus.

Getting around

History and background

Bizerte goes back to Punic times when the natural harbour attracted the Phoenician sailors. The town was destroyed with the fall of Carthage, but later rebuilt by Caesar, and known as **Hippo Diarrythus**. Conquered by the Arabs in 661, Bizerte expanded during the Hafsid Dynasty. The arrival of the Moors from Spain in the 17th century, as in other cities in Tunisia, gave it a new lease of life and guaranteed its fortune. The opening of the Suez Canal in 1869, and the arrival, in 1882, of the French who appreciated its strategically important position and turned the town into a naval arsenal, were other important factors in Bizerte's development.

The arsenal had a key strategic role, controlling the Straits of Sicily. The naval base was the second largest in North Africa, after Mers el Kébir, and was thus a major objective of the Axis armies. The Germans occupied Bizerte in 1942, the Allies took it back again in 1943. At Tunisia's independence, France kept control of the military installations. In the late 1950s, relations between France and Tunisia deteriorated, with the latter angered at the French attack on Algerian nationalists in the Tunisian village of Sakiet Sidi Youssef. France devalued the franc (to which the dinar was linked) without consulting Tunisia.

Populist pressure called for France to evacuate the Bizerte base, which it eventually did on 15 October 1964. Open hostility had broken out in July 1961, with Tunisian civilian lives being lost senselessly in a doomed attack on the base.

Since independence the industrial sector has expanded. There is an oil refinery. A large steelmill, El Fouladh, was set up at Menzel Bourguiba (ex-Ferryville), a few kilometres southwest of the town. Bizerte lies north of the swing bridge over the eight kilometres long canal which joins the inland Lake of Bizerte (111 sq km) to the open sea. Here some commercial fishing takes place, mullet, bream and sole being the main catch. The road from the bridge leads into the regular grid pattern of streets, laid out in the late 19th century, beyond which lies the médina and the old port. The late 1990s saw much new building on the northern and western outskirts of the town, mainly low-cost housing to the west, and villas along the Corniche. Bizerte now also has a special development zone, and it is hoped this will bring in further industrial investment. At the moment many businesses are linked to the port and refineries.

Sights

The old harbour is charming with its blue and white houses overlooking the fishing boats, and in the evening it has a different but equally pleasant atmosphere. From there you can penetrate into the **Kasbah**, the old fortified médina. (Over the modern bridge is another old neighbourhood, the **Ksiba**, or 'little kasbah'). The labyrinth of little streets is fascinating to walk through. It is the sort of place where you should wander through the narrow alleys, 'peeping into doorways where craftsmen can be seen at work using techniques centuries old'. The octagonal minaret of the Grand Mosque was recently over-restored.

Above and behind the town is the **Fort d'Espagne**, built between 1570 and 1573 by the Pacha of Algiers to plans by Gabriel Serbelloni. The fort was completed under the Spaniard. It has been sufficiently repaired to be used, once in a while, as an open-air auditorium.

The new city is pleasant with its squares and cafés. Close to the port is the covered market. In the area are one or two small shops with some desultory craft work. In the **Fort de Sidi el Hani**, in the Ksiba district, Bizerte has a sleepy **Oceanographic Museum**, which sounds most impressive. The 11-storey blue tower block provides an interesting note in the old harbour district, and was originally built as officers' flats.

Bizerte suffered severe damage during the Second World War, and was thus the object of a number of redevelopment schemes during the reconstruction period 1943-48. A whole new town was planned for **Zarzouna**, south of Bizerte. The architecture of this time was firmly based on local models and techniques, given the shortages of steel and concrete. Architecture enthusiasts may want to look out for a couple of interesting buildings from the period, the **Ecole des Jeunes Filles** (arch. J Lecouteur) close to the old harbour on Place Salaheddine Bouchoucha, and the **Contrôle civil de Zarzouna** (arch. J Marmey) high on a hill, overlooking the town, to the south. The **Church of Notre Dame** (arch. R Guy) dates from the same period.

Perhaps the most striking feature on the Bizerte skyline is the great bridge. The channel separating the two halves of the town is 240 metres wide (and 12 metres deep, allowing ships of up to 80,000 tonnes into the port). Until 1904 there was a swing bridge, subsequently replaced by two ferries. The present bridge, Bizerte's answer to Sydney Harbour, climbing 15 metres above the channel, came into service in 1980. A middle section opens up to allow large boats into the port.

There are some good **beaches** on either side of the town, but the most popular one is at **Rmel** (lit: 'sands') over the bridge to the south (try the number eight bus from the Menzel Jamil stop at the bus station). The beach is backed by pine forest, and you have a couple of large wrecked vessels, dating from the Second World War, rusting away in the water just off the beach.

Some 10 km out of Bizerte, you have the headland of **Cap Angela**. North of town, the Corniche runs between coast and a smart neighbourhood with hotels, restaurants and smart residential areas climbing up the hillside (look out for the villa built to look like a ship). Then the road winds upwards and pine forest appears. Turn right down a track through the forest, leave the car at the small village. You have a 20 minute walk up **Cap Blanc**, one of the northernmost points in Africa. There is a radio-station and superb views over the sea, and, to the west, over forest to the beaches at Cap Angela.

Bizerte

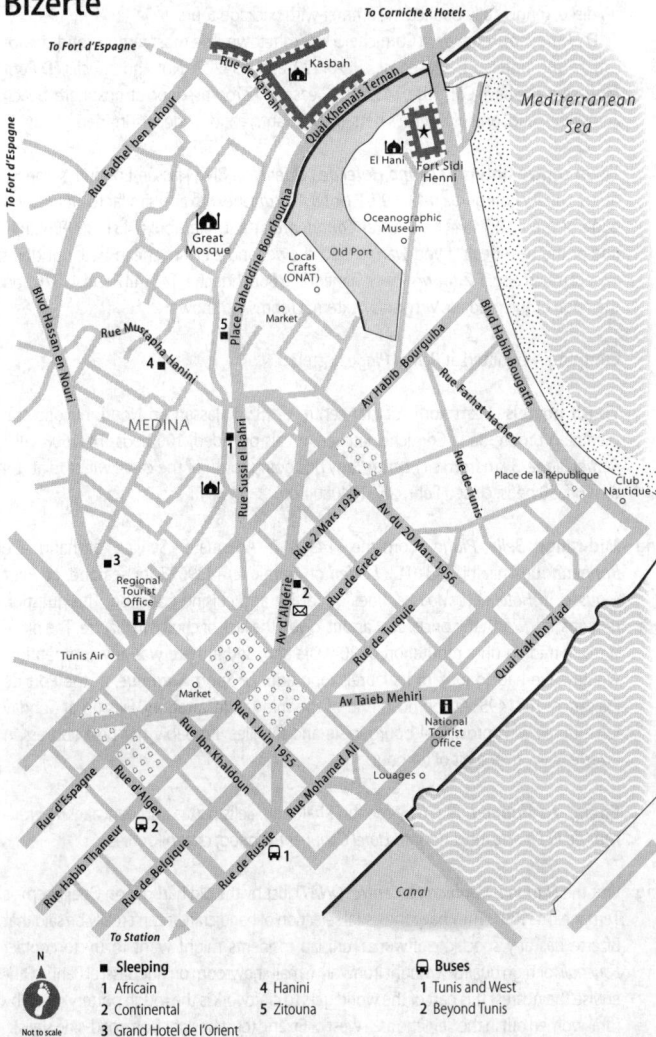

Sleeping
1 Africain
2 Continental
3 Grand Hotel de l'Orient
4 Hanini
5 Zitouna

Buses
1 Tunis and West
2 Beyond Tunis

Northern Tunisia

Festivals Nothing very exciting in this department. The Festival of Bizerte is held in July/August, and will include the same stars doing the summer festival circuit elsewhere in Tunisia. Note that Bizerte is the birthplace of Khemaïs Ternane, one of early 20th century Tunisia's most popular songwriters.

Sleeping
■ *on map*
Price codes:
see inside front cover

The hotels in Bizerte are situated either out on the Corniche, starting about 1 km out of the town, or in the town centre.

Corniche hotels **C** *Apart'hotel Résidence Aïn Meriyem*, T437615/438859, F439712. 296 beds. **C** *Corniche*, route de la Corniche, T431844, F431830, 4 km out of town. Low season prices acceptable, beach, 87 rooms with sea view, fly screens, no a/c, pool, many organized activities, large nightclub. Despite its prime location on the Corniche, this is not a well managed sort of place. **C** *Jalta*, route de la Corniche, T431169/432250, F434277. Next to the Nador, a package sort of place. **C** *Nador*, T431848, F433817. Next to *Corniche*, simpler and much more pleasant, 105 rooms, beach, pool, no disco, tennis, fully booked in summer with package tours

D *El Khayem*, route de la Corniche, 5 km from town. The most remote (and cheapest) of the hotels on the coast, T4321220 and 434277. Nothing special. **D** *Petit Mousse*, route de la Corniche, T432185. Pleasant, 12 rooms, good atmosphere, beach across the road, one of Bizerte's better restaurants, eat outside in summer.

Town centre hotels **D** *Grand Hotel de l'Orient*, on Blvd Hassan Ennouri, some 50 metres off Av Bourguiba, T421499. **F** *Hotel Africain*, next to and similar to *Zitouna*, on edge of médina, T434412. **F** *Hotel Continental*, rue d'Istambul, T431436. Probably one of the best deals if you want a cold shower and a clean, cheap bed, but don't expect much else. **F** *Zitouna*, Place Slaheddine Bouchoucha, T431447 and 438760 on the edge of the médina. Very noisy external rooms, no showers.

Camping Permitted at *Remel Plage* hostel.

Youth hostels 1 km north of city centre up Blvd Hassan en Nouri, beyond the médina on route de la Corniche, kitchen, meals provided, 100 beds, T431608. Also *Remel Plage*, 3 km from city centre, any bus going south of the canal will stop at the turn off, 50 beds, closed February, T440804.

Eating **Mid-range** *Belle Plage*, Corniche, T431817. Adequate. Service off-hand. *De Bonheur*, rue Thaalbi, T431047. *L'Eden* on Corniche, T439023 for seafood. *Le Petit Mousse*, in *Hotel Petit Mousse*, does good fish and cuisine française. The question remains, is it worth the price? Just about, given the lack of choice in Bizerte. The place is really trading on a reputation of 30 years ago, and if there was any competition, would have had to look to its laurels long ago. *Le Sport Nautique*, at the Port de Plaisance, T431495. At the posh end of the mid-range category. Fills up at Sunday lunchtimes with provincial bourgeoisie and families. Probably the best address in Bizerte. View over a bit of harbour.

Cheap *La Mamma*, T433695, rue Ibn Khaldoun. Sells pizzas and pancakes. *Restaurant de la Liberté*, next door to *Hotel Continental*, good, cheap food.

Shopping Visit the *National Handicrafts Centre (ONAT)* just by the old harbour on Quai Khemais Ternane, T431091. They have the usual selection of handicraft. It can't really be said that Bizerte has any specific craftwork. Tunisian residents might want to try to contact *Fouchali* for high quality wrought ironwork (small showroom on Rue Sassi el Bahri). Otherwise the nearest this part of the world gets to craftwork is the rough pottery made by rural women out in the Sejnène area west of Bizerte (best bought from road-side stalls).

Club Nautique, T432262, on the right of the main beach in town, hires out surfboards and does various other watersports. Sub-aqua fishing is very popular. Otherwise try one of the hotels on the Corniche. The *Corniche* hotel organizes water skiing and rents surfboards. Horse riding is offered at some of the hotels. Some of the big hotels and small enterprises hire out bicycles, which is a cheap way of getting to the beach. Municipal swimming pool (heated) on Blvd Hassan en Nouri. Marina for 100 boats. Harbour Master's Office, T431688. **Sports**

Local Bicycles & motorbike hire: *Ben Othman*, Av Habib Bourguiba; *Ben Kilani*, Av Habib Bourguiba, T431622 and *Ben Aleya*, rue Sassi Balıri. **Car hire**: *ABC*, 33 Av Habib Bourguiba, T434624, F436350; *Avis*, 7 rue d'Alger, T433076; *Budget*, 7 rue d'Alger, T432174; *Europcar*, 52 Av d'Algérie, T439018, also at 19 rue Med Rejiba, Place des Martyrs, T431455; *Hertz*, Place des Martyrs, T433679; *Inter Rent*, 19 rue Mohammed Rejiba, T431455; *Mattei*, rue d'Alger, T431508; *Next Car*, 80 Blvd Hassan en Nouri, T433668; *Shipping Co*. *Navitour*, 29 Av d'Algérie, T431440. **Transport**

Long distance Air: the nearest airport is Tunis. Information from Tunis Air, 76 Av Habib Bourguiba, T432201. **Train**: the station is approximately 15 minutes walk southwest along canal out of town. Information on T431070. To Tunis 0540, 0810, 1350, 1835. **Bus**: the main bus station is by the bridge over the canal. Information from *Société Régionale de Transport*, Quai Tarak Ibn Ziad, T431371/736. A short walk north up Av d'Algérie to the town centre. Information from Société Nationale de Transport on T431222/431317. Bus station for places west, as far as Tabarka, is on rue d'Alger. Frequent buses to **Tunis** and **Ras Djebel**; change at Ras Djebel for **Raf Raf** and **Ghar el Melh;** **Aïn Draham** (via Tabarka) leaves early morning. **Louages**: leave by the canal under the bridge to all destinations, but some are harder to obtain if the demand is low. Louages terminate on the Quai Tarak Ibn Ziad under the bridge or at the north end of Av d'Algérie. Sometimes available at the station. **Sea**: Navitour, 29 Av d'Algérie, T431440. Port – Harbour Master's Office, T431688.

Banks The banks arrange a rota so one always stays open later. *BNT*, rue 1er Juin. *STB*, rue Farhat Hached, there is also another branch behind the ONAT, by the old harbour. *CFCT*, Av Habib Bourguiba which takes Eurocheque and Visa. **Communications** Area code: 02. Post Office: main office, 6 Av d'Algérie. Takes parcels as well. Around the back of main building is the telecommunications office, also on rue el Médina and Place Pasteur. **Emergency addresses** Police: T431200/1, rue du 20 Mars 1956. **Medical services** Chemist: all night, *Sparfi*, 28 rue Ali Belhaoane, T439545. **Hospital:** on rue du 3 Août, T431422. **Places of worship** Catholic: 120 Av Habib Bourguiba, T432386. Service Sun at 1030. **Tour companies & travel agents** *International Voyages*, 35 Av Habib Bourguiba, T432885 and 439666, F433547. *Tourafrica*, Av Habib Bourguiba, T432315. *Transtour*, 7 rue d'Alger, T432174. *Tunisia Line*, corner of rue Ibn Khaldoun and Belgique, T431944, F432700. *Via Bizerte*, rue 1er Mai, T432901. **Tourist offices** National Tourist Office (ONTT), 1 rue d'Istambul, T432703/432897. The office is hard to find. It is situated by the canal, about 100m before the bridge, towards the sea. **Directory**

Bizerte to Tabarka

Colour map1, grid A2-4 West of Bizerte, the coastline is wild and remote all the way to Tabarka. The sea is hidden by thick forests noted as a refuge for the last lion (killed 1925) and the last panther (1932) known in Tunisia. The coastline is worth trying to reach, especially if you like deserted beaches, although access is difficult. By car from Bizerte to Tabarka take the road west towards Menzel Bourguiba and turn right five kilometres after Bizerte on the C51, in the direction of Sejnène. This road joins the C57, skirting Lac Ichkeul, before joining up with the main P7 for **Sejnène** (pottery), **Nefza** (storks) and **Tabarka** (red coral).

Sejnène & the northern beaches Closest to Bizerte is the beach at **Ras Angela**. (Note that the GeoCenter world map labels Rass Ben Sekka and Rass el Koran with little precision.) Going west of Bizerte, follow signs for **Bechateur**. There is only one route down to the beach at Ras Angela. If you are tempted to camp out or sleep rough, keep your passport et cetera close to the body. Valuables can be stolen from under your sleeping head.

Moving westwards, the next easily accessible beach is at **Cap Serrat**, some 25 km from **Sejnène**. From Sejnène, the C66, which eventually turns into gravelly/sandy track, takes you down to pale sands backed by meadows green even in summer. A tiny river, banks lined with oleander and cane, flows into the sea. There are showers and a couple of seasonal restaurants.

Sejnène is one of those rural one-street villages which expanded rapidly in the 1999s, becoming the local centre giving vastly improved access to health and education to a once isolated rural population. Sejnène gets packed with Peugeot trucks, the odd mule and women in their colourful best on **Thursday market day**. The area is known for its **hand-modelled pottery**, animals and statuettes, generally sold as 'Berber style' pottery in tourist areas, and you will find small displays of the pottery along the roadside. The most attractive items are the tiny animals, the *kanouns* (braseros) and the wide flat dishes. Note that this pottery is generally fired at quite low temperatures, given that the women have to collect the brushwood for the kiln by hand. This means that the final product is often quite breakable.

After Sejnène, the next easily accessible beach is at **Sidi Mechrig**. Turn right at Tamera, 10 km before Nefza, and follow the narrow metalled road which leads up over the Jbel el Hamar, through great stands of eucalyptus before reaching a wide heathland with views over the sea towards La Galite. Sidi Mechrig has a narrow beach and the ruins of what might be a Roman baths. (The surf and depth of the water as you go in make unsupervised bathing unsuitable for very small children.) Local people set up camp here for the summer. There is a small, unclassified hotel.

Cap Negro (once known as Tamkart) is one of the most inaccessible of the northern beaches. You will definitely need a good four-wheel drive vehicle. Coming from Bizerte, a couple of kilometres before Nefza, there is a badly signposted turn-off right, near the viaduct, for Cap Negro. The drive takes you along earth tracks through cork oak forest, where there are a few isolated farms. After some 10 km, the track gets increasingly stoney. Ordinary cars give up on the climb towards the coast after the *maison forestière*. At the top of an arid, stoney mountain, you come to a steep drop down to Cap Negro. There are a few visitors, and the police post will be delighted to be able to check your passport and car-documents. Back in the 1970s, there was a small seasonal hotel. Now there are just the remains of a few 18th century port buildings.

Northern Tunisia

1741, the fall of the comptoir of Cap Negro

An 18th century historian recounts the fall of Tamkart (Cap Negro) to Younes, son of Ali Pacha. "Before leaving Tabarka, Younes had the message sent from Bizerte to the French community in Tamkart that he wanted to see them on the aforementioned date, to confirm the peace existing between them and the Muslims. I am not certain when the peninsula of Tamkart was occupied by the king of France, but he had a fort and the stores necessary to the trade in wheat, barley, oil, wax and wool built there, for this trade took place there with the whole of Ifrikia. The king established a captain, an interpreter, secretaries and guards, none of whom was allowed to have a woman with him. When Younes arrived at Tamkart with his horsemen, after leaving Tabarka, the French understood that they were in no position to resist, and surrendered. Ships were sent up from Bizerte, and Younes had the Christians embarked and sent to the French consul in Tunis. He set up camp on the peninsula, gathered together everything which could be found, including the canons, and sent everything to Tunis on small boats. The sheikhs of the neighbouring Nefza and Mogods came to him with provisions, horses and presents. Then he left, leaving the Caid Brahim Ben Sassi to represent him, with orders to have all the buildings in this place demolished."

Mohamed Seghir Ben Youssef, Tarikh el mashra'el malaki (1764).

Closer to Tabarka is the **Zouara** beach, only 20 km before the town. Turn right off the Bizerte road before Aïn Sebna (a sign indicates the way) and follow a fairly easy track for five kilometres. This is a beautiful beach with fine sand, but again there is no infrastructure whatsoever, just the odd seasonal shack. (Bathers should note that the currents can be strong.) This is the 'local beach' for inland Béja. The construction of the Sidi el Barrak dam on the Oued Zouara, which brought large amounts of silt down from the mountains to form the beach, may change the area somewhat.

Tabarka   طبرقة

Tabarka, ancient Thabraca, is a pleasant low-key resort in the far northwestern corner of Tunisia. It is a sleepy sort of place, and the appearance of a zone touristique has not disturbed the pace of life. With its port and fishing boats, rocky island set with pines and topped with fort and lighthouse and sand beaches stretching eastwards along the coast, Tabarka would be an ideal setting for a 1950s Italian movie. The town centre is as yet largely unspoiled by new development and many of the new constructions have the red-tiled roofs of the older buildings. Looking inland, there are green forested hills, a welcome relief in the summer after the burnt landscapes of the interior.

Phone code: 08
Colour map 1, grid A2

Ins and outs

Tabarka is easily accessible by bus and louage. From Tunis, buses and louages run from the gare routière at Bab Saâdoun. Arriving in Tabarka, the louage station is on the main street, Av Habib Bourguiba. From the long distance bus station on rue du Peuple, turn left down the hill to the central square. The local bus station is about 50 metres up the hill from the main square.

Getting there

If you are driving, Tabarka is about 4 hours from Tunis. There are several routes, all scenic. The winding GP17 from Jendouba via Aïn Draham is the most spectacular. The GP7 coming in from Nefza to the east has been improved, as has the MC52 north from Béja to Nefza. So take your pick.

The airport lies 9 km east of town at Ras Rajel. Internal flights were expensive, and thus never won the market share to make them viable. In the season, there are charter flights in from various European destinations.

Getting around You may need to take a taxi from the town centre to zone touristique and vice versa. The Musée du Liège (Cork Museum) is also a 25 minute walk out of the town centre, so you might take a taxi for that. Aïn Draham is an easy daytrip by louage.

History and background

The origins of the town can be traced back to Haron (fifth century BC) who is said to have established a trading post here. The Phoenician town was called *Thabraca*, meaning 'place in the shade'. As a third century Roman town it was noted for the export of wild beasts, wood for building, lead and iron from its mines and yellow marble from the quarries of Chemtou.

Thabraca played an important role in developments associated with luxurious buildings – painters, decorators, sculptors and ceramic artists made it the town of 'arts'. Mosaic artists founded a school here whose prestige won wide renown abroad for three centuries. The walls of the staircase in the Bardo Museum which leads from the ground floor to the galleries above are covered with tomb mosaics from Tabarka dating from the fourth and sixth centuries.

The town prospered with the spread of Christianity in the fifth century and especially during the reign of the Fatmids in the 10th century. In the 16th century it regained its status as a strategic harbour for merchant shipping, with the Genoese Lomellini family taking control of the island in 1542. The Genoese were in the Habsburg camp, and throughout the 17th century, the French made no secret of their designs on the Island of Tabarka. They already had an important trading post, Bastion de France, near La Calle, some 30 km to the west, and another at Cap Negro.

The result of much intrigue was an expeditionary force led by Younes, son of Ali Pacha in 1741. Both Tabarka and Cap Negro were taken by the beylical forces. Younes had the town of Tabarka destroyed, although he left the fort intact. The Tabarquins were taken prisoner and transported to Tunis, where they were housed at Bab Souika. Wrote 18th century Tunisian historian Mohamed Seghir Ben Yousef, "Among these prisoners, all the young girls who seemed attractive were taken by the pacha or his sons. The boys were also taken by the pacha to be brought up with the mamlouks; those who showed themselves intelligent were invited to convert to Islam, which they did in general out of fear, after which the pacha had them circumcised, named them Mustapha or Ismail and gave them employment." The other Tabarquins, given their skills, easily settled into life in the city. The destruction of the Genoese settlement and the *comptoir* at Cap Negro had unfortunate side-effects for the region, leading to the decline of Béja.

France became important at Tabarka in 1781 when the Compagnie royale d'Afrique succeeded in gaining exclusive coral-harvesting rights in the waters from Tabarka to Tripoli. A consulate was set up in 1804. The fortress was gradually abandoned. In the Second World War, the fortress was a centre for the Free French, and would have been in the line of fire of Axis forces attempting to enter the Constantinois over the frontier.

Tabarka is known today for its fishing, and lobsters, shrimps, prawns and crayfish form an important part of the catch. For those who wish to look at the fish, the local dive schools organize excursions to the *Grotte des Mérous*, where you can make friends with large cod and other denizens of the deep.

Sights

Tabarka's two main sights are the Genoese fort and a weird, eroded rock formation, Les Aiguilles. The latter is just west of town – walk along the promenade, which follows the bay across which you can see the old fort built by the Genoese. The **Aiguilles** (lit. 'The Needles'), some 20 metres high, are moderately impressive, carved out of the rock by sea and wind. The view from the top of the old fort is impressive and it is worth the effort of walking up the hill. Probably best not to photograph close to, as the military appear to be in residence for the moment.

Tabarka

Northern Tunisia

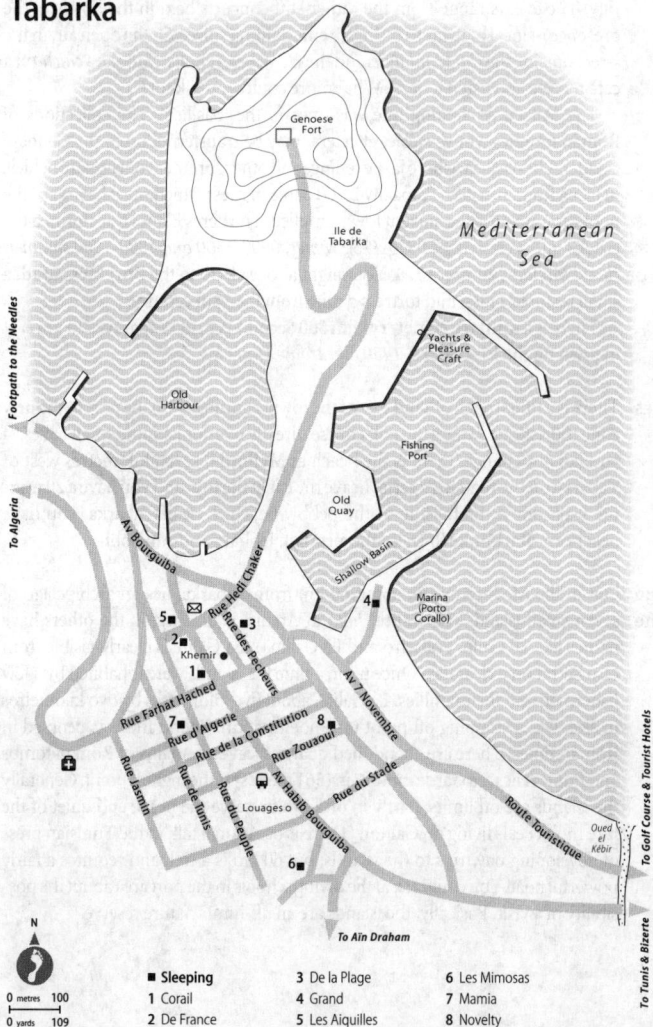

Genoese Fort

Ile de Tabarka

Mediterranean Sea

Footpath to the Needles

Yachts & Pleasure Craft

Old Harbour

Fishing Port

To Algeria

Av Bourguiba

Rue Hedi Chaker

Old Quay

Shallow Basin

Rue des Pecheurs

Marina (Porto Corallo)

5 ■   ⊠   4 ■

2 ■   3 ■

Khemir ●

1 ■

Rue Farhat Hached

Av 7 Novembre

7 ■   Rue d'Algerie   8 ■

Rue de la Constitution

Rue Zouaoui

Rue Jasmin

Rue de Tunis   Av Habib Bourguiba   Rue du Stade

Rue du Peuple

Louages ○

Route Touristique

To Golf Course & Tourist Hotels

Oued el Kébir

6 ■

To Tunis & Bizerte

N

To Aïn Draham

0 metres 100
0 yards 109

■ Sleeping	3 De la Plage	6 Les Mimosas
1 Corail	4 Grand	7 Mamia
2 De France	5 Les Aiguilles	8 Novelty

The fort once dominated an island ruled as a trading strong point by the Lomellini family. The causeway is a 20th century addition.

Tabarka is the centre for **diving** on the north coast and the diving centre in the Yachting Club on the seafront is open all year. The club also organizes other watersport activities including underwater photography. In the autumn, **wild boar hunting** attracts a following of mainly Italian visitors and a few locals. There is now an 18-hole golf course on the route touristique. The course, part of which overlooks the sea, is set in 100 ha of pine and cork oak forest.

In the summer, there is a minor **Jazz Festival**, lasting about a week, which brings together an interesting mix of jazz fans from the capital, tourists from the hotels and bemused locals (almost exclusively male). Back in the 1970s, Tabarka's slogan, invented by energetic young promoter Lotfi Belhassine, was 'Ne bronzez pas idiot' ('You don't have to tan like an idiot', rough translation). The original Jazz Festival was part of this strategy. In recent years, the festival has varied between the end of the summer, and, more recently, late June/early July. The events range from the rather stiff concerts held in the hotels in the presence of local bigwigs to the more entertaining soirées in the open air, in the street outside the *Café Andalous* and the *Hotel Les Aiguilles*. Smoke a *chicha* at a café terrace and listen to jazz. What more could you ask for?

The **Musée Archéologique** was once in the 'basilica'. The collections of Roman mosaics, votive stelae, et cetera, may be transferred up to the Genoese Citadel. The basilica, where jazz evenings and other summer concerts are held, is in fact a Roman cistern (capacity 2,700 cubic metres) which must have kept the public fountains of the ancient town supplied. The Pères Blancs transformed the cistern into a church. ▪ *0830-1730 winter, 0900-1300 and 1500-1900 summer, closed Monday, entrance 1Dt.* You might also walk up to the **Borj Messaoud**, a small restored Husseinid fortress dating from the 18th century.

There is a **military cemetery** with 500 Second World War graves 15 km east of town on the P7. ▪ *0730-1430, Saturday-Thursday.*

Local beaches There is a fine stretch of sand east of the town, running from the port to the new zone touristique, where the golf course directly overlooks some small coves. If you fancy a change, there is the beach at **Melloula**, seven kilometres west of Tabarka on the road to Algeria. Leave the car at the top, and you have a 20 minute walk down the hillside to the pebbly beach. East of Tabarka, you have beaches at **Barkoukech** (near the airport), Jebbara and Aïn Sobh.

The archipelago of La Galite Out in the Mediterranean, about 60 km from Tabarka, lies an archipelago of seven small islands (**La Galite**, *Jalta* in Arabic, is the largest; the others have names like Le Gallo, Pollastro and La Gallina). La Galite is clearly visible from Cap Serrat on a clear day. Once upon a time the islands were inhabited by a few fishermen and their families. La Galite, about five kilometres by two kilometres in size, was a stopping off point for Phoenician mariners, and was peopled in Roman times. There are abandoned quarries, caves, remains of Roman tombs and Punic relics. La Garde mountain (361 metres) is the highest point. Generally the islands are off limits, partly in order to preserve the peace and quiet of the rare monk seals living on Galiton. There is occasional talk in the Tunisian press of developing day trips to the islands, but 60 km is a trek and requires a fairly powerful boat. You could ask at the diving schools in the port area about the possibility of a visit. Basically, the islands are an off-limits nature reserve.

Essentials

Tabarka has a good range of hotels, although demand tends to exceed supply in the summer months. Although new A/B grade hotels along the route touristique have increased the number of beds available, in summer booking is essential. Hotels are listed here according to area: town centre or zone touristique. Note that there is less very cheap accommodation here than in the larger tourist resorts. Good out-of-season bargains are available.

Zone touristique **A** *Abou Nawas Montazah*, T643532/508, F643276. 306 rooms with balcony, phone, heating, no a/c, no fly screens, superb Olympic size pool, beach site, tennis, windsurfing, scuba diving tuition, exercise room and sauna, minimal carpeting so noise echoes through hotel at every step. **A** *Iberotel Méhari*, T670001/3, F643943. 200 rooms, much quieter than Montazah, good restaurant, pool, beach site, tennis. Just across the road is the **B** *Résidence Iberotel Méhari*, self-catering units set in a small pinewood. Safe play area for children, some units with view over golf course. Minimal kitchenware supplied. Residents have use of indoor and outdoor pools in main hotel.

B *Morjane*, on the road behind the sand dunes, T644453, F643888. 160 rooms, the first hotel built on the beach, very convenient. Attractively simple. Staff at reception range from the very unpleasant to the very accommodating. **B** *Paradise Golf*, T643002/440, F643918. **B** *Royal Golf Marhaba*, T644002, F643838. New self-catering accommodation in this price bracket was being built near the golf course in summer 1999.

Town centre **B/C** *Les Mimosas*, on the left as you enter the town, T643018/28, F643276. On top of a hill overlooking the bay, rather nice round pool, 60 rooms with sea view, some in main building, others in an independent wing with balconies. **C** *Hotel Corail*, 76 Av Habib Bourguiba, 50 beds, cheap, but only recommended if funds are low or everything else is full. **C** *Hotel de la Plage*, rue des Pecheurs, T644039. 14 beds. **C** *Hotel Novelty*, Av Habib Bourguiba, T644176/8, F643008. Brand new, 26 rooms, central, very clean. Streetside rooms a little noisy. **C** *Hotel de France*, Av Habib Bourguiba, T644577. 38 beds, restaurant, old fashioned charm, probably the best of the cheap hotels, recently revamped.

Mid-range *Hotel de France*, Av Habib Bourguiba, good food at very decent prices. *Le Pirate*, Porto Corallo, T644061. *Les Arcades*, Porto Corallo, T644069. **Cheap** *Hotel Corail*. *Les Agriculteurs*, T644585, good, cheap, very filling food. *Novelty 66*, Av Habib Bourguiba, T644367.

Deep sea diving: *Scuba Diving Club*, Port de Tabarka, T644478, the first sub-aqua sports centre in Tunisia, open all year, best season April-October. Dive sites only 15 minutes by boat. Diving also at *Mehari Diving Centre*, 'Le Crab', T643136; *Aquamarin*, T643508; *Loisirs de Tabarka*, T643002. The Yachting Club at the Port de Pêche Tabarka is recommended by the Tunisian National Tourist Office as the best place to learn snorkelling and scuba diving. Snorkels can be rented from Magasin Sinbad d'Equipment Marin, at the port. Only those with club membership may participate in diving – in other words you have to join – but the club premises are of a very high standard and the changing facilities are excellent. Rescue equipment is available. **Golf**: 18-hole course, 6,400m, par 72, fees 30-35Dt per day. *El Morjane*, T644028, F644026. **Horse riding**: Can be arranged at the hotels. There may be some horse-trekking available in the near future. **Sailing**: The marina has 50 moorings with planned extension to 280 berths. **Tennis**: At the hotels.

Sleeping
■ *on map*
Price codes:
see inside front cover
Phone code: 08

Eating

Sports

Northern Tunisia

👉 *On the origins of an Italian enclave*

"In 1530, or thereabouts, Jean Doria, commander of four galleys belonging to his uncle and adoptive father, André Doria, having heard that Dragut, the famous pirate of Algiers, was at the island of Corsica with six galleys, set out on the attack and captured him. Doria mocked Dragut about how such a famous pirate had let himself be taken. Dragut, a proud man, replied that the thing which made him most angry was that he had been captured by a ragassou, a mere young man. Doria, angered by this answer, had him clapped in irons, and Dragut was transferred to the galleys of one M Lomellini, of Genoa, who dealt with his ransom. Among a number of things, Dragut promised to give him the island of Tabarka for its coral fishing. He kept his promise, and the gift was confirmed by the firmans of Soliman II, Ottoman emperor who had conquered the kingdom of Tunis. Later Lomellini reached an agreement with Charles V, who agreed to have a citadel built there and maintain a garrison to defend the island, on the condition that the Genoese who traded there pay him five percent on all their trade. The agreement was kept for some time, and Charles V had the castle, which I have just described, constructed. He took stones from ancient Tabraca, and a number of stones with epitaphs can be found in the castle."

Jean-André Peyssonel, Voyage dans les régences de Tunis et d'Alger *(extract from the tenth letter, Cap Nègre, 28 November 1724)* .

Shopping **Market day**: Friday. **Handicrafts**: Little of interest apart from Tabarka briar pipes (although the shop that did these on Av Bourguiba, near the Hotel Novelty, has closed) and the ubiquitous coral. In fact, Mediterranean red coral is now severely endangered, having been collected for jewellery for centuries. Prices reflect the rarity and difficulty of collecting the coral. **Other souvenirs**: you will also find lots of crude arbutus wood carvings of eagles, snakes, stags etc. In the soft toy range, the Select Shop in the port had some rather nice furry wild boars (*hallouf*) along with the more usual camels.

Transport **Local Car hire**: *Hertz*, Port Corallo, T644570. *Interlo*, Blvd de 7 Novembre, T643595; *7 Novembre* at Airport, T640005, F640133.

Long distance Air: T655150, internal flights to Tunis Fri 1600, Sun 1830 take 40 minutes. From Tunis Fri 1450, Sun 1730. **Road**: the long distance **bus** station is in rue du Peuple (1st street on the right going uphill from the central square). Information from Société National de Transport, rue de Peuple, on T444048. Departures **Tunis** (via Mateur) 0400, 0500, 0730, 0900, 1545; **Tunis** (via Béja) 0600, 1000, 1300. The local bus station is 50 metres uphill from the central square. Frequent departures to **Aïn Draham** and **Jendouba**. 2 buses a day to **Bizerte**. Information from Société Régionale de Transport Général de Jendouba, Av Habib Bourguiba, on T644097. **Louages**: the station is at the beginning of Av Habib Bourguiba. Departures for **Jendouba, Aïn Draham, Le Kef** and sometimes **Tunis**. **Tuf tuf**: from tourist hotels to marina/old harbour along tourist road. Leaves on the hour from old harbour. **Sea**: Port – Harbour Master's Office, T644599, F643595.

Directory **Banks** *BNT* and *UIB* on Av Habib Bourguiba. *BNA* on rue de Peuple. **Hospital & medical services** Hospital: on rue de Calle, T644023. **Post & telecommunications** Area code: 08. **Post Office**: Av Hedi Chaker, T644417. Mon-Fri 0830-1230 and 1500-1800, Sat 0830-1330. **Tourist offices** 32 Av Habib Bourguiba, T670111. Open 0900-1200 and 1600-1900, after the main square on the right. Only basic information. **Tour companies & travel agents** *Tabarka Voyages*, Av Ennasr (route d'Aïn Draham), T643740, F643726. *Tunisie Voyages* in *Hotel Mehari*, T643136/325,

F643868. *Ulysse Tour*, Blvd de 7 Novembre, T643582, F643622. *Vaga Tours*, Cité des Arts, T644416, F654803. **Useful addresses Police station:** on rue du Peuple, T644021. Maritime police, Port de Tabarka. **Border police:** Melloula, T632889/860. **Police-Babouche-Algerian border:** T655150.

Southwards from Tabarka

Heading southwards from Tabarka, the road, flanked by tall eucalyptus, runs across flat meadowland. After crossing the Oued Rannagha, you begin the winding climb up towards Aïn Draham. (There are wonderful views back towards the coast.) The vegetation changes, the cork oak replaces the maquis and the oleander. At Babouch (21 km from Tabarka), there is a turning west to **Hammam Bourguiba**, 17 km, a thermal spa greatly prized by the Romans. There are two springs, the lower emerging at 38.5°C and the higher at 50°C. The spa facilities are still managed by the Office national du thermalisme and the ONTT, the Tunisian Tourist Board. The high sulphur levels in the water are good for treating respiratory problems. In the vaporium, the treatment is to inhale vapour from nose cups, the aim being to 'coat' the nasal mucus and sinuses.

C *Hotel Hammam Bourguiba*, T08-632517, F08-632497. Open all year, has 40 rooms and 20 bungalows and is used by Tunisians taking treatment. This road also leads to the Algerian border but the crossing in this area has about 10 km between control posts, a walk not to be undertaken lightly. Border post control at Babouch, T08-647150. — **Sleeping**

Aïn Draham   عين دراهم

Phone code: 08
Colour map 1, grid A2

Aïn Draham is located up in the Khroumirie Mountains. Surrounded by wooded hills, it is a one-street sort of place, focusing on a main road lined with big old trees and whitewashed buildings. The cafés are torpid, the people look poorer than in east-coast Tunisia, on the main 'square' stalls sell local craftwork. Happily, there are signs that prosperity is on its way: newly built housing, all roofed in local red-tiles, spreads out on the surrounding slopes, up-market hotels have appeared in the region. Coming up from the inland plains in summer, the cool air of Aïn Draham is a welcome change. The town is popular as a base for hunters in winter, the wild boar that go rootling through the cork oak forest being the main target. In chilly years, city Tunisians come up to Aïn Draham to see the snow. In summer, you will find some pleasant walks in the surrounding hills, maybe even some horse riding. A short drive south, off the Jendouba road, the Lutyens-style village of Beni M'tin feels like some half-forgotten 1930s hill station.

Ins and outs

Aïn Draham can be reached by public transport from Tabarka and Jendouba. Journey time by louage from Tabarka is about 45 minutes, from Jendouba 80 minutes. — **Getting there**

The town is easily visited on foot. Getting up to Beni M'tin is awkward, although it may be possible to find a louage. — **Getting around**

Northern Tunisia

History and background

To start with some etymology, Aïn Draham means 'spring of the dirhams', the dirham being a long-established currency unit in the Middle East (and official currency in Morocco and the UAE today). And dirham derives from the Greek drachma.

Aïn Draham lies 175 km west of Tunis and 26 km south of Tabarka. The present settlement, stretched out along the main Jendouba to Tabarka road, dates from protectoral times. The steep red-tiled roofs – an indication of snowy winters – make the town feel like some Basque country settlement that fetched up in North Africa. Thick cork-oak forests surround the town, running up to 1,000 metres into the mountains. Aïn Draham is the sort of place where French army officers' wives might have escaped the sticky summer heat of Tunis. In winter, temperatures can get down to freezing, and some years, snow is common. Aïn Draham is also the heart of the wild boar hunting region and it can be difficult to find places in hotels during the season from October to March.

Sights

The Association du Patrimoine Populaire et Historique Aïn Draham is found in a small office where products of the regional arts are displayed. The people there are very welcoming. Just north of Aïn Draham, to the west of the road, is Col des Ruines. This small detour has splendid views as does the terrace of *Hotel Nour el Aïn*.

The local craftwork, although enthusiastically executed, is often of poor quality. You may find some nice large ash-wood bowls. On the roads into Aïn Draham, small children make whooping noises from the side of the road to attract the driver's attention. On sale, according to the season, may be ferns and red-berried *subhan el khallak* in cork-bark pots, shell necklaces, arbutus-wood model wild boar and very Kenyan-looking gazelles.

Beni M'Tin is a spectacular detour off the main road south of Aïn Draham. The reservoir, built in 1955 on the Oued el Lil, a tributary of the Oued Medjerda, is one of Tunisia's largest. The village of Beni M'Tin, built high up among the cork oak woods, is a curious place. The buildings have a 1920s Lutyens feel. There is a church and a mosque, and a large square overlooked by a small café with a fireplace which must have been a pleasant, snug place in its day. Shutters and doors have been given a rather tasteless red-and-black paint job. Beni M'Tin feels like it was built for a population of wealthy weekenders who have not been around for many a year.

Bene M'tir
région d'Aïn Draham

Essentials

B *Hammam Bourguiba*, in Hammam Bourguiba, T647217. **B** *La Forêt*, T655302 **Sleeping**
F655335. The Aïn Draham area's most expensive hotel, (50Dt per person, single supplement 20Dt ; suite at 230Dt). Expensive for what's on offer. Indoor pool being built.
On the road south from the town. **B** *Hotel Rihana* T655391, F655396. 3-star place
under same management as *Les Chênes* (see below). **C** *Hotel Nour el Aïn*, T655000,
F655185. 60 rooms, open all year, covered heated pool, health club, international
menu, busiest in hunting season. **D** *Beau Séjour*, Av Habib Bourguiba, T647005. 30
rooms, an old hunting lodge, restaurant, central, book in summer. **D** *Les Chênes*,
T655211, F655396. 32 rooms, out of town, 7 km towards Jendouba, looking very
worn, good, food, rather secluded, set in the middle of the forest, organizes wild boar
hunting. **D** *Rehana*, T647391. At the south end of the town on the road to Jendouba,
75 rooms, comfortable hotel with a very memorable view overlooking the valley,
within walking distance of the village, book in summer.

Youth hostel Situated at the top of the hill, kitchen, 150 beds, T647087.

Expensive *Grand Maghreb* is good but expensive. **Mid-range** *Café de la* **Eating**
Republique, on Av 7 Novembre is recommended.

Wild boar hunting October-February, and woodcock shooting is advertised for this **Sports**
region in winter, see *Hotel Les Chênes*. Huge new sports complex 6 km south of town.

Road Bus: the bus station is at the bottom of Av Habib Bourguiba, on the right, by **Transport**
the cemetery. Frequent buses to **Tunis**, **Jendouba** and **Tabarka**. **Louages**: the station is situated at the top of Av Habib Bourguiba, on the square. Main routes are to
Jendouba and *Tabarka*.

Banks All on Av Habib Bourguiba. *BNT, STB* are opposite Association du Patrimoine, and *BNA* is **Directory**
beyond the Tourist Office. **Communications** Area code: 08. **Post Office**: Av Habib Bourguiba,
T647118. Further up the road after the Association du Patrimoine. **Emergencies Police:** Av
Habib Bourguiba, T647150. **Medical services Hospital:** is on route de l'Hôpital, T647047.
Tourist offices Syndicat D'Initiative, Av Habib Bourguiba, towards the top, T647115.

South from Aïn Draham

Moving south from Aïn Draham, the road continues to twist up through the
woods, with here and there some superb views across hills and plains. You pass
the Hotel La Forêt with its view looking back up to Aïn Draham and then, more
isolated, the Hotel Les Chênes, shortly after which is the turn off for the
hill-village of **Beni M'tir**. At 45 km from Aïn Draham you reach **Fernana**,
interesting for an anecdote about how the tribes decided to pay their taxes to
the bey. At Fernana (which means 'oak'), the tribal leaders would assemble
under a great oak tree and await the tree's decision on whether they should pay
or not. The movement of the branches meant 'no', and it was a rare year that
the branches did not move. The importance of the story is that it demonstrates
that the tribes were practically independent from central authority, right up
until the development of the Tunisian nation state in the mid-20th century.

After Fernana, it is another 15 km before you come to a cross-roads, just
north of **Jendouba**, where you can opt to go left to **Bulla Regia** (three kilometres) or right to **Chemtou**, ancient Simitthu, some 17 km away.

Bulla Regia بلاريجية

Colour map 1, grid B2

Under the Djebel Rebia, situated on a flat plain, Bulla Regia is one of the most unusual sites in northern Tunisia. This was a town whose wealth was built on cereal farming, for the plains of northern Tunisia came to provide Rome with large quantities of grain. Bulla Regia's wealthy farmers and merchants saw no reason to deprive themselves of pleasant surroundings, and their underground homes, almost unique in the ancient world, were opulent and refined. Some of the building work is still impressive: stone for the Romans seems to have been like butter, they sliced through it to make the most complicated joints and vaults. It is doubtful whether today's concrete and brick homes down the road in Jendouba achieve the same degree of comfort as the trogolodyte villas of Bulla Regia.

Ins and outs

Getting there   Bulla Regia lies 3 km east of the Aïn Draham-Jendouba road. Take a bus from Jendouba and ask to get off at Bulla Regia. The intersection is 6 km north of Jendouba and is signed to Bulla Regia and Bou Salem. You will have to walk or hitch the remaining 3 km.

Getting around   As you drive up from the crossroads, the Antiquarium or museum and guichet is on your right, along with the South Baths and the Church of Alexander. The vast majority of the site is on your left. An hour is the minimum time to allow for exploring the site. Do not miss the House of the Hunt (Maison de la Chasse). There is no accommodation at the site. Visit the museum first (café and toilets), where you may be able to buy a guide book.

History and background

In 2 BC, Bulla Regia was the capital of one of the three small kingdoms set up by the Romans in Numidia after the death of Masinissa. Prosperity was to come under the rule of Hadrian, when the town was raised to the status of *colonia* (117 AD). The economic development of the town was based on its strategic position on trade routes and the fertility of the surrounding plain which produced grain in abundance. The finest houses date from the third century AD. There are the remains of two basilicas dating from Byzantine times.

It is probable that Bulla Regia grew up to serve the needs of the grain trade in the upper Medjerda valley. Italian agriculture was devastated by the Second Punic War and the social uprisings of the last years of the Republic. It was under Numidian ruler Masinissa that the region's potential was revealed. Masinissa, tribal chief of the Massyli, built himself a North African Kingdom. Seizing Carthage's grain lands, he began to export to Rome.

Eventually, the Numidian lands were to come into the imperial system in the mid-first century BC. By the second century BC, Rome had developed a voracious appetite for grain. It is estimated that the empire's capital required 400,000 tonnes per annum,

Bulla Regia

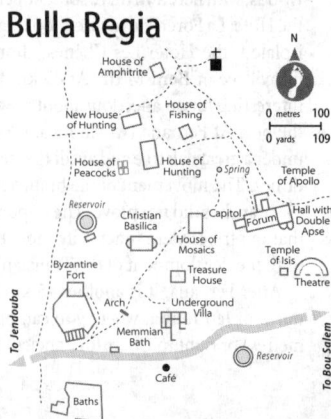

with the army requiring a further 100,000 tonnes. Africa was better placed than Egypt to satsify the demand, being only three to five sailing days from Rome's main port, Ostia, as opposed to 17 to 22 days from Alexandria to Ostia. Risks of shipwreck and transport costs were thus lower. Africa also had climatic advantages: fairly reliable winter rains, mild frost-free springs and good summer sun. The Roman peace did the rest, creating conditions in which irrigation works could be built and towns like Bulla Regia could grow and flourish.

The ruins are laid out on terraces below the steep slopes of Djebel Rebia (647 metres) overlooking a large plain, which is particularly hot in summer and cold in winter. The Roman builders' solution to this climatic problem was to build houses partly underground, a system which can be seen still in use today at Matmata in south-central Tunisia. **Visiting the site**

These **underground villas** are the main attraction in Bulla Regia. Despite earthquake damage to the surface features, many of the villas are well preserved due to their unusual architecture. Like normal, above-ground villas, the general style was to have the eating and sleeping rooms centred around a large underground courtyard, thus giving the owners – wealthy people, judging from the luxurious decoration – the chance to escape the winter cold and the glare and heat of the summers. Despite being underground, these homes were carefully orientated to benefit from the sunlight at different times of day. The villas were no doubt the first really comfortable houses in the region.

The decision to develop underground homes required the right sort of technical solution. In the **Maison de la Chasse**, note that the ceilings are arched. To build these vaults, the inventive Roman builders came up with the hollow terracotta tube. Bottomless bottle-shaped tubes, the neck generally facing upwards, were slotted together to form arches and then sealed with cement. No doubt the inside of the vault was plastered and decorated. Given the materials available perhaps this was the best solution for creating strong but light roofing. Originally, the system was used only for simple barrel vaults. Later it was applied to domes and more complicated forms of vaulting.

Most of the better mosaics have been taken to the Bardo Museum (see Tunis page 90), but in the **House of Fishing** and the **House of Amphitrite** some magnificent mosaics are still in place. Above-ground structures which are still visible include the **Theatre** complete with stage, the **Memmian Baths** near the entrance, the **Forum**, the **Temple of Apollo**, and a Christian Basilica. The **Forum** is a rectangular area with religious and public buildings on all four sides. To the west is the Capitol of which little remains, to the north stands the Temple of Apollo, more ancient than the Forum on to which it opens by means of a small courtyard. A quite remarkable group of statues found here are on display in the Bardo Museum, in particular that of Apollo which gave its name to the temple. A hall with double apse and paved geometric mosaics in very poor condition stands to the east.

The Memmian Baths (some of the walls of the *frigidarium* still standing)

Mosaic of Triton from the Triumph of Venus

are by the entrance to the site. Beneath are basement rooms with groin vaults. In 1942, a hoard of 70 seventh century Byzantine pieces of gold was discovered in an underground villa north of the Memmian Baths, now renamed the Treasure House, indicating occupancy up to that late period. Here an examination of the mosaic pattern shows the arrangement of the dining room. ■ *Open every day except Monday, summer 0800-1900 and winter 0830-1730, closed Monday, entrance 2Dt, photography fee 1Dt.*

Chemtou شمتو

Colour map 1, grid B1

The ancient Simittus, modern Chemtou, is yet another unusual Roman site. Here you can see the impressive results of ancient industrial archaeology, intelligently displayed and interpreted in a superb museum. Simittuss was one of the most important quarries of the Roman world, supplying a unique golden marble to decorate opulent building schemes: imperial propaganda through overblown architecture. Spreading out below a rocky, half-quarried hill, the site of Simittuss, once home to a slave army and Roman overlords, is an unassuming place today. Sheep graze over the lumpy terrain which still conceals a whole town. Children splash in the water by the titanic blocks of the ruined bridge. There are skylarks and redstarts and the occasional hovering bird of prey. To the west, the grey hills rise up towards the Algerian frontier. Do not miss the view from the top of the quarry hill.

Ins and outs

Getting there The C59 is now fully metalled the whole way to Chemtou from the turn-off on the main P17 Aïn Draham to Jendouba road (distance 17 km). If you don't have your own transport, you should be able to get a rural minibus up from Jendouba in the morning, although the minibus may stop at the settlement a few kilometres short of the site. As you come into Chemtou by car, take a left turn and the road will bring you up and over between 2 parts of the hill. You then come down to the car park and museum.

History

The original Numidian settlement of Simittus became a Roman colony under Augustus (27 BC-14 AD), taking on the name Colonia Iulia Augusta Numidica Simmithensium. It was also known by the snappier acronym CIANS.

The colony quickly won fame for its **yellow marble**, *il giallo antico*, which continued to be quarried until Byzantine times. This city was situated at the junction of two important routes: west from Carthage through Bulla Regia and south from Tabarka (*Thabraca*). It covered a large area (about 80 hectares), both on the hilltop by the quarries where there are huge masonry blocks belonging to a ruined Roman temple (perhaps dedicated to Saturn), and below where there are large baths (ruins) and the complicated water system that supplied and connected them to the aqueduct. Here too was a theatre, parts of which have been excavated, a forum, a basilica and a building thought to be a *schola*.

Il giallo antico Yellow marble from Chemtou was to become the height of fashion in Rome. Pliny the Elder tells of elegant Emilius Lepidus ordering a table in thuya wood from the Atlas and having his doorsteps done in yellow Chemtou marble. In 46 BC, the quarries became part of the ruling Iulii family's property. Later they became part of the imperial domains. In 44 BC, when Julius Caesar was assassinated, the Roman plebs erected a column of Chemtou marble to his memory.

In an imperial system where the succession went through periods of turbulence, the ruling caste was ever seeking for new ways to impress its power on the people. Splendid building was one way to do this, fine stone, and in particular marble, helped. From Greece came green Thessalian marble and green porphyry, while Phrygia produced a prized veiny marble. Egypt was the source of pink and grey granite and red porphyry. Africa produced 'the golden rock of the Numidians'. In large pieces, this stone was rather fragile, and so it tended to be used for veneering and occasional columns. The Pantheon built from 118 to 124 under Hadrian made use of it. The colour of Chemtou marble eventually became a poetic commonplace: Martial describes an amphitheatre lion as having 'a mane similar in colour to Numidian marble'. In fact, the colour of the marble quarried at Chemtou varied considerably, from white through veiny yellows to greys and greenish-ochres, as a display of samples in the site museum shows.

Sights

Situated between the craggy hill dominating the site and the River Medjerda, **The museum** the site museum is all that you could ask for. Although the finds are not obviously spectacular, they do tell a story. The displays are excellent, and the place is not too big for children to get bored in. For the English-speaking visitor, there is the slight drawback of displays being labelled in French, German and Arabic only. However, the displays are well-thought out enough for school French and imagination to get you a long way.

There is a good display of the evolution of the **Libyic script**, the first writing system in the region. The geometric forms are well known, and bilingual Libyic and Latin inscriptions have been discovered. Like later Semitic alphabets, ancient Libyic was a consonant-based system, the vowels being left unmarked. Most of the texts known today are from Dougga and Makthar and are funerary inscriptions.

There is a telling panel about the analysis of 337 skeletons from a **Numidian necropolis** discovered under the later Roman forum. Basically, the bone analysis revealed different stages in the local people's development. Prior to 3000 BC, 80 percent of children never got beyond the age of six, and life expectancy was only 50. From 300 to 100 BC, the bones are more resistant, the skeletons better preserved. The men have more distorted skeletons (bow-legged, distorted femurs), possibly as they spent much time as mounted warriors? Finally, in the third period, post-100 BC, the skeletons are in an even better condition, with no fractures due to violence, indicating more settled times.

Despite the limited archaeological discoveries, the museum is interesting on the Numidian Kingdoms, which basically flourished in the second century BC, during the long reigns of Masinissa (202-148 BC) and Micipsisa (148-118 BC.) This was a time of prosperity for the local Massyli tribe, and agriculture developed considerably on the Medjerda plains. (Numidia's independent status later unravelled with dynastic infighting in the first century BC.) The museum has a mock up of the **Numidian monument**, thought to have been built under Micipsa around 130 BC to the glory of Masinissa. This would make the building contemporary to the Dougga monument to Masinissa. The monument, as restituted here, is endearingly eclectic, hung with stone shields and breast plates, the roof defined by an Egyptian cornice-line and supported by Doric pilasters. Later the building became a temple to Saturn, before being switched over to the incense-heavy rites of Byzantine Christianity. (Think of Roman Catholicism grafting itself on to animist rites in contemporary Africa.)

Other interesting items in the museum include ancient tools and explanations of the slave barracks. There is a display of small ornamental statues of

Venus at different stages in their production, and a copy of the unique Baal Saturn plate, of which the original is in the Louvre. All things Hellenic indicated taste in the wealthy Roman household. One might decorate one's villa with copies of fifth century Greek statuary, and the sophisticates of Chemtou were no exception: there is a copy of the Dresden Youth (**Le jeune de Dresde**), from an original by Polycleitus, which no doubt adorned some atrium. In a niche, the results of patient archaeological work are on show in the shape of the partly restored terra-cotta statue of the emperor Commodus as Hercules (recognizable by the skin of the Nemean lion). And there is the inevitable mosaic, a representation of *Dionysos cosmocrator*, Dionysus lord of the universe, a popular theme in African mosaics.

Perhaps the most spectacular discovery at Chemtou was the **hoard** of coins uncovered in May 1993 when the museum was being constructed. An earthenware pot was brought to light containing 1648 gold pieces, weighing over seven kilograms. A careful study of the emperors on these coins indicated that the hoard was buried a few years before the Vandal invasion, towards 420 AD.

■ *Open 1000-1700 October-March, 0900-1800 April-September.*

The site   Ancient Simittus was explored in the 19th century in a limited sort of way. However, it wasn't until 1970 that serious excavations got going, with the Institut National du Patrimoine working with the German archaeological school in Rome, led by F Rakob. The main buildings explored were the workers barracks ('camp des ouvriers') and the Numidian monument at the summit of the hill.

Outside the museum, there is an interesting stretch of Roman road which has been unearthed, and no doubt great plaques of marble were transported along it and down to the river. Leaving the museum, if you turn left down a rough track, you will come to the forum, with remains of its nymphaeum, basilica, and some Numidian tombs. The theatre is straight ahead, and were you to follow the track straight on, and turn right, you come to the remains of the baths.

More impressive, however, are the remaining arches of a huge **bridge**, built by the III Legion in 112 in Trajan's reign, over the Oued Medjerda, then known as the Bagrada. Apparently, the bridge was washed away in serious flooding in the fourth century. The system set up for a **water-driven cornmill** either by or on the bridge (locks, sluices and water channels) can be discerned. This is an unusual feature, the only one of its kind known in Africa, and represents the height of Roman mechanical technology.

The quarries   The overgrown terrain of Chemtou today is still dominated by the craggy hill site of the quarries. Perhaps the most impressive thing is the transport of the marble. Great columns, carved from a single block, were transported over the Khroumirie Mountains and down to Tabarka. The first recorded road, 60 km long, was built under Hadrian in 129. Perhaps prior to then the stone was shipped out down the river. The whole quarrying process was highly organized, with blocks of marble cut to various standard sizes and marked with the name of the reigning Emperor, the proconsul for Africa and the quarry manager. In fact, large numbers of blocks from the first and second centuries AD were discovered stored ready for use in the Marmorata neighbourhood of Rome when it was cleared in the 19th century. But it was not just in the imperial capital where the state was building to impress. Across the provinces of the empire, cities conducted extensive building programmes that demanded costly stone.

If you wish to carry on south from Chemtou, note that the track across the river bed leading to the P6 requires a four-wheel drive vehicle. For real enthusiasts, the track directly west from Chemtou leads to **Thuburnica**, a visit for the really dedicated, but not without interest. (There is a well-preserved Roman bridge.) Thuburnica can also be reached by a right-turn just after Ghardimaou, signposted 'Tubournic 13 km'. The ruins are in a red stone, and there is a post-Second World War mock Roman villa (arch. Paul Herbé), built for a wealthy French farmer.

Thuburnica: another minor Roman site
Colour map 1, grid B1

South from Chemtou to Jendouba

Jendouba is an important crossroads and administrative centre 44 km south of Tabarka and 154 km west of Tunis, providing easy access to Bulla Regia, Chemtou and the Algerian border. All the main banks have branches here.

D *Simithu*, on the right, by the roundabout when arriving from Bulla Regia, T631695, F631743. New hotel, 26 rooms, restaurant, on the main road, not very appealing. **E** *Atlas*, rue du 1er Juin 1955, T633217, F655396. Behind the police station, probably the only decent hotel in town. **Youth hostel**: 60 beds, meals, T631292.

Sleeping
Phone code: 08

Train The train station is off the main square, by the police station. Departures **Tunis** 0554, 1033, 1240, 1515, 1653. **Bus** the bus station is to west of town, past the railway lines. Information on T630411. Frequent local buses to **Tunis**, **Le Kef**, **Tabarka** and **Aïn Draham**, also buses to the border at Ghardimaou. They do not cross the border so you will have to cross on foot. **Louages**: for **Ghardimaou** they leave from the station on Blvd Sakiet Sidi Sousse. For Tunis they leave from rue 1 Juin 1955.

Transport

West from Jendouba : Parc National de Feidja

Ghardimaou, 34 km west of Jendouba, is on the way out towards Algeria. It is not worth a visit on its own account. There is the **E** Hotel *Thubernic*, T08-660043, if you wish to stay on the way to **Parc National de Feidja**, one of Tunisia's six National Parks, 17 km up in the hills near the Algerian frontier, set up to protect the Barbary deer. Take the P6 out of Jendouba and turn north just before the frontier post. You may well be flagged down by border police in any case and asked to show papers. (Border at Ghardimaou T08-645004.)

There is a winding metalled road right up to the tiny settlement of **Aïn Soltane**, and then onto the end of the road, where you have a forest nursery, a semi-abandoned summer youth hostel and a national guard post. Should you wish to continue up into the national park, they will want to take your passport. A four-wheel drive will be necessary if you wish to drive, otherwise you will have to walk from here. No information on the national park was available in the area. Although a wish to develop 'eco-tourism' has been expressed in the Tunisian press, Feidja's location on the frontier with Algeria, where the security situation is delicate, to say the least, would seem to have put the brakes on public investment in park infrastructure, despite the efforts of the GDZ (German International Cooperation).

The Barbary deer was brought back from near extinction by the creation of the reserve in the 1960s, with 420 hectares set aside especially for it. The deer can be heard braying in the rutting period in the late summer. Other features of the park include numerous woodpeckers, a plantation of cedars, that most emblematic tree of the Atlas Mountains, and traces of Libyic and Numidian settlement. If you are very lucky, you might catch a glimpse of the secretive and spotted cerval.

Wildlife

Northern Tunisia

East from Jendouba to Béja

Before proceeding south to Le Kef (below), visitors are recommended to find time to make a journey northeast to **Béja**, either by road or railway. For the first 22 km to Bou Salem, both are alongside the **Oued Medjerda**, the only river in Tunisia which flows all year round. The road crosses the two main tributaries, the Oued Mellègue and Oued Tessa, which can be spectacular in flood and very disappointing at other times, while the railway line from Jendouba to Béja runs along the far side of the main valley.

Bou Salem is a large successful market town dealing with the agricultural produce, mainly cereals but some grapes and livestock, of this fertile valley. You can see why the Romans referred to this area as their 'bread basket'. From Bou Salem the road climbs up wooded slopes to Béja, while the railway crosses and recrosses the main river before turning north to Béja.

Béja   باجة

Phone code: 08
Colour map 1, grid B2

Ancient Vaga (modern Béja) has had an eventful history. Today it is a quietly prosperous market town, overlooked by the usual Husseinid fortifications. It has a pleasant médina with mosques and zaouias, and some very fine early 20th century building. Béja makes a relaxing short halt on the way to the Roman sites of the northwest. It's a shame that there's not more of it to visit.

Ins and outs

Getting there   The bus and train stations are at the bottom of the main street with frequent connections to/from Tunis and Jendouba.

Sights

This town has had a lively history, marked by various unfriendly visitors, including Genseric's Vandals in the mid-fifth century and the Fatimid hordes in the 10th century. Today, fortunately for the residents, there is less excitement, but it is worth a wander round the médina and up towards the keep in the kasbah area for a fine view of the town. Béja has a good location, surrounded by excellent agricultural land and hills to the northwest. It is possible to see from the expanses of cereals why this town was the largest grain market of the Roman Africa. Today, it is still a very busy junction of six important roads.

The old town has the usual mosques and zaouias. From the town centre, leaving the Maison de la Culture (the former church) on your left, head down the bustling rue Kheïreddine with its market stalls and shops. At Bab el Aïn, there is a pleasant small square with an old public fountain. An effort seems to have been made in this part of Béja to avoid jarring modern building. The shop fronts have old-style wooden awnings painted caper-green. Walking around these old neighbourhoods, you can get a feel for life in a Tunisian provincial town. The **Grand Mosque** has a striking red minaret, with Almohad motifs. Look out for the green-domed Zaouia of Sidi Abdel Kader, which today functions as a crèche.

Overlooking the médina area, the Byzantine **Kasbah** was named Theodoriana after the emperor Justinian's wife. It is now used by the army. Though the fortress was remodelled on numerous occasions, it bears witness to the re-establishment of Byzantine authority in Africa in the early sixth century AD.

Ancient intrigue: Sophonisbe, Masinissa, Syphax and the Romans

By 204 BC, Hannibal, despite the elephants and the strategy, had lost all hope of defeating Rome. Tough-nut Roman general Scipio decided to defeat the Carthaginians on their home ground in Africa. He came to a semi-alliance with Syphax, leader of the Masaesyli, a most powerful African clan who ruled over vast expanses of western Numidia. Carthage was threatened but then, inconveniently for Scipio, love intervened.

The ageing Syphax fell for Sophonisbe, daughter of Hasdrubal, the general responsible for Carthage's defence. Hasdrubal gave his daughter's hand in marriage, Syphax changed sides. Scipio was left with the rather more problematic support of Masinissa, young ruler of the other major tribe, the Massyli of eastern Numidia.

The situation was not an easy one. But then things took a surprising turn. Though Masinissa's forces were nearly exterminated by Syphax, Masinissa himself survived. There was a resurgence in support for him, and he headed south to await the arrival of Scipio's armies. Landing near Utica in 204

BC with 30,000 men, Scipio had a slow start. Then he managed to set fire to the Punic-Numidian camp, and defeated Hasdrubal in battle near Carthage. He also took Syphax. Masinissa seized his chance, and invaded Cirta, Syphax' capital.

Masinissa was met by the ravishing Sophonisbe. She begged Masinissa not to hand her over to the Romans. So moving were her appeals, that he fell in love with her, marrying her the same day. Syphax was furious, Scipio worried about the potential loss of an ally. He demanded that Masinissa hand over Sophonisbe, wife of the captive Syphax. But Masinissa remembered his promise that she would never pass into Roman hands. He sent her a cup of poison, which she drank as the only way out.

Masinissa went on to do well, of course: he was given the official title of king by Rome and awarded a triumph. Sophonisbe continued into history as another Punic tragedy queen. With her name attached to the Espace Sophonisbe, an élitist women's club in the modern suburb of Carthage, she is unlikely to be forgotten.

Essentials

Sleeping
Phone code: 08

C *Hotel Vaga*, T450818, F465902. With 36 beds. Has recently moved upmarket. **E** *Hotel Hiba*, 5 Av de la République, a few doors down from the Municipality, T457244, F456299. Not as good as the nearby Phénix. **E** *Hotel Phénix*, Av de la République, almost opposite the Municipality, T450188, F450679. With 30 beds. **E** *Hotel Bou Tefaha*, rue Farhat Hached, street parallel to rue Kheïreddine, opposite the Zaouia de Sidi Bou Tefaha. Basic. **Youth hostel**: T450621. Opposite the bus station, 80 beds, meals available.

Directory

Medical emergencies Hospital on Av Bourguiba. Pharmacie de nuit opposite the cinema behind the former church. **Travel agents** *Vaga Tours*, Av 18 Janvier, T451805.

Short excursions from Béja

Monument to tough Roman engineering, **Trajan's Bridge**, once part of the Roman east-west road network, lies not far from the minor road C76 about 13 km southwest of Béja. To get there locate the Béja bypass, which runs south of the town. If coming from the Tunis direction (east), turn left onto the boulevard de l'Environnement (large sign in central reservation). To your right is the new self-built housing area, Maâgoula. Follow the paved road for around 7.5 km. You come to a point where eucalyptus trees line the road. Go right down a track, lined with eucalyptus. After rainy weather, small cars risk getting

Northern Tunisia

bogged down here. On your left is farmland, much of which can be under water on your right, on high ground, you may see a train go by. After about 4 km, you come to the old railway track, abandoned because of the rising waters of the **Sidi Salem dam lake**. Trajan's bridge is on your left, almost opposite a small obelisk war memorial surrounded by tamarisk trees.

This three-arched Roman bridge, which seemingly has nothing to do with Trajan at all, is still probably in splendid condition. However, thanks to the dam, the bridge now resembles Trajan's hump-backed whale for much of the year – when it is visible at all. If you want to see the top of the bridge, the only time is the late summer/early autumn, when the dam waters are low. With its 70 metre span, the bridge dates from the time of Tiberius.

Even if the bridge is practically invisible, this is a good excursion for bird-watchers. There are all sorts of waders, and the flooded woodland plus narrow mudflats along the lake shores are good terrain for all sorts of birds, including notably waders. About 1 km after Trajan's Bridge, you will come to the old railway bridge (views across the lake), still used by isolated rural communities on the south side.

There are **Second World War cemeteries** in the Béja area. One is just outside the northern limits of Béja with 396 graves. If Dougga is on your itinerary, you could head south-west for **Thibar**. There are two possible approaches: leaving Béja, turn off left about 110 metres after the roadside village of Hammam Siyala, at the sign marked 'Sehili'. Coming from the west, you can turn right, take the better C75, turning off right south of **Bou Salem**. The road winds up to Thibar, and in 1999 was undergoing improvement works. There is another war cemetery at Thibar with some 60 graves about 800 metres north of the village, adjacent to the agricultural college. ■ *Both open 0730-1430 Saturday-Thursday*.

The college was founded by the Pères Blancs in 1895 and was developed as a model farm. Though fertile, the area was unhealthy and malaria-infested (*Dherbet el bounyar, wa la cherbet min Thibar* - 'Better to be stabbed than drink Thibar water' went the local adage), and the region was infested with panthers and hyenas. The Fathers set about developing a model farm, including vineyards – and rather typically of French monks, set about inventing a local speciality, coming up with the tawny **Thibarine liqueur**, available at Carthage Airport in exotically shaped bottles. The White Fathers also developed a strain of sheep, and zebu/cow crosses adapted to the local climate. After independence, the Fathers remained at Thibar until 1975. The Domaine St Joseph still functions as an agricultural college. North of Thibar, follow the signs for Montazah Jebba or Parc Jebba, and head for the **Djebba National Park**, a hilly area with a seasonal waterfall and some caves. The road crosses the plain and climbs up through fig and apple orchards to Djebba village. Eventually you come to a car park under the overhanging cliff, and an area fitted out with Tahiti type parasols.

Djebba was the site of a statue to **Notre Dame de Goraâ**. In 1902, the White Fathers had the idea of setting up a statue to the Virgin. Perhaps they had dreams of creating a sort of African Lourdes, although there doesn't seem to have been any miracles performed. The necessary 450 francs was collected, and in May 1903, the Fathers, equipped with a ladder 16 metres long, placed the statue high up on a ledge, next to a curious wall set with arrow slits perched up in the cliff face. A local legend runs that this is where the Seven Sleepers slept. The small statue, a standard catholic representation of the Virgin Mary – referred to by the locals as Sitt Miriyem – survived until 1998, when someone had the bright idea of stealing it. Surprised by the warden, the thieves dropped the statue, breaking its arm. It is now under lock and key in a concrete bunker under the cliff face.

Another possibility, if you have time, is to climb up to the top of **Djebel Goraâ** (900 metres) which will give you a magnificent view over the region. Steps have been built into the cliff face, so you can get to the stoney plateau above Djebba very easily. From the top there are superb views over the Béja plain. Djebba (and indeed Thibar) are well protected from hot summer south winds by the Djebel Goraâ. The village's tiny houses are set among orchards. In the middle distance, Thibar can be seen, its fields defined by tall dark cypresses, below an Aleppo pine forest.

From Thibar, the C75 winds up and across barren hills to **Teboursouk**. Heading south, there is a left turn off for **Aïn Melliti** (3.5 km), which produces mineral water and is home to the ruins of Roman Henchir Mastria. After this turn off, Teboursouk is 19 km further south.

From Jendouba, head south on the P17 for Le Kef, some 60 km away. You can either head for the main east-west P5 Tunis to Le Kef road, or turn off right for Nebeur, a small town on the Oued Mellegue dam. A minor road will bring you into the northern approaches of Kef.

Southwest from Jendouba to Le Kef

Le Kef   الكاف

Le Kef (from 'el kef', Arabic for 'the crag'), 58 km south of Jendouba, is perched 750 metres up on a rocky hill. It is an attractive place with a long history, mainly military in nature due to its important strategic position. It was settled by the Romans and various Muslim dynasties. In the 18th and 19th centuries, it was the third largest town in Tunisia. Le Kef was taken by France in 1881, and its military role was reinforced. During the Second World War it became the provisional capital of the still free Tunisia. Today the town is an important regional centre, untouched by tourism, but with some interesting sights to visit.

Phone code: 08
Colour map 1, grid B2

Ins and outs

Le Kef can be reached by louage from Tunis, Jendouba, Kalaâ el Khasbah, Kalaât Senam and Tajerouine. There are a couple of daily buses from Kairouan (3 hours 30 minutes), Sakiet Sidi Youssef, Sfax (4 hours 30 minutes), and Sousse, nearly 4 hours away. There are more frequent buses from Béja (2 hours), Makthar, Téboursouk and Testour.

Getting there

The main sights in Le Kef can all easily be done on foot in a couple of hours. If you are thinking of day trips, Kalaât Senam is a good 1 hour 45 minutes drive. By public transport, it might be possible to do this as a day trip with a very early start. (For Kalaât Senam and Haïdra see chapter 6, Central Tunisia.) Another possible trip from Le Kef is out to the tiny hot spring (50°C) at Hammam Mellegue, some 10 km west of the town.

Getting around

History and background

Le Kef has a long history, and in classical times was a major town, known to the Romans as Sicca Veneria. The epithet 'Veneria' was added by the Romans, probably because there was a Carthaginian temple on the site, dedicated to the Phoenician goddess Astarte, identified by the Romans with Venus. Sacred prostitution may have been part of the Punic cult of Astarte. Sicca Veneria had a brief moment centre stage after the First Punic War, when Carthage made the error of sending her mercenaries, called back from Sicily, there. A large number of discontented soldiers assembled in an isolated town inevitably led to rebellion, and the War of the Mercenaries was fought from 240 to 237 BC. Sicca Veneria flourished in the second and third centuries BC. It became the seat of a bishopric, and was the site of a number of monasteries.

Le Kef became an important regional centre once more in the 17th and 18th centuries, due to its strategic location in the marchlands dividing the territories of the Beylik of Tunis and the Beylik of Constantine. Certain Husseinid beys lived in fear that some of their male relatives would try to overthrow them with the support of the Beylik of Algiers. (In conclusion to a complicated episode of dynastic politics, the Bey of Constantine's army conquered Tunis from Ali Bey I in 1756.) Le Kef thus occupied a key geopolitical position. Under the French, the town, although home to a garrison, began to lose ground to the farming towns of the Medjerda plain and the port cities of eastern Tunisia.

Sights

With its steep streets, Le Kef is an atmospheric sort of place. Views open up over the surrounding region. The Roman presence is very real, right in the heart of the town, with the spring and half-excavated ancient baths. The people at the Association de Sauvegarde de la Médina's little office, located on Place de l'Indépendance, can be very helpful. All in all, it's a place for wandering. There is a Mediterranean feel without the crowds of fatally picturesque Sidi Bou Saïd.

Starting your walking tour of Le Kef, you might have a look at **Dar el Kous** behind Avenue Habib Bourguiba. This is a fourth-century Christian basilica dedicated to St Peter. If closed, the warden can normally be contacted through the ASM office. **Ras el Aïn** was/is the spring in the middle of Le Kef which supported the town in Roman times. Evidence of channels and a cistern remain.

The **Kasbah** occupies the highest part of Le Kef. The present fortifications go back to the early 17th century, and were much altered under the Husseinids and the French. Much ancient building material was recycled during the building of the earliest parts. The view is impressive. Entrance 1 Dt. In summer the **Bou Makhlouf Festival** takes place in the courtyard. The Kasbah may be closed if a film crew is in the middle of making some epic or other. There are some nice photo-opportunities from up here.

The **Mosque of Sidi Bou Makhlouf,** a reminder of a half-forgotten saint of Fassi origin, is just below the kasbah. This is a very beautiful mosque with interesting domes and an octagonal minaret. The inside is highly decorated with ceramics and stucco.

The **Regional Museum of Popular Arts and Traditions** is located on the place Sidi Ali Aïssa in the former Zaouia of Sidi Ali Ben Aïssa, of the Rahmaniya *tarika* (order). There are four rooms, the most interesting presents

Mosque of Sidi Bou Makhlouf

elements of the everyday nomadic life, including a large tent of the type seen only occasionally today in the southern regions. There is also some interesting information on the soufi orders. ■ *Open winter 0930-1630 and summer 0900-1300 and 1500-1900, closed Monday, entrance 2Dt.*

Essentials

There is entirely adequate accommodation in Le Kef to suit all budgets. **D** *Hotel Les Pins*, Blvd de l'Environnement. A new address in Le Kef, 27 rooms, T204300/204021. **D** *Hotel Les Remparts*, rue des Remparts, T202100, F224766. In the town centre opposite the PTT. **D** *Hotel Sicca Veneria*, Place de l'Indépendence, T221561. Ugly, 34 rooms, central, relatively cheap, restaurant. Coming up for renovation. **E** *Hotel Résidence Venus*, rue Mouldi Khamessi, but no street name to be seen, T/F204695. 20 rooms, most with bath, good value, helpful owner, organizes wild boar hunting. To get there, head up rue de la Source, then turn right onto rue Ali Belhaouane. Then take second left. With a name like Résidence Vénus, this has to be a reasonable address. **F** *El Médina*, 18 rue Farhat Hached, T220214. Simple, new, fairly clean and welcoming. **F** *La Source*, Place de la Source, T204397. 9 rooms, central, set around a patio next to the Muezzin's loudspeaker, not very clean, slightly shabby.

Sleeping
Phone code: 08

Not too much choice here, but nothing to break your budget either. **Mid-range** *Restaurant Chez Venus*, Av Habib Bourguiba. Very pleasant atmosphere, probably the best food in town, a bit more expensive than the others. This is the restaurant related to the hotel of the same name. **Cheap** *Restaurant el Andalous*, on rue Hédi Chaker opposite the PTT. Perfectly adequate for a fill-up. *Restaurant Chez Nous*, on rue de la Source, next to the Hotel de l'Auberge. Good, cheap Tunisian food. *Restaurant Ed Dyr*, Av Hedi Chaker, near the Esso station. Good value. *Restaurant Les Ruines*, up a side-street near the ASM du Kef's offices.

Eating

Road Bus: the bus station is a 20-minute walk downhill from Place de l'Indépendence. Information on T220105. Frequent buses to **Tunis** and **Jendouba**, connections also to **Sfax**, **Kairouan**, **Nabeul**, **Gafsa**, **Sousse** and **Bizerte**. **Louages**: the louage station is by the bus station.

Transport

Banks STB, Place de l'Indépendence; BT, Av Hedi Chaker. **Communications** Area code: 08. **Post Office**: Av Hedi Chaker. **Emergencies Hospital**: On the Sakiet Sidi Youssef road, T420900. Pharmacie de nuit (all night pharmacy). On rue Souk Ahras, turn right just before PTT. **Tour companies & travel agents** *Nord Ouest Voyages*, rue Essour, T221839.

Directory

Excursions

A minor road, the C72, climbs north to the side of the 1,500 hectares lake held back by the Nebeur Dam. The lake is an impressive 18 km long. A better view is obtained from the dam on the Oued Mellègue by turning off the road to Jendouba after the steep winding road passes Nebeur. You could also head for **Hammam Mellègue**, a thermal spa some 10 km down a piste leading off the P5 road for Sakiet Sidi Youssef west of Le Kef. The bus for Sakiet could drop you at the beginning of the piste, and unless you get lucky with a lift in a Peugeot truck, you'll walk the rest. The spring waters are popular with locals, women having the mornings for bathing, men the afternoons; but there are better places in Tunisia to sample the delights of hot springs. (See Hammam Zriba, Kébili, El Hamma de Gabès and El Hamma du Djérid, for example.)

Northern Tunisia

Northern Tunisia

Know your Romans – who was Emperor Diocletian?

Gaius Aurelius Valerius Diocletianus (245-313 AD) was Emperor of Rome 284-305. Co-emperor Numerian, at that time in charge of eastern areas, died in 284 and Emperor Carinus, in charge of western areas, was assassinated in 285, leaving Diocletian in full control. He was revered as an able soldier and an energetic ruler. Initially he split the empire into two, then four administrative divisions, instituted domestic and fiscal reforms and reorganized the army. He is particularly remembered for his persecution of the Christians (303-305) having them thrown to wild animals, stretched on racks and burned during public demonstrations. He abdicated in 305 and retired to Yugoslavia.

Northeast of Le Kef, some nine km down a piste opposite the entrance to the Presidential Palace, are the remains of a monastery on the Djebel Dyr (*dyr* means 'monastery' in Arabic). The site is now partly occupied by a farm.

East from Le Kef to Dougga (Teboursouk) and Testour

The P5 from Le Kef runs roughly northeastwards towards Tunis, passing through an interesting mixture of small Tunisian towns and ancient remains of Roman and Byzantine origin. This is a rich agricultural area of pasture, cereals and wooded hills. Dougga and Testour are the two must-sees on this route.

Roman **Mustis** is just north of the present-day town of Krib, on the left at Km 119. Here are the ruins of a triumphal arch and a paved Roman street, amongst other things ancient. The site is entered through a green gate and the visit will not take very long. The best of the ruins is the Byzantine citadel, the walls of which are clearly defined. This is constructed of pieces removed from the older buildings. Parts of the Christian basilica with three naves, to the west, are less obvious. There are temples to Apollo, Cérès and Pluto, and to the southeast of the site is the *zaouia* of Sidi Abd Rebba. There is a triumphal arch at each end of the town, the better preserved is along the road towards Teboursouk 300 metres east of the main group of ruins. The original construction date is not known.

Just 10 km further along, ancient world enthusiasts will want to note what remains of a Byzantine fort on a hill to the north of the road. This is the site of the ancient settlement of **Agbia**. There is no sign, just take the track across a field. Immediately beyond, on the left is a turn to **Dougga**. This is a very rough route and a long walk. The best approach is from Teboursouk. A couple of kilometres after Krib, there is a relais-restaurant to the right of the road where you can lunch (with wine) for around 15Dt a head.

On towards Tunis the older part of **Teboursouk**, on a hillside, overlooks the P5, while the modern part of town lies along the main road. Some 10 km before you reach Testour at **Aïn Tounga** are more ancient ruins, immediately to the east of the road. There is an imposing Byzantine

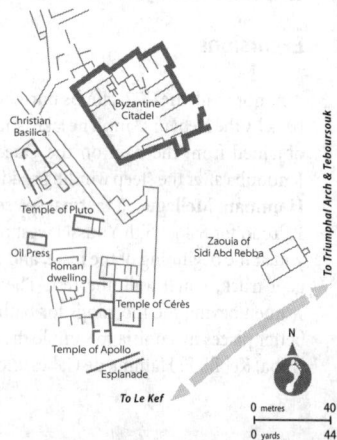

Mustis

after A Beschaouch

fortress (along with the one at remote Ksar Lamsa near Siliana, one of the best preserved in Tunisia), and the remains of Roman Thignica. Next stop is **Testour**, the ancient town of Tichila, home of the Moors driven from Spain in the 17th century.

Dougga   دقة

With an exhilarating view of plain and distant hills, Dougga has the best location of any of Tunisia's ancient cities. It is an alluring place; the grand imperial monuments are improbably intact. The classic views of the site – the theatre, the capitol – are post-card famous. But despite all the columns and pediments, there is plenty of higgledy-piggledy masonry, and children will have a splendid time fighting imaginary battles among the passages and overgrown walls. In fact, the Romans built on an earlier town, and proud Masinissa must surely have held court here. The streets are still Romanly well-paved, and you half expect to look up and find some Numidian beauty and her suite processing to the Licinian Baths. Dougga feels like a confident, healthy place, and complements the picture of the Roman good life inspired by the great mosaics of the Bardo Museum.

Colour map 1, grid B3

Ins and outs

The Roman ruins of Dougga are 100 km west of Tunis, 7 km south from the town of Teboursouk and very clearly signed. Dougga is an easy day trip from the capital by both private and public transport. There are frequent buses from Le Kef and Tunis to Teboursouk. From there, you may find a taxi to take you up to the site.

Getting there

Once at Teboursouk, another option is to take a bus or louage to the new settlement of Dougga (built to house the folk who were living on the site until the 1960s) and walk up a track behind the village. The ruins start 3 km further on along the track.

The ruins cover a considerable area. A short visit would start with the Theatre (near the car park), before moving on to the central forum area (Temple of Mercury, Capitol). Next you would have a look at the Arch of Alexander Severus and the Temple of Caelestis. Heading back to the central area, you could next do the Licinian Baths, and the residential area below them, including the Trifolium House and the House of the Gorgon. The visit would finish at the Libico-Punic Mausoleum below the central part of the town.

Getting around

With more time, a good circuit would take you from the Theatre over the back of the site to the dolmens, Temple of Minerva, Circus and Cisterns of Aïn Mizeb. Then you would come back to the centre of the town, passing via the Arch of Alexander Severus and the Temple of Caelestis. The central forum area is next on this route, to be followed, as for the previous circuit, by Licinian Baths and lower residential area.

History

The Roman ruins known as **Thugga** are spread out across a plateau and on to the steep side of the *djebel* overlooking the Oued Khaled. It was originally a Numidian town allied with Rome against Carthage. As a consequence, after the downfall of Carthage, the town was granted a certain degree of independence. Romanization only started towards 150 AD, after two centuries of coexistence. By the time Carthage had been rebuilt by the Romans, Dougga had become the economic and administrative centre of a very rich agricultural area. It also controlled the route to the coast, and enjoyed great prosperity. Having become a Roman colony by the end of the second century, the town reached the height of its wealth under the rule of Septimius Severus. It was awarded an imposing name – Colonia Licinia Septima Aurelia Alexandriana Thuggenses – to match its importance. Its downfall in the fourth century was caused by the heavy dues paid to the Romans and religious quarrels. When the Vandals invaded, most of the population had moved to Teboursouk.

The ruins

Dougga, at 25 hectares, is one of the largest of the Roman sites in Tunisia and certainly one of the most dramatic. The ruins are on a sloping site, and it is possible to do a superficial visit in an hour or so, although it is really worthwhile spending a great deal more time. On arrival, one of the 'guides' hanging round the entrance will no doubt want to show you around. Most of these guides are not official and do not hold a card issued by the Tourist Office. If you are in a hurry, it can be a good idea to take one, but be careful to agree on the price beforehand. Café and reasonable toilets at entrance.

Dougga

To Teboursouk

Circus

Dolmens

Temple of Minerva

Numidian Walls

Temple of Saturn

Church of Victoria

Cisterns of Aïn Mizeb

Numidian Walls

Amphitheatre

Theatre

Cisterns of Aïn Mizeb

Arch of Severus Alexander

Temple of Mercury

Square of the Winds

Museum

Capitol

Temple of Augustan Piety

Forum

Market Place

Temples of Concordiae, Frugiferi, Liberi Patris

Temple of Pluto

To Columbarium of Remmii

Temple of Caelestis

Temple of Tellus

Arch of Septimus Severus

Dar-el-Acheb

Licinian Baths

Trifolium House

Cyclops' Baths

House of the Gorgon

Nymphaeum

Baths of Aïn Doura

Libyco-Punic Mausoleum

N

0 metres 50
0 yards 54

To Nouvelle Dougga

So what makes Dougga really special? Basically, it is the sheer concentration of well-preserved or well-restored Roman buildings. You have the whole range, buildings for worship, work and leisure, all within a few minutes walk of each other. This, coupled with the panoramic views, must have made Dougga a splendid place to live in. ■ *The site is open 0830-1730 winter and 0700-1900 summer, closed Monday, entrance fee 2Dt, photography 1Dt.*

Touring Dougga

There is a lot to see at Dougga, and to make things more digestible, the city is divided here into seven manageable chunks: the Theatre, the central area, the Arch of Severus Alexander and around, the Licinian baths and around, the lower residential neighbourhood, the Numido-Punic monument, and 'around the back of the theatre'. There are also notes on some miscellaneous buildings.

The Theatre

Close to the car park, the first major monument is the much restored **Theatre,** originally built in 168/9 AD, and a typical example of a Roman theatre. It is quite modest in size, but could nevertheless seat 3,500 people on its 19 semicircular tiers, in three stages, cut into the hill slope. This ensured the stability of the structure and simplified construction. The seating was closed off at the top by a portico, since destroyed, and it is suggested that a temporary screen or blind was erected over the seating to protect the spectators from the sun. Some of the columns have been re-erected on the stage, but now that the back wall of the stage has disappeared a person seated in the *cavea* (seating) obtains a splendid panoramic view of the plain below.

The central area

At the heart of ancient Thugga was the Capitol, with the Temples of Augustan Piety and Mercury adjoining. The Forum and the Market were close by. These were the public buildings and places where the men who ran the city would have been able to meet, arranging to discuss matters at the Forum or participating at the various rituals held in the temples.

Theatre

After Poinssot

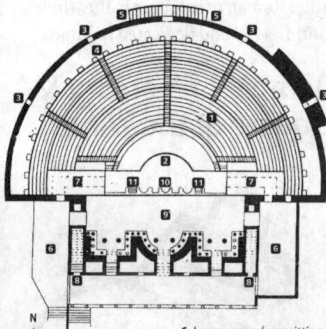

N

0 metres 10
0 yards 11

1 Cavea (19 semicircular tiers of seating)
2 Orchestra
3 Doorway/entrance
4 Staircase (interior)
5 Staircase (exterior)
6 Large room (permitting entrance under orchestra to cavea)
7 Tribunalium (positions for VIPs)
8 Stairs up
9 Proscaenium (stage)
10 Pulpitum (about 1m high with rectangular & semi-circular niches)
11 Stairs from orchestra to stage

The **Temple of Augustan Piety** was a small raised sanctuary with an even smaller vestibule entered from the west by a small stair. The engraving on the architrave supported by columns with Corinthian capitols indicated its name and use.

Approaching the forum and the great mass of the main temple, the visitor comes to the **Square of the Winds** (French: Rose des Vents), which is named after a compass-based inscription naming 12 winds cut into the paving. This square has in fact a semicircular wall at its east end, behind which stands the Temple of Fortune and Temple of Augustan Piety. **Temple of Mercury** This section contains the Temple of Mercury constructed between 180 and 192 AD and composed of three chapels, the rectangular central one being larger; the lateral chapels, much smaller, are almost hemispherical in plan. All three are dedicated to the

Northern Tunisia

👉 *On temple building and Roman piety*

The classic Roman temple as we think of it today owed much to Greek and Etruscan models. Looking at the Capitol at Dougga, you can see Greek columns used on the main entrance but not on all sides of the building, as would have been the case in a Greek temple. Temple buildings like the Capitol were designed to impress, dominating the central area of a town from their raised platforms. They had elegant flights of steps leading to their entrances, ideal to set off the pomp of ritual processions. Note however that these temples were not built like churches to accommodate large congregations: they were places where priests and senior people would officiate at the cults.

Temples were an essential part of the process of Romanization, places symbolizing the power of the Empire where rites in Latin were celebrated. In North Africa, where the cities were new and there was no long tradition of great building, the temples often had a triple dedication to Jupiter, Juno and Minerva. Roman gods were grafted on to local deities, the cult of Saturn taking over that of Punic Baal-Hammon for instance. Temples could also be dedicated to abstract deities, and emperors would show their munificence by building temples. Eventually, temples began to be dedicated to deified emperors. There was a fine temple to Septimius Severus at Djemila in present day Algeria, for example.

same god, Mercury. This temple, dedicated to the god of, among other things, trade, faces towards the market (see also Thuburbo Majus where a similar arrangement exists), donated by the same patron.

The **Market** is bordered on its two longer sides by a series of small shops which were built under the portico – now vanished. Each shop was exactly the same size, 2.8 metres by 2.7 metres. In the centre stood a fountain. The south end held a large alcove which probably held a statue of Mercury. To the right and the left of this alcove, a doorway leads out to separate stairways which descended to rooms below.

You cannot miss the **Capitol**, with its impressive set of steps and six huge fluted monolithic columns over eight metres high on the edge of the portico. It is considered by some to be the most beautiful Roman monument in the whole of North Africa. It was built between 166 and 169 AD and dedicated to Jupiter, Juno and Minerva. The Corinthian capitols on these huge columns support an architraved frieze, bearing a dedication to the Triad for the salvation of the emperors Marcus Aurelius and Lucius Verus. The pediment features a bas-relief of an eagle making off with a human figure. Behind the portico is a *cella* 13 metres by 14 metres, entered by a central doorway and divided into three parts, each with a niche in the end wall. The central, largest niche once held a white marble statue of Jupiter and the smaller side niches statues of the other two deities. Beneath the podium constructed to lift this capitol to its elevated position is a crypt, in three compartments and used at one time as a fort and at another perhaps

Temple of Mercury & Square of the Winds

After Poinssot

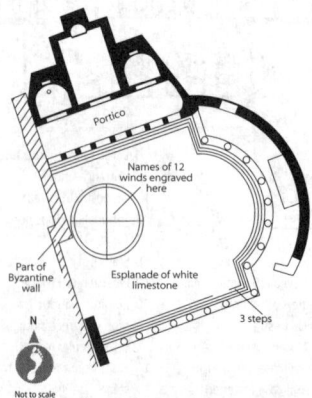

Portico

Names of 12 winds engraved here

Part of Byzantine wall

Esplanade of white limestone

3 steps

N

Not to scale

Public Baths – Roman style

Although the larger private houses had their own bathing facilities, most Roman citizens made use of the public baths – for which a charge was made. The men and women were strictly segregated, using separate facilities or using the baths at different times of the day. Associated with the public baths was the palaestra or exercise room, small shops and sometimes even a library. Visitors to the public hammam in Tunis will find this account very familiar.

The first room in the bathing part was for the removal of outdoor garments – there were niches in the wall for storing the clothes. The body was smoothed with oil, generally olive oil, and then the would-be bather went into the exercise room to get his circulation moving and to raise his body temperature. From there he went to the hot room and steam room, where attendants removed the oil and perspiration with a strigil. The journey then was next to the warm room and then to the cold room which was normally large enough to contain a swimming pool. Fresh oil was smoothed on the body at the end of the operation.

Obviously this smooth operation only worked because of the ingenious and complicated engineering of the building, the organization of water supply and the numerous servants and attendants stoking fires.

as a church. A model of the Capitol area is on display in the Dougga Room at the Bardo Museum.

The open piazza in front of the Capitol (24 metres by 38 metres) at the base of the staircase opens on the west side into an open space which is the **Forum**, also dating from the end of the second century. It was the centre of public life and administration. Few of the original 35 columns (red veined marble from Chemtou with white capitals) and base remains. The floor beneath the porticos which once surrounded three sides of the building was mosaic tiles.

When times became less secure in Byzantine times, the centre of Dougga was extensively remodelled for defensive reasons. At the Forum, traces of the Byzantine fortifications can be seen to the north (a rectangular tower) and south (a rectangular support) of the Forum. The fort covering some 2,800 square metres in fact enclosed both the Forum and the Capitol and the gateways to the north and south. Much of the stone used to construct this fort was taken from older buildings on this site.

Also close to the central area is the small **Temple of Tellus**, the goddess of crop fertility. Close by are the remains of a building referred to today as the **Dar el Acheb** (entry via a grand doorway with two Corinthian columns). It was probably a temple originally. The four rectangular basins enclosed in the larger rectangular building were accessed from a door to the north. Perhaps these basins were for the storage of oil or even for ritual washing.

Temple of Caelestis

After Poinssot

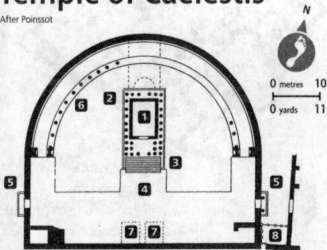

1 Rectangular sanctuary
2 Columns surrounding sanctuary
3 Flight of 11 stairs
4 Semi-circular courtyard
5 Side entrance
6 Remaining columns which supported semi-circular portico
7 Chambers below courtyard
8 Ablutions area

Close to the central area, two pleasant ruins not to be missed are the Arch of Severus Alexander and the Temple of Juno Caelestis. Severus Alexander was an emperor (ruled 222-35 AD), of whom the Latin sources tell us **The Arch of Severus Alexander and around**

little. No doubt he took an interest in African affairs, and his arch, tastefully placed among the olive trees, no doubt commemorates some munificence or other. The arch (four metres wide) spanned a road, paved in herring-bone style which would have been one of the main access points to the city.

Close to the Arch, look out for the **Temple of Caelestis** (Juno?), also constructed during the reign of Alexander Severus, a few years before Christianity began to gain a hold in this part of North Africa. The rectangular sanctuary, once entirely enclosed by columns, is approached by an elegant flight of steps. There is a large, closed semi-circular courtyard with a portico on the curved side.

Licinian Baths and around

This third-century gift to the city by the Licinii family is a very large and complicated building. The furnace room, the hot room with the pipes visible in the walls, the cold room and the *palaestra* or exercise room remain.

The **Temples of Concordia, Frugifer** and **Bacchus (Liber Pater)** were constructed between 128-38 AD. The Temple of Bacchus is the largest and has a large square central area flanked by porticos, while at the northwest side are five rooms, the largest in the centre, while in the opposite direction was a small theatre, seats still present.

Below the Licinian baths, heading away from the Forum, is a complex area of ruined housing where you can also see sections of the ancient **Numidian walls**, part of the same fortifications running north of the Theatre and west of the Temple of Saturn. In this neighbourhood, look out for the well-preserved **House of Dionysus and Ulysses**, where part of the first floor still survives. Now in the Bardo Museum, the great mosaic of Ulysses, tied to the mast of his ship as he sailed past the Sirens, comes from this house.

The lower residential area

Below the Licinian Baths is an area where city homes and a further, smaller, bath complex have been excavated. **The House of the Trifolium** (traditionally presented by guides as Dougga's brothel) dates from the third century and is the best conserved and largest house discovered on the site. It is built on two levels with the entrance at street level and the rooms a floor below. The stairs on the north side of the house lead to a rectangular central garden or *viridium*. There was a small semicircular pool at one end, surrounded by a portico with a mosaic floor. The private quarters to the southwest have the vaulted, trefoil-shaped room from which the house was given its present name.

Next to the House of the Trifolium, the **Cyclops' Baths** are named after the magnificent mosaic taken from the floor of the cold room here and now on display at the Bardo Museum (see page 90). The baths are not in a very good state, except for the communal latrine (good photo opportunity). The extremely realistic mosaic, dated as fourth century, shows the three giants, the Cyclops, working at the forge in the cavern belonging to Vulcan who was the god of Hell. It is unusual to find figures of such gigantic proportions (well, they were giants) or with such dark

Licinian Baths

After Poinssot

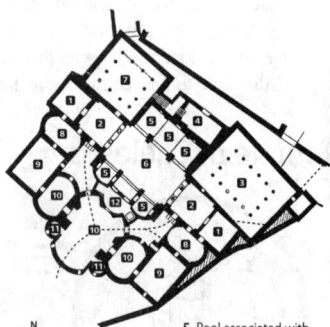

N

0 metres 20
0 yards 22

1 Apodyteria (undressing room)
2 Vestibule
3 Palaestra (exercise room)
4 Ante-room
5 Pool associated with Frigidarium
6 Frigidarium (cold room)
7 Entrance hall
8 Sudatorium (sweating room)
9 Laconicum (hot room - dry)
10 Calidarium (hot room)
11 Boiler room
12 Tepidarium (warm room)

skins depicted on Roman mosaics. Further down towards the Libyco-Punic Mausoleum, the visitor comes to the **House of the Gorgon**, named after the mosaic discovered here showing the Gorgon's head held in the hand of Perseus.

In the lower part of the city, looking for all the world like a lost piece from a giant's chess game, the **Numido-Punic Mausoleum** is perhaps Tunisia's most famous pre-Roman ruin. In its day, it no doubt belonged to a series of similar monuments being put up in the nascent towns of the Numidian tribal monarchy. Dating from the third-second century BC, drawing stylistic inspiration from archaic Greece and ancient Egypt, the monument hints at a faint influence of Hellenistic models. (The third and second centuries BC was a time when massive building works were undertaken in the Hellenistic Kingdoms of Asia Minor.) The mausoleum is dedicated to the Numidian Prince Ateban, son of Iepmatath, son of Pallu, according to the bilingual Libyic and Punic inscription, which also gives the name of the architect as Abarish. It is thought Ateban was a contemporary of Massinissa. The three-storey tower rises from a plinth of five steps and culminates in a pyramid. The central section is reminiscent of a Greek temple. Originally, the pyramidal roof would have been flanked by birds with female faces, all set to guide the deceased's soul through the labyrinths of the afterlife. Take a minute to place this in context: it was a historic building when the Romans were building Dougga.

The Numido-Punic Monument

Having survived over 2000 years, the 21 metres high building was virtually destroyed by the British Consul in Tunis in the 1840s, who took the stones bearing the bilingual inscriptions back in to the British Museum. Happily, Poinssot and his team in 1908-10 were able to reconstruct the mausoleum. With its simple silhouette, today it is one of the most calm and elegant monuments at Dougga. (For mausoleum enthusiasts, a similar building, deassembled by Italian archaeologists, can be seen at Sabratha in Libya.)

Retracing your steps up towards the House of the Trefoil, and turning right, you come to the **Arch of Septimius Severus** (193-211 AD), put up in this emperor's honour in 205 AD after Thugga was made a *municipium* at his command, giving the community at Thugga partial rights of Roman citizenship. The arch marked the eastern entrance to the city, sitting astride a road of some five metres in width made of large limestone pieces set in a herring bone pattern. This was the main road to Carthage.

If you have time, then you could go up to the back of the theatre's seating area, and explore the plateau beyond, tracing a circle to come out close to the Arch of Severus Alexander. The remains here are not spectacular, but give an idea of the extent of the city.

Round the back of the Theatre to the Temple of Caelestis

Moving away from the theatre, there are views on your right towards Teboursouk and the ground drops away in a steep cliff. You will come to the **Sanctuary of Neptune**, a small rectangular sanctuary down off the plateau built near the now non-existent road that led to the Temple of Saturn. (Entrance via a door in the east wall and a niche in the west wall opposite.)

Further on is the **Temple of Saturn** (195 AD), its dominant position overlooking the valley, signalling the importance of the cult. Apparently it was built over the site of an earlier Baal-Hammon-Saturn sanctuary. It is aligned almost east-west. The outer vestibule (some of the original Corinthian columns still stand) leads into the rectangular central courtyard which originally had a gallery on three sides. At the west end are three equal-sized chapels. The central chapel once contained a marble statue of Saturn and that to the left a statue of a man dressed in a toga, the benefactor. Changes in the construction have made the entrance arrangements a little complicated.

☞ *Who were the Severans?*

The names of emperors **Septimius Severus** (193-211) and **Severus Alexander** (222-35) pop up regularly at Roman sites throughout Tunisia. At Dougga, there are triumphal arches to both these rulers. What was special about them? Fast rewind then to the late second century AD, when Rome went through a particularly difficult patch under emperor Commodus. From 180-93, Commodus lived a life of debauchery in Rome, renaming the city Commodiana and spending his time showing off his brute force fighting with wild beasts in the colosseum. Eventually, he was strangled by a wrestling partner. In the power struggle that ensued among the military, one Septimius Severus, an aristocrat from Leptis Magna (in present day Libya), came out on top after four years of civil war.

Septimius Severus was the right strong man at the right time. He realized that the Empire faced some formidable enemies, notably on the eastern frontier, and hence was to rule from the frontier provinces. He added Mesopotamia to Rome's dominions, and expanded the army, adding two new legions and opening up the career structure to soldiers from the ranks. His dying words to his sons are said to have been "Do not quarrel with each other, pay the troops, and despise the rest."

Septimius Severus did not forget his African origins. In 202-203, he overwintered in Africa. He had huge works undertaken at Leptis Magna. Along with Leptis, Carthage and Utica were given immunity from provincial taxes. The emperor had acquired huge properties in Africa Proconsularis, the lands of senators whom he had executed for their support of rival Clodius Albinus. This no doubt gave him the resources for his considerable largesse towards Africa's cities, recognized by the construction of triumphal arches.

Unfortunately, Septimius Severus' sons **Caracalla** and **Geta** were not of the same stuff as their father. Dynastic infighting followed, with Caracalla murdering Geta, only to be murdered by his own troops. **Elagabalus** (218-22) was also murdered after a short reign decadent by even Rome's standards, and his cousin, the young **Severus Alexander**, was to succeed in 222. He too was eventually murdered by the army. The Severan Dynasty disappeared, and 26 emperors followed in 50 years. But though the mid-third century proved to be a time of chaos in Rome, the provinces of Africa continued to prosper. Septimius Severus had broken the power of the warlike desert tribes, Numidia had been made a separate province and the defences reorganized.

Despite the vast sums spent on building programmes and the army, the Severan period saw a development which was to have long-lasting effects for Europe. Septimius Severus named Papinian praetorian prefect. Along with jurists Ulpian and Julius Paulus, he laid the bases of the Roman law which was eventually codifed by the emperor Justinian in the sixth century. And under Caracalla, an edict was issued granting Roman citizenship to virtually all free men in the Empire.

Approaching the Sanctuary of Neptune from the Theatre, to your right you have a small Christian cemetery in which stands the **Christian basilica** (fourth-fifth century AD). Many stones taken from the Theatre and the Temple of Saturn were used in its construction. There are three aisles separated by two rows of columns. The central aisle is wider and longer ending in an altar. Two sets of stairs lead down to the crypt.

From the church return to the top of the plateau and follow the line of the Numidian walls. There is one small section, only 130 metres in length, of very ancient walls with parts of two towers on the outer side. You may also be able to pick out some **dolmens**, stones set up as funerary monuments in some distant pre-Libyic past. Little remains of the **Circus**. This is a very large rectangular area aligned east-west on the edge of the plateau. It is dated at 214 AD with additions some 10 years later. Down the centre is the *spina*, a raised area 190 metres long which ends in semicircles. Did the spectators sit on the rocks to watch the charioteers race round this central strip?

The **Temple of Minerva** (138-61 AD) remains only in outline. Enter by a central door into a large rectangular courtyard with a line of columns at each side. The sanctuary (outer and inner) at the northwest was reached up stairs.

The **Cisterns of Aïn Mizeb** were a vital part of the town's survival. They are made up of seven long reservoirs (each 35 metres by five metres) set one metre apart, which stored water from the spring to the west. The method of construction and the lining to prevent leakage can still be examined where these cisterns are exposed. Having separate compartments prevented total loss if one part was damaged and permitted cleaning and repairs without cutting off the supply. The **Cisterns of Aïn el Hammam** are similar to those further north. There are five parallel reservoirs (each 34 metres by three metres) and one short one across the end all fed from a spring a distance to the southwest.

After the cisterns, the **Arch of Severus Alexander** is clearly visible. The **Temple of Caelestis** is on your right, and turning left, you head back towards the central part of the city.

Down below the Dar el Acheb, there are a number of minor ruins to look out for, including a **private chapel to Juno** (the Exhedra of Juno Regina), the **Columbarium of the Remmii**, a large funerary monument containing the tombs of the Remmii family, and the **Baths of Aïn Doura and cistern**. From these baths, heading towards the House of the Trifolium, you will come to a small **nymphaeum** or fountain on your left. The water for this also came from Aïn el Hammam.

Miscellaneous buildings

Temple of Saturn

After Poinsot

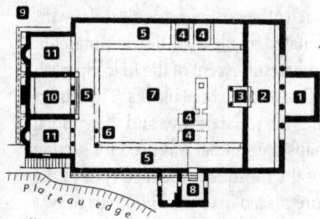

N

| 0 metres | 10 |
| 0 yards | 11 |

1 Outer vestibule
2 Inner vestibule
3 Doorway
4 Cisterns
5 Portico
6 Remaining columns which supported portico
7 Central courtyard
8 Side entrance & annex
9 Waterchannels
10 Central chapel with steps
11 Side chapel with niche

It is possible to stay overnight in **Teboursouk**, although there is only one hotel there. **D** *Hotel Thugga*, on the main road to Tunis, T465713. 66 beds, has obviously seen better days, rather poor quality, used by tour groups for a lunch stop. **Youth hostel**: in Teboursouk, T465095. 40 beds.

Sleeping

Road Bus: there is an hourly bus to **Le Kef** and **Tunis** and many links to **Béja** and **Jendouba**. Info northwestation on T465016.

Transport

Testour تستور

Phone code: 08
Colour map 1, grid B3

Like nearby Slouguia and Medjez el Bab, Testour is a 17th century Andalusian foundation, and a pleasant place for a short stop on the way from Tunis to Dougga. The Great Mosque has an unusual minaret, while the main street lined with one-storey shops with tiled roofs manages to maintain the faintest of Spanish flavours. But for how long? Modern building fashions have arrived, and the remainder of Testour's Andalusian heritage may well be replaced by the usual concrete homes.

Ins and outs

Getting there Testour is about 90 minutes drive from Tunis. There are buses and louages from Tunis, Béja, Medjez el Bab, and Teboursouk.

Background and history

The town of Testour, built on the south bank of the Oued Medjerda, stands halfway between Teboursouk and Medjez el Bab. It stands on the site of Roman Tichilla and small pieces of this are found incorporated into the more modern fabric of the town and apparently into the Grand Mosque. The modern town dates from the flight of the Moors from Andalucía. The Spanish feel is very muted now, there are few women out and about. With the men chatting of weather and farm-produce at the market stalls, swathed in earth-brown *kachabia* cloaks in winter, the feel is very much of a working agricultural town.

The eastern approach to Testour is dominated by the high-flown minaret of the town's great mosque, built in a style faintly reminiscent of the Italo-Spanish renaissance. The square tower is topped with two octagonal blocks. The expert opinion is that the little pinnacles decorating the square tower and the sundial hark back to the mosques of Aragon. Perhaps the sundial was used for getting prayer times right. The other key feature of the mosque is the tiled roof of the prayer hall, set with an unusual dome feature placed over the *mihrab* or prayer niche. In fact, this was not the first mosque on the site, as a ruined square tower in the back streets behind the Great Mosque shows.

The other feature which makes Testour so 'Andalusian' is its regular layout. A long, central street runs into the main square, off which the mosque is located. The main square, surrounded by small shops, would have been the commercial hub of the new settlement back in the 17th century. Perhaps the immigrants sought to recreate the feel of the *plaza mayor* of the towns they had left behind. One early 18th century visitor, F Ximenez, noted that at Testour "the square is in the middle of the village where the Moors who founded it held festivities with bulls in the Spanish manner." Such traditions are long gone.

The importance of the Andalusians The travellers of the 18th century often showed a certain approval of the Morisco villages. After a long period during which the northern part of Tunisia had been dominated by nomad tribes, the Andalusians managed to create new towns, benefiting from the more powerful rule of law established by the Ottoman deys. Wrote traveller Peyssonel in the early 1720s, "the towns and villages were rare in this kingdom before the arrival of the Andalusians. Most of the towns to be seen today owe their foundation or at least their re-foundation to them, because before them the natural or bedouin Moors preferred to live under tents in the countryside, as is still the case."

The flames of passion

The Hara, the Jewish quarter of Tunis, gave the demi-monde of 1920s Tunis a tragic figure in the form of minor diva Habiba Msika (1895-1930), chiefly remembered today for such classics as Ala sarir en-nawm dallani ('On the bed of sleep he spoiled me, he gave me beer and champagne '). Her fan-club, the asakir el-lil, 'soldiers of the night', followed her from concert to concert. She was dubbed habibat el kul, 'beloved of all'.

Habiba also conquered the heart of an elderly Jewish merchant from Testour, one Elyaou Mimouni. The bargain was the usual one: beauty for monied attentions. But Habiba was cruel, and Mimouni found himself rejected by family and home-town. The besotted merchant eventually went wild with jealousy at his diva's varied loves. He burned down Msika's townhouse on the rue de Bône with the expensive songstress inside.

Such a tragedy could not go unfilmed, and in the late 1990s, Tunisian film producer Selma Baccar turned the fiery tale of the diva's life and loves into a film, Habiba Msika ou la danse du feu. The house built by Msika's lover for her in Testour is now the Maison de la Culture, down a side-street on the right as you head away from the Great Mosque.

But Habiba Msika was also touched by the political currents of the time. At La Marsa's Café Saf-Saf, at a famous concert in 1925, she struck a blow for liberty, turning the final song baladi, oh baladi ('my homeland') into baladi tounis ou fiha el hurria ('my homeland is Tunisia, where there is freedom').

Other sights

With time, the Andalusians were absorbed into the rest of the population, and later building lacks the Iberian touch. The other main monument in Testour, the **Zaouia of Sidi Nasser el Baraouachi**, built in 1733, is a standard 18th century building for religious gatherings. It is down a side-street to the left at the far end of the village from the main square. Here you can have a peek at the quiet colonnaded courtyard with its orange tree, and look in at the prayer hall with the saint's catafalque. Local women are said to come here seeking a cure for sterility. The other minor sight at Testour, if still in operation, is the traditional tile and **brick works** above the river bank in the area below the Great Mosque.

An annual Festival of Malouf is generally held at the end of June. *Malouf* is a form of Hispano-Arabic choral music brought from Andalucía by the escaping Moors. (If this is your thing, try to catch a concert by the Rachidia in Tunis, possibly during the Ramadhan Festival de la Médina.) As yet, there are no hotels in Testour. For eating, there are one or two *gargottes* doing fry-ups on the main street. Market day is Friday.

Malouf festival

Medjez El Bab

A market town and an important crossing point of the Oued Medjerda, Medjez el Bab was built on the site of the ancient Membressa. The present town is a creation of the Andalusian immigrants who settled here in 1611. The Great Mosque had a number of Andalusian features but has suffered at the hands of the restorers in recent years. The old bridge over the Medjerda was built between 1675 and 1677 under Mourad II. A new bypass and bridge were constructed in the 1990s. With the improved roads, Medjez is only one hour from Tunis and 40 minutes from Béja by car. (Buses and louages arrive in the central square.)

Phone code: 08
Colour map 1, grid B3

Northern Tunisia

Up in the hills, some 13 km to the northwest of Medjez el Bab, are the villages of **Toukaber** (ancient Thuccabor), **Chaouach** and **Heïdous**, the first two being most easily accessible along narrow climbing roads. Chaouach looks out over the remains of ancient Sua, a settlement which was no doubt prosperous back in the second century AD. Look out for the rock tombs or *haouanet*, as they are known, at both sites. The modern world is catching up with these settlements. Olive trees, wheat and barley are cultivated as of old, but as elsewhere in Tunisia's villages, electricity has arrived.

The British First and Eighth armies suffered losses here in the Second World War, and there are two **military cemeteries** in the area. One is three kilometres southwest of town on the P5 with 2,900 graves and a memorial to soldiers who died in Tunisia and Algeria and have no known grave. The other has 240 graves and is 17 km west of town on the P6 beside the church in the old town of Oued Zarga. Both open 0730-1430 Saturday-Thursday.

Sleeping E *Hotel Membressa*, small, 14 rooms, communal shower, T460121. Not much of a place. Loud and beery bar.

Central Tunisia

6

Central Tunisia

The central regions of Tunisia stretch across steppelands from the rolling grainlands of the north to the pre-Saharan areas. In the east is the Sahel (lit : 'the coast'), a flat region planted with thousands upon thousands of regularly spaced olive trees and home to Tunisia's textile industry. Here are the tourist towns of **Sousse** and **Monastir**, picturesque **Mahdia**, and industrious **Sfax**. Off the coast, there are the soporific **Islands of Kerkennah**. Inland from Sousse lies the holy city of **Kairouan**, centred on its honey-coloured mosque, and the Roman city of **Sbeïtla**, perhaps the best preserved in the country. The great colosseum of **El Djem**, north of Sfax, the third largest in the Roman world, is a spectacular sight. But away from the coast the landscapes open up, and enthusiastic drivers will want to head inland to ancient **Makthar** and hill-crest **La Kessera**, mysterious **Jugurtha's Table** and **Haïdra**, legionary base on a remote Roman frontier.

Background

The *Sahel*, or shoreland, is the low-lying eastern coastal plain of Tunisia extending from the Gulf of Hammamet to the Gulf of Gabès, and inland some 50 km, reaching a maximum altitude of around 275 metres. Because of its good beaches and pleasant climate, tempered in summer by cool sea breezes, the northern Sahel has seen considerable tourist development. North of **Sousse**, the development now extends some 20 km right up to Chott Myriam. **Skanès** and **Monastir**, hometown of Tunisia's first president, were especially favoured in the 1960s and 1970s. The southern Sahel, focusing on **Sfax**, has had a rather different destiny. Sfax is the main port for southern Tunisia, a thriving industrial town, with little to hold the visitor. But just off the coast are the Kerkennah Islands, sleepy and curiously self-contained.

The Sahel region has a long history, going back to the Carthaginians and the Romans, with the amphitheatre in **El Djem** (Thysdrus) being one of the most important ancient sites in North Africa. The médinas in most of the coastal towns have been preserved and there are some very digestible museums. A few hours' drive west from the coast, are some superb Roman cities and some wonderful landscapes.

A large number of visitors to the Sahel come in on packages, staying in either **Sousse** or **Monastir**, although **Mahdia**, south of Monastir, now has some large hotels. If you are based in Sousse or Monastir, you are well placed to see a lot of Tunisia, whether you are travelling by public transport or in a car. Sousse, being larger, has the better onward connections, and **Kairouan**, **Hammamet** and El Djem are all within easy travelling distance. It would be a bit difficult to see the sites of Tunis and area in a day trip, so you might consider an overnight stay. With a few days' car-hire, you can do some splendid circuits into the steppelands of the interior, with overnights at **Kasserine** or **Sbeïtla**. There are some fine landscapes northwest of Kaiouran, around **La Kessera**, a hill-crest village, and **Makthar**, another Roman site.

Based in Sousse or Monastir, you are not too far from the **Djerid**, the south-western oasis area of Tunisia. You could take an organised trip, the so-called 'desert safari', or travel down by public transport, (it is about six hours to Tozeur). This region requires a couple of overnight stays to make it worthwhile.

Sousse سوسة

Phone code: 03
Colour map 1, grid C5

With its beaches of fine sand, turqouise sea and great white hotels, Sousse, Pearl of the Sahel, is everybody's image of a 20th century beach resort. Sousse does not have that faint tinge of decadence that characterizes Hammamet, nor does it have that total slowdown you feel on sleepy Djerba. Sousse is the safe, Mediterranean holiday town par excellence. It would suit young families looking for a quiet all-inclusive type of holiday, or perhaps third-age people looking for an off-season base from which to explore historic médinas and Roman sites.

Ins and outs

Getting there Buses come here from all the major cities to one of the four bus stations, either on **1** Bab el Djedid (from all points south) or **2** by place Farhat Hached, the main square (from the north). Buses from beach areas north of Sousse, arrive at **3** place Sidi Yahia, on the north side of the médina. Finally, coming in from Le Kef and points northwest, you will arrive at **4** the *gare routière* on place Léopold Senghor.

The train station is very convenient, right in the middle of the town on Blvd Hassouna Ayachi. Louages arrive at a station 2 km southwest of the town centre (on the opposite side of town to the hotel strip). If you are arriving from the nearest airport, Skanès/Monastir International, 20 km away, take the regional railway into town (20 minutes ride). A taxi from the airport should certainly cost no more than 8Dt.

Most of the package hotels are located on the Corniche or on the coast north of the town, there being a first concentration immediately north of the centre, and a second concentration around Port el Kantaoui. For moving between the two, taxi is the quickest option. During the day, there is a noddy-train as well and there are buses, too. For a change of scene, Monastir and Mahdia, both beach resorts south of Sousse with historic old quarters are easily accessible by regional railway ('metro') leaving from the station on Av Mohamed V, south of the main Place F Hached in the town centre. Buses for Hergla go from Place Sidi Yahia, on the north side of the médina. **Getting around**

History

Founded in the ninth century BC by the Phoenicians, Sousse is one of the oldest ports in the Mediterranean. In the fourth century BC, when Carthage became the leading city in the area, Sousse entered its sphere of influence. During the second Punic-Roman war, Hannibal used Sousse as his base, but was beaten in 202 BC. During the third Punic-Roman war, Sousse switched allegiance to Rome, thereby avoiding destruction and gaining the status of free town, acquiring the Latin name of **Hadrumetum**. Unfortunately, with the victory of Caesar over the armies of Pompeii in Thapsus (46 BC), just down the coast, Sousse found itself on the wrong side, and Caesar imposed heavy taxation on the town. Nevertheless under the rule of Trajan (98-117 AD) the city became an important commercial centre.

Under Diocletian (284-305), Sousse became capital of the new province of Byzacium, and was the home of a flourishing Christian community – witness the catacombs. Under later invasions, Sousse had a few name changes. Under the Vandals, it was renamed **Hunericopolis**, retaken by the Byzantines, it was redubbed **Justinianopolis**. With the Arab invasions of the seventh century, it was destroyed.

In the ninth century, with the coming of the Aghlabid dynasty to Kairouan, it again prospered, as that inland city's port. It was from Sousse that the Muslim armies heading for Sicily would have embarked. Sousse was taken in the 12th century by the Sicily-based Normans, mid-Mediterranean regional power of the day, and in the 16th century by Spain. With its port installations, the city was a target in the Second World War, and was seriously damaged in 1942-43.

Since the 1960s, Sousse has become a major town, with service industries and tourism important in the local economy. The main north-south autoroute has put Sousse within 100 minutes of the capital, new university buildings and hospitals have been built west of the city. But parhaps the most striking change is in the area north of Sousse: an almost unbroken strip of hotels runs the whole way up to Chott Meriem and Akouda. The area immediately north of the town-centre, all traffic and low-rise blocks topped with oversized neon-lights, is singlularly unattractive. Further north, Port el Kantaoui, Tunisia's first purpose-built marina with self-catering accomodation has been a great success, still popular nearly 20 years after it was opened.

Central Tunisia

Sights

With a population of over 300,000, Sousse is the third largest city in Tunisia after Tunis and Sfax. Situated at the southern end of the long curve in Tunisia's east coastline known as the Gulf of Hammamet, it is a growing town with an important service sector. The city centre, despite the proximity of the port and much industry south of the town, is still very pleasant. The walled médina, looking down towards the sea, contains narrow, winding streets and some interesting sights, at least enough to keep you busy for a day. At Port el Kantaoui, the Tourist information office (T241799) is on the left as you enter through the archway into the marina, the manager Mohammed Lakhdar is very helpful.

Médina First and foremost, there is a fine old médina, still surrounded (unlike Tunis) by long stretches of the original walls, first built in 859 and restored in 1205. The way to enter the médina is either via Bab el Djedid, or through the Place des Martyrs beside the central square which leads to the Great Mosque. The breach in the walls was the result of bombardments during 1943. There are a number of buildings to aim for in the médina to give some direction to your wanderings. Close to the central Place Hached, the most obvious are the **Ribat** (visitable) and the **Grand Mosque**. There are other fine religious buildings viewable from the outside, and a private home restored as a museum. Up at the highest point is the **Kasbah**, its museum housing a small but worthwhile collection of mosaics. Sousse will give you in condensed form what you will be missing if you don't have time to make the trek up to Tunis on a daytrip.

The **Great Mosque** dominates an esplanade leading towards the Ribat. Built in the nineth century by the Aghlabid Emir Abou Abbas Mohammed, it was probably a conversion of a kasbah built a few years earlier. Further renovations and restorations have taken place. On two corners, large, round towers dominate the marble floored courtyard and make it look like the fortress it may originally have been. Overall the monument is very simple, the courtyard being decorated solely by inscriptions around its sides. Only the courtyard can be visited. ■ *Open 0800-1300, closed Friday. Entrance tickets 2Dt can be bought opposite the mosque and at the local ONTT.*

Perhaps the most venerable buildings in Sousse, the **Ribat** was part of a series of nineth century coastal strongpoints built to defend the coast of Ifrikiya from the marauding Christians. It is generally described as 'a sort of fortified monastery', although there is no monastic movement in Islam. Constructed under Aghlabid ruler Ziyedet Allah I, it was completed in 820. No doubt it functioned as a centre for mustering the embryonic Muslim community against outside attacks. Like most other early Islamic buildings in Ifrikiya, the Ribat at Sousse was built using materials from older sites, as can be seen at the entrance where antique columns are placed on either side of the door. There is nothing elaborate about the

Sousse, ruelle dans la Médina

Sousse médina & around

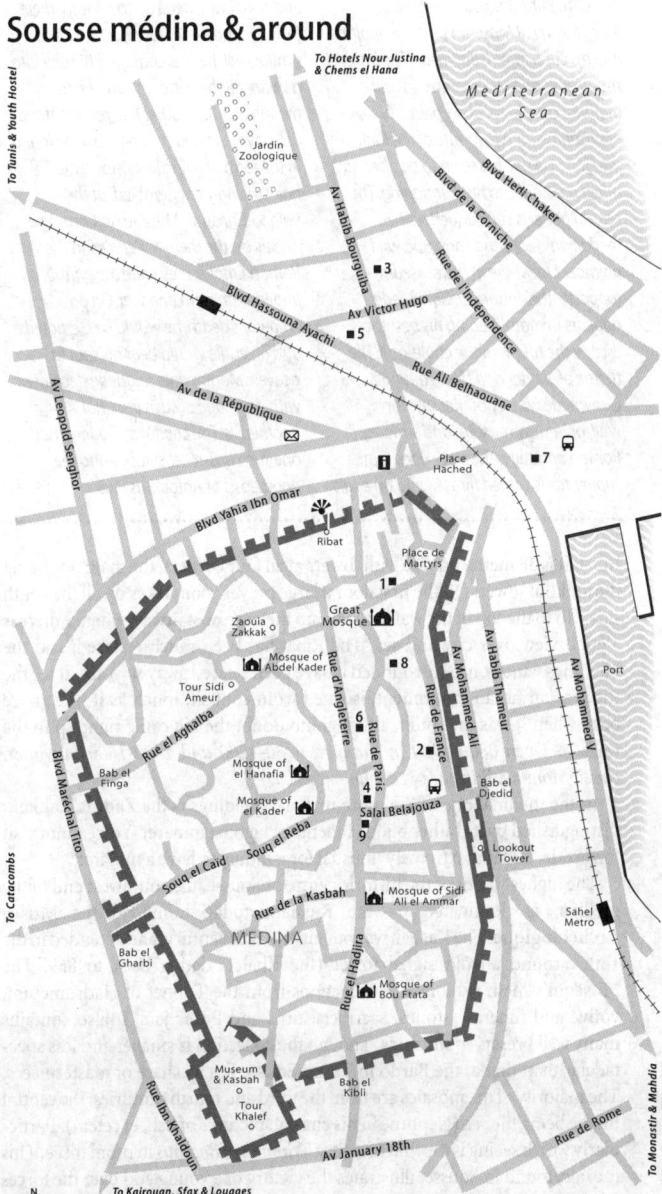

Central Tunisia

Kidnapped by an eagle

One of the finest mosaics at Sousse Archaeological Museum portrays Jupiter and his cupbearer, Ganymede. The latter is shown wearing a Phrygian cap and a minimal cape in royal purple, as is appropriate for a favourite of the King of the Gods. He doesn't seem to be offering much resistance to his kidnapping. The central panel is surrounded with 8 medallions featuring springing wild animals. Elsewhere in the museum, (opposite the entrance), Ganymede appears in marble, doing his best to escape the talons of the eagle-god. The theme of Jupiter and the beautiful Ganymede was a popular one for wall-paintings, mosaics and statuary in Roman antiquity. The story goes that Jupiter transformed himself into an eagle and bore Ganymede up to heaven, there to be his cupbearer. (Jupiter had done a similar trick before, changing himself into a swan, all the better to carry off the nymph Leda). Another fine representation of Ganymede and the eagle can be found in the form of a fine ivory statuette, painstakingly reassembled, at the Palaeo-Christian Museum in Carthage.

Still on the theme of eagles, in the Roman Empire, they were the symbol of imperial strength and war. On an emperor's death, he would be cremated, and an eagle would bear his soul to heaven. Monuments might be decorated with an image of such imperial apotheosis. The capitol at Dougga had one such bas-relief, symbolising the apotheosis of Antoninus Pius.

Ribat: it is 38 metres square with towers at all four corners, the main one being the lookout tower. On the first floor a large prayer room takes up all the south side. Go to the top of the watch tower, up the narrow stairway, whence there is a good view over city and sea. The Ribat has been much restored, and the buildings which once surrounded it have been cleared away so you can see the Ribat as an urban monument, isolated from context, much as it must have been when it was first built, although no doubt the sea came right up to the walls. ■ *Open 0800-1900 in summer, 0930-1200 and 1400-1800 in winter, closed Monday. Entrance 1Dt, photo fee 1Dt.*

In the médina, one of the more unusual buildings is the **Zaouia Zakkak**, distinguished by its rather bijou Hanefite octagonal minaret. You cannot visit the inside, and it is extremely unusual for a zaouia to have a minaret.

The highest point of the historic centre of Sousse, the southwest end of the médina, is dominated by the **Kasbah**, today home to the **Musée Archéologique**. The Kasbah was built in the 11th century, and extended in the 16th, around an old signal tower (the Khalef) dating back to 859. The Museum's main exhibits are collections from the Tophet of Hadrumetum, votive and funerary stones, sacrificial urns and Punic jars. It also contains many well preserved **mosaics**. Though the collection is smaller and less spectacular than that at the Bardo in Tunis, Sousse has its share of masterpieces. The majority of the mosaics are from the third and fourth centuries, the central theme being the sea (Neptune in his chariot, pictures of fish, et cetera). Particularly worth seeing is the third century *Triumph of Bacchus* in room three. This mosaic, found in Sousse, illustrates the victory of a young god over the forces of evil. Another mosaic nearby portrays *Jupiter and Ganymede*. ■ *Open 0800-1200, 1600-1900 summer, 0930-1200, 1400-1800 winter, closed Monday. Entrance 2Dt, photo fee 1Dt, T233695. Entrance via Blvd du Maréchal Tito.* Back in the médina, the **Souqs** are mainly situated around the north end of the rue d'Angleterre. On the west is Souq el Reba, specializing in fabrics and perfume. Again on the right is the Khalaout el Koubba, a building whose original function is unknown but which was probably built in the 19th century.

Mosaic of two fishermen at the Sousse museum

Continue up the Souq el Reba and go out by Bab el Gharbi and turn left along the walls to come to the kasbah and the museum. After visiting the museum re-enter the médina by following the walls to the Bab el Khabli. Following the rue el Hadjira will bring you back to the rue d'Angleterre. Prices in the tourist shops on rue d'Angleterre can be expensive. Do you really want to spend precious swimming time on bargaining for a furry camel or a tooled leather pouf? Either drive a hard bargain or find another activity.

Other sights

Finally, a note on a couple of minor attractions in the médina of Sousse. Starting at Place Farhat Hached, follow the Rue du Rempart-Nord round and up until you come to **Dar Essid**, a restored 20th century house. The owners take great pride in their restored home. The living rooms off the courtyard have their original furnishings, and you can get an idea of how comfortably-off Muslims would have lived in Sousse last century. ■ *Open May-September, 1000-1900, October-April 1000-1800*. The other heritage museum is **Khalouat el Koubba**, just off Souk el Rba in the heart of the médina. The original function of the building is unknown, although *khaloua* is the term used for a saint's retreat or cell (*khalouat el koubba*, 'the domed retreat'). The building is believed to date from 11th/12th centuries. Today it houses a museum of traditional Tunisian marriage customs. The dome, with its zigzag ribbing, is probably unique in North Africa.

On the south side of the médina, the **House of the Tragic Poet** will be worth a visit for people collecting minor Roman sites. (Turn left out of Kasbah, head down Avenue Ibn Khaldoun, fork right after 200 metres).

Back on the north side of the town centre, close to the Place Sidi Boujaâfar, at the start of the Corniche, the **Jardin Zoologique**, has several shaded walkways between the aviaries with birds which range from budgerigars to ostriches. It provides a shaded resting area for entrance 0.25Dt and there is a café and a toilet by the gate.

Catacombs of the Good Shepherd

Visiting catacombs seems a promise of much excitement, and Sousse has five kilometres of catacombs, almost all off limits. **The Catacombs of the Good Shepherd**, are a good 20 minutes walk from the western end of the médina. To get there, take rue Commandant Béjaoui west from the Kasbah, then go first left on rue Abdou Hamed el Ghazali. The Catacombs are on a street on your left after 10 minutes' walk. ■ *Open Tuesday-Sunday 0800-1200, 1500-1900 summer and 0900-1200, 1400-1800 winter.*

☞ Hammam Sousse's most famous son

Besuited, wearing the purple sash of high office, President Ben Ali looks down formally from photographs in government buildings. Since coming to power, Ben Ali and his technocrats have steered Tunisia into a period of unprecedented prosperity. But like his predecessor, Habib Bourguiba, also a native of the Sahel region, there was nothing to suggest that he was destined for the upper reaches of government.

Zine el Abidine Ben Ali was born in 1936 in a modest family in Hammam Sousse, then a tiny village a few kilometres north of Sousse. His father worked at the port and funds were often limited. After the lycée, Ben Ali went on to study at Saint-Cyr, the prestigious French military academy. He took further qualifications at the Châlons-sur-Marne artillery school, and in the USA, at Fort Holabird and Fort Bliss. He developed a deep interest in electronics, which later grew into a passion for information technology. In 1964, President Bourguiba was having security matters reorganized, and Ben Ali was named head of military security at the Ministry of Defence. In 1974, he became naval and air attaché at Tunisia's embassy in Rabat, before being appointed director general of national security in

1977. After a spell as ambassador in Poland, he returned to head national security once more in 1984, becoming minister of national security in 1985. In 1986, he became minister of the interior. In 1987, he became prime-minister. But in 1987, Tunisia faced a growing internal crisis and a loss of international confidence. The ageing president Bourguiba, basically senile, showed no signs of standing down. On 7 November 1987, applying article 57 of Tunisia's constitution, Ben Ali and a group of leading Tunisians had Bourguiba declared unfit to rule.

Since the crisis of the mid-1980s, Tunisia has bounced back, with Ben Ali building teams of highly qualified ministers and civil servants to implement major reforms. After continuing Bourguiba's last mandate, the president was elected for a five year term of office in April 1989, March 1994. He was re-elected for a third term of office in October. Mr Ben Ali enjoys deep-rooted personal popularity with low-income groups. Hammam Sousse's most famous son had a hard start in life, and has worked – and with considerable success – to push through improvement programmes for the poorest parts of the country.

Unlike the Romans, the early Christian communities did not practise cremation. Generally, the Christians were too poor to buy land for burial. For the communities in Rome, Naples, and North Africa, the solution was to dig down into the rock, creating tunnels were shrouded bodies could be placed on ledges (*loculi*) or in niches. In the days of anti-Christian persecution, catacombs provided a gathering place for Christians where they might gather at some martyr's grave. The catacombs might also be attacked by mobs. Later, when Christianity was accepted, basilicas were built above ground on the site of catacombs.

At Sousse, there are more than 250 galleries containing up to 15,000 tombs, testimony to the importance of early Christianity in North Africa. They were built and used between the second and fourth centuries. The catacombs were discovered in 1888, and in the recently restored section, there are few hundred metres open for inspection, and some tombs fronted with glass to reveal the contents within.

Beach The beach of fine sand, cleaned every morning starts in front of the Corniche, but it is much nicer, and less crowded further north. Surfboards can be rented at certain hotels and on the beach. In the evenings, Soussis and tourists enjoy a *paseo* up and down the seafront promenade.

Essentials

There are more than 80 hotels in Sousse, with over 31,500 beds, 20% capacity of all Tunisia. Aim is 50,000 beds in 2001. Most are fully booked in summer. For ease of reference, the hotels are broken down into 4 areas: médina, city centre, the Hammam Sousse/Kantaoui area, and, furthest away from Sousse, Chott Meriem/Hergla.

Sleeping
■ *on maps*
Price codes:
see inside front cover
Phone code: 03

D *Hotel Médina*, behind the Great Mosque on rue de Paris, T221722. Very clean, some rooms with bath, roof terrace, restaurant/bar, no phone bookings, so arrive early in summer. Takes tour groups.

Médina

E *Hotel Ahla*, place de la Grande Mosquée, T200570. Clean and cheap, central location near the Great Mosque. **E** *Hotel Amira*, 52 rue de France, near Bab Djedid in the médina, T226325. Clean, half room have bath, some with view, panoramic roof terrace. **E** *Hotel de Paris*, 15 rue des Remparts, by the walls close to Place Farhat Hached, T220564. Very clean, some rooms on the roof, close to the médina and the new town.

F *Hotel de Gabès*, 12 rue de Paris, T226977. Best of the cheap hotels, very clean, some rooms on roof, good views from terrace, only 14 rooms so book in summer. **F** *Hotel Ezzouhour*, 48 rue de Paris, T228729. Very simple, some rms with bath, otherwise communal shower, very cheap, pleasant manager. **F** *Hotel Perles*, 71 rue de Paris, T224609. In the médina, very small, could be cleaner, communal shower, cheapest hotel in Sousse.

AL *Orient Palace*, 558 beds, T24288, F243345. **A** *Abou Nawas Boujaâfar*, 474 beds, T226030, F226595. Right on the main drag. With thalassotherapy centre. **A** *Hotel Chems el Hana*, T226900, F226076. Elegant, 243 rooms with bath, a/c, phone, TV, terrace, 2 restaurants, 2 pools, fitness centre, tennis, near the sea and quite near the médina, conference room for 150, wheelchair access. Part of the El Hana complex designed by Clément Cacoub. Very 1970s.

City centre

B *Nour Justinia*, on Corniche, T226382. 422 beds, seafront, food and service is reputedly not quite up to scratch. **B** *Riadh Palms*, blvd du 7 novembre, T225700, F228347. Vast package place, marble lobby furnished with pseudo-antiques. **B** *Samara*, blvd Abdelhamid Kadhi, T226699, F226879. **B** *Tej Marhaba*, Av Taïeb Mehiri, T229800, F229815. Large recent hotel next to busy shopping complex (which has a popular upmarket bar). Busy road to cross to get to beach.

C *Hotel Farès*, Blvd Hassouna Ayachi, just off Place Farhat Hached, T227800. 180 beds, central, private beach 200m away, a/c, high rooms with view. **C** *Le Claridge*, Av Habib Bourguiba, T224759. 60 beds, centre of new town. A bit of a Sousse institution in its day. Noisy street side rooms, but clean. **C** *Hotel Karawan*, Av Hédi Chaker, T226139 / 225388, F225307. Package hotel on main drag, close to Nour Justinia. **C** *Hotel du Parc*, rue de Carthage. **C** *Corniche Plaza*, on blvd de la Corniche, T226763. Small, well-run hotel. **C** *Le Printemps*, Blvd de la Corniche, T229335, F224055. 69 rooms for 2/4 persons, with hob, fridge and utensils, bar, tea room, hairdresser, commercial centre, restaurant, 5 minutes walk from town centre. **C** *Royal*, 4 rue de Teboulba, close to the Corniche, T220536. Small pension-type place. **C** *Sousse Azur*, 5 rue Amilcar, off Av Habib Bourguiba, T226960, F228145. 20 rooms, restaurant, coffee lounge, 10 minutes from town centre.

D *Hotel Hadrumète*, Place Assed Ibn el Fourat, T226292. by port, 35 rooms with bath, clean, good restaurant, pool, enclosed terrace café. Once quite chic, now merely a downtown hotel close to sea.

Central Tunisia

Youth hostel T227548. 3 km out along Tunis road, at Plage Boujaâfar, 2 km from station, kitchen, meals available, 90 beds.

Hammam Sousse/ Kantaoui area
NB Don't look for cheap hotels in this area

There are some very large and posh hotels here, especially handy if you're playing golf. **A** *Diar el Andalous* T246200, F246348. Luxurious in its day, built around a network of garden patios. (Won an Agha Khan architecture prize for design). 300 rooms, beach, a/c, indoor and outdoor pools, lots of tennis courts, disco, watersports. **A** *Hannibal Palace* Port el Kantaoui, T241577, F242341. Another oversized 'five star' hotel. Let down by the service. Needs reclassifying. **A** *Hotel Hasdrubal* Port el Kantaoui, T241944, F241969. Better than the Hannibal Palace. **A** *Marhaba Palace* T243633/240200. Just like a palace, 250 splendid rooms, indoor and outdoor pools, tennis, garden.

B *Les Maisons de la Mer* T241799/246266, F241961. Pleasant self-catering accomodation at Port el Kantaoui, ranging from studios for 2 to small flats sleeping 6. Good value out of season. Office is to left of the mock-fortified gate, the main entrance to Kantaoui. **B** *Hotel Résidence Kanta* T240466. Self-catering accomodation at Port el Kantaoui. **B** *Hotel Soviva*, route de Hergla, north of Kantaoui, T246145. Lots of fun to be had on the water slides in the pool complex here.

Sousse North: hotel area

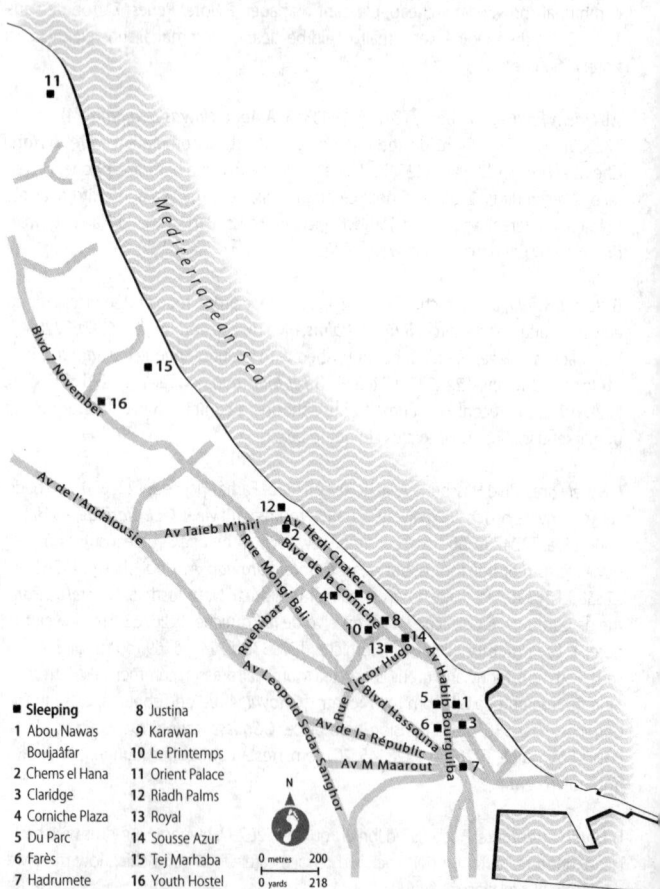

■ Sleeping

1 Abou Nawas Boujaâfar	8 Justina
2 Chems el Hana	9 Karawan
3 Claridge	10 Le Printemps
4 Corniche Plaza	11 Orient Palace
5 Du Parc	12 Riadh Palms
6 Farès	13 Royal
7 Hadrumete	14 Sousse Azur
	15 Tej Marhaba
	16 Youth Hostel

0 metres 200
0 yards 218

C *Tennis Méditerranée*, route de Hergla, Chatt Meriem T248055/56/57, F248060

Good choice available at Port el Kantaoui and Av Habib Bourguiba. Most restaurants cater for tourists, menus in many languages. Small restaurants in the old town may display menus in Arabic only.

Eating

Expensive *Le Bonheur*, T225742, place Farhat Hached, good grilled meat and fish, large terrace on the street. *Restaurant Cherif*, by the harbour, specializes in fish and seafood. *Restaurant des Remparts*, T226326, rue de l'Eglise, by médina walls close to place Farhat Hached, more expensive because it serves alcohol. *Restaurant Malouf*, T226508, place Farhat Hached, excellent food, particularly the fish, large terrace.

Médina and town centre

Mid-range *L'Escargot*, blvd de la Corniche, T224779, space for 65, French cooking; *La Fiesta*, blvd Mongi Slim, better than average. *Restaurant le Golfe*, bve Habib Bourguiba in Boujaâfar complex, clean, good choice.

Cheap *Restaurant Ben Henda*, rue de Paris, in the médina, simple but tasty food. *Restaurant Hassoumi*, rue de Rabat, just off the Corniche, very cheap, good Tunisian food, clean. *Restaurant Populaire*, rue de France, typical médina restaurant. *Restaurant Tunisien*, rue Ali Belhaouane, nice setting, some dishes a bit more expensive, very good fish.

Expensive *Le Beach Club*, T241799. *La Daurade*, T244893 is very good, but very pricey. *Le Yacht Club*, T241799 and *Le Club House*, T241756.

Port el Kantaoui
No cheap eats at Kantaoui. Hotel restaurants also provide (pricey) meals

Mid-range *Neptune VI*, floating restaurant, T241799, giant prawns special. *Les Emirs*, T240865. *L'Escale*, T241791 (one of the best) and *La Méditerranée*, T240788.

Port El Kantaoui Marina

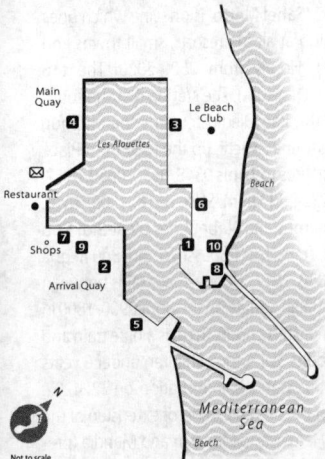

Main Quay
Le Beach Club
Les Alouettes
Beach
Restaurant
Shops
Arrival Quay
Mediterranean Sea
Beach
Not to scale

1 Fuel
2 Harbour Master's Office
3 Quay Amilcar
4 Quay des Sirènes
5 Quay Hannibal
6 Quay Jugurtha
7 Quay President Bourguiba
8 Ramp
9 Ships Chandlers
10 Travel Lift

Casa del Gelato, Blvd du 7 novembre, near the Hotel Hill Diar. Las Vegas kitsch block of mirror glass and marble on the main drag up to Port el Kantaoui. Large amounts of icecream should please the kids. **Nightclubs** Most of the hotels have small, uninteresting nightclubs. Sousse has two large clubs, both at the north end of the town centre, *Maracana* and *Samarra*, at the town end of the Corniche.

Bars, cafés and clubs

Diving *Port el Kantoui International Diving Centre*, Port de Plaisance, T241799, is recognized by the watersport federation and is open all the year. Prices at Diving Centre: First dive 20Dt; Exploration 22Dt; Night dive 25Dt; 6 dives 110Dt; Open water training Dt250. However, if you really want to dive, you should go to Tabarka. **Football** The local team is the Etoile du Sahel, red and white kit, which has done quite well in recent years in African and Arab competitions. **Golf** *Golf El Kantaoui* T231755/6, has a 27 hole tournament golf course, par 108, 9,576m where green fees are 30-40Dt

Sports

Central Tunisia

per round and lessons are available. *Palm Links Golf Course* and *Monastir Golf Course*, shaded by olive trees, are both 18 hole, par 72, 6,140m. **Gym** Beach club near swimming pool at north end of Kantaoui. T241799, 4Dt per session, has weights and organises aerobics, etc. **Sailing and fishing** Yachts and catamarans can be hired from the yacht basin or you can take a trip in an ancient sailing boat. Aquascope trips are available to view underwater life. The harbour has berths for 340 yachts, minimum-maximum draft 2-4m. See piece on Yachting, page , for further details. Organised at quayside are: sailing trip, daily weather permitting at 1000 and 1430, 3 hours, 20Dt – with an hour for swimming and fishing; catamaran trip, daily 1000, 1200, 1400 and 1600, 2 hours, 15Dt; fishing day trip 1000-1800, 80Dt, winter half day for 40Dt, eat what you catch or take it home; Aquascope, 3 vessels operating daily 0700-1800, an hour for 12-15Dt, goes down to 25m – but as sea bed is featureless and the water murky not worth it.

Entertainment **Casino** *El Hana Palace Hotel*, T243000. **Concerts** *Sousse International Festival* in July/August, various venues, including open air theatre.

Shopping Fixed price articles, the usual selection at Socopa in *Hotel Abou Nawas Boujaâfar* and the larger Soula Centre off Place Farhat Hached. *Monoprix*, Place Farhat Hached; *Magasin Général*, rue Khaled Ibn Walid; Blvd de la Corniche, Complex Nejma; Port el Kantaoui. **Thalassotherapy** *Abou Nawas Boujaâfar* offers a range of treatments 'for total well-being' including indoor heated sea-water pool, 2 saunas, Turkish baths, gym, solarium and relaxation room.

Transport **Local Car hire**: Avis, route de la Corniche, T225901; **Ben Jemma Rent a Car**, rue 2 Mars, La Corniche, T224002; **Budget**, 63 Av Habib Bourguiba, T224041; **Europcar**, route de la Corniche, T226252; **Hertz**, Av Habib Bourguiba, T225428; **Inter Rent**, route de la Corniche, T227562; **Touaregs**, 13 route Khezama, T243975; **Tunisia National Rent-a-car**, route de la Corniche, T226333; **Youngcar**, route de la Corniche, T226416.

Long distance Air: Tunis Air, Av Habib Bourguiba, T227955, for details of flights from Skanes/Monastir airport, T260300. **Train**: 'Sahel Metro' is one line which goes all the way to **Mahdia** along the coast stopping at all the resorts, small towns and Monastir international airport (0.6Dt single). Hourly from 0600-2000. The trip **Sousse-Mahdia** takes just under 1$\frac{1}{2}$ hours (3.75Dt return). The station is at the south end of Av Mohammed V, 100m down from the Bab Djedid towards the harbour, T225321. **For Tunis**: The station is on Blvd Hassouna Ayachi, up the road from Place Farhat Hached. Information on T221955. Departures to **Tunis** 0348, 0530, 0650, 0757, 1310, 1418, 1527, 1830, 2012; **Gabès** 0918, 2324; **El Djem/Sfax**, 0918, 1509, 1618, 1935, 2324; **Gafsa/Metlaoui** 2324. For **Hammamet** and **Nabeul** get off at **Sidi Bou Regba** and continue journey by bus or louage. Trains leave Sousse for Sidi Bou Regba at 0348, 0530, 0650, 0757, 1310, 1418, 1527, 1830, 2012. 'Noddy' road trains between Sousse and Port el Kantaoui leaves Place Boujaâfar in Sousse on the hour 0900-1800 in winter 0900-2300 in summer, returning at half past the hour. There is a blue train and a yellow train, tickets cannot be transferred. Adults 3Dt return, children under 8 years 2Dt. Noddy Train, T240353. **Bus**: there are 4 bus stations. Information on T224202. Departures from **Place Sidi Yahia**, north wall of the médina, a sort of extension of the place Farhat Hached, for Port el Kantaoui and Hergla, and Monastir and Mahdia (prefer the metro for the latter two, however). Departures from **Bab el Djedid**, on east side of médina, to all points south, including **Kairouan** (1½ hours, 2.39Dt); **Gabès** (5 hours, 9.27Dt) and **Sfax** (2½ hours, 4.96Dt); **Djerba** (via Zarzis); **Kebili** (7¼ hours, 12.96Dt); **Douz** (7¼ hours, 13.9Dt); **Medenine**; **Matmata** (7 hours, 10.74Dt); **Tataouine** (9 hours, 13Dt. Departures from **place du Port** to **Tunis** (including night departures) and **Bizerte**. Departures from the **gare routière** for points northwest, including Enfida, Le

Kef and El Fahs. **Louages**: the louage station has moved from Bab el Djedid, on rue Mohammed Ali to Souq el Ahad, near camel market on route de Sfax, 2 km out of town centre. Take a taxi as it's a 30-minute walk. **Taxi**: yellow taxis have meters. **Sea** *Compagnie Tunisienne de Navigation (CTN)*, rue Abdallah Ibn Zoubeir, T224861, F224844.

Directory

Banks *STB* on Av Habib Bourguiba. *UIB*, Av Habib Thameur. *BT*, rue Ali Belhaouane. *BNT*, rue de l'Indépendence. Money can also be changed in any of the large hotels. *STB* has an automatic cash dispenser (dinars). **Communications** Area code: 03. **Post Office**: Av de la République, just off Place Farhat Hached, T224750. **Parcel Post**, rue Ali Bey, T225492. **Medical services** Chemist: open nights, 38 Av de la République, T224795. 45 route de la Corniche. Av H Thameur. Chemists display names of those open late. Hospital:*Clinique Les Oliviers*, blvd du 7 novembre, T242711. Probably the first option. *Hôpital universitaire Farhat Hached*, Av Farhat Hached, rue Ibn el Jazzar, T221411. *CHU*, Sahloul, Hammam-Sousse, T241411. *Dialysis Centre*, Blvd du 7 novembre, Route Touristique, T242711. **Police and security** Customs Authority: Place de l'Indépendence, T227700. **National Guard:** Av Leopold Sedar Sanghor, T225588. **Police**: rue Pasteur, T225566. **Tour companies & travel agents**Atlas Voyages, Blvd du 7 Novembre, T240270, F240116. *Carthage Tour*, Av Habib Bourguiba, T227954, F225301. *Chams Tours*, 8 rue Ali Belhaoune, T225357, F227328. *King's Travel*, 10 rue du Caire, T228750, F228307. *Meditours Tunisie*, 95 Blvd Abdelhamid el Cadhi, T227466/7, F223265. *Tourafrica*, rue Khaled Ibn Walid, T224277. *Tunis Air*, Av Habib Bourguiba, T227955. *Tunisian Travel Service*, route des Oranges, T241599, F243499. *Tunisie Voyages*, Blvd du 7 Novembre, T242134, F242664. **Tourist offices** The tourist information offices are at Regional ONTT, 1 Av Habib Bourguiba, by Place Farhat Hached, T225157, open 0730-1930 most days. The local office is opposite, T220431. **Places of Worship** Catholic: *Eglise St Felix*, 1 rue de Constantine, T224596/220554. Service in French, Sat 1815 and Sun 0930. **Evangelical Church:** 16 rue de Malte, T224073. **Synagogue:** in rue Amilcar.

Excursions north of Sousse

If you hire a car, there are some excellent day trips to do from Sousse. One such circuit, north of Sousse, could take you to **Enfidaville** (museum and Second World War graves), the hilltop village of **Takrouna** and the Kène Craft Centre (for these see preceding chapter). You could finish up at **Hergla**, the Roman Horrea Coelia, a cliff village dominated by the mausoleum in honour of Sidi Bou Mendil. Sidi Bou Mendil (literally, 'the saint with the handkerchief') was said to be able to transform any piece of cloth into a magic flying carpet which took him to the Holy Land of Arabia. Hergla also has a go-kart rink. The local craft is esparto grass weaving, as at nearby Takrouna and Jeradou. Originally, woven and plaited esparto grass was the raw material for a whole series of utilitarian products, including donkey bags and *scourtins*, round mats used in the olive oil presses to filter the oil. Today, you can also find decorative fish and table mats.

Finally, **Kalaâ Kebira** (lit: 'the big citadel'), an undistinguished sort of place on the northern outskirts of Sousse, has lost most of its agricultural charm. The Olive Festival in December might be worth a visit if you are an oil fan.

Skanès and Monastir المنستير

Phone code: 03
Colour map 1, grid C6
Arabic script is for
Monastir

Monastir could have been just another sleepy Sahel coastal town. Being the birth-place of independence leader Habib Bourguiba, however, meant that things turned out rather differently. Like leaders elsewhere in Africa who built them-selves concrete capitals in the bush, Tunisia's first president wanted a city to mark his country's accession to nation-state status. So sleepy, walled Monastir, a quiet coastal place, had to be extensively remodelled. But this being Tunisia, the results of the building programme are homely rather than grandiose. The town acquired a gold-domed mausoleum, some impressive modernist public buildings and an esplanade. Along the sandy coastline west of Monastir, some of the first hotels devoted to mass tourism went up, including the Skanès Palace, Tunisia's first five star hotel.

Ins and outs

Getting there A lot of north European visitors fly into the *Aéroport international de Skanès-Monastir*. The airport is 9 km from Monastir. If you are not being met by a tour-company bus, then you can get into Monastir by rail, (the airport has a rail station outside), or by bus or taxi. Taxi-drivers are ready to profit from new arrivals disorientation (so study your banknotes carefully). The ride into Monastir should cost around 5 or 6 Dt maximum. Local shared taxis also do the same run (and considerably cheaper). There are also car-rental companies at the airport, although cheap cars are in demand during high-season, so book in advance.

Getting around The region is served by rail, with the Sahel Metro running from Mahdia to Sousse via the airport and Monastir. The bus, train and louage stations are on Av des Martyrs, next to the rue Mahmoud Bourguiba, the main street leading through the town and just 5 minutes walk from the Ribat.

Background and history

Situated on a headland some 25 km south of Sousse, Monastir is an attractive fishing port with an elegant promenade along the bay. The journey from Sousse improves as you leave the industrial area of Sousse behind. The huge factory on the outskirts makes couscous. The salt pans at Sahline Sebkha are extensive, an unusual sight for visitors from northern Europe but common in these warm Mediterranean areas. The dried salt is collected, purified and exported.

Sponge fishing is carried on here as well as the catching of most indigenous fish and shellfish.

Ancient origins Back in Roman times, Monastir was called **Ruspina**, a corruption of the Punic name Rous Penna, and it served as Julius Caesar's operations base for his Afri-can campaign. Part of the triple ramparts from this time still survive. During the 11th century, when nearby Mahdia was the Fatmid capital and Kairouan was out of favour, Monastir was an important regional centre with a fortress built to defend the Muslim coastal settlements against incursions from the Christian north. The Ribat or fortress was held to have special virtues. It was said that spending three days as part of the garrison in Monastir opened the gates to paradise. After the departure of the Fatimids from Mahdia for Egypt, the town lost its regional importance, although the fortifications were improved in Ottoman times.

Tunisia's first president, **Habib Bourguiba**, was born here in 1903. Presidential interest was a major factor behind the town's post-independence redevelopment. Monastir has a pleasant marina, and there is a whole strip of hotels along the coast running westwards to Skanès and Sousse.

Monastir's most famous citizen

Sights

Monastir's most famous monument is the **Ribat of Harthouma**, whose walls and turrets will be familiar to all who have seen Monty Python's *The Life of Brian*. The much restored fortifications of the Ribat were built in 796 by Harthouma Ibn el Ayoune, as part of the coastal look-out system. One of the oldest and largest of the military structures built by the Arabs in North Africa, it was later refortified and surrounded by an additional wall during the nineth and 11th centuries, which gives the whole edifice an interesting mixture of contrasting styles and shapes but the initial plan remains – a courtyard surrounded by accommodation (primitive) for the defenders and a prayer hall now beautifully set out as the **Islamic Museum**. It is very interesting actually to see the inside of one of these forts. Small children should be watched closely as there are no safety barriers and some of the steps and walks by the walls are unprotected. Note that the building may be off limits if filming is in progress. The Ribat also featured in the 13 episode serial *Jesus of Nazareth* and *Raiders of the Lost Ark*.

The entrance is at the foot of one of the towers, where a corridor flanked by former guard rooms and now used as a ticket office, leads into the central courtyard. There is a good view over the sea from the top of the Nador (look-out tower). The Museum is well laid out, with good details about the exhibits: gravestones, glass, pages of Koran (as seen also in Rakkada Museum), pieces of pottery found here at the Ribat, small pipes, pots and oil lamps, leather covers, exquisite old fabrics, pottery, a display of coins and a unique wooden Arab astrolabe (for measuring altitude), made in Cordoba and dating back to the 10th century.

There are, in the courtyard, more engraved stelae and tombstones dating back from the 11th and 12th centuries. ■ *Open 0800-1900 in summer, 0900-1200 and 1400-1800 in winter. Closed Monday, entrance 2Dt, photography 1Dt, no flash or tripods, T461276. Allow at least an hour to potter about here and get the feel of the place.*

Close to the main Ribat is the smaller **Ribat of Sidi Dhouib**. Also ruins of a similar construction are to be found at the entrance to *Hotel Esplanade*. Plans are to preserve these ruins as they now stand. Another ruined fort stands at the end of Cap Monastir. Also in in the neighbourhood of the Ribat, the **Great Mosque** was built in the nineth century and extended in the 11th century.

The **Habib Bourguiba Mausoleum** at the north end of the cemetery is an imposing affair, a huge square building with a huge golden cupola flanked by two splendid matching minarets. It is approached via a vast paved concourse which cuts through the Sidi el Mazari cemetery at the southern end of which are two new ornate tombs. As one approaches the ornate iron gates (with decorative

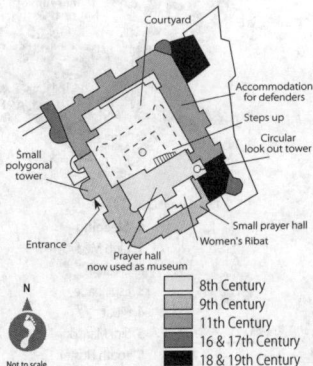

Ribat of Harthouma

Courtyard

Accommodation for defenders

Steps up

Circular look out tower

Small polygonal tower

Small prayer hall

Women's Ribat

Entrance

Prayer hall now used as museum

N

Not to scale

	8th Century
	9th Century
	11th Century
	16 & 17th Century
	18 & 19th Century

Central Tunisia

script on each gate) a man with a key may appear and let you get even nearer – for a tip. This is where former President Habib Bourguiba, currently living in peaceful retirement in Monastir, may well be buried.

In the cemetery near the Habib Bourguiba Mausoleum is the **Koubba of Sidi el Mazari** built in 1149 AD. This can be visited, if respectfully dressed. The Mausoleum was built in 1963 at the same time as the **Habib Bourguiba Mosque**. The mosque (off-limits to non-Muslims) is on rue de l'Indépendence in the old town and was built following the richly decorated 'traditional' style of architecture. The entrance to the prayer hall is through 19 intricately carved teak doors, made by the craftsmen of Kairouan. Once inside, the huge vaulted prayer hall is supported by 86 pink marble columns. There is a large dome before the *mihrab* which is inlaid with golden mosaics and decorated with small onyx columns.

The **médina** has a few suitably picturesque bits and pieces: balconies etc. It was extensively remodelled in the 1960s, and the walls have been restored. It is an interesting area of Monastir with small retail outlets but none of the associated small-scale manufacturing often found in other médinas. There is a small tower on the corner of the médina opposite the post office which seems to have no function now.

Near the mosque and Tourist Office, a **Museum of Traditional Costume** on rue de l'Indépendence has some nice displays of clothing. ■ *Open Monday-Saturday 0900-1200 and 1400-1730, closed Sunday, entrance 1Dt.* For local life, there is the weekly **Saturday market** with the usual goods in Souq Essebt on Place Guedir El Foul and the rue Salem B'Chir near the bus station.

Central Monastir

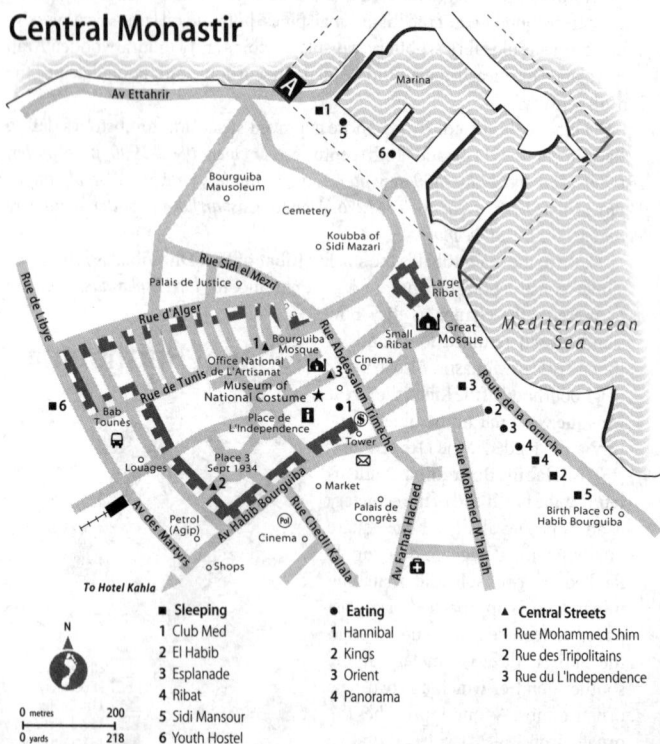

■ Sleeping	● Eating	▲ Central Streets
1 Club Med	1 Hannibal	1 Rue Mohammed Shim
2 El Habib	2 Kings	2 Rue des Tripolitains
3 Esplanade	3 Orient	3 Rue du L'Independence
4 Ribat	4 Panorama	
5 Sidi Mansour		
6 Youth Hostel		

Related maps
A Monastir Marina,
page 248

0 metres	200
0 yards	218

There are a few very minor sights to seek out on the coast, including the **birth** **On the coast** **place of Habib Bourguiba** on Place 3 August, on the route de la Corniche overlooking the old fishing port. It has a blue door and tile work round door and windows. A faded plaque to the right hand side of the door indicates its importance. There are some quite interesting **caves** cut into the sandstone rock which protects the south side of the old fishing harbour as a breakwater. These were used as stores and some still have doors. The shore of the harbour here is covered with many rusty anchors.

From the marina, you can walk out to the **Ile Ghedamsi**. Follow the track at the end of the marina area which leads out to the point and to the small (inaccessible on foot) island beyond. It is a pleasant walk (30 minutes) round the koubba and, surprisingly, three tennis courts. There are good views, close down to the tiny natural harbour with the El Kahlia caves cut into the promontory, where the fishermen pull up their boats and wash their nets and beyond over Monastir or north to Skanès. At the very end of the promontory are the remains of a fort which is being excavated and renovated. The path goes round the edge of this fort and in places there is very limited foot room over a very steep drop.

Day trips can be arranged to the **Kuriat Islands** which lie about 15 km east. For more information, go to the office at end of port. These islands are used by the Cap Monastir diving centre.

Essentials

The number of places to stay in Monastir is quite limited. The hotels are expensive but **Sleeping** not of high quality. Out of season many are closed or are undergoing redecoration. Try Skanès or Mahdia for four-star comfort or Sousse for a wider choice.

The hotels in Monastir are close to the town centre, on the Corniche. The *Sidi Mansour*, **At Monastir** one of the oldest hotels, awaits redevelopment, as does the former *Hayet Regency / Club Med*, close to the Marina.

B *Apart-Hotel Cap Monastir*, reception on the left before you go into the marina, T462305, 464999, www.caesium.fr/capmonastir. Clean and pleasant self-catering accomodation right on the Marina. Attracts lots of Tunisian families in summer. (Flat sleeping 4 costs 125 DDt per night in high season; rates much more reasonable out of season). The Apart-Hotel gives you freedom to do your own thing in a way impossible in the usual 4 star palaces. Kitchen equipment very limited. Recommended. Note that reception will want a 100 Dt caution in cash, returned when apartment has been checked after departure. **B** *El Habib*, T462944, 460214. Has both rooms and small flats. **B** *Kahla*, Av Taïeb Mehiri, T464570, F467881. Self-catering accomodation on offer as well as rooms. **B** *Sidi Mansour*, route de la Corniche, T461311.Currently undergoing redevelopment.

C *Esplanade*, T461146/7, F460050. Very central location with access through garden to Corniche, 7 km from airport, 5 km from international golf course, 130 rooms with bath, telephone, and balcony overlooking pool and within view and sound of the sea, bar, restaurant.

D *Hotel Yasmine*, route de la Falaise T462511. A pleasant small hotel distinguished by the most kitsch façade on the Falaise (whitewashed with lots of blue decorative twiddly bits). 23 beds in 16 rooms, cheap, welcoming, with a beach across the road and down the cliff and a very good restaurant frequented by locals. Pricey in summer.

Central Tunisia

Youth hostel: on rue de Maroc, town centre, T461216. 60 beds, 4Dt per person, only dormitories, no double or family room.

West of Monastir/ Skanès The majority of Monastir's hotels are situated along the beach strip west of Monastir. There is little to fault them, they are all big, concrete and harmless. The beach however, is narrow in places and a bit disappointing.

A *Abou Nawas Sunrise*, T466646, F466282. Bungalow accomodation. **A** *Hotel Kuriat Palace*, T461200, 467000, F460049. The dearest of the hotels in this area. Has all the usual facilities. **A** *Regency*, T460033. **A** *Robinson Club*, T427515. **A** *Sidi Mansour*, T460023. **A** *Skanès El Hana*, T462256. Another big package hotel, part of the El Hana chain. **A** *Skanès Palace*, T461350. Must have been very swish in its day. Unfortunately, the refurbishment brought lots of 'traditional' decorative touches which have destroyed the simplicity of the original design. **A** *Hotel Thalassa*, T520520, F520500. New in 1999. Works mainly with tour-groups. Ill-proportioned entry in a vaguely neo-classical style, vast lobby, etc. Good value out of season. **B** *Sunrise*, T427144. **C** *Hotel Chems*, T466290, F466106, huge and impersonal. **C** *Les Palmiers*, T61151.

Eating **Expensive** *Cap Grill*, T460923. On the left as you enter the marina, attracts a more upmarket sort of clientèle and is used for local business people entertaining. Expect to pay about 30Dt a head. *Le King's* T463394, in the Complexe El Habib, on the Corniche. Good service, has a good reputation. Around 35Dt a head for the full wack. *Marina The Captain*, T461449, F473820. A bar-restaurant and top address in the marina at Monastir (turn left through the main entrance, *The Captain* is on your left at the far end of the quay). Around 30Dt a head. *Le Pirate* in the new fishing port 1.5 km south of town centre. (Take a taxi). High level of service, business takes its clients here. Recommended. Closed on Monday.

Mid-range *El Farik*, about 500m south of the main town beach, right on the coast. The restaurant, which dates back to 1966, is housed in a sort of concrete UFO built on a rocky bit of coast. Basically a boozers' den, with the good sea food and chilled wine which you can find in this sort of eatery in Tunisia. If you sit outside on summer afternoons, the local kids will keep you entertained by diving off the parapet. In its day, El Farik must have been the happening place in Monastir. About 15Dt a head for a really good feed, but you could pay much less. *El Médina*, Place de l'Independence, corner of Av de l'Independence, opposite médina wall, small, clean, pavement tables, friendly staff, menu in English, open 0900-1800. *Restaurant Hannibal* in médina behind Office National de l'Artisanant, T461097. Also on route de la Corniche are *Orient* and *Panorama*. *Restaurant Le Chandelier* T462232 or 462305. Situated at the heart of the marina, on your right as you come in. Highly recommended. Pleasant service, good food. *Restaurant de Tunisie*, Av Ali Belhouane, behind *Hotel Hadrumete*, Dutch owned, Tunisian and Indian food. **Cheap** *La Pizzeria*, T460923, Port de Plaisance, on marina.

Monastir Marina

Night Club · Border Police · Customs · Laundry
Restaurant ·
VIP Quay
Restaurant ·
Restaurant · Marina
Cinema
To Town Centre
Fuel
Arsenal
Main Quay
Resupply Point
National Guard
Boatyard
Outer Harbour

N

0 metres 100
0 yards 109

Cinemas There are a number of cinemas in the town, including one in the marina. **Entertainment**
Hammam In the médina, rue de Tunis.

Office National de l'Artisanat, open 0900-1900 daily, except Sunday 1100-1700, has a **Shopping**
good selection of items to choose from, or from which to learn about prices. On outer
edge of médina facing E towards *Hotel Esplanade*. *Magasin Général*, Place de
l'Independence, in town centre. *Monoprix*, rue de Tunis, opposite médina wall.

Golf *Palm Links* golf course, T466910/2, F466913, 10 km out of town, on road **Sports**
beyond Skanes towards Sousse, 6,140m, 18 holes, par 72, green fees 30-40Dt.
Fishing Excursions from Monastir – weekly mini-cruises to the Kuriat islands. Trip on
El Kahlia for amateur anglers, provision of rods, lines and trolls. For details contact
T461156. **Horse riding** Available, ask at any large hotel for details. Horse racing each
Sunday. **Watersports** Including scuba diving and sailing, at the Cap Monastir.
Underwater diving school, T461156. Monastir Yacht club has 386 berths. Marina
T462305/462509. Cap Marina Monastir – Port de Plaisance Latitude 3546'11" north,
longitude 1050'50" east, T460951/3/5, F462066, nearest airport 8 km, adjacent marinas are Sousse 10 M, Port El Kantaoui 14 M, Mahdia 31 M, 400 moorings, maximum
boat length 45m, depth at entrance channel 6m, harbour 4-5m, outer jetty 7m, moor-
ing rates for an 11 metre boat is 7Dt per day in high season, or 704Dt per year, facilities
include fresh water, electricity on pontoons, toilets, showers, fuel, oil, refuse disposal,
telephone and television to boats exceeding 12m.

Local Car hire: *Avis*, airport, T463031; *Europcar*, airport, T461314; *Hertz*, Av Habib **Transport**
Bourguiba, T461404, and at airport, T461314; *Inter rent*, airport, T461314; *Nova Rent*,
Av Habib Bourguiba, T467826.

Long distance Air: *Tunis Air* at airport, T460300 and in Monastir close to *Hotel Ribat*,
T462550, *Nouvelair*, airport, T460300. Flight information Skanes/Monastir airport on
T461314. **Train**: Opposite the bus station. Information on T460755. **Tunis** (via Sousse)
0610, 1238, 1758 (5Dt). **'Sahel Metro'** goes to the airport and to **Sousse** and **Mahdia**
along the coast every hour from 0600-2000. **Bus**: the bus station is at the south end of
Av de la République. Information on T461059. Departures to **Tunis** 0445; **Sfax** 0500,
0600, 1100. There are also frequent buses to **Sousse** (6Dt). **Louages**: leave from in
front of the bus station. **Taxi**: some taxi drivers take advantage of tourists – check
there is a meter or agree a price.

Banks *STB*, Av Habib Bourguiba, T261383. *UIB*, Av Habib Bourguiba, T261400. *BNT*, Place de **Directory**
l'Indépendence, T261057. *BNT*, Place de l'Indépendence, T261495. Money can also be changed in
large hotels. **Communications Area code**: 03. **Post Office**: Av Habib Bourguiba, by the Palais
des Congrès (conference centre), T260176, also at railway station and airport. **Medical
Services Chemist**: *Charhine* on Av Habib Bourguiba and *Karoui* on Av de la République.
Hospital: *Hôpital Fattouma Bourguiba*, Av Fattouma Bourguiba, T461141. **Places of
worship Catholic**: *Chez les Soeurs*, Zone du Stade, T431931, services Sat 1800 and Sun 0900.
Tour companies & travel agents *ATAC Tour* in *Hotel Rivage*, T230955. *Atlas Voyages* in *Hotel
Chems*, T233350. *B'Chire Voyages*, Av Habib Bourguiba, T261066. *Carthage Tours*, in *Hotel Habib*
on Corniche, T461847. *Skanes Travel Service* in *Hotel Sahara Beach*, rue de 2 Mars 1934, T261088.
Tourafrica, Av Habib Bourguiba, T461381. **Tourist offices** The tourist information office is at
ONTT, Quartier Chraga, in front of the Habib Bourguiba Mosque, T461960. Also in front of the
airport, T461205. **Useful addresses Customs**: at port, T462305. **Fire**: on rue de Libye, T197.
Garage: there are 3 garages on Av Habib Bourguiba. **Petrol**: at Agil, Mobil or Ruspina, all on Av
Habib Bourguiba. **Police**: on rue Chedli Kallala, T461432.

Central Tunisia

☞ *The education of Monastir's most famous son*

Monastir's most famous son is undoubtedly Habib Bourguiba, founder of Tunisia's nationalist movement and first president of the Tunisian Republic (declared 1957). Born on 3 August 1903, he was to leave an indelible mark on Tunisian life, propelling the country from the rank of sleepy Mediterreanean statelet under French protection to that of a pragmatic, modernizing nation with Arab nationalist credentials.

Bourguiba was the product of a particular environment. While Tunis, with its cosmopolitan population, had no difficulty composing with French rule, which in any case brought new business opportunities and improvements in the city, the small farmers of the Sahel had different attitudes. They quickly seized the importance of modern education, and in the early 1900s, began to have their children educated in bilingual private schools. (70 out of the 90 écoles franco-arabes *existing before independence were in the Sahel region*). By the 1930s, sons of ordinary families like the Bourguibas were competing with Tunis notables' children for jobs open to Muslims in the administration. Many, like Habib Bourguiba, were going to France for a university education.

In his memoirs, Habib Bourguiba tended to present himself as belonging to a deprived family. In fact his father, retiring from the Beylical army in 1893, was a notable on the Monastir town council, and held various local posts. The family was wealthy enough to send Habib's two elder brothers to the prestigious Sadiki College in Tunis. Habib almost followed the same track, but having been forced to drop out of the Sadiki through illness in 1920, he returned to schooling at the Lycée Carnot, switching from the establishment which trained members of the Muslim élite to the one dominated by French students. This was a practical move. Through professions like law, accessible to those with a French education, social mobility was possible. In 1924, after completing his baccalauréat, Habib Bourguiba headed for Paris and a law degree. He returned in 1927, marked by French culture, and bringing with him a French wife.

Despite all this education, he was to remain an outsider in all the circles that counted in 1930s Tunis – French administration, traditional Muslim, and cosmopolitan middle-class. The difficulties were both social and professional, and Bourguiba was to move from being a young lawyer trying to build a career to the unstable status of nationalist activist.

South from Monastir to Mahdia

Going south from Monastir, you cross one of the most populated areas in the country, after the capital region. There are many small settlements, some running one into another and the serenity of the rural area, glimpsed at intervals, olive groves and small gardens, has become harder to find.

Unless you have a taste for obscure textile towns, then this route is best done on the Sahel Metro train, which has stations at Khnis, Ksar Hellal and Teboulba in addition to those on the published timetable. Travelling by bus will require changes at Moknine or Ksar Hellal.

If you are driving, the corniche to the south of the old fishing port at Monastir soon loses its attraction and you pass through an area of light industry. Turn right, away from the coast, towards the main road and head south. The small village of **Khnis** stands right on the coast with a small fishing fleet and relaxing views. South of Khnis, agriculture becomes important once more, with olive groves right up to the coast. While the minor road continues along the coast to Saiada, the road to **Ksar Hellal** swings inland, leaving behind the views and becoming increasingly congested. Ksar Hellal has a busy main road, a continuing line of shops, small workshops and the usual concrete housing. This runs on to become **Moknine**, where the road returns us to the coast, with salt flats to the west and the sea to the east. Moknine is connected to Sousse and Mahdia by train (lightrail). Some of this area is used for market garden produce, peppers and melons are common but the main crop is tomatoes for the larger towns. The area of land covered by plastic green houses increases year by year. There are olives under-cultivated with cereals.

On from Moknine, **Teboulba**, a surprisingly large centre, has grown up on agriculture. Fruit trees have more or less replaced the olives here, along with potatoes and tomatoes under plastic cover. The use of prickly pear as hedges adds interest, especially when this cactus blooms. Further south, the small port of **Bekalta** lies near the Byzantine ruins of **Rass Dimass** which stand on the headland. From here, the C82 runs south to Mahdia, one time capital of a Shi'ite dynasty, today a quiet port with a nascent tourist industry.

15 km south of Monastir is **Uzitta** (today called Henchir Makhreba) which was closely associated with Caesar's campaign in Africa. Its ruins are on a slightly elevated position, overlooking the plain. During excavations a residential district was uncovered with a number of villas. Many were very luxurious with private baths and mosaic tiled floors.

Mahdia المهدية

Central Tunisia

Situated on the headland of Cap d'Afrique, the old town is surrounded by sea on three sides. An ancient Punic port, Mahdia followed Carthage and Kairouan as the capital of Tunisia in the 10th century. The city of the Mahdi, 'the rightly guided imam' has fine mosques and homes, chunks of wall crumbling next to the medieval Fatimid port, and a small but busy fishing habour. (One colonial writer, a little grandly perhaps, described Mahdia as the 'African Monaco'). In recent years the dignity and repose of Mahdia has been disturbed by mushrooming beach hotels. The old Mahdois families are deeply attached to their town, however, and it is a pleasant place to visit. The médina has a mediaeval toy town feel: the Spanish fort is neat, not mean and brooding, the Great Mosque feels proudly restored, not the heart of an empire flaring with a crusading mission.

Phone code: 03
Colour map 2, grid A6

Ins and outs

Mahdia is easily accessible by public transport, the best way to get there being the Sahel light rail (Monastir is 1 hour away by train, Sousse 1 hour 30 minutes). Otherwise you have louages in from Sousse, Sfax, Ksar Hellal and El Djem. From Monastir, you have to change louage at Ksar Hellal or Moknine. By road, Mahdia is 100 km from Sfax, 62 km from Sousse and 40 km from El Djem.

Getting there

The train station is conveniently central. The bus and louage station is 3 km west of town on Av Belhaouane. Unless you're a good walker, you'll be getting bus or taxi into the town centre. Note that all hotels, bar one, are in the *zone touristique*, say 1Dt taxi ride from the town centre. There are couple of metro stations for the *zone touristique*, Sidi Messaoud (for the Hotel Mahdia) and Mahdia Zone Touristique.

Getting around

History and background

Mahdia, Tunisia's second largest fishing port, 60 km south of Sousse, and 50 km from the airport, is a charming little town which has (to some extent) escaped the tourist mania of the rest of the coast. The town goes back to the early 10th century, and was founded by the Shi'ite Fatimid dynasty as a jumping off point for their conquest of Egypt. In 969 they successfully conquered the lower Nile valley, and founded Cairo. Mahdia, the town of the Mahdi, as the Shi'ite caliph was called, reverted to a peaceful provincial existence spiced up by a bit of piracy and the occasional invasion. The town, situated on a peninsula, had a fine defensive position, and the Fatimids left behind a perfectly adequate small harbour.

The history of Mahdia is closely linked with the Shi'ite branch of Islam. The Shi'ites believe that the Caliph must descend from Ali and Fatima (the Prophet's daughter). After a seven-year war with the Aghlabids, Ubaydallah, known as El Mehdi ('the rightly guided one'), the founder of the Fatimid Dynasty (followers of Fatima) finally secured victory and sought to establish his own capital. Mahdia was founded in 912 on an easily defended site and El Mehdi settled down in the still unfinished town in 921 in order to reinforce his power and protect himself. However, his cruelty and his enemies' hatred made peace short-lived. In 944 the city was kept under siege for eight months by the army of one Abou Yazid. The siege was unsuccessful. Eventually, the third Fatimid caliph moved the capital to a palace complex closer to Kairouan, Sabra el Mansouriya. The inhabitants of the abandoned capital turned to the sea for their livelihood, with the profits from fishing, commerce and piracy bringing a period of prosperity.

In the medieval Mediterranean world, with its ever-shifting frontiers, reprisals were not slow in coming, with first an unsuccessful Christian expedition to dislodge the pirates in 1088, then the occupation by Roger of Sicily from 1148 to 1160. (The Normans of Sicily also took Djerba, Gabès, Sfax and Tripoli). Later various other attempts were made to rid the town of the pirates, by a joint French-Genoese force in 1390 and in 1550 by Charles V of Spain. The Spanish were finally successful in 1550, but when forced to evacuate in 1554 resorted to blowing up the ramparts.

Eventually, the inhabitants had to revert to more traditional ways of life, such as olive cultivation and the production and weaving of silk. Under the Husseinid beys, the town became home to a cosmopolitan population, with Albanians, Anatolians and Greeks, Italians and French. In the late 19th century, the Sicilians began to come over to Mahdia for the fishing, introducing the *lamparo* night-fishing technique. They nicknamed Mahdia 'the sardine city', and built a new neighbourhood north of the port. Today, Mahdia is one of the largest fishing ports in Tunisia, mackerel and sardines forming a major part of the catch.

The traditional olive cultivation around the town and especially north of Mahdia has been taken over by extensive market gardening – plastic covered, tunnel shaped, head high greenhouses – growing tomatoes, pepper, melons, fennel et cetera. Tourism is now an important employer, too.

Sights

Start your visit to Mahdia by walking right round the edge of the promontory, beginning on the north side, on the Blvd Cap Afrique up to the light-house and back down on the south side. At the tip, you will come to a large **cemetery**. Here on the most exposed part of the peninsula, where nothing grows, the Mahdois have buried their dead for centuries. Wrote local poet Moncef Ghachem, "Nowhere else creates a feeling of peace, a spiritual unwinding like this cemetery beside the sea." On the south side of the peninsula, you will also come across the remains of the **Fatimid port** from which the 11th century invasion of Egypt was launched. It seems that the entrance was defended by two towers, linked by an arch. The port fell to Christian ships in 1088. After passing Mahdia's fortress, the Bordj el Kebir, on your right, you will pass an area of excavations of the Fatimid palace. Before reaching the Great Mosque, call in on the *Café Sidi Salem* to admire the view and possibly swim off the rocks.

Start your visit of the médina with the **Skifa el Kahla** ('The Black Passage'), the monumental gateway to the old town. At the time of El Mehdi only troops and a few, privileged people lived within the walls in order to minimise the risk of rebellion. The people lived outside, but within the walls were their shops and workshops. This meant that starting a rebellion during the day could jeopardize the life of their families outside, while to do so during the night would lead to the loss of their livelihood. The present gate was built in 1554, after El Mehdi's time, following the departure of the Spanish. Outside the gate, the new **Museum of Mahdia**, housed in a superb early 20th century building, is just to the right. The collections are not spectacular or particularly well displayed, but it is nice to see a building of this sort recycled. Eventually some of the finds from the famous Mahdia wreck, a Roman ship loaded with statuary and bronzes discovered off the town in 1907, may be displayed here. For the moment, they can be seen in the Bardo Museum in Tunis when not on international loan.

The **médina** is beautiful even though there are not many specific things to see. Looking through a doorway of one of the numerous weaving workshops, you may see someone at work at foot-operated silk-weaver's loom, producing high quality silk for wedding costumes and cotton *foutas* (towels). Curiously, when it comes to looms, there is a gender divide in Tunisia's cities: men operate horizontal cloth looms, while women work at vertical carpet looms. In the evening, you could spend time on the main square in the médina, Place du Caire, and have a drink in the café under the arcades. This is the local social centre and has a lot of atmosphere.

The honey-coloured walls of the Fatimid **Great Mosque** (founded 921 by Ubaydallah el Mahdi) dominate the Place Kadi Nomen, to your right at the top of the main street. There is something a bit too perfect about the walls, and indeed the mosque was totally rebuilt in 1963 following the original 10th

Central Tunisia

Mahdia

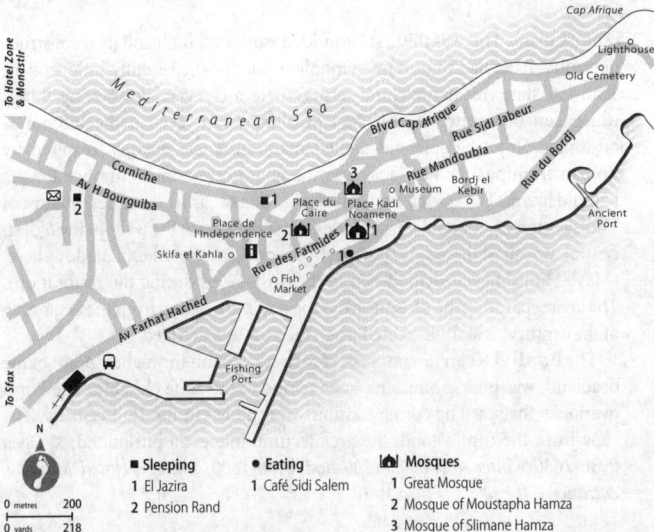

■ **Sleeping**
1 El Jazira
2 Pension Rand

● **Eating**
1 Café Sidi Salem

🕌 **Mosques**
1 Great Mosque
2 Mosque of Moustapha Hamza
3 Mosque of Slimane Hamza

☛ *Muslim cemeteries*

One of the lasting monuments in Islam is the maqbara or graveyard. All are different, ranging from undefined rocky areas near villages, where unnamed head and foot stones are barely distinguishable from the deserts surrounding them, to the elaborate necropoli of Cairo where a veritable city of the dead grew up. In all cemeteries bodies are interred with head towards the qibla – Mecca.

In Tunisia graveyards often contain a series of simple whitewashed mud brick tombs of holy men or marabouts, around which his disciples and their descendants are laid. At Mahdia, there is a large and complex example of a long-used cemetery beyond the town, where stylized marble mausoleums, tombs and graves are densely packed in. Similarly ornate and walled cemeteries occur in cities elsewhere, there is a fine one at Monastir with the mausoleum of the late President Habib Bourguiba adjacent to it. Muslim graveyards in Tunisia have no flowers unless they grow wild and by chance. Instead of buying flowers to ornament family graves on a routine visit, relatives will often give a simple dish to the poor to provide a meal for the children.

Important or noble families have private cemeteries called tourbet. Tourbet

are sometimes part of a complex of religious buildings – schools or mosques – with separate rooms or a distinct domed area. In Tunis the most well-known are the Tourbet el Bey, mausoleum of the Husseinid sultans of the 18th-20th centuries located in the central section and the Tourbet Aziza Othmana of the médina (see page 71).

Death and funerals are times for noisy outbreaks of wailing and crying. In traditional families, the approach of a person's death is signified by wailing, increased on actual death by the addition of the mourning neighbours and relatives. Occasionally in villages the body is laid in a large room. Corpses are washed and wrapped in a simple shroud for interment. Male mourners follow the cortege to the cemetery often in large crowds since every person who walks 40 paces in the procession has one sin remitted. At the graveside a shedda or declaration of Islamic faith is recited. Women visit the grave on the days following burial.

There is a strictly observed sequence of occasions to commemorate the deceased: el fazk el awal (lit: the first separation), el fazk el thani, and the fortieth day. All family members and close friends will be there.

century plans. This was the first Fatimid mosque ever built and its reconstruction must have had important symbolic value for the recently independent Tunisian state. In architectural terms, there are several interesting things which can be spotted by the non-Muslim visitor, even if the interior is off-limits. Note the splendid arched main entrance, possibly inspired by Roman triumphal arches? This was the grand ceremonial entrance for the Fatimid imam. The spirit is very different to that of earlier mosques. In most of Tunisia's towns, the souks and houses come right up to the walls of the oldest, central mosques; there is no perspective looking across an esplanade as here. (Maybe housing was demolished in the early 1960s during the restoration). The area separating the Mosque from the new port, dating from the beginning of the century, is landfill created when the port was dredged.

The **Bordj el Kebir**, an impressive fortress built on the highest point of the headland, was built around the same period as the Skifa el Kahla. The Bordj overlooks the sea. The corner bastions were added in the 18th century. The view from the top is good, the architectural interest a bit limited. ■ *Open 0930-1630 winter and 0900-1200 and 1400-1800 summer, closed Monday, entrance 1Dt.*

Around the town, the coast is rocky and the water clear. The best beaches are north of the town, out towards the new hotels. The zone touristique is five kiometres north, served by local bus 36B, or take a taxi.

Some 14 km south of Mahdia, just beyond the small town of **Ksour Essaf**, you have the remains of Roman Sullecthum at the coastal village of **Salakta**. The **Salakta Museum,** situated on the site of Sullectum, next to the ancient cemetery, has some interesting items. There is a splendid mosaic showing a lion, the emblem of a rich shipowner of the city at that time, and a funerary breastplate of a Carthaginian general. As English archaeologists did a lot of work on Roman pottery here, there are English captions in the museum. Nevertheless, this is a site of rather specialist interest. To get to Salakta, take a louage from Ksour Essaf. ■ *Museum open daily (not Monday) 0930-1630 winter and 0900-1200 and 1400-1800 summer.*

Essentials

Mahdia now has large numbers of hotels up in its new beach *zone touristique*, and some are very posh indeed. For the budget traveller, some of these might be just about accessible for a night of comfort off-season. Otherwise, there is only one hotel in the old town, the *Hotel Jazira*. Also outside the beach zone, in the new town, is the *Pension Rand*.

A *Abou Nawas Bordj (club luxe)*, route de la Corniche, T694602, 694677, F696632. Extensive grounds, the usual effectively managed Abou Nawas hotel. **A** *Mahdia Palace*, along route Touristique, T696777, F696810. A very dear do, but good pools.

B *Club Cap Mahdia*, along route touristique, T681. **B** *Abou Nawas Cap Mahdia*, route touristique, T680300, F680405. Horse riding and water sports. **B** *Club Cap Mahdia*, along route touristique, T681725, F680405. 250 rooms, beautiful, newly built, beach, quality service, pool, nightclub, tennis, horse-riding and all watersports, closed November and Decemeber, value for money. **B** *Cap Sérail*, along route touristique, T695011. Smaller than your average *palace touristik*. **B** *El Mehdi*, route de la Corniche, T681300, F680309. On a beach of fine sand, 260 a/c rooms with bath, telephone and balcony, some family rooms, restaurants with local and international dishes, bar, Moorish café, TV room, indoor and outdoor pools, disco.

D *Corniche*, Av 7 Novembre, T694201, F694190. 16 rooms with bath, small, cheap, clean, good restaurant, 2 km from town, not on beach side. **D** *Sables d'Or*, 3 km north out of town, along the Corniche, T681137, F681431. By the sea, beach, 68 rooms are individual bungalows, sea view, most watersports. Could do with a refit

E *Pension Rand*, 20 Av Taieb M'Hiri, T680525. 22 rooms with bath, breakfast included, no restaurant, clean, pleasant staff and owner. Main drawback is that it's a long walk from both railway station and médina. **E** *Hotel el Jazira*, rue Ibn el Fourat, not far from Skifa el Kahla, on north side of médina, T681629. Only hotel in the médina, very simple, clean, communal bath/ toilet rather antiquated, not very inviting, some rooms with sea view.

Youth hostel In Mahdia, T681559. 60 beds, meals available, family rooms, very clean, good view from roof, signposted from train station, about 5 minutes walk. Another at Chebba, T683815. 37 km from Mahdia, 60 beds, convenient for those taking the coast road C82 south to Sfax.

Camping El Asfour, close to *Sables d'Or*, large, well organized site.

··

☞ *The Mahdia wreck*

Archaeologists Merlin and Poinssot describe the wreck spotted by sponge divers nearly five kilometres off the coast of Mahdia in 1907.

"39 metres down we noted some 60 columns of different sizes, lying on top of each other, in 7 rows running from north to south for 24 metres … These were the main item of freight in the ship which sank at this place. They were not, however, the sole or most sensational item … digging into the muddy sand which partially covered the columns, after cutting through a 20 centimetre thick

layer of wood, which was the bridge of the lost ship, items of far greater value were discovered, the objects which filled the hold: noble effigies, fine statuettes and reliefs in bronze and marble, fragments of containers or utensils with delicate fittings, fragments of luxury decorative marble pieces, a whole set of items indicative of skilled craft techniques, thanks to which we have a reflection of high Hellenic art."

A Merlin and L Poinssot, Cratères et candélabres de marbre trouvés en mer près de Mahdia (1930)

··

Eating **Mid-range** *Restaurant Pizzeria Italia*, on Av Tahar Sfar, route de la Corniche, T695296. *Neptune*, Av 7 Novembre, start of *Corniche*, T681927. Clean, fish dishes sold by weight before cooking, seats 40. *Restaurant Le Lido*, Av Farhat Hached, by harbour, very good fish, T681867.

Cheap *L' Espadon*, near *Hotel Corniche*, T681476. Small, pleasant decor, close to beach, cheap, seats 26. *Restaurant de la Médina*, in the market building, excellent for fish. *Restaurant el Moez*, between main gate and market, very cheap, good food, typical local restaurant, no alcohol. *Café Sidi Salem*, see map, hardly matters about the food, the views are excellent. All along the side of the harbour there are small cafés, fish appearing frequently on the menu. The **Market** on the east side of port sells fish daily and other fresh produce and general goods on Friday.

Sports **Yachting** 20 yacht berths, minimum-maximum draft 3-6m.

Transport **Local Car hire**: *Avis*, T696342; *Hertz*, T695255; *Jet Car Loisirs*, T681796; *Self Drive*, T/F696863. All on Av Habib Bourguiba. **Taxis**: *Abou Nawas*, T695900.

Long distance Train: 'Sahel metro' train every hour 0500-1800 to **Monastir**, **Skanes/Monastir airport** and **Sousse**. Train station, T680177, is down the street from the bus station, by the harbour. **Tunis** (via Sousse) 1135, 1645. Takes 4 hours. **Bus**: the bus station, T680372, is by the harbour on Place 1st May. Frequent buses to **Sousse** and **Monastir**. Less frequent buses to **Tunis**, **Sfax**, **Gabès** and **Kairouan**. **Louages**: a long hot walk out of the town centre (circa 3km), take a taxi. Louages run to **El Djem**, **Kairouan**, **Monastir**, **Sfax** and **Sousse**.

Directory **Banks** *BNT* on Place de l'Indépendence. *BT* and *STB* on Av Habib Bourguiba. **Communications Post Office**: in the new part of town on Av Habib Bourguiba. **Tour companies & travel agents** *Abou Nawas Travel*, Av Tahar Sfar, La Corniche, T696222, F696224. *Cap Voyages*, 196 Av Habib Bourguiba, T680355, F680629. *Fatimides Voyages*, 191 Av Habib Bourguiba, T680763, F694590. **Tourist offices** The tourist information office is inside the médina's main gate, Skifa el Kahla, on the right in rue el Moez, T681098. Friendly but uninformative. **Useful addresses Taxis**: T695900. **Police**: Av Habib Bourguiba, near supermarket. **Port**: Harbour Master's Office, T681595.

Southwest from Mahdia to El Djem

South of Mahdia are a few small coastal settlements, Er Zgana and Rejiche being the main ones. **Ksour Essaf**, seven kilometres inland and 10 km from Mahdia is larger, its prosperity built on agriculture. From Ksour Essaf, the C87 takes you on to El Djem, an essential stop for all those interested in imperial Rome's taste for violent sports.

El Djem الجم

A small town of around 10,000 people in the middle of a plain of olive trees, El Djem would be of little interest if it were not for its imposing Roman amphitheatre, one of the most surprising sights in Tunisia. The sheer bulk of the building, largest of all Roman monuments in Africa, is breathtaking. The sheer size of the ochre stone walls and arches and a thought for the simple technology in use in Roman times to build them makes this a breathtaking monument. But it was also a setting for mass entertainment of the cruellest kind: watching men fight each other to the death, or the slaughter wild beasts, was the ancient equivalent of a Hollywood spectacular.

Phone code: 03
Colour map 2, grid A5

Ins and outs

The train station on main Tunis-Sousse-Sfax line is 10 minutes east of the amphitheatre and SRT bus station is by the museum, 500m from the amphitheatre. In summer the buses are full and it is difficult to find a place. The louages and SNTRI buses terminate in the street by the station. Tunis is a 3 hour train ride from El Djem, and there are frequent louages from Sousse and Mehdia.

Getting there

The entrance to El Djem from the east is graced by three columns, part of the town's great heritage and on the other side of the road is a workshop which produces mosaics. Does nothing change?

Getting around

History

The ancient town of Thysdrus was probably founded in Punic times, but it was only under the Romans, in particular the rule of Hadrian (117-138), that the town prospered. Hadrian encouraged the continued cultivation of olive trees and the town became an important centre for the manufacture and export of olive oil. By the third century the town reached its peak, as the ruins of luxurious villas testify. The population was over 30,000. In addition to the owners of the villas there was a large rural population. But, due to political rivalries within the Empire, El Djem's fortunes gradually decreased, and were finally brought to an end during the Arab invasion, when the olive groves were set on fire, definitively ending El Djem's commercial prosperity.

Sights

Thysdrus covered an area of between 150 hectares and 200 hectares, the size of the remaining monuments gives a clear indication of the size of the original city. The huge **Amphitheatre**, 148 metres long by 122 metres wide, has a perimeter of over 425 metres. The long axis of the arena is 65 metres and the shorter axis 39 metres. The tiers rose to more than 35 metres providing seating for a capacity of 45,000 spectators. It was the third largest amphitheatre in the

Main amphitheatre

Central Tunisia

Roman Empire and the most famous and best preserved in Africa. Lack of inscriptions prevents accurate dating but construction, which is attributed to Emperor Gordien I who owned land and property in the area, began in the second century between 230 and 238 AD and when one considers that the nearest quarries were over 30 km away, the task must have been enormous. The building was never completed due to lack of funds and political instability. The stone was too soft for fine sculpture – hence the simplicity of the decoration. The theatre was used for some of the spectacular shows so dear to the heart of Emperor Gordien – wild beasts fighting to the death, martyrs or prisoners being thrown to the wild animals, good family viewing. Some of the scenes were recorded in the mosaics found here.

In later life, the Amphitheatre was used as a rebel stronghold. The legend of the underground tunnels leading from El Djem to the sea refers back to Kahena, a Berber princess who rebelled against Islam and used the amphitheatre as a fortress. She is said to have waved wriggling fish at the troops surrounding her stronghold, taunting them with her freedom of movement. In 1695, Mohammed Bey ordered a hole to be made in the amphitheatre's walls to prevent its use during any further uprisings by the local population who protested about his heavy taxation. The breach in the walls was further enlarged in 1850 during another tax revolt. The theatre was thereafter used as a convenient supply of building stones by the inhabitants of the town. Nevertheless the bulk of the original building remains and it is a truly impressive sight.
■ *Open daily from dawn till dusk. Entrance 2Dt. Photography permit 1Dt includes visit to museum.*

El Djem

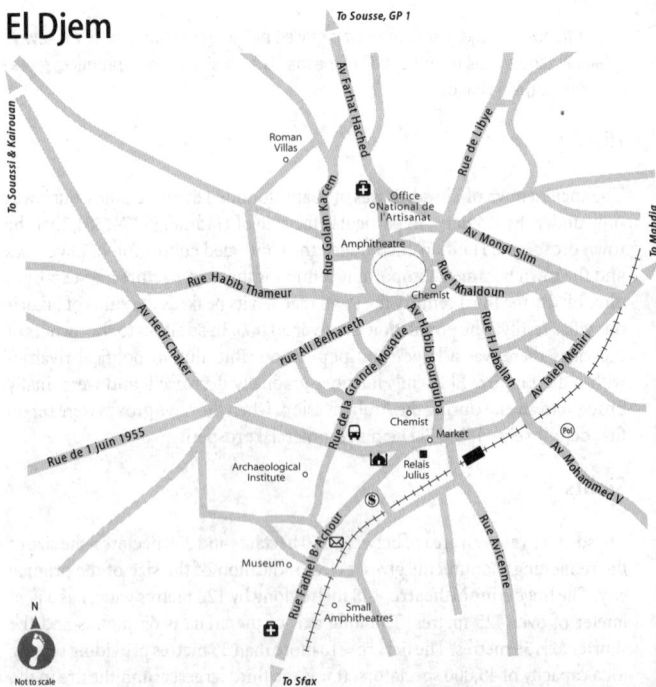

Carnage under the sun – thumbs up for the great amphitheatre of El Djem

A good guide to the level of the 'Romanity' of a city was the presence of an amphitheatre. These great buildings for public entertainment existed right across the Roman Empire. The amphitheatre of Thysdrus in the sleepy modern town of El Djem was, after the Colosseum in Rome and the amphitheatre in Capua, the largest in the Empire.

It is difficult to see where the Roman practice of public slaughter came from. The Greeks were certainly too refined for such practices. Yet the populace of the Empire developed a taste for the munera, the bloody spectacles provided as bounty by the magistrates or as a tribute to the deceased. Pliny in his Natural History tells the tale of the origin of the amphitheatre. In 53 BC, in Italy, a candidate for the tribune's office in search of votes, devised a new electioneering technique. Two semi-circular wooden theatres were set up back to back, mounted on a swivel. Thus two plays could be put on at the same time. But the gimmick was revealed in the afternoon, when the two theatres were swung round on their pivots to form a circle where a munus or gladiatorial show was held.

Under Augustus the munus became an important (and sinister) way for rulers to interact with those they ruled. The primitive wooden structures gave way to magnificent stone buildings and the word amphitheatrum was coined to describe these settings for various brutish 'sports' depicted in gory graphic detail in the mosaic floors of the ancient Thysdritan home. In addition to the hoplomachia or gladiatorial fights there were re-enactments of various myths (Pasiphae and the bull, amongst others) and in the later Empire, the followers of Christianity, then viewed as a dangerous sect with secret ceremonies, were a particular target. Blood spilling on to the ground and disguising of Christian martyrs as initiates of Caelestis would transform torture into sacrifice. Damnatio ad bestias (being condemned to the beasts), however, was reserved for common criminals and certain prisoners of war. The huge resources devoted to the shipping of rare beasts to Rome for slaughter is testimony to the importance of the amphitheatre shows and also evidence of the wealth of the Empire and the extent to which this wealth could be squandered.

The inhabitants of the province of Africa, to go by the evidence of the mosaics, preferred venationes or the exhibition and 'hunting' of big cats and other wild beasts. (See the tiger attacking two wild asses in the El Djem museum.) For a long time it was thought that mock sea battles were a feature of Thysdritan entertainment but unfortunately archaeology has laid this particular myth firmly to rest.

Today's visitor to Thysdrus can clamber up into the highest parts of the seating and look down into the arena just as the Roman spectator would have done. Mercifully the slaughter of people and beasts is no longer considered great entertainment and little disturbs the quiet of the great building apart from the clicking of camera shutters and cooing of pigeons nesting in the crumbling stonework.

Central Tunisia

El Djem has two smaller amphitheatres, one built on top of the other. These are just a short distance to the south of the main amphitheatre and can be found on the other side of the road to Sfax. The older, more primitive one, dating from the first century, was simply cut into the rock and the second one, which was to last until the building of the large amphitheatre was erected against the hillside on top of the remains of the first. Behind the museum, about 250 metres to the west of the small amphitheatre, there is a group of villas bounded by a Roman **necropolis** to the south and a well preserved, paved street to the east. The houses are of the classic Roman style with a garden surrounded by a peristyle with richly decorated rooms.

Smaller amphitheatres and other excavations

The large number of fine **Roman villas** excavated at El Djem are indicative of the considerable wealth of the town. The dwellings, built round an inner courtyard and surrounded by a colonnaded gallery, were paved with colourful mosaics depicting mythological themes. **Mosaics** from the earlier excavations of these villas are now displayed in the Bardo National Museum in Tunis, in Sousse and in the local museum in el Djem. In the more recently discovered villas the mosaics have been left in situ. The baths, covering a surface area of over 2,000 square metres revealed some fine mosaics too.

The **Archaeological Museum**, clearly signed, is 500 metres from the amphitheatre on the road to Sfax, set in a replica of a Roman villa. Here are yet more magnificent mosaics. In the main room is a famous mosaic showing Orpheus charming the beasts with his music, while in the end room are two lively mosaic scenes, *Lions devouring a wild boar* and next to it *Tiger attacking two wild asses*. These were found in a villa which once stood beside the museum. ■ *Open 0700-1900 in summer and 0730-1730 in winter, entrance included with ticket to amphitheatre. Clean toilets.*

Basically, wealthy Romans liked to display their taste and status, and one way to do this was with **wall-paintings** (which do not seem to have been widespread in ancient Africa) and mosaic pavings. Certain themes were more popular than others. The inhabitants of El Djem seem to have been good-time people, and liked scenes with the muses, to remind them of the arts, of animals and of boozy romps, liberally decorated with vineleaves and cupids. There is Minerva judging the musical contest between Apollo and Marsyas, for example. The careful detail of the mosaics is impressive: for example, in one Dionysian mosaic, you have a border full of lurking grasshoppers, frogs, rats, snails and lizards. The entire pavement is trellised with vines and set with tiny birds, animals and cupids. There is a ladder-carrying cupid, off to the grape harvest. In the central medallion, three chubby *putti*, urged on by a naked woman, are tying up a bald, bearded and pot-bellied Silenus (Bacchus' father) with floral garlands.

Another theme dear to villa owners was the four seasons. The countryside was close by, and the wealth of the city depended on farming. A small mosaic with a central medallion containing the bust of a bearded old man is a good example of this concern. Six circles contain the Sun (Apollo), the Moon (Artemis) and the four seasons, Spring in green, Summer in red, bare breasted and vine draped Autumn and darkly cloaked Winter.

Music in the Ampitheatre

First held in 1986, El Djem's small scale annual **International Music Festival** takes place in late July / early August in the Amphitheatre. The festival tends to feature European symphony and chamber orchestras, although there have been concerts of lyric music and the occasional opera too. Thousands of candles light the building. The nightime noises of El Djem (the last call to prayer, amplified music from a distant marriage, the braying of a donkey) are the exotic backdrop for concerts which can range from Mozart to jazz.

Mosaic of a young woman, symbol of Spring

Essentials

C *Hotel Club el Ksar*, 5 km from El Djem on route de Sousse, 35 rooms, bar, restaurant, **Sleeping**
3 pools, should be complete by autumn 1999. **E** *Relais Julius*, off the main square by
train station and near bus stop, T03-690044. Simple, clean, cheap, 15 double rooms
with bath round the courtyard, restaurant, ask for a room with a view of the amphitheatre. On the noisy side, given proximity to the railway line.

The cafés in front of the amphitheatre offer simple fare. The menu generally com- **Eating**
prises *mechoui* (barbecued lamb) and salad of some kind. Check prices when you
order. Café Bacchus (no alcohol despite name) opposite site, distinctive blue and
white décor, shaded terrace, good coffee, mint tea, basic toilet. A meal at **2** *Relais Jul-*
ius is slightly better value for money. This is the only place in El Djem where you're
going to get a beer.

Surprisingly, El Djem has some quite interesting shopping opportunities. Look out for **Shopping**
the slightly odd puppet-type wooden animals with the articulated joints. You can also
find newly manufactured ancient carvings or metal statuettes, old agricultural implements and cooking pots which no-one wants in the age of plastic and stainless steel.
Supermarket: On Av Habib Bourguiba. Market day Monday, opposite train station.
Also make a visit to the mosaic workshop on the by-pass.

Train Departures for **Tunis** (via Sousse) 0701, 1323, 1425, 1915, 0252; **Sfax** 1014, **Transport**
1604, 1712, 2033, 0018; **Gabès** (via Sfax) 1014, 0018; **Gafsa** and **Metlaoui**, 1014.
Bus The SNTRI bus station and the louage stop is opposite the train station. SRT
buses go from near the museum. Frequent buses to **Sfax**, **Sousse**, **Gabès** and **Tunis**.

Kairouan القيروان

Isolated on featureless steppe and founded in the seventh century by nomad Arab   Phone code: 07
conquerors, Kairouan is a tough, puritan place. Winter is bitter and summer   Colour map 2, grid A4
turns the region into a frying pan. Blonde and brazen beaches, kidney-shaped
hotel pools, discos and casinos are a world away. See the Great Mosque of Okba
Ibn Nafi, built of tawny brick and pillaged ancient masonry, appreciate the much
restored Aghlabid reservoirs and wander the sculptural streets of the médina,
explore the sleepy souks, observe the industrious girl carpet-weavers, buy some
sticky date cakes and meditate on vanished dynasties at the museum of Rakkada.
But there is little else that will draw the visitor in: the town has neither pleasant
oasis nor restaurants for the chattering classes. Half-forgotten capital, Kairouan
and its threadbare splendours are now just a place on the way to somewhere.

Ins and outs

Buses and louages go from Le Kef, Makthar, and El Fahs, Tunis, Sousse, Sfax and Gabès. **Getting there**
The main bus and louage station is located a good 20 minutes walk from the médina.

If you are looking for a cheap hotel, you need to get to the Bab ech Chouhada area and **Getting around**
the new town south of the médina (the bus station is northwest of the médina). Turn
left out of bus station, then left again onto a wide street after 100 metres. When you
come to Av Zama el Belaoui, turn right. Follow over roundabout onto rue de la Victoire
(Agil station on right). A left onto rue de Gafsa will bring you to Bab ech Chouhada.
This is a long walk on a hot day maybe best to get a taxi.

Central Kairouan is small enough to be visited on foot. If you want to get out to the Museum of Islamic Art at Rakkada, a short taxi trip will be necessary to save time, although there is a bus leaving at 15 minutes past the hour from Av Haffouz. Ask to be let off for the museum, which is a 15 minute walk from the stop.

Background

The spiritual and religious capital of Tunisia, the city was the first base for the conquering Arab Muslim armies from the east, back in the seventh century. Still surrounded by the historic walls, the town has a strong character. Kairouan is also the capital of traditional carpet manufacture and the market town for Tunisia's main fruit growing area. It stands at the junction of roads to Tunis, Sousse and Gafsa.

Kairouan is the city where the visitor can get a feel for the evolution Islam in North Africa. Getting a hold on names of places and rulers, you begin to understand how the Muslim religion took root, developing with the dynasties into the religion as it is lived today. The city is also a lesson in just how small and fragile the mediaeval Muslim state was in North Africa. For a leading city, it was actually very small but totally dominated by its vast mosque, rather as English wool towns developed in the shadow of huge churches.

History

The Romans, who knew a thing or two about city building, never considered the plain at Kairouan as a location. Siting a city at such an inhospitable location takes some explanation, and fortunately, there is a founding legend for just this purpose. Back in 671, a few decades after the Muslim Arabs had conquered the Middle East and Egypt, Okba ibn Nafi, companion of the prophet Mohamed and warrior leader, was leading an army into Byzantine Africa. He halted his troops at the edge of an arid, wild-beast infested valley (which no longer seems to exist), and called out "Inhabitants of the valley, depart, for we are stopping here." At which, all the various snakes, scorpions and creepy-crawlies emerged from their hiding places and headed out of the valley where Okba's troops were able to camp in complete safety.

Founding Kairouan Extra reassurance was provided for the Muslim forces when Okba's horse stumbled across a goblet which had been lost in Mecca. Water flowed from this miraculous cup, directly from the sacred spring of Zemzem in Mecca. The site was clearly ripe for a holy city, and Kairouan was founded. In fact, there were other more pressing reasons for the choice of the location. The early Arab armies were rapid light cavalry, well able to harry slower infantry forces, but worried about attacks from troops which could be landed by the Byzantine fleet. The interior and its strategic water points was dominated by Christian towns with strong forts, while up in the mountains, the tiny Berber communities had no reason to accept a marauding army from Arabia. Any major base-camp for the eastern Maghreb had to take these potential threats into account.

In the event, the Berbers counter-attacked, winning two significant victories, the more important in 688. The hostilities did not last long, however, with the Berbers gradually converting to Islam.

Aghlabid prosperity During the ninth century, Kairouan prospered as home to the local Aghlabid Dynasty, achieving independence from the Caliphate of Baghdad. The city saw much building activity under the Aghlabid emirs, notably Ziyadet Allah I. (They also undertook extensive building works elsewhere, notably at Tunis where the

Zitouna Mosque was extended). Two major issues dominated politics in Aghlabid Kairouan: the relationship with the military (a well-established Arab army or *jund*), and matters theological. Kairouan also developed into something of a medical research centre, with Jews and Muslims working to develop a heritage of medical knowledge passed down from ancient Greece.

How did Kairouan come to be such a centre of Islamic learning under the Aghlabid princes? The prophet Mohamed had left behind him a scattered body of teachings, which had to be codified. This was the work of religious scholars, sponsored by the caliphs, rulers of the Middle Eastern Islamic state, to whom all other Muslim rulers owed allegiance. And then the codified teachings had to be disseminated across the Islamic lands – hence the importance of regional centres like Kairouan in fringe areas of the Islamic world.

Malikite Islam

One of the leading scholars of the eighth century was Malik ibn Anas (d.795). Many Ifrikiyans travelled to the East to attend his seminars. With Islam laying down so many rules for life, it was inevitable that a major body of legal knowledge should emerge to interpret the grey areas. At Kairouan, the a Malikite school emerged, winning the support of the people through its rigourous approach: only Koranic prescriptions and the traditions of the Prophet could be valid bases for law. The scholarly Imam Sahnoun produced a comprehensive digest of Malikite law, *Al Mudawwana*.

There was a social point to all this legal activity. The Aghlabid princes, who followed the more intellectual Hanafite school of Islam, were seen by the people as a decadent, oppressive lot. Criticism started with their tax policy, and then went on to their lifestyle, which included lots of carousing and singing-girls. (They obviously tolerated wine production). On the whole, however, they were able to avoid major friction with the people and the Malikite scholars. After all, they spent generously on new religious buildings, and built new fortifications to protect the coasts from marauding Christians (see the Ribat at Sousse in particular).

Things all went horribly wrong, however, in the late eighth century. Mohamed II (864-75) who came to the throne aged 13, quickly developed a taste for dissipation and frivolity and died prematurely. His governor in Kairouan (the future Ibrahim II, emir from 875-902), won a reputation for fairness. But he later turned into a tyrant, massacring members of the Arab military caste and crucifying an Arab aristocrat. In 876, he began building a vast royal residence at Rakkada, near Kairouan, recruiting a corps of black slave troops. The military aristocracy saw its influence declining, and this, combined with various exactions, explains the success of the Shi'ite Fatimids in overthrowing the last Aghlabids in 910. Aghlabid rule had lasted little more than a century.

A royal capital

Without going into the obscure intricacies of Shi'ite politics in early 10th century North Africa, the Aghlabid rulers had made themselves sufficiently detested to be easily overthrown. Shi'ite preacher Abu Abdallah created a movement which won popular support, and in 909 Shi'ite leader Ubaydallah Saïd made his triumphant entry into Rakkada. He claimed to be the *mahdi*, claiming descent from the Prophet's daughter Fatima, hence the name of his dynasty, the Fatimids. But establishing a state in Ifrikiya was just a stepping stone to conquests further east, and in 915 he began building a new capital at Mahdiya on the coast.

The Fatimid interlude

Fatimid rule was to weigh heavily on the Sunni Muslims of Ifrikiya. The Malikites were persecuted, and although the Fatimids were not a decadent lot, nor did they spend on religious buildings. Tax revenues went into campaigns against the Sunni caliphate in Egypt. Rebellion was inevitable, and came in the form of Kharijite leader Abou Yazid, who easily won control of Kairouan with Sunni support. All of Ifrikiya – bar Mahdiya – was lost in 944. Abu Yazid failed to take the Fatimid capital, and the revolt failed, with a new Fatimid caliph, El-Mansour ('the victorious') defeating Abu Yazid at Kairouan in 947. In 953, he began the construction of a new capital, Sabra el-Mansouriya, just two kilometres away from Kairouan. This meant the older settlement was bypassed commercially, most trade being done in the new city.

The curse of the Fatimids The real decline of Kairouan came with the invasion from Egypt in 1050s, when the city changed its allegiance from the Fatimids in Cairo to the Sunni Abbasids in Baghdad. By way of vengeance, the Shi'ite Fatimids allotted Ifrikiya as booty to the warlike Banu Hilal, who had been stirring up trouble in southern Egypt for some time. Opinions are divided as to the actual extent of the devastation caused by the **Hilalian invasion**: Ibn Khaldoun, for one, who was writing in the following century, attributes a severe economic decline in Ifrikiya to the havoc caused by the Banu Hilal. One result of the arrival of large numbers of Arab-speaking nomads was the arabisation of the countryside, which had no doubt continued to be home to Berber and Latin-speaking communities. Berber communities were to remain intact further west, and in isolated inland pockets in Ifrikiya.

Kairouan in Hafsid and Husseinid times Under the Hafsids, the centre of power shifted in Ifrikiya. Relations changed with Europe, trade with the Italian merchant cities developed, it was important for the capital to be on the coast. Kairouan was thus left by the Hafsid court in favour of Tunis, which after all had a far more agreeable climate. The development of the coastal cities continued in the 17th and 18th centuries, as first Ottoman deys and beys, and subsequently Husseinid beys became involved in profitable piracy. Kairouan thus became a backwater, albeit an important one. It maintained a holy aura, and the tradition (spurious?) went that seven visits to Kairouan were equivalent to the hajj, the pilgrimage to Mecca which every Muslim is supposed to perform once in their lifetime. Wrote traveller Peyssonel in 1724, "The Arabs' veneration for Cairouan is so great that the beys of Tunis have always exempted the inhabitants of this city from all taxes and have granted them so many privileges Jews and Christians are not allowed to live there lest they pollute their sanctuary". When French troops arrived in 1881, however, the town surrendered without a shot being fired. No doubt rumours of what the French had done in Algeria's cities were fresh in the minds of Kairouan's notables.

The invasion of the Arab tribes C10 and C12 AD

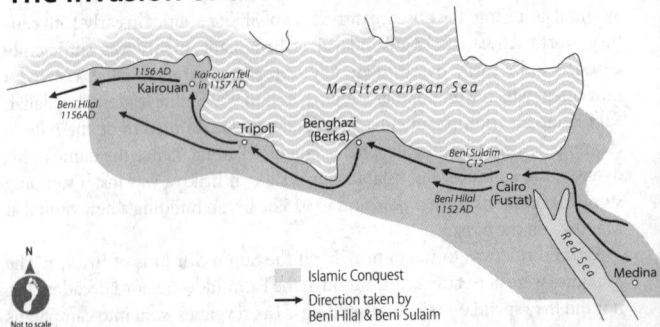

Mediterranean Sea

1156 AD
Kairouan — Kairouan fell in 1157 AD
Beni Hilal 1156AD

Tripoli

Benghazi (Berka)

Beni Sulaim C12

Beni Hilal 1152 AD

Cairo (Fustat)

Red Sea

Medina

N
Not to scale

▨ Islamic Conquest
→ Direction taken by
Beni Hilal & Beni Sulaim

Based on its bygone theological glories, Kairouan today has some claims to be an important **religious centre**, the leading holy city in the Maghreb region, preceded in status only by Mecca, Médina and Jerusalem. Islamic intellectual debate is probably more alive in Morocco, however, where the great Karaouiyine University at Fès (originally founded by migrants from Kairouan) is a focus for a certain modernist brand of Muslim thought.

Today, Kairouan is a rapidly expanding town, with a major university at Rakkada, carpet manufacture, some light industry and food processing. The large amounts of new building around the town are testimony to present-day economic buoyancy. There is also considerable interest on the part of the authorities in the city's built heritage. International Islamic organisations, mainly funded by the oil states, are impressed by the amount of ancient Muslim building, while the Tunisian authorities are keen to be seen conserving anything which will reinforce their Islamic credentials. Much restoration work has been undertaken, and the main monuments are now labelled and visitable. The main street is animated in a pleasant, provincial way. Ultimately, however, all the religious heritage gives the town has a ponderous atmosphere, and it is nice to get back to Mediterranean pleasures of the coastal towns.

Kairouan the pious?

Sights

If time is short, you might consider a guided tour of the town. These can be booked at the tourist office. However, the sights are actually quite limited, and for many people, a look at the Great Mosque, a wander down the main street to take in the atmosphere and Bir Barouta, and a peek in at the zaouia house which today houses the Association Sauvegarde de la Médina de Kairouan will be sufficient. You probably need two hours to take in something of Kairouan, adding a further one and a half hours for a trip out to the Museum of Islamic Art at Rakkada.

There can be some confusion with street names in Kairouan, some have two names and the locals you ask will recognize neither unless you get the pronunciation spot on. Accept this as a challenge which adds to the charm of the place.

For visiting Kairouan, you should equip yourself with a **multi-sight ticket** from the tourist office next to the Aghlabid Pools. Valid for a day, it costs 4.2Dt for seven sites (French names in brackets): 1. the Great Mosque (*Mosquée Okba ibn Nafi*); 2. the (so-called) Barber's Mosque (*Zaouia Sidi Sahab*); 3. the Aghlabid Pools (*Bassins aghlabites*); 4. Zaouia of Sidi Amor Abbada (*Mausolée de Sidi Abbada*); 5. Zaouia of Sidi Abid el Ghariani (*Mausolée de Sidi Abid*); 6. National Museum of Islamic Art (*Musée de Rakkada*); 7. Bir Barouta. Note that the Great Mosque is closed as of 1400 every day, and from midday on Friday. The Museum of Islamic Art (closed Monday), opens 0900-1600. There is a supplementary photo fee of 1Dt for the Great Mosque and the Sidi Sahab Mosque. Official guides can also be recruited at the tourist office, and at 15Dt (maximum) for a good two hours, this option might be worth it if you have a small group. Note that of these sights, three (the Aghlabid Pools, the Barber's Mosque, and the museum at Rakkada) are some way off centre. Try to check whether the Rakkada Museum is actually open if you call in at the tourist office.

A large part of the médina's walls have survived, notably the section near the Great Mosque. In fact, compared with Tunis or Sousse, the médina is small, so it is fairly difficult to get totally lost. There is a main street which leads from Bab ech Chouhada to Bab Tunis, on which you will find stalls selling *makroud*, (sticky date cakes), various everyday shops, carpet emporia, and Bir Barouta, after which, on the right, there is a small covered souq. Further up, again on the right

The médina

following the signs for the *Hotel Marhala*, is a small busy market. If you have time, there are a number of minor sights not to miss in the médina, including the headquarters of the ASM de Kairouan, and the Mosquée des Trois Portes.

If you go into the médina at Bab ech Chouhada, you might start your culture hunt with a look in at the **Zaouia of Sidi Abid el Ghariani**, (second street on the right after the main gate, look for fine doorway on your right). This burial place of Sidi Abid, a 13th century saint, was constructed in the 14th century. Of particular interest is the room with the mausoleum. The ceiling is extremely finely worked wood, with fine plasterwork all around. The building is a good example the courtyard style building which dominated in Kairouan, used for both religious buildings and homes. Today the zaouia houses the office of the Association Sauveguarde de la Médina (an organization dedicated to helping to preserve the médina) and the regional office of the National Art and Archaeology Institute. ■ *Open for a quick look around during office hours.*

Continuing up the main drag, turn right just before Bir Barouta, up the rue de la Mosquée des Trois Portes, and you will eventually come to the **Mosque of the Three Doors**, (Jamaâ Thelethe Bibene) on your right. Founded by an immigrant from Córdoba in 866, the mosque has an interesting façade with carved inscriptions. At the end of this street, turn left down a narrow street, and you will come to rue Tahar Zarrouk. Turn right, and you will come out on a wide street (Boulevard Ibrahim ibn Aghlab), which if you go left will bring you to the imposing buttressed ochre walls of the Great Mosque.

The Great Mosque of Okba ibn Nafi

The **Great Mosque** was founded with the city by Okba ibn Nafi in 671. The building includes much ancient masonry, recycled from earlier Roman and Byzantine buildings. It is the oldest mosque in western Islam. It was severely damaged during the rebellion of 688, was virtually rebuilt in the nineth century and later enlarged in the same severe style. The age of the minaret is open to debate, although the bottom section is thought to date from 730. The main dome is of ribbed brick in a herring-bone design.

Although this is not obvious to the visitor, both prayer hall and courtyard are trapezoid in shape. The shorter sides of the mosque measure 70 metres and 74 metres and the longer sides 124 metres and 125 metres. For the courtyard, the shorter sides are 52.45 metres and 50.25 metres, the longer sides are both 67 metres. Here there are pillared cloisters with easily missed wooden ceilings. Both the east and west porticoes have two aisles supported by three lines of arches. The **vast courtyard**, one of the largest in any mosque in Tunisia, is half-paved in white marble, the remainder paved with limestone blocks in which there is a differentiated path, not quite central, which leads to the minaret. Towards one corner is a sundial indicating the times of the five daily prayers. Close to the sundial the rain water was collected in a cistern for use in ritual ablutions.

Minaret of Great Mosque

The **square minaret** is 31.5 metres high, built in three successively smaller sections. The first is 10.7 metres square and 19 metres high, the next 7.7 metres square and five metres high and the smallest 5.5 metres square with a ribbed dome. It is thought to date from 836. (Enquire if it is possible to climb up the 128 steps for a superb view). One theory goes that the minaret was inspired by the pharos of Alexandria.

The **prayer hall** is filled with numerous imposing granite and marble columns brought from older sites in other parts of the country. Unfortunately non-Muslims are unable to view the internal wooden ceilings, the lavishly decorated and carved doors, woodcarving on the pulpit nor the nineth century tiles from Baghdad in the niche which faces Mecca.

So why is the the Great Mosque laid out like it is? Compared with the Byzantine basilicas which the Arab conquerors would have found when they took towns like Sbeïtla, the mosque marks a sharp break. Gone are the high vaulted ceilings of the basilicas as the Roman building technology got lost in the conquest. Rather the new occupiers needed a large, ritually pure space. Islamic worship is based on the principle of facing Mecca. The worshippers

Kairouan Mosque

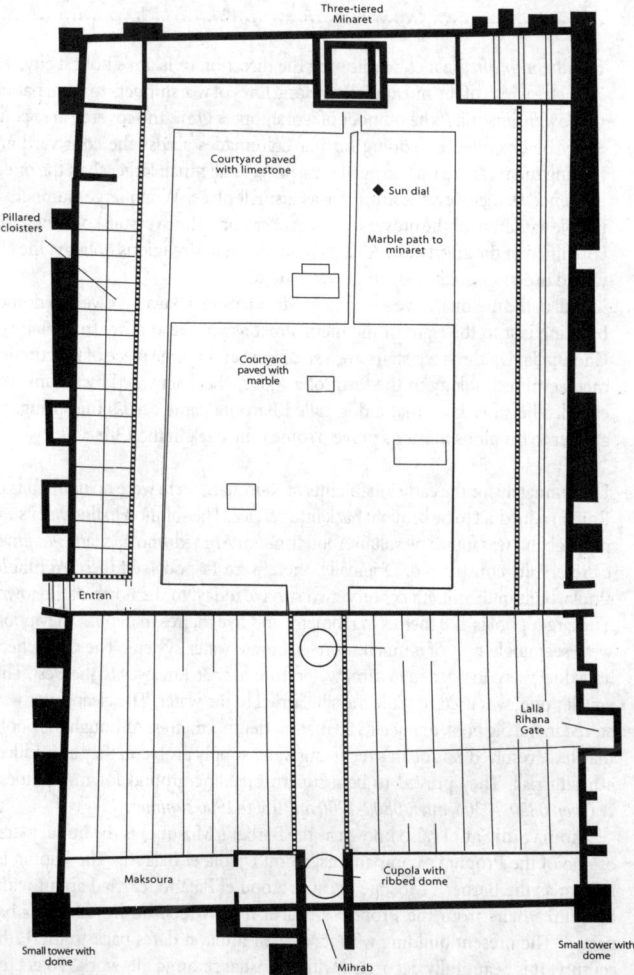

Three-tiered Minaret

Courtyard paved with limestone

◆ Sun dial

Marble path to minaret

Pillared cloisters

Courtyard paved with marble

Entran

Lalla Rihana Gate

Maksoura

Cupola with ribbed dome

Small tower with dome

Mihrab

Small tower with dome

👈 *Ifrikiya, Kairouan and turbulent dynasties: a name check*

The term **Ifrikiya**, an Arabisation of the Latin 'Africa' came to be used for what is now eastern Algeria and Tunisia under the **Aghlabid** dynasty (founded by one Ibrahim el Aghlab), who ruled from **Kairouan** from 800 to 909. Simplifying grossly, the Aghlabids were eventually replaced in Ifrikiya by the **Fatimids**, a Shi'ite dyanasty who ruled from **Mahdiya** before moving on to conquer Egypt in 970. The new city of Cairo became the Fatimid capital in 973. To rule Ifrikiya, they left behind them viceroys, who established an independent Sunni dynasty, the **Zirids**, who finally broke with the Fatimids in 1044. By way of vengeance, the latter unleashed the **Hilalian tribes** on Ifrikiya in the 1050s. In the 12th century, Sicily flourished under a **Norman dynasty**, and a number of Ifrikiyan coastal towns came under Norman rule. In the late 1100s, the Berber **Almohad** dynasty conquered Andalusia and the Maghreb. The Almohads' hold over Ifrikiya declined in the early 1200s. They appointed one Abdul Wahid, son of Abu Hafs Umar, a leading Almohad figure, as viceroy. The cycle repeated itself as a new dynasty, the **Hafsids**, established itself at Tunis, ruling until the early 16th century.

face the *mihrab*, the niche indicating the direction of Islam's holiest city. The 70 metre width of the mosque allows long lines of worshippers to form parallel to the *mihrab* wall. If the number of worshippers grew, the covered area could easily be extended by adding further colonnades across the courtyard and roofing them. There was no need for a prayer hall much larger than the one in existence as mediaeval Kairouan was a small place. When large numbers of people gathered for the prayers on great occasions, the overspill could be easily contained in the courtyard. And then on any major religious holiday, the city would use its *musalla* or open prayer ground.

Still in the médina, have a look in at **Bir Barouta**, (Barouta's well), a domed building just to the right of the main street as you head away from Bab ech Chouhada. Up the steep stairs are a small café and a large piece of functioning mediaeval technology in the form of a water wheel activated by a blinkered camel. The story goes that a dog called Barouta came across the spring, an answer to his pious master's prayers some time back in the 13th century.

Other sights Unfortunately for the early inhabitants of Kairouan, there were no useful bits of Roman aqueduct to be brought back into service. The solution to the water supply problem was found by sultan Abou Ibrahim Ahmed who had large *fesquiyet* or reservoirs constructed. Originally, there were 14 pools. Of these **Aghlabid Pools**, built in the ninth century, two survive today, to the north of the town. The larger pool is 128 metres in diameter and five metres in depth. They pools were seemingly part of a much more elaborate water system. The Cherichera aqueduct was constructed to carry water from over 36 km away to the west. The smaller pool was used to settle the silt carried in the water. The clear water was stored in the big pool, diameter 128 metres, depth 5 metres. Although the pools may have resolved Kairouan's recurring water supply problem, they also added a health risk. They proved to be a superb breeding ground for mosquitoes.
■ *Open 0830-1730 winter, 0800-1200 and 1500-1900 summer.*

Zaouia Sidi Sahbi (also known as the Barber's Mosque) is the burial place of one of the Prophet's companions, Abou Djama el Balaoui. The Zaouia is known as the Barber's Mosque because Abou el Balaoui carried about with him three hairs from the Prophet's beard, from which he would never be parted. The present building with its elegant minaret dates back to the 17th century. It is beautifully decorated with the usual ceramic tile-work. To get to the mausoleum, you first pass through a small room and continue along an open air corridor. The next small room with a finely worked plaster ceiling opens on to the delightful main courtyard (square in shape and bordered on three sides by colonnades), with the mausoleum which houses the tomb. A small room off to one side houses the tomb of **Sidi Cherif ibn Hindu**, master-builder of the great mosque. Access to the mausoleum is reserved to Muslims. Notice the painted wooden ceilings under the arcade surrounding the courtyard. On Friday when circumcision ceremonies take place and during the Mouled (the Prophet's birthday), there are numerous pilgrims.

Another fairly peripheral monument is the **Zaouia of Sidi Amor Abbada**, a 19th century blacksmith who had a penchant for designing large Tolkienesque metal objects, including huge anchors (to hold Tunisia to the land?), and immense swords fit for a dragon slayer. A number of these items are on display in his seven-domed tomb, although some seem to have been stolen. It's all rather curious, and there is little to tell you about how and why such an obviously expensive building was put up by a blacksmith around 1860. The lack of

Kairouan

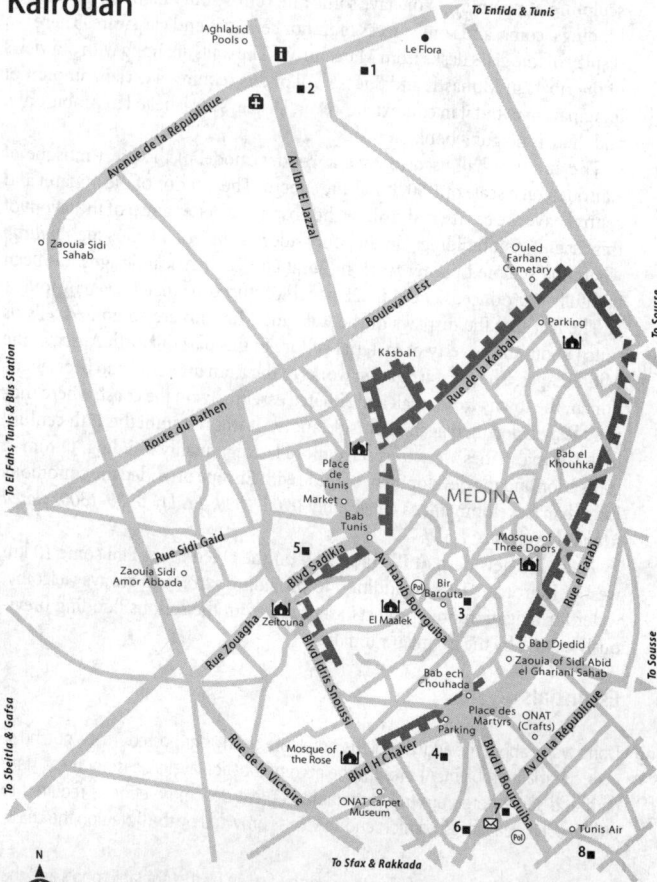

To Enfida & Tunis

Aghlabid Pools

Le Flora

Avenue de la République

Av Ibn El Jazzar

Zaouia Sidi Sahab

Ouled Farhane Cemetary

To El Fahs, Tunis & Bus Station

Boulevard Est

Parking

To Sousse

Kasbah

Rue de la Kasbah

Route du Bathen

Bab el Khoukha

Place de Tunis
Market

MEDINA

Rue Sidi Gaid

Bab Tunis

Zaouia Sidi Amor Abbada

Mosque of Three Doors

Blvd Sadikia

Av Habib Bourguiba

Bir Barouta

Rue el Farabi

Rue Zouagha

Zeitouna

El Maalek

Bab Djedid

Zaouia of Sidi Abid el Ghariani Sahab

To Sousse

Blvd Idris Snoussi

Bab ech Chouhada

Place des Martyrs

ONAT (Crafts)

To Sheitla & Gafsa

Rue de la Victoire

Mosque of the Rose

Blvd H Chaker

Parking

Av de la République

Blvd H Bourguiba

ONAT Carpet Museum

Tunis Air

To Sfax & Rakkada

N

| 0 metres | 150 |
| 0 yards | 163 |

■ **Sleeping**
1 Amina
2 Continental
3 Marhala
4 Sabra
5 Sidi Bel Hassan
6 Splendid
7 Tunisia
8 Youth Hostel

information tells you something about Tunisian attitudes to saints' shrines in the post-independence period. In the 19th century, the beys and their ministers frequently sponsored the construction of new zaouias. In the 1960s, with Tunisia becoming a modern nation state, the practice of visiting saints to seek blessing was severely stigmatised.

National Museum of Islamic Art and Culture

The **Palace of Rakkada**, 11 km southwest of Kairouan on the P2, was ex-president Habib Bourguiba's official Kairouan residence and today houses Tunisia's most important collections of Islamic Art. The palace was designed by architect Jacques Marmey, proponent of a style of architecture derived from the simplest of traditional forms. Why Bourguiba chose to have a palace on this site is open to debate. As Rakkada was the second royal town of the Aghlabid Dynasty, perhaps he was seeking to confirm his place in the pantheon of Tunisian rulers. As a former royal complex, the site has archaeological importance in its own right.

The collections are not as spectacular, however, as those at the Bardo. Islamic culture rejects representations of the living form, so there is neither sculpture nor painting. You have some fine 10th century manuscripts, leather bindings, coins, and some pieces of minor ceramics and glassware. There is a display of fine glass flasks from Mansouriya. The walls are hung with old views of the ribats in Monastir and Sousse. All of this requires a certain amount of imagination to put it in context, however. Displays are labelled in Arabic only, and there is no guidebook on sale.

The entrance hall used to have a wooden model of the great mosque of Kairouan on a scale of 1:50. It is quite superb. The interior of the minaret and central nave are exposed and allow the observer a better grasp of the layout of this magnificent building. On the other side is a copy of the mosque's *mihrab* where the sculpted plaster work of floral and geometrical designs has been faithfully reproduced. There are 28 panels of stucco arranged seven by four.

The fact that the displays of the Rakkada Museum are so limited tells us much about the poverty of material culture in this part of North Africa in the Middle Ages. The great irrigation works of the Roman period had been abandoned, the towns were small and situated essentially on the coast, where they were heavily fortified against outside attack. It was not until the 17th century that Tunisia's cities were to receive more lasting, quality building. Ottoman protection and the development of trade with Europe provided the conditions for urban development. ■ *Open daily 0900-1600, Friday 0900-1300, closed Monday. Entrance 1.5Dt.*

There is a new **dam at El Haouareb** on the Oued Merg Ellil some 10 km west of Kairouan. This, in addition to providing extra, and always welcome, water for irrigation now protects Kairouan from the serious flooding previously caused by the irregular rainfall.

Essentials

Sleeping
■ *on map*
Price codes:
see inside front cover
Phone code: 07

Don't worry about the address, all the hotels are clearly signposted. This is not, however, the main problem. At present the accommodation available is not up to standard and some hotels are truly miserable. A great deal more effort is required to produce the cleanliness, comfort and service as provided by the hotels on the coast.

B *Hotel Continental*, route de Tunis, to north of town by the Aghlabid pools and the tourist office, T220607, 175 rooms, a/c, large pool, garden, restaurant, visitors could be forgiven for turning round and leaving, thinking they had arrived at the wrong place, which given the current state of the hotel is probably the best thing to do.

C *Hotel Amina*, route de Tunis, GP2, 300 Kairouan, T226555, F225411. 3 minutes from city centre, 62 rooms and 5 suites all with bath and balconies, telephone, a/c, 2 restaurants, coffee shop, bar, large pool, garden, near Tourist office and Aghlabid pools, disco each evening, good lunch for 7Dt served from 1230, hence popular with coach parties, at present this is the best hotel in town, but then there is no competition.

D *Le Splendid*, T220522. Rue du 9 Avril, 28 rooms with bath, a/c, clean, basic, bar and busy restaurant, slightly over-priced. **D** *Tunisia*, T221855. Av Farhat Hached, 44 rooms with bath, breakfast, no restaurant, comfortable, very clean, no a/c but fans on ceiling.

F *Hotel Marhala*, T220736, F229527. 35 Souq El Bey in the médina near Bir Barouta, 30 rooms, fairly pleasant, well run, small, view from top room, roof terrace, no lift. **F** *Hotel Sabra*, Rue Ali Belhaouane, by place des Martyrs, T220260. Clean, pleasant, friendly staff, roof terrace, 30 room, room at back are quieter, *hammam* next door highly recommended but men only.

Youth hostel Ave de Fès, T220309. In the new town, kitchen, 70 beds, reports say noisy and not clean.

Mid-range *Le Flora*, route de Tunis; *Raschid*, Ouled Farhane; *Hotel Amina*. **Eating**

Cheap *Restaurant des Sportifs*, Place de la Victoire, couscous speciality; *Restaurant El Karawan*, rue Souqeina Ben El-Houssein, behind *Tunisia Hotel*, typical Tunisian cooking, family run. *Restaurant Fairouz*, signposted off Av Habib Bourguiba in the médina, good food, cheap. *Restaurant Sabra*, Av Farhat Hached, an excellent, cheap place to eat typical Tunisian food. *Roi du Couscous*, Place du 7 Novembre, Tunisian food at cheap prices, closes in late afternoon, best for lunch or early dinner. *Restaurant La Tabouna*, off Place des Martyrs, another, just about adequate cheap eating place, plenty of chips.

Kairouan is one of the major centres for **carpets** in the country. Visit first the display of **Shopping** old and new carpets at the ONAT on Av Ali Zouaoui, to get an idea of real prices even though carpets can be cheaper elsewhere. Be careful when walking around, the term *musée du tapis* (lit. carpet museum) does not indicate a museum, but rather a shop with carpets on display and the hard sell. For an experience of purchasing carpets try *Société Tapis Sabra*, rue Sidi Abid, T223068 or *Centre Kairouanais du Tapis*, 35 Souq des Tamis, T226223. An arched doorway in a plain wall leads into what was once a private dwelling. Sunlight filters down onto hundreds of carpets, spread on floors, hung on walls and piled in rolls at every turn. In one room there is a loom and a woman or women will appear to demonstrate how a carpet is woven. Seating is provided in the largest room where any carpet you would like to see is rolled out for inspection.

If carpets are not your thing, then you could look out for some of **beaten copper** kitchen pans and dishes for which Kairouan is also known. Items covered in zinc (*tekezdeer* is the technique) are attractive but expensive. Otherwise, the best buy in Kairouan are **makroudh**, sweet date cakes basted in oil and coated in syrup and sesame seeds. Appropriately packaged in boxes labelled *pâtisserie tunisienne* they make a sticky, calorific gift.

Local Car hire: *Budget*, Av de la République, T220528; *Hertz*, Av Ibn el Jazzar, **Transport** T224529.

Long distance Bus: the station is northwest of the town centre, a good 20 minute walk from the médina. For information T220125. Departures to **Tunis**; **Kebili/Douz**; **Gafsa**; **Tozeur**; **Djerba**; **Zarzis**; **Medenine** and **Nefta**. **Louages**: departures from bus station. To **El Djem** possible by louage, requires changes and patience.

Central Tunisia

Early medicine in Kairouan : the Jewish contribution

One of the high points of Aghlabid rule in Kairouan was the development of medical knowledge. The early Aghlabid princes built hospitals in the main towns. Medicine in these far off times was above all a family affair. In the troubled years of the late 10th century, Ziyadet Allah III had Jewish physicians brought over from Egypt, among them Ishak ben Imran al-Israili and Abou Yacoub Ishak ben Suleyman (later known as Isaac Judaeus in Europe). Both studied in Baghdad, and won fame in Kairouan, teaching medicine and treating the Aghlabid princes.

Ishak ben Imran earned the nickname 'the prince of physicians'. He is said to have written 13 works, the most famous of which is his Anatomy of Melancholy, which refers to ancient Greek sources. Wrote Ishak ben Imran: "I have not read a single satisfactory book by an Ancient writer on the subject of melancholy …

Rufus of Ephesus limits his study to a single type, the hypochondriac form … Hypochondria originates at the mouth of the stomach; other forms are born in the brain itself." Ben Imran also wrote treatises on fevers and urines. His work, while drawing on the Greeks, is also filled with a wealth of personal observation.

Kairouan's greatest Muslim physician of the 10th century was Ahmad ibn al Jazzar (d.980). His father and uncle were doctors, and he studied under Ishak ben Suleyman. He was also a pharmacologist, developing an advanced selection of plant remedies. His most famous work, Zad el Mousafir (Provision for the Traveller), is a 156 chapter work describing all the illnesses known to Al Jazzar, giving their names in Persian, Greek, Syriac and spoken Arabic. He proposes three types of treatment: minor surgery, phytotherapy and minerals.

Directory **Banks** *BDS*, *UIB* and *BT* on Place de l'Indépendence. *STB* has automatic cash dispenser for Visa and Mastercard. **Communications** Area code: 07. **Post Office:** Place du 7 Novembre, rue Farhat Hached. **Emergency numbers** Police: T220577. **Hammam:** *Sabra*, next to the hotel of the same name, close to the tourist office by Bab Ech-Chouhada. Immaculately clean. Men only, closes around 1600. **Medical services** Hospital: Hopital Ibn Jazzar by the Aghlabid pools, T230036. **Pharmacie de nuit** (all-night chemists) near the centre on Av Ali Zouaoui, between junction with Av Hédi Chaker and Bab Jedid. **Tourist offices** The tourist information office is opposite *Hotel Continental*, near Aghlabid pools. There are 2 offices, turn left for information and right to buy tickets for the monuments. Welcoming, competent staff will organize you a tour or an official guide if requested. Open 0800-1730 daily except Sunday 0800-1200, T220452-221797.

South from Kairouan to Gabès

Colour map 2, grid A/C4

If you want to get south fast, avoiding Sousse and Sfax, there is the busy P2 running directly south to Skhira, where it joins the P1 coast road for Gabès. Leaving Kairouan, you pass the National Museum of Islamic Art at **Rakkada**. Further south where the P2 crosses Oued Zeroud and the railway line and where the C86 cuts off to to the southwest is **Zaâfrane**, a small settlement with a large clean café set back off the road. Eucalyptus trees provide welcome shade, although their number has been reduced by road widening. Further south, olives stretch as far as the eye can see.

Some 35 km south of Kairouan, **Bouhajla** is a small crossroads settlement. Here you will find the National Guard, yet another square-faced clock on a central pillar, chemist, bread shop, louage and bus stop. There is a café by the bus stop and a slightly better café to the north of village by the new mosque and petrol station.

Djebel Khechem closes in on the west and Djebel Kordj on the east. At the road junction P13 and P2 are two fairly basic cafés. Sebkhet Mecheguig, to the west, in right conditions a very large expanse of water, supports a rich bird life.

Bir Ali Ben Khalifat, 49 km north of the Skhirat / P1 junction, is a government resettlement project. There is a hotel and café, very popular at lunch times with welcoming staff. Hotel has eight reasonable rooms.

On the routes north of Kairouan

The road north from Kairouan towards Tunis (P2) is in poor condition in parts, although there is a rolling improvement programme. The journey can be slow.

Colour map 1, grid A/C4

The wildlife reserve of **Lake Kelbia** lies about 30 km northeast of Kairouan, spreading to the southwest of the P2, the main road to Enfida which eventually merges with the P1 for Tunis. The best way to view the lake is to walk around the shore, but clear paths and viewing points are rare as the water level of the lake changes during the year. There is no other way to the lake but through fields or olive groves. However, at 25 km from Kairouan a small loop to the east takes one nearer to the water. In summer it is dry. It is an important wildlife reserve, with a wide variety of birds. During the summer you may spot squacco herons, purple gallinules or the fantailed warbler. In the winter, migrating birds such as flamingoes and cranes pass through.

Bird watching at Lake Kelbia

A more interesting route from Kairouan takes you along the C99 towards Siliana, passing between the Djebel Ousselat and Djebel Bou Dabouss. At Aïn Djelloula, you pass a fine field of ruins. Before reaching remote Ouesslatia, turn right on the C46. The ruins of Ksar Lemsa lie some 23 km to the north. (After Ksar Lemsa, you can continue on to El Fahs, 50 km further north. Some fine scenery here).

Ksar Lamsa, a remote Byzantine fort

Like all Roman cities Ksar Lamsa was situated in a position of strategic importance. It overlooked the valleys of the Oued el Kebir and the smaller, nearer Oued Maarouf. It controlled movement from the plains of the west to the coast and was itself protected by its position on a low plateau backed by the Djebel Bargou. The fortress (hence the modern Arabic name *ksar*) dates from the sixth century BC, (the reign of Justinian) though re-use of older building stones complicate the issue. The battlements of the well-conserved fortress (29 metres by 31 metres) remain. Entrance was through a gate on the north side. Inside the fortress was a large, deep water cistern fed by a conduit from outside – a supply in times of siege. Around the fortress are many ruins, few excavated. On the opposite side of the road to the fortress is a pocket-sized amphitheatre. Even Ksar Lamsa must have had its entertainments.

Northwest of Kairouan: the road to Siliana

Following the same route out of Kairouan as for Ksar Lamsa, and eventually El Fahs, you could continue at Ouesslatia on the C73 northwards for Siliana. The road will take you past **Djebel Serj**, the second highest mountain in Tunisia (1360 metres, Djebel Chaâmbi near Kasserine being highest at 1554 metres). The road climbs up through the moutains to Siliana, now capital of a governorate.

Colour map 1, grid B3

West of Kairouan: La Kessera and Makthar

Driving west of Kairouan, head for Chebika (not to be confused with Chebika in the Djerid region), on the P3. Branch right off the P3 onto the the P12 for Makthar and Le Kef. Here you are heading into *la Tunisie profonde*, the remote interior of Tunisia, although this was a region settled by the Romans too, as the

Phone code: 08
Colour map 1, grid C3

Central Tunisia

☞ **Fortifying Africa: the Byzantine defences**

In the 6th century, under the leadership of the energetic emperor Justinian, Africa returned to the Byzantine fold. The Vandals were defeated, and the province once more became part of the Eastern Roman Empire. But things could not be as they had been before. The Roman peace had been shattered forever. During the Vandal interregnum, security had been shaken, and a new factor had appeared: roaming nomad tribes, highly mobile on their camels.

Justinian wanted to see the restoration of the old Roman frontier of Hadrian's day. His governor Solomon realised that the enemy was now within, not in the lands south of the limes. A new approach to defence was necessary, it was no longer a matter of stationing a legion on the frontier. Forts and citadels were therefore put up wherever important towns needed protection. Some eighty fortified sites have been identified, and there are thought to be many more. Towns which once had no need of a garrison were heavily fortified – Dougga and Mactaris, for example.

Remote villages were given look out posts – see La Kessera, while even quite minor settlements received solid square forts (Ksar Lemsa).

Huge energies were put into protecting the reconquered province's settlements. There was a good deal of dismantling/rebuilding, and at times, older Roman buildings were integrated into the new fortifications (the capitol at Dougga became part of the new walls). The aim was to ensure that Africa remained under Byzantine rule. Ultimately, however, Byzantium's efforts to maintain its hold on the province failed. Despite all the best efforts of the empire's military engineers, the province fell to the Muslim armies in the second half of the 7th century. The fortifications which survive are often spectacular – as can be seen at Haïdra, unequalled in scale and sophistication until the 16th century and the coming of Renaissance military technology (see the fort at La Goulette and 17th century forts at Ghar el Melh).

number of ancient sites shows. It was also a region of settlement in prehistoric times. In contemporary Tunisian political jargon, large parts of the interior are the *zones d'ombre*, the 'regions in the shadow', untouched by the prosperity of the east coast in the first decades of Tunisian independence. Since the early 1990s, the government has made major efforts to develop the isolated parts of the interior, and the results are evident to even the casual visitor: pistes replaced by metalled roads, power lines, schools, post offices, the odd bit of light industry.

Heading for the northwest, you could combine the scenic drive from Kairouan to Le Kef with visits to the hill-crest village of **La Kessera** and the remains of Roman **Mactaris**, at **Makthar**, roughly halfway between Kairouan and Le Kef. Driving time to Le Kairouan to Makthar is roughly two hours, from Makthar to Le Kef 90 minutes.

Some 17 km before you reach Makthar, the village of La Kessera is up on your right on a loop off the P12. At 1,078 metres altitude, the village is in a magnificent defensive position. The houses are grouped below the plateau, sheltered by cliff from the prevailing winds. Originally built of local stone, the houses blended into the landscape, perfect protection from marauders. Although chosen for defensive reasons, the site had the additional plus of plentiful water (there is a spring in the middle of the village). Above the village, on the plateau, was grazing, and there was plentiful wood in the Aleppo pine forests.

The origins of La Kessera are lost, as you might expect, in the mists of time. Was there a settlement called Chusira, named for distant Chosroes, king of the Persians? Or does the name derive from the Latin 'caesar'? Some slight remains of a Byzantine watch tower overlook the village. Stelae and stones of ancient origins can be found integrated into the walls of the houses. During the French protectorate, La Kessera, was the seat of a caïdat, and its zaouia, Sidi Ameur, a place of local pilgrimage. In the 1960s, policy was to bring isolated communities into line. A new village was built below the village, with standard concrete houses, facilities were moved down next to the main road. The village people refused to move, however, remaining attached to their homes. Whereas in many hill-crest villages Zriba, near Zaghouan for example, people moved down to the plain, the advantages of ancient La Kessera were too good be lost.

In recent years, signs of a new prosperity have appeared, with constructions in the usual concrete style being lodged on top of older stone dwellings. There has also been much new building down below the village. The village lives on agriculture, government employment, and some weaving. Heavy wool *kachabia* cloaks for men, essential gear for the cold winters of the interior, are a local speciality.

Out on the Makthar side of La Kessera, you come to the only accommodation option here, the *Hotel des Chasseurs*, which may be open in the near future. The bar should be in operation.

Next stop on the P12, **Makthar**, (population 7,500), lies 900 metres above sea level and 114 km west of Kairouan. Though the new town was built by the French in 1887, the Roman city of Mactaris, dating from around AD 200, was built on the site of an earlier Numidian defensive position. Makthar town lies to the north of the site and at an altitude of over 900 metres is refreshingly cool. The town is built on the hillside and the buses stop at the lower end of the town while the louages stop higher up the main street. Market day is Monday. Make sure you don't miss the **dolmen**, a megalithic tomb near the town centre, on the left as you come in from Kairouan. (If you have a car, and have a yen for things prehistoric, you might want to head for **Elles**, a left turn down a minor road some 30 km north of Makthar on the P12 for Le Kef.)

Ancient Mactaris

The ruins of ancient Mactaris are fairly scattered, so you will probably need at least an hour. Start with a look at the triumphal arch of Bab el Aïn right in the middle of town. You get tickets for the site at the museum. ■ *The site is open winter 0830-1730, summer 0800-1200 and 1500-1900, entrance 2Dt, photography 1dt.*

See map next page

The remains of the **amphitheatre** lie to the left and further left, across the Roman road are the remains of a **temple** dedicated to the Carthaginian god Hathor Miskar. Follow the Roman street towards the central section of the site where there is the main forum and the remains of Trajan's Arch, looking less triumphal than in its heyday of 115 AD. Beyond are the foundations of the fifth century **Basilica of Hildeguns** and after another 100 metres are the **southern baths**, built around 200 AD, considered among the best preserved in Africa. Much of the splendour is in the mosaics. The building was changed into a fort in the more troubled Byzantine times. The walls are 20 metres high in places, unfortunately the vaulting failed to survive.

To the west, lies the **Schola Juvenum**, one of the most charming ruins in Tunisia, once a sort of club-house come educational establishment for young men. Close by is the old forum, and just across the street, a temple dedicated to Bacchus.

If you are on the look out for the more **obscure Roman sites**, then on the C80 road to Siliana (turn off right 24 km north of Makthar on the P12) you will be rewarded with **Kbor Klib**, a large mausoleum, similar to the Numidian mausoleum at Chemtou. Further on, at **Ksar Toual Zammel**, are yet more remains.

Sleeping Not too much choice at Makthar. Try **C** *Mactaris*, T08-876014, 20 rooms, reasonable standard, bar.

Transport There are **buses** from Tunis (2 a day), Kasserine (2 daily) and Le Kef (also 2 daily).

Makthar to Sbeïtla: across deepest Tunisia

The 75 kilometre journey south from Makthar to Sbeïtla is along winding minor roads through the Dorsal region. Within two km of leaving Makthar, there is a magnificent view north to the mountains and as the P4 climbs through the **Djebel Skarna** (1,076 metres), the Tunisia seen here is in sharp contrast to the level plains of the Sahel. As the road descends, the ruins of the ancient settlement of **Sufes** at Sbiba lie to the left and 40 km further on is the magnificent Roman site at Sbeïtla.

Across the steppe: routes for Le Kef, Kalaât Senam and Haïdra

From Makthar, there are a number of options for continuing your exploration of central Tunisia. The obvious choice is to overnight in Le Kef (covered in the previous chapter, Northern Tunisia). Then, if you have a car, you can easily cover the Roman site of **Haïdra** and **Kalaât Senam** in a day, pushing on south to overnight in **Kasserine** or **Sbeïtla** (for which see below). Without your own transport, getting to Haïdra will be fairly time consuming, requiring a louage or bus to Kalaât Khasaba, and then hitching or country mini-bus to Haïdra. For Kalaât Senam, you will need to take a louage or bus from Le Kef to Tajerouine, a minor town on the P17, 37 km south of Le Kef. There you change louage for Kalaât Senam. An early start would be a good thing.

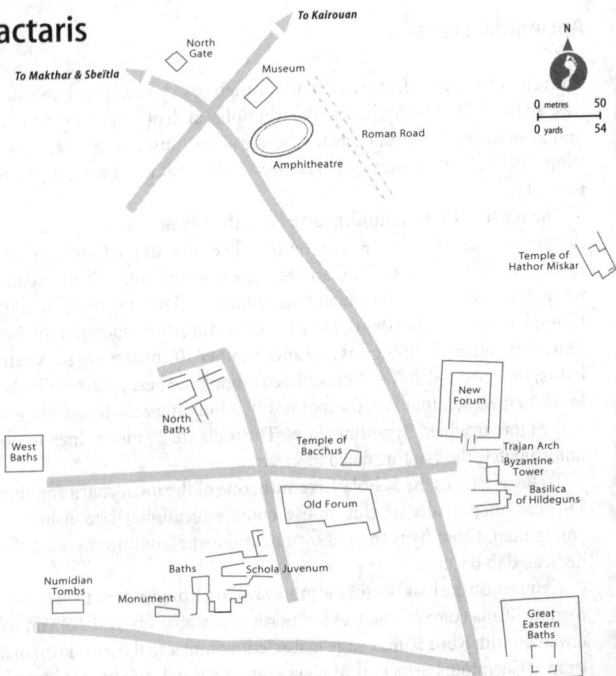

Mactaris

A more obscure route from Makthar would take you from the turn off at Henchir Lorbeuss (left off the P12, 38 km north of Makthar). A minor road takes you down to **Dahmani**, whence the C18 takes you across to the former mining town of **Jerissa** and the P17 just south of Tajerouine.

Kalaât Senam, Senam's Citadel, is one of the more rewarding out-of-the-way corners of Tunisia. It is a strange, flat-topped mountain which rises up out of the surrounding steppelands. The settlement below has grown considerably in recent years, with electricity being brought in. From the village, you have a 90 minute hike up the top of the citadel. Small children may offer to show you the way. The walk is not difficult, and you have one steep climb up a flight of steps carved out of the rock. After passing through an ancient gatehouse, you are on the plateau, which must have been one of the most impregnable sites in pre-modern Tunisia. There are remains of a village, some cisterns, and an eerie *zaouia*, white-domed, the interior blackened with candle smoke.

Kalaât Senam

The tale goes that the table mountain is named for one Senam, a brigand who lived in more heroic times. When the bey's army passed through these remote marchlands to collect taxes, Kalaât Senam was a port of call. The inhabitants of the region would shut themselves off with their flocks in their rocky citadel, flinging down a bit of rotting carrion to show their indifference to the tax collecting army, which would go on its way empty handed. Local people still take goats and cows up onto the plateau to graze.

You might like to spend an hour exploring the desolation of Kalaât Senam. There are wonderful views, and even non-birdwatchers will be impressed by the number of birds of prey soaring around the cliff faces. Aleppo pine woods can be seen away to the south. At the western end of the plateau are some rock chimneys. The local story is that a few years ago, a lad from the village climbed to the top of one of these pillars for a bet. Unfortunately, he couldn't get down. Given the sheer drops on all sides, children shouldn't be left unaccompanied. In fact, the 'table' is not flat at all. It hollows towards the middle, and is actually quite large. One can easily lose sight of other members of one's group – the plateau takes on a mysterious feel – shades of the Blair Witch Project *à la tunisienne*.

Haïdra ﺣﻴﺪﺭﺓ

Haïdra, ancient Ammaedara, is well off the main tourist track . It lies a short distance from the Algerian frontier, on the way to nowhere (at the moment), although when Algeria reopens for tourism, you will be able to combine visiting Haïdra with ancient Theveste. The site is lonely, the ruins scattered over an arid hillside sloping down to a river. On the far side, Aleppo pines contrast green with the stoney ground. There are all the usual features, including triumphal arch and basilicas, and the massive masonry of Byzantine forts. In Roman times, either the climate must have been wetter, or the water infrastructure very efficient to support such a grand military base on this stoney site.

Colour map 2, grid A1

Ins and outs

Haïdra can be easily reached by louage from Kalaâ Khasbah, about 18 km to the northeast.

Getting there

The main site lies to the southeast of the modern town of Haïdra. The old Roman road runs parallel to the P4 from which many ruins can be seen.

Getting around

History and background

Ammaedara stood at the western end of one of the oldest Roman roads in Africa, running inland from Tacapae, (modern Gabès) on the coast. Inscriptions record it has having been built in 14 AD. Later, a road from Carthage to Theveste, some 40 km to the southwest and a major military base, passed through Ammaedara. (Theveste became the Third Augustan Legion's Head Quarters in the first century AD, under Augustus or Tiberius. Later, when the legionary base was moved west to Theveste, a colony of veterans was settled at Ammaedara at the end of the first century.

In Christian times, Ammaedara remained an important centre, and there are the remains of no less than five basilicas to visit on the site. Under Justinian in the sixth century, with Africa temporarily reconquered by the Byzantines, the town acquired a vast citadel, which in all probability continued in use under the early Arab rulers. It was in part restored and altered in Husseinid times.

Visiting the site

The remains at Haïdra are located to the north and south of the main road, the more spectacular sights being on the south side. For the moment there is no entrance charge, but someone might emerge into the sunbaked field of ruins to show you around (you will probably need about an hour). In summer, given the shadeless nature of the site, an early start is advisable. At the time of writing, a museum was planned for the site, to be housed in a former customs building dating from last century.

Ruins south of the road Coming from the east, one first encounters the **Triumphal Arch of Septimius Severus** which once spanned the Roman road to Carthage. The arch was dedicated in 195 AD as can be seen from the frieze. Having been incorporated in a small Byzantine fort at a later stage, it is not exactly in pristine condition.

Haïdra

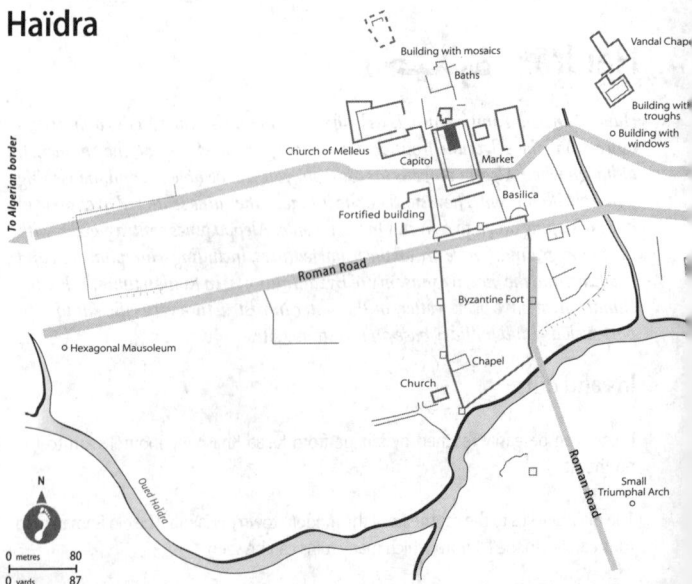

Church of Bishop Melleus

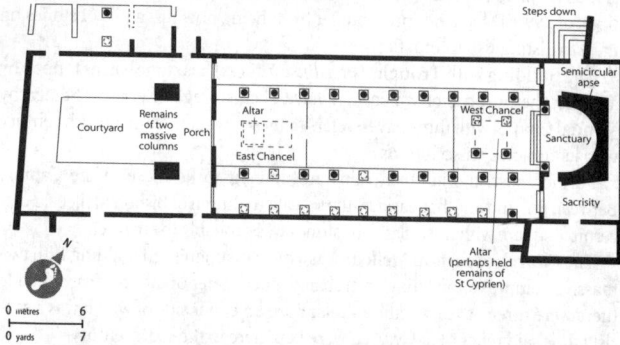

See text next page

Southeast of the arch are the remains of a **Byzantine church** with three naves. Excavations show that this covers a more ancient church. In both the apse faced east. This church is dedicated to the martyrs who perished under the persecution of Diocletian. A small chapel there is dedicated to these unfortunates.

About 300 metres to the south, not far from the *oued*, is a beautiful **mausoleum** with portico. It is well preserved, still having a second storey. The upper floor is in the style of a small temple and the façade of four columns supporting a pediment gives it its name. Any statues which stood between the columns have long since been removed.

The building of greatest distinction at Haïdra is without doubt the **Byzantine Fort**, built at the time of Justinian (527-565 AD). It has claims to be the largest Byzantine fort in Africa. The massive fortifications measured 200 metres by 110 metres, and had walls 10 metres high. Nine square towers can be clearly seen. Halfway down the east wall was a circular tower. The main north-south route actually passed through this fortress and at the south end led to a bridge over the Oued Haïdra. A small chapel with three naves was incorporated into part of the west wall against one of the towers. There was a side aisle on the south side and a high tower, as high as the wall. Parts of the ribbed vaulting are still preserved. Renovations to the north elevation of this fortress were undertaken by the Turkish beys. And just outside the walls of this fortress to the southwest is yet another small basilica.

Ruins north of the road

On the north side of the main road, the ruins are rather less legible than the spectacular Byzantine citadel. Nevertheless, there are one or two points of interest which enthusiasts will want to look at.

At 200 metres north of the road and in line with the **Church of the Martyrs** is the **square mausoleum**

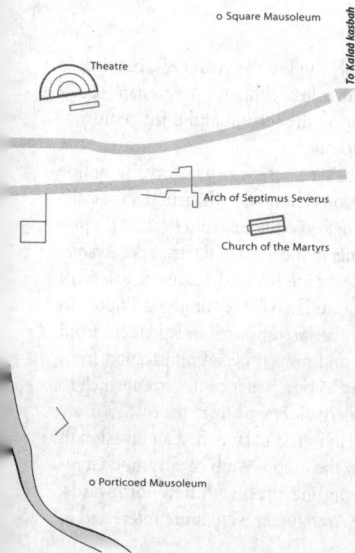

Central Tunisia

decorated with Corinthian pillars and stylized garlands. The **Theatre** also stands to the north of the road. This is a great disappointment as the restorations of 299 AD have not prevented it from being now just a pile of stones on hard to distinguish foundations.

The **Building with Troughs** (Fr: *edifice à auges*) has stone basins topped by arcades, the purpose of which may have been storage of grain. The nearby **Vandal Chapel** with three naves, refers to these invaders from the fifth century who left funerary inscriptions.

Further west, the jumbled ruins are thought to be those of the Capitol. Between this and another basilica, the so-called Church of Bishop Melleus, a discernible square with miscellaneous stones was probably the market.

See plan on previous page

The **Church of Bishop Melleus** was a most distinguished building with two massive columns supporting an arch at the perimeter of the courtyard. Inside there were three naves, a semi-circular apse on either side of which was a sacristy. It is said relics of St Cyprien were kept here in the sixth century.

Sbeïtla سبيطلة

Phone code: 07
Colour map 1, grid A2

The golden-stone ruins of Sbeïtla have an other worldly feel to them. This is the most distant major site from Carthage, and also one of the best preserved. Whereas many Roman cities were quarried for building stone down the centuries, Sbeïtla has remained relatively untouched, apart from a little refortifying under the Byzantines. For a short time, it was an imperial Christian capital. In 646, the exarch Gregory had himself proclaimed emperor and moved from Carthage to Sbeïtla to better defend Africa against the Arab invasions.

Ins and outs

Getting there The bus station is in the centre of the new town and the louages are next to it. Many buses come here from Kasserine, Gafsa, Tunis and Kairouan. The train station is on rue Habib Thameur to south of town.

History and background

The Roman town of Sufetula was probably built in the year 3 BC, but little is known about it until the period under the rule of Emperor Vespasian (69-79 AD). The town was very prosperous during the second and third centuries, judging by the remains of the public buildings.

It is in the early seventh century that Sbeïtla emerges into history. Byzantine Africa was supplying corn and olive oil to Constantinople, which under the leadership of the emperor Heraclius (d.641), defeated the Sassanid Persian Empire in the East. But a new enemy was emerging, in the form of the tribes of Arabia, united by a new revealed religion, Islam. Egypt was invaded, leading to a flood of refugees. In 642, the Arabs took Cyrenaica, and in 643 they besieged Tripoli. In 646, the exarch Gregory, in a bold move, declared himself independent from Constantinople, called himself Emperor and moved his administration from Carthage to Sufetula, which he considered to be a better centre from which to defend the country against the new and energetic enemy from the east.

This proved not to be the case. Abdallah ibn Saâd launched an invasion in 647. Gregory's forces were annihilated by the mobile Arab cavalry, and Gregory himself was killed. The remaining Byzantine forces withdrew northwards, abandoning southern Byzacena. But the Arab forces were more interested in booty than siege warfare.

The Byzantines, however, made a fatal error after their defeat. They offered a huge bribe to the Arabs to leave. Abdallah ibn Saâd, surprised by the quantity of coins put before him, asked where all this wealth came from. The Byzantine representatives explained that it came from the sale of olive oil to Constantinople. Such a rich territory would clearly have to be conquered on a more long term basis. Though the Arabs headed back to Egypt, they were to return and conquer the whole of North Africa in the late seventh century.

No modern city was grafted onto ancient Sufetula, and the result is one of the best preserved Roman street layouts in Tunisia. Nearby modern Sbeïtla, a minor agricultural centre, is not too exciting, though it does have all the necessary facilities a traveller could require and looks its best on a Wednesday when there is the weekly market.

Visiting the site

The best time to visit this impressive ruined town is early in the morning or in the evening when the soft sunlight is particularly beautiful on the stones of the temples (and there are fewer visitors.) ■ *Open 0830-1730 winter and 0600-2000 in summer. Closed Monday, entrance 2Dt, photo fee 1Dt. Most of the site is accessible in a wheelchair.*

Opposite the ruins (adjacent to the Coca-cola stall and coach park) is a **museum** containing artefacts and photographs of Sbeïtla divided into five sections covering prehistory, Roman sculptures, ceramics, Christian/Byzantine and Muslim periods. A visit to the museum first may make the site visit more valuable. ■ *Open daily 0600-2000. Entrance included in fee for ruins. There are toilets beside the museum.*

Central Tunisia

Sbeïtla

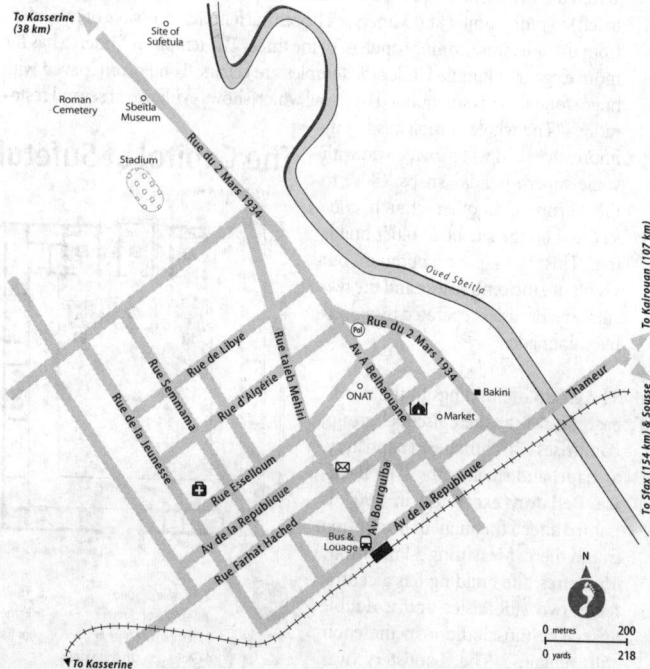

Map of Sbeïtla showing roads and landmarks including: To Kasserine (38 km), Site of Sufetula, Roman Cemetery, Sbeïtla Museum, Stadium, Rue du 2 Mars 1934, Oued Sbeïtla, To Kairouan (107 km), Rue de Libye, Rue Sennmana, Rue d'Algérie, Rue taïeb Mehiri, Rue de la Jeunesse, Rue Esselloum, ONAT, Bakini, Market, Thameur, Rue Farhat Hached, Av de la Republique, Av Bourguiba, Av A Belhaouane, Bus & Louage, To Sfax (154 km) & Sousse, To Kasserine

As you drive up from Sbeïtla town, the first evidence of the site is the **Arch of Diocletian** which formed part of the old walls to the south of the site. You start your visit opposite the museum going into the Byzantine quarter where there are remains of three forts/dwellings constructed of materials taken from older buildings. The nearby **Byzantine church** is dedicated to Saints Gervais, Protais and Tryphon; and there are **baths** badly damaged and partially rebuilt with a mosaic of fish and crustaceans and an oil press (originally there were two presses and a windmill).

Turning right, down the street taking you towards the central area is a large cistern which supplied water to the city, the rainwater being perhaps supplemented by an underground canal. Close by are the remains of a large **public baths**, with hot and cold rooms and a geometric mosaic decorating the room dedicated to exercise. You can see evidence of the hypocaust underfloor heating system very clearly. The nearby fountain is one of three public fountains dating from the fourth century.

To the right here, overlooking the Oued Sbeïtla, is the **theatre**, a shadow of its glorious past. The tiers are in ruins but the orchestra pit is clearly visible as are the colonnades round the stage. Worth the detour if only for the magnificent view over the dry river course. Turn back to the baths and head towards the main temples. The **Church of St Servus**, built in the courtyard of a Roman temple, is on your right. Now only four columns of stone mark the corners of the building.

The capitol Head along the street originally with shops on either side to the magnificent capitol entered through the **Arch of Antonius Pius**. This gateway was built in the style of a triumphal arch and formed part of the ancient walls. This arch can be dated between 138 and 161 AD thanks to an inscription which refers to the Emperor Antonius Pius and his two adopted sons, Marcus Aurelius and Lucius Verus. The **three massive temples** which stand side by side opposite this gate, across the vast, almost square, **Forum** are assumed to be dedicated (from right to left) to Juno, Jupiter and Minerva. The central temple, accessible only by steps from the side, was the more opulent of the three. The temple of Minerva has the more elegant columns. Under the temples are cellars. The Forum, paved with huge stone slabs, is surrounded by a wall which shows evidence of several restorations. The whole complex is highly impressive, and will provide you with some superb holiday snaps. Close to the Forum is another church constructed on the site of an older building. This is in poor condition but visible are the central aisle and the two smaller side aisles separated by a double colonnade.

The Capitol at Sufetula

After H Saladin & A Merlin

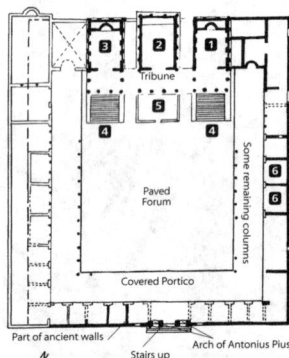

The 'episcopal group' The group of buildings to the northeast, known as the episcopal group, comprises two churches, a baptistery, a chapel and small baths. The **Basilica Bellator**, excavated in 1907 is named after a fragment of inscription found there. Measuring 34 metres by 15 metres, the building has a central nave, two side aisles and a double apse. The mosaic floor in the choir still remains. The baptistery was

1 Temple of Juno	5 Tribune
2 Temple of Jupiter	6 Large room
3 Temple of Minerva	or hall
4 Stairs up with wide steps	

0 metres 10
0 yards 11

converted into a chapel dedicated to Bishop Juncundus (fifth century) who is believed to have been martyred by the Vandals. The adjacent **Basilica Vitalis** is a later, larger building. It has five naves and double apses and like the Basilica Bellator has evidence of long occupation. A marble table decorated with biblical themes found here is now in the Bardo Museum. (The museum on the site has only a photograph).

If time and enthusiasm permit, you could explore the northwest of the site through the houses and unidentified temple to the amphitheatre and across to the much restored bridge.

The recently constructed museum at Sbeïtla is well worth a look. **Room one** contains local material from Sufetula accompanied by maps and plans. The Libyan period is represented by megalithic tombs from Djebel Selloum and Thala and by an inscription from the region of Djediliane-Rouhia to the north

The museum

Central Tunisia

Sufetula

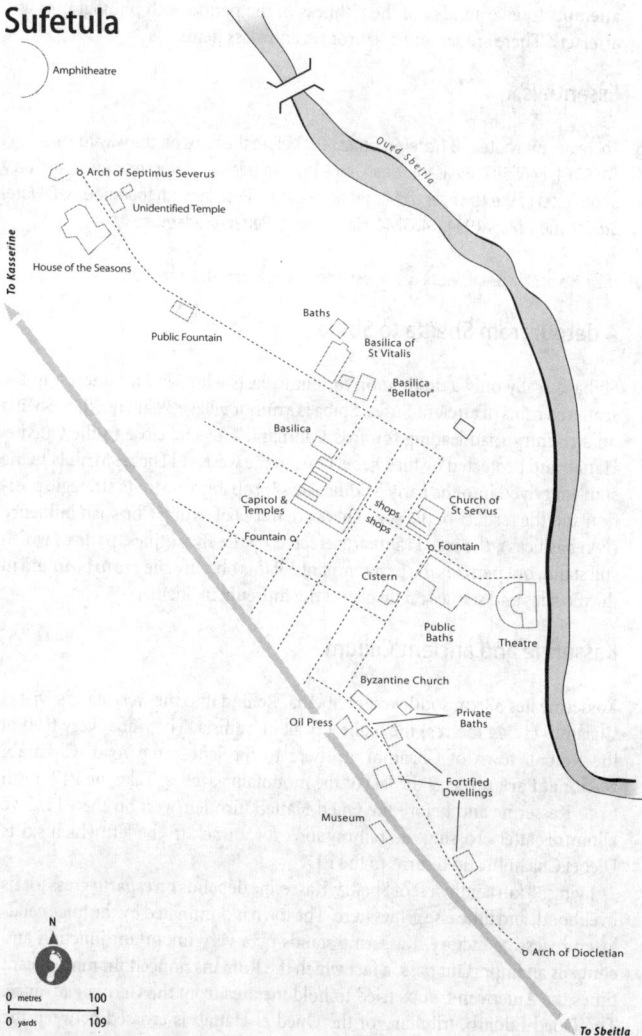

Amphitheatre

Oued Sbeitla

To Kasserine

Arch of Septimus Severus
Unidentified Temple
House of the Seasons
Baths
Public Fountain
Basilica of St Vitalis
Basilica "Bellator"
Basilica
Capitol & Temples
shops
shops
Church of St Servus
Fountain
Fountain
Cistern
Public Baths
Theatre
Byzantine Church
Oil Press
Private Baths
Fortified Dwellings
Museum
Arch of Diocletian

N

0 metres 100
0 yards 109

To Sbeitla

of Sbeïtla. The early Roman period is represented here by a series of votive and funerary steles.

In **Room 2**, you have marble statues and busts including a statue found at Sufetula, Bacchus, god of wine, accompanied by a panther from whose open mouth once came a fountain of water. From Kasserine came the statue of a female figure, perhaps Diana the huntress. Look too for the female bust from Haïdra and a smaller statue from Sbiba.

In **Rooms 3** and **4** there are two important mosaics, from Sufetula and Sbiba. The rest of the space is given over to the economic life of the region at that time which was firmly based on olive oil. There are presses, containers for carrying the oil, lamps, plates and dishes. The marble head of Mercury from Sufetula is on display here and a special piece of very ancient leather from Sbiba.

Room 5 is devoted to Christian and Byzantine exhibits. From the second century the Christian religion was expanding its influence. Here in Tunisia there were many churches, as many as six at Sufetula and Haïdra. The display attempts to give an idea of the richness of the period with photographs and artefacts. There are sarcophagi, bronze, and glass items.

Essentials

Sleeping
Phone code: 07

There are two hotels. **B** *Hotel Sufetula*, just before the ruins on the way to Kasserine, T465074, F465582. Pleasant, clean, nice pool (available to non-residents), the only good hotel in the town, and charges accordingly. Popular with tour groups. **D** *Hotel Bakini*, rue 2 Mars 1934, T465244. Has 80 beds. Perfectly adequate.

Directory There is a bank, a telephone booth, a post office and sufficient shops at Sbeïtla.

A detour from Sbeïtla to Sbiba

Colour map 2, grid A2

Sbiba is really only a destination for enthusiasts who will find interest in the scattered ruins of **ancient Sufes**. Sbiba is a minor village 39 km north of Sbeïtla on a country road leading towards Dahmani. The site, close to the Oued el Hattab and protected by the Djebel Oust to the west and Djebel Mrihila to the south survived into the early Middle Ages, probably due to its strategic position and the fertility of the soil. There are traces of strong Christian influence (two basilicas), the usual ramparts erected by the Byzantines, parts of which still stand, but perhaps the best remnants of this obscure site are to be found in the mosaics and statues on display at the museum in Sbeïtla.

Kasserine and ancient Cillium

Phone code: 07
Colour map 2, grid A2

Kasserine lies 38 km southwest of Sbeïtla. Behind it to the west stands Djebel Chaâmbi (1,544 metres) the highest peak in Tunisia. The ruins (very few) of the Roman town of Chaâmbi are here to the left of the road. **Chamâbi National Park** protects the last of the mountain gazelles. Take the P17 north from Kasserine and before the Oued Hattab turn left/west on the P13. Five kilomtres after crossing the railway look for a track to the left which skirts Djebel Chaâmbi and returns to the P17.

Lying 38 km southwest of Sbeïtla, Kasserine depends on esparto grass for its livelihood, and little else grows here. The town is dominated by the huge cellulose processing factory. Kasserine stands by a very important junction and controls an important pass, a fact which the Romans noticed. In more recent times the American troops tried to hold the area from the German advance. The Oued Eddarb, tributary of the Oued el Hattab is crossed between the junction and the town proper. There are plenty of banks, small and medium size shops, a chemist and a hospital. It is large enough to have two of the regulation issue square-faced clock monuments, confusing when getting directions, but the central monument is a hand clutching a few stalks of cereal (or is it esparto grass?). Bus and louages stop in middle of town. The main ruins are a good walk or a short taxi ride to the west, past two more interesting pieces of public art: an oversized concrete candle with garlands of apples, on a roundabout, and a Tunisian horseman, up on your left.

Cillium is the most important Roman site in this region, strategically located to control routes both north-south and east-west. Once the local nomads were subdued it was settled by the Romans. The site is on a plateau overlooking the Oued Derb, a tributary of the much larger Oued el Hattab. As the present town of Kasserine was built on the far side of the *oued* much of the site has been preserved though the necropolis was unnecessarily destroyed when the *Hotel Cillium* was built. So what is there to see? You have two mausolea which would seem to have given Kasserine its name (lit: 'the two palaces'). Next to the main road, you have the three-storey **Mausoleum of the Flavii**. On its main façade, Latinists will be able to pick out a long poem in memory of one Flavius Secondus. Further on is the distinctly ruined **Mausoleum of the Petroni**. Continuing on the road to Gafsa, just after the *Hotel Cillium*, you will see more confusing ruins (signposted), including the Triumphal Arch (third century AD) with a dedication mentioning the Colonia Cillitana from which the town gets its name. Also in the area is a dam on the Oued Derb and a number of small Byzantine forts.

Cillium was a fairly prosperous sort of place to judge from mosaics discovered there, some of which are now in the Bardo. These were found in the houses which stood about 100 metres west of the Triumphal Arch. Best known is a panel with Venus, surrounded by tritons, nereids on sea-monsters and putti on dolphins.

For those searching for finer details – the water for the baths was supplied from the *oued* and there is a small channel which leads from there to the baths . At present the water in the *oued* is some 50 metres below the channel entrance, so no baths today.

Just five kilometres south of Cillium, near the tiny settlement of Henchir el-Guellali is the remains of a reservoir, to provide water for Cillium and irrigation water for the nearby fields.

Ancient Cillium

Central Tunisia

On the Kasserine to Gafsa road

The road runs across a high and lonely plateau, with Djebel Chaâmbi to the west/right. There are stretches of Aleppo pine, and occasional settlements. Before reaching **Fériana**, you pass faint traces of ancient Thelepte and some pitched roof houses dating from colonial times. If you get stuck in Fériana try **E** *Hotel Mabrouk* T485202 near bus and louage stop. In the future, if things continue to calm in Algeria, it may be possible to cross the frontier to visit the ruins of **Tébessa**, ancient Theveste, once an important legionary base.

Further on, **Mejel ben Abbès** has some interesting pieces of recent public art, including a wild grey leopard outside the municipality, and a sort of viking ship with an eagle prow and a giant figure seven in place of a sail.

Phone code: 07

C *Hotel Cillium*, T474406. 5 km from town centre, just before the ruins en route from Kasserine, interesting 1960s circular design, 72 beds, all rooms have bath, 770 metres above sea level, splendid views, pleasant, clean hotel, pool, a/c, it is the only good

Sleeping

hotel in Kasserine (although it has seen better days) and charges accordingly. Very popular for lunches (7Dt), can organize wild boar hunting in the vicinity. **D** *Hotel de la Paix*, T471465, Av Habib Bourguiba. **D** *Hotel Pinus*, T470164. **E** *Hotel Ben Abdallah*, next to the Magasin Général. **Youth hostels** in *Kasserine*, 3 km from Kasserine centre, T470053. 92 beds, meals available.

Transport Moving on to Gafsa by louage will require changes at Fériana and Mejel Ben Abbès each leg costing about 1.5Dt. Louages also run to Tunis, Sbeïtla, and Thala, but not as far as Le Kef. Tunis is a good 4 hours 30 minutes to 5 hours drive away, Le Kef about 2 hours. The SNTRI has buses for Fahs, Gabès, Gafsa, Sbeïtla and Tunis.

Sfax   صفاقس

Phone code: 04
Colour map 2, grid B6

Sfax ought to be an entertaining Mediterranean city, and it certainly has all the right pieces: a historic old town with mosques and perfectly preserved walls, and a new town with boulevards and some fine pieces of neo-Moorish wedding cake architecture. Once upon a time it was a multi-ethnic place, with large Jewish and European communities. But multiculturalism is not the buzz-word in today's Sfax. The city, second largest in Tunisia, is entrepreneurial and energetic. There are industrial zones, phosphate processing and olive oil plants – which give a characteristic odour to the air and none of this goes to make Sfax a magnet for tourists. The médina and the new town nevertheless merit a couple of hours on your way south (or north). And if you are heading for the Kerkennah Islands, you will be getting the ferry from the port of Sfax.

Ins and outs

Getting there Sfax can be reached by rail and road. If you arrive in Tunis, and want to head south, a train down to Sfax might be a good way to start your journey. Although slower than road, it avoids a trip down the autoroute in a lunatic louage. The airport, 6 km to the southwest, T241700. Handles a few international and internal flights.

Getting around The main bus station is at the east side of Av Habib Bourguiba, in front of the train station. There is another bus station at the other end of Av Habib Bourguiba at Ibn Chabat, beyond the market, for services to Gabès and all destinations south. The train from Tunis takes 4 hours. Louages (Tunis-Sfax, slightly under 4 hours) stop on Place de la République. The airport is a 4Dt taxi ride, or take bus 14 from rue Abou Kacem Chabbi, Bab Bhar (town centre). To get to the Kerkennah boat station, head down rue Hédi Chaker, going away from the médina. Turn right the boat station is 400m on your left. If stuck in Sfax, you might want to go to the beach. Head for Chaffar, 13km away from louage station at start of route de l'Aéroport.

Bypassing Sfax Those wishing, perhaps understandably, to avoid Sfax can use the clearly signed by-pass (*rocade*) which skirts the town centre to the west. It is a dual carriageway with the main storm drain down the middle. There are numerous, slow junctions with lights. In places it is three lanes wide and the turn to Sfax generally has a filter. Try to avoid getting into the wrong lane.

Background

With a population of well over 500,000, Sfax is the second largest city in Tunisia and is an important agricultural, industrial and commercial centre. The older part of the city has, however, retained a lot of its charm. Sfax is a thriving city with a city centre composed of two distinct parts: the new town, built on a geometric pattern, and the médina, still surrounded by its original walls. It is a delight for tired visitors for it is absolutely flat.

The fact that the city is absolutely flat also explains the presence of mopeds. During the evening rush hour, thousands of these squealing mobylettes take their owners homewards. But by nine in the evening, the streets are empty. Sfax, a hard working city, goes to bed early. In the rest of Tunisia, the business sense (and the supposed avarice) of worthy Sfax's people are legendary. One of the country's biggest banks, the BIAT, is very much dominated by Sfaxians, and it is true to say that Sfaxians are active in all areas of the economy. Rumour has it that Sfax produces the best students although the cynics say that this is because that as soon as pupils show signs of failing, they are withdrawn from school to go into the family business. Solidarity across the extended family continues to play an important role in everyday life. So Sfax is not a town which offers much to the outsider. It has no pleasant eccentricities, no late night cafés or cabarets. Sure of its entrepreneurial capacities, the city of Sfax devotes itself to the making of money.

History

Sfax has its founding legend. The Arabic name of the town, Safakus, derives from the name of an Aghlabid prince's groom, Safa, and the Arabic verb *kus*, 'to cut'. 'Cut, Safa', said the prince, 'cut the cow hide into fine strips and mark out the limits of the city.' This, of course, is a repeat of the myth which recounts how Dido outsmarted the local tribes to found Carthage. More prosaically, however, it would seem that the name Safakus is of Berber origin.

There was an ancient town called Taparura on the site of present day Sfax, apparently with a strong commercial tradition. In the seventh century the town was already a trade centre, exporting olive oil to Italy. By the 10th century, Sfax declared itself an independent state, only to be conquered by Roger of Sicily in 1148. It later fought off the Venetians in 1785 and only surrendered to the French in 1881 after some fierce fighting, one of the few Tunisian towns to bother putting up any resistance at all. In the early years of French rule, the new Bab el Bhar neighbourhood replaced the old Rbat el Qibli, the Frankish and Jewish quarter A number of fine public buildings in the neo-Moorish style went up, including the town hall, with its minaret, the now demolished municipal theatre, and the Hotel des Oliviers. A modern port was completed in 1891.

Bombardment during Second World War destroyed a large part of the town centre. This created an opportunity to re-plan the city centre. Neighbourhoods close to the médina's walls were cleared. The resulting open spaces give central Sfax the feel of a Moroccan city, where new European areas were always built separately from the old médinas. The walls give a monumental feel to the boulevards.

Today, Sfax has Tunisia's second largest port. Activities include exporting phosphates, and olive oil processing continues to be a major industry. The city has expanded far beyond the original dual core. Until the mid-20th century, Sfax was surrounded by orchards and market gardens, and every wealthy Sfax family would have its *saniya* or orchard, complete with summer residence (*borj*). The city is constantly expanding. To the north of the médina, the new quarter of Sfax el Jedida is nearing completion, dominated by the minaret of the Sidi el Lakhimi mosque.

Sights

Sfax probably has enough sites to keep you busy for a half a day, without rushing. In the new town, you have the Archaeological Museum and some nice bits of architecture, in the médina, likewise, you have a museum (Dar Jellouli), and more architecture, plus some interesting atmospheres and workshops.

The **Archaeological Museum** is in the ville nouvelle on Place Hedi Chaker (in the new town), T229744, (off Avenue Habib Bourguiba), housed in the town hall building with its mock minaret. This small museum of seven rooms displays Islamic, early Christian and Roman exhibits, mostly mosaics, manuscripts and pottery. There is a third century Roman painted funeral artefact. ■ *Open 0900-1200 and 1500-1830 in summer, 1400-1730 in winter, closed Sunday, entrance 3Dt.*

The **médina** is one of the best preserved and most authentic in Tunisia. Unlike the souks of Tunis and Sousse, it is primarily aimed at the locals, who do a lot of their shopping there. Many artisans and craftsmen still work here and earn a living in a traditional way. This all makes the médina very interesting for visitors, particularly as its walls are still intact and the difference in atmosphere between the old and new cities is clear. You should try to visit the **Dar Jellouli** museum, climb up onto the battlements at the **Kasbah**, and have a look at the **Great Mosque** (from the outside).

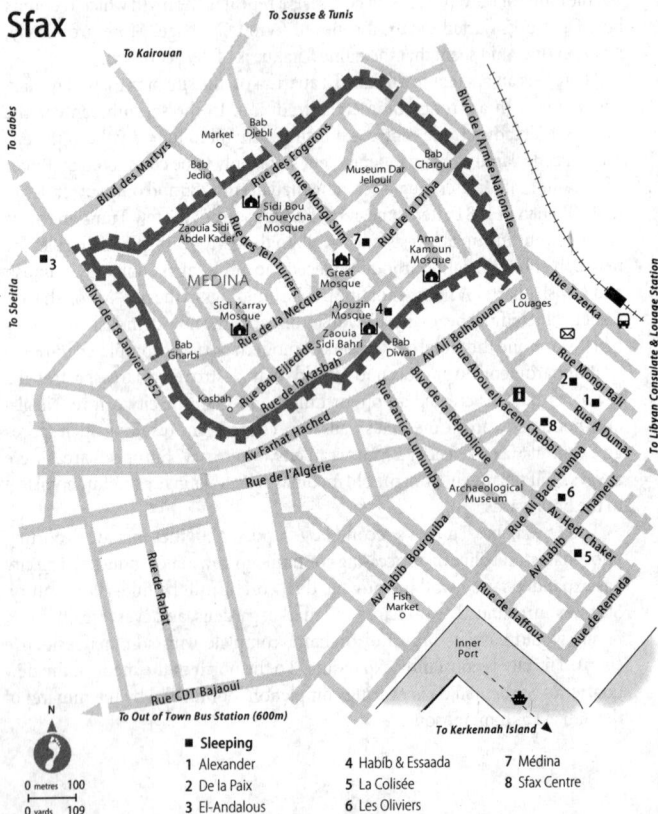

Sfax

To Sousse & Tunis
To Kairouan
To Gabès
To Sbeïtla
To Libyan Consulate & Louage Station
To Kerkennah Island
To Out of Town Bus Station (600m)

Bab Djebli
Market
Bab Jedid
Museum Dar Jellouli
Bab Chargui
Rue des Fogerons
Rue Mongi Slim
Sidi Bou Choueycha Mosque
Zaouïa Sidi Abdel Kader
Rue des Teinturiers
Rue de la Driba
Amar Kamoun Mosque
MEDINA
Great Mosque
Rue Tazerka
Sidi Karray Mosque
Rue de la Mecque
Ajouzin Mosque
Zaouïa Sidi Bahri
Louages
Bab Gharbi
Rue Bab Ejjedid
Bab Diwan
Av Ali Belhaouane
Rue Mongi Bali
Kasbah
Rue de la Kasbah
Blvd de la République
Rue A Dumas
Av Farhat Hached
Rue Patrice Lumumba
Rue Abou el Kacem Chebbi
Archaeological Museum
Rue de l'Algérie
Av Habib Bourguiba
Av Ali Bach Hamba
Av Hedi Chaker
Thameur
Rue de Rabat
Fish Market
Av Habib
Rue de Haffouz
Rue de Remada
Inner Port
Rue CDT Bajaoui
Blvd des Martyrs
Blvd de 18 Janvier 1952
Blvd de l'Armée Nationale

N
0 metres 100
0 yards 109

■ **Sleeping**
1 Alexander
2 De la Paix
3 El-Andalous
4 Habíb & Essaada
5 La Colisée
6 Les Oliviers
7 Médina
8 Sfax Centre

Central Tunisia

Very fishy

Today in Tunisia the sign of the fish is still a sign of a blessing. Look around now and see delicate pendants of gold and silver fishes in jeweller's windows, fish above shops, dangling fish rather than dangling dice in the taxi, fish-shaped amulets on babies' clothes, fish-shaped biscuits at a feast, fish motifs on mosaics and fish on every menu. After all, the fish was the symbol of early Tunisian Christians. In Sfax the bride and groom still step seven times over a large fish elaborately decorated with ribbons which is afterwards part of the wedding feast. Listen for the blessing Al hoot aleekum meaning the blessing of the fish be on you. For a country with 1,600 km of fishy coastline – why not?

Visiting the médina

Entering the médina by the main gate, **Bab Diwan**, there are two roads leading straight ahead, the rue de la Grande Mosquée to the left, and the rue Mongi Slim, on the right. You could head straight up the rue de la Grande Mosquée, and have a look at Sfax's oldest mosque, situated bang in the middle of the médina. You might catch some glimpses of the interior, closed to non-Muslims, Then continue down rue des Etoffes, which merges into rue des Teinturiers. Within the souqs, one can find everything from clothes and meat to saddles for donkeys. At the end of this street are the city walls and the rue des Forgerons (blacksmiths). Opposite is the **Bab Djebli**, a gate looking over a recently built market, where food is generally sold. This can be worth a visit. In the rue des Forgerons, artisans can be seen at work in cramped workshops. Go back in the direction you crossed the médina, but on the rue Mongi Slim. There are some fine doorways here. This street takes you back towards Bab el Diwan. Take a left onto rue de la Driba and on the left is the **Dar Jellouli Museum**.

Also of note is Place de la Kasbah, to the west of Bab Diwan. The **kasbah** itself is of no great interest, but there is a beautiful private building on the square. In the streets leading into the médina from here notice the iron grilles on the first floors of most houses. Also notable is a beautiful 17th century private house on Place Barberousse.

Médina monuments

The main gate of the médina, **Bab Diwan**, dates back to 1306. However, it was reconstructed in the 17th and 18th centuries. The last reconstruction was after the bombardments of 1943.

Dar Jellouli, T221186, is a fine city residence dating back to the 17th century and now housing the **Regional Museum of Popular Arts and Traditions** at 5 rue Sidi Ali Nour, off rue de la Driba. On the ground floor the rooms are organized around a small courtyard. Each contains well-explained life-size pictures of traditional Tunisian living. In one room is a kitchen complete with implements, in another living rooms with all the furniture and so on. On the first floor is a display of traditional clothes and jewellery. ■ *Open 0930-1630, except Monday and public holidays, entrance 2Dt.*

The **Great Mosque** was built in the late nineth century, and altered in 988 and 1035. From the outside you can have a look at the minaret, made of three superimposed square sections. There are similarities with the minaret of the Great Mosque of Kairouan. There is far more decoration, however, including horizontal bands and religious inscriptions. Unfortunately, the interior is closed to non-Muslims. As elsewhere, there is a large courtyard, which is considerably smaller than it once was, part of it having been built upon during an extension of the prayer hall. On the eastern outside façade of the mosque are some niches decorated with a tooth motif. Can the influence of the Norman dog-tooth style be detected here?

Central Tunisia

Visiting El Djem and Sfax in the 1920s

"About El Djem is no trace of the city that once sent its tens of thousands of shouting spectators to the games, that gave rise to the mighty coliseum that now alone remains. The gaunt relic stands, solitary, and native huts have nested in its broken columns and porticoes.

A little overwhelmed you turn toward Sfax – think of a city called 'Cucumber'. But cucumbers are a lordly vegetable in the East, quite worthy to name a town. Gardens spread about its walls. It is a merry town, this Cucumber, a garrison town, full of gay uniforms and their attendant brightly gowned ladies. No wonder there are beauty salons in the square, henna plantations close by, and groves of almonds for protection salves. A

garrison town where all the colourful Colonials are seen at their most resplendent. Chasseurs d'Afrique, in sky blue tunics and voluminous scarlet trousers. Swaggering Spahis with crimson capes to the ground. Black Tirailleurs from Senegal in high tarboosh and khaki – all the welter of savage tribes that serve the tri-color of France. Patrols just in from the desert mingle with their nomad friends in an irresistible jumble. Here, at his best and his worst, you may see the horse dealer and learn of the ways of that marvel, the Arab horse, for the army takes great pride in its cavalry and rightly so."

From a 1923 brochure entitled Tunisia, *produced by the French Line (Compagnie générale transatlantique).*

Essentials

Sleeping
■ on maps
Price codes:
see inside front cover
Phone code: 04

A *Hotel Sfax Centre*, Av Habib Bourguiba, T225700, F225521. 115 rooms, 8 suites, brand new, very little character, all mod cons.

B *Syphax Novotel*, route Souqra, T243333, F245226. 127 room. Recommended. 65Dt a night, low season.

C *Hotel el Andalous*, Blvd des Martyrs, T 299100, F299425. 90 a/c rooms, bar, 2 restaurants, on busy street but quiet inside and in rear rooms, free underground parking. **C** *Hotel Donia*, route de l'Aéroport, T247391, F223594. Used by tourist groups. **C** *Hotel Etoile*, 9 rue Mohamed Jamoussi T296091. West of town centre. **C** *Hotel Les Oliviers*, Av Habib Thameur, new town centre, T225188. Charming, 50 rooms, old style, currently undergoing renovation – reopening soon?

D *Hotel Alexander*, rue Alexandre Dumas, T221911. Extremely well kept, 30 rooms, clean, very good restaurant. **D** *Hotel Amine*, 40 rooms, T245601. Out of town centre on the Tunis road, on blvd du 5 août, has been recommended. **D** *La Colisée*, rue Taieb M'Hiri, T277800, F299350. 40 rooms with bath, a/c, heating, restaurant.

F *Hotel de la Paix*, rue Alexandre Dumas, T296437/221436. In new town, 30 room, pay showers, very clean. Good value next door the Hotel Alexander. **F** *Hotel El Habib*, rue Borj Ennar, T221373. In médina, 22 rooms, clean, communal showers. **F** *Hotel Essaada*, rue Borj Ennar, T220892, opposite *El Habib*, 43 beds, small, clean. Communal showers. Just about OK. **F** *Hotel Médina*, 53 rue Mongi Slim, T220354. 32 beds, in médina (not surprisingly!), small, clean, pay shower.

Youth hostel On the road to the airport, T243207, 126 beds, train station 1 km.

Eating
Expensive *Le Baghdad*, T223085. Av Farhat Hached, fine Tunisian food, if a bit expensive. Around 35Dt a head. Sfax's number 2 restaurant. *Le Corail*, T227301. Av Habib Maazoun. The top address. Very comfortable restaurant, excellent seafood,

very expensive, you could pay as much as 50Dt a head. *Le Printemps*, 55 Av Habib Bourguiba, T226973. Wide choice of French food. **Mid-range** *Chez Nous*, rue Patrice Lumumba, good choice at a good price. **Cheap** *La Renaissance*, 77 Av Hedi Chaker, T220439. Choice of fish and meat dishes, clean. There are a number of very reasonably priced eateries just inside Bab Diwan. Note that cheap restaurants are practically all closed by 1900.

For a **drink** go to Place de l'Indépendence and the surrounding streets, or to the **Cafés** médina. Recommended. is the *Café Diwan*, on the left after the main gates (Bab Diwan) following the walls. Nice terrace with views. Pleasant in the evening.

Markets Central Market on Av Habib Bourguiba; Fish market Bab Jedid to southwest **Shopping** of town; also route de Gabès/Ave Farhat Hached. Monoprix, 12 rue Abou el Kacem, open daily 0800-1900.

Fitness centre Samorail, route Sidi Mansour, near beach. **Sports**

Local Car hire: *Avis*, rue Tahar Sfar, T224605; *Budget Immeuble Taparura*, T222253; **Transport** *Europacar*, 40 rue Tahar Sfar, T226680; *Hertz*, 47 Av Habib Bourguiba, T228626; *Locar*, rue Habib Maazoun, T223738; *Mabruk Car*, 46 rue Mohammed Ali, T297064; *Rent a Car*, rue Habib Maazoun, T227738; *Solvos*, rue Remada, T229882.

Long distance Air: *Tunis Air*, 4 Av de l'Armée, opposite the Post Office, T228028, F299573; *Air France*, rue Taieb Mehiri, T224847. The airport, T241700, is about 6 km southwest on the road to Gafsa. **Train**: Information on T221999. Departures for **Tunis** (via Sousse) 0555, 1225, 1325, 1825, 0145; **Gabès** 1128, 0210; **Metlaoui** (via Gafsa) 0143. 2nd class return Sousse 7Dt plus 650 mills fee each way. Takes 2 hours. **Bus**: services for **Gabès**, **Djerba**, **Zarzis**, **Tataouine**, **Ben Ghardane** and **Tunis** leave from the bus station on Av Habib Bourguiba, by the train station. Information on T22355. All other destinations are served from the bus station at the other end of Av Habib Bourguiba. **Louages**: leave from Place de la République. **Ferry**: information on ferries for the **Kerkennah islands** can be found in the back pages of *La Presse*. Departures are evidently more frequent in summer, with first boat leaving at 0500. Winter 4 boats per day 0700-1700. Foot passengers 0.5Dt, motorbikes and cars 4Dt and the crossing lasts just over 1 hour. For further information contact Sonatrak, Av Hedi Khefacha, T222216.

Banks *STB* and *UIB*, Av Hedi Chaker. *BIAT*, rue Salem Harzallah. *BT*, Av Habib Bourguiba. *BNT*, rue **Directory** Taieb Mehiri. *UBCI* and *BS*, rue Abou el Kacem Chebbi. *BC*, Place de l'Indépendence. *STB* has automatic cash dispenser for Visa and Mastercard users. **Communications** Area code: 04. **Post Office:** large building at east end of Av Habib Bourguiba, T224722. Emergency numbers Customs: rue Mongi Bali, T229184. **Police:** rue Victor Hugo T229710. **Hospitals & medical services** Chemist: all night, *Rekik*, 25 rue Alexandre Dumas. *Kilani*, Av Habib Bourguiba, T220740. **Hospital:** *Hôpital Hedi Chaker*, route d'El Aïn, T244422. *Polyclinique Ettaoufik*, T241105. Places of worship **Catholic:** 4 rue Dag Hammarskjold, T210253, Sat at 1830 and Sun at 0930. **Tour companies & travel agents** *Bahri Travel Agency*, 32 bis Av Habib Bourguiba, T228654. *General Voyage*, Av Hedi Chaker, T221067. *Siwar Voyages*, 26 bis rue Habib Thameur, T226400. *Tourafrica*, Av Hedi Chaker, T229089. *Tunisia Line Service*, 16 rue Habib Maazoun, T296983. *Univers Tours*, Av Habib Bourguiba, T222029. **Tourist offices** The tourist information office is at Place de l'Indépendence, in a little kiosk, T224606.

Central Tunisia

The Kerkennah Islands

Phone code: 04
Colour map 2, grid B6

Little has happened in history to disturb the tranquility of the Kerkennah Islands. They are flat, planted with palm trees, and somnolent. The legend goes that they are named for the nymph Circe who had a try at keeping Greek hero Odysseus here during his Mediterranean travels. Other famous exiles on Kerkennah include Hannibal and Habib Bourguiba. There are two main islands, Gharbi (western) and Chargui (eastern), a few hotels, and rumour has it that further tourist development is on the way. Until then, the Kerkennah Islands go quietly about their business. The people are welcoming in a reticent sort of way, and you could have a pleasant few days on the archipelago, cycling, birdwatching, and splashing in the shallows. Note that Kerkennah is one of the few places on the planet where you can buy stretches of sea.

Ins and outs

Getting there Daily crossings from Sfax, 6 in summer, 4 in winter (ticket 560mills). Crossings take 45 minutes. For information contact **Sonatrak**, Av Hedi Khefacha, Sfax, T222216. Most hotels in Sfax have SNTKS timetables available, or you can look in *La Presse* (back pages). In Kerkennah the ferry lands at Sidi Youssef, at the southwestern end of Gharbi, about 20 km from the hotel zone. as you leave Sfax on the *loud* (ferry), you have a good view of the city, and you may even see some dolphins.

Getting around The two main islands are linked by a Roman causeway. A minibus service is provided and will meet the incoming ferries, though this costs more than the service bus. A bus will go directly to the hotels, so be sure to take the right one! All buses go to Remla. For El Attaya, there are a few buses a day, but they tend to stop early, so check the times. Buses for the ferries leave about an hour before ferry departure time. Times can be checked at the bus station in Remla, beside *Hotel el Jazira*. All other hotels should have this information. Otherwise, rent a bike (try the *Hotel Farhat*), especially as the islands are very flat.

Kerkennah Islands

Background and history

There are seven islands in the group with a total area of 15,000 hectares made up of 6,000 hectares of agriculture, 4,000 hectares of palm trees and the rest uncultivated salt flats. The two large inhabited islands, Gharbi to the west and Chergui to the east, lie 20 km from the mainland.

The islands are almost flat (maximum altitude 13 metres) and covered in palm trees and with many lagoons. (Birdwatchers should find something of interest). At the moment tourism is just developing with most of the hotels concentrated around the *zone des hôtels* in Sidi Frej, with a few in Remla.

The rest of the island is almost untouched, making it quite easy to 'get away from it all'. A good way to get around is to rent a bicycle from *Hotel Farhat*. Some of the beaches are difficult to get to without transport as the buses only go through the main villages. The inhabitants have the reputation of being the most hospitable in Tunisia. The people live largely off fishing and now tourism. As there are few sights on Kerkennah, activity is restricted to lying on the beach and taking life easy. In Remla it is possible to visit a carpet factory, without the anxiety of sales pressure as here they don't sell, but ship them to the mainland for retail.

At low tide it is possible to walk for several kilometres out into the sea from the islands, the water lapping round one's ankles. At high tide, the water rises up to chest height. The result of this natural feature is that the people of Kerkennah have developed unique fishing techniques. The island's men have a great reputation as skilled fishermen, being recruited by mainland fishing fleets, and people were sent to Kerkennah as apprentices to learn how to fish. When the men are out at sea, it is the women who continue fishing off the islands (and ensure that the land gets cultivated), using some unusual local methods.

Fishing on Kerkennah

Kerkennians own sections of sea. Using palm branches and fronds, they construct fences out into the water which form a sort of hedge, curving or zigzaging away from the coast. At high tide, shoals of fish swim in between hedge and beach. When the tide goes out, it becomes impossible for them to swim back, and they are stuck in the increasingly shallow water, where they take refuge in special fish-traps (*drina* in Arabic, *nasse* in French). Another fishing technique, primitive but fairly efficient, involves a team of people and a sort of floating barrier made of *dhriaâ* sea weed (*Posidonia oceanica*). The team walks slowly through the shallows, moving away from the coast, each individual pushing a floating section of twisted seaweed. The frightened fish swim back landwards between the individual fishers. A kilometre from the shore, the team turns backwards, gradually moving closer together. The fish are trapped in the shallows. Fishing for octopus is another activity, with the tentacular beasts unwisely taking up residence overnight in specially planted pot traps. Once upon a time, sponge fishing was important on the islands.

Fishing on Kerkennah has suffered considerably since the early 1990s. Pollution and competition from other regions are the main culprits. In the early 1990s, pollution, possibly caused by phosphate processing in Sfax and Gabès, had severe side effects, leading to a sharp reduction in the fish stock. It is also thought that the Cap Bon fishing fleet, under severe competition from Italian boats illegally fishing with more sophisticated methods in Tunisian waters, has begun to fish further south, in areas traditionally fished by Kerkennah's people. Modern trawling methods are harmful. The heavy weights used on trawler nets rake up the sea bottom, destroying the weed, source of food for the fish.

If you want to go out fishing, many fishermen, for a small fee, will take a passenger with them. It is also possible to rent a *felouka* (traditional fishing boat)

Central Tunisia

with a captain and go either for a day trip round part of the island and probably a quiet lunch out at sea. ■ *Prices between 12Dt to 15Dt for a half-day per person. Information for these trips at either El Attaya, a small fishing village in the north of the island, or at one of the two larger hotels, the Grand Hotel and the Hotel Farhat, in Sidi Frej.*

Sights

Kerkennah has little in terms of sights. Up at the northeastern end of Chergui, there used to be a small museum commemorating Bourguiba's escape by *loud* (traditional fishing boat) to Libya in 1945. You can see the shack he hid in and his boat. The *Festival des Sirènes* takes place in August.

Birdwatching Keen birdwatchers will find some points of interest on Kerkennah. It has a unique sub-species, Thekla's crested lark, the *cochevis de Thekla* in French. There are lots of great grey shrikes but no birds of prey. It is also a place to observe migrant cranes (Fr: *grue cendrée*). Whereas this bird is practically never seen out of shallow water, on Kerkennah it can be seen among the palm groves.

Essentials

Sleeping
Many hotels are closed in winter and those that remain open are often poorly heated.

C *Appart-Hotel Aziz*, Sidi Frej, T 215884. Self-catering an option. **C** *Grand Hotel*, Sidi Frej, T281266, F281485. Large hotel, 114 rooms on 2 floors, half with sea view, a/c dining room, pool, tennis, organized watersports, cycle hire, nightclub, beach restaurant, open all year. Has the best stretch of beach at Sidi Frej. **C** *Hotel Farhat*, Sidi Frej, T281240, F281237. Next to *Grand Hotel*, 308 beds, well decorated, pleasant, pool, tennis, beach virtually non-existent. **D** *Hotel Cercina*, Sidi Frej, T281228, F281262. Very good, beach, 70 beds, half rooms have bath, most rooms are bungalows, some have sea view, restaurant has typical Kerkennian fish specialities. **F** *Hotel el Jazira*, Remla, T281058. Well kept, small, 24 rooms, communal bath/toilet, bar, good restaurant open all year but cold in winter. Try also the unclassified *Aziz*, 88 beds, T259405, F259404; and *Kastil*, 32 beds, T281212. **Youth hostel** Remla, just behind the stadium, T281148, 80 beds, meals available, family room. **Camping** El Attaya.

Eating **Mid-range**: *Restaurant La Sirène* T481118, by the bank in Remla, very good fish and seafood, alcohol available, shaded terrace. **Cheap**: *Le Régal*, at El Attaya, north of Remla, by the harbour, very good simple, cheap food, welcoming owner. Try the special Kerkennah sauce of tomato and garlic which is excellent on shellfish.

Sports All watersports including windsurfing and octopus fishing, horse and camel riding and tennis. Try a camel ride from Sidi Frej to the ruined tower at Borj el Hissar.

Yachting El Attaya has berths for 10 yachts, minimum-maximum draft 3-4m.

Transport **Ferry**: office on Av Hedi Khefacha, T223615, frequent ferries summer 0600-2000 about every 2 hours and winter 0700-1700 4 return journeys. Car 3.5Dt, passengers 0.5Dt, motorbike 1Dt.

Northwards from Sfax to El Djem

This road, a journey of 64 km, runs through farming land, The small settle- *Phone code: 04* ments providing ample petrol stations, local cafés and the occasional baker *Colour map 2, grid A5* and small shop. **El Hencha** is an exception, a larger linear settlement with a small industrial zone, bricks, cement as well as the usual metalwork and car repair outfits. There are more cafés, one or two of better quality and small stores. The station is two kilometres to the west. Here and there, as the road rises, you have views across vast olive groves.

Banks *UIB* is in centre of Remla, beside *Hotel el Jazira.* **Hospital & medical services** Chemist: **Directory** *Behiri* in centre of Remla, T281074. **Hospital:** Remla, T281119. **Communications** Post Office: T281000. Centre of Remla. There are a few other branches, the closest to the hotel zone being in Ouled Kacem. **Useful addresses** Police: in Remla and El Attaya, T281053. Maritime police, Mellita, T223615.

Routes southwards: Sfax to Gabès

Heading south of Sfax on the P1, you enter road-movie territory. You pass *Colour map 2, grid B5* through an industrial zone with a tentacular phosphate works covering the land between the road and the coast. Then it is flat landscape all the way to Gabès. There is little dual carriageway, so if driving, you will be faced with thundering lorries and louage drivers with suicidal tendencies.

The saltpans of the region immediately south of Sfax are of interest for bird-watchers. At 10 km south of Sfax, the Roman ruins of **Thaenae** near present day Thyna, fairly well signposted, are of minor interest. There is a sign at the south end of Thyna pointing to the land between the coast and the road. Follow the track through a small agricultural area to the coast beside the lighthouse.

Thaenae was at the coastal end of the line marking the limit between Numidian **Ruins of** and Roman territories. It has suffered from thoughtless pillage and the **Thaenae** necropoli on the town's periphery were 'turned over' for profit. Later excavations produced evidence of a huge square enclosure having a side over two kilometres long with semicircular towers. A baths was discovered nearer the coast, and it was suggested that the bathing facilities, originally of individual ownership, had been changed into public use. Mosaics and painted frescoes are recorded. The Baths of the Months excavated in 1961 had walls several metres high, roofing with groin and barrel vaults. There were some notewor-thy mosaics but to cheer the workers a treasure hoard of gold coins was discov-ered dating back to the third century AD. The better objects were taken to the Bardo and to Sfax Museum where they are on display.

Maharès

The roadside town of Maharès, 24 km south of Sfax, has a reputation for public *Phone code: 04* art. From the four-lane main street (Avenue Habib Bourguiba, as usual) metal *Colour map 2, grid B5* fun structures can be seen on the beach-side gardens. On a long car journey, children will appreciate a stop to have a look at the reconstructed skeleton of a small whale in the sculpture promenade near the harbour. There are numer-ous petrol stations (Mobile, Shell, Esso), repairs of cars, tyre repairs, metal-workers, mini-supermarket, chemists, and bakers. A new mosque is set back at the south end of town while the older mosque is right on the road.

Market day is Monday and the carpets for sale in large quantities are laid out along the harbour wall. All very colourful. Should you have time for a swim, prefer the beach at Chafaar, 15mins drive away (head north out of Mahares, turn right after level crossing, follow the track).

Sleeping   D *Hotel Marzouk*, Av Habib Bourguiba, T290261, F290866. 20 rms, restaurant, pool, clean, good restaurant for evening meals, café, snacks all day, pleasant management. D *Hotel Tamaris*, Av Habib Bourguiba, T290950, F290494. Next to *Hotel Marzouk*, 60 beds, popular with safari tour groups. E *Hotel Younga*, T290334. 20 beds.

Eating   Not much going on here try the *Caféteria du Festival* for a break from driving, or eat at the *Hotel Younga*.

Transport   Public transport for Sfax leaves from next to the Hotel Younga, and there is a train station inland, with two trains a day for destinations north and Gabès, and one train to Gafsa / Metlaoui.

Skhira

Phone code: 04
Colour map 2, grid C4

Skhira, 45 km down the P1, (and 42 km north of Gabès), is southern Tunisia's largest oil terminal. The town is a major junction heading north, you have the choice of the P1 for Sfax and the coast, or the inland P2 direct to Kairouan. Skhira has good cafés both sides of road dealing with tour coaches, petrol, car repairs, bakers. The agriculture here consists of beans and moderate grazing land. Perhaps there is more money to be made out of selling food and drink to passing lorry drivers.

Southwestern Tunisia

7

Southwestern Tunisia

In southwestern Tunisia, the landscapes are arid and often spectacular. There are canyons and a vast low-lying region of salt lakes, the **Chott el Djerid**. Beyond this is the colossal Sahara desert. At oasis towns with poetic names like **Tozeur**, **Nefta** and **Douz**, civilization's hold over nature becomes distinctly shaky. Once upon a time, life depended solely on the palm tree and pack animals, whose survival was possible thanks to painstakingly managed spring-water. From the palm tree, the region around Tozeur takes its name, 'El Djerid', 'palm' in Arabic. Like the Nefzaoua, to the south of the Chott el Djerid, this area is best visited in spring or autumn, when the great vault of the desert sky is clear and temperatures are lower. (In high summer, temperatures of 50°C are not uncommon.) The 'date harvest' finishes in early winter, and there is a festival in Douz. Today, southwest Tunisia is easily visited by car and public transport. (There are also some ersatz 'safaris' by four-wheel drive running from the main coastal resorts.) But the peace of the desert is best experienced by travelling by camel. From remoter settlements like **Zaâfrane** it is sometimes possible to head off with a local guide to explore the white dunes of the **Grand Erg Oriental**.

The Djerid and the Nefzaoua

Heading down from the Sahel, Gafsa is the first oasis town you come across. With its backdrop of arid hills, it provides a foretaste of the barren landscapes to the southwest. The Djerid and the Nefzaoua regions have a range of spectacular scenery a few hours travel by road from the crowded towns of the Sahel. The two areas are divided by a vast expanse of salt lake, the **Chott el Djerid** and the **Chott el Fedjaj**. The Djerid, to the north, centres on the important oasis town of **Tozeur**, strategically located at the western end of the Djebel Cherb and between two main seasonal salt lakes or chotts, the vast Chott el Djerid (to the south) and the Chott el Gharsa. A regional capital with an expanding tourist industry, Tozeur sits 22 km east of **Nefta**, important as a centre for the cult of Islamic saints until the mid-20th century. Here again there is an old oasis, set in a deep natural hollow surrounded by cliffs.

Hill villages & phosphate towns North of Tozeur and Nefta lies the **Chott el Gharsa**, and within an easy day trip distance of Tozeur (60 km north), close to the border with Algeria, is a hilly area, just west of the Djebel en Negueb, with the much touted mountain oases of **Chebika**, **Tamerza** and **Midès**. From Chebika there are superb views westwards. The old village of Tamerza has been abandoned but there is an upmarket hotel. Midès is perhaps the most attractive of the three, its abandoned village overlooking a deep gorge. The oasis is still very much under cultivation. You can continue on east from the hill oases to the phosphate towns of **Redeyef** and **Moularès**, joining the main GP3 road at Metlaoui, from where it is 42 km east to Gafsa and 50 km southwest to Tozeur.

Douz & dune desert In the old days, crossing the Chott el Djerid was a risky business. Today the 86 km from Degache, close to Tozeur, to Kebili are fully tarmacked road. There is little risk of tourist buses being swallowed up in the great salt waste, as was the case for caravans in earlier times. South of the Djerid is the **Nefzaoua**. **Kebili** is the regional capital, **Douz** is the second largest town, scene of an annual Festival of the Desert in late December. The east-west range of the **Djebel Tebaga** separates the Chott el Fedjaj from the arid lands to the south. In the Nefzaoua, you are at the eastern edge of the **Grand Erg Oriental**, the true dune desert of heroic films. The oases appear as tiny spots of green in a white sand waste – a 'leopard skin' in the eyes of the region's poets.

Changing lifestyles Both the Djerid and the Nefzaoua have felt the impact of the modern world. The process began back in Protectorate days when the French made Kebili an important base. Today, the pure nomad lifestyle is very much a thing of the past. The attractions of a settled life are too great and the government has made efforts to stabilize the nomads and enable them to enjoy the benefits of modernity. Although you can still see old-style oasis cultivation with vegetables and fruit trees growing in the shade of great palms, the region has vast new agri-business oases, notably near Nefta and at Rejim Maâtoug, where the succulent Deglet en Nour, 'finger of light', dates are cultivated for export.

In the 1990s tourism arrived in a big way with new *zones touristiques* at Douz, Nefta and Tozeur. The expensive Saharan hotels have found it difficult to break even, however, as visitors come in overnight rather than stay a week. Nevertheless, the tourist is now very much part of the local scene. At the main sights, you are as likely to see large numbers of visitors, decked out in mock-Touareg dress, as you are to see real nomad tents. The desert lifestyle of the M'razig and the Adhara, perfectly adapted to a difficult environment, did not survive the 20th century unadulterated, but it could yet provide the basis for a new, ecologically friendly tourism based in the local communities. For the moment, four-wheel drive safaris are the main 'product' on offer.

Gafsa   قفصة

Gafsa may well be your first taste of a southern Tunisian town. Not quite the desert, it nevertheless has the midday somnolence of a desert settlement. You approach Gafsa from the northeast via a long straight road shaded with eucalyptus, followed by a view of the deep course of the oued Baïech. The modern town centre has an undistinguished Eastern Bloc feel to it, but the médina with its narrow streets and doorways feels suitably ancient, though decay and demolition have set in. However, there is the superbly restored Dar Loungo to visit, and the piscines romaines. André Gide in crumpled linen suit can be imagined watching the local lads diving from a great height into the ancient waters if restoration work on the pools has been completed.

Phone code: 06
Colour map 2, grid B2
population 60,000

Ins and outs

Gafsa is very much a meeting of the ways, and coming from Sfax, Kairouan, Kasserine or Gabès, you will no doubt pass through Gafsa on your way to and from the Djerid. The train station is 3 km east of town in the new suburb of Gafsa Gare. Buses and louages come into the main square, in front of *Hotel Gafsa*. If you are driving, you are 369 km from Tunis, 149 km from Gabès, and 93 km from Tozeur. Once you get beyond Kairouan, the P3 is a quiet road. Note, however, that after heavy rains, there may be

Getting there

Southwestern Tunisia

Gafsa

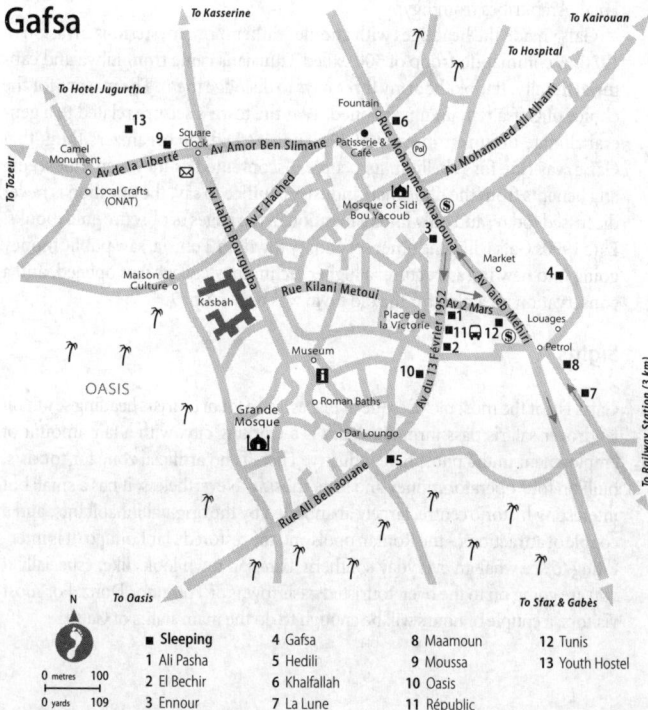

To Kasserine
To Kairouan
To Hospital
To Hotel Jugurtha
To Tozeur

Fountain
Square Clock
Camel Monument
Av Amor Ben Slimane
Av de la Liberté
Patisserie & Café
Local Crafts (ONAT)
Av Habib Bourguiba
Av F Hached
Av Mohammed Khadouna
Av Mohammed Ali Alhami
Pol
Mosque of Sidi Bou Yacoub
Maison de Culture
Kasbah
Rue Kilani Metoui
Market
Place de la Victoire
Av du 13 Février 1952
Av Tajeb Mehiri
Louages
Petrol
Museum
OASIS
Grande Mosque
Roman Baths
Dar Loungo
Rue Ali Belhaouane
To Railway Station (3 km)
To Oasis
To Sfax & Gabès

N
0 metres 100
0 yards 109

■ Sleeping			
1 Ali Pasha	4 Gafsa	8 Maamoun	12 Tunis
2 El Bechir	5 Hedili	9 Moussa	13 Youth Hostel
3 Ennour	6 Khalfallah	10 Oasis	
	7 La Lune	11 République	

flooding on the plain around Bir el Hafey (30 km northeast of the P3/P13 junction), which could mean a detour, approaching Gafsa via Sbeïtla, Kasserine and Feriana, on the P13 and P15 over higher plateau lands.

Getting around Shared taxis to and from the train station, terminate in the town centre next to the *Hotel Maamoun*.

History and background

Gafsa (Roman Capsa), the most northerly of the oasis towns, is also the chief town of the southern steppe region. It stands at the junction of the P3, P14 and P15, the crossroads between southwestern Tunisia and the central plains. Gafsa has a long history going back to prehistoric times. A Proto-Mediterranean people left traces of a civilization referred to as Capsian by archaeologists. The main find in the Gafsa area has been mounds of waste, containing a lot of snailshells – hence the French technical term *escargotière* for this kind of prehistoric remains. Capsian Stone Age tools can be seen in the Gafsa Museum.

Gafsa comes into written history with the Romans. Capsa was an important town on the road linking the III Augustan Legion's base at Haïdra to Gabès on the coast. Although some way back from the southern frontier or *limes* controlling tribal movements, it had a role as regional tax collection centre. Under the Byzantines, the fortifications were developed and Capsa was renamed Felicissima Justiniana. For a short while it was capital of the province of Byzacium. It fell to the invading Arabs in 668. Any trivia quiz on Gafsa should include a question on its 12th century inhabitants: Arab historian El Idrissi reports that they spoke a Berbero-Latin, and that many were still Christian. This is surprising, given the supposed impact of the 11th century invasion by Hilali Arab tribes from Egypt.

Gafsa made the headlines with another rather more mysterious invasion in 1980. A commando troop of 300 exiled Tunisians came from Libya and captured the city. It took the army three days to dislodge them. The reasons for the choice of Gafsa remain unexplained. Was the town's seizure related to a general climate of unrest in early-1980s Tunisia? Did the organizers think that Gafsa was ripe for rebellion, its people discontented as they were not seeing any benefits from the phosphate industry? Suffice to say, the question is never discussed today, and only finds a mention in the pages of obscure guidebooks. Late 1990s Gafsa, like the other secondary towns in Tunisia, saw public money going into new infrastructure: a higher technology college was opened, and a conservation area plan for the old town was drawn up.

Sights

Gafsa is not the most picturesque of places and a lot of tourists heading south on landrover safaris pass through. Gafsa is a working city, with a fair amount of employment in the phosphate industry. There is no artificial zone for tourists, built on tour operator money and state subsidy. Nevertheless, it has a small but interesting historic centre, largely abandoned by the original inhabitants, and a couple of attractions – the Roman pools and the restored Dar Loungo. It is interesting to see what an everyday southern Tunisian town looks like, especially if you are going on to the over-touristed oasis towns of Tozeur or Douz. For most visitors, a couple of hours will be enough to do the main sights of Gafsa.

If you just wander in the old quarter, you will eventually come across most of **Old quarter** the historic sights of Gafsa. Proceeding in a more orderly manner, you could head down the Avenue Ali Belhaouane, passing the *Hotel de l'Oasis* on your left. Second turn right will lead you to Dar Loungo, on your left. Continue down the street and you will come to Roman pools, a museum, and the arcades of Dar el Bey. The Kasbah is just beyond, off the Avenue Habib Bourguiba.

The restored **Dar Loungo** gives you an idea of what a patrician residence of the 18th/19th centuries looked like. There is an entrance passage, lined with seating, and no doubt the clients and tenant farmers of the master of the house would wait here to be received. Inside there is a large courtyard, and some splendid apartments upstairs. There are good views over the town from the roof terrace. Dar Loungo may become open to the public with tickets; for the moment, though, you need to hope that there is a warden around to let you in. (*Où est le gardien ? / wayn el assas ?* you could ask.)

To reach the **Piscines Romaines** (Roman baths) turn left out of Dar Loungo. They are some 50 metres away and consist of two deep rectangular pools. Nearby there is an ancient but non too salubrious *hammam*. ■ *Open 0800-1200 and 1500-1900 in summer, 1930-1630 in winter, closed Monday, fee 1Dt*. These pools are the only major building to have survived from Roman Capsa. In the summer, youths jump from the side into the water. The diving used to be even more spectacular when there was a particularly tall palm tree overlooking the pools. Watch the diving, but remember that a tip may well be expected. Young Gafsans have played this game since the dawn of tourism. The square surrounding the pools has recently been carefully redeveloped and has a small café. The tourist information office and the small museum are also here. At the time of writing, there were works underway to improve the pools. The water level had fallen, so maybe they will be returned to their former glory.

The **Museum** of Gafsa has the sort of local artefacts you would expect, along with two absolutely superb mosaics of sporting activities. The better one shows an athletics tournament from the start to the prize-giving ceremony. ■ *Open 0930-1630, closed Monday*.

Near to the pools, on Avenue Habib Bourguiba, is the **Kasbah**, which from a distance looks like a splendid fortress. It was built by the Hafsids, on the foundations of the usual Byzantine fortress. Under the energetic Ottoman beys, it was partly rebuilt in 1663: artillery bastions were added, and the curtain walls adapted to firearms. There were further major works in the 19th century. Unfortunately, in 1943, ammunition stored in the Kasbah exploded, destroying one side. The **Palais de Justice**, which fits into part of the site, was built in 1963. Note that under the walls of the Kasbah, there is a tiny ancient hammam.

The oasis starts just beyond the Kasbah, and has over 100,000 palm trees and **Oasis** numerous pomegranate and some citrus trees. Follow the extension of rue Ali Belhaouane into the oasis. This is a pleasant ride/walk with numerous side turnings. The direct road through the oasis emerges at the P3 about seven km west of town. The dates are of poor quality, and the oasis is better known for its fruit trees and vines. The pistachios and apricots are held to be among the best in Tunisia.

Southwestern Tunisia

Essentials

Sleeping
■ *on map*
Price codes:
see inside front cover
Phone code: 06

B *Hotel Jugurtha*, 4 km west of town, in the oasis of Sidi Ahmed Zarroug which is now a built up suburb of Gafsa, T221467 or 221315. An impressive site, 78 rooms, pool, tennis, unfortunate approach via used car/bus dump, still closed for refurbishment, may be upgraded when completed.

C *Hotel Maamoun*, Av Taïeb Mehiri, T222433, F226490. Central, modern, relatively nondescript building, 46 a/c rooms, pool, restaurant used by tour companies, indifferent service but all modcons. Very handy for louage station.

D *Hotel Gafsa*, rue Ahmed Snoussi, street behind cinema parallel to rue Jamel Abdel Nasser, and close to market and louage station, T224000, F224747. Modern, very communist East European, a/c. Restaurant opposite.

E *Khalfallah*, Av Taïeb Mehiri, by police station, T221468. Clean, on a noisy road, rather expensive for what is provided. **E** *La Lune*, rue Jamel Abdel Nasser, T222212. South out of town on left beyond *Maamoun*. Has a good reputation. **E** *Hotel Moussa*, Av de la Liberté, T223333. Clean and cheerful, a little out of town which makes it quieter.

F *Ennour*, Av du 13 Février 1952, T220620. Very cheap, outside showers, close to bus station. **F** *Hotel de la République*, Av Ali Belhouane, T221807. Quite new, clean, 20 rooms, probably the best of the cheap hotels, sign-posted in Arabic only. Other hotels worth trying are: **F** *Ali Pasha*, 4 rue Ali Belhaouane, T220231, which is more than adequate. **F** *El Bechir*, 40 rue Ali Belhaouane, T223239. Reported as 'cosy'. Rooms on the small side. **F** *Tunis*, Av 2 Mars, T221660. Overlooking place du 7 novembre and very near to bus station, perhaps a bit too near. Also try *Hotel de l'Oasis*, on Av Ali Belhaouane, T222338. Handy for the bus station.

Youth hostel 2 km from station, T220268. Kitchen, meals provided, 56 beds, north side of Av de la Liberté, beyond *Hotel Moussa*.

Eating
Mid-range *Restaurant Semiramis*, rue Ahmed Senoussi, T221009. By *Hotel Gafsa*, one of the best places in town for French and Tunisian cooking, a bit expensive. **Cheap** *Restaurant de Carthage* on the main square. Basic Tunisian fare. Try also the Restaurant du Paradis, on Av Taïeb Mehiri.

Entertainment
Hammam There is a clean hammam on rue Hassouna Ismaïl, women till late afternoon, men from late afternoon till 2000.

Shopping
Excellent fruit shops on south side of Av 2 Mars, fruit is beautifully arranged.

Handicrafts The craft centre is clearly signposted at the north end of Av Habib Bourguiba. This is a school set up by the ONAT to train people in the art of carpet making. Make a visit to the workshops. The best buys are the striped and geometrically patterned woollen blankets and woollen rugs and shawls.

Transport
Bus the bus station is by the main square, just off the Av du 2 mars. Information on T221587. Frequent departures to **Tozeur** and **Nefta**, also buses to **Kairouan, Sfax, Sousse, Gabès** and **Sbeitla. Tunis** 0730, 1030, 1230 (4Dt). **Louages** on the Av Abou el Kacem Chabbi. (Turn left at the *Hotel Mamoun* coming from the town centre.) **Train** The station is rather inconveniently situated 3 km outside the town in the suburb of Gafsa Gare, along the road to Gabès. One train daily at 2056 goes on to Tunis (via Sfax and Sousse) and 1 to Metlaoui at 0526.

Banks *BDS* is on the main square, under *Hotel Gafsa*. *STB* nearby. **Communications** Post Office: Av Habib Bourguiba north of the kasbah. **Places of worship** Catholic: Chez les Soeurs, Quartier Doualy, T223785. Ring for details of services. **Tourist offices** The tourist information office is by Piscines Romaines at the end of Av Habib Bourguiba, T221644. Has limited written information, but very willing to talk, open 0900-1700.

Gafsa to Sfax

The road south out of Gafsa crosses the **Oued Sidi Aïch** and turns northeast. *Colour map 2, grid B2-6* The road to Tunis continues in this direction while that to Sfax takes a right turn. Just at this junction is the **wildlife park**, very popular in the evening and at weekends. Visitors at other times may find the gates firmly locked. Here gazelle and ostriches roam in enclosures. There is a small café.

The road runs adjacent to the railway for much of the journey. Around **Zannouch** is a richer, government settlement area with expanses of plastic greenhouses and wells at intervals for the irrigation. This availability of water encourages plasticulture which is not perhaps the most economic return for such an expensive commodity.

There are small settlements as far as the eye can see, not villages but individual hamlets. Esparto grass grows on the poorer land.

Sened Gare has grown up round the railway station. The small *oued* which runs through the village is dammed for small-scale irrigation. Djebel Majoura, 874 metres, stands to the north. Old **Sened** is a Berber village about 10 km south of here along the track to the west of the station. It nestles into the north slope of Djebel Biada (1,163 metres) into which caves have been cut. Some of the houses make use of caves and are semi-troglodyte in nature. At about three km east of Senned Gare, where change of governorate is indicated, look out for railway lines which are raised well above the level of the road. These could cost a tyre or two.

At slightly greater altitudes, where the soil is thinner and less fertile, there is no cultivation. This is an amazing contrast to the abundant green of the cereals. Then down to another fertile basin and the regular arrangement of olive groves. New olive orchards have been planted, as yet these are too young to produce a harvest. There are a few small settlements on the road – don't run short of petrol – few buses and few louages.

Maknassy, 80 km from Gafsa, is the first settlement of size. The main street, Avenue Habib Bourguiba, is a dual carriageway and the main square is Place

The Djerid

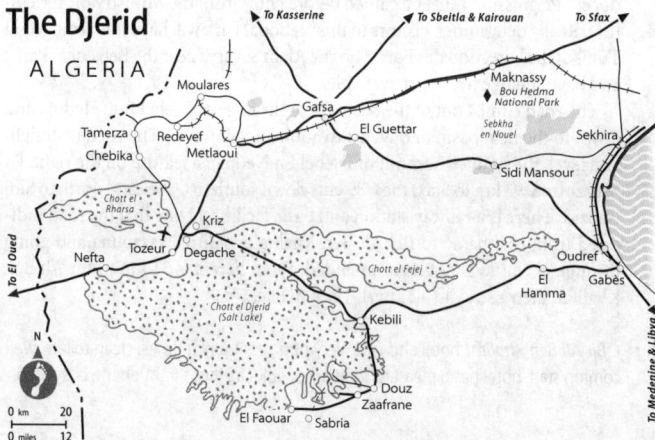

Mirages – illusions in the desert

A mirage is a type of optical illusion, caused by the refraction (bending) of rays of light as they pass through air layers of varying temperatures and densities. The most common mirage occurs in the desert where what appears to be a distant pool of water, perhaps surrounded by palm trees, turns out, to the disappointment of the thirsty traveller, to be only another area of dry sand.

The rays of light that come directly to the eye show the palm trees in their correct position. The rays of light that travel through the warmer, less dense air travel faster as they meet less resistance and change their direction. They bend nearer to the ground, but are assumed to have come directly to the eye so the brain records the trees and the blue sky as reflections in a pool of water.

The rays are real, just misinterpreted, thus a mirage can be photographed; but that does not, alas, make the shimmering 'water' available to quench the thirst.

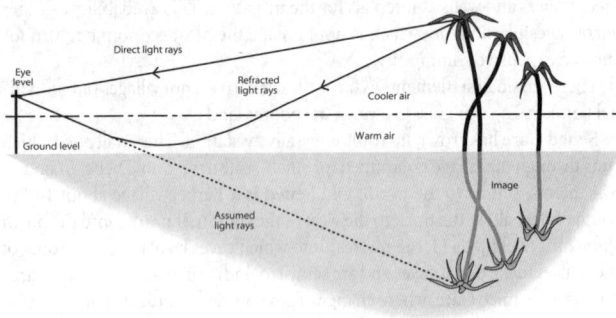

des Martyrs complete with blue square-faced clock, chemist, post office and petrol. There is a bus station with an unpleasant café and at the east end a training school for those employed in tourism. The C83, of good quality road, goes north from here to Sidi Bouzid, and a track suitable only for walkers or mountain bikes goes south round Djebel Bou Hedma to Bou Hedma National Park, though this is better accessed from Gafsa via the C124.

Bou Hedma National Park is an area of pre-desert steppe, where Dorcas gazelles, sabre-horned oryx, Addax antelopes and ostriches have been reintroduced. Permission must be gained before entry from the Ministry of Agriculture. Really determined visitors to this National Park will have this arranged in Tunis at the Direction des Forêts on rue Alain Savary (near the Belvédère Park) and have suitable transport available.

The road climbs out of the basin on to the edge of Djebel Bou Hedma and down to the next basin of olive cultivation and almonds. The road is straight and level, the pointed summit of Djebel En Nedjilet a feature on the right. At **Mezzouna**, 93 km to Sfax, the C89 cuts down south to Gabès and north to Sidi Bouzid. There is a railway station and basic facilities. Note that the road indicated from Maknassy to Bir Ali Ben Khelifa avoiding Mazzouna and going through el Ghriss is not recommended. From here it is 31 km to Bir Ali Ben Khalifat, then a straight 42 km run east to Sfax.

Sleeping C *Bir Ali Ben Khalifat* hotel and café, very popular at lunch times, clean toilets, welcoming staff, hotel has 8 pleasant rooms, not quiet as this is right on the busy road.

Gafsa to Gabès

This journey along the P15 is 146 km. The first recommended stop is the oasis of **Lalla**, clearly signposted to the east of the road, five km out of Gafsa. Turn left after crossing the railway track. This thriving oasis community is very pleasant here after the bustle of Gafsa and very popular at weekends. **Lares**, 18 km from the Gafsa turn-off south on a good surfaced road, is much quieter, its oasis planted with a mixture of palm, olives, figs, almond trees and prickly pear hedges. The road through the oasis rejoins the main road after 5-6 km.

Colour map 2, grid C2-4

The C124 goes off east at **El Guettar**, taking advantage of the lower land between the Djebel Orbata and the Djebel Ank, and is a road of variable quality. There is a turn-off for the isolated village of **Sakket** 13 km from El Guettar. **Djebel Bou Hedma National Park** is 63 km from Gafsa.

El Guettar is a small settlement of about 15,000 inhabitants on the foothills of the Djebel Orbata, 1,165 metres. It owes its existence, and evidence shows there has been a settlement here some thousands of years, to the unusual (for Tunisia) system of water supply to the oasis. The water source was within rock layers in the foothills and was lead by gravity to the fields of the oasis. At one time 28 *khattara* were recorded providing between 5-6 litres of water per second, and this supply was shared between the fields on a six hourly basis. Unfortunately these do not function today, though in places remnants of the shafts to the underground channel can be distinguished.

El Guettar

At 37 km out of Gafsa along the P15, there is a turning south to Kebili (68 km) across the Chott el Fedjadj. It is wise to check this road (C103) is open after the winter rains, some parts are very low-lying; 56 km across the Chott you reach the tiny oasis of **Stiftimia**.

Gafsa to Kasserine

In Gafsa, at the junction with the square-faced clock, take the road north to Kasserine. At **Barroucka**, on the left, set well back off the road, is a huge ornate mosque. The road runs close to the Oued el Kebir, with open plain used as grazing land on the east and Djebel Bou Ramli to the southwest, reaching a height of 1,128 metres. There are a few settlements on the road. At 32 km from Gafsa you cross the Oued el Kebir which is very very wide. It is hard to imagine such a valley full of rushing water. The only settlement of any size is **Maajen Bel Abbès**, which has developed due to its position by the railway station. It has some spectacular pieces of public art, including a galley with eagle prow and a leaping leopard.

Colour map 2, grid A/B2

The road and rail now run parallel all the way north to **Fériana** (72 km from Gafsa). Alterations to the centre of this long narrow settlement may make some improvement but it has little to recommend it. All services are available, plenty of petrol and small shops selling basic supplies.

F *Hotel Mabrouk*, T485202, in town centre, directly opposite bus station and adjacent to louages.

Sleeping

There are Roman ruins on the west side of the road just south of Thélepte; the ruins and the village have the same name. There is not much to see except ruined walls of dressed stone. Thélepte itself has a splendid air of decay. Some of the original bungalows remain, and with their pitched roofs would not look out of place in a French suburb. From Fériana to Kasserine there are very few settlements, an expanse of sparse grazing land, cereal, fruit trees and olive plantations. Djebel Chaâmbi, Tunisia's highest mountain, can be seen to the west.

Fériana to Kasserine

Southwestern Tunisia

☞ *Water technology of yesteryear*

Tunisia, like other North African countries, benefited in the past from the introduction of the khattara or foggara (or mkeil as they are known locally in south Tunisia), which is an underground water channel that taps the water table in alluvial fans of hill areas. The technology was brought probably from as far away as eastern Iran or western Afghanistan in the mediaeval period, though Roman systems with well-engineered and large diameter channels also exist in Libya. Water can be transported to fields and villages over considerable distances. The mkeil in south Tunisia was formed by a narrow diameter inclined channel, with 20-30 metre deep vertical shafts spaced at 15-20 metre intervals for the removal of detritus during building or maintenance and for ventilation afterwards (see illustration). In the villages in El Guettar, located on the P15 between Gabès and Gafsa, the remnants of the mkeil can still be seen but are sadly not in current use.

The mkeil illustrates the virtues of traditional technology. It has a generally long life cycle. Once it has been completed, it will keep flowing, given adequate maintenance. It will run continuously day and night and, except in a few cases, throughout the four seasons. The mkeil needs no power other than that provided by gravity. The mkeil is a friendly influence on the water table.

Despite these major advantages, the mkeil and its traces, as with so many other kinds of traditional technologies, are now at great risk of complete extinction.

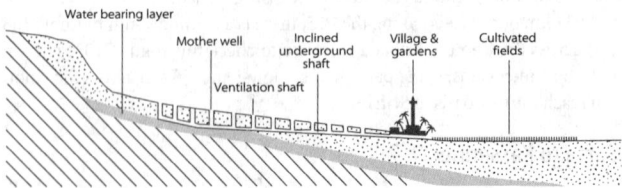

Water bearing layer — Mother well — Inclined underground shaft — Ventilation shaft — Village & gardens — Cultivated fields

Into the Djerid: from Gafsa to Tozeur via Metlaoui

Colour map 2, grid B2-C1
From the square-faced clock at the centre of Gafsa, take the road west to Tozeur, 93 km to the southwest. A junction to the north should indicate *Hotel Jugurtha*. At seven km from town, the road from the oasis joins on the left. The route is pleasant, lined with stands of young eucalyptus trees. After crossing the Oued el Melah (Salty River), the major *oued* of the region, the railway accompanies the road and the *djebel* on the right and gradually closes in until Metlaoui is reached, 42 km from Gafsa.

Metlaoui
Phone code: 06
Thanks to the phosphate industry, the village of Metlaoui has grown into a minor regional centre. Unless you chose to stop, you will see little more than ribbon development along the busy tree-lined main road. Elsewhere, in the shadow of conveyor belts and industrial buildings, the visitor can spot French-built staff houses with their pitched roofs. After the hospital, over the railway line up the Moularès road, there is the **National Mining Museum** (*Musée national des mines*), recently revamped, housing various fossils and prehistoric remains.

By the railway station, there is a restaurant and a number of small cafés used by tour buses and safari four-wheel drive vehicles. There is a large mosque with a striking bright green dome at the centre, and all the usual facilities, including petrol and chemists. The bus station and louages are in the town centre. At the square-face clock is the junction with the road running north to the mining town of **Moularés** and the **hill oasis towns**, as well as to the station from which the Red Lizard train departs daily at 1100 except Monday. Here too you will find the STB bank, a chemist, the police and *Restaurant Ellafi*.

Sleeping D *Hotel Ennacim* (lit: 'the breeze') is situated out of the town centre on the Tozeur side, T240271. Bar.

Eating At the *Hotel Ennacim* or the *Restaurant Ellafi*.

Transport Louages: run out of a station up the Moulares road. **Train**: the station is to the east of the town. One train daily to **Tunis** (via Gafsa and Sfax) at 1915; **Redeyef** at 1555; **Moularés** at 1505.

Once through the town the junction west to the **Seldja Gorges** is clearly signed by the Mobil petrol station. At this junction is *Café Seldja*, busy when the tourist coaches arrive.

Seldja Gorges

The gorges, with their sandstone cliffs rising to 200 metres in places, are best seen from the train to Moulares and Redeyef which departs daily from Metlaoui. This is the former royal train, now used for touristic purposes and called the **Lézard rouge**, the 'red lizard'. It comes complete with the original fittings which on the whole have seen better days. ■ *It does the journey in about two hours and leaves daily at 1100, except Monday, 20Dt. A fascinating trip, which gets a bit full on some days. Information on T/F06-241469.* The train does not run if there aren't enough people.

Alternatively, take an ordinary train which is advertised to leave at 1505 to Moulares and Redeyef at 1555. This is much cheaper but less appealing. Both trains return to Metlaoui at 1830.

You can also access the Gorges by car. Leave Metlaoui on the P3 heading for Tozeur, and take the track right across the plain for five km until you reach a narrow defile called the *coup de sabre*, the 'Sword cut'. Walk through into the Gorges. There are two narrow tunnels. It is best to do this in the morning before the temperature gets too high. Note, however, that this is a potentially dangerous activity. You do not want to be caught in a tunnel by a speeding phosphate train. The Oued Seldja is also subject to flash floods, so the gorges are best left alone after heavy rains.

Continuing south to Tozeur, the P3 is a well surfaced, straight road. Watch your speed, however, and do not overtake on a continuous line. The Garde nationale will be watching just around the corner. This region is still used by the nomads and their black tents and grazing dromedaries can on occasion be seen out on the barren plain.

Southwestern Tunisia

Tozeur توزر

Phone code: 06
Colour map 4, grid A1

Capital of the Djerid, Tozeur is everybody's ideal oasis. There are thousands of palm trees, and a chance to see a disappearing rural way of life in action. In the narrow streets of the old Ouled el Hadaf neighbourhood, the houses have patterned façades carefully executed in narrow mustard brick. Many of the women still wear an all-enveloping black wrap, decorated with a white band. Tourism has come to stay in Tozeur: landrover safaris from the coastal resorts and vast hotels overlook the oasis. This is not Marrakech, however. It is all rather low key and few stay more than a couple of nights, but Tozeur is a good base from which to explore the region. With a hire car or by public transport you can reach Nefta and the hill oases, and at El Hamma du Djerid you can enjoy a bath with the locals at the hot springs.

Ins and outs

Getting there Tozeur is accessible by air and road. You can also get the overnight train from Tunis and Sfax as far as Metlaoui, whence you complete the remaining 93 km journey by bus or louage. The bus station on Av Farhat Hached is used by buses from Tunis, Nefta, Gafsa and Kebili. The louage station is opposite.

Getting around The airport is 4 km out of town, and there will generally be taxis available for the short run to the nearby *zone touristique*. Bus and louage stations are 800m from the Hotel Splendid, other cheap hotels being nearer. Turn left out of the bus station onto Av Farhat Hached, then right onto Av Bourguiba.

The town is easily explored on foot. The central area (Av Bourguiba plus old quarter Ouled el Hadef) is linked to the upmarket tourist hotels by the 1,500m long Av Chabbi, along which is a sprinkling of other hotels.

History and background

Human settlement at Tozeur goes back at least to Roman times. The small oasis settlement of Bled el Haddar has a minaret built on Roman foundations, and is thought to be the site of Roman Tusuros. Tozeur was conquered by the Muslim Berber dynasties which came out of Morocco in the early Middle Ages. It was the key town in a region known as Kastiliya, perhaps from the number of abandoned Roman forts or *castella*. Tozeur basically remained an independent statelet, until brought under Hafsid rule in the later Middle Ages. The village was dominated by rivalry between different groups, which often erupted into open feuding. In the 18th and 19th centuries, Tozeur was the final stop on the bey's annual tax-gathering expedition or *mahalla*.

Under the Protectorate, Tozeur remained an independent minded sort of place. Charles Lallemand, propagandist for French rule in the late 1800s, noted that there was little interest in modern education, unlike the rest of Tunisia where there was a huge demand. Traditional forms of learning remained strong in Tozeur, and it is hardly surprising that the town produced Abou Kacem Chabbi, romantic poet who wrote of love and freedom and was adopted as Tunisia's national bard after independence. (His portrait can be seen on the 30Dt banknotes.)

Traditionally, the oasis was the mainstay of Tozeur life. Dates were the main **Managing the** crop, with fruit trees and vegetables being grown in the shade of the palms. A **oasis** carefully worked-out system ensured irrigation water for all. Written by one Ibn Chabbat back in the 13th century, the regulations were designed to avoid waste of the oasis' scarcest resource, water. Straight from the spring, water was channelled into the palm groves to irrigate the trees and market gardens. Water flowed along hollowed out palm trunks and out through holes which were blocked with clay when irrigation time allowed was over. Time was calculated by means of a *kadouss*, a water container with a hole in it which took just over an hour to empty. Each landowner would be allotted so many *kadouss* units.

With the growing need for water to support more modern lifestyles, the water table has fallen in the oasis, and water is pumped up from deep underground. Thanks to the increasing depth of the boreholes, the area of palms under cultivation has been expanded dramatically. The new *périmètres irrigués* (see the Ibn Chabbat area south of the Chott el Gharsa) are planted with high quality date palms. The traditional cultivation and labour systems have given way to advanced agri-business.

Tozeur is now well established as the political and commercial centre of the **Tourism in** Djerid. With its new international airport it is starting to develop a significant **Tozeur** tourist industry, and hotel developers benefit from considerable state subsidies and preferential loans. Of course tourist development has a social dimension, too. Bringing large numbers of visitors to Tozeur, both local and international, is a way of showing the conservative oasis people that they are part of Tunisia's republic and its values, that women can actually go around unveiled outside films.

The difficulty for the hotels is to try and build a clientèle prepared to stay more than a couple of nights. Many of Tozeur's visitors at present just stay overnight as part of a four-wheel drive excursion round the South. To attract people with money and taste for the exotic, *à la Marrakech*, Tozeur will need some proper restaurants and smaller, classier hotels. The development of more intelligent, less tacky attractions would also be a step in the right direction. A Jardin des 5 Continents is planned, basically a themed oasis garden designed by top French landscapers. Developments like this will help Tozeur build a reputation as something more than just a stopover.

Sights

To cover the sights of Tozeur, you will probably need little more than a day. Two days would allow you to really take in the atmosphere of the oasis, while with three days, you could do a trip to the other main Djerid town of Nefta, 25 minutes down the road towards Algeria. Another day trip, easily done with a hire car, takes you up to the hill oases (*les oasis de montagne*) of Chebika, Tamerza and Midès. Four days in Tozeur, and you will really be unwinding, your body clock slowing to the rhythm of oasis life.

Tozeur is a three-street sort of place. The Avenue Farhat Hached (bus and **The town** louage station) takes traffic through the town. The Avenue Abou Kacem Chabbi runs along the edge of the oasis, and has some of the older tourist hotels. The Avenue Habib Bourguiba, with its arcades and market, links the two. Here are the main cheap hotels and restaurants, and male Tozeuris come out for their evening paseo here. In Ramadhan there is some mild animation on the market place.

Central Tozeur is rendered exotic by local **brick work** on the arcades, strung here and there with colourful klims – and by the town council's recent improvement scheme. There are large onion-shaped wrought iron grills along Avenue Abou Kacem Chabbi, and some moderately dramatic pieces of **public art**, not least of which is an oversized fountain type structure on the market place. Irrigation expert Ibn Chabbat, water-saver extraordinary, must be turning in his grave.

The Ouled el Hadaf neighbourhood

North of the Avenue Habib Bourguiba is the Ouled el Hadaf neighbourhood. (Turn left off Av Bourguiba before the market into Avenue Ibn Chabbat.) Down this street on the right, follow rue de Kairouan (signposted to the museum) which passes under an arch. This is the oldest part of the town with many archways and intriguing side streets. Some of the houses date back to the 14th century. They are decorated with geometric patterns executed in earthen bricks in an elaborate decorative style particular to this region. Notice that few houses have windows on to the street, light for the rooms coming from a central courtyard. The doors are decorated with nails and three door knockers. The explanation (for tourists?) is that the one on the left is for women, on the right for men and the lowest for children. Each knocker emits a different sound, that is deeper for men, enabling residents to recognize who is at the door. Sounds fair enough.

The small **Museum of Popular Arts and Traditions** in rue de Kairouan has some interesting displays, housed in the former Zaouia of Sidi Aissa. Everyday objects are on view, giving insight into daily life in Tozeur. There are diverse objects, including traditional clothes for celebrations, jewellery, oil lamps, cooking implements and weapons. Also on show are manuscripts written by Ibn Chabbat in the 13th century, setting out the complex water distribution system in the oasis. In the courtyard you can see one of the doors with the three knockers. The museum, though simple, has a certain charm, and shouldn't be missed. It certainly tells you more about a vanishing way of life than the ersatz Dar Cheraït. ◾ *Open 0900-1200 and 1500-1800 in summer, closes 1700 in winter. Closed Monday. Entrance 1Dt includes services of guide.*

The Oasis

Tozeur's raison d'être is of course the oasis. It is beautifully fresh in summer, due to the large number of irrigation canals fed by more than 200 springs. Get there by following the signposts to the 'Jardin du Paradis' or take the road leading to the Belvédère, on the left after the Tourist Office. If the peace of the oasis is to be appreciated the well advertised tour by *calèche* is to be avoided. Problems with water supply and neglect have resulted in the loss of some of the palm trees.

One oasis activity is to take a dip in one of the springs. Ras el Aïn is well known, a spring emerging at 30°C at the foot of a low buff. (The water flow may have fallen off considerably with hotel development). Water from the springs is subsequently diverted for irrigation. The oasis definitely merits exploration: vegetation is surprisingly dense and the palm groves large enough to enable you to escape the crowds.

The name the **Belvédère** suggests a large cliff overlooking the oasis. In fact, you are dealing with a couple of large boulders, which do however give you some nice views over the palms and the arid plain and salt flats beyond. At night the Belvédère boulders may be illuminated to provide a view for those in the *zone touristique* hotels. The road to the Belvédère (three km) goes through one of the most picturesque parts of the oasis. It is a long, but nevertheless very pleasant, walk starting on the left along Avenue Abou Kacem Chabbi, beyond the Tourist Office, and following the oued.

'Come explore the oasis, my gazelle'

Metaphor for grace and beauty in classical Arabic poetry, symbol of speed on the tailfins of national carrier Tunisair, the gazelle is a rare animal in North Africa today. The main species is the Dorcas gazelle, rim in Arabic, easily distinguished by the black stripe along its flank, separating fawn back from pale underbelly. Within living memory, the gazelle could be found in the central steppes. The spread of settlement and cultivation, and above all hunting, have limited its range to the southern wastes. The gazelle is easily frightened, taking flight at the approach of humans. It is also known for its ability to shake off hunters, who then get lost in the desert emptiness without capturing their prey. Hence the unattainable, graceful gazelle becomes a metaphor for female beauty. Courtly Arab poets often refer to the eyes, neck, nose and gait of the gazelle in descriptions of

exquisite concubines. (The beautiful tourist may be addressed with a bonjour, la gazelle.) From gazelle horns, as from ram's horns, fish tails and pointed pieces of red coral, emanates protective force. Today, the hunting of the Dorcas gazelle is strictly controlled. Once upon a time, the nomads would rear gazelles. Captured young enough, the gazelle fawn becomes very tame.

Today, there are two national parks east of Gafsa: Djebel Bou Hedma, south of Meknassy, and Hadaj, where an attempt is being made to reintroduce the Dorcas gazelle into an unusual micro-environment, the last surviving area of natural savanah in Tunisia. Also included in the reintroduction programme are the oryx and addax antelopes, along with the ostrich. Gazelle can also be seen at the Orbata Zoo outside Gafsa on the Tunis road.

Tozeur has three establishments with caged animals, **Le Jardin du Paradis**, the **Zoo du désert** and the **Zoo de Tijani** (once a snake farm). *Le Jardin du Paradis* is through the oasis (about three km), following the well signposted road which starts just before the *Hotel Continental*. (The *Zoo du désert* is just next door.) The *Zoo de Tijani* is near the old train station. At the Jardin du Paradis, the camel may perform, swigging coke straight from the bottle. They also do some unique natural syrups. Flavours include pistachio, rose and pomegranate. Next to the Jardin is the *Zoo du désert* (open 0800 till dusk, entry 1Dt), with examples of desert animals and reptiles including snakes and scorpions. Beasts in both places are kept trapped in minute cages. Hell for animals, basically, in the gardens of Paradise. ■ *Open 0800 till dusk, entry 1Dt.*

Zoos

Dar Cherait Museum

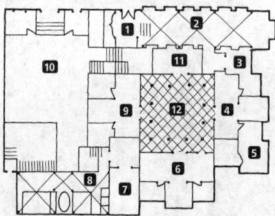

1 Entrance	7 Koranic school
2 Reception hall	8 Hamman
3 Wiseman's chamber	9 Ladies' chamber
4 Bey's chamber	10 Art gallery
5 Kitchen	11 Glassware room
6 Bridal chamber	12 Courtyard

At the end of the Av Abou Kacem Chabbi, the road veers to the right. The *zone touristique* begins here, and on your left is the **Dar Cherait Museum**. Dar Cherait is easy to find: look for the groups of parked tour coaches just beyond on the left or the tourist-trap shops on the opposite side of the road. This private museum is located in a mock-up of an upper-crust Tunis house, a sort of cross between Dar Lasram and Dar Ben Abdallah, the Museum of Popular Arts and Traditions in Tunis. The displays are clearly inspired by those at Dar Ben Abdallah, and there are

Heritage sights

areas set up as kitchens, living rooms and even a *hammam*. There are some very flashy pieces of Damascus furniture with mother-of-pearl inlay, and some highly decorative fire-arms. There is also a small collection of modern Tunisian painting. ■ *Open 0800-2400. Entrance 3Dt. Photography fee 1.5Dt, video recorder 10Dt.*

The display rooms are located round a spacious central courtyard, complete with star-shaped fountain and an L-shaped hallway that opens on to a grand staircase. Grand houses in Tunisia's main cities had a number of vestibules, the greater the family's importance, the greater their number. Suppliers and tradesmen never progressed beyond the first, distant relatives would reach the second, but only very close friends and members of the family would reach the last which opened out on to the patio. Of the display rooms, the old-fashioned kitchen is of particular interest. Kitchens of this kind, with wood or charcoal used as a source of heat, were common 50 years ago. The red-copper utensils, each with a special role, were made in Kairouan.

Tozeur

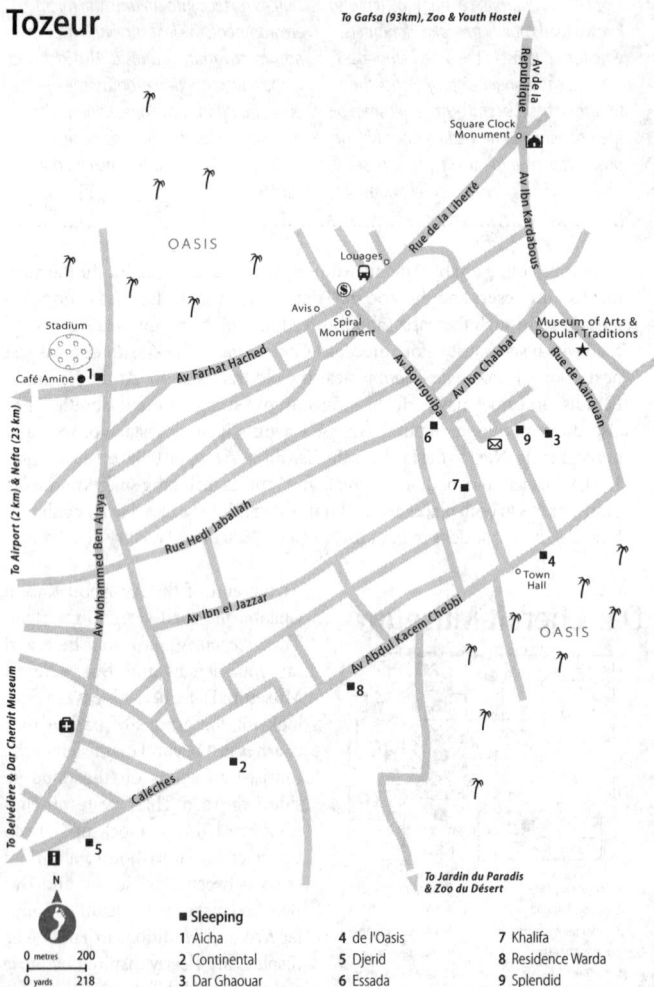

Sleeping

1 Aicha	4 de l'Oasis	7 Khalifa
2 Continental	5 Djerid	8 Residence Warda
3 Dar Ghaouar	6 Essada	9 Splendid

In addition to the main museum area, Dar Cherait has some Disneyfied attractions, including a tacky Arabian Nights grotto and a 3,000 years of Tunisian history experience. Love it or hate it, nowhere else in Tunisia offers such a concentration of processed heritage. It is disappointing, however, that the same effort has not been put into presenting the culture and history of the Djerid region.

Essentials

In Tozeur, there is cheap accommodation in the town centre or along the rue Abou Kacem Chabbi, or something altogether more plush in the recent *zone touristique*. Unfortunately for the budget traveller, the amount of over-elaborate accommodation far exceeds the basic.

Sleeping
Phone code: 06

Zone touristique A *Hotel Abou Nawas*, T452700, F452686. One of the leading hotels in the Abou Nawas chain. **A** *Hotel Dar Cherait*, T454888, F452399. Too big to be intimate, but tacky decoration adds a certain charm. Styles itself as Tozeur's premier address. **A** *Hotel Palm Beach*, T453111, F453911. Has neither beach nor that many palms for an oasis hotel. An upscale establishment, nevertheless, with entrance fountain decorated by artist Rachid Koreïchi. Impeccable. Highly recommended if you have the funds.

B *Hotel Basma*, T452488, F452799. **B** *Hotel El Hafsi*, past the Tourist Office, T452966, F451577, very pleasant, restaurant, pool. A good standard maintained. **B** *Hotel Ksar Jerid*, T454357, F454515. One of the newest *route touristique* hotels. All the usual facilities, including organized excursions. **B** *Hotel Ksar Rouge*, T454933, F453163. One of the best appointed *route touristique* hotels, rather more tasteful than most. A hotel built on 3 levels with views over the oasis. Few palm trees, however. Indoor and outdoor pools, tennis courts. A good address if there is a special seasonal offer. Managed by Eldorador. **B** *Hotel Palmyre*, T451588. Has a fine pool with palm trees planted round the edge.

C *Hotel Phedra*, T452185, F452799. Yet another route touristique special. **C** *Hotel Ras el Aïn*, T452003, F452189. For a while this was Club Med territory. Pleasant grounds with lots of green, next to the oasis.

Town centre and around C *Hotel Continental*, Av Abou Kacem Chabbi, F452109, 150 rooms, 1970s hotel, part of the Fourati Hotels group, which must have been something in its day. The pool is surrounded by palms, and the back of the hotel abuts onto the oasis. Could be a fine place, but rundown and awaiting refurbishment. Less expensive than *l'Oasis*. **C** *Hotel de l'Oasis*, on Av Habib Bourguiba, T450522, 125 a/c rooms, popular with tour groups. A good address. Clean and well-managed. Small pool.

D *Hotel Dar Ghaouar*, rue de Kairouan, T452782, F452666, beside *Hotel Splendid*, opened 1993. Despite ugly entrance and reception, a good cheapish address. Chiefly famed for its bar. Large terrace area round pool. Clean, a/c. **D** *Hotel El Djerid*, Av Abou Kacem Chabbi, T450488, F451160, has definitely known better days, pool, 50 rooms, clean, slightly over-priced. May be closed for refurbishment.

E *Hotel Aïcha*, rue Farhat Hached, T450988, F452873, some rooms with bath and a/c. Handily located 300m from louage and bus station. **E** *Hotel Splendid*, behind the central market, near the Post Office, T450053, extremely faded charm, requires some attention, clean, most rooms with bath, pool, restaurant. **E** *Résidence Warda*, T450597. Off Av Abou Kacem Chabbi, just before road to oasis. Not particularly attractive, but cheap. Simple, very clean rooms, very welcoming, dry your laundry on the roof.

Southwestern Tunisia

F *Résidence Niffer*, Bab el Hawa, T460555/460610, F461900, on the square at the bus station end of Av Habib Bourguiba. New in late 1998. Clean and simple, although Av Farhat Hached facing rooms may be noisy. Best of the cheapies and only 300m from bus/louage station. **F** *Hotel Essaâda*, Av Habib Bourguiba, opposite the market, T450097, very simple, noisy, communal bath/toilets, 1Dt for a hot shower.

Youth hostel Av de la République, close to the station, T450235/450213, 47 beds.

Camping At Degache, 10 km north of Tozeur on the C106. *Bedouin Camping*, down the track opposite the piscine municipale, clean facilities, food available, shady sites. 5Dt for 2 people, 1 car and 1 tent – rates pro rata. *Camping les Beaux Rêves* – turn left at Tourist office into the palmery.

Eating Tozeur's non-too-exciting restaurants are all on or around Av Habib Bourguiba. The entrepreneur who does an upscale restaurant here will find the field open.

Mid-range *Restaurant Diamanta*, on Av Abou Kacem Chabbi. The usual traditional fare. *Restaurant Le Petit Prince*, signposted off Av Abou Kacem Chabbi, near Hotel Oasis. Given the lack of competition, this passes for a good restaurant. Fairly pleasant surroundings. In need of an upscale place to dine, you might also check to see if there is a restaurant in the *Dar Cheraït* museum complex.

Cheap *Restaurant de la République*, in an arcade a few metres off Av Habib Bourguiba, good standard fare. *Restaurant du Paradis*, by the *Hotel Essaada*, off Av Habib Bourguiba, very good, cheap, a few pleasant tables outside. *Restaurant du Soleil*, Av Abou Kacem Chabbi, slightly more upmarket than the Av Bourguiba eateries.

Entertainment **Hammam** 1 minute from *Hotel Essaâda*. Signposted.

Shopping In season, go for the fresh dates. If you are Tunis-based and can arrange transport, there is a small workshop doing palm-branch furniture on the Av Abou Kacem Chabbi.

Sports **Hot air ballooning** *Aeroasis Club* offers a trip in a floating balloon every day of the year, weather permitting. Trips last about 2 ½ hours and are a very peaceful way to see the Sahara. The club has 3 balloons and can cater for 15-18 people at a time. Time your trip to coincide with the sunrise, early morning or sunset (remembering to include something warm to wear). Too little or too much wind and extreme heat prevent the programme going ahead, for safety reasons. Expect to pay about 85Dt and be as flexible as possible in your arrangements, T452361. (**NB** At time of writing, it seemed that the balloon company might eventually cease activity.) **Sand yachting** On the Chott el Djerid is organized by *Hotel El Jerid*. The best season is from November to May after which it is too hot.

Transport **Local Car hire**: *Avis* and *Car Tours*, 3 Av Farhat Hached, T453547; *Europacar*, Av Abou Kacem Chabbi, T450119; *Hertz*, Av Farhat Hached, T/F450214.

Long distance Air: *Tunis Air*, Av Farhat Hached, T452127; at the airport, T450388. The airport is 4 km along the road to Nefta, T450345. Flights to **Tunis**, Monday, Tuesday, Thursday, Saturday and Sunday 0615; **Djerba** (30Dt), Thursday and Saturday 0710; **Monastir**, Tuesday 0710; **Brussels**, Tuesday 0710; **Lyon**, Thursday 0840; **Paris**, Monday 0930 and Friday 1625; **Zurich**, Saturday 0710. There are seasonal changes, always check. **Bus**: frequent buses to **Tunis**, **Nefta**, **Gafsa** and **Kebili**. A few buses a day to **Gabès**, **Kairouan** and the north. Information on T451557. **Louages**: opposite the bus station. Louages have destinations marked only in Arabic, ask for your destination. Be early at

The Talisman

The 'evil eye' is a powerful force in the local societies of North Africa. It is believed that certain people have the power to damage their victims, sometimes inadvertently. Even a camera can be considered as an alien agent carrying an evil eye – so only take photographs of country people where they are comfortable with the idea and be exceptionally careful in showing a camera at weddings and above all funerals. Envy too is a component of the evil eye and most conversations where any praise of a person or object is concerned will include a tabark allah ('blessing of God') as protection against the evil spirits that surround human kind. Likely victims of the evil eye are the young, females and the weak. Vulnerability to it is seen to be worst in marriage, pregnancy and childbirth, so that women in particular must shelter themselves from the evil eye. Uttering the name of Allah is a good defence against the evil eye. Alternatively amulets are used, this practice originating from the wearing of quotations from the Koran written onto strips of cloth which were bound into a leather case, which was then strapped to the arm. The amulet developed as a form in its own right, made of beads, pearls, horn or stone brought back from a pilgrimage. Amulets also have the power to heal as well as to protect against the occult.

The Romans too were keen to fend off the effects of the evil eye and incorporated in the mosaics at the threshold of their dwellings, 'good' components to fight off the 'evil'. The mosaic from Moknine and now in the museum at Sousse shows the 'good' fish and snake keeping an 'evil' eye in bounds.

For Tunisians particular talismans are the hand of Fatima, the five fingers known as the khamsa, and the fish symbol, which is regarded as very effective as a protection for women and new-born infants.

In contemporary North Africa, medicine, superstition and ornament combine to give a wonderful array of amulets and decorations worn for both everyday and specific use.

---

the stop and be sharp, as locals with less luggage slip quickly into the seats. Plenty every day to Kebili, none direct to Chebika, go via Redeyef (or hitchhike).

Banks *STB* and *BDS* on Av Habib Bourguiba, *BNT* and *BIAT* on Av Farhat Hached. *STB* has **Directory** automatic cash dispenser (dinars) for Visa and Mastercard holders. **Communications Post Office:** on the main square off Av Habib Bourguiba. **Medical services Chemists:** on Av Abou Kacem Chabbi, T450491. Av Farhat Hached, T450370. Av Habib Bourguiba, T450153. **Hospital:** *Hôpital Régional de Tozeur*, Cité de l'Hôpital, T450400. **Tour companies** Most of these are to be found on Av Farhat Hached going out towards the airport. From the junction with Av Habib Bourguiba, they are in order on the right: *Tozeur Voyages*, T452439, F451440. *Cartours*, T450547, F451077. *Tunis Air* on the right beyond the stadium, then on the left *Meheri Voyages*, T450387, F451211. *Passion Voyages*. *Etoile du Sud*, T451055. *Carthage Tours*, T541300. *Europ Tours*. In addition there is *Abdelmoula Voyages*, route de Degache, T451130, and *Voyages Chaabane*, Av Abou Kacem Chabbi, T451011. **Tourist offices** The tourist information office is *ONTT*, Av Abou Kacem Chabbi, close to *Hotel Jerid*, T450503. Organizes camel trips from Tozeur. There is an official price list for all excursions. *Pension Warda* and *Hotel de l'Oasis* offer four-wheel drive tours to Nefta, Tamerza and Seldja Gorge. **Useful addresses** Police: T450126, 1 km down road to Gafsa.

Tozeur to the hill oasis via Metlaoui

The much-advertised *oasis de montagne* provides a wonderful day's excursion   *Colour map 4, grid A1* for those with own transport. (For those without, there are plenty of four-wheel drive excursions.) **Chebika**, **Tamerza** and **Midès** are at some of the most beautiful sites in the Tunisian south, and if you have time, should not be missed. An ideal circuit would be anti-clockwise from Tozeur via Metlaoui,

Southwestern Tunisia

giving you some fantastic views and getting most of the boring driving out of the way first. Total distance: 185 km. Accommodation on this route is extremely limited, there being only two hotels in the oases, both at Tamerza: one upmarket (the *Tamerza Palace*), and the basic *Les Cascades*.

Leave Tozeur on the GP3 heading northeast for **Metlaoui**, where you turn left at the junction with the square-faced clock for Moulares. The area to the north of town is like a moonscape. Spin-offs from the phosphate industry include piles of dark gritty material, huge lorries, and dust. Driving here is dangerous, as the lorry drivers must be on piece-work and few give consideration to other road travellers. There is also much heavy industrial plant being moved. The road runs adjacent to the conveyor belt for a while, interesting but not scenic, and then winds up slowly into the *djebel*. The Michelin map has a green line on this road to indicate a scenic route, which is only part of the story. The road surface is poor in parts.

At the top, after 16 km of grime, everything changes. Turn left to Moulares going directly west through barren plain with Djebel Bou Ramli to the north, Djebel Mrata (948 metres) and Algeria directly ahead. **Moulares** means 'mother of the bride'. The settlement grew up thanks to the phosphate industry, and today includes a collection of government buildings, small shops and petrol stations. Phosphate wagons trundle along the railway line running through the middle of town. A few palm trees struggle to brighten the environment. From Moulares to Redeyef is 18 km. There is a bypass round **Redeyef** which means you miss seeing the bus station and the regulation issue square-faced clock.

After Redeyef, the road gets more interesting. Although the road surface is quite rough, there is very little traffic apart from tourist four-wheel drives and the occasional Peugeot pickup truck. This road crosses many *oueds* and the engineering is erratic. At times the dip down to the *oued* bed is very steep, not something to meet at speed. At **Aïn el Ouchika**, there is the turn off for **Midès**, five km away, and, in normal times, you can get your papers checked before continuing into Algeria.

The road to Midès (ancient Madès), eight km from Tamerza, is on a good surfaced road as it goes on to Algeria. You approach through a very beautiful, working oasis, the old system of tiered cultivation still in operation, with palm trees under-planted with pomegranates and vegetables. Park near the village, now essentially abandoned, and no doubt you will be greeted by kids hoping to take you to the canyon, to take you round the old town, to take you to the oasis.

Midès (Djérid)

The Marabout

The North African landscape is dotted with small white painted buildings scattered about the hillsides, hilltops and cemeteries. These are the burial places of the holy men or marabouts (marabit in Arabic). The marabout was a religious teacher who gained credibility by gathering disciples around him and getting acknowledgement as a man of piety and good works. Marabouts were in many cases migrant preachers travelling to and from Mecca or were organizers of sufi schools. Place names of marabout sites are mainly after the names of the holy man interred there, usually prefixed by the word 'sidi'. Some sites are very modest, comprising a small raised tomb surrounded by a low wall, all whitewashed. Other marabouts have a higher tomb several metres square topped by a dome (koubba). In some instances, marabout tombs are large house-like structures acting as mausoleums and shrines. Most tombs in rural areas can carry stakes bearing flags in green cloth as symbols of the piety of their donors and as a token of continuing protection from the marabout.

In Libya annual processions are made to the marabout shrines for good luck, fertility and protection against the evil spirits. This is particularly the case where the area around is occupied by a tribe claiming descent from the holy man in question.

Tamezret

The village clings to the mountainside, surrounded by canyons on three sides. Flints and other traces of prehistoric occupation have been found in the area. The Berbers who founded Midès really knew what they were doing – a site with better natural defences would be difficult to imagine. Rumour has it that the Club Med was interested in developing the old settlement as a holiday village. Buying out the multiple-owners would be an estate agents nightmare, however, so Midès looks safe for the time being.

There is no other road out of Midès so you backtrack to the junction and turn right for Tamerza, eight km from Midès. Go carefully, the road dips down to the Oued el Horchane and four-wheel drive vehicles sometimes go faster than they really should.

Ancient Ad Turres, today's **Tamerza**, was part of the Limes Tripolitanus fortifications. Here again the old village has been abandoned. Tamerza, situated on lower lying ground than Midès, suffered heavy flood damage. Now often used for film shoots, the walls have been restored in places. The marabouts are kept in good repair, too. In the old village walk down the deserted main street from the highest point, the *kalaâ*, to the lowest point around the mosque and *marabout*. The extensive oasis with abundant water produces excellent dates as well as vegetables. The valley is full of stands of giant cane which apparently provide a refuge for wild boar, unwelcome visitors to the oasis gardens. The new village is a standard Tunisian rural settlement. From new Tamerza you access the main attraction, the **cascades**. Given the shortage of such sites in the Tunisian south, they are a bit of a tourist trap, attracting lots of local visitors too.

A possible walk is back up to Midès via the canyon. Take plenty of water and provisions – there are no shops in Midès. Also work out how you're going to get back if you're not going to walk. It might be better to do this trip with a mule and guide arranged via the Hotel des Cascades. On no account attempt this excursion if rain looks like a possibility. Flash floods are extremely dangerous, and carry everything in front of them.

Sleeping
Phone code: 06

The area's only hotels are here. **B** *Tamerza Palace*, T/F453722, stone-built in a vaguely kasbah style, 65 spacious rooms, a/c, heating, bar, good restaurant, panoramic views over old village, pool, conference room, tennis. Looks classy in the tour brochures, but lacks real elegance and the personal touch. Seems to make most of its money doing lunches for tour groups and safari tours overnight. The rooms with views over old Tamerza are fine. **D** *L'Hotel des Cascades*, T445365, 150 beds, outdoor restaurant, pool, beautiful location to the east of the palm groves. Follow the signs to the cascades about 100m from the main road, 50 individual 'bungalows' are made out of palm fronds. Mosquitoes are a major presence, so don't forget your jungle gel. A cheaper and more pleasant alternative is to rent a tent from the locals at the entrance to the village (5Dt per person) and spend the night in the oasis by the river. This is not an official camping area.

Eating

Tamerza Palace is a good but expensive choice. Down by the *Hotel des Cascades* are a couple of cheap restaurants.

The road from Tamerza to Chebika has been improved considerably. There are splendid views over Chott el Gharsa and over the plain to Algeria. There are occasional service buses to Tozeur, but very little traffic otherwise. Between Tamerza and Chebika the waters of the Oued el Horchane actually run across the road.

Some eight km on from Tamerza lies **Chebika**, Ad Speculum in classical times and also part of the Limes Tripolitanus fortifications, a small oasis of palms and vegetables in a narrow gorge. The name Ad Speculum derives from an ancient Roman communication method. Roman outposts and troops on the move could signal to each other by mirror (Latin: *speculum*). Later the village became known as Ksar ech Chems, 'palace of the sun'. Chebika has a

Chebika

Change at Chebika

Reached by little more than a rough piste, Chebika was one of the remotest places in Tunisia in the mid-20th century. It wasn't until the early 1990s that the piste was turned into road. Back in the 1960s, Chebika was the focus of a study which was to become a classic of social anthropology. Academic Jean Duvignaud was looking for a place to undertake research into the impact of development on isolated rural communities. At Chebika, he and his team of young Tunisian researchers were to enter into the daily lives of a community with its own deep-rooted values. The messages of the modern world (and the new Tunisia) were only just beginning to arrive via the transistor radio.

Duvignaud and his team found an oasis community regulated by complex unwritten rules of conduct. There was little money circulating in the oasis, but a complex exchange economy, services and favours being constantly traded. Contacts with the outside world were limited, though certain Chebikans were working in the mines at Redeyef, and marriages were arranged with the sister village of El Hamma du Djerid. But it was oasis cultivation which was the centre of Chebika's existence. For the village's people,

the oasis was a divine creation, more than just land cultivated to produce profit. But the Chebikans had lost control over their palmgroves: acquiring sheep and goats from the nomads, they had been forced to exchange land ownership to cover their debts.

Chebika in the 1960s was already beginning to change. A local official declared that "the people of Chebika belong to the past, they will be swept away if they don't adapt."

While the older people saw themselves as part of fictional family trees going back to the land of the Prophet, the children, beginning to go to school, could place their village in the south of the new Tunisian nation state. Today, the old ways of thinking are gone for ever. Chebika has become picturesque, providing the rushed tourist with a place where 'the old ways of life continue unchanged'. But how are Chebika's people doing beyond the façade of 'desert serenity'?

Duvignaud's research was translated into English as Change at Chebika *(University of Texas Press), but is unfortunately out of print. A cheap paperback edition of the French original is available in Tunis bookshops, published by Cérès Editions.*

beautiful location looking out over arid plain to the west and south to Chott el Gharsa. The old, abandoned village clings to the rocky hillside, while its residents have moved out to the new village. New Chebika is a small village, just a mosque, shop and a post office. There is parking at the top with a café over-**looking the palm trees and gorge. If you arrive at the wrong moment, there will** be 20 or so four-wheel drives jostling for parking space. Walk up into the old village. Hordes of excited kids will probably accompany you, ready to sell various minerals and poor necklaces made of tiny coloured flour beads. The spring comes trickling out of a narrow defile below the old village.

Nefta   نفطة

Phone code: 06
Colour map 4, grid A1

While Tozeur had a reputation for its men of letters, the sister oasis town of Nefta was famed across the Sahara as a spiritual place. Arriving in Nefta today, one's initial impression is more of a dust-blown outpost town. From the cliffs above the Corbeille (surely the only oasis to be set in what looks like a large crater), there is a panoramic view of Nefta. On its cliff top, there is the brooding mass of the Sahara Palace. Opposite, across the Corbeille, is the El Bayadha quarter. Here and there among the low sand-brown buildings are domes signalling the tombs of holy men. Explore the alleyways, still suffused by a certain spirituality, but better still, head off into the palm groves, where, at the right time of year, it will be possible to get a taste of the local 'palm wine' or the dates for which Nefta is famous.

Southwestern Tunisia

Nefta

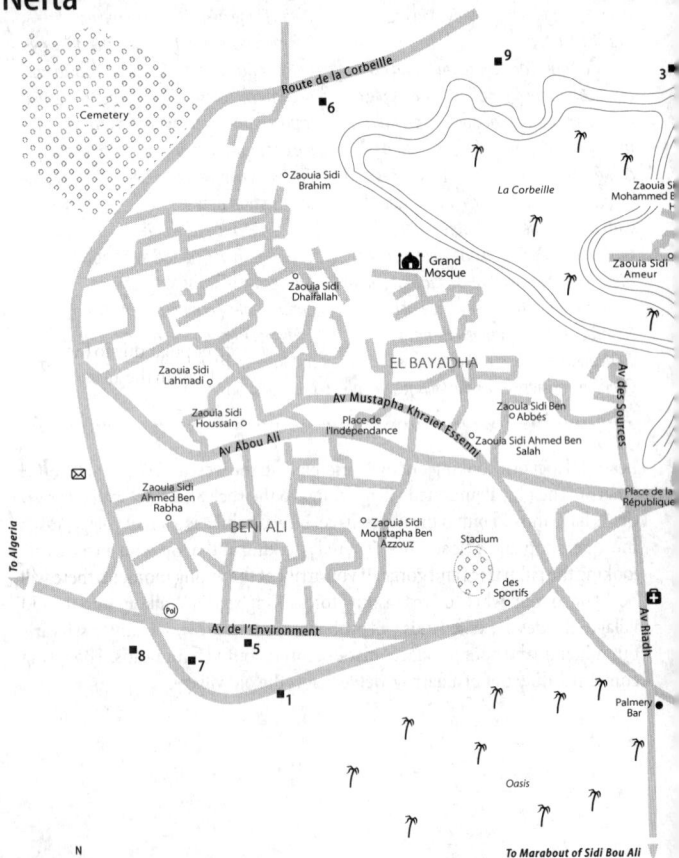

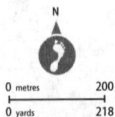

| 0 metres | 200 |
| 0 yards | 218 |

■ Sleeping

1 Caravanserail	4 de la Liberté	7 Neptus
2 el Habib	5 Marhala	8 La Rose
3 Horizon	6 Mirage	9 Sahara Palace

Ins and outs

The bus station is on the north side of the main street, Av Habib Bourguiba. The louages stop opposite. Journey time from Tozeur, just 23 km down the GP3, is 20 minutes. Hazoua on the Algerian border is only 36 km away.

History and background

Nefta was settled back in ancient times, when it was known as Aggersel Nepte. In the 11th century, the town was destroyed for refusing to pay taxes to Tunis. Rebuilt, Nefta became an important sufi centre by the 16th century. The cult of saints fell into disrepute after independence, and Nefta no doubt suffered.

Like other fringe areas of the Islamic world (Iran and Turkey), North Africa was to prove fertile ground for the cult of saints. Shrines of earlier animist Berber or Roman deities tended to take on Islamic identities, but why Nefta in particular should have proved such a centre for mystic Islam is something of a mystery. There are said to be over 125 shrines in the area. Some, such as the Zaouia of Sidi Bou Ali, were extremely important, attracting adepts from far afield.

It may be that sufism held a greater attraction for the peoples of the peripheral Islamic regions where there were deep rooted forms of religious practice. Sufism offers spiritual development through means other than the study of the Koran. Only a few adepts actually achieve the highest stages of sufi practice. Sufism was rejected by orthodox Islam but became quite popular due to the freedom it offered within the austere confines of mainstream Sunni Islam.

Sights

The oasis in Nefta has about 400,000 palm trees which produce some of the best dates in Tunisia. The **Corbeille**, a wide, deep basin which originally had springs flowing from its sides, must be seen as well as the old town. This large depression is situated to the north of Avenue Habib Bourguiba, and from the ridge surrounding it there is an excellent view over the **oasis** below and towards the Chott el Djerid in the distance to the east. The best view is from the *Café de la Corbeille*, which is reached by taking the road north from the Tourist Office or by foot through the old town north of the Place de la République.

Walk down into the oasis. Natural springs used to flow from the sides of the Corbeille. Children will want to act as guides but this is not necessary. The Tourist Office provides guides who are both competent and friendly.

Nefta has two main neighbourhoods: **Ouled ech Cherif**, on your right as you arrive from Tozeur, and **El Bayadha** to the west side of the Corbeille. It is recorded as having 24 mosques. The neighbourhoods are well worth strolling around, particularly as not that many tourists make the effort. In the narrow streets, you may come across women wearing the traditional black wrap, here enlivened with a blue stripe.

The **Zaouia of Sidi Brahim** (his tomb) is at the head of the Corbeille adjacent to *Café de la Corbeille*. **Sidi Salem's Mosque**, also known as the Great Mosque, is on the ridge above the Corbeille.

Brick making

On the western outskirts of Nefta, you may come across a rudimentary brick (*yajour*) factory. As in mediaeval Europe, bricks are hand made according to the needs of a building project. The craftsmen create good stodgy mixes of clay and sand, which is then used to make the bricks, shaped in rough wooden moulds and left to dry in the sun. The sun-dried bricks are then covered in ash and kiln fired.

Originally, brick must have been the perfect construction material for the region, given that other naturally occurring materials are poor. Today, hand-made bricks are increasingly in demand. Though concrete post-construction with red-brick infill has pushed traditional brick into second place in the Djerid, the realization has grown that local brick provides far better insulation against the extremes of the desert climate. Yellow brick decorative work can be found in many of the new hotels, too, providing that essential 'traditional touch'.

How brick-making technology reached the Djerid is unknown. Could it be a survival from classical times? The Romans, after all, were a dab hand at making thin bricks or *tegulae*. Or was it brought from the Middle East, where decorative brickwork was used for many buildings in Iraq and Iran? Maybe the skill filtered in from Europe thanks to some renegade converted to Islam. Whatever the case, the ochre imperfections of brickwork lend texture to a façade. When used to create patterning, geometric brickwork animates a wall with geometric detail. With so many Tunisian towns losing the last fragile vestiges of their local architecture, it is nice to see that at least one technique is still surviving down in the Djerid as people rediscover the benefits of brickwork.

The oasis

You might try a walk down into the oasis, heading for the **Zaouia of Sidi Bou Ali**. From the junction where the Avenue Bourguiba meets Avenue des Sources, head towards the hospital on Avenue Riadh. (Some 200 metres after the hospital, the Palmery Bar is on your left.) Carry on for the Zaouia, some 300 metres further on. This is a good chance to have a look at the palm gardens.

The Zaouia of Sidi Bou Ali is one of the most important in Nefta, mausoleum to a holy man who came from Morocco in the 13th century. The zaouia is visited to ask the saint's blessing on important family occasions: pregnancy, circumcision, marriage. The annual pilgrimage, the *dakhla*, attracts pilgrims from both the Djerid and across the border in Algeria. Unlike many other zaouias, that of Sidi Bou Ali has managed to maintain its prestige. The family guarding saintly prestige has managed to win the favours of the authorities. With the tourist industry in search of picturesque places, the folklorish side of zaouia life will no doubt become part of the tourist attractions of the region.

Essentials

Nefta is entering the age of mass tourism, albeit more slowly than Tozeur. New hotels are springing up along the *route touristique*, although given the financial difficulties facing the Saharan hotels which mushroomed in the mid-1990s, construction may be slower. Nefta's hotels come in 3 main areas. There are 2 posh locations, overlooking the Corbeille, and the inevitable *route touristique*, next to the oasis, on the road west of town. There are only a couple of cheapies in the town centre. However, Nefta is near enough to Tozeur for you to nip back if you can't find a room.

Sleeping
Phone code:06
■ *on maps*
Price codes:
see inside front cover

Overlooking the Corbeille A *Sahara Palace*, just behind the Corbeille, T457046, 100 a/c rooms and 9 suites, luxurious, large pool, disco, well situated overlooking the oasis. The hotel, now part of the Sangho group, has been beautifully refurbished and merits at least a look. There is a distinct smell of drains, however, in the reception. The rooms are very smart indeed. Coach tours stop in for buffet lunch and a look at the view. **B** *Hotel Bel Horizon*, T430088, F430500. Close to the Sahara Palace. The decorators made an effort here, with liberty lamps and Berber bits and pieces. Lacks the style of the Sahara Palace, however. Pool and a/c in rooms. **B** *Le Mirage*, T430622, F430644, further round the Corbeille, close to the Café de la Corbeille. Acceptable but dull.

Next to the oasis B *Caravanserail*, T430355/430416, F430344. Part of a chain which also has a hotel in Douz. Quite attractive stone built hotel, right next to the oasis. **B** *Neptus*, T457378/430698, F457447. **B** *La Rose*, T430697, F430385. **C** *Hotel Marhala*, T430027, F430511, an old address, with choice of accommodation in older wing or newer 3-star wing. Pool, restaurant, simple decoration.

Ouled ech Cherif neighbourhood and around E *Hotel Les Nomades*, at the entrance to town on the left, T430052. In its day, this must have been a fine address, just 'typical' enough. There are a couple of older wings with vaulted rooms and beds on built-in platforms, and a new block under construction. All rooms have shower. The hotel, about as far from the old town and its marabouts as you can get in Nefta, also has a bar, which is its main raison d'être. Maybe the refurbishment will be completed. **F** *Hotel El Habib*, the 3-storey block on the main square in Ouled ech Cherif. Signposted, T430497, clean and very basic, some rooms with bath, rooftop rooms. Go for rooms giving onto the back, as the square can be noisy with traffic. Handy for early morning bus departures. **F** *Hotel de la Liberté*, eccentric little place built around a patio, at the heart of the Ouled ech Cherif neighbourhood. Not terribly clean, but if you have a sleeping bag, you can kip out on the roof terrace.

Cheap *Restaurant du Sud*, Av Habib Bourguiba, good, cheap Tunisian food; *Restaurant la Source*, by the Tourist Office on Av Habib Bourguiba, Tunisian specialities; *Café du Stade*, for local flavour.

Eating

Best buys *Roses des sables*, 'desert sand roses', are found a few metres under the desert surface, are unusual and attractive objects. They are formed due to evaporation from the mineral barites and are created in beautiful patterns. The only problem might be transport as they come in all sizes, the biggest being really big.

Shopping

Bus Departures to **Tunis** (takes 8 hours); **Sfax**; **Kairouan**; **Gafsa**; **Hazoua** and the Algerian border. Buses do not cross the border but taxis do, otherwise you are faced with a 5 km stretch of no-man's land to get to the Algerian border post. From the other side, it is an 80 km stretch to the first town, El Oued, but louages are available. **Louages** Depart frequently to Tozeur (takes 20 minutes). There is a service to Hazoua and the Algerian border.

Transport

Southwestern Tunisia

West from Nefta into Algeria

The Tuniso-Algerian border is only 35 km west of Nefta and El Oued another 64 km. In the 1990s, Algeria was most definitely off-limits to tourists, who, like foreign workers, were a target for Islamist groups. In late 1999, the situation in Algeria looked like settling under newly elected President Bouteflika. Time will tell, but maybe by 2002 southern Algeria will be a viable onward destination from the Djerid. For the moment, it is still risky.

Directory **Banks** *BDS* and *UIB* on Av Habib Bourguiba. **Communications** *Post Office:* Av Habib Bourguiba, 150m beyond the Tourist Office. **Emergency numbers Police:** T457134. On Av Habib Bourguiba. **Hospitals & medical services Hospital:** Hôpital Local de Nefta, rue des Martyrs, T457193. **Chemist:** on Av Habib Bourguiba, T457159. **Tourist offices** The main tourist information office is on Av Habib Bourguiba, on the right as you enter the town, T457184. It organizes *calèche* and camel rides round the oasis. They also organize excursions into the desert and the dunes. Guides are available. Open daily 0800-1800.

Southeast from Tozeur to Kebili

Phone code: 05
Colour map 4, grid A1/2

This is a worthwhile route to follow. It goes via the small oases of Degache and Kriz right through the centre of the massive salt lake, Chott El Djerid. It is a most impressive sight, a single black line of road cutting through the white salt deposits. Mirages and interesting optical illusions are frequent. The Chott begins about 20 km from Tozeur where the road dips down. The west side of the Chott is not so tidy, with abandoned vehicles, split tyres and old oil cans. There are occasional small palm thatched huts at the side of the road at about the centre point, all with the same facilities, selling *roses des sables* (some dyed garish hues), cups of tea and coffee, and providing a primitive toilet a few steps across the salt flat. These are frequented by coach tours.

Where the chott is at its lowest salt is extracted. At each side of a road a channel, about one metre wide, has been dug in the white sand. In winter and spring this is full of water which will evaporate and leave a deposit of salt. Occasionally work with mechanical diggers is in progress lifting this salt.

About 40 km from Kriz, the land begins to rise and you come onto a peninsula sprinkled with small oases. The small settlement of **Souk Lahad** (lit: 'Sunday souk'), 75 km from Tozeur, has the usual services, banks, chemist, two or three cafés, of which *Café Salam* by the bus stop and the municipal garden is perhaps the best.

For an area sitting next to a salt sea, there is a gratifying amount of vegetation as you approach Kebili. There are recently planted palm groves to the south of the road, and elsewhere the trees are almost mature, with underplanting of olives and cereals. In less fertile places the scrub provides grazing land. Just after the Chott el Djerid, at **Zaouia**, 20 km before Kebili, is **C** *L'Hotel les Dunes*, T480711, F480563, 89 rooms, built 1991, exchange and boutique, very well decorated, pool, entertainment includes *mechoui* outside under the tents with traditional dancing and music. Turn off opposite the petrol station. **Menchia** has cafés for a rest en route.

At **Mansoura** (turn left off the main road at Tombar) you are at another Roman outpost. Here was one of the key strong points on the southern frontier, the legionary base of Turris Tamalleni, controlling access to the narrowest point across the Chott el Djerid, just west of the Djebel Tebaga which provided a natural rampart running eastwards to El Hamma (Acquae Tacapitanae) and Gabès (Tacapae). All that survives are a couple of Roman pools. **Telmine** is another compact oasis seven km before **Kebili**.

Kebili قبلي

Phone code: 05
Colour map 3, grid A1

Never really more than a stop-off on the route to Douz, Kebili has a certain charm. A late 19th century French creation, the town has a pleasant shady central square. There are hot springs, too, on the Douz side of town. Old Kebili, a few kilometres from the new town, definitely merits a visit. The village, abandoned after flooding, is still largely intact, its marabouts perfectly preserved. The oasis gardens are extremely beautiful, definitely worth a visit.

Ins & outs

There are buses to Kebili from Douz, Gabès, Blidet, Nouail, Tozeur and Tunis. Two bus companies operate services: the SRT and the SNTRI. Louages run from all these towns, too. Note that buses from Tunis may run via Tozeur or Gabès. Buses come into the main street, stopping by the Magasin Général. The louage station is central, just behind the Magasin Général.

Sights

Modern Kebili, founded in 1892, is a small regional town of considerable military importance under the French. It is strategically situated at a meeting of the ways from Tozeur, Gabès and the desert settlements further south. There are few specific sights to see, but plenty of interest in the oasis surrounding the abandoned settlement of old Kebili, half forgotten in the midst of a beautiful oasis. You could also relax at the **hot springs** to the left of the main road on the west side of town. Originally, the locals could bathe in splendid open air pools, said to go back to Roman times. The authorities decided that this was an unfitting spectacle, so they had the pool replaced with a large fountain. The hammam buildings are a few metres back from the road, separate sections for men and women.

Old Kebili

The old village of Kebili is not to be missed; it is certainly as interesting as the new one and much more peaceful to say the least. Follow the signs more or less opposite the fountain on the road to Douz and take the track which winds through the oasis. The **oasis gardens** under the palm trees are well cared for and have a prosperous air. The oasis is said to produce a unique variety of fig. The irrigation system is in good order. Yet the houses in the village are deserted and decaying. In places roofs have fallen in and walls collapsed. Only 20-30 years ago it was a busy centre but the people moved into more modern accommodation. The village has no inhabitants but is not deserted. The market gardens are tended by both men and women, and men still come to pray at the mosque. The blue painted koubba in the village is in good repair.

Southwestern Tunisia

Kebili

Sleeping

C *Fort des Autruches*, signposted off the road to Douz, T490737, F490933, 96 rooms, recently renovated, pool, bar on a terrace overlooking the oasis and the Chott, clean, views over oasis, can organize rides and tours, a good place as stop-over, but in summer it is advisable to book. The name for this hotel derived from a time when ostrich feathers were in fashion and an abortive attempt was made here to breed ostriches. **C *Hotel Dar Oasis***, zone touristique, close to the Fort des Autruches, T491436, F491295, 1 km from town centre, has 256 beds in 124 rooms, all with bath, good view,

■ **Sleeping**
1 Ben Said
2 Fort des Autruches
3 Kitam
4 Oasis
5 Youth Hostel

Not to scale

telephone with direct line. Reception has change facilities, takes major credit cards, will book you on four-wheel drive excursions, camel treks, car hire, restaurant, large pool with 2 different levels joined by a waterfall, conference centre for 300, disco, mini souk, *hammam*, sauna, provision for disabled visitors. **D** *Hotel Kitam*, near town entrance from Gabès, T491338, 32 rooms, a/c, telephone, restaurant, exchange, open all year, 2 pools – small one for children, disco. **F** *Hotel Ben Said*, Av Habib Bourguiba, T491573, on left of road to Douz, near centre of town and louage stop, clean rooms, shared bathroom. A highly recommended cheapie. **Youth hostel** T490635, 60 beds, bathrooms awful, meals available, catch bus in town centre towards Tozeur to Total petrol station.

Shopping Museum of Kebili near spring-fed pool on way to Douz is really a shop selling *kilims*, where someone will work a loom as a demonstration. The quality of the produce is not high.

From Kebili to Douz

Colour map 3, grid A1 **Bazma**, four km south of Kebili on the east side of the road, has an old *ksar* and minaret, among the palm trees, both abandoned. M'Said, 10 km south of Kebili, and a further five km from the road to the west, is a rather more pleasant place than Bazma, with the advantage of being on slightly elevated land and completely encircled by a cool and inviting palm oasis. The squat minaret, with a small cupola on the top, is in the centre of the new settlement, the old settlement of mud bricks being completely abandoned.

Djemma, 16 km from Kebili, shows a bright face to the passing traveller, the road edges are painted, trees have been planted at intervals along the way and the settlement is just big enough to offer most services. Set back from the road, the newly settled areas still have a raw appearance. It is noted for the water in the public fountain which, unlike most water in the area, is not brackish.

El Golaâ is really a suburb of Douz, north of the main settlement. The town centre is marked by a square-faced clock (another!) on brick pillars. The oasis covers a large area and a wide road, running parallel to the C206, takes one along a pleasant ride into Douz, a possible alternative to the main road.

Douz دوز

Phone code: 05
Colour map 3, grid B1

Hard by the oasis town of Douz are the dunes you find in the Tunisian holiday brochures: rolling expanses of smooth sand, searing white in the day, golden-brown at sunset. Douz also has plenty of palm trees, camel rides, hot springs, an interesting desert museum – and a lot of charm. At year's end, there is even a folkloric festival. There are mammoth hotels lined up along the desert edge like so many UFOs – and some rough and ready places in town. Douz, or nearby Zaâfrane, could be your base for a couple of nights in the desert, crunching across the sand in the company of the dromedaries and a hard-bitten former nomad. Far from any urban glow, the desert sky at night is unbeatable for star gazers.

Ins and outs

Getting there Douz is 35 km south of Kebili and 122 km from Tozeur (via Chott el Djerid). Gabès is the nearest large town, 155 km to the east via Kebili and El Hamma. The town is easily accessible by bus and louage. By bus, journey time from Gabès is around 2½ hours, from Tozeur, 2½, generally with a change at Kebili. Louage times may be somewhat shorter.

You can do mostly everything on foot. The dunes by the zone touristique are a 3 km walk from the centre. If you want to go down to Zaâfrane (12 km west), you have louages/rural transport running from just opposite the inter-city louage station. **Getting around**

History

At the beginning of the 20th century, Douz was an isolated oasis. Today it is a small town, witness to the attractions of a settled life. The nomad lifestyle is an ancient one and tribal roots still run deep though. The main tribe in Douz are the M'razuig. To the southwest, the Adhara are essentially based in Zaâfrane, and practise a form of seasonal nomadism, migrating with their flocks across to Ksar Ghilane. Then there are the Sabria, centring on the village of the same name. Originally, the distinctions between the tribes would have been obvious from their tents and tatoos. (Until the 20th century, men as well as women had tatoos.) Today, however, true nomadism is more or less a thing of the past. French observers of 70 years ago report encampments of up to 30 tents, something never seen today. The nomad populations have been settled, giving up their ancestral myths. Sidi Marzoug, 15th century founder of the M'razuig, is said to have declared "I will lead my sons far from the rainy lands which turn a man into a slave stifled under insults. Better to keep their honour, even if their stomachs are half-empty, rather than have full stomachs at the price of humiliation."

Today the settled way of life is gaining ground and the combined population of Douz and the villages in the region must be around 50,000. Douz is

Southwestern Tunisia

Douz

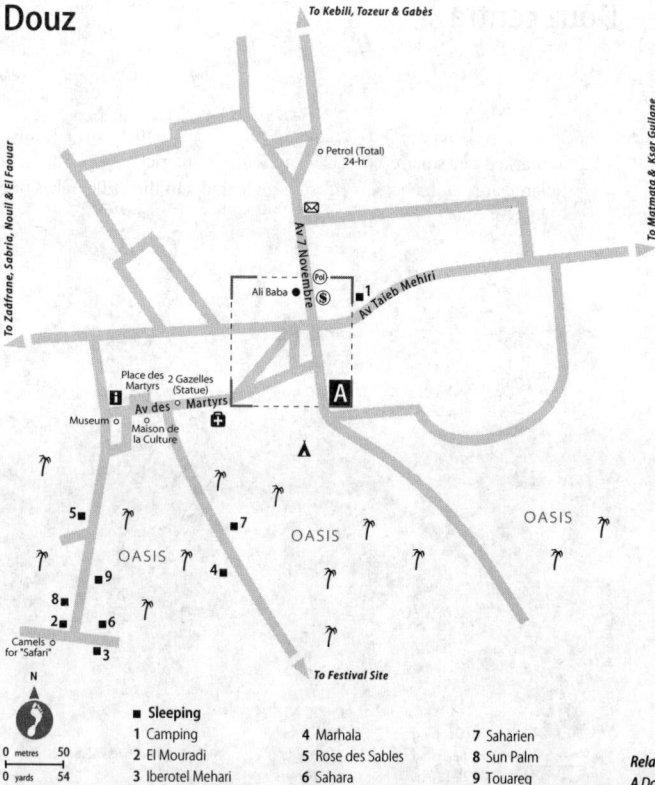

To Kebili, Tozeur & Gabès

To Zaâfrane, Sabria, Nouil & El Faouar

To Matmata & Ksar Guilane

o Petrol (Total) 24-hr

Av 7 Novembre

Ali Baba ●

Av Taïeb Mehiri ■ 1

Place des Martyrs · 2 Gazelles (Statue)
Av des · Martyrs
Museum o
Maison de la Culture

A

OASIS

OASIS

5 ■

· 7

OASIS

9 ■

4 ■

8 ■

· 6

2 ■

· 3

Camels o
for "Safari"

N

To Festival Site

0 metres 50
0 yards 54

■ **Sleeping**		
1 Camping	4 Marhala	7 Saharien
2 El Mouradi	5 Rose des Sables	8 Sun Palm
3 Iberotel Mehari	6 Sahara	9 Touareg

Related map
A Douz centre, next page

where nomads and oasis dwellers meet. But though there are very few purely nomadic families left, the desert is all around Douz and just a few kilometres out of town the road is hemmed in by dunes. The harsh environment maintains its hold on visitors' imaginations, no doubt through images maintained in Hollywood myth, of which *The English Patient* is the most recent example.

Sights

The centre of Douz does not have very many sights as such. The **place du Souk** with its arcades somehow feels like 40 years ago with some small, locally run shops. There is no trace of shopping malls here – but you will find pretty desert boots and beautifully soft camel-wool cloaks and blankets. Central Douz has not been subject to the 'beautification' programme with unlikely pieces of urban street art that has afflicted Tozeur. There are a couple of pieces of statuary, handy for directions, notably the camel and rider at the north entrance to the town, and the twin gazelles on the road towards the oasis.

The **Ofra sand dune** is one of the largest easily accessible sand dunes. Take the road towards the hotels and park by one of them or, alternatively, hire a camel by the Tourist Office. The official prices are posted in the Tourist Office. Further on is the village of **Glissia**, now largely covered by the shifting sands.

There is a **market** each Thursday attended by many nomads. (Douz is a centre for the now largely settled M'razuig nomads.) There is also an animal market which sometimes has camels. Buyers and sellers collect in the designated area off Avenue des Martyrs, beside the oasis.

Douz centre

To Kebili

Ali Baba

Square Clock

Café Sahara
Man on Camel Statue

Café Amel
Travel Agents

Chemist

Rue de la Liberté

Louage Station

Rue de la Liberté

Books & Cards Shop

Av Taïeb Mehiri

2

3

Rue Ghara Jawal

4

La Rosa

Av 7 Novembre

Café 20 Mars

Secondary Market Area

Av de la République

Christian/Craft Shops

Market

1

Av Mongi Slim

To Zaafrane

Chemist

Av des Martyrs

Animal Market

5

Av Farhat Hached

Av 7 Novembre

To Tourist Hotels

OASIS

Camping

To Matmata, Ksar Guilane, Camping & Picnic area

N

	Sleeping		
1	Bel Habib	3 Essada	5 Sahara & Restaurant
2	de la Tente	4 20 mars	

0 metres 50
0 yards 54

Douz International Festival, also known as **Festival du Sahara**, is generally held roundabout Christmas. Lasting three days, the festival is centred on a large stadium overlooking the dunes a couple of kilometres down the road from the Hotel Saharien. Here there are horse races, demonstrations by acrobatic riders, camel races and mock camel combat, and the ever popular *sloughis* (desert greyhounds), only bred in the Douz region, who go racing after unfortunate hares. There will be finely turned out horsemen from Libya, and a *jahfa*, a camel topped with a bridal palanquin accompanied by musicians. In the evening, there may be poetic jousting in the nomad tradition at the **Maison de la Culture**. Various traders set up their stalls on the main road in the villages. There are some fierce contests for position and at times it's a problem to find a way through the throng. Douz families' friends and relatives swell the crowds. The posh hotels organize displays of traditional costume and the like, while downtown, some of the lads may get a bit excitable after a few too many beers. On the day after the festival, all along the road back to Kebili, are dromedaries, Arabian horses and their owners.

Douz International Festival

There is also a **Folklore Festival** in March. Check exact dates with the Tourist Office. At peak festival periods, be sure to have booked a hotel room. Cheap hotels in particular can fill up at popular times of year.

The Museum of the Sahara is housed in a large building at the end of the village, just before you turn left onto place des Martyrs and down towards the hammam. Recently revamped, the museum has displays on textiles and tents, desert plants (and their uses), domestic items and even tatoos. It illustrates the difficulty of making a good museum around what was a frugal way of life, perfectly adapted to a difficult environment. It would be nice to know how nomad life evolved as the French brought the Sahara into their orbit, and how life has changed in the last 20 years. An audio-visual display on nomad music and poetry might be a good thing, too. ■ *Open 0830-1300 and 1500-1800.* (If you want to know more about nomads in southern Tunisia, try to get hold of Louis André's *Nomades d'hier et d'aujourd'hui dans le Sud tunisien* (Aix-en-Provence, Edisud, 1979).)

Museum of the Sahara

Essentials

New hotels appeared at a vertiginous rate in the late 1990s in Douz, all of them out of the town with views over the desert. They sit on the edge of the dunes the way hotels at Sousse are all lined up along the beach. The older, more modest hotels are in town or in the oasis. Although the big hotels are most comfortable, you might have more fun and find out more about the local people in one of the town centre cheapies.

Sleeping
■ *on map*
Price codes:
see inside front cover
Phone code: 05

Zone touristique B *Iberotel Mehari*, T495088, F495589, 127 rooms, pool, opened 1989, built to look like a ribat, so plain stone exterior but inside a cool environment, luxury, all rooms telephone, a/c, heating, 2 pools. The outside pool has sulphurous hot spring at a temperature of 25°C spilling down a sort of stone column. Hotel also has nightclub, boutiques, conference facilities. B *Oasis El Mouradi*, T470303, F470905, another large hotel, used by safari tours, 342 beds in 180 rooms with a/c, outdoor pool and indoor covered pool with a solarium, *hammam*, sauna, and a 'fitness centre', conference facilities, well appointed restaurant with a good choice of food.

C *Le Sahara Douz*, T495246, F495566, 300 beds, opened in 1990, all with balcony, covered heated pool. C *Sun Palm* (was *Caravanserai*), T495123, 172 beds, opened 1992. C *Touareg*, T470057, F470313, 315 beds.

Southwestern Tunisia

D *Hotel Rose du Sable*, route Touristique, T495484, not quite as nice a position as *Saharien*, recently renovated and enlarged, 200 beds in 90 rooms, all with bath and a/c and heating, pool, restaurant.

Town centre and oasis D *Hotel Saharien*, T495337, F495339. Turn left into the oasis, just before the Maison de la Culture. Accommodation in bungalows, most with bath, among the palms. Pool, delightful setting, rooms spacious but a little dusty, a/c and heating, hot water, not much choice for dinner. Bar lively with tour groups in evening. Continuing a couple of kilometres down the road, you come to the stadium where the festival parade and displays are held.

F *Hotel Bel Habib*, on the Av du 7 novembre near Place du Souk, T495309, clean, very cheap, welcoming owners, communal bath/toilet, large breakfast, interesting views from terrace over fruit and vegetable market. Owner will organize lifts – eg Ksar Ghilane in four-wheel drive for 5Dt. **F** *Hotel de la Tente*, T470468, next to louage station, dormitories, bath with hot water, sleep on the roof in a bedouin tent for 2Dt, manager very kind. Recommended. *Hotel du 20 Mars*, on rue du 20 mars, unsurprisingly enough, T470269, in town, unclassified, 7Dt per night.

Eating Nothing to get very excited about here, although you should try the local 'desert pizza', *m'tebeg*. When eating in cheap restaurants, remember to calculate your bill. It may be tempting for an underpaid cashier to add on an extra 5Dt.

Expensive *Hotel El Mouradi*, good standard buffet evening meal in upmarket surroundings. **Mid-range** *Restaurant Ali Baba*, by the police station to north of town, keeps the backpackers happy. Their *merguez* (spicey sausages) turned out to be chipolata sausages. Full marks for trying. The hospitable son of the original owner runs the place with panache. *Restaurant Le Petit Prince*, between the 2 tourist offices on Place des Martyrs; *Restaurant La Rosa*, in the town centre, has been recommended. **Cheap** *El Kods*, 100m from Tourist Office, good simple food, cheap.

Cafés Stop in at the *Café du Théâtre* of an evening. This is where generations of amateur theatre groups have performed, and there are pictures on the walls to prove it. Generally, the place functions as a blokey chicha café. Pleasant service. Busy during the Douz Festival, but not with theatre.

Entertainment **Hammam** Unfortunately, a couple of the big hotels seem to have tapped most of the hot spring water for their clients. For the locals, there remains a small hammam located down the hill to the left after the museum. Mornings for men, afternoons for women. There is a covered pool to soak in, and individual cubicles with baths. Bring your own towels, no extras like massages.

Shopping Surprisingly perhaps, there are some really nice buys to be had in Douz. Have a look round the Place du Souk. You could go for a pair of Douz shoes, which have some coloured embroidery and high backs, or a pair of *ni'al* sandals, very Ali-Baba with their pointed toes. Other good buys include camel hair cloaks and blankets.

Transport **Bus**: from the station near the junction by the cemetery there are frequent buses to Kebili; **Tunis** 0600 (via Kairouan) and 2030 (via Gabès and Sfax); **Gabès** 0700, 1000, 1430; **Tozeur** 0630; **El Faouar** (via Zaâfrane) 0645, 0800, 0900. The **local buses** are absolutely jammed – a problem to get on and even worse to get off. **Louages**: are based near the bus station in the centre of town. Louages to Kebili 1.8Dt, to Gabès 6Dt. Almost opposite the louage station, you have the *nakl rifi* (rural transport) for Zaâfrane and places west.

Douz is an important point of departure for trips into the desert. In spring you could try a week's camping trip through the desert to Ksar Ghilane by camel. In summer the desert gets much too hot for these trips. Camel Trekking is organized by *Douz Voyages*, T495179, and by *Abdelmoula Voyages*, T495484, F495336. Douz to Ksar Ghilane (8 days) or Douz to Sabria (3 days). Price of 21Dt per day includes camels and drivers, cooks, blankets, sleeping bags, breakfast, lunch and dinner.

Desert trips

Banks Douz has the STB, just opposite the bus station on Taïeb Mehiri. **Communications** Post Office: in the centre of the town. **Tourist offices** The tourist information office *ONTT*, Place des Martyrs, route de Zaâfrane, T495350, is in the same building as the local tourist office. They are separated by a café. Local office, T470351, where Mr Amor Boukris has very little information to hand out but everything you want to know in his head. He is most helpful. Open 0830-1400 and 1500-1800 every day. They organize excursions into the desert on camels. **Tour operators** Douz Voyages, Av Taïeb Mehiri, T470178, and Abdelmoula Voyages, Av des Martyrs, T495484. Can set up desert excursions of various kinds.

Directory

From Douz into the desert

The metalled road from Douz takes you to Zaâfrane, about 10 km away, and on to the once remote oases of Sabria and El Faouar. You head out through new concrete housing and small palm gardens, neatly laid out, carefully irrigated, protected from the elements and the blowing sand by palm frond fences. But soon the barren land appears and small salt lakes, which may provide birdwatchers with some interest. Lines of palm fronds stick out of the top of the dunes, the sand gleams almost white due to the high salt content, the road is a thin black line and the sky an amazing blue. Young eucalyptus trees line the road.

Southwest from Douz

Zaâfrane is accessible by bus, louage or hitchhiking from Douz. The old village, west of the modern village has been abandoned and is slowly being covered by the sand. The surrounding landscape of endless dunes and sand with the occasional palm tree is very impressive. New Zaâfrane is a linear settlement with the palm gardens to the north. It has a police station, a water tower, a school, two bakeries, a butcher, taxiphone and post office.

Zaâfrane
Phone code: 05

Tourist activity takes place on the El Faouar side of the town, where there are photogenic dunes and the remains of the original village. The tourist office is open only in 'the season', unspecified, and is situated by the café and the dromedaries. There are many dromedaries here, already harnessed to take the tourists a very short ride to see the sand. The settlement has increased in size very rapidly as the nomads have been settled. The new village has modest housing. Each property has a square house with a window on each side of the central door and three half cylinders making up the roof, and store built round a courtyard. All to the same plan, but modified by the individuals.

Sleeping E *Hotel Zaâfrane*, T491720/495074, small, simple hotel, café, beers. Excursions by camel are available 25Dt per day, following a circuit around the water holes and eating desert bread, cooked in the sand.

Camel trips There are plenty of beasts available for short rides into the desert from opposite the Hotel Zaâfrane. More interesting would be a few nights in the desert, walking/riding camels. One way to organize this is via the tourist office in Douz. Another option could be to ask in the local shops on the Douz side of Zaâfrane. This is very much at your own risk, however. The best times of year are spring and autumn. Remember to have a warm sleeping bag, as desert nights can be bitingly cold. The

Southwestern Tunisia

☛ *The tribes of Nefzaoua*

The region is called the Nefzaoua region and in it there are five tribes. These are the M'razuig of the Douz area numbering around 29,000; the Adara of the Zaâfrane region numbering around 5,000; the 7,000 Sabria in the region of the same name; the Ghribs of the Faouar region numbering

3,000; and a final 3,000 Aoulad Yaghoub. While to the visitor they may seem all alike there are obvious distinctions, clear to themselves, and each tribe can be recognized by the clothes, the bags, the tents and domestic objects and, on the women, their head and face coverings.

really courageous might want to travel south to isolated oases with magical names like Aïn Mansour, Bir Bel Kacem, Bir Touil el Adhara and Tembaïn.

Zaâfrane to Sabria and El Faouar

Colour map 3, grid B1 The land south of Zaâfrane is very flat, the bed of a dried lake. You could turn off left to visit Sabria, three km south off the C206. The palms begin at one km off the main road. The road which bends sharply through the palms to the village soon deteriorates into a track. Although the settlement has spread the palm trees have been retained beside the houses, tempering the starkness of the settlement. Sabria goes about its daily rural business, there are chickens in the streets, goats by the houses, women by the well. Though a poor sort of place (hence investment by the National Solidarity Fund in the late-1990s), it has a certain charm. The children here are less used to tourists, and if you come by car, may lob the odd stone or follow you around. Nevertheless, it is worth putting up with the pestering.

El Faouar Approaching El Faouar, the flat dried lake bed gives way to small dunes which
Phone code: 05 have been stabilized with palm fronds and planted with mimosa and acacia. Moving the ever-encroaching sand seems to be a major occupation here, either with bulldozers or shovels and mule carts.

El Faouar is also accessible by bus, louage or hitchhiking. (In the winter there is a steady stream of four-wheel drive vehicles on the road west of Douz.) This is the last major village on the road. Try and see the **market** on Friday when any nomads and locals assemble. It is at its most interesting when dates are in season. Go early in the morning as many goods have disappeared by 1000. El Faouar is surprisingly large and busy with a police station, a clinic, a large school and oasis. The *Café de Tunis* stands at the entrance to the town on the south of the road, the chairs and tables are set up across the street. The central square, from which the buses and louages leave, is marked by the mosque and a square-faced clock. Here stands *Restaurant Salam*. The first bus of the day (good quality but exceedingly crowded) leaves about 1000 from El Faouar.

Sleeping D *Hotel El Faouar*, T460531, F460576, international telephones, satellite TV, 106 rooms with 300 beds, a/c and heating, comfortable shady lounge area, bar, sand skiing, folklore during dinner under tents, is virtually built in the desert, with pool, restaurant. The hotel organizes four-wheel drive and camel trips (two-three hours) in the desert and you can learn dune skiing! The palm groves close round the village to the west.

West of El Until recently, the surfaced road ended at El Faouar. By 1999, the road had
Faouar been surfaced all the way round the western end of the Chott el Djerid, enabling the visitor to complete a circuit on to Tozeur. The State has ploughed

The Roman frontier

In the second and third centuries AD, the Roman province of Africa prospered in peace. While the northern provinces of the empire faced invasion from Germanic tribes, the Rome's southern African frontier was a different matter. The pre-Saharan and Saharan regions were peopled by Berber nomads, who no doubt moved northwards in the summer when the scarce desert pasture for their flocks ran out. They may also have participated in the annual grain harvest, much as nomads continued to do well into the 20th century. To keep a check on the nomads, the Romans, with their usual efficiency, developed a frontier defence system referred to as the limes. Unlike massive works like Hadrian's Wall in the province of Britain, it was designed more as a filter than a linear frontier.

Part of the more extensive limes Tripolitanus, a defensive zone varying from 50 km to 100 km in width, the limes in Africa had two main parts. The northern line of defence ran east-west from Tacapae (Gabès), via Thelepte to Haïdra. Eventually, as Romanization advanced, it was extended to Teveste (Tebessa) and Lambaesis, both in contemporary Algeria. The southern limit of the limes, completed under the Severan emperors, ran from Leptis Magna (in Libya) across to Turris Tamalleni (Telmine), just north of modern Kebili. The frontier was designated by forts and camps, watchtowers (equipped with mirrors for signalling) and short sections of wall and ditch (fossatum). The whole system made good use of natural features such as the chotts, which became impassable in winter and spring after the rains. Scholars believe that the whole point was to regulate pastoral tribes, ensuring that their beasts did not stray into Roman farmlands when the crops were young. The limes was practical, no doubt permitting the taxing of the nomads as well.

More than 140 sites forming part of the limes have been identified. Some of the most important ones – Turris Tamalleni, Talalati (Ras el Ain Tlalit, near Tataouine) – are little more than heaps of stones today. The outpost of Ksar Ghilane has survived, witness to Roman tenacity.

considerable sums of money into developing the oasis at **Rejim Maâtoug** to the west, with the army involved in land preparation and construction work.

Another possibility from El Faouar is to return to Kebili (54 km) via the isolated settlements of **Blidet** and **Touiba**. Returning up the main Zaâfrane to Douz P206, you would turn off left on the metalled road which runs to Blidet via Noueil. There are regular daily buses from Kebili to Blidet and Noueil. The old settlement of Blidet, visible from the road, has been abandoned to crumble away around its whitewashed marabout. In the school holidays, hordes of children will emerge to show you round the ruined village.

East to Ksar Ghilane

Remote Ksar Ghilane is a long uncomfortable slog across the desert. A four-wheel drive safari from Djerba will probably take you there via Matmata and Tamezret. The short stretch from Matmata to Tamezret is a little rough, while from Tamezret, you take a rough track for 18 km to join the pipeline track. With the pipeline on your right, head southwards for 59 km. Then turn right for Ksar Ghilane, which is 13 km down a rough track. Another possible approach is via a piste from Chenini. This is not to be recommended unless you are a very good navigator and have a tough four-wheel drive. The route from Douz, 124 km, really does not warrant doing unless you have a yen for flat stoney landscapes. Note that the Douz to Matmata route is now fully surfaced.

Colour map 3, grid B3

☞ *On Nefzaoua desert roads*

There was a good deal of road improvement in the Nefzaoua in the late 1990s. Unfortunately, the maps available in Tunisia (Geo-Center and Freytag and Berndt) are not always accurate, especially for the area west of Douz. The maps show the P210 from Blidet as joining a road between Sabria and El Faouar. This is not the case – unless it was completed in late 1999. Sabria is shown as being on the P952 Douz to El Faouar road, when it is actually 3 km south of the road, etc. Be aware of the official map deficiencies when travelling in the area, and be prepared to ask. (Ettarik mekeyyes walla piste? *Is the road tarmacked or track?*)

If you pick up a hitchhiker at a remote settlement, they may advise you to take shortcuts across sandy piste. Such shortcuts are not to be attempted lightly in a hire car. You need to have confidence in your skills as an off-road driver and a spade. Getting stuck in the middle of nowhere with night coming on is tedious, to say the least. And you will probably be in breach of your hire car contract.

Ksar Ghilane (Roman Tisvar) is the most isolated of the oases, a small settlement right out in the desert, recently discovered by tourism. There are numerous tamarisk trees, a little cultivation, a few nomad shacks, and three camp-type hotels. The outstanding feature of Ksar Ghilane, however, is the nearby remains of an ancient fort.

The Roman fort or *castellum* of Tisvar is on a low rise looking out over the dunes. The scenery is totally Beau Geste; the military objective was control of an important watering point mid-way between the Nefzaoua and the *castrum* (camp) at Remada (ancient Tillibari), in the far south of modern Tunisia. The fort is thought to have been built under the emperor Commodus in the second century AD. It may well have continued in use into the Middle Ages, and was excavated by the French, who discovered an altar to the spirit of Tisvar. The fort was an outpost of the main *limes* which lay further north. No doubt its solid construction and Roman garrison effectively intimidated the nomads. The commander would have been responsible for providing intelligence on nomad movements.

Until the 1990s, the drive to Ksar Ghilane was the ultimate adventure of the Tunisian South. It is still sold as such by the four-wheel drive safari operators. Today there are three tourist campsites, including the extremely pricey **B Pansea** which even has a pool. Reservations via SITH in Tunis on T01-893275, F01-846129 or T/F05-900521. Also via Paris on T1-42275431, F1-42275434. The Pansea is sold as a harbour of peace and tranquillity, et cetera. There is a watchtower for looking out over the oasis, and the reception areas and bar are built with vaults like the *ghorfa* granaries of the Tunisian South. People from the other campsites will not hesitate to come trooping through, however, just to have a peek at the rising sun. The catering has had some very mixed reports.

Southwestern Tunisia

Southeastern Tunisia

8

Southeastern Tunisia

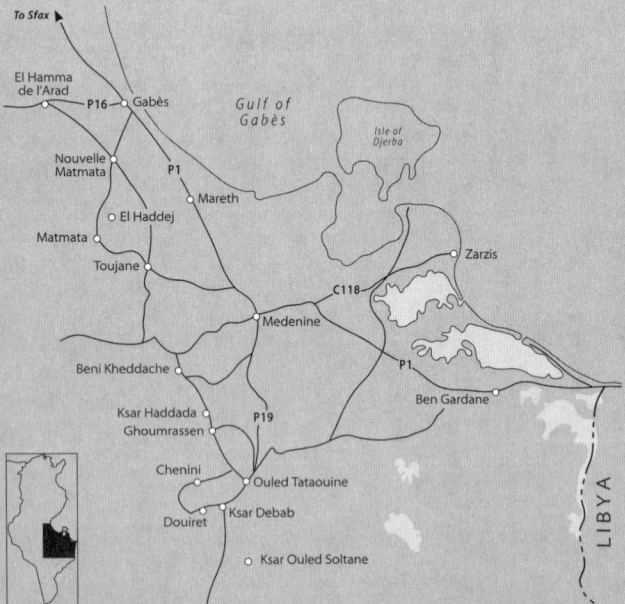

*Heading south from Sfax, the olive plantations gradually give way to an arid monotony. At **Gabès**, the visitor has a first taste of the South. Right next to the sea is a great oasis. Inland, the landscape soon turns mountainous, and here at the northern end of the **Djebel Dahar** are villages of pit homes at **Matmata** and hilltop Berber outposts. Further south in the Dahar, near **Tataouine**, the traveller will come across another type of settlement: the citadel villages of **Chenini**, **Guermessa** and **Douiret**. This is also the land of the ksour, the fortified granaries which once played such a key part in the lives of the region's tribes. East from **Medenine**, the coast is quickly reached again. **Zarzis** has the usual hotels and sandy beach, while towards the Libyan frontier, the remote **Bhiret el Bibane lagoon** will provide opportunities for birdwatching.*

Background

Under the French protectorate, Tunisia was seen as a land which divided into a rich, fertile, well-watered North, around Tunis, Sousse and Sfax and the cereal growing lands of Béja, and an arid South which had to be administered, in part, to keep Italian colonial ambitions at bay. In the decades following independence, there was considerable migration from the arid South to the northern cities and on to France. Investment in modern agriculture and industry tended to be on the northeastern seabord, reinforcing the pull. In the 1990s, tourism and petroleum-based manufacturing slightly redressed the balance, though almost all of this kind of employment has tended to be on the coast. One unexpected factor did help the development of southeast Tunisia, however – the UN-imposed embargo on Libya, which created a huge amount of business. The result today is a scattering of increasingly developed towns – industrial and military Gabès, desert Tataouine, regional centre Medinine, tourist-oriented Zarzis – and inland areas left with low productivity agriculture.

1990s prosperity The bustling air of incipient prosperity in the southern towns is based on a number of factors: phosphate processing, petroleum exploration, tourism and new agricultural ventures. Petroleum exploration is mainly offshore but workers in the industry come mainly from the South, given their tolerance for the heat and the fact that they have no qualms about spending long periods working away from home. In the late 1990s, a large number of new hotels went up along the northeast coast of Djerba, catering mainly for the European package market (see next chapter). These hotels – and the building sites – on Djerba are an important source of employment, too. Inland from Gabès too, new hotels at Matmata have made this a comfortable overnight stop, and the completion of the direct road from Matmata to Douz has created a southern tourist circuit in the desert for European visitors, most of whom would never have found their way to this region. Four-wheel drive tourism is getting (perhaps unfortunately) to be big business and a major source of income for local people.

Agriculture The changes in agriculture in the South are less dramatically visible than the convoys of four-wheel drive vehicles. In addition to the age-old export of dates, the warm, sunny winters of the South are now used to grow crops demanded out of season in prosperous industrialized states of the EU. Recently, melon and soft fruit have been grown for the French market and there is scope for much more intensive development using new technology and newly found underground water supplies. The signature in 1995 of an arrangement with the EU for free trade will further open up this market, provided the high rewards of tourism do not draw labour away from the land. The coastal area must not be overlooked either: in addition to the tourist beaches of Djerba the sea itself contributes to the region's economy. King prawns, octopus, squid and cuttlefish found in the region of Gabès are all valuable exports.

Effects of the Libyan embargo The UN embargo on Libya provided an unexpected impetus to the region's economy. Libyans travelling abroad were obliged to transit either via Djerba (or Malta). The black market in the Libyan currency made products subsidized by the Libyan State incredibly cheap, and large amounts of electrical goods, foodstuffs and household essentials found their way into Tunisia to be sold in the informal 'Libyan souks' on the outskirts of the main towns. The embargo ended in 1999, and it remains to be seen how this will effect the informal Libyan trade that gave a boost to so many households' incomes.

Libyan traffic

Until 1999, Libya was under UN sanctions arising from the Lockerbie bombing in 1988 and the shooting down of a French airliner over the Sahara in 1989. The sanctions began on 15 April 1992 and were subsequently renewed in 1993, 1994 and 1995, despite last ditch attempts by the Libyan authorities to stave them off. The sanctions included the banning of all civil aviation connections with Libya.

Thus the only routes into and out of Libya are by sea or land. A principal land route is via Tunisia (travellers take international flights from Djerba or other Tunisian airports and then go overland into Libya). Consequently, there is a strong flow of traffic at the border at Ras Ajdir. (This is in addition to the high level of commercial goods that have always been
moved between the two countries at that border crossing.)

Visitors to southern Tunisia can spot a Libyan vehicle by the colouring of the number plates. Libyan trucks and taxis carry a yellow number plate, government vehicles red and private cars green. For those who can read Arabic, Libyan private plated vehicles also have their town of origin marked. The number of Libyan cars travelling to Tunisia is limited by shortages of foreign exchange and occasional arbitrary official constraints on movements of Libyan nationals by their government. Libyan drivers are not always versed in international traffic conventions and the conduct of vehicles is often erratic. So, when you see Libyan number plates on vehicles, take extra care!

The south of Tunisia, including the Djerid, can no longer be dismissed as economically irrelevant to the fate of the country as a whole. Djerba has changed from being a somewhat exclusive and sleepy island resort into a major package destination, especially popular with Germans. The knock-on effects of the jobs generated are felt across the South and can be seen in the vast amount of new building. It remains to be seen whether tourism in the south of Tunisia is sustainable and this depends principally on the development of something more challenging for the tourist than being driven across stoney wastes in an air-conditioned four-wheel drive vehicle.

Visiting the southeast

Visitors heading to southeast Tunisia do so mainly for the landscapes. There are some extraordinary forms of local habitat to see, too. With plenty of time, you would want to have a look at the the pit-dwellings and Berber villages of the Matmata region, 40 km west of Gabès (say one day, though two would be better), and some of the hill-crest villages and fortified granaries (*ksour*) in the Tataouine region. Here again, two days would be best. Note that Gabès to Tataouine is 135 km, say two and a half hours driving time. Another minor attraction is the Mareth line military museum, some 40 km south of Gabès.

The Land Rover safari packages are organized to cover the main villages and most striking landscapes. For the full desert experience, you could take a package to one of the tent hotels out in the desert at Ksar Ghilane (dealt with in this book in the Djerid and Nefzaoua chapter). Whether the hours of piste driving are really worth it is another matter.

Basically, in the Matmata region, you should see old Matmata and Tamezret, and if there is enough time, Toujane and Techine (rough tracks to these destinations). South of Tataouine, Douiret and Chenini de Tataouine should not be missed, along with isolated Ksar Ouled Soltane (perhaps the best preserved *ksar*). Guermessa, Ghomrassen and Ksar Haddada are worth a look if there is time. Most of the remaining *ksour* are for enthusiasts only.

Note that although the distances are not enormous, in the summer, the hot sun takes it out of you, meaning that not as much gets covered as you would like. If you are driving down from Tunis to Gabès, a good journey time (without stops) is five hours and fifteen minutes, Sfax to Gabès, just over two hours, and Sousse to Gabès, three hours and 40 minutes, in clear road conditions.

Gabès قابس

Phone code: 05
Colour map 3, grid A4

As you head south from Sfax, Gabès is the first town where you really feel 'the South'. The pace seems slower, the traffic more erratic. Despite much industry both north and south of the town, the oasis, the only seabord oasis in Tunisia, remains an important presence. There is a garrison, a reminder that Gabès sits strategically on the easiest north-south route. Tourism is a minor activity – there is a small souk catering for the four-wheel drive trade. But Gabès merits more than just a cursory halt. It is also well situated for day trips to troglodyte Matmata and reminders of the Second World War Mareth line.

Ins and outs

Getting there Strategically located Gabès can be reached by road and rail. It is a transport hub with buses coming in from all over the country. Journey time from Tunis by louage, if the motorway is not too crowded, is around 6 hours, including short stops.

Gabès

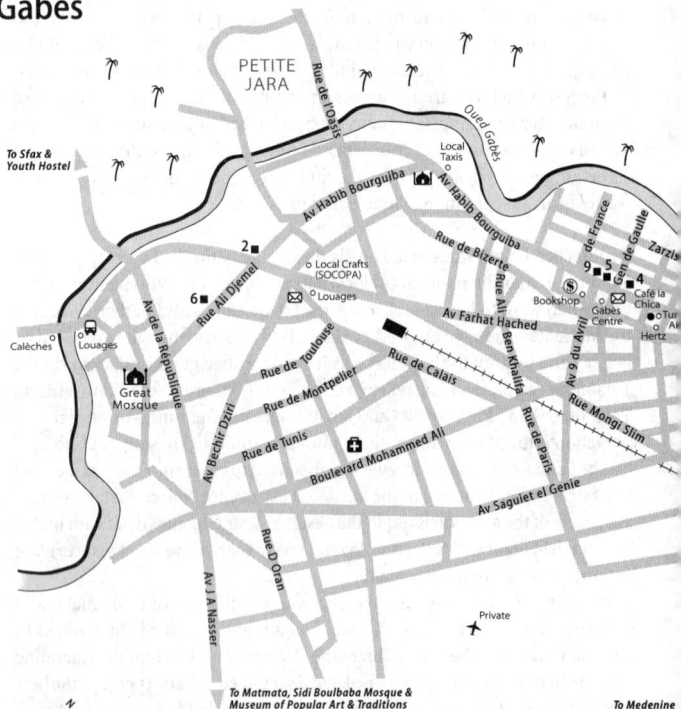

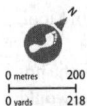

■ Sleeping		
1 Atlantic	4 de la Poste	7 Nejib
2 Ben Nejima	5 Khenini	8 Oasis
3 Chems	6 Medina	9 Régina

If you are driving, the Sfax to Gabès road (138 km) is single lane all the way. Journey time around 2¼ hours. Heavy traffic in Sfax's southern suburbs and lorries will slow you down. Remember to slow at roadside settlements – the Garde Nationale may be lurking to catch speeders; 95 km out of Sfax, Bou Saïd with its numerous butchers is a good place for a pause and a barbecue lunch.

Getting around

The bus station is on the main street, Av Farhat Hached, at the west end, where the Sfax road comes into town. Walk east to the town centre. There are a number of louage stations, the main 1 being next to the main bus station. Louages for local destinations like Mareth and Matmata leave from next to the Great Mosque opposite the tourist souk. Louages for Matmata also leave from the Av Farhat Hached, almost opposite the Hotels Ben Nejma and Marhaba.

Trains from Tunis and the coastal resorts, Gafsa and Metlaoui, arrive at the station on Av 1er Juin, in the centre of town.

Bypassing Gabès

Coming down from Kairouan or Sfax, you may be tempted to avoid Gabès altogether and head on for more southerly destinations. The town can be bypassed by a route to the west. There is a turn-off 16 km north of Gabès near Oudref, signposted to Kebili. This turning is alongside the military zone (guard posts with armed guards – definitely not the place to take photographs). You will know you are on the right road if you almost immediately cross the railway. Take a right turn to Oudref (a bit confusing when you know you want to be going south) and then left on to the C208. On the road south ignore the industrial pollution from the cement works to the west of Gabès and note the ruined ksar up on the hillside to the east of the road instead. In this area you may see a number of black tents, depending on the season and the grazing available. The nomads are not fully settled and these tents are erected adjacent to pasture for the herds. Note that very little of this route is lit at night.

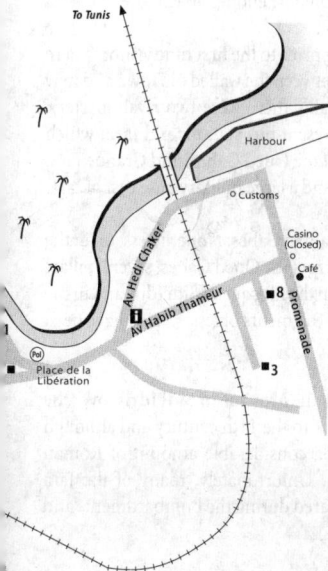

To Tunis
Harbour
Customs
Casino (Closed)
Café
Av Hedi Chaker
Av Habib Thameur
Promenade
Place de la Libération
Pol
■ 8
■ 3

History

Thought to be of Phoenician origins, by 161 BC Gabès was part of the Carthage domains, an important trading link with the South. It later came under Roman influence when it was known as Tacapae and was destroyed during the Arab invasion. The rebirth of the town is linked to the arrival of Sidi Boulbaba, the Prophet's companion, in the seventh century. He is now revered as the town's patron saint. Gabès later became an important halt on the caravan routes from the South.

The French turned Gabès into a garrison town. Concerned about potential Italian interference from neighbouring Libya, they set up their largest base in the south. During the

Second World War, the Afrika Korps set up headquarters in Gabès, using it as a strategic point on their supply lines back to Libya. The town was retaken in March 1943 by British and French troops, but only after extensive damage had been done.

Modern Gabès is a relatively new city, much of it having been rebuilt after the Second World War and the serious floods in 1962. Despite the long beaches and fine sand, the coast is not very appealing. Today, apart from traditional industries such as fishing and agriculture based on fruit from the oasis and the 300,000 palm trees, Gabès has become highly industrialized with a massive cement and brick factory, an oil refinery, harbour and projects for petro-chemical industries. Oil and gas wells have been drilled offshore in the Gulf of Gabès. Fortunately, though, the industries are dispersed over the surrounding suburbs, making them less conspicuous. There are two ports, the small harbour in town and the industrial port six km away.

The amount of industry probably means that the sea at Gabès is polluted, but it is nevertheless worth a stop to enjoy the coolness of the oasis. In summer, local people tend to head south of town to Teboulbou to swim.

Sights

Despite having a population of nearly 100,000, Gabès has a definite sleepy small-town feel. It originally grew up as a minor settlement where the Oued Gabès runs into the sea. The main attraction is the very large oasis which comes right down to the sea. A full day should be enough to explore the main sights of Gabès and take in the atmosphere.

Downtown Gabès can seem a confusing place to the first time visitor. There is no readily comprehensible distinction between the walled old town and new 19th century neighbourhoods. Traditionally, there were two rival quarters: **Menzel**, basically the area south of the present bus station; and **Jara**, which divides into two parts: Petite Jara, north of the Oued Gabès, and Grande Jara. The French established a small new town and a large military base east of Jara, towards their new port.

Practically no ancient monuments remain in Gabès. Nonetheless, up in the oasis there are traces of the Roman dam across the Oued Gabès, several pillars and capitols that have been incorporated in the mosque of Sidi Idris and in the mausoleum of Sidi Boulbaba. Some other fragments of lesser value have been used in buildings in the older quarters.

North of the Oued Gabès: Petite Jara One of the most important old buildings is the **Mosque of Sidi Idris**, over the oued in Petite Jara. The building goes back to the 11th century and although you will not be able to see the interior, a considerable amount of Roman masonry was recycled into the building. Unfortunately, many of the Jara neighbourhood's older buildings disappeared during the bombardments and fighting of the Second World War.

Menzel In the Menzel district, you might look out for the **Great Mosque** at the junction of Avenue de la République and Avenue Bechir Dziri, dating back to 1938. The neighbourhood has its own market on rue Omar el Mokhtar. The **Zaouia of Sidi Ben Isa** is another interesting old building to look out for in Menzel.

More spectacular is the **mosque** on avenue Bourguiba in Grande Jara. It is currently undergoing major extension works, and very spectacular they are. Opposite the mosque is a **souk** which attracts plenty of tourists. Local handicrafts include numerous items of basketwork and hats made of plaited palm. There are stalls selling jewellery, food and spices. Both spices and plaited items

Henna for the future husband

are very good buys. However, Gabès' real speciality is **henna** and you can see powdery green volcanoes of this powerful dye in the souk. There are three strengths, 'neutral', red and black. The strength of the henna depends on how long the leaves were left on the plant. Neutral henna strengthens the hair. Red henna is used as hair dye, while black is used for geometric temporary bridal tatooes. In the souk, you may find a stall able to do you a quick scorpion design.

The Oasis

The maritime **oasis** of Gabès is very large, covering 10 sq km, and has more than 300,000 palm trees which shelter hundreds of olive and fruit trees, in addition to numerous vegetable gardens. To get to the more attractive parts of the oasis you can go by car towards the village of **Chenini** by taking the main road towards Sfax, turning left in the direction of Kebili, then left again, signposted Chenini. Alternatively, go on foot from the other end of the oasis, by the bus station, crossing the little bridge. Following the road it is seven km to Chenini, but it is not necessary to go that far since there are pleasant walks along the small, shaded paths between the palm trees, especially in summer. A more picturesque way to see the oasis is to take a *calèche* from the end of Avenue Farhat Hached. The price from a travel agent is lower. It takes one hour and fifteen minutes to make the whole tour. The price, 12Dt, for up to four people, is set by the Tourist Office which is close to the louage and bus station.

The oasis has a couple of sights in the form of a small **zoo** (entrance 0.5Dt) complete with crocodiles and scorpions. At the end of the oasis, towards the source of the river, are located the **Sidi Ali el Bahloul Mausoleum** and a very small waterfall. The area attracts a very high proportion of tourists but the oasis is large, and it is easy to get away from the crowds.

Boulbaba neighbourhood

South of town, about 30 minutes on foot, is the third of Gabès historic areas, the Boulbaba neighbourhood. The **Mosque of Sidi Boulbaba**, which dates back to the seventh century, is one of the most important religious monuments in the area. This is the burial place of Sidi Boulbaba, who was the Prophet's barber after he came from Kairouan. The building is very elegant, with beautiful arcades. Only the inner courtyard is open to visitors. The saint is still the object of much veneration, and on Friday afternoon the smell of incense wafts around the mausoleum. The portico is crowded by people drinking tea kept hot on small charcoal fires. Women come to ask Sidi Boulbaba's intercession for success in exams, a happy marriage or to bring about a much-awaited pregnancy.

Also in the Boulbaba neighbourhood is the **Museum of Popular Arts and Traditions**, housed in a former medersa next to the Sidi Boulbaba mosque. The medersa was built during the reign of Mohammed Bey. The rooms around the courtyard were once student accommodation. Nowadays, those rooms constitute the main part of the museum which has a collection of everyday objects demonstrating the traditional way of life in Gabès. The material is well displayed but unfortunately there is a disappointing lack of information.

There may be a guide on hand who will explain them to you. The museum's exhibits have been divided into four sections, namely domestic crafts, marriage, cultivation in the oasis and preparing and storing food. Although the items on show are not without interest, the best thing is really the building.

Inside the building, the first room on the left begins with **domestic crafts**. This section focuses on women's traditional home-based handicrafts, notably weaving and embroidering. There are different kinds of wool on display, together with the spinning, combing and dyeing tools, jars with different vegetable dyes (tannin, henna, et cetera), a vertical loom and examples of typical textiles (*hambel*, *bettaniya* and *ferrashiya*). Also on display are different veils: on the right the white veil typical of Gabès, in the centre the veil decorated for wedding ceremonies at Gabès, on the left the Matmata veil. There are also displays of cushions, blankets, kilims and a selection of embroidery.

In the room opposite the main entrance, originally the prayer hall of the medersa, **marriage** is the theme. Here the trousseau, traditionally given to the bride by the groom, and the dowry are on display. In the middle of the room, three different bridal dresses are displayed; the first to be worn during the ceremony, the second when she was introduced to relatives, the third for the last day of the wedding feast (the seventh day).

In the section on **agriculture in the oasis** there are displays of different tools, jars to transport foodstuffs, along with information on irrigation and cultivation patterns.

The section on **food preparation and storage** has jars and boxes with vegetables and cereals, photographs of 10 different types of dates, oil-press, mortar, millstones, jars and pots.

Leaving the display areas, turn right into the small garden where, among the fruit trees, you can find Roman and Punic capitols. At the end of the garden it is possible to see the old minaret of the medersa. ■ *Open daily 0800-1300 and 1600-1900 in summer, 0930-1630 in winter. Closed Monday, entrance 1.10Dt plus 1Dt photograph fee, flash prohibited, T281111.*

Essentials

Sleeping
Phone code: 05
■ *on map*
Price codes:
see inside front cover

C *Hotel Chems*, end of Av Habib Thameur, 1st on the right after the railway line, 5-mins walk from the centre, just beyond *Hotel de l'Oasis*; T270547, F274485, 1 min to beach. Over 200 a/c rooms with telephone, each with a small terrace, some with sea view, small pool, childrens' pool, 500 seat restaurant. A standard 3-star hotel, clean but dull. Ugly tiles and 1970s décor, obliging reception but pitiful breakfast. The hotel is situated right next door to the *Foire Internationale de Gabès*, much used for weddings in summer. Heavily amplified music means you will be sleeping with windows closed and air-conditioning on – unless you go and invite yourself to a wedding. C *Hotel de l'Oasis*, at the end of Av Habib Thameur, 2nd turn right after railway line, T270381, F273834, just 5 mins walk from town centre and 1 min from beach.

Museum of Popular Arts & Traditions

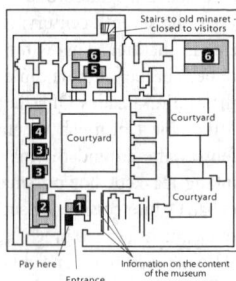

Displays of
1 Wool & associated crafts
2 Veils
3 Cushions, blankets, kilims & embroidery
4 Embroidered blouses & embroidered motifs
5 Wedding dresses & finery
6 Agriculture in the Oasis

Fingers of light – or the dates of Tunisia

In Tunisian cities, the feathery foliage of the date palm waves majestically over squares and avenues. In the southern oases of Tunisia, it is the tree of life: its fruit, leaves and wood the basis of the local economy. The Swedish naturalist Carl Linnaeus rendered homage to the beauty and generosity of the palm tree when he classified it in the order of Principes. The Latin name of the date palm, Phoenix dactylifera, may be translated as "the Phoenician tree with fruit resembling fingers" and Tunisia's top variety of date, the famed Deglet Nour, are also referred to as doigts de lumière.

The date palm is a close relation of the grasses. Its trunk is in fact a stem with no branches. It has no bark, being simply covered by the base of the old fallen leaves. A cross section of a palm trunk reveals a multitude of rigid tubes containing sap bearing vessels, rather than annual growth rings.

In the wild state, the young palm tree tends to resemble a hedgehog due to the uncontrolled development of buds at the base of the initial trunk. If severed with skill, these buds can be planted elsewhere. There are both male and female trees. Broadly speaking, a male tree can pollinate some 50 female trees but to ensure maximum fruit production, the farmer will place a sprig of male flowers next to the female flowers.

In March or April, the tiny green date is round like a marble. Its future is uncertain for if the sand winds are too fierce, it may be blown from the tree before its time. During the summer, the date reaches full size, becoming smooth and yellow, rich in vitamins but bitter to taste. In the heat of the summer and autumn, the fruit slowly matures on the tree, softening and turning an amber colour, deep brown or black, depending on the variety. The date sugars change as well and little by little, the date dries out and becomes a preserved fruit while still on the tree.

Each country has its top varieties of date. As well as Deglet Nour, Tunisia produces the Kuwat, a rather dry dessert date; Kentra which is very sweet; Menakher, the robust Allig and Ftimi; and Kentichi, a dry date stored in jars and which does not harden.

The date is no longer a providential food for oasis dwellers. The date palm orchard, now limited to the top producing varieties, has become more fragile. The market economy now regulates the palm grove with all that this implies in terms of processing and packaging. Whereas in the traditional palm grove, apricots, pomegranates, figs and oranges were grown in the shade of the palms, newly planted groves are laid out to permit greater mechanization. Whereas once there were tiny allotments between the irrigation channels, the modern palm grove is devoted to dates alone.

112 a/c rooms with bath, private terrace, telephone, sea view, also 9 luxury apartments, safe car parking, conference facilities for 20-200 persons, small pool and some garden. Gabès' number one address, which must have been very stylish in the 1970s, now needs a low-key facelift.

D *Chellah Club* (Village de Vacances), in Chenini in the oasis, 20 minutes from the beach and 300m from the zoo, T270442, T/F227446, clearly signposted. Accommodation in 50 small bungalows (damp in winter and spring), ask for hot water as heating runs independently in each bungalow, indoor restaurant only fair, outdoor restaurant under vine arbour marred by overamplified music, pool small and mucky, no credit cards, no money change, from Gabès yellow taxi to Chenini around 1.5Dt. Must have been very pleasant in its day, but basically now functions as locals' drinking den. Nothing wrong with that – but the food could be improved. Bungalows have pitched roofs, and are hot in summer, though they provide you with a fan. Bring your insect repellant. **D** *Hotel Anis*, about 3 km from town on road to Medenine, T278744. Very new. **D** *Hotel Nejib*, corner of Av Habib Bourguiba and Av Farhat Hached, T271686. 56 rooms, all modcons, a/c, noisy due to main streets on both sides, slightly over-priced but very comfortable and convenient, showing signs of age.

E *Hotel Atlantic*, 4 Av Habib Bourguiba, T220034. Old hotel retains some charm but needs decorating, clean, all 64 rooms have bath, restaurant, good value, recommended. **E** *Hotel Khenini*, Blvd Mohammed Ali, T270320. 34 rooms with bath, breakfast only 1.5Dt. *Hotel Médina*, near Great Mosque, T274271. 40 rooms. **E** *Régina*, 135 Av Habib Bourguiba, T272095. Only 14 rooms with bath, arranged around central courtyard back from the street, clean, restaurant, food is served on the patio, best of the cheap hotels. However, in summer the patio is used for weddings, which means no sleep until the small hours. A good opportunity for a free invitation.

F *Ben Nejima*, 68 rue Ali Djemel, near train station, T271591. Clean, quite pleasant and very simple, hot communal showers, rooms at front rather noisy, good restaurant; **F** *Hotel de la Poste*, 116 Av Habib Bourguiba, T270718. Very cheap but not really very clean, communal bath and toilets.

Youth hostel   Known as *Sanit el Bey* or *Centre de stages et de vacances*, Rue de l'Oasis, T270271, F275035. In quarter called 'Petite Jara' north of the souk. Small rooms, 80 beds, 60 beds, clean, 4Dt per night, breakfast 1Dt, dinner 3Dt.

Camping   On main road, follow sign opposite Agil petrol station. Cheap and adequate, also at Youth Hostel, 2Dt per person, 1Dt per tent, per car and per van. Palm trees here provide some shade.

Eating   **Expensive** *Restaurant Chez Amori*, 82 Av Habib Bourguiba. Has good, simple Tunisian food, choose the fish before it is cooked, very friendly. *Restaurant l'Oasis*, 15-17 Av Farhat Hached, T270098. A very popular restaurant especially for locals at lunch time, evenings are quieter, more expensive than the others. *Restaurant* in *Hotel Chems*, serves international and some Tunisian food, buffet 11Dt, menu 7.5Dt. Try also restaurant *El Mazar*, Av Farhat Hached, T272065.

Mid-range *Restaurant A la bonne table*, Av Habib Bourguiba. Very reasonably priced. *Le Pacha*, Av Farhat Hached. Filling food, served by welcoming people. *Pizzaria Pino*, 114 Av Habib Bourguiba, T272010. Standard Tunisian version of Italian grub. Clean, no booze.

There are also several very small, very cheap restaurants beside the daily vegetable market off Av Farhat Hached

Cheap *La Ruche*, on the road to Sfax, T270369; *El Khalij*, Av Farhat Hached, T221412. *Chez Amori*, 82 Av Habib Bourguiba. Is not quite as good as it used to be, choose the fish before it is cooked. The restaurant in *Hotel Ben Nejima* has good, well presented food.

Shopping   **Bargains** *SOCOPA* (part of ONAT) on Blvd Farhat Hached by post office has a range of quality goods. Open 0900-1300 and 1600-1900 in summer; 0830-1230 and 1500-1830 in winter, closed Sunday afternoon. Gabès is well known for its straw work and Berber jewellery, which can be bought in the souk or the markets. Gabès is the last town where you can buy a European newspaper, although it will probably be several days old. The daily vegetable market gives a good insight into Tunisian life. **Books** The bookshop marked on map has a very good selection. **Crafts** The ONAT school/workshop on Av Farhat Hached, T270775, is worth a visit to see all the local handicrafts on display, closed afternoons on Friday and Saturday. This is where the various craft techniques are taught. The course lasts 2-3 years for jewellery making, the majority of the young artisans opening their own shops on completing the course. There are courses, too, on palm frond weaving and carpet making and the demonstrations show how these skills are taught. **Food** In the area of the Sidi Boulbaba mosque and the museum, on the corner on the right there is a baker who sells lovely fresh bread and mouthwatering Tunisian sweets. The baker by the tourist information office sells excellent bread with seeds on. **General** The *Gabès Centre* on Av Habib Bourguiba is only a collection of small and noisy boutiques, not for any serious shopping. There is, however, a public internet centre on the 1st floor.

Sailing 20 yacht berths min-max draft 2-4½m, T270367. **Sponge fishing** Also fishing for tuna fish, king shrimps, octopus. **Sports**

Local Car hire: Hire here as there are no facilities in Medenine or Foum Tataouine. *Avis*, rue du 9 Avril, T270210; *Budget*, 57 Av Farhat Hached, T270930; *Europcar*, 12 Av Farhat Hached, T274720; *Economic Rent-a-Car*, 159 Av Farhat Hached, T257515; *Express*, 154 Av Farhat Hached, T274222, F276211; *Hertz*, 30 rue Ibn el Jazzar, T270525. **Cycle hire**: enquire at the Youth hostel or at *Hotel de la Poste*. **Transport**

Long distance Air: nearest airport is Sfax 137 km north or Houmt-Souq on Djerba 106 km east. *Tunis Air*, Av Habib Bourguiba, T270697; *Tunis Avia*, route de Sfax, T272501. **Train**: the train station is off rue Farhat Hached. Information on T270744. Departures as follows: Tunis (via Sfax and Sousse) 1535, 2310. **Bus**: the bus station is at the end of Av Farhat Hached, by the entrance to the oasis. Information on T270008. In Gabès there are 3 bus companies, all in the same place. *Sotregames* (timetable only in Arabic) **Tunis** via **Sfax** and **Sousse** at 0600, 0945, 1230, 1235, 2115, 2200, 2215, 2250 and 2350; **Medenine** 0600, 0730, 0800, 1000, 1700, 1730; **Matmata** 1015, 1100, 1200, 1400; **Djerba** 0930, 1345, 1530. *Entri* **Tunis** 0600, 0945, 1230, 1235; **Sousse** 0815, 0915; **Djerba** 0930, 1345, 1530; **Zarzis** 1345; **El Hamma** 1400; **Sfax** 1500; **Tataouine** 1615; **Ben Gardane** 1735. *STE* **Tataouine** via Medenine 1000; **Zarzis** via Medenine 1100, 1330; **Djerba** via Djorf 0945; **Ras Ajdir** and **Libyan border** via Medenine and Ben Gardane 1145, 1530. **Louages**: the louage station is close to the bus station. Sample fares Tunis 14Dt, takes 6 hours; Djerba 5Dt; Sousse 10Dt; Medenine 3.5Dt; Tripoli (Libya) 25Dt. It is possible to get a round trip visiting all the villages and the area surrounding Gabès. Tour operators offer a variety of options, including travel by four-wheel drive vehicle with a group of 5-10 people (see Travel agents).

Banks *BCT*, rue Mohammed Ali, T271203. *BIAT*, Av Farhat Hached, T270459. *BNA*, Av Habib Bourguiba, T272323, with cash machine. *BS*, 131 Av Habib Bourguiba, T271499; *BT*, Av Habib Bourguiba, T270093. *UIB*, Av Habib Bourguiba, T274881, open 0800-1200 and 1400-1700. On Sat and Sun there is always one bank open at 0930. *STB* has an automatic cash dispenser (dinars) for Visa and Mastercard holders. **Communications** Post Office: T270544, Av Habib Bourguiba, opposite *Hotel Régina*, exchange available. **Internet:** *Publinet Gabès* on Av Habib Bourguiba, Gabès Centre building, 1st floor, unit 146-7, T275724. Quite easy to find in a large shopping precinct. One of the few places for you to check your email in southern Tunisia. **Hammam** There are 4 to try, in the souk, on Av Mohammed Ali, by the *calèche* station and close to the Sidi Idris mosque. Open morning and evening for men, afternoon for women, entrance 1Dt. **Hospitals & medical services** Chemist: all night, 2 in Av Habib Bourguiba. Hospital: *Hôpital Universitaire*, Cité M'Torrech, T282700. *Clinic Bon Sécours*, 10 rue Mongi Slim, T277700. *Dialysis Centre*, 112 rue Mongi Slim, T273200, F275822. **Places of worship** Catholic: 25 rue d'Alger, T270326, service Sat at 1830. **Tour companies & travel agents** *Etoile du Sud*, Av Farhat Hached (same office as Express Rent), T650244, F651076. *Voyage Najar Chabane*, Av Farhat Hached, T272158, F277555. *Europtours*, Av Farhat Hached, T274720. *Sahara Tours*, Av Farhat Hached, T270930. *Gabès Voyage*, Av Farhat Hached, T270797. *Carthage Tours*, Av Habib Bourguiba, T270840. **Tourist offices** The tourist information office is at Place de la Libération, T220254, open 0830-1300 and 1500-1745, closed Fri, Sat and Sun afternoon. **Directory**

Southeastern Tunisia

Gabès to Medenine via Mareth

Colour map 3, grid A/B4

Driving southeast to Medenine there is little of major interest to keep the traveller. Military history buffs will want to take a look at a small museum south of Mareth, which was the scene of some very fierce battles during the Second World War.

Just four km from Gabès, on the right in Teboulbou, is the *Restaurant Les Lanternes*. Gabès people tend to head out to the shore at Teboulbou to swim. Some 20 km further is the village of Kettana on the Oued El Ferch. On the right under the shadow of the palm trees, a permanent market of small shops sell local handicrafts. (All-night opening too!) The main market day is Wednesday.

Mareth
Phone code: 05
Colour map 3, grid A4

Mareth is 37 km from Gabès and 39 km from Medenine. The name survives in the annals of military history. If you have time, take a look at **The Military Museum of the Mareth line**, located out of Mareth on the road to Medenine. The museum has information in English and you will be able to see some of the original bunkers. ■ *Open from 0900 to 1645. Closed on Monday. Entrance 1Dt, permission to take photographs 2Dt. Free entrance for students, children (less than 8 years old) and disabled.*

The **Mareth Defensive line** was built between 1936 and 1940 by the French forces in response to a possible Italian offensive on Tunisia from Libya, which was at that time an Italian colony. The Mareth line was also called the 'desert Maginot line'. It played an important role in the development of operations in

The Mareth Defensive Line

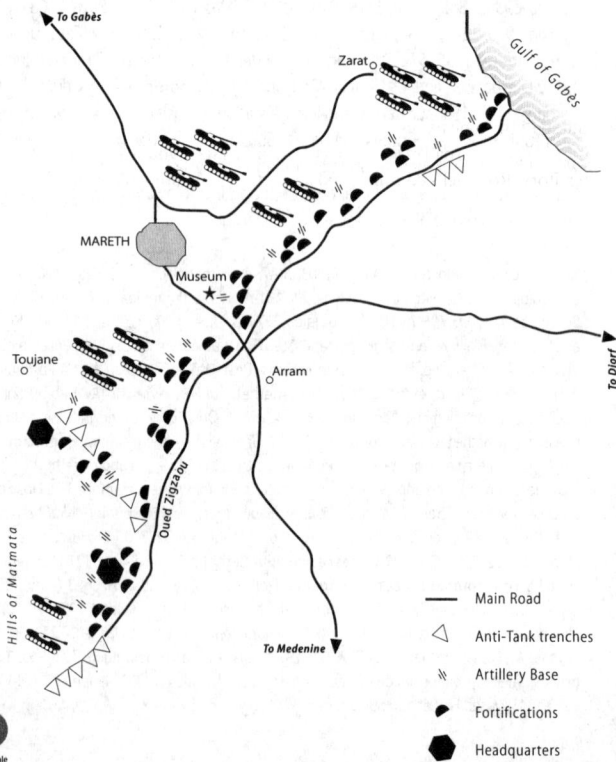

The Battle of Mareth, March 1943

After the occupation of French territories by the Germans in 1940 and the Franco-German and Franco-Italian armistice treaties, a German-Italian commission proceeded to demilitarize the Mareth line. The German-Italian troops commanded by Field Marshall Rommel withdrew from Tunisia via Tripolitania as a consequence of their defeat against the British Eighth Army led by General Montgomery (4 October 1942, Battle of El Alamein). In order to enable Rommel's forces to hold up the British advance, the Mareth line was rearmed and reinforced by the Axis High Command. This rearming took place between November 1942 and March 1943. As a result, the Mareth line became an insurmountable obstacle, especially during the flood season.

The Battle of Mareth took place in March 1943. It coincided with the pressure exerted on the Axis forces – led by General Von Arnim – in central and northern Tunisia, and with the start of maritime and aerial supremacy in the Mediterranean Sea of the Allied Forces – led by General Anderson. The battle began on 16 March 1943 when the British attacked the Mareth line on two fronts, the first along the coastal area between Mareth and the shore, the second across the Dahar plateau. On the 20 and 21 March the British attempted to cross the Oued Zigzaou, but met the fierce resistance of the Axis forces led by General Messe. The battle ended on 28 March 1943 following the British success in crossing the El Hamma-Tebaga gap. The Axis forces were forced to abandon their defensive positions on the Mareth line and withdrew northwards.

the Tunisian Campaign of November 1942 to May 1943. This line stretched 45 km from the sea to the Matmata mountains and lay alongside the Oued Zigzaou. The line fortifications comprised 40 infantry emplacements, eight large artillery bunkers, 15 command posts and 28 support points.

With your own transport, after visiting the museum, you could always head out to inspect the territory fought over by Allied and Axis armies. Head south on the Toujane road, and at the village of **Lazaiza**, you will be in Mareth line territory. Rommel's command post is a couple of kilometres from the village.

Should you need to stay overnight in Mareth, there is not too much choice. Try the F *Hotel du Golfe*, T236135. There are some restaurants and banks, notably the BNA (on the right arriving from Gabès) and the STB (on the left).

Moving on from Mareth, you pass through the village of **Koutine** (24 km) where there are some handy cafés located on the main road. Try *Restaurant 7 Novembre* which is just at the beginning of Koutine on the left or *Restaurant l'Olivier*, T05-630017. A few kilometres before Medenine, **Metameur** is signposted to your right. Coming from the North, you will see your first *ghorfa* or fortified granary here, a hive of vaulted cells built round three courtyards. One section used to function tourist accommodation, the personably run E *Hotel des Ghorfas*, T05-640128, which also does good food. Maybe it will reopen. The manager, Hachmi Drifi, is very talkative and knowledgeable on the neighbourhood and local culture. Try to arrive early or make a reservation, as he lives a distance from the hotel and might leave before you arrive. Bring sleeping bag as sheets and blankets are not provided. Good place to meet people either driving to Libya or to the desert.

Note that there is a rough piste from Metameur northwest to Toujane, which would be extremely slow and painful going in a standard hire car, but feasible by four-wheel drive.

Mareth to Medenine

Southeastern Tunisia

Tunisia and Libya in the Second World War

The physical marks of the destruction wrought by the Second World War are still very apparent in Tunisia and Libya – if mainly now in the large cemeteries of war dead.

Italy, the colonial power in Libya at the outbreak of the Second World War, invaded British-held Egypt in the closing weeks of 1940, mistakenly believing that the campaign there would be brief and successful. In reality, the war raged, with many changes of fortune for the combatants, until May 1943. The prize of winning Egypt from the British was the destruction of British lines of communication to the Middle East, India and the Far East, together with access for the Italian and German commands to the rich oil fields of Iran and the Arabian peninsula. Great Britain and the Commonwealth countries, for their part, desperately needed to hold their grip on Egypt, their lines of communication such as the Suez Canal and the natural resources of the region. Scarcely surprising, therefore, that the battle for control of North Africa should be so protracted and bitter.

The local populations were for the most part unwilling spectators of the desert war, though their suffering was considerable. In Libya, the Senusi movement backed the British against the colonial Italy, and Libyan troops did ultimately have a hand in the re-conquest of their country. In Francophone North Africa there was uncertainty and confusion in the ranks of the French colonial authorities and their colonial peoples as a result of the Pétain régime's accommodation with the Nazis.

Although the Italian armies made some progress in Egypt in 1940, they were soon expelled. Faced with what appeared to be

War in the desert 1940-43

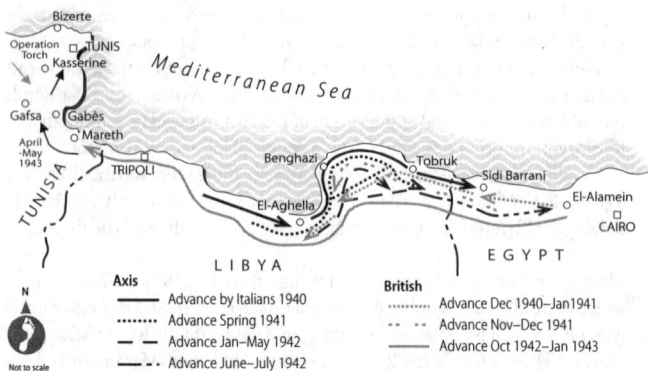

- Axis
  - —— Advance by Italians 1940
  - ····· Advance Spring 1941
  - — — Advance Jan–May 1942
  - —··— Advance June–July 1942
- British
  - ·········· Advance Dec 1940–Jan1941
  - – · – · Advance Nov–Dec 1941
  - —— Advance Oct 1942–Jan 1943

N
Not to scale

Gabès to Kebili via El Hamma de l'Arad

Colour map 3, grid A1-4 Four kilometres north out of Gabès, the P16 west to Kebili is clearly signed. This first part is through the pleasant oasis region. At Maqsef, where the C208 'Gabès bypass' crosses, the route is a government subsidized agricultural estate with surprisingly large grain silos, large areas under plastic, olives and a few date palms. About five km before El Hamma on the north side is an area used by coaches and safari tours, *Station Chincou Tourisme*, a good place for a coffee. This is decorated with huge desert roses and is impossible to miss. It is here that the gas pipeline crosses the route and where a number of tracks lead out north across the sebkha.

an Italian collapse, German troops and armour were moved into Tripolitania in February 1941. The combined German and Italian army pushed back the British to the Egyptian frontier by April. The Axis army was led by General Rommel with skill and audacity, supported by a strong air force. Rommel's eastwards advance was slowed by the protracted resistance of the garrisons – first Australian, then British and Polish – at Tobruk. Meanwhile, the main armies fought pitched battles around the Libyan-Egyptian frontier until Rommel withdrew temporarily in December 1941. Once back in Libyan territory, Rommel reorganized and, taking advantage of improved lines of communication, prepared a counter attack which pushed the British back as far as Gazala, near Derna, in January and February 1942 and, after a pause, into Tobruk and deep into Egypt in June, though this advance was finally held at El-Alamein after a fierce battle. Rommel made a final attempt at Alam Halfa, east of El-Alamein, to push aside British and Commonwealth forces and break through to the Nile Valley in August 1942, but failed in the face of a strong Allied defensive effort and his own growing losses of men and equipment.

The balance in the desert war changed in mid-1942. The Allies gradually won superiority in the air and gained freedom of movement at sea. The Germans and Italians increasingly lacked adequate armour, reinforcements and strategy as Rommel's personal health also deteriorated. On the Allied side, General Montgomery took over leadership and began a build-up of the Eighth Army sufficient to overwhelm the well-trained and experienced Afrika Korps. Montgomery opened his attack at El-Alamein on 23 October 1942 and, after 11 days of hard fighting, the Axis army was beaten back and retreated by rapid stages to the west to make a last stand in Tunisia.

The German attempt to hold on in North Africa was made difficult by sea and airborne landings by Allied, including American, troops in Morocco and Algeria in November 1942. These two countries were liberated with comparative ease when French Vichy units, formerly collaborating with the Germans, were brought round to support the invasion. German and Italian reinforcements were rushed to Tunis, and a battle began to stop the advance of Allied units from the west as they fought their way in from Algeria and from the south through Libya. German attacks in the Battle of Kasserine in the hills north of Gafsa during January and February 1943 almost succeeded in halting the Allied progress. Rommel's final assault against Montgomery's advancing Eighth Army arriving from Libya failed in early March. Axis troops retreated northwards behind the Mareth Line on the Gulf of Gabès (see page), before being outflanked and being forced to withdraw by Montgomery's troops. A concluding series of battles in northern Tunisia saw the Allies push through the Medjerda Valley to Tunis and Bizerte in May 1943, effectively ending Axis resistance in North Africa.

Southeastern Tunisia

The settlement of El Hamma de l'Arad, 32 km west of Gabès, has grown up round the hotsprings. (Note that there is another El Hamma, also with hotsprings, near Tozeur, called El Hamma du Djerid.) The town is situated between the salt flats to the north and the foothills of Djebel Tebaga to the south. The Romans called it *Aquae Tacapitanae*. The hot water in the springs which feed the hot baths is very sulphurous. The road in through the triumphal arch just beyond the *oued*, by the hospital and the grain stores, leads past a few villas to the date palm oasis. The road into the oasis turns off north and the dual carriageway, complete with smart double globe lights, goes right through the town. Here you will find plenty of shops (try *Ulysses* for size), tyre and car repairs, pâtisseries, chemist, petrol, calor gas, cafés, three banks near the square-faced clock and even the opportunity for photo development. The

El Hamma de l'Arad
Phone code: 05
Colour map 3, grid A3

souk has a good selection of spices, market day is Monday. The louages gather near the Shell station while the post office is opposite the road to Matmata.

In El Hamma there are several thermal springs and three **hammams**. Unlike many hammams which use the same facilities and divide out the time, here the bathing areas and entrances for men and women are quite separate so no timetable is needed. The hammams here differ in condition of the buildings, some less pleasant than others. Hot showers are available in all.

From Place 7 Novembre go towards the banks and turn right. On the left is **Hammam Aïn el Borj**, entrance 0.250Dt, four pools for women and four for men. This is probably the most friendly and most colourful hammam. At the women's entrance, soaps, panties and bras, combs, shampoo, henna and *suak* (walnut bark to clean the teeth) are sold.

The hammam on the road to Gabès is not clearly signed, though there is a white label with a red arrow and the name of the bath house in Arabic script. Turn right before the hospital into a nameless and dusty road. At the very end there is the **Hammam Esghaier**, entrance 0.500Dt. This is the cleanest and the most expensive hammam in town and also the least crowded, probably because it is a 15-minute walk from the centre. The building is well kept, with blue columns and a light blue ceiling. Both the women's and the men's areas are provided with lockers, one big and one small pool, and a hall with benches for resting before leaving. The toilets are pretty unpleasant, however.

Situated near the souk is **Hammam Abd el Kader**, entrance 0.12Dt. This is the most crowded *hammam*. There are two big pools for women and one for men, high ceilings but unpleasant atmosphere and the usual grotty toilets.

Sleeping F *Hotel Hammam*, 80 Av Habib Bourguiba in front of Banque de Tunisie, 8 rooms small and mostly dark, extremely cheap (3Dt without breakfast). The only hotel in town, management don't speak much French, so smile and do your best.

Eating **Mid-range** *Restaurant de Tunis*, Av Habib Bourguiba/Place 7 Novembre near Bank de Tunisie. Couscous with lamb is better than elsewhere. For dessert try *makroudh* (date cakes) from the nearby patisserie. **Cheap** *Restaurant Amel*, in the commercial centre. Has food on display, good chicken kebab, very cheap, no tables. There are some other cheap eateries at the western end of town. Coffee shops and restaurants are found on both sides of the main street.

Transport **Bus**: plenty of buses to Gabès, just 30 minutes away, and 6 to Kebili (1hr 45mins). Also **louages** from Av Habib Bourguiba.

Directory **Banks** BT and BNA in Av Habib Bourguiba near *Restaurant de Tunis*. **Communications** Post Office on the right in Place 7 Novembre. **Hammam**: see details below. **Festival** of the *hammam* each Mar. **Hospital & medical services** Chemist: on Place 7 Novembre. **Hospital:** on the road to Gabès in a very new building, T234127. **Useful information** Police: T234141.

El Hamma de L'Arad

To Gabès

Oued el Hamma

Triumphal Arch

Sign to Hammam (red & white)

Hammam Esghaier

Café Chicha
Louages

Shell Petrol & Calor Gas

School

Amel

COMMERCIAL CENTRE

Chemist

Place du 7 Novembre

Hammam de Tunis

Pâtisserie

Kodak Film Processing

Hammam Aïn el Borj

Av Habib Bourguiba

Hammam Abdel Kader

Oued el Morteba

Chemist

To Matmata (35 km)

Total Petrol

N

Not to scale

Café

To Kebili

Southeastern Tunisia

A 19th century tourist at the baths of El Hamma

"It was late in the evening, near ten o'clock, and I was about to retire to rest, when Ali noticed that I had caught a slight cold. He insisted that I should at once go down to the wonderful healing waters of the warm spring, declaring that in a quarter of an hour I should be perfectly well.

It was pitch dark when Hamed, Ali and I, carrying lanterns, strolled through the village to the spring near the ruined old 'Borj'. We descended a stone stair which ended in a dark, paved lower room, from the opening into which steam issued into the cold outer air. By the light of the lantern I saw that the water rose within the room, through which it flowed, and was discharged through a small opening into a basin outside. In the centre of the room stood a clumsy pillar supporting the roof, and surrounding the fountains were tanks built of stone.

The room was full of choking hot steam, as in a Roman or Moorish bath; I began to perspire before I got into the water. Counting 1, 2, 3, I scrambled in. Over my whole body I felt an icy sensation, just as though I had plunged into cold water, but immediately after followed a feeling as of being scalded, and I sprang back to the stone verge. Twice I repeated my endeavours to bear the burning heat of the water, but each time had to jump out quickly; so I remained seated on the stones, throwing the water over my body, and even that I could hardly bear.

With Hamed it was the same, but he was able to remain longer in the water. But Ali astonished us by quietly enjoying himself sitting in the water, the temperature of which was at least 113° Fahrenheit."

From The Cave Dwellers of Southern Tunisia by Daniel Bruun, (London, 1898).

El Hamma to Kebili

Just after El Hamma de l'Arad, **Sembat** is basically a continuation of the main settlement with the same central reservation with double globed lights. There is low-income housing with half cylinder roofs and a huge brick works colouring everywhere around bright red. In contrast, immediately after the *oued* is the oasis, with good quality soil and adequate water providing good crops, particularly pomegranates. From here to Kebili it is a very long straight road, with the serrated summits of the **Djebel Tebaga** visible across scrub land to the South. To the North is low grade grazing land. Watch out for the white posts with red writing. The sign says 'danger, death' but only in Arabic script. **Don't check**. **Don't enter**. The few small settlements in this region can be spotted by their tall water towers.

Keep a watch at 57 km from Kebili for a restaurant on the north side of the road, and reward yourself with a coffee. The 'feature' marked on the Michelin map at **Saïdane** was a fort, then a hotel and now a police post, so no photographs. Finally the road turns south and cuts up through the Djebel Tabaga to take you to Kebili.

El Hamma to Nouvelle Matmata

Rather than get to the Matmata on the direct newly resurfaced road from Gabès, Matmata Nouvelle can be reached from El Hamma via a track (34 km) clearly signposted in the town centre. A normal car will do it (very slowly) in good weather conditions and with daylight. At the six km crossroad, go straight ahead. In El Magcem, at 12 km, drive carefully as there is a school and children usually try to get a lift. At 15 km, El Magcem ends, there are some houses on the left and a crossroads with a fountain in the centre. Take the road on the left. From here the route to Nouvelle Matmata is straightforward.

Southeastern Tunisia

Matmata مطماطة

Phone code: 05
Colour map 3, grid A3

Nothing really destined the Matmata, southwest of Gabès, to become a major daytripper destination: there was merely the mild curiosity of the underground pit-homes and some arid hills, and many of the villagers moved to Nouvelle Matmata in the 1970s. Then came Star Wars, and the famous bar scene with bizarre denizens of the galaxy, enough to put Matmata firmly on the tourist trail. Roads across the area have been improved, and it is now possible to cut westwards right across to Douz via the outpost Berber village of Tamezret. Tracks to other villages – notably scenic Toujane – look set to be improved in the near future, too. Although sometimes swamped by herds of four-wheel drive vehicles, the landscapes of Matmata nevertheless merit more than just a flying visit.

Ins and outs

Getting there Matmata is most easily accessed from Gabès, 44 km away. There are buses and louages, from next to the big minaret by the tourist market in downtown Gabès. Journey time, depending on traffic and roadworks, just under an hour. Note that most louages only go to Nouvelle Matmata. You have to take a 2nd louage or minibus for the final leg of the journey from the main street of Nouvelle Matmata. This leaves when it is full.

The Gabès to Matmata road is being upgraded, and eventually the section Gabès to Nouvelle Matmata (28 km) will be very good indeed. After Nouvelle Matmata, the road begins to wind up into the hills. You pass Tijma and the turn-off for another troglodyte village, Haddej, 10 km after Nouvelle Matmata. A further 6 km on you climb over a small col and into the Matmata Valley.

With your own transport, Matmata can also be approached from Douz to the west on a newly built road. Journey time is around 2 hours and 45 minutes, depending on traffic. The approach to Matmata from Medenine (via Toujane) to the east is only to be contemplated with a good four-wheel drive.

Getting around From the main road junction, you can have a good wander around Matmata on foot, discovering the underground Hotel Sidi Driss and the nearby museum (market day is Tuesday). Without your own transport, things get more difficult if you are pressed for time and want to get to the nearby villages such as Tamezret (13 km on metalled road) and Toujane (23 km on rough piste). Neither has accommodation, and both are too far for a comfortable day walk in the heat. There is a mini-bus once a day to Tamezret from the centre of Matmata. For Toujane there is no public transport.

Should you have your own transport, there is a poorly surfaced road to Toujane from Nouvelle Matmata via Beni Zeltene and Aïn Tounine.

Matmata

To Gabès

● Rim

(Pol)

✉

ℹ 🚌

Pâtisserie ●   Chemist ○

Café   Ouled
Hamadi ●   Aziz   ○ Bread Shop

■3   Café

                           ■1   To Toujane

■2   ■5 ■4

        ■6

To Tamezret

N
Not to scale

■ **Sleeping**

1 Kousseïla   4 Marhala
2 Ksar el Amazigh   5 Matmata
3 Les Berbères   6 Sidi Driss

History and background

The appearance of the Matmata Valley is generally described as 'lunar', the arid yellow landscape being scattered wth numerous pit-dwellings. Until 15 years ago, the only visible signs of habitation above ground were the TV aerials. But increasing prosperity and new means of construction have enabled the people of Matmata to build themselves concrete houses next to their troglodyte homes. The other features of the area are the numerous *marabouts* or saints' tombs, speckling hillside and valley with their white domes.

The village has a population of around 3,500. As in many poor southern Mediterranean communities, there is a tradition of migrating to the cities of Europe for work. At one time, many Matmatans would set up as bakers in northern Tunisia's towns. Money earned elsewhere funds new building. A section of the population still live in the underground dwellings, but their number is slowly decreasing. If you want to see the inside of one of the underground houses it isn't really necessary to take a guide, but doing so is one way of obtaining entry. The fee should be negotiated but is generally very reasonable, about 1-2 Dt.

The people of Matmata have been living in these houses for over 700 years. The population may originally have lived in more defensible hill villages like the ones at Tamezret and Toujane. When times became more secure, the underground home was the ideal building solution in a region of great extremes of temperature. The soft ground made the construction of homes underground possible. Provided there was no excssive rainfall, troglodyte living provided the best protection from heat and marauders.

There is little scope for agriculture in Matmata due to the climate and the lack of water, which explains the tendency to migrate. Traditionally, each family would have olive and almond trees and date palms, as well as a few animals and fowl. There was a little dry farming. Water was carefully husbanded in cisterns. A carefully constructed system of terraces (the *jessour*), visible here and there off the road as you approach Matmata from Gabès, increasing the area available for agriculture. Today, however, jobs in the ever-expanding tourist sector provide a new source of income for low-skilled labour.

Sights

Matmata has few sights. Obviously, you will want to see one of the famous **underground dwellings.** On arriving in Matmata it is unclear where to go since nothing is visible, but walking around will reveal one of the 700 underground houses. Many of these can be visited in return for a small payment at the end of the tour. You could start with a look in at the underground **Hotel Sidi Driss**, down the road to the right just after the café at the central crossroads. Sort of 'behind' the hotel is a small **museum** in a typical, though rather tumbledown, troglodyte dwelling. There is a bridal chamber with a rather stylish built-in bed made from white-plastered branches. In another chamber, you can see some local girls at their looms weaving mergoum carpets. Note also the way the tunnelled entrance passage is carefully roofed with supporting flat stones. ■ *Opening hours and entry fee (say 1Dt a head) are erratic.*

And of course there are **camel rides** to be had from just by the Hotel Sidi Driss. Probably best to pay all the fee when you get down or it may cost you more. More camels and guides can be found on the way to Toujane.

The **underground dwellings** really are rather special. The basic layout centres on a large excavated area or *houch*, in the local parlance, which will have a tunnel or occasionally stairs leading to the surface. The houch is often as much as seven metres below ground level, with a diameter of between 10 to 15

Southeastern Tunisia

A bridal baton

"One custom is universal amongst these people; it is that at the wedding the bridegroom shows his bride a heavy stick, of which one end that he holds to her nose is thoroughly and sweetly scented. The interpretation of this custom being that so long as she conducts herself

properly, her life will be mild and pleasant like the scent; but, on the other hand, should she misbehave she may be sure of being well punished. I saw one of these sticks at Tatauin."

From The Cave Dwellers of Southern Tunisia *by Daniel Bruun (London, 1898).*

metres. It functions like the courtyard in the Tunisian townhouse, providing light and air for the rooms joining onto it. Large dwellings for an extended family will have several *ahouach*, connected by tunnels.

Troglodyte dwellings are kept impeccably clean. Traditionally, they would have whitewashed walls, shelving cut out of the soft rock and tiny excavated cuboards. Sleeping rooms would have small curtained niches for washing. In the village of Techine, near Matmata, the houses have built-in furniture, constructed from branches coated with a white plaster finish. Some dwellings have been modernized, and have electricity and water. With the successful conversion of some underground homes to hotel use, the troglodyte dwelling in Matmata looks set to survive well into the 21st century.

Overlooking the village, off the Toujane road, is a small fort which unfortunately cannot be visited because it is occupied by the military.

Excursions **Nouvelle Matmata**, 15 km away, is often ignored, but a visit here will help explain the reasons why the villagers moved. By car there is a variety of places to visit. Going southeast towards Medinine, you can reach Toujane via a poorly metalled road.

Essentials

Sleeping
■ *on map*
Price codes:
see inside front cover
Phone code: 05

All the water in Matmata has a distinct yellow hue. Accept it as part of the excursion. There are no upmarket hotels, but some of the cheaper underground places would be great fun for a school excursion.

C *Hotel Ksar el Amazigh* (ex-*Hotel Les Troglodytes*), T230062, F230173, 1 km down road to Tamezret on left. Small but pleasant pool, 50 a/c rooms, opened 1993, during the late evening and night water is not very hot, no credit cards, private parking, most expensive hotel in the village, but reasonable nevertheless. Views over the fierce sunburnt hills.
C *Hotel Kousseïla*, arriving from Gabès take Toujane exit at Matmata's central roundabout. The hotel, a large brown concrete structure with some vaguely Berber designs, is on your right, T230303, F230265. 34 rooms, 100 beds, a/c, no pool, no credit cards, clean. Opened 1995. Not a very inspirational place, but would do for an air-conditioned night. Makes its money by feeding tour groups in a viewless restaurant.

D *Hotel Matmata*, F230177, beyond the *Kousseïla*, turn right off the Toujane road. Quite small, above ground (so no troglodyte charm), all 32 rooms have bath, a/c, comfortable, clean, small pool, restaurant, management offers large discounts to groups of over 10, be warned.

E *Hotel Marhala*, T230015, slightly out of the village, up the Toujane road towards the fort. The best of the 3 underground hotels, very clean, very basic (bed, door without lock, light bulb), communal bath/toilet, quiet, Tunisian food in restaurant, book in summer, composed of 5 holes around which the rooms are located, neither humid/cold in winter, nor hot in summer, cheap, friendly management. **E** *Hotel Les Berbères*, T230024, F230097, on Tamezret road, on left before *Ksar el Amazigh*. Most recent and smallest underground hotel, communal bath/toilet, restaurant, book in season, a curious experience, 13 rooms, 120 beds (some rooms have 9 beds), the holes in which the hotel is built are less deep than usual and are therefore less impressive, watch your head! **E** *Hotel Sidi Driss*, T230005, close to the centre of the village. Turn right immediately after Toujane exit on main roundabout by café. Largest and most touristy of the underground hotels, endless corridors and courtyards, communal bath/toilet, bar, restaurant, fairly clean, not all the management can speak English or French.

Eating

For a reasonable feed, it is probably best to eat in the hotels, open to all visitors, although there are a few restaurants in the market place.

Mid-range *Hotel Ksar el Amazigh*. Try the warming barley soup (winter only) and as a dessert the *mehchi Tataouine*, a pancake filled with almonds, sesame seeds and peanuts, lunch 7.5Dt.

Cheap *Café Restaurant Ouled Aziz*, at the centre of Matmata more or less opposite the tourist office. Has the traditional Tunisian restaurant staples (salade tunisienne, chicken or lamb couscous, etc). Full meal (salad, main course, dessert or fruit) is 5Dt. No menu on display, so check prices when you order. *Café Hamadi*, near *Restaurant Ouled Aziz*. Has good cakes. Try also *Café Restaurant Rim*, arriving from Gabès at the beginning of Matmata on the left, T230023. Opened 1996. *Café de la Victoire* has only coffee, tea and soft drinks.

Transport

Bus the buses come to a halt in Matmata's main square, on the Toujane road just below the main junction. No buses to Medenine. Tunis 1930 running via Sousse; Gabès 0530, 0730, 0900, 1100, 1230, 1330, 1400, 1600, 1730, 2000; Tamezret 1400. Also a couple of minibuses to Techine. **Louages** on main road in town centre but very few cars. Matmata to Matmata Nouvelle is 800 miles.

Directory

Banks Banks are situated in Matmata Nouvelle, 15 km along the road to Gabès. **Communications** Post Office: in the centre of town, changes money. **Hospitals & medical services** Chemist: on the main road in front of bus station. **Tourist offices** The tourist information office (the Syndicat d'initiative, T230114) is right on the crossroads in the middle of Matmata. They are helpful, and will allow you to leave your rucksack in the office while you explore. Closes at 1715. **Useful addresses** Police: on road to Medenine, T270390.

Around Matmata

If you have time, there are a number of small villages to visit around Matmata. Without your own transport, getting to these settlements, although not especially difficult, takes time with waits for louages or buses. **El Haddej**, off the main Matmata Nouvelle to Matmata road, is similar to Matmata, though much less visited. West of Matmata, stone-built hillcrest **Tamezret** and **Taoujout** are different kinds of village altogether, as are **Techine** and **Toujane** to the east. **Beni Aissa** and hilltop **Beni Zelten** are probably for enthusiasts only.

El Haddej

Inconveniently, El Haddej is not very clearly signposted off the Nouvelle Matmata to Matmata road. Coming up from Matmata, look out for signs for **Tijma**, a tiny roadside settlement with some troglodyte dwellings. This village

Phone code: 05
Colour map 3, grid A3

is located on the road to Gabès. After six km north from Matmata, turn right where the tourist shop and the *Relais Touristique des Troglodytes* are situated. The *Relais* is a restaurant with a circular courtyard and, around it, 10 small dining rooms, T230129, prices from 4Dt to 6Dt (better to book as in low season they do not cook every day, suitable for groups). After the *Relais* the paved road goes on, full of curves and ups and downs, for two km to El Haddej. (Takes one hour to walk.) El Haddej is made up of cave dwellings hidden in the ground. Many have partly collapsed, some have been abandoned. Though similar to Matmata, El Haddej has been less involved with tourism so it is possible to see what Matmata must have been like before the tourist influx. Nonetheless, guides are easy to find. There are three main things to see: the oil-press, the marriage cave and the typical troglodyte house. Bargain and arrange the tour price in advance.

Going around in El Haddej may seem familiar as this landscape was used to great effect in famous films such as *Star Wars* and *Raiders of the Lost Ark*.

Sights The **oil-press** is made of a huge stone trough and an enormous mill wheel once turned by a camel. The **marriage cave** is a troglodyte dwelling used only for wedding ceremonies. Around the courtyard are several rather derelict rooms. One of them was the bridal kitchen, where the food for the guests of the marriage ceremony was prepared. Another was the wedding room, where the bride and the groom consummated their marriage. In this room there was a hole in the ceiling connected to the upper surface. Through this hole the groom threw a foulard and some sweets. The bride waited here, sitting below the hole in the wedding room and if the foulard and the sweet touched her, it was considered good luck. In the wedding room there was a window from

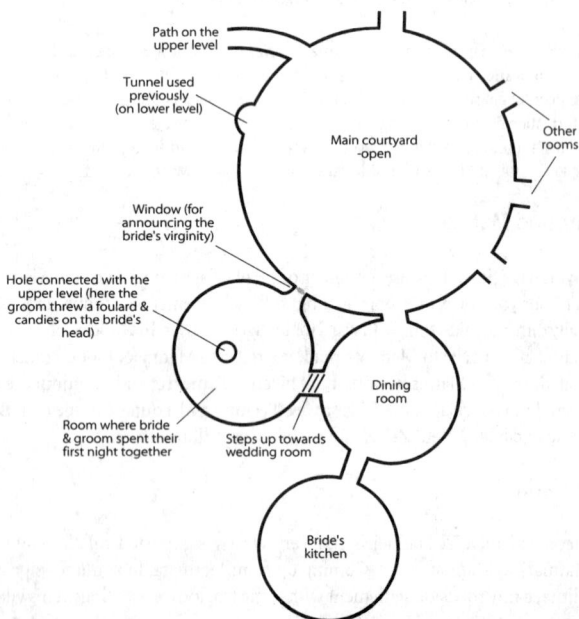

Haddej: rooms set aside for the wedding ceremony

Path on the upper level

Tunnel used previously (on lower level)

Main courtyard -open

Other rooms

Window (for announcing the bride's virginity)

Hole connected with the upper level (here the groom threw a foulard & candies on the bride's head)

Dining room

Room where bride & groom spent their first night together

Steps up towards wedding room

Bride's kitchen

where the groom shot his rifle, signifying the bride was a virgin. The rifle fire meant that the wedding feast could start and that dinner could be served to the guests waiting in the courtyard. Watch your head when you enter the rooms.

Note that in Haddej, many of the troglodyte houses are inhabited. Tourists will only be welcome with a guide.

Northwest of Matmata to Beni Aissa

Beni Aissa is a sleepy troglodyte settlement seven km from Matmata. Few tourists come here, and it could give you a feel for what the area was like before the arrival of the four-wheel drive brigade. To get there, take the Tamezret road from the centre of Matmata. Measure the journey. After one km turn right towards El Hamma. After another 500 metres you pass a troglodyte dwelling on the left. After a few hundred metres more the road condition becomes very poor and there is, unfortunately, a lot of litter here. After six km, turn left at the crossroads and on both sides are troglodyte houses almost hidden (of course) and still inhabited, although their owners might be with their sheep and goats. At seven km on the right there are two *marabouts*. The track ends here.

Colour map 3, grid A3

West of Matmata: Tamezret, Taoujout and Zeraoua

You should certainly try to make a side-trip to **Tamezret** from Matmata, given that it occupies a striking position – and thanks to the much improved road, easily accessible by car (only 13 km west of Matmata). The road here from Matmata is black top. The first section out of Matmata, past the *Hotel Ksar Amazigh*, is narrow and in need of some attention – which doubtless it will get

Surrounding area of Matmata

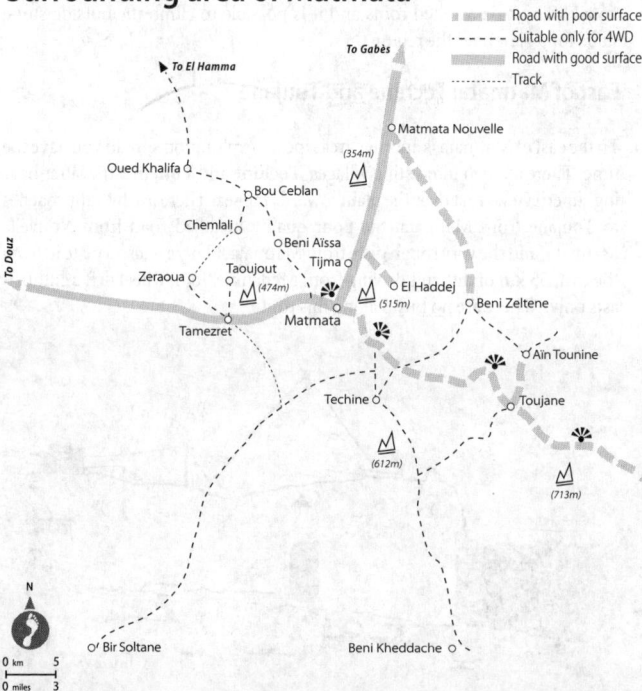

Legend	
▦ ▦ ▦	Road with poor surface
- - - -	Suitable only for 4WD
▦▦▦▦	Road with good surface
··········	Track

To El Hamma
To Gabès
Matmata Nouvelle
(354m)
Oued Khalifa
Bou Ceblan
Chemlali
Beni Aïssa
Tijma
To Douz
Zeraoua
Taoujout (474m)
El Haddej (515m)
Beni Zeltene
Tamezret
Matmata
Ain Tounine
Techine
Toujane
(612m)
To Medenine
(713m)
N
0 km 5
0 miles 3
Bir Soltane
Beni Kheddache

Southeastern Tunisia

in the near future. Further on, works were in full swing in summer 1999, and parts of the road are now very good. The scenery on this route is a mixture of the moon and the Grand Canyon, if the telephone and electricity supply lines are ignored. Troglodyte houses can be seen at three km and four and a half km on the left, and, if you look down, at six and a half km on the right. Tamezret eventually comes into view, its neighbourhoods built over the hillsides. The stone-built houses (see illiustration) blend in perfectly with the scenery. Though many houses have been abandoned, the village seems to be enjoying a minor revival, thanks to its position on the new Matmata to Douz road. The State has put money into paving the narrow streets and repairing once tumbledown walls. There is even the most touristic *Café Mamou le Berbère*, on your left on the main road as you arrive from Matmata. Stroll around the narrow, winding streets and walk up to the top of the village. To reward your efforts, there is a small chicha café and marvellous views across the desert. Tamezret, along with neighbouring Taoujout, is one of the few places in Tunisia where Berber is still spoken. The relative isolation of the village enabled the language to survive the 20th century. Although it is not politically correct to mention ethnic difference in contemporary Tunisia, the language has been the object of recent ethnographic research.

Taoujout, four km on from Tamezret, and also a hilltop community where Berber has survived, is more a destination for enthusiasts only. The black top goes as far as the village, but no further. With a four-wheel drive or motorcycle, plus good navigating skills, it might be possible to drive from Taoujout to Beni Aïssa.

Finally, just six km by piste northwest of Tamezret, lies **Old Zeraoua**, an abandoned Berber village. The inhabitants have moved to Nouvelle Zeraoua. Feel free to wander through the streets and look into the houses which have survived better than those at, for example, Tamerza as they are stone constructions. Many have vaulted roofs and it is possible to climb the outside stone stairs for a view over the region.

East of Matmata: Techine and Toujane

Colour map 3, grid A3-4 To the east of Matmata is another area ripe for exploration should you have the time. There are two interesting villages, **Techine** and **Toujane**, the latter having superb views east over the plain towards the sea. There are two approaches to Toujane from Matmata, the poor quality metalled road from Nouvelle Matmata, and the very rough piste from Matmata. (There is also a piste in from the east, 35 km of difficult driving from Medenine, four-wheel drive enthusiasts only.) There are no buses along this route.

Tamezret

With the Khalifa of Haddej in the 1890s

"Said-ben Mansur-Fatush, as Khalifa of the mountains, exercises authority over the villages of the Matmata range. His is born of the tribe of Uled Sliman, of which his son is a tribal sheikh.

The Khalifa is between 60 and 70 years of age, and has three wives, Mena, Fatima and Sasia. By the first he has two sons, Amar and Mansur. By the second, one son, Mohamed … the Khalifa's family, therefore, consists of about a score of souls, who, as will be seen further on, live together; but to these must be added other members of the household, negroes and servants with their children, and a number of near relatives and a number of men who attach themselves to the Khalifa's service. Many of the latter have homes of their own, and possess palms, olive trees and cattle, which they farm on their own account, but being dependants

of the Khalifa, must help him sow and reap his corn, prune his palms, gather the dates and olives, press the oil, and, in short, do any work of which they are capable.

The Khalifa is very rich. He owns many underground dwellings, barns, stables and oil mills, but a large proportion of the profits of all these must be expended in providing food and shelter for the infinity of people whom he protects. The Khalifa's property is valued at some 200,000 francs – a pretty penny for a mountaineer living amongst barren hills devoid of either springs or wells, but where the cliffs and valleys are furrowed with channels to conduct the rain water to cisterns, and where every tree must have earth banked about it that the water may lie at its foot."

From The Cave Dwellers of Southern Tunisia by Daniel Bruun (London, 1898).

Heading east out of Matmata, **Techine**, another troglodyte settlement, could be your first destination. The road is metalled most of the 12 km to Techine. After one km on the right is a military fort while to the left is a panoramic view over the plain below. On a clear day it is apparently possible to see as far as Djerba! (**NB** No photographs here, as this is all a military area.) Look out for the birds of prey and the ground squirrels. After five km on the right is a *marabout* and, two km further on (on the right again), some troglodyte houses. At Km 8 is a crossroads, left for Toujane and straight on for Techine, which is noted for the built-in furniture in the dwellings, carefully constructed out of branches which are covered in decorative plaster. This furniture looks fragile, but no doubt replacement is not a problem as all the materials are close to hand

After visiting Techine, the track is not very easy (be sure to have a good spare tyre) but a normal car could do just about do it. The asphalt returns at a T-junction one km from Toujane. At 10 km more crossroads (right to Zriba, Techine and Beni Kheddache), go straight on here and also at the next cross-roads (left to Beni Zelten and Mzata). Keep an eye on the track as its condition gets worse and worse, and look down on the right at the small lakes (during spring) or at the *oued* (during winter and autumn). The landscape is gorgeous. At 14 km on the right is a troglodyte house. At 20 km you will be on the edge of the mountain.

At 24 km is another T-junction where you can turn right to Cheguine or left to start the descent to **Toujane**, which will suddenly appear, apparently clinging to the mountain side. It is a beautiful village on an exceptional site. Wander around – there may be locally made carpets and weavings for sale. Purchases can be made at *Chez Laroussi* on the road. At the end of the village, after Chez Laroussi, on the left is the *Relais Mohammed Esnani*; kilims, *smen* (cooked butter used on couscous), honey and tea herbs are sold here. Drinks, coffee and tea available too, unpleasant toilet.

☞ **Jouant à la Kherbga** *or playing draughts Tunisian style*

This popular game requires no board or manufactured counters. Everything required is readily available. A small pile of earth, sand or roadside dust is scraped together with the foot and patted flat with the hand. Seven rows of seven holes are impressed into the surface and the playing area is ready. Pieces used in the game are small pebbles, date stones or dried dates, all to hand.

The aim of the game is to eliminate the

pieces of the other player in a style similar to draughts. Although this is a 'game for two', everyone around takes part with well-meaning advice or noisy criticism about the mode of play.

The game can be set up so that the players and spectators can also watch the activities in the village street, while the shepherds organize their games in a position from which they can watch over their flocks.

Toujane to Nouvelle Matmata

Colour map 3, grid A3-4 To avoid repeating the boneshaking piste from Matmata to Toujane, you could head for Nouvelle Matmata, following a poorly surfaced road which runs via Aïn Tounine (six km from Toujane) and Beni Zelten.

Toujane to Beni Kheddache After the café in Toujane take the C104 towards Medenine. After seven km is the new village of Dekhilet Toujane. This is not an interesting place but has *Café du 7 Novembre* on the left and a post office on the right. After five km a paved road goes north to Mareth (36 km), while the main road (unsurfaced) goes on to Medenine (25 km). The truly adventurous, equipped with four-wheel drive, could turn right and head for Ksar El Hallouf and Beni Kheddache. The track is good at the beginning but soon deteriorates. There are some herders' huts, magnificent views and plenty of holes in the road. Really a trek for the desert navigator with plenty of time.

Matmata to Douz via the desert road

Colour map 3, grid B1-A3 There is now a fully metalled road from Matmata to Douz, running via Tamezret. This is 60 km shorter than the route via El Hamma-Kebili, although not necessarily faster. From here on it is more or less a straight 43 km to Douz.

Medenine مدنين

*Phone code: 05
Colour map 3, grid B4* *An important crossroads in the South, through which you will probably pass on your way to Tataouine and the ksour, Medenine has little of interest for the visitor. Of the once vast fortified granary complex, only a rump courtyard remains. With the usual concrete buildings, Medenine bears witness to the huge changes in the life of the Tunisian South in the last quarter of the 20th century.*

Ins and outs

Getting there Medenine is accessible by bus and louage. Journey time from Gabès (73 km) is about 1½ hours. There are overnight buses from Tunis, 7 hours 45 minutes away, and plenty of buses from Tataouine (55 km) and Ghoumrassen, Djerba, Zarzis (62 km away) and Ben Gardane.

The bus station is on rue du 18 Janvier and the louages stop in a small street opposite. All the main hotels are within walking distance of these. If you want to go to Beni Kheddache, once an important ksar, there are louages leaving from near the Agil station on the Av Bourguiba.

Background and history

Medenine is at the northern end of what might be called the **ksour** area, a region whose economy once centred on nomad stock raising and some cereal cultivation. The harvests were stored in characteristic fortified granaries or *ksour*. The region is a frontier between two cultures, the nomads and the settled people. Once the area was totally controlled by nomads, but today the tents have been replaced by small concrete houses and the camel by a Peugeot or Isuzu truck. Market days at Medenine are Saturday afternoon and Sunday.

Medenine was once a centre where tribal groups belonging to the Ouerghama confederation stored their harvests. It was probably the largest ksar in the South, and early photographs show a vast network of interlinked courtyards. After independence, however, everything changed. Settlement was the order of the day; the *ksour* of Medenine were almost completely demolished. What remains – a single courtyard – is an attraction of day-trippers.

Medenine is a not a bad place for the start of excursions towards Metameur and the surrounding area, where there are some *ksour* in a far better state of preservation than in Medenine. Nevertheless, given the choice, Tataouine, 55 km farther south, is a much better choice as a base, being close to both hill-crest villages and *ksour*.

Essentials

C *Hotel Ibis*, place du 7 Novembre in the centre of town, 200m from the *ksour*, T643878/9, F640550. 44 rooms, all a/c, some rooms with terrace, conference room, clean, sometimes a bit lively as sports teams usually stay here, opened 1994. F *Hotel Essaada*, Av Habib Bourguiba, T640300. 28 rooms, 6 rooms with shower but none with toilet. *Hotel El Vazira*, off Av 7 Novembre, near the *ksar*. Clean and cheap. F *Hotel Hana*, T640690, in Av Habib Bourguiba. Quite noisy, but well placed, central. **Youth hostel**: rue des Palmiers, on the road to Djorf, T640338. 60 beds.

Mid-range *Restaurant* of the *Hotel Ibis*. **Cheap** *Restaurant Echana*, Av Habib Bourguiba, T640690. Good food and cheap, parking available. *Restaurant de la Liberté*, in front of *Hotel Ibis*. Good and cheap. *Pizzeria Plaza*, Av Habib Bourguiba. *Restaurant Carthage*, rue du 18 Janvier, across the road from the bus station. *Restaurant* in *Hotel Hana*, Av Habib Bourguiba. Out of town, you have the *Restaurant l'Olivier*, road to Gabès (Km 14, Koutine), T630017.

Bus information on T640427. Buses to Tunis; Djerba, Tataouine, Zarzis, Ben Gardane, Gabès, Gafsa and Sfax.

Banks *BS*, Av Habib Bourguiba, T640087; *STB*, rue 2 Mai, T640053; *BNT*, Av Habib Bourguiba, T640088; *Banque Centrale*, at the crossroads to Foum Tataouine; *Amen Bank*, behind *Hotel Ibis* in Place du Festival. **Communications Post Office**: on place des Martyrs, off Av Habib Bourguiba, near the crossroads towards Foum Tataouine, where the Gouvernorat and public gardens are to be found. **Tour companies & travel agents** 52 rue de 18 Janvier, T640817. **Useful addresses Police**: T640033.

☞ *Homes and citadels in southern Tunisia*

Southern Tunisia has a characteristic selection of local architectures – and a precise terminology in Arabic to name the different forms of building. A **kalaâ** is a citadel, the fortified village in a mountain strongpoint. A **ksar** (pl. **ksour**) is also a fortress, the Arabic giving the modern Spanish Alcazar. In southern Tunisia, the term refers to a courtyard made up of **ghorfat**, vaulted cells built to store grain, oil and fodder. Each tribe would have its ksar, inhabited only by a caretaker and family. As times became more settled, **ksour** were constructed on the plains.

The nomads and semi-nomad family would spend the spring and autumn months living in a tent or **khayma**. In summer, when the tent was too hot, they might live in a roughly constructed hut or **zriba**. Eventually, the hut would turn into something more permanent, a **raguba**, a stone-walled enclosure roofed over with olive branches and alfa grass – preferable to the zriba as the fire risk was less.

In the citadel villages, homes may be composed of a **houch** (courtyard) and a **ghar**, a cave-like inner area excavated out of the hillside. In coastal areas, homes are different again. On Djerba, the **menzel**, a courtyard building surrounded by fields, was the typical home. In the orchards round Sfax, city families traditionally had a **borj** (lit: 'a tower'), a place where they could spend the hot summer months. Matmata has the most original form of housing in the South, the famous pit-dwellings – the only place where 'the living live below the dead', to quote the local saying.

Excursions around Medenine

On the Djerba road If heading north to Djerba, the ancient site of **Gightis** (*Colour map 3, grid A5*) will attract archaeology enthusiasts. Located on the coast 27 km north of Medenine on the road to Djorf, Gightis has remains of Romano-African style buildings, capitol, forum, temples, and baths. ■ *Museum open 0830-1730 in winter and 0900-1300 and 1500-1900 in summer, closed Friday, entrance 1Dt.*

The ksour west of Medenine Heading southwest from Medenine, the C113 takes you to the ksar villages of **Djoumaa** and **Beni Kheddache**. Located 36 km southwest of Medenine, **Djoumaa** is composed of a new village and the original ksar. Situated at the top of a hill, old Djoumaa is crumbling back to nature. There are buses here from Medenine at 0815 and 1000, returning at 1000 and 1400. It is worth a trip to this most attractive hill top village with splendid views. The *ksar* has only recently been abandoned.

Beni Kheddache, beyond Djoumaa, 65 km from Ksar Guilane and 14 km from Ksar Hallouf, can be reached by the same buses from Medenine at 0815 and 1000. The village is of little interest in itself except on Thursday which is market day, but from here you can take the road south to Ksar Haddada and on to Tataouine (see below). From Ksar Haddada there is occasional public transport on to Ghromrassen and Tataouine. South of Beni Khaddache is surprisingly fertile area planted with olive groves and fig trees, but if you want to stay the night out this way, the only option is at Zamour, where there is the **F** *Hotel Zamour*, on a track a few kilometres after the Beni Kheddache post office and the hospital (better ask), T05-647196, F05-647197, 13 rooms, 40 beds, very basic (bring your own sleeping bag and be prepared to sleep on a mattress on the floor), built in a cave structure, therefore no windows, communal toilets and showers, clean, very quiet as you are surrounded by the mountains, excellent restaurant. The hotel also has a restaurant (best to ring to book).

Roadside sales

The produce of the local countryside can often be deduced by the items on sale by the roadside. Containers of unrefined olive oil, cans of olives, live geese and turkeys and chickens held by their legs, nuts, grapes, oranges even fresh fish. It is certainly an interesting and effective method of retail. Fossils, amethysts and huge desert roses are on display and often held in the hand of determined and foolhardy youths who stand in the road, so take care. Look out too for the can and the plastic funnel advertising fuel for sale. The small motor bikes have a very small tank and need frequent replenishment. On the main road south of Gabès, onwards towards the Libyan border, bundles of green notes are waved at the face of the driver – Libyan dinars – the best exchange rate is here but perhaps the best opportunity is for a fresh sheep skin, still warm.

Beni Kheddache has basic facilities, including: **Hospital**: 05647010. **Post & telecommunications Post Office**: in the centre of town, close to the hospital and behind louage. **Useful addresses Police**: T05647025.

Directory

This 77 km of road is very busy as goods go into Libya this way. You could hitch, but there are plenty of louages and 3-4 buses daily. See box on page 341.

Medenine to Ben Gardane

Tataouine   تطاوين

Established by the French as an administrative centre for the villages and nomad tribes, Tataouine still has something of a frontier feel to it. Though fleets of four-wheel drives pass through on their way to Berber villages and ksour, life goes on unperturbed, with local people, settled, semi-nomads or government employees, coming in for the jolly weekly markets. The area has gained in prosperity – witness the amount of new construction – and tourism may yet bring benefits in the form of a rural life museum. Tataouine makes a good base for exploring the hill villages to the west and ksour of the Djebel Abiadh.

Phone code: 05
Colour map 3, grid B4

Ins and outs

Tatouine is accessible by public transport from Medenine. There are direct buses morning and evening from Tunis via Gabès. Journey time from Tunis is around 9 hours, from Gabès 2½ hours. If you are driving from Medenine to Tataouine, be prepared for numerous police checkpoints – unsurprising given the security problems in Algeria. Slow right down and be prepared to smile and show your papers.

Getting there

Buses from Tunis arrive at the SNTRI station on Av Habib Bourguiba. Buses from Medenine, Zarzis, Houmt Souk, Ghoumrassen and other southern places arrive at the SRTGM bus station on the corner of Av du 1 juin 1955 and Av Ahmed Tlili. The louage station is on Av du 1 juin as well. For getting out to Chenini and Douiret, pick-ups run from Rue du 2 mars, a street parallel to Av du 1 juin.

Getting around

History and background

At first glance, Tataouine is not the most interesting of towns. It is more charming than Medenine, and there is a lively market on Monday and Thursday. Discussions with locals will give you some insight into the way the area has changed.

In fact the changes wrought by the 20th century were enormous. Nothing really destined Tataouine to become centre for the most southerly inhabited region of Tunisia. The town's name points to Berber origins, however. (Tataouine is the plural of the Berber *tit*, meaning 'spring', and the town used to be referred to as Foum Tataouine, 'mouth of the springs'.)

Following the declaration of the French Protectorate over Tunisia, the southern tribes initially accepted the rule of the new authorities. As there was only a small garrison left in Medenine, dissident tribes were not slow to revolt in 1882. In 1883, the tribes submitted once more, with the Touazine and Ouderna being given the status of *makhzen* tribes, that is, exempt from taxation provided they protected the South from outside incursions and rebellion. In 1888, the French created a *bureau de renseignements* at Douiret, the largest settlement in the region. But Douiret was too isolated, and the office was moved to Tataouine, where there was a military camp. After discussion with local leaders, a market was set up in 1892. An infirmary followed in 1914 and a primary school in 1916. A recruitment centre for the French *goumier* regiments was set up. The French military authorities asked tribal notables to settle at Tataouine – which the cheikhs did. They built houses which they then entrusted to Jewish or Muslim traders, preferring to live close to their *ksour* as they had always done. Later Tataouine was a garrison for one of the penal regiments, the *bataillons d'Afrique*. Originally set up in Algeria, the *bat d'Af* recruited men condemned for minor felonies.

Tataouine thus started life as a military town, and like many southern towns, it still has a major garrison. Although generally rather drab, it does have a life of its own. With four-wheel drive excursions from Djerba now popular, Tataouine is a stop-off for tourists. There is even a *Festival des Ksours* in April – not terribly spectacular, but an occasion for local people to gather. Desert culture does not lend itself to public display, but visitors will probably get to observe a mock marriage procession complete with bride riding in a *jahfa*, a camel-back palanquin heavily covered with cloth. This tradition is still alive and well in rural communities like Douiret.

Tataouine

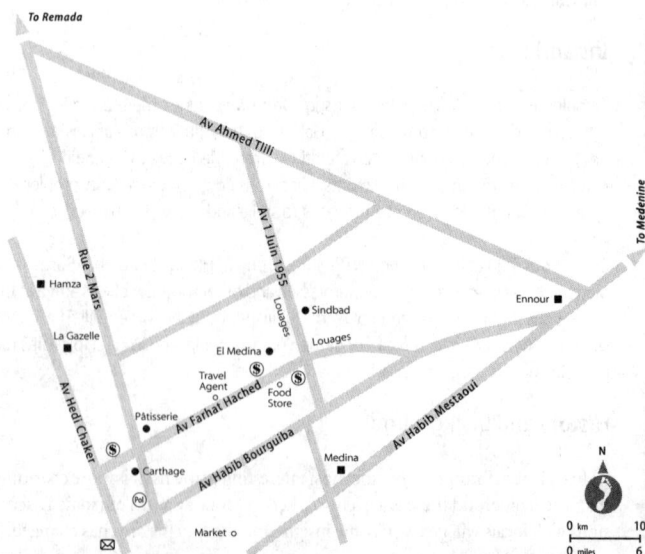

Essentials

B *Hotel Dakyanus*, 6 km from Tataouine on the road to Chenini. Turn right at the crossroad towards Ghoumrassen, the hotel is an earth-coloured building on the left next to the Oued El Ferch, T862932, F862932. 100 beds, pool with water if supplies permit. **B** *Sangho*, T860124, F862177, 62 rooms, 3 km south of Tataouine near the turn-off for Chenini and Ghoumrassen. Turn right towards Ghoumrassen el Bled. The hotel Is clearly signed, spotlessly clean, tastefully decorated. Pool, tennis, restaurant, opened July 1993. Recommended, if you can afford it.

Sleeping
The choice is pretty limited. If going for 1 of the upmarket hotels, try to ring ahead, as they can fill up with tour groups

D *La Gazelle*, Av Hedi Chaker, T860009, F862860. A/c, all 23 rooms have bath, could be better looked after and cleaner, decent restaurant, 62 rooms, definitely over-priced and not very welcoming, but unfortunately one of the few suitable hotels in town.

F *Hotel Médina*, Av Habib Mestaoui, T860999. 20 rooms with sink, hot showers, restaurant, breakfast 1.5Dt. **F** *Hotel Ennour*, Av Habib Bourguiba, T860131, by the main road to Remada. Not very clean and quite noisy. **F** *Hotel Residence Hamza*, Av Hedi Chaker, T863506. 9 rooms, communal toilet and shower every 3 rooms, very cheap and clean, ask for hot water because the heating has to be switched on, nice management. The woman on duty in the morning speaks only Arabic, in the afternoon somebody can speak French. Recommended.

Cheap *Restaurant Carthage*, rue 20 Mars, T863167. Good and cheap, try the grilled meat, the owner speaks only Arabic but his young son can get by in French. Recommended. *Restaurant El Médina*, near Iouage, T861978. Very cheap. *Restaurant Sindbad*, 13 Av 1 Jun 1955, near bus station and Iouage. Varied menu. If you need a beer, then you will be heading for the *Hotel Gazelle*.

Eating

The **market** is held Monday and Thursday on Av Farhat Hached. Among the stands selling plastic goods and clothing, you might just find a bargain in the shape of a nice piece of locally woven cloth. You could also look out for the rather nice slippers made in Tataouine, combining leather and pieces of klim-type wool weaving.

Shopping

Bus: buses to Medenine at 0630, 1000, 1300; to Gabès at 0630 and 1000. **Louage**: on the corner between Av Farhat Hached and Av 1 Jun 1955. Fare to Medenine is 2Dt, to Gabès 5Dt.

Transport

Banks Banque du Sud close to Post Office, in the centre of town, and Amen Bank, on the corner between Rue Farhat Hached and Av 1 Jun 1955. **Communications** **Post office**: in the centre of town, close to *Café de Paris*. **Medical services** **Emergencies** Infirmary behind Garde nationale on Av Hedi Chaker, T860902. **Hospital:** on the road to Medenine, T860114. **Private clinic:** near *Hotel Hamza* and *Hotel La Gazelle*, T860710. **Tourist information** The ONTT has an office on Av Bourguiba, and there is a Syndicat d'initiative on Av Hedi Chaker, almost opposite the Hotel Hamza, T850850. **Useful addresses** **Police**: rue 20 Mars near *Restaurant Carthage*, T860871, ask here how to apply for permission to drive from Remada onward in the desert (the *Gouvernorat* is the authority that gives such permits).

Directory

Hillcrest villages and fortified granaries around Tataouine

The region round Tataouine has two main draws for the tourist: the landscapes and some surprising vernacular architecture, some of it in impressively good condition. Happily, the two attractions combine rather well and some of the best views can be had from the once isolated hill-crest villages. A couple of good day trips, easily done with own transport, will give the visitor a feel for the region: one day could be spent exploring the villages of **Ksar Ouled Debab**,

Colour map 3, grid B4

Douiret and **Chenini**, while another could be devoted to a circuit south and east of Tatatouine, taking in one of the best preserved *ghorfa* complexes, Ksar Ouled Soltane. A third possibility is to do **Guermessa**, **Ghomrassen** and **Ksar Haddada**, all of which lie to the northwest of Tataouine.

If you have limited time, then Douiret and Chenini are a must, even if the former is now pretty heavily visited. Without your own transport, one possibility is to get an early-morning pick-up truck out to the villages. There is also a twice daily local bus to Chenini.

South & east of
Tataouine – the
Ksar Ouled
Soltane circuit
Colour map 3, grid B4

If you have your own transport, then there is an interesting tour to do into 'ksar land' south of Tataouine. The road is blacktop all the way, and you have well-preserved ksar at Ksar Ouled Soltane and at Ezzahra. If doing this excursion by public transport, there is no link between Ksar Ouled Soltane and Ezzahra. If you have to chose, go for Ksar Ouled Soltane, served by at least a couple of daily buses from Tataouine and by the odd pick-up.

Take the road directly south of Tataouine, to the left of the main road to Remada, in the direction of Maztouria where on the right are three *ksour*, and overall some splendid views.

On the way to Ksar Ouled Soltane there are some small villages in which it is possible to buy bread and drinks. In **Tamelest**, on the right, you have a small shop (bread, vegetables and drinks) and, after the mosque on the left, another one stocking bread and yoghurt. There is a café in the square in Ksar Ouled Soltane, but neither a hotel nor a restaurant as the inhabitants apparently have been opposed to catering for mass tourism. People are, nonetheless, very nice and knowledgeable about the history of their *ksar*.

Ksar Ouled Soltane is one of the best preserved *ksour* in Tunisia. The circular outer wall of the *ksar* is still virtually intact. The *ksar* is built on a slight rise allowing good views across the desert towards Libya. The people stored their grain in *ghorfas*, and two superb courtyards of them survive, the older dating from the 15th or 16th century. Standing on the hillside below this ksar, you can understand how easily defensible it must have been, at least against pillagers armed only with light firearms.

From Ksar Ouled Soltane the blacktop road snakes off across the arid land. After Ksar Ouled Soltane, you come to **Mghit**, where you need to go right at the junction. Next on the road is **Ezzahra**, 10 km from Ksar Ouled Soltane, which used to be called Ksar Retbet or El Krachaoua. It is an impressive village on the top of a hill. The village itself is a *ksar* built around a square in the middle of which two eucalyptus give shade. From the main square pass through the arch which joins a second square, which looks rather like a courtyard and where the third and fourth floor *ghorfas* are still in use. The people of Ezzahra voted against a tourist development project which would have meant the opening of restaurants, cafés and hotels.

From Ezzahra to Tataouine is a further 21 km drive. Leaving Ezzahra after 500 metres on the right there is a *marabout*. At three km on the right is the tiny village of Bir Yekzer, at five km Khatma, and at six km on the left Maaned. More interestingly, at 10 km from Ezzahra you come to the villages of **Beni Blel** and **Guettoufa**. Ksar Jelidat on the left is worth a look. After 500 metres crossroad (Beni Mhira 23 km away on the right), turn left to admire the *ksar*. After 300 metres, there is another crossroad, turn right for a panoramic view. Drive carefully as the road is up and down and there are many curves. Just keep to the surfaced road and Tataouine will appear.

To the south and west of Tataouine, you have the hill-crest villages of **Chenini** and **Douiret** to explore. Once home to self-sufficient Berber communities who lived in close contact with the Arab nomads, they are now on the tourist trail. Nevertheless, their impressive hill top sites make them among the most impressive sights in the Tataouine region. Visiting them with your own transport is easy enough, Douiret being only 17 km from Tataouine, Chenini around 20 km. There is a rough piste linking the two. From Tataouine, both villages can be reached by pick-ups running from the rue du 2 mars.

Southwest of Tataouine: Ksar Ouled Debbab, Chenini and Douiret
Colour map 3, grid B4

For Douiret, leave Tataouine on the P19 and head out in the Remada direction. **Ksar Ouled Debbab** is about 10 km south along the road. Arriving in the new village at the foot of the hill, walk left towards the mosque. You will find a path on the left. If you have your own transport it is possible to drive up to the hill. This beautiful hilltop *ksar*, now abandoned and falling into ruin, blends into the surrounding landscape. Steps and arches can still be identified. It looks like a lonely place, but actually many boys and men spend their lazy days on the top of the dwellings. Their presence is almost concealed and they might reveal it by banging on something in a rhythmic way.

For **Douiret**, head west from the centre of Ksar Ouled Debbab; the road runs for nine km through land cultivated after the winter rains but barren in the summer. Drive with care as the road has many bends and drivers may be looking at the view. The old, almost abandoned village is perched on the hillside two km further along the track. Only five families remain here. Even with tourists, the place feels quite eerie and has a faint mystical air. The white mosque attracts attention while the dun-coloured houses tone in with the hillside. There is a small *marabout* on the left on the way into the village. Watch out for dogs. Notice the inscriptionless tomb stones. There is a youth hostel with four large rooms and four tents.

For the the bold equipped with a four-wheel drive, there is a possible route on to **Chenini** via a scenic track north through the mountains. Take the usual precautions regarding water and spare tyres. (An ordinary car driven with care will just about do it.) Cross the new village of Douiret and take the track on to the west. It is best to check with one of the villagers to make sure the route is not closed by floods. The other road to Chenini is south of Tataouine. Heading south out of Tataouine, turn right after two km on the C207 to Ghoumrassen el Bled and three km further on keep straight ahead when the main route swings right. Total distance 20 km. There is no need to stop in the new town, rather follow the road round the hill to the only restaurant.

Chenini Tataouine

Southeastern Tunisia

Ghorfas

Throughout the south of Tunisia grain was stored in small stone cells known as ghorfas. They were each about two metres high and 6-10 metres in length. More units were added as required both at either side and above, sometimes reaching up to five units in height. Eventually the whole formed a courtyard, the blank outside walls deterring raiders.

A skill you might just require – how to make a ghorfa:

1. Build two walls of rock and mud about two metres apart and one and a half metres high.

2. Place vertically between the walls two straw grain baskets packed with earth. These must fit exactly between the walls to support them. Place a third straw grain basket of earth horizontally on top of the first two.

3. Over this place a previously manufactured plaited reed/straw mat to make an arch.

4. An arched roof of rocks held by a fine clay and gypsum mortar can then be gradually constructed, using the matting and grain baskets as support.

5. Construct a rear wall if necessary. Remove the supporting baskets and plaster the internal walls with lime and mud. Decorate if required with figures and handprints or fish to ward off the evil eye.

6. Construct a front wall with a wooden access door of palm.

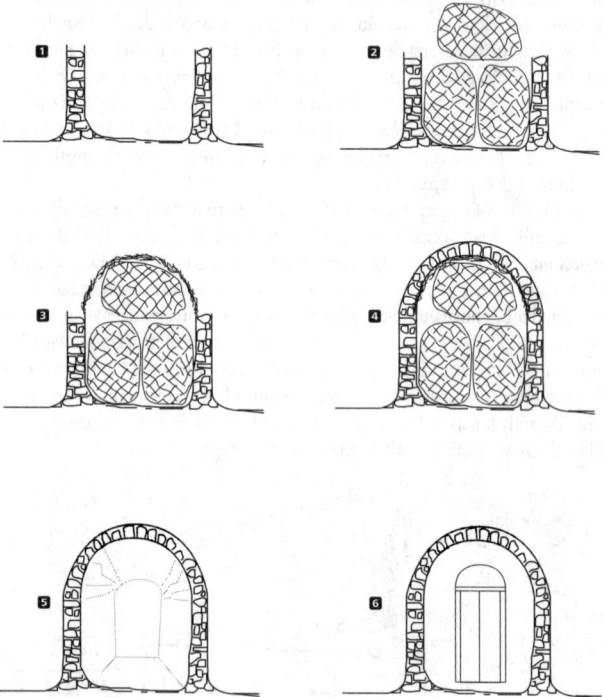

Walkers will be pleased that Chenini is only five and a half km from Douiret over the top past the highest houses. It takes one and a half hours to walk. Seek a guide at least for the first half of the walk as the only people en route will be girls herding goats. Leave Douiret early and wear strong shoes since the path is, in some parts, rocky. You will arrive in Chenini Nouvelle, where it is possible to visit the old mosque on the top of the hill. Near the mosque on the right there are

Taking out a contract at the ksar

The ksar region was a complex mosaic of nomad and semi-nomad tribes, some Arab, some Arabised Berbers and sedentary communities, some Berber. These groups had to make use of the scarce resources of the region to the best advantage, and there was a sort of ethnic division of labour. The Berbers were not nomads, having neither horses nor camels. Living in their citadel villages, they cultivated their ghabat, meagre parcels of land, maximizing water resources by constructing jessour dams. They grew olives, figs. The Berbers 'cut their hair, wear the burnous and eat couscous', went the saying. If they had herds, they would entrust them to an Arab neighbour.

The desert Arabs were always on the move, following their herds. They were masters of both grazing areas and cultivated land on the plains. But given their nomadism, they needed Berber produce – olives, dried figs and dates – and above all, woven cloth for garments. The nomad women, being always on the move, were unable to produce fine weavings. Thus the nomads would give the wool from their flocks to the Berbers who would produce cloth for them.

A sort of service-exchange system had developed over time, formalized by sahaba ('friendship') contracts. The nomad Arab needed the Berber – and vice versa. Times were often unsettled – as the Berber villages' locations show. The nomads thus offered to protect the Berbers from raids. The Berber would pay a sort of fee in kind, while the Arab would provide protection and bring an annual gift, either wool from the flock or smen (salt melted butter).

After the arrival of the French in the southern regions, 'protection contracts' gradually fell into disuse. Raiding became a thing of the past, life became more settled. Today, they are very much a thing of the past. The distinction between the different groups remains, however. Marriages in isolated areas are often still within the tribal community.

a *marabout* once inhabited by a woman and graves covered by stones and grass. If you do not have your own transport don't leave it too late to look for a lift back.

Located high above the arid plain, **Chenini** is an impressive sight. The houses which are built into the rock have a small courtyard, where animals are kept. There are some *ghorfas* at the top of the village, but only a few are still in use. Like the men of the other Berber villages, Chenini men began to migrate to the cities in the 20th century, where they became established as newspaper sellers. Visit the underground Mosque of the Seven Sleepers with its particularly intriguing long tomb stones. Chenini has become part of the tourist route but, despite the crowds climbing up and down the village, it is worth seeing for the extraordinary setting. The streets here are just ledges, scarcely wide enough for two people to pass! The restaurant *Relais de Chenini* at the bottom of the hill has good, reasonably-priced food. At lunch (5Dt) service can be slow since many groups call in here. With a packed lunch and a drink you will have more time for the sights.

Another 'ksar circuit' takes you through the arid landscapes northwest of Tataouine. **Ghoumrassen** is a largish market centre with much modern building and some underground dwellings. **Guermessa** is the least visited of the hill-crest villages, while at **Ksar Haddada** a small hotel has been fitted into the old ghorfa complex.

Travelling by public transport, there are buses from Tataouine and Medenine to Ghoumrassen. Ksar Haddada, just five km north of Ghoumrassen, is served by local bus, or you could try hitching. There is blacktop road to Guermessa, eight kilometres south of Ghoumrassen. Try to get a local pick-up truck out to the village, or again, hitch.

Northwest of Tataòuine: Ghoumrassen, Guermessa & Ksar Haddada
Colour map 3, grid B4

With your own transport, heading out of Tataouine, you have two choices for getting to Ghoumrassen: there is the direct route, moving north along the GP19 for Medenine and branching left for Ghoumrassen on the C221; for the scenic route, head south out of town on the GP19 and take the C207 on the right. You will be looking for a left hand turn-off for **Guermessa**. The new village is of no interest but behind, along a dirt track to the west, is the old village. It is similar to Chenini, but without the tourists. From the top, (half an hour climb up a paved path), the panorama of the surrounding area is breathtaking.

Ghoumrassen is only eight km further on to the north from Guermessa. The most interesting part is towards the centre of the town. Behind the town, to the north, you can see the old abandoned village clinging to the cliff topped by a small mosque, as if watching over the inhabitants. If you have the energy, it is worthwhile going up to the mosque. From here you will see the old *ghorfas* and the rest of the old town. There has been a considerable amount of new building. To walk to the top to the old mosque on top of the hill, ask in the centre of town where the path starts. It is not very clear. It is a stiff climb but rather dangerous. The mosque is small and its plan is quite irregular. On Thursday evenings many people walk up to the old mosque. Friday is market day.

The story goes that the people of Ghoumrassen are famous throughout Tunisia for their **fritters**, *ftayer* in Arabic. (Note also the Tunis saying, *wajhek kee fatira*, 'fritter face'.) Despite this culinary skill, there aren't too many restaurants in Ghoumrassen. Nonetheless, the *pâtisserie* in Avenue Habib Bourguiba and, in the same road, the baker can provide some basic food. Avoid the restaurant in the small road close to the police station as it is neither good nor cheap.

The Deep South

If you want to spend the night in this area, there are as yet no hotels in Ghoumrassen. **Sleeping** Your option (apart from back-tracking to Tataouine) is to stay in **Ksar Haddada**, a small settlement just 5 km north along the road after Ghoumrassen el Bled. The only *ghorfas* left have been beautifully conserved and transformed into a hotel. The **E** *Hotel Ksar Haddada*, T05-869605, is very cheap, 26 simple rooms, with bath/toilets which could be cleaner, restaurant serving good, traditional meals at reasonable prices, even if the comforts are limited and the management not very cordial; a night in the hotel could be an experience.Some rooms have 3 floors and up to 7 beds. Anti-mosquito gel will come in handy. In the main square by the hotel, there is the rather touristic *Café Etoile*.

Banks & money changers *BS*, Av Habib Bourguiba, T869147. *STB*, Av Habib Bourguiba, **Directory** T869115. **Post & telecommunications Post Office**: Av Habib Bourguiba. **Useful addresses Police**: Rue Ibn Arfa (in front of post office), T869175.

North of Ksar Haddada, the road runs on for 22 km (soon to be fully surfaced) **North of Ksar** towards **Beni Kheddache**. There is as yet no public transport between these **Haddada** two settlements. Real ksar enthusiasts might want to try for **Ksar Kerafcha**, which lies east of the Ksar Haddada to Ben Kheddache road.

Into the Deep South

In Tunisia's southern cone, the only major settlement is **Remada,** a military *Colour map 4* town 78 km south of Tataouine. This can be the starting point for travelling west to the military posts of **Borj Bourguiba** (ex-Fort Saint, and also shown as Borj el Hattaba on some maps) (41 km) or southeast to **Dehibat**, where there is a border post with Libya (50 km). Heading south, you come to Lorzot (75 km), Bir Zar, still further south on the Libyan border. Travelling on from Remada, either in the desert or to the Algerian or Libyan borders, requires special permission. The competent authority is the Governorate in Tataouine. Tents and sleeping bags are required, as there are no hotels in the area. The Governorate is unlikely to grant the necessary papers to everyday travellers, however – at least, not without prolonged consultations with the Ministry of the Interior in Tunis. Should you wish to go on into Libya, the border post up at Ras Ajdir is by far the easiest option. **Borj el Khadra** is the southernmost point in Tunisia.

Zarzis   جرجيس

On the mainland a stone's throw from Djerba Island, Zarzis is Tunisia's most *Phone code: 05* *southerly resort town. Nothing remains of the town's previous life as a Roman* *Colour map 3, grid A5* *outpost. Under the French, the town had a small military garrison and there was much planting of olive trees in the region. In recent years, a few more hotels have sprung up along the beach, and there is now a tax-free industrial zone. A Zarzis hotel could make a nice base camp before driving off round various remote southern villages. Local antiquities: the ruins of ancient Zitha.*

Ins and outs

Zarzis can be reached by public transport from Djerba (8 buses a day) and Medenine **Getting there** (8 buses). There are buses and louages from certain northern towns too, journey time from Tunis, with stops, around 9 hours. There are buses from Ben Gardane and Gabès, too, and 1 daily bus from Tataouine.

Getting around Buses and louages arrive some 300m from the central square, at a station off the Av Habib Thameur. If you need to get out to the *zone touristique* and its beach, and the outlying resort area of Sangho, then bus No 1 from the town centre will get you there.

Background

The town has long been associated with Djerba as a tourist resort, and there are certain similarities. The architecture is quite similar and the landscape, with large olive groves and long, white beaches, is indeed very reminiscent of Djerba. The town, originally the market town for the area, is highly developed for tourism and generally well organized. The main point of interest in the town, apart from the market on Monday and Friday, is the **Sponge Festival** (15 July-15 August) which is celebrated with traditional dances and music, fishing boat competitions and, of course, sponge fishing. Zarzis is probably best enjoyed as a low key beach resort, with the additional plus for birdwatchers of being near the **Bahiret el Bibane** lagoon to the southeast, a little awkward to get to without you own transport, however.

Zarzis is close to the road access to **Djerba**, across the causeway which was originally built by the Carthaginians and later rebuilt by the Romans. The road as

Zarzis

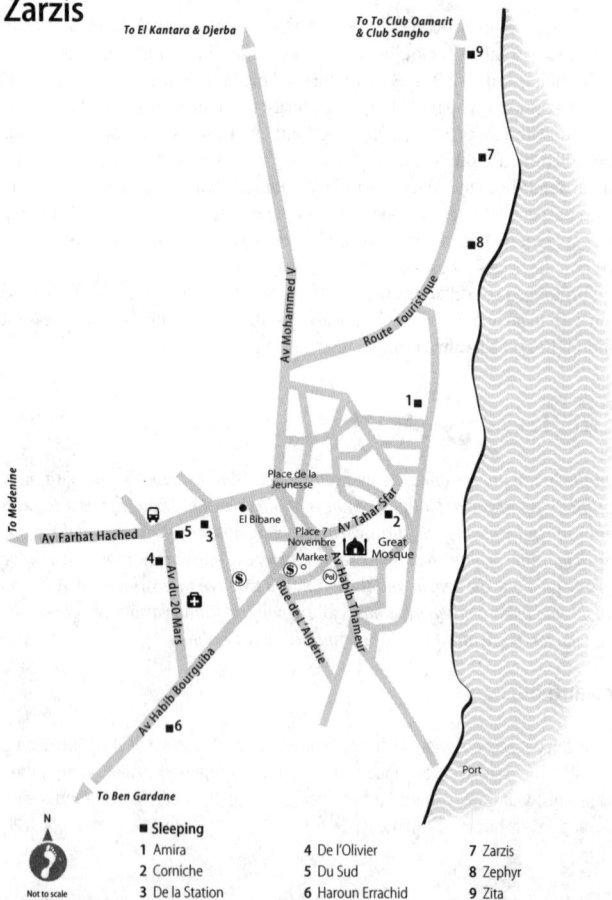

Not to scale

■ **Sleeping**

1 Amira
2 Corniche
3 De la Station

4 De l'Olivier
5 Du Sud
6 Haroun Errachid

7 Zarzis
8 Zephyr
9 Zita

Ralia of Zarzis

The independent-minded E Pellissier had a North African career in the 1830s and 1840s. France was interested in building a picture of all things North African, and Pellisier, who had a reputation as a historian, was a member of the Commission for the Scientific Exploration of Algeria. From 1843 to 1848, Pellissier was French consul in Sousse, a post which gave him the leisure to gather the material for his Description de la Régence de Tunis, published in 1853. Here are his reflections on Zarzis.

"Zarzis is a small maritime town with fairly fertile land producing lots of palms and olive trees. It has a small castle with a few men to garrison it. It has a cheik, like all the other villages, but, at the moment, this authority is effectively exercised by a woman. She is called Ralia. At the height of her youth and beauty, the remains of which are still remarkable, this woman played a certain role in the troubles at Tripoli. Brave as a man, she was often seen in the midst of the fighting, displaying the greatest courage. However, immoral as a woman of the Orient who has thrown down her veil, she had many lovers, whose generosity provided her with a fortune which she has managed well. Retiring to Zarzis, she married a quiet man there, who is known merely as Ralia's husband, as is the common destiny of all those who marry famous women. I met Ralia, who was a generous host in her village, where she has the influence which a strong and resolute mind can always exercise over the Arabs, no matter what the sex. Her manners are polite and quite distinguished, her conversation interesting and her good sense remarkable. Finally, she was of enough interest for me to devote these few lines to her in a book where all kinds of observations must find a place."

From Description de la Régence de Tunis by E Pellissier (Paris: Imprimerie Impériale, 1853)

it stands today was rebuilt in 1953. (The only other access to Djerba is by the Djorf ferry). Given this easy access to Djerba and its airport, plus the good beaches, Zarzis looks set for major hotel development in the near future. Further hotel construction on Djerba has been stopped – there are now over 85 hotels on the island – so the developers and tour companies will be looking for somewhere new. *Rebbi yestur*, 'May God provide protection', as they say in Tunisian.

Essentials

Zone touristique D *Hotel Amira*, T680188. 22 beds, small beach hotel. **C** *Zarzis Hotel*, T680160, F680292. 600 beds. Large package hotel. **C** *Hotel Zephyr*, T681027, F681026. 652 beds. One of the older package hotels. Not one of the best – visitors have noted noisy building works at the height of the season. **C** *Hotel Zita*, T680246, F680359. 600 rooms, a/c, adequate restaurant, coffee shop, an old building. Another of the original package places. **Sangho C** *Club Sangho*, T680124, F680715. 722 beds. The best of the Zarzis beach hotels. **C** *Club Oamarit*, T680770, F680685. 844 beds. **Town centre E** *Hotel Anis*, T681409. 36 beds. **E** *Hotel Corniche*, Av Tahar Sfar, T682833. Pleasant cheap hotel. **F** *Hotel Haroun Errachid*, T681332. 20 beds. **E** *Hotel Médina*, T681861. 40 beds. **F** *Hotel du Port*, T680777. 24 beds. **F** *Hotel Soltana*. 20 beds. **F** *Hotel de la Station*, T680667. 51 beds. Handy for the SNTRI bus station, as its name suggests. *Hotel du Sud*, 18 Av Farhat Hached, almost opposite the Hotel Médina. 20 beds. **F** *Hotel de l'Olivier*, close to the bus station, T680637. 20 beds, simple, clean, probably the best of the cheap hotels. **Youth hostel**: rue de l'Algérie. 40 beds, T681599. **Camping**: Sonia site recommended.

Sleeping
Out of season, there may be some bargains in the beach strip. There is another small area of hotels 12 km north of Zarzis at Sangho

Eating   **Expensive** *Restaurant Abou Nawas*, route des hotels, T680583. **Mid-range** *Restaurant El Borj*, route des hotels, T680928. *Restaurant El Bibane*, Av Farhat Hached near Place de la Jeunesse, T681344. Very good fish (choose the fish you like before they cook it), good, cheap and clean. Recommended. *Restaurant l'Oasis*, on the road to *Club Sangho*, T680124. *Restaurant Les Palmiers*, town centre, T680114. *Restaurant Le Pacha*, route des hotels, T680497. Has a good name. *Restaurant Nozha*, route de Sonia Plage Municipale, T681593. *Restaurant République*, town centre. **Cheap** *Restaurant l'Olivier*, Av Farhat Hached after *Restaurant El Bibane* on the same side of the road, T680721. Try lamb steak or chicken, cheap.

Sports   Zarzis is a typical resort town with provision for watersports such as swimming, windsurfing and water skiing at all the large hotels along the beach. Harbour has 60 yacht berths, min-max draft 2-4½m. Sponge fishing is advertised. Tennis can be practised at *Club Sangho*, T680124.

Transport   **Local Car hire**: *Africar*, T680152; *Avis*, T681706; *Europcar*, T680562; *Hertz*, T680284, all on route des Hotels; *Express*, in *Club Oamarit*, T680770; *Mattei*, next to *Club Sangho*, T680124; *Zarzis Loisirs*, Hotel Zita, T680246. **Long distance Bus**: Tunis 2100; **Sousse** 1300 (via Medenine); there are about 4 buses a day to Medenine and Ben Gardane, 1.7Dt, more frequent departures towards Djerba, 2.1Dt. Information on T680661. **Louage**: Av Farhat Hached, T680078; **Taxi**: Av Mohammed V, T680063.

Directory   **Banks** *STB*, town centre, T680082; *BNT*, rue de Palestine, T680020; *BT*, rue de Palestine and rue d'Algérie, T680024; *BDS*, town centre; *Bank el Amen*, ex-CFCT, Av Mohammed V, T680818; *BS*, town centre, T680318. There are also bureaux de change along route Touristique, 100m beyond the Tourist office. One takes VISA and Eurocheques. **Communications Post Office:** is in Av Habib Bourguiba, T680125. There is another Post Office/ telephone centre in the hotel zone, about 1 km north of the Tourist Office. **Hospital & medical services** Hospital: Av du 20 Mars, in town centre, T680302. **Chemist:** all night, Av Farhat Hached, T681124. **Clinic:** on the road to Djerba, T682240. **Tour companies & travel agents** *Agency Globus*, T/F668288. *Majus Voyages*, T680666. *Syndabad Tours*, Zarzis, Av Mohammed V, T681896. *Tunisirama* at *Club Sangho*, T680124. *Zarzis Loisirs* at *Hotel Zita*, T680246. *Zarzis Travel Service*, route de Djerba, T681072. *Zarzis Voyage*, route de Ben Gardane, T680654. **Tourist offices** The tourist information office is at route des Hotels, route du Port, close to the *Hotel Zarzis*, T680445. **Useful addresses** Police: Av du 20 Mars, T680063 and Av Farhat Hached, T680745. **Port:** route de Porte, T681827.

Zarzis to Ben Gardane

Phone code: 05
Colour map 3, grid B6

If you have your own transport, drive on the C109, which follows the coast, skirts the salt lakes and reaches Ben Gardane 46 km away. Otherwise take the bus (the bus station is near the port). The ticket costs 1.7Dt and the trip should take one hour, but it might take more as stops are on request. As you arrive in **Ben Gardane**, the market, held on Saturday, is on the right. The bus station is 100 metres from the louage stand.

Sleeping, eating & transport   Should you need to spend the night in Ben Gardane, there are a good few hotels, including the **E** *Pavilion Vert*, T05-665103, **E** *Hotel de l'Algerie*, rue 20 Mars, T05-665279, **E** *Hotel El Ouns*, rue de Medenine T05-665920, 20 rooms, most with bath, fairly clean, good views over town from terrace on upper storey. **F** *Baghdad*, rue de Zarzis, T05-666123, next to bus station, clean, shared toilet facilities. For food in Ben Gardane, try the *Restaurant de l'Espoir*, in front of *Hotel Baghdad*, rue de Zarzis, a very good unofficial exchange rate for Libyan dinars is available here, and you are now just 33 km away from the Libyan border. Going to the Libyan border at Ras Ajdir by louage costs 10Dt, and there are plenty of buses doing the run as well.

Djerba

9

Djerba

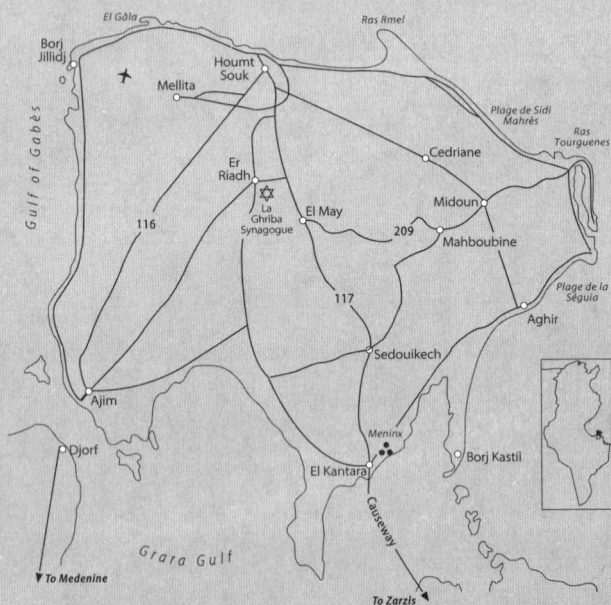

A low-lying expanse of sand and palm trees moored off Tunisia's southern coast, Djerba is the perfect holiday island. It is a slow-moving, seductive place – you can feel that life pulses quite a few beats slower than on the mainland. There are long stretches of sandy beach, mainly along the northern and eastern coasts, fringed with palms and backed by tourist hotels.

Coming to Djerba on a package, you could quite easily spend the entire holiday between beach and hotel compound. The island does, however, merit some exploring. Architecture buffs will find the white vernacular building of the countryside fascinating (there are some nice walks to do near **Midoun** and **Mahboubine**), while birdwatchers could nip out to **Ras Rmel** to see the wading birds. There is an ancient community of potters at **Guellala** in the southwest of the island, a large synagogue at **Er Riadh** (Hara Sghira), and some scattered Roman remains at **Meninx**, in the southeast, close to the causeway.

Ins and outs

Getting there There are 3 points of access to the island. There is a 6 km causeway leaving the mainland near Zarzis, or the ferry from Djorf to Ajim. Coming from Gabès, the ferry saves a lot of time but in summer be prepared to queue. The crossing only takes 15 minutes. The ferry runs every 30 minutes until 2000. From then it sails hourly through the night. Free for foot passengers and motorbikes, 1Dt for cars by day and 1.5Dt at night. All buses arrive at the bus station in the centre of Houmt Souk. The 3rd way in is via Djerba's international airport (T650233) in the northwest of the island, near Houmt Souk. It receives scheduled flights from Frankfurt, Lyon, Geneva, Zürich, Brussels and Paris, and regular internal flights from Tunis (1 way 46Dt), Sfax and Tozeur.

Getting around You will probably be staying in a hotel either in Houmt Souk or the *zone touristique* on the northeast coast. Distances are not great – the beach hotels start 6 km to the east of Houmt Souk and run round the coast for over 12 km. The energetic could hire a bike to get around the villages of 'the interior', otherwise there are taxis and local buses. A taxi ride from Houmt Souk to hotels should cost around 3.5 to 4Dt.

Background

History Djerban history begins in mythic times with Greek hero Odysseus. In the Homeric epic, Odysseus lands in Djerba and has great difficulty in leaving again, not least because of the attractions of the lotus flower he found on the island. Back in real history, Djerba was in turn Phoenician, Carthaginian and Roman. To the Carthaginians, it was the island of Meninx, much appreciated for the safe anchorage it offered. The Romans were not about to leave such a pleasant island unsettled and they established a city in the southeast part of the island, close to where their causeway touched land. Djerba was finally conquered by the Arabs in 667, but was later involved in the rivalries between the Kharijite sect and the orthodox Muslims.

By the 15th century, Djerba had become a den of pirates and various efforts were made to dislodge them, the most fateful being in 1560 when an attempt was made to fight off the pirate Dragut. This failed and Dragut built a tower with the skulls of the slain Christians. The unpleasant monument was fortunately demolished in 1848, but survives in early prints. In the late 19th century, the French arrived. In fact, the commercially minded Djerbans were actually quite happy to see the French come, fearing attacks from rebellious inland tribes which would upset trade and the making of money. The arrival of French authority imposed order on the southern regions and created new souks. Djerbans were quick to seize the opportunities for commerce.

Djerba's people The population of Djerba has always been quite isolated from the mainland. The effect has been the development of a unique style of life and architecture. The population is now mostly Berber in origin but, until recently, there was also a significant Jewish population on the island, one of the oldest communities in the world, dating back to 566 BC and the fall of Jerusalem to Nebuchadnezzar. Now there are only about 1,000 Jewish people left here, a large number having emigrated to Israel and France. The Muslim population numbers over 100,000, and a small percentage belong to the Ibadite branch of Islam, which derives from the rigorous and austere Kharijite sect, established shortly after the Arab invasion. It is possible that the Djerban Berbers adopted this form of Islam in order to keep some independence from the mainstream Islam preached by the Arab invaders.

Today, the population is faced with the new problems of tourism and the influence of western culture. Having lived for so long in isolation, they were perhaps less well equipped than other places for the large influx of tourists. The industry is having an adverse effect on the island's population and way of life since many of the traditional occupations such as agriculture and fishing are being abandoned for easier and better paid jobs in the tourist industry. Other residents have been forced to change jobs or leave due to the ever increasing cost of living, making Djerba an island with a very high emigration rate. In major French towns, the ever open corner grocer is often *un Djerbien*. However, after years abroad, this grocer will usually return to his native island to live out retirement among family and friends.

Traditionally, Djerba's main resources were agriculture, fishing and certain handicrafts, including weaving and pottery. Given the lack of rainfall, agriculture required the cultivation of a drought-tolerant species of tree (date palm, olive and pomegranate), and the careful management of water. Every farmstead has both wells and cistern. Though there are many palm trees, they produce poor quality dates, due to the high salt content of the water. Olive trees are more successful and olive oil is an important industry. Over 80 varieties of fish inhabit the sea around Djerba including shark, skate and swordfish, but fishing is an occupation that is slowly declining, due to the continued use of traditional fishing methods and the preference for employment in hotels, usually for a bigger salary. Of the crafts, some pottery making continues at Guellala.

Traditional activities

The arrival of mass tourism since the mid-1980s has brought about a huge change in the life of the island. In the second half of the 1990s, development outpaced expectations. There are now close on 100 hotels and 35,000 beds, usually occupied mainly by Germans. (German tour operator Neckerman is set to buy hotels.) The authorities have tried to encourage a more upmarket form of tourism than that at Hammamet and Sousse. The most recent hotels are all four or five star, and there are a number of new attractions (including a 27-hole golf course and a casino, opened in March 1998) which aim to encourage a higher spending clientèle. The austere Ibadite ancestors of today's Djerbans must be turning in their graves at such tack. Thalassotherapy is another area in which Djerba's hoteliers have invested their money, and there is an elaborate centre at the *Hotel Hasdrubal*.

Tourism on Djerba

Whether Djerba will be successful in attracting the upscale traveller remains to be seen. Many hotels were built by investors attracted by the tax breaks for putting money into the tourist industry. Hotel investment companies need to fill beds and pay back loans, and the major European tour operators have huge leverage on prices, being able to buy large numbers of bed nights at very cheap rates years in advance, or take over the management of whole hotels. The result is of course that while the overall standard is good, service is often poor.

There are other, more basic problems. Djerba produces very little, so everything the tourist (and those working for them) needs has to be imported. Further State investment in infrastructure will be essential. The airport, which saw traffic grow with the embargo on Libya, is being extended, the causeway will need widening, further water and waste treatment plants will have to be built. The tourist industry has created a huge demand for unskilled and semi-skilled labour, almost all of which has to come from outside. The effects of the arrival of large numbers of outsiders could change the face of the island.

Djerba

Houmt Souk حومة السوق

Phone code: 05
Colour map 3, grid A5

*Up in the northwest of the island, Houmt Souk is the only real town, and is there-
fore referred to as its capital. The town has around 20,000 inhabitants and gets a
huge number of visitors, but nevertheless manages to maintain its charm. The
Association Sauvegarde de Djerba is ever vigilant, and with luck the town will not
be swamped by lurid neon signs and traffic like downtown Hammamet. The town
struggles to maintain a careful balance and so far has not been totally destroyed
by tourism. There are, however, gaudy souks where an enthusiastic lad will dress
you up as an Arab for a photograph, with venerable traders and craftsmen selling
textiles and jewellery, and some of the old fondouks where merchants would
spend the night have been tastefully turned into small hotels. (The town's name
means 'market quarter'.) And to return to Djerba's traditions, there is a small
museum of traditional life.*

Ins and outs

Getting there As above for Djerba. The airport is a short taxi ride from Houmt Souk (around 3Dt by
day, 4.5Dt at night). Most buses coming to Djerba terminate at Houmt Souk.

Getting around At Houmt Souk you are well placed for exploring the Jewish centre of Hara Sghira (Er
Riadh) and Hara Kebira. There are local buses to the big hotels at Sidi Mahares and to
Midoun. Try renting a bike or scooter to get around.

Sights

The souk The souk is in the centre of the town. The main souq, not to be missed, is covered
and has many small shops selling mainly silver, brass, leather goods, shoes,
material and clothes. Prices tend to be high, shop around to get an idea of the
going rates. Djerba is noted for its straw mats, blankets, jewellery (until recently,
much was still made by the Jews) and pottery, particularly from Guellala. Typical
Djerban pottery was made for utilitarian purposes such as storing water or foodstuffs. There is no glaze, but the pottery has a special whitish colour obtained by
soaking the clay in sea water. The market is held around the souk every Monday
and Thursday. The pottery and straw mats are sold on the main square, by Avenue Habib Bourguiba. Walking around the town will not take very long as it is
quite small. Little streets lead on to charming squares with cafés. Notice the large
doorways indicating an old *fondouk* or merchants' hostel.

**Religious
buildings** The austere 17th century **Zaouia of Sidi Brahim** (works started in 1674) was a
centre of religious learning. It still contains the saint's tomb, and is off limits to
non-Muslims. Across the road is the **Mosquée des Etrangers** (the **Outsiders'
Mosque**), distinguished by the large number of small domes around the main
one. The **Mosque of the Turks**, further north, is interesting due to its splendid
pointy minaret, recalling those built by the Ottomans further round the coast
in Tripoli. Unfortunately, all these monuments are closed to non-Muslims.
You could, however, have a look in at the former **catholic church**, down a
side-street near the cinema. In the 19th and first half of the 20th centuries,
Djerba, like other southern ports, had a fair-sized European population, of
Greek, Maltese and Sicilian origin, who were involved in fishing (for both
sponges and fish) and trade.

On the seafront by the harbour north of Houmt Souk is the **Bordj el Kebir** (the Great Tower). This largely 16th century fort goes back to the 13th century (although it is likely that there was a Roman construction here), when Roger de Lluria, King of Sicily, then extending his influence along the Ifrikiyan coast, needed to build his forces a strongpoint on Djerba. Later, in the 16th century, with Habsburg Spain and Ottoman Turkey fighting for Mediterranean supremacy, the fort was occupied by the Spaniards. In 1560, Ottoman sea supremo Dragut wiped out a Spanish fleet, and a large number of Spanish troops were left defending the fort. When the *bordj* fell, the Turks massacred the Spaniards, building a tower with their skulls – now marked by a small monument – as the

Houmt Souk

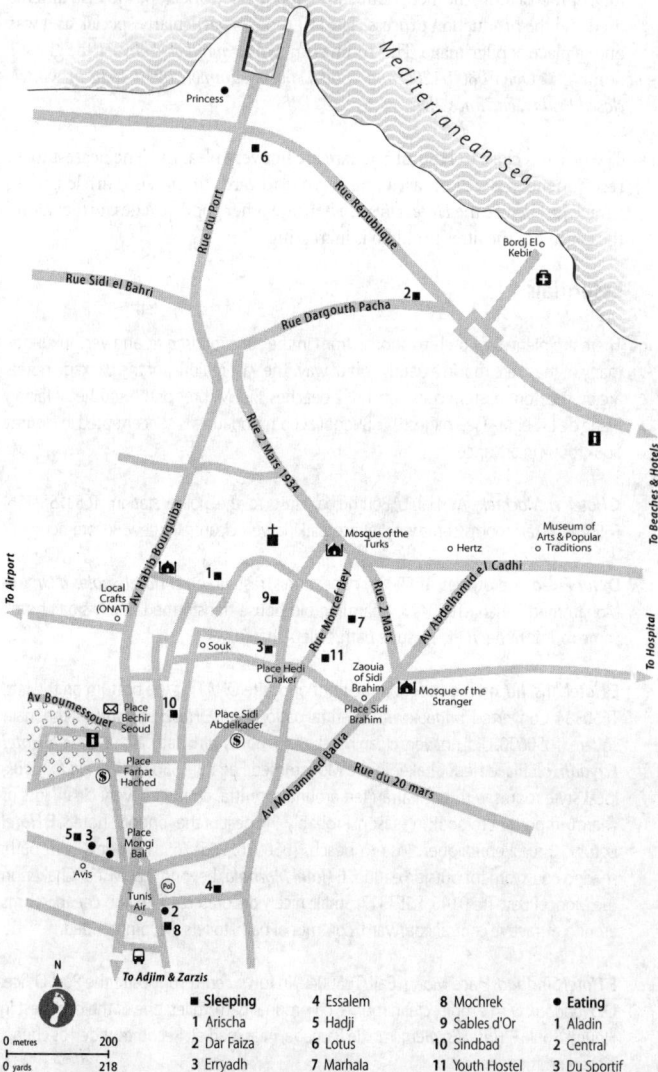

Djerba

■ Sleeping	4 Essalem	8 Mochrek	● Eating
1 Arischa	5 Hadji	9 Sables d'Or	1 Aladin
2 Dar Faiza	6 Lotus	10 Sindbad	2 Central
3 Erryadh	7 Marhala	11 Youth Hostel	3 Du Sportif

0 metres 200
0 yards 218

Princess
Mediterranean Sea
Rue du Port
Rue République
Bordj El Kebir
Rue Sidi el Bahri
Rue Dargouth Pacha
Rue 2 Mars 1934
To Beaches & Hotels
Av Habib Bourguiba
Mosque of the Turks
Museum of Arts & Popular Traditions
Hertz
Av Abdelhamid el Cadhi
Local Crafts (ONAT)
Souk
Rue Moncef Bey
Rue 2 Mars
To Airport
Zaouia of Sidi Brahim
Place Hedi Chaker
Mosque of the Stranger
Av Boumessouer
Place Bechir Seoud
Place Sidi Abdelkader
Place Sidi Brahim
To Hospital
Place Farhat Hached
Av Mohammed Badra
Rue du 20 mars
Place Mongi Bali
Avis
Tunis Air
To Adjim & Zarzis
N

tower was demolished in 1848. The fort is sometimes referred to as Bordj Ghazi Mustapha, after the Turk who supervised its reconstruction.

Inside the fort it is possible to see the ruins of an earlier fort built in the 13th century, though the site goes back further to Roman times. ■*Open 0800-1200 and 1500-1900 summer, 0830-1730 winter, closed Friday. Entrance 3Dt.* From the top of the fort is a wonderful view over the sea and harbour. There is the **market** by the harbour held every Monday and Thursday. The fish auction is particularly interesting.

The musuem
The **Museum of Popular Arts and Traditions** on Avenue Abdelhamid El Cadhi is set in an old *zaouia*, dedicated to Sidi Zitouni who used to come here and heal the mentally ill. The collection is interesting and well labelled. The first room displays traditional Djerban costumes and jewellery and explains the history of the island. Another room shows a pottery workshop, the instruments used and the production process. The last room is particularly special, as it was once a place of pilgrimage. This room is known as *quoubet el khyal* ('the ghost's dome'). ■ *Open 0800-1200 and 1500-1900 in summer, 0930-1630 in winter, closed Friday, entrance 2Dt.*

Beaches
The beaches close to Houmt Soukare are not very pleasant. The nearest to be recommended is six km east along the road towards the hotels. Turn left along a track just before the *Hotel Ulysse*. There are other good beaches further along the coast, but the litter problem is increasing.

Essentials

Sleeping
Prices are generally higher on Djerba than in the rest of Tunisia and there is little budget accommodation

There are plenty of hotels to choose from in the *zone touristique*, and very luxurious many of them are too, in a gaudy sort of way. The vast majority of the package hotels are on the northeastern coast, on 1 of 2 beaches, Sidi Mahres or the southeast facing Plage de la Séguia (see page 392). Budget accommodation is concentrated in Houmt Souk, book in advance.

C *Hotel el Machrek*, Av Habib Bourguiba, close to the police station, T653155/156, F650717. 40 a/c rooms, some with terrace, parking, very clean, fairly new. Recommended.

D *Dar Faiza*, rue Ulysses, T650083, pool, tennis, restaurant. **D** *Hotel Sables d'Or*, rue Mohammed Ferjani, T650423. Charming old house transformed into a small hotel, some rooms rather dark. En suite bath, toilets shared.

E *Hotel Arischa*, on the street on the right opposite ONAT, at the bottom on the left, T650384. Converted *fondouk* with a central patio, clean. **E** *Hotel Le Hadji*, off the main square, T650630. Old, not very clean hotel, all 45 rooms with bath, 17 have a/c. **E** *Hotel Erryadh*, off Place Hedi Chaker in rue Mohammed Ferjani, T650756. An old *fondouk*, local style rooms with bath arranged around a central courtyard, very clean, lots of charm, important to book in season. Probably the best of the fondouk hotels. **E** *Hotel Lotus*, 18 rue Republique, close to beach, T650026, F651765. 17 rooms with bath, shaded courtyard for outside eating. **E** *Hotel Marhala*, beyond Place Hedi Chaker on rue Moncef Bey, T650146, F653317. Small, nicely decorated, clean and cheap, rooms around attractive central courtyard, communal bath/toilets. Recommended.

F *Hotel Sindbad*, Place Mongi Bali, T650047, in town centre, opposite the Post Office. Old *fondouk* with simple, clean rooms, communal bath/toilet, one of the cheapest in Houmt Souk. **F** *Hotel Essalem*, rue de Ramada, near market. Recommended as cheap, clean and friendly.

Djerba

Youth hostels 11 rue Moncef Bey, T650619, 120 beds, exceedingly basic.

There is a small but good range of restaurants to suite all budgets. The larger hotels all **Eating** have the usual à la carte restaurants, which tend to be expensive for the level of service provided.

Expensive *Restaurant La Princesse d'Haroun*, T650488, by the harbour. Specializes in fish, cosy atmosphere and decor. *Restaurant Ettebsi*, Avee Abdel Hamid El Cadhi. Pleasant. Folklore-type entertainment some evenings.

Mid-range *Restaurant Blue Moon*, place Hédi Chaker, T650559. Tables in both the inner courtyard and inside. Pleasant, one of the better restaurants in this category. *Pizzeria Dar*, 161 Av Abdel Hamid El Cadhi. Good value pizzas. *Restaurant Dar Faïza*, rue de la République, T650083. Good set menu. Perhaps the best of the hotel restaurants. *Restaurant El Hana*, place Mohamed Ali, T650568, near 1 of the entrances to the marché central. *Restaurant de l'Ile*, place Hédi Chaker, T650575. Set menu or à la carte. *Restaurant Jerbanova*, place Sidi Ibrahim, next to the Restaurant de l'Ile. *Restaurant Sidi Bou Saïd*, in the souk at Midoun, 1st floor terrace.

Cheap *Restaurant Aladin*, Av Mohamed Badra. Small and cheap. *Restaurant Berbère*, place Farhat Hached. Small eatery with good couscous. *Restaurant Le Carthage*, 11 Av Mohamed Badra. Tunisian home cooking, including dishes like *kamounia* (meat in a tomato and onion stew with cumin) and an excellent couscous. *Restaurant Central*, 128 Av Habib Bourguiba. Good, cheap food. Handy for the bus station, closes late. *Le Mediterranéen*, 5 rue Moncef Bey. Seafood and Tunisian food. *Restaurant Les Palmiers*, place d'Algérie. *Restaurant du Sud*, Place Sidi Ibrahim. A bit touristy but the food is good. *Restaurant Chez Salem*, marché central. Near the fish auction. Buy your fish or meat at the market, then head for Chez Salem who will cook them for you. Get there before midday. Lunches only. *Restaurant du Sportif, 147 Av Habib Bourguiba. Tunisian food at budget prices.*

Delicatessen *M'Hirsi*, rue Abdelhamid Belkadhi, T651206. Best but most expensive. *Boukhris Marina*, also in rue Adbelhamid Belkadhi. Good, sells pancakes too.

Handicrafts The main ONAT craft shop is on Av Habib Bourguiba, where the work- **Shopping** shops and training centre are open for viewing.

Aerobics and Martial Arts can be practised in the gymnasium in Place Aricha, **Sports** which used to be a church. **Golf** by the sea shore, 18 holes, T659055, F659051. **Harbour** 10 yacht berths, min-max draft 1-3m. All watersports. Tennis. Fishing (see box, page 388). Scuba diving and undersea fishing (with permit) are allowed, though there are no facilities.

Local Bus: Djerba has a good public bus service to most parts of the island. There is **Transport** also a bus link with most major Tunisian towns. The bus station, through which all buses pass, is in the centre of Houmt Souk. Information on T650076. Buses No 10 and 11 go hourly round the island, along the coast past the major hotels; No 12 goes to Ajim and the Djorf ferry; No 13 to Beni Maquel; No 14 to Guellala and No 16 to Sedouikech. **Car hire**: although cars can be rented they are expensive and there is a minimum 24 hr rental. However it is a good idea if you intend to go down to the south. Be careful in Houmt Souk when you park, as the police have clamps (same problem as in Tunis: the difficulty is not the fine but finding the person with the keys to come and remove the clamp!). *Avis*, Av Mohammed Badra, T650151; *Budget*, rue du 20 Mars 1934, T650185; *Europacar*, Av Abdelhamid el Cadhi, T650357; *Hertz*, Av

Djerba

☞ *Fishing in Djerba*

Djerba's coastline is composed of rocky shallows, sandy ledges and clay banks. It is occasionally cut by oueds which meander through vast fields of eelgrass. There are approximately 86 fish species living off the shores of Djerba. Generally speaking, bass and mackerel can be found off the northern coast (Borj Jellij, Houmt Souk, Ras Rmel and Ras Tourgueness), made up of limestone tables and sandbanks constantly beaten by waves and by the eastern Barrani wind. Mullet, carangidae and flat fish off the south coast (Ajim, Guellala, El Kantara and Aghir), deep and sandy, where the Ghibli wind blows. The east and west coasts are both rocky and dotted with lagoons. Off the east coast are perch, bass and dace. Off the western coast are weevers and dogfish. Fishing methods widespread in the island of Djerba are hook fishing, la palangrotte (hook fishing from the shore), rod fishing, troll fishing (nocturnal and winter only), long line fishing, fishing à la lenza in shallow waters, net fishing and fishing à la sautade.

Abdelhamid el Cadhi, T/F650039, highly recommended; *Topcar*, rue du 20 Mars 1934, T650536. **Cycle hire**: the island is small and flat making bicycles, which can be rented at most large hotels and in Houmt Souk, an attractive means of transport. In the tourist area to the east of Houmt Souk try Holiday Bikes Tunisie, close to *Hotel Médina*. At *Hotel Arischa* half day hire (0900-1300 or 1400-1900) is 6Dt, all day is 10Dt. **Moped**: from Location Cycles, Av Abdelhamid el Cadhi, in front of Shell petrol station, T650303, 15-20Dt per day. **Taxis** are a good way of getting around but can be hard to find, particularly at night, on market day or away from main routes. Taxi to airport costs 5Dt. Taxis from airport to Tripoli, Libya take 4-5 hrs. The route to Libya is from Djerba to El Kantara, Zarzis, Ben Gardane, Ras Ajdir and over the border, cost is 100Dt.

Long distance Air: T650233/650408, Tunis Air, Av Habib Bourguiba, T650586; Air France, Av Abdelhamid el Cadhi, T650461. The airport is 8 km from Houmt Souk, served by a bus from town, but be sure to check the times beforehand. Flight information on T650233. In the summer there are many more flights in addition to those listed below. **Bus**: the bus station is in the centre of Houmt Souk. Information on T650399/650475/652239. Departures to: Sfax; Gabès; Medenine; Tataouine (2½ hrs); Zarzis and Tunis. **Louages**: by the bus station. **Ferries**: Ajim to Djorf run by CTN.

Banks Plenty of banks in the centre of Houmt Souk, on Av Bourguiba and around. *STB*, Place **Directory**
Farhat Hached, T650140. *BNT*, Place Ben Daamech, T650025. *BT*, rue du 20 Mars, T650004. *BTS*, Av
Habib Bourguiba, T650729. There are also many bureau de change offices around the town which
accept credit cards and are open more flexible hours. Even better, *STB* now has an automatic cash
dispenser for Visa and Mastercard holders. **Communications Area code:** 05. **International
exchange:** on the side of the Post Office. **Post Office:** Av Habib Bourguiba, after the main square.
Hammams Try the 1 next to the zaouia on place Sidi Ibrahim in Houmt Souk (men mornings,
women afternoons). **Hospitals and medical services Hospital:** main hospital on Av Habib
Bourguiba, T650018. Private hospital El Yasmin on Av Mohammed Badra. **Places of
worship** Catholic: 2 rue de l'Eglise, Houmt Souk, T650215, service Sun and holy days at 1000.
Tour companies and travel agents All can organize 2-4 day tours of the desert and into the
towns and villages of southern Tunisia. *Carthage Tours*, centre of town, T650308. *Djerba Voyage*,
Av Habib Bourguiba, T650071. *Evatour*, 653172, on airport road. *Malik Voyagec*, rue Habib
Thameur, T650235. *Sahara Tours*, Av Taleb Mehiri, T652646, F652822. *Tourafricac*, 146 Av Habib
Bourguiba, T650104, F653240. *Voyages Najor Chabane*, Av Habib Bourguiba, T652633, F652632.
Tourist offices The local information office is on Av Habib Bourguiba, just before the Post Office,
T650157. Main office at the start of route Touristique, slightly out of town, T650016, Tx651956.
Closed on Sat afternoon, Fri, Sun and public holidays.

Exploring Djerba

Southwest Djerba

If you opt to head north from Medenine on the C108, you will be crossing over
to the island from **Djorf,** departure point for ferries to **Ajim** (foot passengers
go free, car only 1Dt). Ajim was once an important sponge fishing harbour
although this activity is now virtually abandoned, due to the difficulties and
dangers of the job. Today, Ajim is an important fishing port.

Ajim village itself is of minimal interest, but there are a few cafés and restaurants with large terraces and long rows of street stalls. Arriving from Houmt
Souk or Borj Jellij, in Avenue Habib Bourguiba, on the left is the medium
priced *Restaurant Ouled-M'barak*, the fish here is excellent and is served with
fried rice or chips, choose your fish and bargain, the meal is as cheap as you can
get it! Towards the port are a couple of cheap eateries, on the right, *Café du Port
Fafi*, and on the *Fast Food Fethi*, serving spaghetti, fish and chicken.

Guellala, called Haribus in classical times, is renowned for its **pottery**, particularly the typical Djerban white
coloured ware. The clay for the pottery comes from galleries cut into the
small hill nearby, on the road to
Sedouikech. After a brief soaking in
seawater the clay goes white. Guellala
has over 500 artisans making pottery,
now mostly selling to the tourists.
Indeed it has shops from one end of
the village to the other. Another village once well known for its pottery is
Sedouikech, three km east of
Guellala on the road to Midoun.
Today all that remains of this craft are
long underground stores. Other
crafts still plied include alfa-grass
plaiting for baskets of various styles.

Potier   Djerba
(Guellala)

The west coast

The west coast of Djerba is still untouched by tourism – and looks set to remain this way, as it is rocky and there are few beaches. It is, however, ideal for walks, or a trip along the coast. To get there, take the road to the airport and continue straight on towards **Borj Jellij**, until the road goes right. Here you should take the track to the left. You can follow it south, all the way to Ajim. A few kilometres along the track, on the right, there are a few beautiful houses and a mosque by the sea. Allow half a day to Borj Jellij and all day to Ajim. At Borj Jellij there is a small port with a few simple fishermen's houses and a small lighthouse. The fishermen spend from 3-15 days here in the huts and then return to their village and their family elsewhere on the island. There is no organized transport here, no facilities and certainly nowhere to buy food. If you have made an arrangement with a taxi, make sure the driver knows where and when to pick you up.

On your way out of Houmt Souk heading for the coast, you might stop off in **Melita**, a village near the airport. There is a white block shaped mosque with a very low minaret. Most of the older houses in the village have vaulted roofs. There are two cafés here. Drinks are cheaper here than in Houmt Souk. In a small street on the left is a Tunisian takeaway.

South of Houmt Souk

A few kilometres south of Houmt Souk, there are some final examples of Djerban religious architecture. El May has a fine mosque, while at Er Riadh, formerly Hara Esseghira, is a major Jewish shrine. Hara Kebira, the other main Jewish village, is within walking distance from Houmt Souk.

Er Riadh was originally known as **Hara Sghira** or 'Little Neighbourhood'. It was here that most Jews moved after the introduction of Islam to the area. They were treated with tolerance and became famous for their jewellery. In the village a signposted road on the left leads to the **Synagogue of El Ghriba**. The original synagogue is said to have been built at the time of the first Jewish settlement in 586 BC, shortly after the destruction of King Solomon's temple in Jerusalem. The story goes that the place for the first synagogue was marked by a sacred stone falling from heaven and by the arrival of a strange woman to supervise the construction. Should the Jews ever abandon Djerba, then the key to the Synagogue will be hurled back up to Heaven.

Ghriba means 'miracle' and there is an annual procession on the 33rd day after the Passover – called *Lag be Omer* to commemorate the miracles. The congregation, including many pilgrims, bear the holy books through the streets on a covered platform. The Synagogue has become a spiritual centre for the study of the Torah and makes an interesting stop in an Islamic country. Inside the synagogue heads will have to be covered (head covers provided).

The Ghriba synagogue is a smart building, freshly whitewashed each year. The present building was constructed in the 1920s, and is neither really beautiful nor wholly kitsch. The huge studded wooden doors open into the large, rectangular main room. The marble-paved floor is covered with rush matting. The walls are faced with blue tiles, the columns have had a good dose of pale blue gloss paint, and there is coloured glass in the windows filtering the sun onto dark, heavy wooden furniture. Aged men recite from the holy books. Some of the older men wear baggy trousers which fasten at a black band below the knee. The black signifies mourning for the destruction of Solomon's temple. The second room holds what is said to be one of the oldest Torahs in the world. ■ *Open 0700-1800 except Sat. A small contribution (say 1Dt) is appreciated.*

Djerba

Looking for lotus fruit

George Woodberry goes looking for lotus fruit on Djerba …

"Yes, there was a jujubier in the neighbourhood. The old man, who had an alert, breezy way about him … seemed to wonder that I had come to see it, but said nothing; he was for the time more intent on rites of hospitality, and I went about examining the curiosities. His wife and a little girl came in with a great pitcher and tall glasses and set them down before us, and the old man poured out generous draughts of bright-brown cider. I smiled to think into what a vintage my dreamed-of juice of the enchanted stem had resolved itself – a glass of russet cider … It was excellent cider … On inquiry I found it was not even of the fruit of Djerba, but brewed from a preparation made at Paris, somewhat as root beer is with us. Meanwhile, we had tales of the sea and old adventures on 'the climbing wave', pleasant talk, till I brought the conversation round to the jujubier. It bore a hard, brown fruit, I learned, sweetish, and a drink was made from it, like lemonade; and, yes, it had a sleepy effect. No, it was not bottled. So, talking incidentally of many things, my host showed me the rest of the house, the little bedroom with his photograph of other days, and with a last health we went out into the garden, where

the little girl was waiting with a bunch of spring flowers, and we walked off to see the jujubier.

It was at the end wall of a small, shut-up Arab house near by, against which it was trained. It was shoulder-high, and grew in stout, hardy stocks. The blithe old man told me it must be more than two hundred years old. I said it was very small for its age; but he added that its growth was very slow, almost imperceptible. It was just showing signs of leaving out; a naked, rough, shrub-like tree, with neither leaf, nor flower, nor fruit; but it was alive, and I still have hopes that in the case of a tree so long-lived I shall some time find it in its season, and eat of it, and perhaps drink of its sleepy soul. I went back to the garden and said goodbye to my kind and gentle host, and I was really almost as glad to have had this tranquil hospitality and Crusoe memory as if I had met with better luck in my search. I walked back over the rough fields content; and as we drove slowly through the sand in the wide prospect of scattered palm and olive, with the little white domes, quiet in the universal sun, I thought the lotus land was very good as it was."

From George Woodberry's North Africa and the Desert, scenes and moods *(London, 1914).*

The **Jewish population** on Djerba today is down to a couple of thousand, although numbers are said to be on the increase. They practise their religion unhindered. Attitudes are tolerant. Although there is latent anti-Jewish prejudice in some everyday sayings, this never spills over into violence. Many older Tunisians have fond memories of departed Jewish neighbours. The Tunisian Muslim viewpoint includes a respect for local Jews (accepted as part of a way of life now almost vanished) and a strong opposition to continued Zionist colonization of Palestine. (See box, following page.)

After visiting El Ghriba, you might want to continue south to **El May**, home to the Mosque of Um Etturkia, a typical Djerban mosque with thick walls and a low, rounded minaret, resembling a fort. On Friday afternoon and Saturday morning, a small local **market** takes place here. There is a livestock market too. *Restaurant Aladin*, rue Salah ben Youssef in front of the market place, is small, good and cheap, take a small cup of strong tea at the end of the meal to wake you up. There are few tourists here.

Heading northeast from El May towards the Plage Sidi Mahres, you pass through **Cedriane**, also spelt **Cedghyène**. Going straight through the village, you reach the main Houmt Souk to Midoun road after about 2,500 metres.

👉 *The Jews of Tunisia: ancient community, modern diaspora*

The Jews were the first non-Hamitic people to settle in the Maghreb, and their presence goes back 26 centuries to the time of King Solomon and his friend and son-in-law, King Hiram of Tyre. The two kings worked together in establishing trading posts in the western Mediterranean. Recent (1991) archaeological discoveries at Carthage confirm this. After the Arab conquest in the early eighth century, the Jews remained important in the region: across the Maghreb there were Jewish communities (the hypothesis that the majority of these communities were Judaized Berbers is supported by most writers), and the historian El Idrissi was struck by the importance of Judaism on Djerba. (Hara Sghira was founded in 586 BC on Djerba after the destruction of the first temple in Jerusalem (see page 390). In the 16th century, Testour became a leading centre of the megorashim, the Jews expelled from Andalusia.

In the 17th and 18th centuries, with Tunisia a regency of the Ottoman Empire,

the Jews came to play an important role in the developing trade with Europe. In the 18th century, numerous Jews of Iberian origin, established in Livorno, took up residence in Tunis, forming the core of the Grana community, as opposed to the Twansa or Tunis Jewish community. As of 1741, each community had its own synagogues and institutions. An 1846 agreement with Tuscany allowed the Grana Jews to settle in Tunisia while retaining their original nationality. Under the protection of the Tuscan consul, the community grew rapidly.

As elsewhere in the Mediterranean, the Jews were quick to understand the importance of modern education. In 1878, the United Israelite Alliance opened a school with a modern French curriculum. The coming of the French Protectorate in 1881 opened new possibilities for an increasingly educated, energetic group. As they prospered they left their insalubrious quarters in the médina for new areas like

Note that south of Cedriane is a ruined 18th century palace, the **Qasr Hamida Ben Ayed**. East off the road to Midoun are palm groves where the huge *menzels* (now abandoned and in disrepair) can be seen. The oasis has ample water and produces pomegranates as well as citrus.

Plage Sidi Mahres and Plage de la Séguia: the tourist coast

Hotel development has been concentrated on the island's two best stretches of beach, the Plage Sidi Mahres, running from Ras Rmel to Taguermess, and the Plage de la Séguia, running from Taguermess to Borj Kastil. The beaches are kept clean – but can get very crowded in summer. Surfboards can be rented and various other watersports are organized in all the major hotels. If you want some peace, however, head for the west coast.

Outside summer, there is a longish beach walk, taking around three hours, from Aghir to Borj Kastil, a fort falling slowly into ruins on the southeast point of the island. There are interesting views, especially south across the mainland and the causeway. A very primitive overnight stop, if necessary, is available at the fisherman's cottage at the end of the walk.

Sleeping
Phone code: 05

Many of the large beach hotels are run by foreign tour operators, including the large German TUI group. The Club Med, with 3 very high standard holiday villages, is another important presence. Club Robinson is a sort of Club Med run by TUI. The best rated hotels are on the beach. There is now almost a complete '2nd line' of hotels off the beach in the Sidi Mahres part of the *zone touristique*.

Lafayette – where the community's wealth is reflected in the great Art Déco synagogue on Av de la Liberté.

With a tradition of publishing religious works, the Jews were active in the press. Popular literature in Judaeo-Arabic was published along with newspapers like La Justice. Unlike Algeria's Jews, who received French nationality en masse, Tunisia's Jews remained subjects of the bey in their great majority – which by no means stopped them from joining the Communist Party and the Nationalist Movement. By 1950, the community was at its peak with 120,000 members, of whom 25,000 had foreign nationality.

After independence in 1956, Tunisia's Jews voted to elect the Constituent Assembly on equal footing with their Muslim fellow citizens. Again in contrast with Algeria, most felt secure enough to remain in their newly independent country, even if the new government aimed to remove any trace of separatism. Hence, in 1957, the Rabbinical Courts were dissolved, followed by the Community Council in 1958. More serious, however, was the transformation of the main Jewish cemetery into a public park, today's Jardin Habib Thameur. Anti-Semitic incidents took place during the 1961 Bizerte crisis and the 1967 Six Day War which saw Jewish property ransacked. With the co-operative movement under super-minister Ben Salah, the climate for private enterprise continued to deteriorate.

A spiritual people, deeply attached to their traditions, the Tunisian Jews were almost too well prepared to receive the ideology of the 'Promised Land'. Some 50,000 opted for Israel, in the years after independence, a further 35,000 for France. Today, the community numbers a few thousand, with a handful of families still important in business. Nevertheless, the sacred books are still carried in procession during the annual pilgrimage to the El Ghriba Synagogue on Djerba, the oldest synagogue in the world.

A *Hotel Athénée Palace*, T600600, F601601. A truly luxurious place, closest to Houmt Souk on the Plage de Sidi Mahares. **A** *Hotel Hasdrubal*, T657650, F657730. Another luxurious establishment, on Plage de Sidi Mahares, towards Ras Taguermes end. **A** *Hotel Ulysse*, T657422. 300 rooms all a/c, on beach, pool, restaurant, nightclub, sports activities, 10 km from Houmt Souk.

B *Abou Nawas Djerba*, on the beach, central section of Sidi Mahares beach, T657022, F657700. **B** *Aquarius Club*, T657790, 600 beds, and *Meridiana*, 400 beds, both beach hotels at Taguermes 28 km from Houmt Souk. **B** *Hotel Dar Midoun*, T658168, F658169. Another luxurious place. Overwrought lobby decoration with tonnes of marble, carved plasterwork and bathroom tiles. All the usual features. **B** *Hotel Djerba Orient*, T657440, opposite *Hotel Ulysse*, 56 beds, 10 km from Houmt Souk, not on beach. **B** *Hotel Djerba Plaza*, T658230, F658229. A large hotel, close to golf course at Ras Taguermes end of Sidi Mahares. **B** *Djerba La Douce*, T657129, F657161. On the Plage de la Séguia. Very comfortable Club Med holiday village.

C *Hotel El Djazira*, T657300/657304, F657015. Plage de Sidi Mahares, on the beach after the Hotel Ulysse. One of the oldest hotels in the zone touristique.

Midoun

Djerba's second largest town, Midoun is 12 kilometres from Houmt Souk. (The term 'town' is being a little generous perhaps for a sort of road-junction village.) A large black community, descendants of slaves brought from sub-Saharan Africa, still exists here. Midoun has a particularly good weekly

market each Thursday afternoon and Friday. To see an interesting **olive press** take the road towards Houmt Souk and turn right at the crossroads, rue Salah Ben Youssef. The press is about 400 metres on the left by the well and hidden by an olive tree. A mule or camel was used to turn the stone roller to crush the olives which were then transferred to a sieve where a large palm tree trunk squeezed out the oil into a jar underneath. All around are chambers once used for stocking olives. This particular piece of ancient technology is said to be more than 300 years old.

Sleeping
Phone code: 05

The only hotel is the **E** *Hotel El Jawhara*, completely refurbished, T600467. Midoun is close to the beach hotels, however.

Eating

Expensive *Restaurant Le Khalife*, route du Phare, Midoun. Tunisian specialities. **Mid-range** *Restaurant El Guestile*, T657724, 21 rue Marsa Ettefah, near the place du Marché. Typically Tunisian, eat on the terrace, on the verandah or the upper floor in one of the small dining rooms. Fish specialities. Menzel-type building. **Cheap** *Restaurant de l'Orient* on central roundabout. Tunisian food. There is also the cheap *Restaurant Constantine*, Av Badra, less smart, food good.

Banks

STB, T657723. *Bank El Amen* (ex-CFCT), T657493, both in town centre.

Around Midoun

From Midoun, there are some pleasant excursions to be done, either by bike or on foot, into the countryside of central Djerba. Heading south or west of Midoun, you are in a landscape of olive and palm groves dotted with *menzels*, the fortified farmsteads typical of the island. The tracks, perfect for walking or cycling, run between high earth banks planted with agaves and prickly pears.

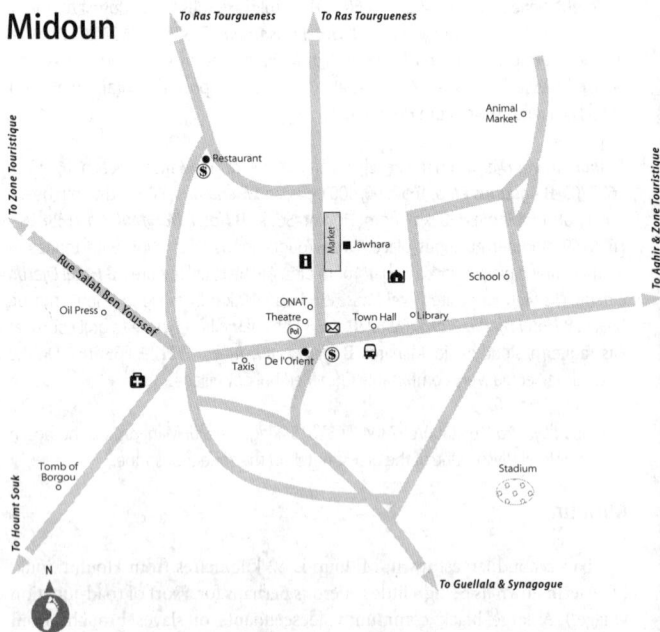

Midoun

To Ras Tourgueness · To Ras Tourgueness

To Zone Touristique

To Aghir & Zone Touristique

Animal Market

Restaurant

Rue Salah Ben Youssef

Market · Jawhara

School

Oil Press

ONAT
Theatre

Town Hall · Library

Taxis · De l'Orient

Tomb of Borgou

Stadium

To Houmt Souk

N

To Guellala & Synagogue

Sketch map: not to scale

Djerban vernacular, an austere architecture

Farming was difficult on Djerba, and the menzels, the small landholdings of the Djerbans, each focusing on a whitewashed courtyard dwelling, are scattered, seemingly randomly, across the countryside. With their high, windowless walls and corner tower rooms or ghorfas, they were so constructed to maintain the intimacy of family life and protect valuable stores of grain and other foodstuffs. Every house would have a well and cisterns, either a fasguia, an underground cistern with vaults and columns, or a magen, a bottle-shaped underground water storage system. Precious rainwater would run off from the roof terraces into these cisterns. A typical menzel would have a main houch (courtyard), onto which gave living and sleeping areas and the kitchen and stores. Upstairs, in one of the corner 'tower rooms', would be adult sleeping areas. There would also be a sort of bathroom equipped with large amphorae of water for washing.

The Djerban house was built with stones from the fields, roughly cemented together. Roofs were either flat terraces, vaults or, more rarely, domes. The rooms were rarely wider than 2.5 metres, given the springiness of the split palm trunks used for roofing. The roof was rendered waterproof with a layer of dried seaweed, on top of which was spread a layer of clay and pebbles, topped with lime mortar and whitewash. Barrel

vaults, ideal for roofing narrow oblong rooms, were made with small pieces of masonry built with formwork.

Though Djerba was not the easiest place to farm in the Mediterranean, its people built themselves homes perfectly at one with their biotope. (The contrast with the new palace hotels of the coast could hardly be greater.) All the materials were local; the overall impression is one of simple, pure design. There is rarely any emphasis on the building materials used, nothing to indicate the stone or brick under the whitewash. Tiny windows emphasize the sculptural feel. However, despite this apparent austerity, Djerban menzel building is very much at a human scale. Thanks to the courtyard, each family had a private square of Mediterranean sky to enjoy. They could sit outside on reed mats or carpets to eat and chat. In the narrow rooms, the beds were built in masonry platforms or doukkana. There would even be a special entrance for the cat.

Note that this form of Djerban domestic architecture differs only slightly from that used for religious buildings. (There are as many as 200 small mosques.) With their rounded entrance doors, barrel-vaulted outbuildings, buttressed whitewashed façades and inward-looking plan, the average menzel hardly differs from the country mosques of the island.

One option is to explore the countryside west of Midoun, heading for **Mahboubine** and **Khasroun**. The aim is to keep off the roads as far as possible, following the sandy tracks. Mahboubine lies three km west of Midoun. From there, a track will take you north towards Khasroun. Take the blacktop road east from Khasroun, and after one km, turn right. After a further kilometre, a piste leads to the left to take you back to Midoun.

If walking, you could always break at **Mahboubine**, which is half an hour by bus from Houmt Souk. The village has an interesting mosque, a picturesque and peaceful village square and could provide an opportunity to become acquainted with the real people of Djerba. Said a taxi-driver, 'At Mahboubine there is nothing' – or at least nothing more enjoyable than this visit. Certainly don't expect to find a hotel or a restaurant. There is only the café in the main square, alongside the mosque and the bus stop.

Another option is to explore the area south of Midoun, heading for the village of **Arkou**. Leaving Midoun on the road for El Hdada, turn right down a piste after half a kilometre. A piste runs south for two km. As you approach Arkou, there is a small grocer's on your left. At the cross-roads, go right. After five km you cross the main Midoun-Aghir road. You are on the track for Mahboubine. After about 2,500 metres, head right down another track crossing an area of farmsteads. Eventually, you reach the main Mahboubine to Midoun road. Head right for Midoun. This is a particularly good route if you want to have a look at the *menzel* farm buildings.

Heading for the causeway: Meninx

Leaving Djerba (or arriving) from the southeast you will drive over the seven km of causeway originally built by the Romans. At the Djerba end of the causeway is **El Kantara** (lit: 'the bridge'). If you are coming from El Aghir and the Plage de la Séguia, then you will see the remains of ancient Meninx on the left (eastern) side of the road. The settlement, founded by the Carthaginians, was refounded in Roman times, and was no doubt an important trading post, especially given its proximity to the great city of Leptis Magna, near modern Tripoli in Libya.

Djerba
mosquée fortifiée
près de Houmt Souk

Background

10

Background

History

Greeks, Phoenicians and Carthaginians

Like other parts of the Mediterranean, the North African coastal regions became an area for competition between the Greeks and the Phoenicians. The power of both peoples was based on their maritime technology. In order to trade in the commodities of Africa, they established settlements on the coast of present day Libya, entering into relations with the nomadic communities of the desert, notably the Garamantes around the Fezzan. The **Garamantes** appear to have specialized in warfare based on charioteering and they began to raid the new coastal settlements. At the same time, they also controlled trans-Saharan commerce, one of the major reasons why the Phoenicians, at least, were so interested in North Africa.

The **Greeks** had begun to colonize the Egyptian and eastern Libyan coastline as part of their attempt to control Egyptian maritime trade. Cyrene, the first of five Greek colonies in Cyrenaica, Libya, was founded about 625 BC and, a little earlier, three **Phoenician** colonies were created in western Libya, on the coast of what is today Tripolitania, in order to exploit new commercial opportunities – the Phoenicians were first-and-foremost traders. Eventually more important, however, was the major Phoenician settlement at **Carthage**, on the coast of northern Tunisia, close to the modern capital of Tunis, founded in the late ninth century BC, in order to control access to Sicily and the western Mediterranean basin.

Greeks and Phoenicians competed for control of the coastal areas in Libya and eventually created an uneasy division of the region between themselves. The Greeks took over Egypt after the creation of the **Ptolemaic Kingdom** on the death of **Alexander the Great** in 323 BC and incorporated Cyrenaica into the new kingdom. The Phoenicians, harried in their original Lebanese home of Tyre by the Assyrians and Persians, created a commercial empire based on Carthage, with outlying colonies to the west, right round to the Atlantic coast near Larache in present day Morocco. Traditionally, Carthage was founded in 814 BC when princess Dido led part of Tyre's population to settle in a safe place on the North African coast, founding Qart Hadasht, the 'new city', which was to become the leading maritime power in the western Mediterranean.

In the seventh century BC, Carthage had trading posts in the Balearic Islands, Sardinia and the western end of Sicily. In the sixth century BC, they achieved footholds in Corsica, with Etruscan aid. In 481, they organized a great expedition to extend their influence in Sicily – with disastrous results. At the Battle of Himera, the Carthaginian forces were crushed by the rulers of Agrigentum and Syracuse. It was a huge disaster for the ruling Magonid family. (Carthaginian compensation payments probably funded a Hellenic renaissance in Sicily.) Henceforth, Carthage restricted her efforts to maintaining her valuable network of trading posts. From the fifth to the third centuries BC trade flourished, with Punic merchants providing the link between Africa and the Mediterranean. They traded in gold, ivory (highly prized for statues of the gods), and slaves from Africa, silver from Spain, copper from Sardinia and olive oil from Sicily, exchanging them against manufactured products from the eastern Mediterranean: Greek pottery and textiles. Explorers were sent to prospect distant coasts: Himilcon reached Finistère, while Hannon sailed along the western coast of Africa, possibly as far as the Gulf of Guinea. Commerce with remote peoples was based on barter – the Carthaginians first struck coins in the late fourth century.

The late fourth century was a time of strife in Sicily as the Syracusan state fell apart. In 310-308, Syracuse's ruler Agathocles took an army into the Carthaginian heartlands, landing on the Cap Bon and causing considerable damage. (The round town of

The rise of Carthage

Background

👉 *Chronology of Tunisian history*

Date	Event
circa 1100 BC	Phoenician city of Utica is founded.
814 BC	Carthage founded by Queen Dido of Tyre.
264-241 BC	First Punic War (Carthage versus Rome). Loss of Sicilian, Sardinian and Corsican trading towns by Carthaginians.
219 BC	Second Punic War begins.
218 BC	Hannibal invades Italy.
205 BC	Carthaginians defeated in Iberia.
202 BC	Hannibal defeated by Roman general Scipio.
201 BC	End of Second Punic War.
149-146 BC	Third and final Punic War. Carthage is destroyed by Romans.
47-46 BC	Roman military campaign in North Africa.
29 BC	Establishment of Pro-Consular Africa and the reconstruction of a settlement at the site of Carthage.
29 BC–AD 225	Rapid growth of Roman territorial control in Tunisia with colonization and thriving agrarian and trading economy.
AD 235	End of rule of the Severus Emperors.
AD 238	Revolt by Thysdrus (of El Djem) and weakening of imperial control.
AD 439	Carthage captured by the Vandals. Disruption and decay of city life.
AD 534	Tunisia taken by Byzantine Empire. Christian religious buildings become important part of the urban architectural heritage.
AD 647	Islamic conquest reaches Tunisia.
AD 670	Founding of Islamic city of Kairouan by Aqba ibn Naffi.
AD 671	Founding of the Great Mosque at Kairouan, developed by succeeding Aghlabites.
AD 800-909	Aghlabid dynasty with capital at Kairouan later moved to Mahdia.
AD 909-973	Fatimid dynasty. Shi'ite Islam in ascendant.
AD 973	Fatimids conquer Egypt and leave Tunis in hands of Berber Zirid dynasty.
AD 1041	Invasion of North Africa by the Arab Beni Hilal tribe.
AD 1051	Tunisia under Beni Hilal domination.
AD 1159	Tunisia under Almohads rule from Morocco.

Background

Kerkouane may well have been abandoned after being sacked by his army.) When Carthage attempted to make the most of the situation, extending her hold by setting up a garrison at Messina in 270, she found herself faced with a new enemy, Rome.

Roman Africa

The Roman conquest Conflict between Carthage and the expanding Roman state was inevitable. Both had interests in Sicily which, for Rome, was of vital strategic importance. Three conflicts between the two powers ensued: the **Punic Wars**. Although Carthage was expelled from Sicily in 201 BC, Rome still feared Carthaginian power and the city was eventually razed to the ground in 146 BC, after three years of warfare. The fertile plains around the city were then converted into a Roman province. A hundred years after the fall of Punic Carthage, **Julius Caesar** defeated the last of his political adversaries at Thapsus (modern Ras Dimas), an event which signified the end of the Roman republic as well as the end of the independent Numidian states. The Kingdom of Juba I was annexed and renamed as the province of Africa Nova. Subsequently, **Augustus** was to rebuild Carthage as a Roman colony. The city became headquarters of the proconsul and capital of Africa Proconsularis.

AD 1228	*Hafsid dynasty makes Tunisia independent: first as Governorate, then as a kingdom. A period of great prosperity and cultural splendour.*
1534	*Hafsids deposed by pirate chiefs Barbarossa and Kheireddine.*
1535	*Spanish conquest by Charles V.*
1574	*Ottoman Turks take Tunis.*
1590	*Revolt of the Janissaries, Dey becomes governor.*
1631	*Beys of Tunis take the title of* Pasha.
1705	*Hussein Ben Ali Bey seizes power as hereditary Pasha of Tunis.*
1837-1855	*Ahmad Bey. Abolished slavery and introduced modern industry into Tunisia.*
1869	*France enforces control over Tunisian financial affairs for European creditors of Bey.*
1881	*Treaty of Bardo, following invasion by French army from Algeria, ratifies a permanent French interest in the running of Tunisian foreign and defence affairs.*
1883	*Convention of La Marsa gives French rights effectively to manage the government of Tunisia.*
1920	*Start of an organized Tunisian independence movement with founding of the Destour Party.*
1934	*Activists break from Destour Party to form the Neo-Destour Party under leadership of Habib Bourguiba.*
1942-43	*Axis control in Tunisia with Bey collaborating with Germans.*
1943	*Moncef Bey deposed by French.*
1945-49	*Habib Bourguiba in exile organizing campaign for Tunisian independence.*
1946	*Trade Union founded.*
1956	*France grants independence to Tunisia.*
1957	*Habib Bourguiba made first President of the new Republic of Tunisia.*
1963	*Final withdrawal of French troops from Bizerte military base.*
1987	*Ageing President Bourguiba is removed from office, declared unfit to rule, Zine El-Abidine Ben Ali becomes second president.*

Background

Roman administrators in the new North African province faced a problem of border security, with nomad tribes and local dynasties constantly threatening stability. The problem was solved by creating the *limes*, a border region along the desert edge which was settled with former legionaries as a militarized farming population. Thus, although the border region was permeable to trade, resistance to tribal incursion could be rapidly mobilized from the resident population, while regular forces were brought to the scene. As Roman power and influence grew, the *limes* spread westwards from Egypt as far as the Moroccan Atlantic coast. In southern Tunisia, the frontier was reinforced by a ditch – the *fossa regia*.

The Roman peace

Under Roman rule, Carthage quickly became one of the most important cities of the empire. In the first century AD, the twin African provinces were a major source of wheat for Rome. From the reign of Nero, two-thirds of Rome's total grain supply came from Africa, with the remaining third coming from Egypt. Other farming activities developed, notably the cultivation of olives and vines, thanks to the establishment of irrigation programmes. Indigenous villages and Roman settlements (*coloniae*) became prosperous towns. The most fortunate became fully fledged *municipiae*, managed by Roman magistrates and embellished with fine temples, baths and market squares.

Towards the end of the second century AD, a number of men of African origin reached important posts in the empire: 15 percent of the knights and senators were from Africa, and the province produced several emperors too, notably **Clodius Albinus** (AD 196-197) and **Septimius Severus** (AD 193-211). The African provinces also produced intellectuals, including **Fronto**, tutor to the Emperor Marcus Aurelius, and the poet **Apuleius**, author of *The Golden Ass*.

By the beginning of the Christian era, North Africa had been organized into five Roman provinces: Africa Vetus and Africa Nova, Numidia, Mauritania Caesariana and Mauritania Tingitania. The sedentary Berber populations were largely Romanized in

Archaeological sites of Tunisia

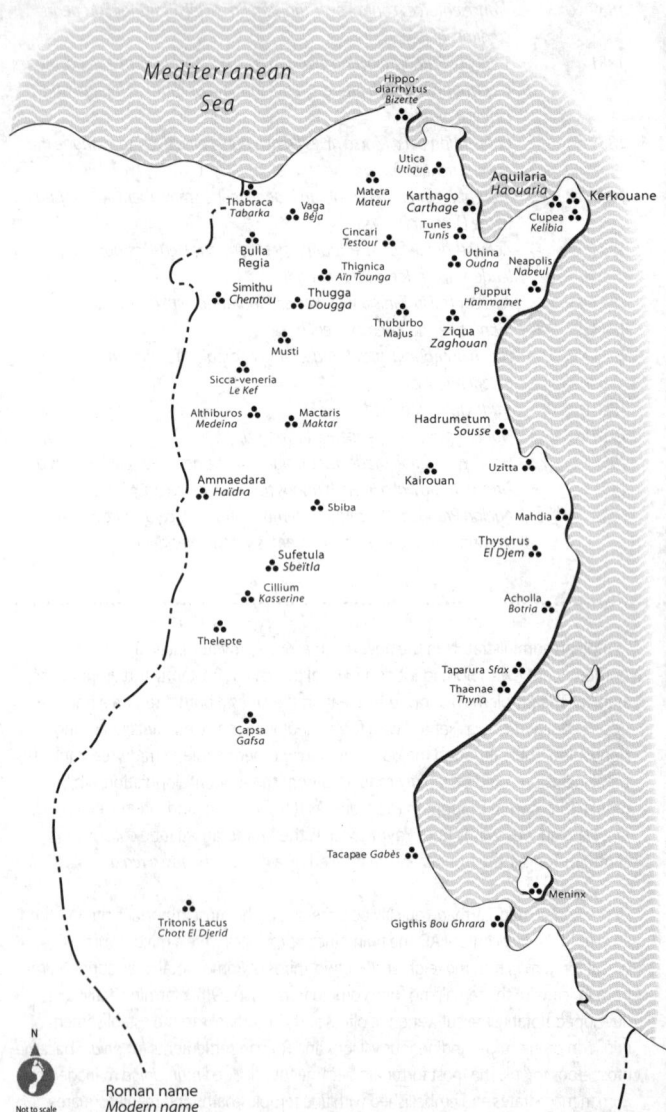

Mediterranean Sea

Hippo-diarrhytus
Bizerte

Utica
Utique

Aquilaria
Haouaria

Kerkouane

Thabraca
Tabarka

Vaga
Béja

Matera
Mateur

Karthago
Carthage

Clupea
Kelibia

Cincari
Testour

Tunes
Tunis

Bulla Regia

Thignica
Aïn Tounga

Uthina
Oudna

Neapolis
Nabeul

Simithu
Chemtou

Thugga
Dougga

Pupput
Hammamet

Thuburbo Majus

Ziqua
Zaghouan

Musti

Sicca-veneria
Le Kef

Althiburos
Medeina

Mactaris
Maktar

Hadrumetum
Sousse

Ammaedara
Haïdra

Kairouan

Uzitta

Sbiba

Mahdia

Thysdrus
El Djem

Sufetula
Sbeïtla

Cillium
Kasserine

Acholla
Botria

Thelepte

Taparura *Sfax*

Thaenae
Thyna

Capsa
Gafsa

Tacapae *Gabès*

Meninx

Tritonis Lacus
Chott El Djerid

Gigthis *Bou Ghrara*

N

Roman name
Modern name

Not to scale

The Tophet, centre of Carthaginian child sacrifice

From the mid-1800s, numerous ancient stelae ('stone markers') were discovered at Carthage around the Punic harbours and near Byrsa Hill, many incorporated into Roman or Byzantine structures. The discovery of the sacred precinct, known today as the Tophet, in 1921, was an important archaeological event. Initial excavations were supported by one Count Byron Kuhn de Prorok, a Maecenas figure who sponsored various archaeological projects in Carthage in the 1920s.

All those who excavated the site have supported the view that the Phoenicians practised child sacrifice. A Greek writer, the 3rd century BC Alexandrian Clitarchus, tells us how the Carthaginians would sacrifice a child to Cronus every time they needed a big favour. Other ancient sources say or imply that child sacrifice was a feature of Carthaginian religious life. Centuries later, the sources appeared to have been vindicated with the discovery of a sacred precinct in Carthage. Dedicated to Tanit Pene Baal and her consort Baal Hammon, the area contained numerous stelae and burial urns, filled with the cremated bones

of infants, lambs and kids, along with amulets, beads and jewellery.

Biblical evidence also attests to child sacrifice among the Canaanites, as the Bible calls the Phoenicians. Both children and animals were votive offerings, made because the sacrificer's wish had been fulfilled ('Because the gods heard my voice and blessed me', Carthaginian inscription formula). It may be that the first born was sacrificed – see the near sacrifice of Isaac by Abraham. Another possibility is that Carthaginian child sacrifice functioned as a ritual method for disposing of unwanted children. Digs in the 1970s suggest that in the later Carthaginian city, the number of cremated infants increased, and animal sacrifices decreased. The practice seems to have survived into Roman times, if Christian author Tertullian, writing around AD 200, is to be believed. In any event, the similarity of the literary sources suggests that child sacrifice was a very real part of Carthaginian religious practice. Today the Tophet, hidden away in the suburb of Salammbô, remains a place of morbid fascination.

See box next page

the coastal and agricultural regions and North Africa, in cultural terms, was now part of the Mediterranean world, its gods and goddesses assimilated to imported Roman deities: Baal Hammon had become Saturn, Punic Tanit was Caelestis, and fertility god Shadrapa was the dionysiac Liber Pater.

In addition to the commercial and cultural interpenetration of North Africa and Rome, this cultural interaction was intensified by two other factors. First, the region had long been in contact with **Greek culture** and, indeed, through the Phoenicians, with **Levantine culture**. Secondly, as a result of the destruction of the Kingdom of Judea in AD 70, large numbers of Jews migrated into North Africa and **Judaism** intermixed with **Berber culture** to a significant extent, as the surviving contemporary Jewish traditions in Tunisia show.

The eastern part of North Africa, and in particular the provinces of Africa Vetus and Africa Nova (Byzacium in the late Roman period), was the site of major developments in the early history of the Christian church. In the early days, the church was much persecuted by the Roman emperors, who had a tendency to blame the Christians for the various problems facing their vast empire. But Christianity spread across the empire. There were invaders threatening on all sides, and the gods of the Roman pantheon seemed to have abandoned the people.

By the mid-third century AD, Carthage had become the seat of an important bishopric. The forceful **Cyprian**, one of the great figures of the early church, became bishop there in AD 249. Cyprian led the African church at a time when Trajan had increased the level of persecution. He was eventually to die a martyr in AD 258. The

Background

Early Christianity

The Tophet, place of ritual and piety

Carthaginian rites of child sacrifice were described by many ancient writers. Diodorus, 1st century BC Sicilian Greek historian, describes the Carthaginians' reaction when Agathocles of Syracuse' army menaced the city: "They were filled with superstitious dread, for they believed they had neglected to honour the gods in the way established by their ancestors. In their zeal to make amends for the omission, they chose 200 of the noblest children and sacrificed them in public ... There was in their city a bronze image of Cronus, extending its hands, palms up and sloping toward the ground, so that each of the children when placed thereon rolled down and fell into a sort of gaping pit filled with fire." Other sources say or imply that the infants were roasted alive.

The Greek and Latin authors' view of the Carthaginians as child sacrificers seems totally untenable. Both Biblical and Classical sources are sensationalistic, and the latter really amount to little more than anti-Punic propaganda. It is more likely that the Tophet was a child cemetery. No doubt infant mortality was high in ancient Carthage, and stillborn children or those who died soon after birth were buried here. Purificatory offerings of lambs or kids accompanied the infants to the afterlife. Given the vagaries of pre-industrial health care, life expectancy was short in ancient

Carthage. (Could they sterilize those terracotta feeding bottles?) Infant sacrifice would have endangered the very existence of the community. With a network of scattered trading posts around the Mediterranean, the Carthaginian empire would have had to avoid any unnecessary loss of human life. Nevertheless, the myth of Carthaginian child sacrifice dies hard – and was kept alive by Flaubert in a vivid description in his orientalist fresco of a novel, Salammbô.

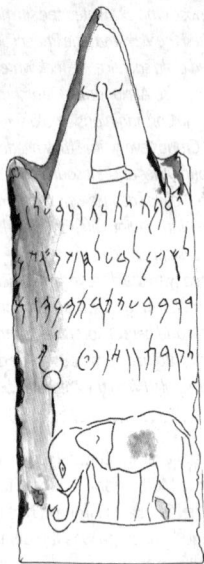

church, however, continued to attract numerous new adepts and to divide into warring factions supporting different theological positions.

Under **Diocletian** in the early fourth century, the empire was split up to be ruled by four leaders, a tetrarchy. Africa Proconsularis was divided into two, the southern and southeastern areas being renamed Byzacenium. The province became the theatre of the **Donatist** heresy – far too complicated to go into here. However, the emperor **Constantine** came to believe that the only hope for the survival of the empire was for Christianity to become the official religion – and he became the first emperor to embrace it. In AD 313, his **Edict of Milan** proclaimed religious tolerance throughout the empire. He also relocated the capital from Rome to Constantinople.

By the late fourth century, the problems created by the Donatist heresy had largely disappeared. One of the great figures of the early church, **St Augustine** rose to prominence in Africa. Son of a pagan father and a Christian mother, he misspent his youth at Carthage, where he studied and taught, before leaving for Milan. In his *Confessions*, he wrote of his life as a young man in the cosmopolitan capital of Africa, describing it as 'a hotbed of sinful desires.' He had a mistress and a thoroughly hedonistic time – but once converted to Christianity he criticized the licentiousness

St Augustine and the decline of Rome

The future St Augustine of Hippo was born in the province of Numidia. In his early 30s, he converted to Christianity, and by 395 he had become the Bishop of Hippo (Annaba, ex-Bône, in modern Algeria, close to the Tunisian frontier). Like most Romans, he was horrified by the sack of Rome in 410 by Alaric and the Goths. He had a deep-felt belief that the Roman empire had been created by God as an instrument for the spread of Christianity. He thus sought to understand how God had allowed such terrible things to happen to the empire.

This is the theme of his work, The City of God. For Augustine, history moves forward according to the purposes of God. However, he came to consider that God's instrument on earth was not a city or an empire. Rather it was the community of believers; it was they who formed 'the city of God.' Unbelievers were of course excluded. Thus it was that the decline and fall of the Roman empire did not really matter in the long run, for the community of believers would survive. St Augustine was to live long enough to see North Africa ravaged by Vandal invaders.

of Carthage's student population. The town was obviously a highly entertaining place, both a fun city and a centre of scholarship and high learning.

The Vandals and the Byzantine reconquest

Augustine died in AD 429. In hindsight, the early fifth century was to prove the high point of the Christian presence in Africa. The Roman Empire was crumbling under external threats, and North Africa was invaded by a Teutonic tribe based in Spain: the **Vandals**, who by AD 429 had conquered as far as eastern Cyrenaica. The Vandal ruler Gaiseric's aim was clear: a rich homeland for his people and independence from the Roman Empire. The Vandals' capture of Africa deprived Rome of corn supplies – and created a dangerous precedent: the Vandal Kingdom was the first independent state actually within the borders of the empire. Feeble attempts at liberating the North African provinces were launched from Constantinople in the 440s, but to little avail. The Vandals were able to use the captured Byzantine fleet for raids on Italy and Sicily, and in 455 **King Gaiseric**, benefiting from the chaos left behind in northern Italy and Gaul by Attila and his Huns, succeeded in looting Rome itself, carrying off empress Eudoxia and her daughters. The eastern emperors feared that the Vandals would expand into the vital corn-growing lands of Egypt. However, the Byzantine expeditionary force launched against them in 468 was a total disaster. As a result, Gaiseric was able to take Sicily, Rome's oldest province. In fact the end of the Roman Empire in western Europe was nigh (in 476 to be exact). Central power collapsed, and Roman populations came to co-exist with Visigoth and other Germanic settler populations.

However, the Vandals were not efficient managers in their new North African homeland. Although they have gone down in history as the most destructive people of the ancient Mediterranean world, certain contemporary writers left a rather different image. Wrote Byzantine historian Procopius: "Of all the nations I know, the most effeminate are the Vandals. They spend all their days in the baths and in consuming sumptuous repasts ... Covered with gold ornaments and clothed in Oriental silks, they pass their time in spectacles, circus games and amusements. They especially like to hunt. ... They like to locate their homes in the middle of well-irrigated orchards with abundant trees. Finally being lovers of the earth, they deliver themselves without reservation to the pursuit of love making."

All of which gave the Byzantines time to get organized. The Eastern Empire re-asserted its control under Emperor **Justinian** and his general, Belisarius, in AD 533.

However, this was to prove unpopular, not least because of the onerous taxation system necessary to cover Byzantium's heavy military expenditure as it tried to confront the Sassanids in Asia as well as maintain its position in the Mediterranean. A little more than a century later, when Byzantine rule in Africa was threatened once more, this time by the expansion of Islam, local populations showed little enthusiasm for supporting Constantinople's continued hegemony in the region.

Despite the supposedly destructive presence of the Vandals, there are numerous remains in contemporary Tunisia from the period of the third to seventh century. Carthage has the ruins of one of the largest early churches, the great Damous El Karita basilica, while up and down the country are the remains of Byzantine fortresses – see for example Aïn Tounga, near Dougga, Oudna and Ksar Lemsa, south of El Fahs. Sbeïtla, ancient Sufetula, where Byzantine prefect Gregorius made a stand in 646 against the invading Arabs, has basilicas too.

The Islamic conquest

In the first half of the seventh century, Semitic tribes of the western Arabian desert, under the sway of a new revealed religion, Islam, were able to make considerable conquests in the Fertile Crescent. The tribes' sudden unity under the charismatic leadership of the Prophet **Mohammad** came at a time when the two great powers of the region, the **Sassanian Empire** (centring on what is now Iran and Irak), and the **Byzantines** in Syro-Palestine, were weak after years of fighting. The Muslim Arabs were not to stop at the Middle East, however, and continued their conquests westwards into Byzantine North Africa.

In AD 642, 10 years after the death of the Prophet Mohammad, Arab armies, acting as the vanguard of Islam, conquered Egypt. To secure his conquest, the Arab commander, Amr Ibn al-As, immediately decided to move westwards into Cyrenaica where the local Berber population submitted to the new invaders. Despite a constant pattern of disturbance, the Arab conquerers of Egypt and their successors did not ignore the potential of the region to the south. Nubia was invaded in AD 641-42 and again 10 years later. Arab merchants and later, bedouin tribes from Arabia were able to move freely throughout the southern regions. However, until AD 665, no real attempt was actually made to complete the conquest, largely because of internal problems within the new Islamic Empire. Then, after two feints southwestwards towards the Fezzan, an army under **Okba Ibn Nafi'** conquered what is now Tunisia and set up the first Islamic centre there at **Kairouan** in AD 670. Four years later, the Arabs in Kairouan were able to persuade **Kusayla**, the leader of the Berber confederation which spread right across Tunisia and modern Algeria as far as the Oued Muluwiya in Morocco, to convert to Islam. Shortly afterwards, Okba Ibn Nafi', in a famous expeditionary raid to scout the unvanquished areas to the west, swept across North Africa along the northern edge of the Sahara desert as far as the Atlantic coast of Morocco, into the land of the Sanhadja Berbers who dominated the major Western trans-Saharan trade routes.

These early conquests were ephemeral, being based on two mistaken assumptions: the first was that the new conquerors could afford to ignore the isolated Byzantine garrisons along the North African coast, because they would eventually collapse due to their isolation (the Byzantine navy, in fact, supplied them by sea); the second was that the Umayad Arab commanders and administrators now imposed on North Africa ignored the promises of equality of treatment given to Berber converts and thus encouraged a major rebellion, led by Kusayla. Arab control of Kairouan was lost and the Arabs had to reconquer the **Maghreb**, the Land of the West, as they called North Africa.

North Africa and Shi'ite Islam

Islam, one of three great revealed religions emanating from the Middle East, remained solidly united only for the brief period, AD 632-661, under the rule of the early Caliphs. The succession was contested, however, after the reign of the prophet's son-in-law Ali (656-661) and led to a divide in Islam. The followers of Ali and his son Hussein became known as shi'at Ali ('the party of Ali'). They believed that Ali, as nephew and son-in-law of the Prophet Mohammad, was the true heir to the Islamic Caliphate. They held that only his direct male descendants could be supreme religio-political leaders or imams for the Muslim community. The Umayyad rulers of the early Islamic empire (late seventh/eighth centuries) were usurpers for these Shi'ites.

The development of Shi'ism is complex. The Shi'ites held their imams to be divinely inspired – and hence infallible. Things got complicated when sixth imam Ja'far el Sadik died. His son, Ismail, had died before him, and a group of Shi'ites held that Ismail had not died, but merely been occulted. As the Mahdi ('rightly guided one'), he would return from his hiding place to lead the Islamic world and restore justice.

The Shi'ites also understood that communication with God could be done in individual ways, and importantly, through God's interpreters on earth – the eminent authorities of the Islamic teaching schools at Karbala, Najaf, Qom and Meshed. The Shi'ites rejected the formal teachings of the Islamic jurists and the religious consensus

of Sunni Islam. One reason for the survival of Shi'ism in the face of an all-powerful Sunni tradition and military supremacy was that the Persians adopted Shi'ism and incorporated it into their cultural and political resistance to the Arabs and gave the religion a geographical base in what is present day Iran.

It is strange to reflect that present-day Tunisia could have been one of the main Shi'ite centres. The Ismaili Shi'ites sent preachers across the Abbasid empire to convert people to their cause. The creed of these Ismailis was one of humanity and equality, and proved attractive to the North African Berber communities. In AD 893 one such preacher, Abu Abdallah, converted the powerful Katama Berbers of what is now eastern Algeria. This eventually led to the Ismaili leadership's move to North Africa. A certain Ubaydallah Saïd claimed the imamate for himself and founded the Fatimid state (so-called because of the succession in the caliphate from Fatima, the prophet's daughter).

Tunisia served as a base for the Fatimids for the period 909-973 after which time their ambitions to convert the Islamic world back to Shi'ism led them successfully to attack Egypt, found Cairo in 969 and give up their hold on Mahdia. Tunisia was thus a mere stepping stone for the Fatimids. Shi'ite Islam all but died out in North Africa under the impact of Arab invasions by the Beni Hilal and Beni Sulaim beginning in AD 1050.

The first Arab move was against Kusayla, who was killed in AD 688 or 689. Then after a further delay caused, once again, by unrest in the Levant, a new army moved northwards against Byzantine centres in Carthage and Bizerte, where the last remaining garrison was defeated in AD 690. The Arab conquest came up against determined Berber resistance, this time in the Algerian Aurès where the core of the Berber Zenata confederation was led by the **Kahina**, a Judaized or Christianized Berber priestess. Once again the Arabs retreated to Cyrenaica, returning to the attack only in AD 693. In AD 697, the Kahina was killed and her forces defeated in a battle at **Tubna** in the Aurèsm, marking the start of a permanent Arab presence in North Africa.

The city of **Tunis** was founded to prevent further Byzantine encroachment at neighbouring Carthage and, under **Musa Ibn Nusayr**, Arab armies swept westwards to conquer **Tanger** in AD 704. There they came to terms with the sole remaining Byzantine governor in North Africa, **Julian of Ceuta**, a Christian potentate who paid tribute to the new Muslim governor of neighbouring Tanger,

Tariq Ibn Ziyad, in order to be confirmed in his post. Seven years later, Ziyad, with help from Julian, who had maintained links with the Visigoth rulers of Spain, organized the Muslim invasion of the Iberian peninsula. By AD 732, Muslim forces had conquered virtually all of Spain and Portugal and had even crossed the Pyrenees. The Muslim advance was stopped near Poitiers by **Charles Martel**. Although for the next four years Provence was ravaged by marauding Muslim armies, the Muslim presence in Europe had reached its limits at the Pyrenees.

Early Islamic rule

As it was the governors of Egypt who had piloted the conquest of the Maghreb, these areas remained initially attached to that province. In 704, the eastern Maghreb was constituted as a separate province, the **wilaya of Ifrikiya**, an Arabic version of the Latin Africa. The term was initially used to cover what is now Tripolitania, Tunisia and eastern Algeria. With the conquest of Morocco, the wilaya extended right across to the Atlantic, and its capital was at Kairouan. The emirs of Ifrikiya thus represented the person of the caliph, the leading authority in Islam, across a vast expanse of territory. Unfortunately, authority was not easily imposed, and the Arabs, by imposing extensive taxes beyond what Islam allowed on the Berbers, created much resentment. Heavy taxation was no doubt levied because of an exaggerated idea of the wealth of the Maghreb held in the Middle East. The inferior status given to Berber warriors in the Arab armies which conquered Spain was another factor in fuelling resentment.

In the event, major **Berber rebellions** broke out. In the seventh century, Islam was yet to develop the set of all-encompassing set of rules for an ideal, pious society which it was to have thanks to the great theological and legal scholars of later centuries. A challenge arose in the Maghreb in the form of the **Kharijites**, who rejected the hereditary succession of the caliphate, insisting that an imam should be chosen by the community on the basis of his learning and religiosity. They also adopted a severer approach to sin than mainstream Muslims. The movement grew out of Berber feelings of resentment. In 741, a Kharijite Berber army defeated an Arab army in a major battle. In 742, the position was reversed when the Umayyad governor of Egypt defeated the Kharijites in two battles near Kairouan.

In political terms, much of the remainder of the seventh century in Ifrikya was dominated by clan rivalry. The **Fihrids**, descendants of Okba Ibn Nafi', created a principality based on the interests of the Arab warriors. In 750, a new dynasty assumed the caliphate in the Middle East. The **Abbasids** were open to non-Arab cultures, Greek, Persian, and other, and during their rule, the Maghreb became a full part of the Islamic cultural domain. The Fihrids were overthrown, an Ibadite (Kharijite) state came into being for a short while – and then an Abbasid army imposed its authority on the eastern Maghreb in 761. Further west, three autonomous dynasties appeared, the most important of which was the **Idrissids** who were eventually to found Fès and enable Islam to take root in the western Maghreb. Ifrikiya thus gradually shrunk back to the eastern segment of the Maghreb, ruled from Kairouan by a series of able governors with the co-operation of the Arab warrior caste.

The Aghlabids

The clan rule which typified North Africa in the late eighth century was ended in AD 800 when **Ibrahim Ibn Al-Aghlab** was made the ruler of the Muslim province of Ifrikiya, based in Tunis. He came from the Middle Eastern lands of the central Caliphate and had been a successful governor for the Abbasid Caliphs in Baghdad. His brief was to manage Abbasid possessions in North Africa without relying on Baghdad for financial support. In practice, granting Ifriqiya to Ibn Al-Aghlab was to lead to the establishment of a local dynasty.

Ibrahim Ibn Al-Aghlab began his reign by imposing peace on the turbulent Berber and Arab tribes of Tunisia. There was a great deal of opposition, not least from the vested interests of the Islamic jurists in Tunis and Kairouan and the Arab garrisons in the main towns who had grown slack and oppressive. In a short time, regional groups were put down and order restored.

Ibrahim Ibn Al-Aghlab's successors kept up the peace and there began a period of **artistic** and **architectural development**. Under Abu Ibrahim Ahmad (AD 856-863) the great mosque in Tunis was restored. In water storage and irrigation the Aghlabids were particularly active, the large storage pounds at Kairouan were their work and are still known as the *Bassins aghlabites*. The pools were fed by springs 36 km to the west. Impurities were allowed to settle in a first pond before the water was transferred into elaborate and ornate long term storage pools. The royal city of **Rakkada** near Kairouan was the work of the Aghlabids, built in the tradition of Islamic dynasties, as a strongly fortified palace complex complete with water pools, mosques and housing areas.

The Aghlabid contribution

The Aghlabids retained independence from Baghdad but eventually fell to the rising power of the Berber Katama tribes, converted to Shi'ism, and the emergence of the Fatimid state. The Aghlabid contribution to Tunisian technology and welfare was considerable, bringing artistic and architectural techniques from the eastern Caliphate to mix with Mediterranean and local traditions.

Local dynasties like the Aghlabids were able to dominate the Maghreb from a few small cities, and much of the population was converted to Islam. Nevertheless, **Christian** and **Jewish** communities survived, the former until the 11th century, the latter until the present day. Arabic only took hold slowly, and 10th century writers observed that the bulk of the population spoke no Arabic.

Fatimids, Zirids and the Beni Hilal

The 10th to the 11th centuries in Tunisia were a period of complex dynastic manoeuvrings, with the creation of new royal capitals and a great nomad tribal invasion which was to have long lasting ethnic and linguistic impact on the eastern part of North Africa.

The beginning of the 10th century saw the arrival in the Maghreb of one **'Ubaydallah**, arch enemy of the Abbasid caliphs in Baghdad and leader of a dissident branch of Islam, the **Ismaïli** sect. (The Ismaïlis were a branch of Shi'ite Islam, that of the *shi'a* or party of 'Ali, the prophet Mohammad's son-in-law.) Aghlabid rule in the eastern Maghreb collapsed, and in 909 'Ubaydallah made a triumphant entry into the royal capital of Raqqada. He immediately proclaimed himself the *mahdi*, and the dynasty he founded was to be called the **Fatimid**, after the Prophet's daughter Fatima from whom all Shi'ite religious leaders claim descent. In 915, 'Ubaydallah moved to the coast, and began work on a new royal capital at **Mahdiya**, indicating the start of a new political leadership.

The relations between the Shi'ite Fatimids in their Mahdiya stronghold and the Sunni Muslim majority in cities like Tunis and Kairouan were strained, not only for theological reasons. Taxation and money from the sale of government posts was spent on numerous campaigns against the Sunnite caliphate. Eventually, however, in 969, the Fatimids successfully conquered Egypt, leaving behind a tribal chief named **Buluggin** as viceroy. He was to create a dynasty of viceroys, referred to as the **Zirids**, who came to view themselves as the rightful rulers of Ifriqiya. They took up residence in yet another palace-city, **Sabra al Mansouriya**, located just outside Kairouan. Sunnite influence was growing all the time, however, and in 1016 there were major anti-Shi'ite riots. Eventually, in 1044, the Zirid ruler, **Al Mu'izz** (1016-51) broke with the Fatimids – with disastrous results.

The curse of the Fatimids: two tribes go to war

Both Tunisia and Libya were deeply affected in ethnic origin, religion and culture by two invasions of Arab groups from the east – the Beni Hilal and the Beni Sulaim. The Beni Hilal confederation consisted of the three tribes, the Atbeg, the Riah and the Zoghba, which originated in central Arabia before moving to Egypt. A parallel tribal group, the Beni Sulaim, had similar origins and structure. Both tribes had created security problems in southern Egypt, being constantly involved in uprisings against central authority. When in 1047 the Zirid successors to the Fatimid rulers in Tunisia changed their allegiance from the Shi'ite branch of Islam to Sunni and recognized the Abbasid Caliphs, the Fatimids retaliated by bequeathing their former territories in North Africa on the unruly tribes.

The Beni Hilal began their journey west in AD 1050-51 and first settled in Cyrenaica before moving, first, into Tripolitania where the Zoghba took control, then second, into Tunisia in the 11th century. They defeated the Zirid governors of Tunisia at Gabès in 1052 and by 1057 Kairouan fell to the nomadic invaders. The Beni Hilal fought the ruling Muslim rulers in North Africa, fought amongst themselves and were a thoroughly disruptive force in the eastern

Maghreb. It took the tough Moroccan Almohads to contain both them and the Beni Sulaim.

It appears that both tribes were essentially marauders looking for loot and land rather than soldiers of Islam. Little was done on behalf of the Fatimids in the religious domain and the two tribes remained as nomads and herders entirely unabsorbed into the city and its civilization, often making bedouins of the more settled populations.

The Hilalian invasion is celebrated in the Saga of the Beni Hilal, which tells of love, conquests and tales of derring-do. On the other hand, Arab historians remember the two tribes of nomadic invaders as 'no better than a cloud of locusts.' After the invasions, the surviving cities in the eastern Maghreb were foreign bodies in a sea of nomadic backwardness. Cultivation was largely abandoned and irrigation systems fell into disrepair.

But though the Fatimid curse on North Africa destroyed urban life, it didn't do the Fatimids much good either. It took many years before the towns were repeopled, and in many cases it wasn't until Hafsid rule in the 13th century that some degree of prosperity was re-established.

As a punishment, the Fatimids directed two great tribal groups, the **Beni Hilal** and the **Beni Sulayman**, against the Maghreb. (Both tribes had been creating considerable problems in Egypt.) Fatimid caliph Al Mustansir actually 'granted' towns and provinces to these tribal groups. Over 50,000 tribal warriors headed northwestwards into Ifriqiya, pillaging the countryside. The Zirid state collapsed, and a large number of local emirates – the Khorassanids in Tunis, for example – emerged to fill the power vacuum. **Malikite Islam**, centring on the Kairouan school of legal theology, had emerged as a strong force, underpinned by the belief that the life of the Muslim community should be governed according the principles of Islamic law. Such a concept was to be crucial to the success of the great tribal based dynasties which emerged in the late 11th and 12th centuries.

Almoravids and Almohads

And now over to the High Atlas, the mountains dominating the western part of North Africa. The Saharan gold trade, in the 11th century, was to be dominated by a nomad Berber group, based in fortified religious settlements or *ribat* – hence their name, *el-murabitoun*, which transposes as **Almoravid**, as the dynasty is called in English. Based in the northern Sahara, they founded a capital at **Marrakech** in 1062. Their empire was to expand to include much of Spain and present day Algeria.

A second tribal group, also given cohesion by a strong sense of religious mission, was to unite the Maghreb. In the 12th century, the Almoravids were overthrown by the **Almohads**, *el-muwahhidoun* or 'unitarians', whose power base lay in the Berber tribes of the High Atlas. United by their common religious cause, the Almohads took Sijilmassa, the 'gold port', and their empire expanded to include the whole of present day Morocco, Algeria and Tunisia, along with Andalusia. This political unity, lasting from c.1160 to 1260 brought cultural and economic development. The cities expanded and distinctive mosques were built, along the lines of the Koutoubia at Marrakech (see the mosques at the Kasbah and Bab Jazira in Tunis). Trade grew with the merchant cities of Europe. Arabic took root as the language of urban areas.

The Almohad Dynasty disintegrated towards the end of the 13th century. The ruling tribal élite lost its sense of cohesion – and the feudal Christian lands of Spain were quick to react: Seville fell to the Christians in 1248, and Granada became a sort of protectorate. The Almohad Empire split into three separate kingdoms – roughly corresponding to the independent states of today's central Maghreb. Ifrikiya (presently Tunisia), was ruled by the Hafsids, who initially ruled in the name of the Almohads; other regional kingdoms were centred on Tlemcen and Fès.

The Hafsids

The new Hafsid state saw itself as the legitimate successor to the Almohads and its ruler as caliph. The claim was widely accepted, even in the Middle East, because the strength of the Hafsids coincided with the Mongol invasions which destroyed Baghdad and the last vestiges of the Abbasid caliphate in 1250. But in reality, the Hafsid state lacked the social and political cohesion of its predecessor. Thus its long history was marked by the constant interplay of internal conflict between different members of the Hafsid family and with Arab and other tribal leaders who sought supreme power. Like the Merinid state, based in Fès, it also had to integrate increasing numbers of Muslims and Jews emigrating from Al Andalus.

The Hafsids had to deal with an ever greater **Christian threat**. This came in two forms: direct aggression, such as the eighth crusade, led by the French King Louis IX, which besieged Tunis unsuccessfully in 1270, and commercial penetration. In the early part of the 13th century, the great Italian trading cities of Pisa, Genoa and Venice, together with the French of Provence, obtained trading and residence rights in Ifriquiya. The most important dynamic trading state was Aragón. The Aragonese had created a major commercial empire in the western Mediterranean and, after 1246, Aragón had an ambassador in Tunis, the Hafsid capital. Mercantile representation was established in 1253. After Aragón annexed Sicily in 1282, this commercial hegemony was backed by military dominance as well.

By 1318, Aragonese influence was on the wane and Hafsid fortunes revived. The Hafsid state was, nonetheless, a Mediterranean state rather than one with its attention directed towards Africa or the Middle East – in part, its finances increasingly depended on piracy. By the end of the 15th century Hafsid influence had declined once again. Spain, the new threat to the Mediterranean Muslim world, annexed Tripoli in Libya and Bejaïa in modern Algeria in 1510, as the first move in a widening penetration into the Maghreb. The Hafsids lingered on until 1574, when Tunis and its lands were integrated into the Ottoman Empire.

Hafsid rule left an important socio-religious legacy, however. Their predecessors, the Almohads, had been reforming crusaders, conquering Spain and North Africa in the name of a puritan doctrine. The first Hafsid ruler at Tunis, **Abdul Wahid**, son of Abu Hafs Umar, a governor for the Almohads. His successors developed an independent state in Ifriqiya while retaining the strong religious bent of their ancestors. In conjunction with native Tunisian scholars, this led to the development of **Malikite law** as the foundation for the social life of Tunis. This trend became particularly marked under three strong rulers from the late 14th to the late 15th centuries (Abu Al Abbas, Abu Faris and Abu 'Amr Othman). Malikite scholars in official posts legitimized Hafsid authority in the eyes of the city populations. The developing Malikite religious awareness also counterbalanced the influence of saints, which although it led to stability in rural areas, could also create centres of dissidence. The Hafsid rulers thus founded numerous *medersas* (colleges), which although at first intended for the study of Almohad doctrine, later came to give instruction in Malikite law. This strong interest in the law, and the idea that *'urf*, local customary law, could have legal validity as long as it did not contradict the *shari'a*, was to prove a distinctive and longlasting trait in Tunisian Islam.

Ottoman rule

The Hafsid Dynasty came to an end in the middle of the 16th century. A succession of weak rulers proved no match for the ambitious Habsburgs and Ottomans, for whom the Mediterranean with its ports and islands was to be the setting for an imperial struggle for most of the 16th century. Tunis was captured by a Turkish-Algerian pirate, Kheïreddine Barbarossa (Red Beard) in 1534. The city subsequently fell to Charles V of Spain in 1535, who was to reinstate the Habsburgs as puppet rulers. Then in 1574, the Ottomans finally retook La Goulette and Tunis (Tunis suffered considerable destruction during these mid-16th century conflicts).

Once the Spaniards had been driven out of Tunisia and the remnants of the Hafsid Dynasty had been eliminated, the Ottoman commander, **Sinan Pasha**, was given a mandate to organize the administration of Tunis and its region. From the conquest until the 1620s, the Ottoman military controlled government and army. A corps of often rowdy janissary troops was stationed in the city, while leadership often came from the renegades, dynamic Christians who converted to Islam in order to be able to rise to positions of importance. The task of bringing nomad tribes to heel and collecting of taxes from the countryside was entrusted to the *bey*, a post which was to rival the power of the military leader, the *dey* by the late 17th century. The political subordination of Tunis and other cities to the Ottoman Empire took the form of payment of annual tribute to Istanbul and the important place given to the Hanefite school of Sunni Islam (the dominant form of Islam at court in Istanbul.)

The early 1600s in Tunis were marked by two soldiers of fortune, **Othman Dey** (1598-1610) and **Youssef Dey** (1610-37). (Dey was an Ottoman military title, and the deys based in Tunis elected one of their number as leader.) As neither Othman nor Youssef had much taste for luxury, the influence of Tunis was reinforced. The turbulent soldiery was disciplined, and Djerba, run by Tripoli, was brought under Tunis' authority. Mosques, fortifications and barracks were constructed. Under Youssef Dey in particular, piracy became an important source of revenue, and the Tunisian fleet had around 20 ships.

More importantly in the long term, large numbers of Andalusians fleeing Catholic persecution in the Iberian peninsula were allowed to settle in Tunisia. Othman Dey gave favourable treatment to the new arrivals. Unlike earlier Andalusian immigrants, many were poor folk. They were given tax exemption for three years, and land grants in the Medjerda River valley and the Cap Bon, where they established their own villages. They contributed greatly to the development of agriculture, as well as to the *chéchia* or felt cap industry. The export of this characteristic piece of headgear, so useful for winding a turban on, was to become an important source of revenue for Tunis.

A further source of dynamism were the European Jewish immigrants, the *Yahoud el Grana*. (The term is a corruption of the Ladino/Hebrew term *Gornim*, itself a corruption of Livornese.) The first wave of these Sephardic Jews, originally pushed out of Spain to settle in Livorno and Ancona, migrated to Tunis in 1675.

In the mid-17th century a renegade of Corsican origin, one **Murad Bey**, rose to prominence, building a power base by using local troops to collect taxes in rural areas. His son Hammouda was to rule from 1631-66. Both these beys received the title of pasha from Istanbul, in recognition for their capacity to maintain order in the countryside. Their capacity to mobilize taxation revenue enabled them to reduce the power of the deys, and after 1665, they controlled customs revenues from European trade as well. **Murad II** (1666-75) succeeded his father, further reinforcing the hereditary principle. The situation in the late 17th century deteriorated, however, with often bloody struggles for influence between deys and beys.

There is no space here to go into the complex political infighting of the first years of the 18th century. The last Muradite bey, Murad Ben Ali, was assassinated in 1702. In 1705, the exasperated notables of Tunis requested one Husseïn Ben Ali, a local member of the Ottoman military caste of Greek origins, to take control. He had been deputy bey, and understood the weakness of the situation. Through the creation of a local military force, part Tunis citizens, part tribal warriors, he was able to stabilize the situation, and eventually turned out to be the founder of a hereditary dynasty, the Husseïnids, around whom some semblance of a nation state was to begin to take shape in the late 18th century.

A strong hereditary dynasty: the Husseïnids

After defeating an attempt by the Regency of Algiers to conquer Tunisia in 1705, Husseïn Ben Ali acquired considerable prestige, and was able to reorganize the adminstration and army to suit him. The Turkish military group or *jund* ceased to have any governmental authority, becoming an army corps providing ultimate protection for the bey. The dey became just another official post. Leading Tunisian families and Malikite religious leaders were brought into the spheres of government. The rural areas were administered by local notables or *qaids*, a sort of mix between governor and tax-farmer.

Tunisia was now effectively independent and came to be referred to as the *Iyalet Tunis*, generally translated as the Regency of Tunis to denote the fact that allegiance was still owed to the Sultan-Caliph in Istanbul. The Ottoman Empire, covering vast territories with often poor communications, was a loosely organized sort of affair, and could easily tolerate such arrangements.

Thus, in the course of the 18th century, the Husseïnids, despite a certain amount of strife, appeared as hereditary rulers of a nascent Tunisian state. Djerba marked the southeastern limit of their domains, while the northwestern limit was somewhere up in the Khroumirie Mountains. This region of the eastern Maghreb had a number of advantages for an emerging dynasty: fertile agricultural lands and a series of well-fortified coastal towns, within a couple of days' horse ride of each other; the population was relatively homogeneous, comprising a settled Malekite urban Muslim population and nomad tribes; minorities (Jewish, Kharijite in Djerba) were small and unlikely to threaten the dynasty. Thus the Husseïnids were able to carve out a role for themselves as intermediaries between the rural and urban subsistence economies and the expanding trade of the Mediterranean. The only people who could have really opposed the Husseïnids, the urban populations, benefited from the prosperity brought by this trade, especially in the latter half of the 18th century.

Under Ali II (1759-82) and more especially his son, Hammouda Bey (1782-1814), the **Regency of Tunis** emerged as something of a Mediterranean power, albeit only a minor one. The encroachments of the restive and powerful Regency of Algiers was resisted as necessary, the Ottomans' wishes regarding Tripolitania were defied, and annual tributes were extorted from various minor European states by using the threat of piracy. Hammouda Bey inherited a prosperous state, and fully intended things to stay that way. (An indication of the prosperity of Tunis at the time are the large palatial homes of government officials like the Dar Lasram in the Médina of Tunis.) He encouraged subordinates to express opinions, and came to rule with the assistance of a super-minister, the vizir and lord of the seal, Youssef Sahib al-Tabi'a. Hammouda also spent considerable time and energy in reinforcing his Turkish and Zouawa army corps.

The 19th century: rising European influence

Hammouda Bey's reign was the last during which the Regency of Tunis was treated as an equal of the European powers. No one in Tunis seems to have foreseen the coming change. The context, of course, had been favourable to an increasingly independent Regency. The Europeans were too embroiled in the Napoleonic Wars to be bothered about North Africa. Their military and administrative technologies were developing, however. France was finally defeated in 1815, and eventually was to turn a colonizing gaze southwards, partly as a way of rebuilding smashed prestige. Dying in 1815, Hammouda Bey was not to live to see the change.

In the 17th century, and right up to the 1740s, it had been the custom for visiting European dignitaries to kiss the bey's hand at audiences. However, in the early 19th century, there was a huge shift in the balance of power. A series of new factors weakened the Regency of Tunis' position in the Mediterranean and strengthened the European powers of the northern shore. In 1816, **Lord Exmouth** and his fleet had successfully put pressure on the Algiers' beys to end Christian slavery. A similar concession was exacted from Tunis. In 1827, the Greek War of Independence was at its height. The Ottoman fleet, with Tunisian ships, was destroyed at the **Battle of Navarino**. In 1830, the French took Algiers; Constantine fell in 1837. To the southeast, the Ottomans re-conquered Tripoli from the Karamanlis. Tunis now had strong and potentially dangerous neighbours.

Internally, things were little better. The Turkish army corps revolted twice, in 1811 and 1816. The second revolt left the Husseïnids with reduced military support. A terrible plague epidemic swept the country in 1829. France was strengthening her presence. In 1829, Husseïn Bey signed a capitulation treaty giving the French consul the right to try cases involving French nationals in Tunisia. The government was increasingly forced to borrow from foreign banks, and manufactured goods were beginning to appear, sold far more cheaply than the handmade goods produced in Tunisia. In short, by the 1830s, the writing was on the wall.

In 1837, an energetic ruler, **Ahmed II**, came to the throne. Son of a Sardinian mother, Ahmed Bey (who ruled to 1855) was determined to reform his country. He sought to reduce European domination in trade. Institutional reforms aimed at increasing taxation on agricultural produce were introduced, monopolies were established, and soap and tobacco factories built in Tunis.

Reacting to the increased military strength of the European nations Ahmed Bey was the founder of the modern Tunisian army based on the Ottoman model. Keen on all things military, he had headed the army under his father Mustapha Bey's short reign (1835-37). He was very close to the troops, which enabled him to see where changes were needed. On coming to power in 1837, he implemented a number of reforms: the move from a small army of Turks and Zouaves to a larger professional army was accomplished. In 1840, the Bardo military academy was opened. By the end of the first decade of Ahmed's reign, a *nizami* or regular army with a strength of 27,000 men had been created. There were seven infantry regiments, and a Tunisian expeditionary force was participating in the Crimean War (1855-56) at the time of Ahmed's death in 1855.

The schemes, very much in line with the *tanzimat* reforms taking place in Mohammad Ali's Egypt and in the Ottoman Empire, were unfortunately not very successful. The tax farmers turned out to be unscrupulous, and massive spending was needed for the steamship fleet and a large new palace complex at Mohamedia, south of Tunis. The agricultural sector, heavily dependent on the vagaries of Tunisia's rainfall, could not always produce harvests good enough to meet extortionate tax demands. Thus the following year's activities could not be financed, and farming went into decline. Major epidemics – cholera and smallpox – took their toll. In 1853, a new burden appeared. As an Ottoman vassal, the Regency of Tunis was obliged to contribute an expeditionary force to fight alongside the Turks (and France and Britain) in the Crimean War – 10,000 troops were sent, of which 4,000 died from sickness (but none in the fighting).

Ahmed Bey's successor, **Mohammad** (1855-59) attempted legislative reform too. It was during his reign that the *Ahd al Aman*, the Pledge of Security, a sort of constitutional pact, was drawn up, a unique document for the time.

The 1860s were a difficult decade for Tunisia: the doubling of the poll tax in 1864 led to a rebellion which was fiercely suppressed; there followed drought, a cholera epidemic in 1865 and typhus in 1868. Burdened with debts, the country was reduced to a state of misery which the reforming minister Kheïreddine was to find difficult to overcome. The general depression was reflected in the situation of the country's armed forces, for example. The Bardo military academy was disbanded, the supply factories closed, and the number of soldiers (and their salaries) reduced. Increasing debts brought Tunisia's finances under the control of an international financial commission, an early version of the IMF. The events of the 1870s which eventually brought the Regency of Tunis under French 'protection' in 1881 are too complicated to recount here, but involved corrupt super-ministers, scheming European consuls jockeying for influence, and unscrupulous banking houses.

The cosmopolitan regency of Tunisia

From 1881 and until around 1960, the cities of Tunisia were cosmopolitan places. When the protectorate was declared, the country's cities already had sizeable Italian and Maltese populations. This was swelled by an influx of civil servants from France. In the early 20th century, there were further arrivals fleeing the wars of Europe. After the Russian Revolution, a small White Russian community arrived at Bizerte aboard Admiral Wrengel's fleet, escaping the Bolsheviks. There were Greeks involved in sponge fishing. Later came Italians and Spaniards fleeing fascism in their homelands.

In numerical terms, the **Italian** community was initially the most important. As the largest European group, they had to be handled carefully by the French administration, especially as Italy considered Tunisia as *terra perduta*, the colony which should have been. In the 1930s, to counteract the growing influence of fascism, French nationality was granted extensively to Italians resident in Tunisia. The Tunisian Jewish community also became increasingly gallicized during the 75 years of the French protectorate. Education spread rapidly, and the growing wealth of both Twansa and Grana Jews was reflected in a move from the médinas to new, well-planned neighbourhoods.

Today, the cosmopolitan towns of the 1950s are a memory of the older generation, recalled with nostalgia in films like Férid Boughedir's *Un été à La Goulette*, memorial to a Mediterranean mix of peoples. On a tree-lined avenue, the visitor may come across a synagogue; the cafés and the bi-lingual street plaques, the grand old apartment buildings and the surviving terrace tables of a restaurant speak of a Mediterranean sociability. French politicians, comics and artists born in Tunisia now return for visits, as the tensions of the decolonization period have receded from the public memory. The 1990s official slogan *Tunisia, Land of Tolerance*, no doubt owes much to a multi-religion, multi-cultural period which with hindsight seems like a cosmopolitan interlude.

Background

☞ *The Tunisian film industry: bold new cinema?*

Back in the Fifties, the ingredients for a good Arab film were a dose of kitsch, lots of sentimentality and plenty of singing under the stars on the banks of the Nile. Things changed with the return home in the 1970s of young European-trained directors. Films by Tunisian directors have won a number of international prizes: one recent success was Moufida Tlatli's 1994 Les Silences du Palais, a maid's-eye view of a mid-1950s Tunis aristocratic home.

Independent Tunisia set up its first film laboratories, the SATPEC, in 1967. However, it was President Bourguiba's wife's nephew, the flamboyant Tarak Ben Ammar, who got Tunisia on the international directors' circuit. In the ex-president's home town of Monastir, he set up a studio complex where Polanski filmed part of Pirates and (curiously) a number of films figuring Christ were made, including Life of Brian and Zeffirelli's Jesus of Nazareth. A further stimulus to the nascent Tunisian film industry was the creation of the Carthage Film Festival in 1966, which provides a bi-annual meeting point for the African and Arab film industries.

In the mid-1970s a few Tunisian films were taken on by international distribution companies, including Naceur Ktari's Les Ambassadeurs (1976), a sharp critique of the conditions of migrant workers in Europe, and Rida Behi's sardonic look at the side effects of tourism, Le Soleil des Hyènes (1977).

In the 1980s a new generation of local film makers and production companies like Carthage Film and International Monastir Film reached maturity, putting the experience from international productions to good use. A series of highly individual films gained the respect of the local public, among them Nacer Khemir's aesthetic reworkings of the theme of lost Andalucía, Les baliseurs du désert (1984) and Le Collier perdu de la colombe (1991)) and Mahmoud Ben Mahmoud's Traversées.

At the end of the decade, producer Ahmed Attia's Cinétéléfilm came up with three highly successful art house films: L'Homme de cendres in 1986, Les Sabots en or in 1989 (both by Nouri Bouzid), and Férid Boughedir's Halfaouine in 1990. With 500,000 entries, Halfaouine, a loving and sometimes whimsical portrayal of growing

Moving to independence

In the immediate aftermath of the installation of the French Protectorate, Tunisian resistance was confined to tribal groups in the south of the country. Opposition to colonial occupation gradually began to gather strength reflecting popular opposition to the growing, and predominantly Italian, European settler colony in Tunisia, a colony totalling around 100,000 people and controlling some 800,000 hectares of Tunisia's best agricultural land.

Initially, the opposition was diffuse, with a focus on the **Destour** or Constitution party, which reflected the thinking of the educated urban intelligentsia. The Destour was founded in 1919 by one Abdelaziz Thaâlabi. Its basic idea was that Tunisia should become a constitutional monarchy based on on the 1861 *destour* or constitution. The fact that there was a French protectorate was no reason for not applying a valid local code of law. In 1921, the Destour Party proposed a reform package, including the creation of a Franco-Tunisian assembly.

All this was to little effect. French commercial interests had become too important, and the depression and strikes of the 1930s meant that no one was willing to give way. The poorer members of the French community, minor officials and government employees, and the poor Italians had too much to lose.

A more radical current was taking shape in the Destour Party, however, under a bright, charismatic French-trained lawyer, **Habib Bourguiba**. At a conference held in the movement's regional fief of Ksar Hellal in 1934, the Destour split, with Habib

up in Tunis in the 1960s beat all the records for a film in Tunisia. The sensitive treatment of sexuality and the separation of the sexes in the still codefied world of an old part of the city ensured the film's success.

For its bold treatment of prostitution, the effects of child abuse and the relations between the Muslim and Jewish communities, Bouzid's L'Homme de cendres *was condemned by critics. (Tolerance and the coexistence of different communities is central to Mahmoud Ben Mahmoud's symbolic* Chichkhan *and Férid Boughedir's 1996 film* TGM.) *Bouzid's* Les Sabots en or *grew out of his experience as a political prisoner in the 1970s. The subject matter, imprisonment and the effects of torture, drew in the audiences, and the public clearly wanted more. In his third film,* Bezness, *Bouzid went on to attack 'sexual tourism' while* Une fille de bonne famille *tackles that old chestnut, marital breakdown.*

Tunis seems unlikely to become the Hollywood of the Mediterranean, though. For many years, Tunisian cinema came somewhere between the private Moroccan film industry and the state-dominated Algerian industry. It is not easy producing for a market of only 8 million people, and in the early 1990s co-productions between European TV stations such as Channel 4 and Tunisian companies dominated. Will the production of the films d'auteur *which have made Tunisia's name on the international festival circuit continue? Various forms of French government funding directed at African cinema can no longer be taken for granted, and the American way of life is clearly on its way (70 percent of films shown on the Tunisian pay channel Canal Plus Horizons are US produced) and the capital's cinemas specialize in Hindi melodramas, soft porn and Jean-Claude Van Damme. Art house films need ideas, and what passes for an original idea in Tunisia is often a cliché elsewhere. Tunisia's films please the local public and seduce festival juries. Whether the laws of international distribution will allow them to reach a wider audience is another question. Mahmoud Ben Mahmoud's 1999* Les siestes grenadine, *also a look at identity and the individual, may mark a renewal in what was one of Tunisia's most flourishing arts.*

Bourguiba taking over the more radical wing, now renamed the **Neo-Destour**. This part of the movement had its power base in the small towns of the Sahel and the growing urban proletariat of Tunis. Many of its leaders had risen thanks to the Franco-Arab schools and university education in France, where they had studied law and medicine. The old urban élite of Tunis, the *beldia*, were little represented. For the first time, a political movement was taking shape independently of both the beylical establishment and the leading city families.

The French authorities did their best to stamp out the Neo-Destour, but to no avail. Time and the general trend of history was on the nationalists' side. The early 1930s was a time of poor harvests. The Depression led to a huge fall in the price of olive oil, Tunisia's staple agricultural export. Much marginal land was abandoned; drought had terrible effects on nomads, who had lost their ancestral grazing rights, as land was enclosed for modern agriculture. The mechanization of farms also put many out of work. There was a drift towards the towns – severely repressed by the police.

A package of reforms was put forward in 1938, but too late. Developments in Europe meant that such schemes had to be shelved, and the Neo-Destour's leaders were imprisoned. A chance for France and Tunisia to move towards a working relationship had been missed.

When the Second World War came, France lost considerable face, and the monarchy under Moncef Bey was not slow to exploit this weakness. Tunisia came under Axis occupation from 1941 to 1942. When the French returned with Allied support, however, nationalist bey Moncef was exiled and replaced by Amine Bey, an

Tunisian Museums

Tunisia has a very rich and diversified archaeological history. The museums throughout the country have on display some of the richest artifacts ranging from Punic and Roman times to the present day. There are over 40 museums under the management of the Institut National du Patrimoine and another 15 managed by a number of official and private institutions. Exhibits are housed in old palaces (Bardo, Rakkada), in forts (Monastir), government buildings (Sfax), purpose-built mansions (Dar Cherait, Tozeur) and on Punic/Roman sites (Kerkouane, Dougga).

elderly be-spectacled monarch unlikely to provide a figurehead for the nationalist cause. Moncef Bey died in exile in Pau, fate was clearly on the side of the Destourians. In the wake of the war and growing agitation, it became clear that some concessions to nationalist sentiment would have to be made.

Before this was done, France tried to enforce its position in Tunisia by requiring the Bey to accept the idea of 'co-sovereignty', whereby France would gain permanent rights to Tunisian territory. Following this attempt by France in 1950 to gain a firmer foothold inside North Africa, the nationalist movement under Habib Bourguiba took on the characteristics of a mass movement. As a result, Habib Bourguiba was able to negotiate autonomy for Tunisia in 1955 and in 1956, when Morocco was granted Independence, Tunisia soon followed suit. The situation elsewhere in the French Empire was favourable to such a development. France had been defeated in Indochina and was facing simmering disturbances in Algeria, then considered as an integral part of France. The mid-1950s were clearly the wrong time to become bogged down in some sort of guerrilla warfare in a minor possession like Tunisia. In any case, France's economic interests and influence could be protected by other means.

See page 445 for Tunisia's more recent history

Land and environment

Geography

The Republic of Tunisia has a surface area of 163,610 sq km. It measures 750 km from north to south and averages 150 km from west to east. The Gulf of Tunis is included in the northern coastal (330 km) zone while to the south, forming part of the east facing coast (1,270 km), are the Gulfs of Hammamet and Gabès, the latter lying between the islands of Djerba in the south and Kerkennah in the north. It is not a mountainous land: less than one percent of the land is over 1,000 metres and more than 65 percent is under 350 metres; the highest land is in the north and west. Nor is it a land of rivers: the one major river is the Oued Medjerda, in the north.

Borders Tunisia has a long land border with Algeria, with a multiplicity of crossing points. It has a short land border with Libya, the crossing point at Ras Jedir being well used at present – although this may change now that air links have been resumed with the ending of the embargo. The Tunisia/Libya offshore boundary dispute over the Bouri oilfield in the Gulf of Gabès was arbitrated in favour of Libya. Tunisia and Libya are, however, contemplating joint development of other oilfields lying across their offshore boundary. The creation of the Union du Maghreb Arabe has made other potential border disputes with neighbours less likely in the short term. Travel between UMA states also helps all UMA and other Arab travellers and tends to make it slightly easier for non-Arab tourists to get through border crossings in Tunisia and other North African countries.

Background

Tunisians tend to be deeply attached to their home regions, and even when they move away for work, they return home frequently. The most populated area is the economically dominant eastern seabord. Regions with strong identities include Tunis, the Cap Bon, the Sahel, the Djerid and Djerba, all of which are well defined in geographic terms.

Three main physical regions can be distinguished. **Northern Tunisia** has a rugged north-facing coastline – an extension of the mainly sandstone Algerian Atlas which rises into a distinctive range known as the Northern Tell. In places these uplands with altitudes exceeding 1,000 metres are covered with cork oak and pine. The southern flanks of the Tell in the Béja region are lower, more open and more fertile. To the east are the rich alluvial plains around Bizerte. The Oued Medjerda, Tunisia's only major perennial flow, cuts a wide fertile valley to the south of these ranges flowing northeastwards to enter the sea in the Gulf of Tunis. This is the major agricultural region noted particularly for cereals. Further south, aligned southwest-northeast, is an extension of the higher, broader and mainly limestone Saharan Atlas. This forms the distinctive Dorsal/High Tell region with its harsher climate and sparser vegetation. The Dorsal range, including Tunisia's highest point, Djebel Chaâmbi at 1,544 metres, ends in the northeast at the Cap Bon peninsula, Tunisia's richest region, with a mild climate, fertile soils and a dense population.

Central Tunisia is a lower central plateau of semi-arid steppe land. Its harsh environment renders the area bleak and barren, especially in the west. Only the lower, eastern steppe offers opportunities for stock raising and cereal cultivation. The Sahel, a low-lying and flat westward extension of the coastal plain, has seasonal salt lakes and sandy soils with a widespread, dense cover of olive groves which are supported by light rainfall, heavy dews and the tempering influence of the Mediterranean Sea.

Southern Tunisia, lying south of the steppes and stretching from the Algerian border to the sea, is an area of low-lying salt lakes or *chotts*, some below sea level, which are flooded during the winter and which dry to give extensive seasonal salt flats. Other depressions, where the water table is exposed or very close to the surface, produce the spectacular green oases of date palms. The depressions in the north and the level summits of the Djebel Dahar to the east give way to the sand dunes of the Great Eastern Erg and rocky wastes.

Tunisia's largest river is the **Oued Medjerda**, the Bagrada of the Romans, which runs across northern Tunisia from the Souq Ahras area in Algeria to the Gulf of Tunis. It has been heavily engineered for irrigation purposes and carries only a moderate flow in its easterly reaches. Elsewhere the streams are short *oueds* which often drain internally into seasonal **salt lakes**, the largest complex being in the Chott El Djerid, south of Gafsa. *Oueds* in spate are dangerous and in recent memory heavy floods in the south have carried away whole villages. Travellers should not attempt to cross *oueds* in flood and should certainly not camp in stream beds.

Climate

The climate of the northern region is archetypically Mediterranean with hot dry summers and warm, wet, westerly winds in winter. To the south, the influences of the Sahara increase and the aridity of the landscape intensifies. Rainfall is irregular and decreases progressively to the south with annual averages ranging from 1,000 millimetres in northern regions to 200-400 millimetres on the central plateau and less than 200 millimetres in the south. Rainfall, nowhere reliable, is most regular in the north. There was heavy rainfall in 1995/96 winter season, suggesting the start of a run of wetter years. Humidity is generally low, especially away from the coast and towards the south. High temperatures and high relative humidity are an unpleasant combination, especially in July and August.

The prevailing wind is from the west, though in summer northeast winds also occur. A fierce, hot sirocco-type wind from the Sahara, the *shihili*, takes temperatures into the mid 40°C range, relative humidity to 10 percent and has serious effects on human and plant life. Temperatures are influenced by proximity to the coast. Average temperatures increase to the south and extremes of temperature between day and night occur in the desert. For the visitor, summers can be hot by day and over warm at night on the coast and unbearably hot (45°C) by day and surprisingly cool (10°C) by night inland. Winters are pleasantly mild in the north in the lowlands but temperatures fall quickly with altitude, while high daytime desert temperatures plummet at night making it 'too cold to sleep'.

The natural vegetation and farm crops are strongly influenced by the climate. The cork oak and pine forests of the wetter cooler north give way to thin pastures and esparto grass cover and eventually to desert in the south where the oases, supplied by natural springs, contrast sharply with the surrounding barren sands.

Flora and fauna

Tunisia has a wide variety of natural habitats. The **Mediterranean coastline** is varied, with rugged inaccessible cliffs and smooth sandy bays. Coastal wetlands include deltas, salt marsh and estuaries, while inland lakes and reservoirs provide freshwater sites. The **maquis** and the **garrigue** contrast with the agricultural areas, while **mountain ranges** such as the Atlas provide their own climate, delaying flowering and shortening seasons. Even the **desert** areas provide contrasts with the sands (erg), gravels (reg) and rock (hammada) set with the occasional oasis.

However, many habitats are under threat, either from pollution, urbanization, desertification or advanced farming techniques. Fortunately, in Tunisia, awareness of conservation issues is growing and many National Parks and Nature Reserves have been created and programmes of environmental education set up.

In both the Mediterranean and desert regions, wildlife faces the problem of adapting to drought and the accompanying heat. The periods without rain may vary from four months on the shores of the Mediterranean to several years in some parts of the Sahara. Plants and animals have, therefore, evolved numerous methods of coping with drought and water loss. Some plants have extensive root systems; others have hard, shiny leaves or an oily surface to reduce water loss through transpiration. Plants such as the broom have small, sparse leaves, relying on stems and thorns to attract sunlight and produce food. Animals such as the addax and gazelle obtain all their moisture requirements from vegetation and never need to drink. Where rain is a rare occurrence, plants and animals have developed a short life cycle combined with years of dormancy. When rain does arrive, the desert can burst into life: plants seed, flower and disperse within a few weeks, or even days.

Many animals in the desert areas are nocturnal, benefiting from the cooler night temperatures, their tracks and footprints revealed in the morning. Another adaption is provided by the sandfish, which is a type of skink (lizard) which 'swims' through the sand in the cooler depths during the day. Perhaps the most remarkable example of adaption is shown by the camel. Apart from its spreading feet which enable it to walk on sand, the camel is able to adjust its body temperature to prevent sweating, reduce urination fluid loss and store body fat to provide food for up to six months.

Mammals   Mammals have a difficult existence throughout Tunisia, due to human disturbance and the fact that many of the species are not well adapted to drought. Many have, therefore, become nocturnal and their presence may only be indicated by droppings and tracks. Some mammals common in northern Europe can, nevertheless, be seen in the Mediterranean environments and these include fox, rabbit, hare, Red, Fallow and Roe deer and at least three species of hedgehog. Despite widespread hunting, wild boar are common wherever there is enough cover in deciduous woodlands. Hyenas and jackals still thrive in many areas but the attractive fennec, whilst still fairly common in Tunisia is frequently illegally trapped. Typical woodland species include the red squirrel (the grey variety from North America has not been introduced), garden dormouse, which readily hibernates in houses, pine and beech martens and the polecat. The cat family, once common, is now rare, but the lynx hangs on in some areas. The leopard, formerly common, is now extinct. There are at least three species of gazelle in North Africa, the Dorcas gazelle preferring the steppes, the mountain gazelle inhabiting locations over 2,000 square metres especially where there is juniper forest, and the desert gazelle locating in the region of the northern Sahara. The latter is often hunted by horse or vehicle, its only defence being its speed. There are also many species of bat, all of them insectivorous. Recent ringing has shown that bats will migrate according to the season and to exploit changing food sources. Many species have declined in recent years due to insecticides and disturbance of roosting sites. Desert rodents include the large-eyed sand rat, the gerbil and the jerboa.

Tortoises are widespread in North Africa. The best distributed is Hermann's tortoise which can reach a maximum size of 30 centimetres. Pond terrapins are small freshwater tortoises and can be found in all the Mediterranean habitats. Both tortoises and terrapins are unfortunately taken in large numbers for the pet trade, and may be seen, along with chameleons, on sale in the souks. There are over 30 species of lizard in the area, the most common being the wall lizard, which often lives close to houses. Sand racers are frequently seen on coastal dunes, while sand fish and sand swimmers take advantage of deep sand to avoid predators and find cooler temperatures in the desert. The ocellated lizard is impressive in size, growing to 20 centimetres. Geckoes are plump, soft-skinned, nocturnal lizards with adhesive pads on their toes and are frequently noted on house walls. The chameleon is a reptile with a prehensile tail and a long sticky tongue for catching insects. Although basically green, it can change colour to match its surroundings.

Reptiles & amphibians

There are some 30 species of snakes in the Mediterranean areas alone, but only the viperine types are dangerous. These can be identified by their triangular heads, short plump bodies and zig-zag markings. The horned viper lies just below the surface of sand, with its horns projecting, waiting for prey. Sand boas stay underground most of the time, while other species twine themselves around the branches of trees. Most snakes will instinctively avoid contact with human beings and will only strike if disturbed or threatened.

The Mediterranean is a land-locked sea and it is only in the extreme west that there is any significant tidal range. Without strong tides and currents bringing nutrients, the Mediterranean is somewhat impoverished in terms of marine life. Fish and shell fish, nevertheless, have figured prominently in the diet of the coastal people for centuries, with sardines, anchovies, mullet, sole, squid and prawns being particularly popular. Tuna and swordfish are also widely caught. Over-fishing, leading to the depletion of stocks, has become increasingly problematic, especially with incursions by the well-equipped Italian fishing fleet into Tunisian waters. Of the sea mammals, Tunisia has a small colony of Mediterranean monk seals on the outlying northern archipelago of La Galite. Dolphins are also occasionally seen off the coast.

Marine life

Because of the lack of vegetation on which to lay eggs, butterflies are scarce in the steppe and desert areas. The Mediterranean fringe, in contrast, is often rich in species, some quite exotic. The life cycle – mating, egg production, caterpillar, pupa,

Butterflies & moths

Background

butterfly – can be swift, with some species having three cycles in one year. Some of the butterflies are large and colourful, such as the swallowtail and the two-tailed pasha. The most common butterflies in the early spring are the painted ladies, which migrate from North Africa northwards, often reaching as far as Britain. Other familiar species include the Moroccan orange tip, festoon, Cleopatra and clouded yellow. Moths are also widely represented, but as they are largely nocturnal they are rarely seen. Day flying moths include the Burnet and hummingbird hawk moths. The largest moth of the area is the giant peacock moth, with a wingspan of up to 15 cm.

Birds Neither the Mediterranean nor the desert areas is particularly rich in resident bird species, but both can be swollen temporarily by birds on passage. Four categories of birds may be noted. Firstly, there are the **resident** birds which are found throughout the year, such as the crested lark and the Sardinian warbler. Secondly, there are the **summer visitors**, such as the swift and swallow, which spend the winter months south of the Equator. **Winter visitors**, on the other hand, breed in northern Europe but come south to escape the worst of the winter and include many varieties of wader and wildfowl.

Passage migrants fly through the area northwards in spring and then return southwards in increased numbers after breeding in the autumn. Small birds tend to migrate on a broad front, often crossing the desert and the Mediterranean Sea without stopping. Such migrants include the whitethroat, plus less common species such as the nightjar and wryneck. Larger birds, including eagles, storks and vultures, must adopt a different strategy, as they depend on soaring, rather than sustained flight. As they rely on thermals created over land, they must opt for short sea crossings such as the route running via Tunisia, Malta and Sicily, where birds run the gauntlet of the guns of so-called 'sportsmen'.

Tunisia has a number of **typical habitats** each with its own assemblage of birds. The Mediterranean itself has a poor selection of sea birds, although oceanic birds such as gannets and shearwaters will enter the Mediterranean during the winter. Wetland areas, such as Lac Ichkeul (see page 187) contain numerous varieties of the heron family such as the night heron and squacco heron, while spoonbill, ibis and both little and cattle egrets are common. Flamingoes breed in a number of locations when conditions are right. Waders such as the avocet and black winged stilt are also typical wetland birds. The wetland species are augmented in the winter by a vast collection of wildfowl. Resident ducks, however, are confined to specialities such as the white-headed duck, marbled teal and ferruginous duck. On roadsides, the crested lark is frequently seen, while overhead wires often contain corn buntings, with their jangling song, and the colonial bee-eaters. Mountain areas are ideal for searching out raptors. There are numerous varieties of eagle, including Bonelli's, booted, short toed and golden. Of the vultures, the griffon is the most widely encountered. The black kite is more catholic in its choice of habitat, but the Montagu's harrier prefers open farmland.

The desert and steppe areas have their own specialist resident birds which have developed survival strategies. Raptors include the long-legged buzzard and the lanner, which prefer mountain areas. Among the ground-habitat birds are the Houbara bustard and the cream coloured courser. Dupont's lark is also reluctant to fly, except during its spectacular courtship display. The trumpeter finch is frequently seen at oases, while the insectivorous desert wheatear is a typical bird of the erg and reg regions.

Scorpions – the original sting in the tail

Scorpions really deserve a better press. They are fascinating creatures, provided they no not lurk in your shoe or shelter in your clothes.

Scorpions are not insects. They belong to the class Arachnida as do spiders and daddy longlegs. There are about 750 different kinds of scorpions. The average size is a cosy 6 centimetres but the largest, Pandinus imperator, the black Emperor scorpion of West Africa, is a terrifying 20 centimetres long. The good news is that only a few are really dangerous. The bad news is that some of these are found in North Africa.

They really are remarkable creatures with the ability to endure the hottest desert climates, revive after being frozen in ice, and survive for over a year without food or water. They have a remarkable resistance to nuclear radiation, a characteristic yet to be proved of great use.

Scorpions are nocturnal. They shelter during the heat of the day and to keep cool wave their legs in the air. They feed on insects and spiders, grasping their prey with their large claw-like pincers, tearing it apart and sucking the juices. Larger scorpions can devour lizards and small mammals.

Their shiny appearance is due to an impervious wax coating over their hard outer shell which protects them from any water loss. They have very small eyes and depend on their better developed senses of touch and smell. The sensitive bristles on the legs point in all directions and pick up vibrations of movements of potential prey or enemies. This sensitivity gives them ample warning to avoid being seen by heavy-footed humans.

The oft reported 'courtship dance' before mating is merely repeated instinctive actions. The grasping of claws and the jerky 'dance' movements from side to side are a prelude to copulation during which the male produces spermatozoa in a drop of sticky fluid to which the female is led so that they may enter her body. The male departs speedily after the 'dance' to avoid being attacked and devoured.

Scorpions bear live young. After hatching, the young crawl on to the female's back and are carried there for two or three weeks until their first moult. They gradually drop off after that time and have to fend for themselves.

Most scorpions retreat rather than attack. They sting in self-defence. The sting is a hard spine and the poison is made in the swelling at the base. The sole of the bare foot, not surprisingly, is most often the site of a sting, and the advice in the section on Health (see page 59) is not to be ignored. The African fat-tailed scorpion (we do not recommend measuring the size) is described as aggressive and quick-tempered. It is responsible for most of the reported stings to humans and most of the human fatalities in North Africa. The beautifully named Buthus occitanus, the small Mediterranean yellow scorpion and Leirus quinquestriatus, the African golden scorpion, also have neurotoxic stings that can be fatal.

Background

Flora

Most of northern Tunisia, as mentioned above, is in the Mediterranean region, and was covered by evergreen forest. Man has intervened extensively since then and there is a variety of plant life for the visitor to discover – many of the larger species having been imported from elsewhere in the world. The spring flowers which cover the fields, hillsides and ancient ruins of the north are a particular attraction for people from lands where farming relies more heavily on pesticides.

Hotel & villa gardens The visitor's first contact with Tunisian plant life will probably be the hotel garden. Here there will be plants introduced from other Mediterranean climate regions, but now firmly established in North Africa. That great and colourful climber, the **bougainvillaea**, smothering walls with its sprays of purple, red, yellow and white 'paper flowers' will inevitably make an appearance. Bougainvillaea was introduced to Europe from Brazil in 1829, and in fact it is the papery bracts which surround the tiny white flowers which provide the colour. Hotel and villa gardens are also home to **hibiscus**, an import from China particularly popular for hedges. Among the climbers there will be pale-blue flowering plumbago, and various red and orange 'trumpet-flowering' climbers from the USA. **Datura**, originally from South America, and easily recognized by its great white bell flowers is elegant – and poisonous. Both datura and *Cestrum parqui* are highly scented. The latter, called *misk el lil* ('musk of the night') in Tunisian Arabic, has highly perfumed creamy yellow flowers. **Jasmine** is also essential to hotel and private gardens. Two pinkish-white flowering varieties are popular, *Jasminum officinale*, and the *Jasminum grandiflorum*, which – as its name indicates – has big flowers and larger, more rounded leaves. Both are used to make the *mashmoum*, the jasmine bouquet which is an indispensable fashion accessory for a Tunisian summer evening, worn jauntily behind the ear or in a corsage (see illustration below). Making a mashmoum involves carefully inserting jasmine buds on fine stems of alfa grass. The stems are bound together with a cotton thread, an orange or fig leaf provides a cradle for the unopened buds, which are held together with another thread, which, once removed, allows the flowers to open during the evening.

Streets & roadsides Tunisia's city streets are planted with shade trees doing daily battle with the vehicle pollution. Varieties of hardy **ficus** are popular, which cut into a box shape on maturity, provide shade. They also provide an evening roost for great flocks of starlings (*asfour ez zitoun*, 'olive tree birds') in winter, unpopular with the local authorities for the large amounts of guano they leave behind. Palm trees are also popular for urban avenues, where both the ordinary date palm and the elegant *Washingtonia*, which grows to great heights, can be seen. Look out too for the **Norfolk Island pine** (*Araucaria heterophylla*), a relative of the monkey puzzle tree from Chile, with its distinctive frond-like branches. It gives an exotic touch to residential neighbourhoods by the sea. Its original home, Norfolk Island, is way down in the Pacific, between New Zealand and New Caledonia. Back on the city streets, there are plane trees, which provide leafy shade in summer, but let in the light in summer, and purple flowering **jacaranda** with delicate foliage and great sprays of pale mauve flowers.

Mashmoun

Of the roadside trees, the eucalyptus is the most popular, although sadly many have been ripped out due to road widening schemes. **Eucalyptus** originally come from Australia, where they grow in open savannah. Tunisia has some old stands of eucalyptus forest (see the approach to Sidi Mechrig in the north), but most eucalyptus are roadside trees (see the M'saken to Sfax road). The tree grows fast, and many species have two types of leaves, broader on saplings, slender, green and dangling on the mature tree. Another characteristic tree is the rapid growing black poplar, seen in the north.

Approaches to towns and autoroute verges are often planted with **oleander**, (Arabic: *defla*) an attractive shrub which flowers white and pink, and can grow to some height in the right conditions. It is highly poisonous to beasts. In spring, you may notice low-growing flowering shrubs on the roadside. These may be **acacias**, another Australian import. The blue-leaved wattle has hanging branches and strong-smelling flowers, while the silver wattle, better known as the **mimosa**, has long branches of tiny yellow pompom flowers. A rarer species is the Persian acacia, easily identified by the long, silky, reddish stamens of its flowers. All the wattles are tough and drought resistant, and some can be found on sandy land close to the sea, like the tamarisk, used also as an ornamental tree in the southern oasis settlements. The tamarisk has delicate feathery branches with tiny leaves, and its flowers, pink or white, grow in dense bouquets.

In the interior, the **prickly pear cactus** (*Opuntia ficus indica*) is much used along with the **agave** to hedge in olive and almond groves. Both are naturalized imports from the Americas. With its wide flat thorny 'leaves', the prickly pear forms great barriers which dissuade foraging goats and sheep. You may see the new plantations of prickly pear where chunks of the plant have been pushed into the earth to take root. The pear shaped fruit, an attractive yellow-orange colour, is collected by small boys with long canes. Ripe at summer's end, it is known as *sultan el ghilla*, the 'sultan of fruit', and is both delicious and constipating.

The Cap Bon region and the Mornag plain, south of Tunis, have some of Tunisia's most fertile fruit growing regions. The orchards or *sweni* can easily be picked out: very often they are surrounded by lines of slender, dark **cypress** trees which protect the trees in blossom time from spring winds and driving rain. **Almond** are the earliest trees to flower, followed by **pear** and **peach**. Then come the citrus trees, filling the air with fragrance. The Beni Khaled area, lowlying land close to the sea, is famed for its citrus trees. In fact, **oranges** and **lemons** were unknown in the ancient Mediterranean, and were probably brought from China in the early Middle Ages. Today, Tunisia produces a large number of citrus fruits, and is especially known for the Maltaise juice orange. Rarer citrus fruits include the *lime beldi*, a small green lime, the *bergamote*, a small sweet lemon with a slightly soapy taste, and the grapefruit (Fr: *pamplemousse*, Ar: *zimba'*).

Orchards (sweni)

Older residential areas often have some interesting fruit trees. The **mulberry** is often grown. Black mulberry is a sweet, deep mauve *fruit*, while the white mulberry was originally planted both for fruit and as food for silkworms. The production of **silk** was a Chinese state secret until the mid-sixth century. Then the Emperor Justinian managed to get two Persian monks to smuggle silkworms out of the Celestial Empire in their hollow bamboo walking sticks. Silk production then took root in the Middle East and Europe. A tree unfamiliar to European eyes is the **loquat** (*Eriobotrya japonica*) medlar – *nèfle*, in French. This is an evergreen tree with coarse dark green leaves. The fruit have smooth orange skin and deep yellow flesh, and are plum-like in size and shape. Loquat trees are grown extensively in residential areas.

Background

☞ *Gnarly, resilient and productive : the olive tree*

The olive branch, synonymous with peace, was Noah's first indication of the receding flood. It is a phoenix among trees. Gnarly and dead-looking, it will quickly produce fresh sprouts when cut back. It was Athena's gift to ancient Athens, the mother of all trees. When the Athenians climbed up to the Acropolis in 480 BC, the day after the Persians had sacked their city, they found that the remains of Athena's sacred olive tree had already sent out a new branch.

The olive is a subtropical, broad-leaved, evergreen tree, both fire and drought resistant. It grows 3-12 metres high and many trees are said to be between 50-100 years old. The leathery, lance-shaped leaves, growing in pairs are dark green above and silvery underneath. From the tiny white flowers the green olives develop, later maturing through shades of purple to black.

The toughness of the olive tree is one of its most notable features. The tree can survive the odd frost, and grows right down on the edge of the Sahara, drawing its moisture from the dew. Modern archaeology has shown that in Roman times, the tree's southern limit was much further south than it is today. During its lifetime, the tree is often roughly treated, pruned and shaken, even beaten to bring down the fruit, though this is not recommended. In some places, the pickers claw through the trees with goats' horns on their fingers to take off the olives.

Although table olives are a great delicacy, it is the oil which is the glory of the tree, a rich liquid which ranges from the cloudy green to the smooth golden. Its value is esteemed by all the peoples of the Mediterranean – in the Koran, it is referred to as "oil so luminous it seems to shine, though no fire has touched it." But the oil is as fragile as the trees are resilient. If the crushing and filtering process is too rough, the delicate smell of the oil is in part destroyed. The oil also quickly takes on surrounding aromas, which makes it ideal for cooking, but implies great care in the processing.

The olive tree carries much symbolism. For northern Europeans, its oil is synonymous with southern cuisine and the sunfilled landscapes of the Mediterranean. In Tunisia, the well-planted groves symbolize the wealth of an entire region – and this was the case back under the Romans, when olive trees were planted in their thousands, more profitable and less labour intensive than wheat. Visiting El Djem and Sfax, you have the strong impression that the landscape has not changed in a very long time.

Northwestern forests Evergreen forest can be found in the Khroumirie Mountains south of the coastal resort of Tabarka. Evergreen **holm oak** and **cork oak** are the characteristic trees, and there is a dense undergrowth, home of the wild boar amongst other animals, of various thorn trees and juniper. In places, this forest grows quite high, and there are small areas of **sweet chestnut** trees. Another tree found in the north is the **carob** or locust tree (*Ceratonia siliqua*), which like many Mediterranean trees has coarse foliage and waxy leaves. The tree produces long, chocolate-coloured pods containing three or four big seeds, which are used for cattle fodder and as 'country chocolate'. Carob pods are also an ingredient in a Boga Cidra, a Tunisian fizzy drink with a passing resemblance to Pepsi or Coke.

Further south, in the mountainous parts of the interior (the Dorsal Range), the climate is drier, and the forest is mainly composed of **Aleppo pines**. This tree thrives on dry hillsides, regenerating after fire. It has long needles, which make great splashes of bright green on the landscape in the spring. The La Kessera region south of Makthar has particularly fine pine forest.

In many areas once covered with Aleppo pine, overgrazing and wood cutting have destroyed the forest. Vegetation becomes a dense, fragrant brush a few metres high, referred to in French as the *maquis*. **Tree heather**, **juniper**, **lentisc** and **broom**, along with **rosemary**, **sage** and **thyme** are the main plants. In such dry regions, the only plants to survive have special adaptive features: some have extensive root systems; others have hard, shiny leaves or an oily surface to reduce water loss through transpiration. Plants such as the broom have small, sparse leaves, relying on stems and thorns to attract sunlight. The herbs all smell strongly, which seemingly makes them less attractive to animals. (Maquis regions produce splendid **honey** on account of these herbs.) Where the maquis is overused by people, the vegetation becomes sparse and stunted, rocky outcrops more pronounced as the soil is eroded away. This plant cover is the *garrigue* in French, bright with annual flowers in spring, but an arid place in summer. Further south in central Tunisia, the garrigue turns to **alfa grass** steppe land. Salt bushes and the grasses which come up after the spring rains provide seasonal grazing. In the steppes too, modern agriculture is at work. Thanks to the irrigation water available from tiny hill dams and bore holes, there are new fruit orchards and plantations of prickly pear, acacia, and eucalyptus. Efforts are being made to upgrade the open grazing lands, the *terres de parcours*, with new varieties of artemisia. The process of reversing the impact of several thousand years of deforestation would seem to be underway at last.

Brush *(maquis)*, garrigue & steppe lands

Arts and architecture

Tunisia, as the visitor will quickly notice, has a wealth of characteristic buildings and craft forms. Though in certain areas, traditional architecture is giving way to less aesthetic – and less climatically adapted forms of buildings – there is a huge amount of interesting building to see. Regarding traditional crafts and art forms, some of the best examples can be found in city museums. Collections of traditional arts and crafts from recent centuries are held at the Dar Ben Abdallah in Tunis, the Dar Djellouli in Sfax, the Kène collection at Bou Ficha near Hammamet, and various smaller museums elsewhere. The great museums of Carthage and the Bardo have the finest collection of objects from ancient times, however. Disappointingly, there is no national carpet and textile collection, nor any national gallery of contemporary painting. The visitor will have to visit souks to see textiles, and small private galleries for painting. Architecture buffs are spoiled, though, and will find a huge selection of 19th and 20th century building styles in Tunisia's city centres.

Prehistory

The earliest traces of human settlement in Tunisia go back to 800,000 BC. Towards 5000 BC, new populations, probably the ancestors of today's Berbers, are thought to have arrived. They brought with them a nomadic form of pastoralism. There are prehistoric remains at **Elles**, near **Makthar** (tombs), and in the **Oueslatia** region west of Kairouan (a few isolated rock paintings and tombs).

Carthaginian and Numidian period

When Rome was founded in 753 BC, the coast of Tunisia was already on the trade routes of Phoenician merchants. Inland areas were inhabited by a people called the *Numides* by the Romans – hence the name Numidia for the Roman province covering part of what is now Tunisia. There were a number of Berber kingdoms with zones of influence, and there were alliances and conflicts with the Numidian people

Background

during the Punic Wars which pitted Rome against Carthage. Important Numidian towns included the settlements which were to become Roman **Chemtou**, close to Jendouba, and **Dougga**. Evidence of Numidian artistic skills has survived in the form of a funerary monument at the latter site, the famous Libyco-Punic mausoleum, dating from the first half of the second century BC. The building features Egyptian cornices and Greek-style Ionic columns.

Little has survived of Punic building – apart from the remains of some sturdy housing on Byrsa Hill, **Carthage**, and ground floor walls in the round town of **Kerkouane**. History has looked on the Carthaginians with a rather cruel eye, partly because of anti-Punic Roman propaganda, partly because they left little in material terms, unlike the Greeks with their temples and the elegant Etruscans. Carthaginian pottery bears no comparison with Greek black figureware, and there is practically no statuary. Nevertheless, Carthaginian graves have produced numerous items left as funerary offerings: small plates, jars and containers, incense burners, jewellery and amulets of various kinds. Among the more intriguing items discovered are ostrich eggshells with painted faces, probably a symbol of new life. Tiny glass pendants featuring human faces were also popular. Sacred razors, incised with varied motifs and scenes, and also part of the offerings left with the deceased, bear witness to Carthaginian skill in metal working, as does the display of Punic jewellery in the Bardo Museum.

*Libyco-Punic
mausoleum at
Dougga*

Roman period

In contrast to Punic times, the Roman period has left the visitor to Tunisia with a wealth of sites to visit – and the finest collection of Roman mosaics in the world, housed in the Bardo Museum. The Romans were a practical lot, and so careful was their engineering that some of their greatest buildings – sections of the **Zaghouan to Tunis aqueduct** (originally 80 km long), the great amphitheatre of **El Djem** – have survived in an amazingly intact state down to the present day.

Some of the remains of the Roman towns in northern Tunisia are truly impressive – and there are still more across the border in Algeria, for the moment off limits. To the Romans, as later on to the Muslim Arabs, the city represented the home of civilization, and across their African territories the Romans laid out new towns on a grid iron pattern (see Haïdra) or overbuilt existing settlements – as at **Dougga** and **Carthage**.) The typical town which the visitor can see today centres on a forum and temples, and has extensive public facilities, including baths, a circus, a theatre and basilicas. There is also generally a triumphal arch or two, reminder of some benefactor emperor.

Temples   The temples are generally the most impressive feature – especially at Dougga and **Sbeïtla** – and were derived from Greek and Etruscan models. Greek columns were the fashion from the second century onwards, but only covered the front of the temple, not all four sides, as in the Hellenic world. Accessible by steps, set at the heart of the Roman towns, the temples are the most striking buildings to have survived, even in their ruined state. Initially, temples were built to a trinity of gods, Jupiter, Juno and Minerva. Later in the empire, they were dedicated to deified emperors. When Christianity took root, they fell into disuse, as they were too small to house congregations, being built for ceremonies carried out by leading citizens and a priesthood. Great basilicas took their place, and remains of these can be seen in many of the Roman cities.

The influence of the Greek-speaking eastern Mediterranean was marked in another domain, that of statuary, samples of which (often minus head and limbs) can be seen in museums and archaeological sites across Tunisia. Perhaps we are a little blasé today when we look at Roman statuary. It is easy to forget that the Romans lived in a world without the instant images of today. Statuary, in stone and clay, played important social functions.

Statuary

The bust was one of the most widespread forms of statuary. Portraits in stone were a way of spreading one's influence, of building family prestige. It was through statues that emperors could make their authority felt. The great families of the empire, old and *nouveaux riches*: any leading member of a major family would be immediately portrayed after his death. A death mask would be made, to be carried in procession at the funeral – along with the death masks of other members of the family. Thus ancient lineage could be displayed and a pecking order of important families maintained.

The emperors used busts and other statuary for propaganda purposes. Statues of Augustus and his successors, often larger than life, showed them as athletic men in the prime of life. Examples of such statuary can be seen in the museums at the Bardo and Carthage. Growing Greek influence can be observed at work in the fashions here as well. In earlier times, emperors are shown clothed. Later, with the mode for all things Greek, they were portrayed nude, with bodies that suggest gym workouts on a regular basis. The truth of the matter? Sculptors had a range of models, and practice was to add a lifelike portrait head to a standard body.

Statuary would have been displayed in niches on the triumphal arches which were very much a feature of Roman towns, and Africa is the province where the largest number have survived Good examples can be seen at **Dougga**, **Haïdra**, **Macthar** and **Sbeïtla**, while at **Tripoli**, (ancient Oea) in Libya, an arch to Marcus Aurelius survives on the edge of the old town. Although both the Egyptians and Greeks were familiar with the arch, they made no wide-scale use of it in building. The Romans, with their well-honed engineering skills, were able to build large arches without using mortar.

Street furniture: the honorific arch

Urban arches of triumph were originally built to celebrate great military achievements. They were not related to the city walls, but were generally built on the street along which the victor's procession was to pass. Sometimes they are located outside the city. Later, arches would be dedicated by a city to an emperor who had been particularly generous. Basically, the Roman triumphal arch was a spectacular piece of street furniture – functioning rather like the Arc de Triomphe on the Champs Elysées, or the Porte de France in Tunis, an 18th century arch which is all that remains of the walls on the east side of Muslim Tunis. One of the most spectacular arches is in Libya at **Leptis Magna**, a great four-way construction decorated with reliefs commemorating the imperial family and military successes.

The Roman villa, built to a courtyard plan with colonnades and tiled roofs, was a cut above the Carthaginian dwelling in elegance and comfort. Wealthy citizens of Roman Tunisia liked to impress their neighbours, as the mosaics and statuary found in their villas clearly indicate. They also had elegant furniture including couches, bronze oil lamps and tripods and objets d'art, although little of this has survived and in all likelihood, there were wall paintings, although none of these have survived.

Villas

It is the mosaics which are the clear indicator of the existence of disposable incomes for elaborate interior decoration in second and third century Africa.

The art of the mosaic   In modern Tunisia, the finest survival of ancient times is undoubtedly the mosaic. The earliest mosaics go back to ancient Greece. In its most primitive form, mosaics of pebbles were used to cover floors. The earliest figurative mosaics date from fourth century BC Greece. The first mosaics made from specially cut stone cubes (*tesselae*) date from the early second century BC. The new more refined technique – known as *opus tessellatum* – created a smoother, more compact surface and meant that objects could be portrayed in much greater detail. It quickly became popular right across the Greek-speaking lands of the eastern Mediterranean. It also became increasingly sophisticated: fine lines of coloured stone allowed the artists to reproduce a huge range of tone and colour, to the point that certain ancient writers referred to the technique as *opus vermiculatum*, literally 'worm-style technique' (from the Latin *vermiculum*, 'little worm'), so fine were the lines.

The mosaic became popular in Italy, and fine mosaics dating from the second and first centuries BC have been discovered at Pompei. By the first century AD, the mosaic was a decorative technique used right across the empire, used along with the painted wall-fresco and statuary of Greek inspiration to decorate private homes and public buildings. Local schools of mosaic work grew up. Italy, for example, was known for its black and white mosaics. Africa, however, was to develop large and elaborate multi-coloured mosaics.

The oldest figurative mosaics in Tunisia date from the beginning of the second century AD. The early figurative mosaics were composed by artists who were brought over from the Hellenistic regions of the eastern Mediterranean. These mosaics have a number of Hellenistic traits: they rival wall paintings in their subtle tones and detail; the themes – Nile landscapes, rural idylls, and the post-banquet 'unswept floor' motif – were popular in the East. Later, towards the end of the second century AD, strong regional schools of mosaic work emerged. New themes became popular, generally inspired by daily life in Roman Africa: hunting, the sea, the amphitheatre games and life on the farm. Sometimes these mosaics have captions. In the later third century, technique declines, becoming cruder. Mosaics become more abstract, and some, executed for early Christian buildings, have a strong symbolic charge, only obvious to the initiated observer, given that the Christian communities were initially persecuted. In the mid-fourth century, Christian mosaic work emerges. From this period date a fine portrait of a female saint (today in the Museum of Carthage) and more naïve work such as that from certain Tabarka Christian tombs.

It is generally thought that mosaic work largely disappeared in the sixth century under the Vandals. However, recent finds at Thuburbo Majus contradict this view. After the Arab invasions of the seventh century, mosaic work disappeared from Africa, although the Fatimid caliph of Mahdia called in mosaicists to decorate his palace in the 10th century.

The buildings of Islam

In 682, the Arab general Okba Ibn Nafi' and his army crossed the Maghreb, bringing with them a new revealed religion, Islam. This religion was to engender new architectural forms, shaped by the requirements of prayer and the Muslim urban lifestyle. The key building of Islam is of course the mosque, which evolved considerably from its humble beginnings as a sort of low platform from which the call to prayer could be made, becoming an elaborate tower designed to demonstrate the power and piety of ruling dynasties.

Mosques   Cannot generally be visited in Tunisia by the non-Muslim visitor, with some notable exceptions, including the colonnade of the Zitouna Mosque in Tunis and the Great Mosque of Okba Ibn Nafi' in Kairouan. Minarets, visible from afar, are not always easy to photograph close to, being surrounded by narrow streets and densely built up

Mosque terminology

jami' mosque
minaret tower from which the call to
prayer is made
mihrab door-sized niche in wall of
mosque, indicating the direction of Mecca
minbar preacher's chair, often elaborate

midha ablutions area
muezzin the man who performs the call
to prayer from the minaret
medresa institute of higher education in
classical Islam
taleb student

areas. Tunisian minarets are generally a simple square tower, with a small 'lantern' feature on the top, from which the muezzin makes the call to prayer. There are unusual exceptions, however, including the octagonal minarets of the Hanefite mosques (see Yousef Dey and Hamouda Pacha mosques in Tunis) and some of the simple whitewashed vernacular structures on Djerba (see El May near Houmt Souk). Some mosques bear witness to Almohad origins – the Kasbah Mosque in Tunis, for example – and are characterized by an interlinked lozenge pattern, executed in stone. (The Giralda tower of the Cathedral of Seville started life as an Almohad minaret.) Minarets tend to feature blind horseshoe arches and a small dome on the topmost 'lantern' room. On top of the dome is an ornamental feature resembling three metal spheres on a pole, topped by a crescent. This is the *jammour*: tourist guides have several entertaining explanations for this, for example, that the spheres represent the basic ingredients of bread (flour, water and salt).

Mosques tend to have large covered prayer halls, comprising a series of narrow transepts, created by lines of arches supporting flat roof terraces or, more rarely, pitched roofs (see Testour). There will be a main 'aisle' leading towards the *mihrab* (prayer niche) which indicates the direction of Mecca, and for prayer. The main nave in the traditional Tunisian mosque does not however have the same dimensions as the main nave of a Christian cathedral. Note that Islam does not favour representation of the human form. The oldest mosques make extensive use of masonry, including columns and their elaborately carved capitals, recycled from Roman sites. Later mosques, (18th and 19th century) may have much elaborate marble marquetry, carved plaster work and ceramic tiling. (See the beylical tombs, Tourbet el Bey, in the Médina of Tunis.) There is no religious pictorial art. The same dense decoration can be found in upper class 18th and 19th century domestic architecture too. A mosque will also have an open courtyard, occasionally with a decorative fountain. Modern mosques often adopt hybrid styles. In the Cap Bon, tall space rocket minarets are popular.

Medersas

The non-Muslim visitor can get a very good idea of Muslim sacred architecture by visiting one of the medresas, the colleges which were an essential part of the Tunisian Muslim education system from mediaeval times onward. Perhaps the most spectacular are at the three medresas complex near the Zitouna Mosque in Tunis: the oldest medresa, the Nakhla or Palm Tree Medresa is simple; the latest in the series, the Slimaniya (mid-18th century) features tiles, stucco and black-and-white horseshoe arches. Here the austere students' rooms come as something of a shock after the elaborate decoration of the courtyard.

Historic médinas

Perhaps the most easily photographed of the old mosques is the Mosque of Okba Ibn Nafi' in Kairouan, set close to the walls of the old town. However, this great building, one of the finest early mosques, is an exception in that it stands towards the edge of the city. Mosques and medresas are generally surrounded by buildings. The visitor to Tunisia quickly has to learn to navigate through the narrow streets of the médinas or old towns to reach the monument or museum to be visited.

Background

In much 19th century writing, the médinas of the Maghreb – and of the Arab world in general – were seen as chaotic places, which although harbouring exotically clothed populations, were also home to disease and ignorance. The médina was taken as a metaphor for the backwardness of the *indigène*. In fact, the tangled streets of the average Tunisian médina are no more disorganized than many a European mediaeval town. Today's visitor will immediately be struck by the external walls in *pisé* (sun-dried clay, gravel and lime mix). Disorientation due to narrow alleys and high walls sets in later, perhaps after leaving the main souks.

Logic of the médina

The médinas of Tunisia do, however, obey a logic, satisfying architectural requirements arising from climatic and religious factors. The climate is hot in summer, but often very cold in winter. In the coastal towns, damp sea air is a problem, while inland there are hot summer winds from the South. The city therefore has to provide protection from this climate, and networks of narrow streets are the ideal solution. Streets could be narrow as there was no wheeled transport, there being plenty of pack animals for carrying goods around. Narrow streets also ensured that precious land within the city walls was not wasted.

The traditional city house

For housing the Muslim family, the courtyard house was the ideal solution. This of course is an architectural model which goes back to Mesopotamia, Greece and Rome. For Islamic family life, with its insistence on gender separation in the public domain, the courtyard house provides a high level of family privacy. In densely built up cities, the roof terraces also provided a place for women to perform household tasks – and to share news and gossip. The biggest houses would have several patios, the main one having arcades on two levels. Thus extended families could be accommodated in dwellings with large open areas. Old Tunisian courtyard homes are not generally easy to visit, however. In Tunis and Sousse, there are houses which have been restored and altered to function as upmarket restaurants (see the late 19th century Dar Jeld and the overwhelmingly kitsch Saraya in the Kasbah district of Tunis, for examples) or private museums (Dar Essid in Sousse.) In Tunis, the visitor can discover a good concentration of Tunisian artefacts in a lovingly restored patrician house, the Dar Ben Abdallah, in the central Médina. You may well be invited into ordinary homes, however, where fridges and pressure cookers are in use alongside traditional braseros in the main courtyard.

Vernacular architectures

The **courtyard home** is the most characteristic building in Tunisia's cities, discrete and anonymous to all but a neighbourhood's inhabitants from the outside, spectacularly decorated in its patrician form on the inside. There are other, more rustic, building traditions which have only recently fallen out of use, however, the best known being the **fortified granaries** or *ksours* of the areas south and east of Tataouine, and the stone-built citadel villages (*kalaât*) in the same region and over in the Matmata Hills. The latter region also has the **underground dwellings** made famous by the Star Wars films. Tozeur has its characteristic yellow brick work, while the Djerba countryside is dotted with the austerely beautiful *menzels*, whitewashed courtyard dwellings totally in harmony with the natural environment.

Beautiful though they often are, the vernacular building styles are under threat. They are often more vulnerable to the weather than modern buildings, and despite excellent qualities in terms of temperature regulation, they need maintenance. Reinforced concrete building is becoming popular, and carries the prestige of being 'modern'. However, in the southern regions, mock vernacular architecture is often used for hotel buildings. Vaults and decorative detailing of vaguely Berber inspiration can be found on hotels and restaurants. The tourist industry may yet fuel some sort of return to traditional – and more ecological – building typologies.

Dar Lasram, a traditional city home

Early 19th century Dar Lasram, once home to the family which provided the Husseïnid beys with numerous private secretaries, is a good example of a patrician city residence. The house now houses design offices for an architectural conservation association. All houses such as Dar Lasram had a central courtyard or wast al-dar (1) with perhaps a colonnade, and even a central fountain, which was reached indirectly through an angled corridor from the street. The house entrance was usually via a studded door (2) to a lobby or pair of small rooms (3), designed to ensure that no-one from the street could either view or easily enter the inner courtyard or rooms. Around the central courtyard were clustered all the principal rooms, including in large houses a bit bel kebu (4), a set of family rooms set around a main living space or an area to give family privacy from visitors. Libraries (5) were important in the houses of public figures, and no truly great house could be without its hammam (6) or bath area. Naturally, there was a large staff with appropriate housing for it (7). In the case of Dar Lasram, the house was considerably remodelled in the 20th century, and part of the building now houses an exhibition area (8). Kitchens, stores, water well/storage, stables (9) and accommodation for servants took up considerable space (7). Tunisian great houses of the 18th and 19th centuries would often have an upper storey. Roof areas were accessed by stairways (10) and used for laundry, the drying of grain and fruit. Rainwater ran off the roof into cisterns under the house. Open space within the house was often generous in scale (11 and 12). In lower class dwellings this same format was repeated but on a much smaller scale.

1 Courtyard 1	7 Service area
2 Door	8 Harem
3 Entry rooms	9 Stables/yard
4 Apartment area	10 Stairways
5 Library	11 Open space
6 Hammam (bath)	12 Courtyard 2

Plan of Dar Lasram, Tunis médina

Coastal strong-points

On the coasts of Tunisia can be found interesting forms of military architecture. **Monastir** and **Sousse** have their *rbats*, early mediaeval fortresses built to defend the Muslim communities of the Sahel. And at coastal towns, there are numerous fortifications of early modern European inspiration. In the 16th century, the southern Mediterranean coasts were targets for expansionist Spain. Coastal strong-points such as **Bizerte**, **La Goulette**, **Porto Farina**, and **Tabarka** were occupied, all the better to control the Mediterranean. In the 16th century, Hapsburg Spain was still at the height of its glory as an imperial power, and the Nova Arx, a particularly elaborate piece of military architecture, was erected outside Tunis, equipped with all the most up-to-date features of the military architecture of the day. There were monumental gateways, cannons, watchtowers and sharp-angled bastions. When the Ottomans finally triumphed in Tunis, they continued to build and extend existing fortifications, notably at **Kélibia**, **Le Kef** and **Porto Farina**, as well as on **Djerba**.

20th-century architecture

The heart of the contemporary Tunisian city is very much a late 19th century achievement, and there is a good variety of interesting architectural styles to observe. Except in the case of Tunis, old city walls were not totally demolished and re-used as development land, but kept as part of a buffer zone between old and new. The new areas had large open spaces planted with regular rows of trees, while a system of avenues in the new neighbourhoods (*villes nouvelles*) provided a grid for new apartment building and villa developments, as well as linking into a system of highways leading in and out of the city. After the destruction of the Second World War, the French became interested in preserving the aesthetic face of the city – witness the replanning of the area around the walls of Sfax.

In Algeria, the French had caused considerable destruction in the old cities, demolishing and pillaging entire neighbourhoods. In Tunisia, they wished to present themselves as protectors of the former Ottoman regency. Part of this policy was to display a respect for traditional building styles and crafts – hence the development of the *style arabisant* or neo-Moorish style for public buildings. The style, which involved extensive use of mock minarets, domes and horse-shoe shaped windows, originated in Algeria, were it was known as the *style Jonnart*, after the prefect who promoted it. In Tunisia, the *style arabisant* appeared in private villas, mainly the work of one Victor Valensi, and official buildings, designed by **Raphaël Guy**. Tunis and its suburbs, Sfax, Sousse and Bizerte all have fine examples of the style.

In the 1930s, most official commissions for buildings tended to go to French architects – which meant that architects from Tunisia's big Italian community had to look to the private sector. The result was some very fine Art Déco and modernist apartment buildings in the Lafayette and Passage districts. Among the architects active at the time were **René Audineau** (Hotel Ritza, 1929-30), the **Maltese Joss G. Ellul** (Villa Boublil, rue d'Autriche, 1931-32), and **Georges Piollenc** and **Marcel Royer** (the Colisée cinema complex in downtown Tunis, also dating from the early 1930s.) **Victor Valensi** designed the Synagogue Daniel Osiris on avenue de la Liberté. One of the most surprising buildings of this period is the **Villa Zodiac**, a modernist country house built to a perfectly radiocentric plan situated in the countryside south of Grombalia near Hammamet. The story goes that the villa was built as a present from a leading member of the Italian community to **Mussolini**.

The post-Second World War period in Tunisia produced some interesting building. All construction materials were in short supply, and for a short period, 1943 to 1948, a strong team of architects, many of whom had started their careers in Morocco, were in charge of seeing that the country got new public buildings. The vernacular building style of the **Sahel**, with its whitewashed courtyard houses with their vaulted rooms was the model adopted for schools, training centres and administrative buildings across Tunisia, many of which can still be seen today. One of the team's leading architects, **Jacques Marmey**, was to stay in Tunisia where he continued to build. The former presidential palace at Rakkada, Kairouan is a Marmey building.

In the 1960s, Tunisia was proving to itself and the world that it was a modern nation. **Olivier Clément Cacoub** emerged as the leading architect, favoured by the President Bourguiba – and a number of other African presidents too – for the design of official buildings and hotels. The Hotel Aïn Oktor is a Cacoub building, as are many buildings in Monastir, President Bourguiba's hometown which was also redesigned by Cacoub.

In the late 1990s, new official building and hotels across Tunisia often incorporated features of traditional architecture in a throw-back to the neo-Moorish style of the early 20th century. The attention to the styling of more workaday buildings which was such a feature of protectoral architecture seems to have disappeared. Much of the new building in Tunisia's town centres relies on marble or mirror glass for effect. In the suburbs, very little building is architect-designed at all. Local builders make use of their imaginations, often with surprising results – for example the pagoda roof atop suburban villas in the Cap Bon towns.

Contemporary painting

Given Tunisia's proximity to Europe, easel painting soon took root after the arrival of the French protectorate. (A stay in North Africa had already been a popular source of inspiration for numerous European painters, for whom Algiers or Tangiers was all exotic street scenes, cavalcades in movement, and sharp, often violent colour contrast.) A number of European artists passed through, the most important being **Paul Klee** and **Auguste Macke**. Struck by the light of the intense light and the forms and colours of St Germain (today's Tunis suburb of Ezzahra) and Kairouan, Klee was to draw on his experience in Tunisia for the rest of his career. **Alexandre Roubtzoff**, a White Russian who chose to settle in Tunis, documented local life with his line drawings and oils, while **Rodophe Baron d'Erlanger** painted oils of his adopted village, Sidi Bou Saïd, and its people. In the 1940s and 1950s, a number of self-taught Tunisian painters emerged, the so-called Ecole de Tunis. Some of these artists were self-taught, others trained at the Tunis Ecole des beaux arts or abroad. Some chose to imitate European styles, while others opted to illustrate the rich heritage of oral literature and the streetlife of their hometowns.

After independence in 1956, a generation of Tunisian painters came to the fore, working in a number of registers – calligraphic, abstract, naïve. Nja Mehdaoui produces vast expanses of calligraphic signs, while Rachid Koreïchi, an Algerian based in Tunis, works with a repertoire of talismanic symbols and Arabic script in a variety of materials. Adel Megdiche produces scenes of strangely distorted voluptuous figures, often inspired by ancient Arab myth. Rafik El Kamel tries to capture daily life, the street scene, in a semi-abstract form while self-taught Ahmed El Hajeri creates a dream-like universe of swelling, supple forms where humans have an almost feline, animal appearance. Gouider Triki and Abderrazak Sahli, both of whom have withdrawn to their home villages, produce canvases filled with objects and figures of a strong hieroglyphic quality. Among the younger generation of painters, born in the 1960s and now coming to the fore, are Meriem Bouderbala, Rim Karaoui and Asma M'naouar.

Unfortunately, there is as yet no museum of contemporary art, but there are frequent exhibitions in galleries in Tunis, Sousse and Hammamet. A national museum of contemporary art may yet be opened in the restored Palais de l'Abdaliya in the up-market Tunis suburb of La Marsa.

Urban and rural crafts

Although Tunisia does not have the same reputation as Morocco for its craft industry, the visitor will find much of interest. In the souks of the historic cities, interesting ceramics and vivid carpets can be found. There is the delicate tracery of wrought iron, painted wood products and some fine basket work. Basically, the traditional arts divide into two categories, rural and urban. Urban crafts are generally taken to be more refined, displaying an Andalusian influence, while rural crafts, especially textiles, are very popular with visitors.

But rural and urban crafts are different in many other ways too. Rural craft items – carpets and woven items such as saddle bags and tent strips, pottery, jewellery – were, and still are to a great extent produced in very different conditions to urban items. Rural craftwork is solid, practical, made to stand up to long years of use in places of harsh climatic extremes. Carpets and pottery are made by women, while jewellery and metal utensils by men in small country settlements. The signs and symbols used to decorate these items are generally geometric, arranged in simple,

Background

repetitive combinations to pleasing effect. Lines, dots and dashes, lozenges and squares are combined to cover surfaces made from clay, metal and wool. Sometimes these decorative forms are linked to the tribal marks tatooed on women's faces and arms. The isolation of rural communities meant that the peoples of different areas could develop very individual styles of craftwork. This is apparent in weaving, clothing and women's jewellery. But given the fact that craft-made items were subject to harsh conditions of use, few pieces can be safely said to be more than 100 years old.

Striking colour and form are often features of rural crafts. The *bakhnoug* and the *ta'jira* were the traditional veils woven by rural women. Dyed deep bordeaux or indigo, these pieces of textile may be decorated with dense white geometric forms or naïve silk embroidery. Flat weave carpets from the Gafsa region often display strong colourful forms. The jewellery of southern communities was once made by Jewish craftsmen based in Djerba. It is always silver; necklaces include silver tubes and spheres, mixed in with rings and sometimes amber. Pottery once varied greatly from region to region, each area having very individual forms. With the spread of cheap plastic and hard-wearing enamelled utensils, most of the local forms have disappeared.

In contrast, urban craft items are generally produced by men, often working in structured corporations. While the women folk of nomad tribes produced for their own use, men in towns were working to sell their produce. They did not, however, build up sufficient capital to develop production on a large scale. City craftsmen produced carpets, jewellery, pottery, leather items, and metal utensils. They worked the raw materials for their production. Urban jewellery is in gold, often set with precious stones, and very finely worked. Pottery was enamelled and decorated with designs flowing and floral as well as geometric. The leather workers produced footwear (*belgha*) and high quality bindings for the sacred texts. Traditional copper work included cooking pots and trays. Wooden items were often very elaborate in their decoration – witness the painted marriage chests and *porte-armes*. Mahdia had a great reputation for fine quality silk weaving.

Within living memory, Tunisia's cities had very locally specific forms of craft production. Today, certain craft items are mass-produced for the tourist market. However, older items can only be found in the antique shops of Tunis, where they go for very high prices – the aesthetic qualities of the finest Tunisian craftwork are much appreciated by collectors. Unfortunately, there is little new craft production of any great quality – with some notable exceptions, one of which is the art of ceramic tile making, a craft which has been established in Tunis since the 16th century and possibly earlier.

Tiles from Tunis *Zlliz* or multi-coloured ceramic tiles were traditionally used to decorate the walls of the Tunisian city home. The fashion probably came from Andalusia in the 17th century – or possibly with the 'integration' of Tunis into that most loosely articulated of empires, the Ottoman Empire, as of the late 16th century. (The great Sidi Mehrez mosque in the Médina of Tunis had red, green and blue Iznik-type wall tiles until its restoration in the late 1970s.)

In folk memory, the holy man named **Sidi Kacem Ezzilizi** (the tilemaker) is generally cited as having brought tilemaking to Tunis. Little is known about him except that he was a tile maker for part of his life and that he was highly esteemed by the Hafsid sultans. In 1496, he was buried at his home on the western edge of the Médina, overlooking the Sedjoumi saltflats. Today it houses a small museum of Tunisian ceramics, with a fine collection of both urban and rural pottery. Transformed into a museum with Spanish help in the 1970s, the building, situated on the Place du Leader, is instantly recognizable with its pyramid-shaped green-tiled roof, recalling the palaces of Morocco and Andalusia.

Where to see (and buy) tiles and pots

After a visit to the potters of Kallaine, Georges Duhamel wrote "I looked for potters, I found poets". The traditional ateliers and kilns of the Médina of Tunis have long since vanished, and there is not much poetry about a visit to Nabeul, although this is definitely the place with the most ceramic showrooms – something for all tastes. In Tunis, some of the shops on rue de la Zitouna have good selections of contemporary Tunisian pottery, ranging from the neo-Habitat to the natural browns and reds of Sejnène pottery from the North. For fans of old ceramic panels, the Café Mnouchi (at the intersection of souk es-Sekkajine and souk el-Kebabjiya) has a fine collection, many with figurative designs. Older collectors' pieces may

sometimes be found at the antique dealers on the rue des Glacières (street to the right of the British Embassy) and in any of the antique shops in the La Marsa/Le Kram zone. (Look out for work by the Chemla brothers). Perhaps the most reliable craft emporium is Driba, near the TGM station and opposite Arthé restaurant in Marsa Plage. On occasion they also have some interesting contemporary pieces.

Some of the finest tiled interiors are in the Médina of Tunis, notably at Dar Lasram (rue du Tribunal), Dar Husseïn and Dar Ben Abdallah, which also houses museum displays of traditional life in the Médina. Fine tile detailing can also be seen on many buildings in parts of the city dating from Protectorate (1881-1956).

From the late 16th century, **Tunis'** potters and tilemakers set up their kilns and workshops close to Bab Souika on the eastern side of the Médina, in an area which even today is still known as *Kallaline* (the plural form of *kallal*, potter.) Three influences were at work in Kallaline pottery – Andalusian, Ottoman and Italian, and the result was a uniquely Tunisian style. The *cuerda seca* or dry cord technique was used to imitate the geometric designs of Hispano-Moorish ceramic mosaic: fine lines of manganese and oil were used to define a pattern on the tile and isolate areas to be filled in later with coloured ceramic. **Cuerda seca** tiles are rather rare (the technique must have required considerable skill and was therefore expensive.) In the 18th century homes which have survived with their decoration intact – notably Dar Lasram, the preference is to cover large surfaces with small (12 centimetres x 12 centimetres) tiles in two or three colours.

Exuberant floral motifs, stylized cypresses, minarets and domes, and occasionally animals too, feature in large panels executed in harmonious shades of green, blue and yellow on a white ground. Tile manufacture at Iznik in Turkey was at its apogee in the 16th century and the stylized yet fluid lines of the tulips and carnations of the Perso-Turkish decorative vocabulary came to feature in Kallaline tiles. Some of the best examples can be seen at the 17th century palace Dar Othman. The craftsmen of Kallaline were never able to imitate the celebrated Iznik red, however.

In the 18th century, Kallaline products were in high demand. The increasing prosperity of Tunisia under two strong Husaynid rulers, Ali II (1759-82) and Hammouda Pacha (1782-1814) saw the development of a pronounced taste for richly decorated interiors which was to the great benefit of the ceramic tile industry. Great expanses of interior walls were covered with tiles in luminous shades of green and blue, egg yolk yellow contrasted with black and white, the whole set between the grey white of marble flooring and bands of elaborately carved white stucco.

In the early 19th century, Tunisois or *beldi* taste was to move towards the more naturalistic leaves and flowers of Italianate tiles. Large quantities of *zelliz* were imported from Italy, and to satisfy market demand, Hammouda Pacha created new workshops at Gammarth on the coast north of Tunis, employing foreign artisans.

Background

To deal with the Italian competition, the artisans of Kallaline were to make use of Italianate motifs, adapting them to local taste. Times were changing, however, and large Italian and Spanish 18 centimetres x 18 centimetres tiles came to be used before giving way to modern industrial tiles with a fine biscuit, more suitable for the modern apartment. As the way of life changed, the demand for traditional pots fell as well. Kallaline was unable to compete, and by the 1960s, the workshops and kilns had completely disappeared.

The Tunisian ceramic industry is still very much alive in the holiday town of Nabeul. As tourism developed, some bright spark realized that large quantities of blue and white plates and dishes were what the visitor wanted to buy in a Mediterranean resort. (Observing the mountains of pots sold to tourists, Jean Genet expressed the fear that in a few decades time there would be nothing left of Tunisia.) Today, the traditional subtle greens, yellows and aubergine have practically disappeared – except for a few of the larger *khabia* type jars. The higher quality traditional pots, often with metal decoration, are imported from Morocco. However, there is some rather nice contemporary Nabeul stoneware, and German expertise has established *La Rose des sables*, a company manufacturing fine porcelain for the up-market dinner table.

Culture

The Tunisian people

Population Tunisia's population has undergone enormous changes since independence. In 1961, the population stood at just over four million. In 1994, it topped the 8.7 million mark. The growth rate has slowed dramatically, however, from 2.75 percent per annum in 1961 to 1.85 percent per annum in 1993. This is the result of sustained family planning programmes. In a part of the world where population growth rates of three percent and above were current, Tunisia exercised a rare control over its population, with an average 2.2 percent growth for the period. A real improvement in purchasing power, nutrition, and a move by women into formal employment has accompanied this demographic slowdown. In 1994, average annual income was 23 times higher than in 1961, 1,706Dt as against 74Dt.

So what does a typical Tunisian look like? The question is not an easy one to answer, as the population of contemporary Tunisia is the result of a long history during which various settlers passed through the country. While the earliest populations of northwestern Africa were probably of Hamitic stock, the ancestors of today's Berbers, there have been numerous other inputs (including Phoenicians and Romans, and in particular the **Arabs**, who first began to arrive in the eighth century.) The mid-11th century Hilalian invasions strengthened the Arab component, removing Arabising the **Berber**-speaking countryside, and removing the Arab/Berber divide which has remained so important in Algeria and Morocco. Until the mid-20th century, there was an important and ancient **Jewish** community, based in Tunis, Kairouan and the southern island of Djerba. This was reinforced, particularly in the 18th century, by highly educated and talented groups Jews from Livorno in Italy. Many Jews left Tunisia after the foundation of the State of Israel in 1948. As of the late 18th century, a **European** population settled in the coastal towns, and was particularly numerous in the mid-20th century. This population was mainly of French, Italian and Maltese origin, with a few Greeks and even the odd White Russian. There is a **sub-Saharan** African component to Tunisia's population, originally the result of the slave trade. In physical terms, then, an average room-full of Tunisians at, say, a business meeting will not look very different from Brazilian or Spanish counterparts.

Background

European travellers to Tunisia in the 19th century distinguished between three groups: the **Turks**, the **Moors** and the **Arabs**. The Turks were the ruling and military élite, and Ottoman Turkish was their prestige language. In court circles, it was practice to take wives of southern European origin, often captured in pirate raids on Italian islands or brought over from Istanbul. Travellers wrote of the Moorish population of the cities, who were described as being refined and polite. Seventeenth-century immigrants from Andalusia were a component of this population, but had been absorbed into the mass of Arabic-speakers.

The most important divide, however, was that between **townspeople**, sedentary countryfolk, and **nomads** ('the Arabs'.) There was a clear split in ways between the city people, the *beldia* (a term meaning 'people from the *balad* or town') and the nomads (*el 'arab*). Mannerisms, speech, and dress were highly different.

These socio-ethnic divisions have long since disappeared with the abolition of the monarchy and massive rural exodus after independence. Certain regional types can still be distinguished, however. The inhabitants of Sfax tend to be pale skinned, and have a distinctly Iberian look. People from coastal towns like Kélibia, Haouaria and Bizerte tend to look very Mediterranean, too. There are certain faces which to the insider look very Sfaxi or Djerbian, and others which are distinctly *'aroubi* ('from the country') – something in the shape of the face, perhaps. The older generation of Tunisians, particularly the country people, are shorter than their European counterparts. However, lifestyle for the urban middle classes differs little from that of southern Europeans. The rural regions, until recently fairly behind, are catching up fast. There are now very few parts of the countryside without electricity. Basic infrastructure is being put in everywhere, and as a result, life expectancy will rise.

Tunisians differ greatly from northern Europeans in the way their lives are focused, however. The **family** is of primary importance, determining a person's life chances to a great degree. Family loyalty is of great importance, with the father seemingly the dominant figure – although very often wives rule the roost. Islam is a strong force, laying down the limits of what can and cannot be done. The home is a private place – but strangers, when a friendship forms, are readily invited in. On the whole, however, men meet their friends in cafés, while women socialize in each others' homes. In some of the larger cities, there are places where young people of both sexes mix in cafés and restaurants – the Makni Centre and the Arcades in the El Manar area of Tunis, for example.

Tunisian society is changing rapidly. Today, just over 60 percent of the population is urban. The main cities have expanded enormously over the last 20 years. Tunisia's old families, and the brightest and best connected of the university educated élite, have done very well for themselves since independence from France in 1956. The second generation urban populations have new aspirations, however, and expect (and indeed are getting) some part of the national cake. Affluence is growing and Tunisia's people have seen their society transformed in the 45 years since independence. Education, some form of health care and consumer goods are available in a way unthinkable a couple of generations ago. Tunisia is well on the way to achieving the egalitarian society of which those who fought for its independence dreamed.

Language

Who speaks what language? when? and to whom? The visitor to Tunisia will quickly become aware of the range of languages on offer. Street signs and official notices are in Arabic, French and occasionally in English, people talk to each other in Tunisian Arabic, but seem to throw in a bewildering number of French terms. In tourist areas, souk salesmen can blarney their way in English, German, Spanish and many other tongues.

Background

The use of different language styles depends upon social, professional and geographic factors. **Spoken Arabic** is the everyday language of the cities, with the dialect of Tunis the most prestigious. Classical or **formal written Arabic** is the language of law, religion, official government activities and political speeches. A 'halfway form' of Arabic, *darija muhadhaba* ('educated dialect') is spoken in the school room to facilitate communication. Dialect is also used in advertising. **French** is the language of business, science and higher education, and while a mixed language, **Franco-Arabe**, is used by much of the urban educated élite on many occasions. **Italian** – in part thanks to the availability of Italian television – is often understood in the north. **Berber** is spoken in tiny rural communities in the Matmata region (Tamezret), near Tataouine (Douiret) and in some villages on Djerba. It is not a linguistic hot potato in the way it is in Algeria and Morocco – reference is never made to Berber identity in the other North African states in Tunisian media. When relations are tense with France, then shopfront signs in Latin letters may be temporarily painted out or covered in black plastic bags, generally part of a knee-jerk reaction to criticism of Tunisian internal policy in the French press.

Historically, Berber is the oldest language in North Africa. Latin was obviously the educated urban language in Roman times, and before that Punic, a Semitic language, was in use in Carthage and its satellite trading posts. In the 10th century, a characteristic Maghrebi form of spoken Arabic appeared. Fourteenth century historian Ibn Khaldoun tells us that the mixing of Berbers with the Arab invaders led to the development of a form of Arabic very different to that current in the Middle East. Present day spoken Tunisian Arabic goes back to the linguistic interaction between Arabs and Berbers in early medieval times. Arabic has a huge word stock, and the choice of basic lexical items, including the main verbs, is often completely different to those in use in Egypt and the Near East. Added to this, Tunisian urban Arabic took on massive numbers of French and Italian terms from the 19th century onwards. While Tunisians will easily understand educated Middle Eastern Arabic dialects, especially Egyptian, thanks to the film industry, the reverse is not true.

Today the Tunisian language situation is complex – and changing. Behind the multi-lingual screen lie a range of personal attitudes and aspirations. How you get on in life is linked to your language ability, and few Tunisians have any doubt that mastery of at least one European language is essential for access to science and technology. French is certainly vital for achieving a useful university degree and indispensable for a well paid job. At the same time, there is an oft expressed will to 'Arabise', cultivated by the generation which passed through the university system in the 1970s and early 1980s. (The future of the Berber-speaking communities will be interesting to observe.) Arabization has become bogged down in the process of creating terminology, and several competing national language academies, notably in Baghdad, Cairo and Damascus, are involved in trying to keep up with the flood of new words in the main world languages. The truth is that Arabic has lacked the effective language policy which updated Hebrew, for example, and transformed it into the language of the State of Israel in a generation. In any case, Tunisians are a pragmatic lot, and a Gadhafi style Arabic-only stance is unlikely: it would interfere with the making of money far too much. For the moment basic literacy in classical Arabic, *al 'arabiya al fusha*, the language of Islam, looks set to maintain its position in the education system, especially at primary level, alongside French for technical and commercial purposes.

Religion

The people Tunisia, and of North Africa, for that matter, follow Islam in the main, a religion similar to Judaism and Christianity in its philosophical content. Muslims recognize that these three revealed religions have a common basis, and Jews and Christians are referred to as *ahl al-kitab*, 'people of the book'. (Both Moses and Jesus are prophets for Muslims.) There are considerable differences in ritual, public observance of religious customs and the role of religion in daily life between the revealed religions, and when travelling in Tunisia it is as well to be aware of this. Note, however, that although the Islamic revivalist movement has in recent years been a force in neighbouring Algeria, in Tunisia, the situation, for historic and social reasons, is very different.

Islam is an Arabic word literally meaning 'submission to God'. As Muslims often point out, it is not just a religion, but a way of life. The main Islamic scripture is the Koran (often also spelt Quran in English), again an Arabic term meaning 'the recitation'. Islam appeared in the desert oases of western Arabia in the early seventh century AD. The isolated communities of this region were Jewish, Christian or animist, existing on oasis cultivation and the trade in beasts of burden. There was considerable inter-tribal warfare. It was in this context that the third great revealed religion was to emerge. Its prophet Mohammad was a member of the aristocratic Meccan tribe of Quraysh, born c.570.

The **Koran** divides into 114 souras or chapters, placed in order of length running from the longest to the shortest. Muslim and western scholars disagree on the nature of the Koran. For the true Muslim, it is the word of God, sent down via the Prophet Mohammad. The Koran appeared in this way in segments, some in Mecca, some after the Prophet was forced to leave Mecca for Médina. The later souras tend to have a more practical content, and relate to family and inheritance law, for during the period in Médina, an embryonic Muslim community was taking shape. Western scholars, however, have opened up more critical approaches to the Koranic text and the way it was assembled. During the Prophet's lifetime, nothing was written down. After his death, fragments of the text, noted in simple script on parchment or flat bones, were assembled at the order of Abu Bakr, Mohammad's successor or *khalifa*. In fact, the Arabic script was not fully codified at the time. the language of the Koran was to eventually to become the base reference point for the Arabic language.

The Koran does not cover all aspects of the Muslim's life – and it became apparent to early Islamic rulers that they would need another source. The *hadith*, short statements which recount what the Prophet is supposed to have said about various issues, were assembled to provide a crucial supplement to the main scripture.

The practice of Islam is based on five central points, the **Pillars of Islam**, namely the *shahada* or profession of faith, *salat* or prayer, *sawm* or fasting during the month of Ramadhan, *zakat* or giving charity, and the *hajj* or pilgrimage to Mecca which every Muslim is supposed to accomplish at least once in their lifetime. The **mosque** is the centre of religious activity. There is no clergy in Islam, although major mosques will have an *imam* to lead prayers. In principle, the *mesjed*, a small neighbourhood mosque, will have someone chosen from the area with enough religious knowledge to conduct prayers correctly.

The ***shahada*** is the testament of faith, and involves reciting, in all sincerity, the statement, "There is no god but God, and Mohammad is the Messenger of God." A Muslim will do this at ***salat***, the prayer ritual performed five times a day, including at sunrise, midday and sunset. There is also the important Friday noon prayers, which include a sermon or *khutba*. When praying, Muslims bow and then kneel down and prostrate themselves in the direction of Mecca, indicated in a mosque by a door-sized niche in the wall called the *qibla*. The voice of the *muezzin* calling the faithful to prayer five times a day from the minaret provides Muslim cities with their characteristic soundscape. Note that a Muslim must be ritually pure to worship. This involves washing in a ritual manner, either at the *hammam* (local bathhouse) or the *midha*, the ablutions area of the mosque.

A third essential part of Islam is the giving of ***zakat*** or alms. A Muslim was supposed to give surplus revenues to the community. With time, the practice of *zakat* was codified. Today, however, zakat has largely disappeared to be replaced by

Background

☞ *On being a good Tunisian*

Coming to Tunisia, the visitor from the anglophone world is immediately struck by how responsive Tunisians are to friendly greetings. The polite Tunisian walks into the local shop and says sabah el khir ('good morning') or a more formal salam alaykum ('peace be upon you'), and a long exchange of greetings and hand shaking will follow. You certainly can't leave the country without learning the phrase ça va la bes? ('How are you, OK?'). Plenty of time is taken to greet friends and acquaintances, and being skilled in the niceties of greetings and small talk is a key part of being a good Tunisian.

Greetings and ways of thanking often include a religious formula (yaishek, 'may God give you long life', rebbi fadhlek). Tunisians are not however austerely religious. During Ramadhan, almost everyone fasts during daylight hours – but mosque-going is not a majority activity. Many Tunisians learn some of the Koran by heart at the local kuttab, when they are small. All will know the basic precepts of Islam, and newspapers run articles on the difficulties of certain points of observance. Islamic rules provide a valued basis for daily conduct.

Other valued characteristics include being metrebbi (well brought up), 'akil (calm) and ndhif – literally 'clean' but used to mean something approaching 'of good family'. A son of a long established family is an ould 'aila. Memories run deep, and belonging to a dar kebira, a big family is another plus point. Tunisians are very much family people. They adore children, and fathers can be frequently seen proudly showing off their children to their friends at the café. Everyone seems to know everyone somewhere along the line,

even in Tunis. Knowing all your relations – and being au fait with the intricacies of family politics – is another skill the good Tunisian naturally masters.

Getting on well in Tunisia calls for ability to manipulate the family links when necessary. You will have ktef (lit: 'shoulder') or piston to help you get essential papers or a job for a cousin. (The system roughly approximates the British old boy network). You have to be a little hallouf (lit: 'a pig'), ie sharp and a bit roguish. (The phrase inti hallouf, depending on context, means 'you're a clever bastard – and I know what you're at'). Tadbir ra's, 'getting by', is crucial. The effective Tunisian – and in particular the male – is a fixer, someone who is able to yakdhi, to use the verb, equally able to command good service from a tired café waiter or make sure that the dossier is in the right place for the right signature at the right time. Even if money is short, Tunisians appear as immaculately turned out as possible. Women, who shoulder most of the domestic tasks, have to be able to conjure up good meals out of whatever is in the kitchen or come up with magnificent garments from the friperie, the second hand clothes market.

Above all, the good Tunisian is generous, karim, able to give time to help out relatives, stand a round in the café or ferry friends around. This, along with a seemingly ready friendliness is perhaps the characteristic which will stay in the visitor's mind longest. In most of Europe, no-one seems to have the Tunisian generosity with time anymore. Hopefully, this characteristic, along with the vivaciousness of the children and a general staunch humanity will survive the damping effects of globalization.

modern taxation systems. The practice of zakat al fitr, giving alms at 'Id El Fitr, the Muslim holiday which marks the end of Ramadhan, is still current, however.

The fourth pillar of Islam is **sawm** or fasting during Ramadhan. The daytime month-long fast of Ramadhan is a time of contemplation, worship and piety – the Islamic equivalent of Lent. Muslims are expected to read 1/30 of the Koran each night. Muslims who are ill or on a journey, as well as women breast-feeding are exempt from fasting. Otherwise, eating, drinking and sexual activity is only permitted at night, until "so much of the dawn appears that a white thread can be distinguished from a black one."

The **hajj** or pilgrimage to the holy city of Mecca in Arabia is required of all physically-able Muslims at least once in their lifetime. The *hajj* takes place during the month of Dhu al Hijja. The 'lesser pilgrimage' to the holy places of Islam is referred to as the *'umra*, and can be performed at any time of year. Needless to say, the journey to Mecca is not within every Muslim's financial grasp – fortunately, perhaps, as the mosques would probably be unable to cope with the millions involved, despite the extension works of recent years.

The Koran and the hadith also lay down a number of other practices and customs, some of which are close to the practices of Judaism. Sexuality, provided it is within marriage, is seen as positive, and there is no category of religious personnel for whom marriage is forbidden. Sensuality and seduction, between the married couple, are encouraged, without any guilt being involved. Eating pork is out, as is drinking alcohol and gambling. In the matter of dress, habits have changed hugely in recent years. Young women no longer automatically cover their heads as their mothers did. (The veil disappeared after independence.) Even the 'headscarf and long dress', the modern version of Islamic dress, widespread in Egypt, for example, is rarely seen. Tunisian Islam, and indeed North African Islam as a whole, is a long way from the more extreme forms practised in Saudi Arabia, where women are forbidden from driving and are all but invisible in the public sphere. While in traditional families the women's domain is most definitely the home, Islam does not stop the overwhelming trend for Tunisian women to get themselves educated and into jobs once thought of as being exclusively for men. In any case, with the rising cost of living in the 1990s, urban professional families came to consider two salaries essential.

Gender issues

The **status of women** in Tunisia underwent huge changes after independence, although the debates had begun back in the 1930s, notably through the writings of Tunis intellectual Tahar Haddad. In the early 20th century, Tunisian women of enlightened Muslim families began to go to the Jewish and Catholic schools, and at independence there was already a small core of literate urban women – unlike Morocco, for example, which has had great difficulties in building female literacy.

For the moment, Tunisia is the most advanced Muslim country in terms of legislation aimed at removing discrimination against women – and is a model often referred to by people in other Arab and Muslim states working for women's rights. The Tunisian *Code du statut personnel*, promulgated on 13 August 1956, was part of a package of reforms pushed through by Tunisia's first president, Habib Bourguiba, who considered that a radical improvement in women's status was vital for achieving progress and material wealth. The code was a great step forward, a single piece of legislation creating a unified personal status system applicable to all Tunisians, Muslims as well as Jews. It abolished both **polygamy** and **talaq** (Islamic repudiation by the male partner), a step which women's movements elsewhere in North Africa would still like to see taken. The Tunisian code did not, however, touch the issue of Islamic **inheritance** rules which favour male over female descendants, although laying down strict rules for the division of property. It did set a minimum age for marriage though: 18 for men and 15 for women.

The *Code du statut personnel*, like other codes in the North African states, affirms the importance of the family as the basis of society. The family is **patrilinear**, that is to say, takes its name from the father, although maternal filiation is recognized. Although permitted by the Code, practice means that a Muslim woman may not marry a non-Muslim man. He must convert to Islam, even if this is only for form's sake, and the process is a long one. Non-Muslim women marrying Tunisians do not have to convert, however. **Divorce** can be initiated by both parties, and both can be accused of adultery.

Background

The availability of **education** was perhaps the key factor in improving women's conditions. In 1959, a 10-year programme was launched with the aim of achieving universal primary education by 1969. Educated women can better understand reproductive health issues, and Tunisia early on launched mass birth-control campaigns. This continues today through the work of specially trained health workers who cover even the most isolated rural areas.

With the number of educated women increasing year by year, attitudes will continue to develop, and the coming generations will no doubt demand further changes. Back in the 1970s, there was an active women's movement with its own magazine *Nissa'* ('Women'.) Urban based, it had little reach into the countryside. Today, a government-sponsored organization, the Crédif (*Centre de documentation et information sur la femme*), provides a focus for research on women's issues.

Long established practices went overboard surprisingly quickly in the post-independence period, even though Tunisia, like the rest of the Maghreb and much of southern Europe, is in many ways a macho land, and the young girls of the house are the object of jealous surveillance. Although the Koranic texts are basically clear on the principle of equality between men and women, certain *souras* and *hadith* stress women's weakness, the need for women to serve men, and mention the need for male protection. The way ordinary daily relations between the sexes run is the result of a long history in which economic, religious and traditional social factors are interlinked. While essentially regulated by Islam, the nature of women/men relations differs between social classes and regional groups. And very often, in traditional areas, it is the women who seem to be the most vigilant guardians of the status quo.

However, in this system, although women rarely have direct authority, they have very definite space of their own. All is not repression – far from it. While weddings are still very often a matter of alliances between families, loving marriages certainly develop in this traditional context. Women are now present in most areas of the country's economic and professional life. There are frequent television programmes on women who have succeeded in new domains, as train drivers, pilots and physicists, in stockbroking, advertising, the catering business and the like. Although the legal status has improved since the 1950s, it will have to change even more to keep up with the new responsibilities taken on by women. The reduction of inequalities links in with the image which Tunisia wishes to project for itself and for the outside world. Women's quest for new identities is a legitimate one – and probably inseparable from the evolving identity of the modern nation.

Modern Tunisia

The kingdom of Tunisia which became independent in 1956 was very different from the Beylicate of the 1861 Destour (Constitution.) The new constitution, the type of state (a republic was proclaimed in 1957), administrative organization and practice made it firmly a modern state, very much in the French centralizing tradition. Further huge changes were on the way, however, to produce the prospering little North African nation that Tunisia had become by the end of the 1990s. Many commentators have seen these changes as being largely due to the energy and ambition of one man, Habib Bourguiba, Tunisia's leader from independence until 1987. The dynamism built up in the first decades of independence was continued under the country's second (and current) president, Zine el Abidine Ben Ali. Both figures led/lead the country as wise and enlightened father figures. However, this is a superficial similarity, for there are in fact considerable differences in their leadership styles.

Recent history

Post-independence changes: 1956-1959

Post-independence Tunisia, unlike neighbouring Algeria (independent in 1962), had the advantage of having a strong, single-minded leadership with a clear vision of the future. For Habib Bourguiba, Tunisia had fallen under French domination thanks to the decadence and corruption of the beys. Radical changes, if necessary removing the country's traditional institutions, would be necessary to bring about progress to the benefit of all. Bourguiba made use of his immense personal prestige and the fact that the constitution was being revised to push forward major reforms in the period 1956-1959.

Tunisia prides itself on having the most progressive attitude towards gender relations of the Arab states. In 1956, a **Personal Status Code** became law, replacing Islamic law and the Rabbinic courts in all matters of personal status. The new unified code abolished polygamy and introduced equality before the law between the sexes with regard to divorce. Minimum marriage ages were introduced, the marriage of non-Muslim men to Muslim women was legalized.

In hindsight, the vast expansion of **education** in the 1960s was a key element behind Tunisia's later economic success. The principle of free and universal primary education was accepted. The Sadiki College model, with sciences taught in French and humanities in Arabic, was extended to the rest of the educational system. The University of Tunis was set up in 1960. Tunisia, unlike her neighbours, had a small core of educated, urban women in the 1950s. Women's education was expanded rapidly, and by 1961 there were over 200,000 girls in school.

Land reform was a further key area. The country had large amounts of property, and notably agricultural land, held under the traditional Islamic mortmain system or *habous*. (The use and product of land could be left for future generations by the founder of the *habous*.) The system was abolished, and 175,000 hectares of land was sold off between 1956 and 1961. Choice property went to reward loyal party followers. A futher 150,000 hectares went into the cooperative system introduced in 1963.

The 1960s: Ben Salah & the socialist experiment

Bourguiba faced considerable pressure to achieve results for the poorer members of Tunisian society, and it this pressure which may have led him to introduce a rather limited version of socialist development in the 1960s. The concept of socialism entered Bourguiba's speeches, and the party was renamed the *Parti Socialiste Destourien* (PSD) in 1964. Agricultural cooperatives were set up to manage the former habous lands – and the farms confiscated from French and Italian farmers in 1964. The socialist experiment was managed by Ahmed Ben Salah, one time secretary-general of the UGTT, the main labour union, who gradually became a sort of super-minister, and for a time seemed to be being groomed to succeed Bourguiba.

But Ben Salah ran up against well established interests. When it began to look as though privately owned estates, (some belonging to members of old Tunisois families close to the presidency), might be nationalized, opposition began to Ben Salah began to grow. Sahel landholders were unhappy about risking the loss of their profitable olive groves, while other families in trade had suffered from import restrictions. The final straw was a World Bank report in 1969 criticizing Ben Salah's management of the economy. Bourguiba decided that the cooperative movement had had its day – and dismissed Ben Salah. He was charged with treason and condemned to 10 years imprisonment. (Three years later he was to escape and fled into exile.)

The 1970s: the return to capitalism

The year 1970 saw the old guard of the party under the leadership of the new premier, Bahi Ladgham, regain ground. Bourguiba was suffering from ill health, and spent increasing periods of time abroad for treatment. Ladgham was in office for barely a year, replaced by technocrat Hédi Nouira. A new constitution was promulgated in 1976, reflecting the leader's increasing inability to control all areas

Background

of policy. The new constitution entrusted executive authority to the cabinet headed by the prime minister, although the President retained the ultimate veto on policy.

The end of the socialist experiment coincided with a notable improvement in Tunisia's economic situation. Older Tunisians look back on the 1970s with nostalgia. It was a time of technocratic rule, when business became legitimate. Hédi Nouira, in his cold, efficient way, presided the liberalization of the Tunisian economy. Fortunes were made – not all of them honestly, and consumer goods returned to the market. Education continued to expand, and there were plenty of jobs in the civil service and new import substitution industries. Incentives were set up to bring investment into Tunisia, including the famous Loi 72, which offered a range of tax breaks to foreign investors willing to put money into export-oriented businesses.

During the 1970s, Nouira and his cabinet effectively governed, and came to replace Bourguiba in the Tunisian public's mind. This situation was not to last, however. Victim of a heart attack, Nouira was forced to retire from public life in 1980. One of his decisions was to have far-reaching effects years later: a hardworking military man from Hammam Sousse, one Zine el Abidine Ben Ali, was put in charge of national security .

The 1980s: Mzali & Arabism

The 1980s saw prime minister **Mohammad M'zali** emerge as President Bourguiba's successor until his spectacular fall from grace in 1986. The period was marked by growing domestic unrest, with the Islamic fundamentalist movements gaining ground in the suburbs. Official rhetoric was marked by a strong pan-Arab line.

Tunisia's performance during the Vth Economic and Social Development Plan (1982-1986) was mediocre, to say the least. M'zali, a former Arabic teacher, proved to be a demagogue and was nicknamed 'Bozo le clown' on account of his haircut. The government gained a reputation for corruption and nepotism. (The premier's wife, Fathia M'zali became Tunisia's first Minister for Women.) In such a political climate, there was no room for the opposition in the National Assembly. Left wing groups, which during the 1970s had been under considerable repression, were replaced by a growing radical Islamic movement as the main source of opposition to the régime.

The crisis was at its most acute by August 1986, when a carefully worked out structural adjustment plan was adopted. The aim was twinfold: the reduction of macro-economic imbalances and the creation of a stable basis for growth.

1986-1994: structural adjustment & a big change

The World Bank sponsored structural adjustment plan put forward a number of fast-working remedies, as well as providing for a number of long term strategies to help the Tunisian economy on its way to achieving faster growth. Shortly after the reforms had been launched, there was a change of president. Habib Bourguiba, increasingly out of touch with the mood in the country, demanded the retrial of some Islamic revivalist dissidents, in an attempt to ensure their conviction. It was clear that the president had lost his grip. The prime minister, **Zine el Abidine Ben Ali**, stepped in, and on 7 November 1987, President Bourguiba was declared medically unfit to govern. Ben Ali took over as president until elections could be organized.

The early Ben Ali years, broadly speaking 1987 to 1994, were devoted to ensuring stability, implementing the structural adjustment programme and making major institutional reforms, notably in education and investment legislation. The challenge from the revivalist Islamic movement was removed, and a number of major political reforms implemented. Life presidency was abolished, parties with a regional or religious basis outlawed. Political exiles were allowed to return. National reconciliation was the order of the day, in order to ensure favourable ground for *et taghyir, le Changement*, as the shift in social, economic and political life is referred to in Tunisian newspeak.

Why the Tunisian monarchy was abolished

Ruler from 1859 to 1883, Sadok Bey and his mamlouk ministers (some of considerable incompetence) proved incapable of preventing the country from passing under French "protection". From 1881, the beys lived a rather pleasant bourgeois existence, moving with the seasons from one suburban palace to another. The uprisings and murders of 18th century court life gave way to Ruritanian ceremonial. No longer did a mauvais café sort out the succession. Rubber stamping the decisions of the resident general, the bey (and his entourage) benefited from the prosperity generated by France's 'informal colonization'. The Bardo Palace was heavily remodelled at the beginning of the 20th century, Nasser Bey built himself a new palace at Sidi Bou Saïd.

However, living in settings worthy of an exotic opera, the beys proved unable to follow the rising demands of Tunisia's nascent independence movement. (The 1930 eucharistic congress at Carthage, partly sponsored by the bey, helped fire nationalist sentiment). Moncef Bey, the one ruler who openly challenged the power of the residence, exploiting French weakness during the Axis occupation of 1942-43) was exiled by the victorious allies, accused of collaboration with the Nazis. His successor, Sidi Lamine, was a kind old man who was no match for the nationalist leader, the wily Monastir lawyer, Habib Bourguiba. Unlike the Moroccan sultan who returned in triumph from exile as liberator of his people, the bey had lost all legitimacy. Undefended, the monarchy was eventually abolished on 25 July 1957. Its fall was lamented by very few.

Simplifying greatly, by the mid-1990s, Tunisia had come through the period of structural investment successfully. There was no longer any risk of violent internal political upheaval. The process of building an investment-oriented economy was well under way, based on closer links with Europe. A friendly business environment and improved legislation was attracting investors. Whether incoming foreign capital flows will be sufficient for Tunisia's ambitions remains to be seen. As compared with its North African neighbours, Tunisia was easily the least problematic state of the region.

The Maghreb

Tunisia forms part of a block of North African countries generally referred to in Arabic and French as the Maghreb, the Arab west, as opposed to the Middle East, known as the Machrek. Four of the Maghreb countries, Algeria, Mauritania, Morocco and Tunisia, were colonized by France, while Libya came under Italian rule for a brief but fraught period. A United Arab Maghreb, free of outside domination, was a dream of those working for independence back in colonial days. In February 1947 the Committee for the Liberation of the Maghreb was set up. In 1958, at the time when th European Community was being established, Algerian, Moroccan and Tunisian representatives met at Tanger to discuss the prospects for Maghreb unity. On 17 and 18 February 1989, a united Maghreb seemed to be on the way to becoming reality. At Marrakech, the leaders of the five states, King Hassan II of Morocco, President Chedli Bendjedid of Algeria, President Ben Ali of Tunisia, Colonel Muammar Gadhafi of Libya and President Ould Sidi Ahmad Al Taya of Mauritania signed the founding act of the Union du Maghreb Arabe, whose acronym, UMA, recalls the Arabic word umma or nation. The new union was to be presided by each nation in turn for six month periods. In October 1990, a document was drawn up providing for the creation of a free exchange zone before the end of 1992 and the establishment of a customs union in 1995.

Background

Very quickly, however, the new union ran into problems. With Bendjedid removed from power in Algeria, there was a cooling of Algero-Moroccan relations. Libya proved to be a difficult member of the team, and neither Morocco nor Tunisia were keen on Gadhafi's unpredictable style in international relations. The security situation deteriorated rapidly in Algeria, with guerrilla warfare and appalling massacres in certain regions. Thousands of Algerians began looking to emigrate. In 1994, after a terrorist attack on a Marrakech hotel, Morocco sought to limit any risk of Islamic fundamentalist contagion and introduced a visa for Algerian visitors. Algeria replied by closing the frontier. In response, Morocco put its activities in the UMA on hold. While relations between Algeria, Tunisia and Libya remained generally good, there was little move to develop things at UMA level. Tunisia was increasingly drawn in the orbit of the European Union, while maintaining good relations with Libya. The borders between the two countries were defined.

For the moment, the UMA is more or less stalled, although the bilateral contacts improved in1999. Good personal contacts seemed to have been established between the new king of Morocco, Mohammad VI, and Algerian president Bouteflika. Any progress in the UMA will have to be based on the settlement of Algero-Moroccan differences over the latter's Saharan provinces. Without this, there seems little hope for any advance. In any case, for Tunisia, like Morocco, commercial relations with the European Union have taken on great importance.

Tunisia and the European Union

As of the late 1980s, Tunisia opted to intensify its ties with Europe, although never going so far as Morocco, which in 1987 requested membership of the EEC, perhaps more as a symbolic gesture than anything else. Relations are generally excellent, for Europe and Tunisia have too much in common for the two sides not to work together. Algerian gas transits over Tunisian territory on its way to the Italian peninsula, European companies – and notably French, German and Italian ones – have relocated to Tunisia in recent years, benefiting from the favourable tax legislation. The current privatization programme and the recent, albeit timid, development of the Tunis stock exchange will no doubt maintain European business interest. Tunisia's credentials as a stable country, close to Europe, will doubtless continue to make it favourable terrain for business relocation.

Continuity and trends

Tunisian political life since independence has shown a remarkable degree of stability, notably in terms of the direction and application of policy. In Tunisia, as in neighbouring Libya, the political leadership, right from independence, has always followed the line that the improvement of the majority's living conditions was the way forward. Education and health, infrastructure and housing, and in recent years, leisure facilities have always been the focus for investment. (The army, which in both Morocco and Algeria, for different reasons, absorbed large amounts of state finance, has always been a negligible factor.) The result has been the creation of an educated work force, able to satisfy the needs of relocating manufacturing industry. Islamic fundamentalism has little attraction for this large and stable group in society, content to work and enjoy the prosperity brought by the policies of the technocratic élite.

Under Bourguiba, there was little room for public debate on the policy line adopted by the government. He had himself referred to as *al Mujahid al Akbar*, translated into French as *le Suprême Combattant*. In Arabic, the term carries a hint of *jihad* or holy war. Bourguiba considered himself to be leading a *jihad* against ignorance and poverty; only the application of reason could bring about development and well-being. The leadership style was paternalist, to say the least. The National Assembly essentially functioned as a forum for announcing decisions already taken at presidential level, the country was run by a growing body of university graduates who supported the modernizing policies of the Bourguiba's prime ministers because they were a product of them. The improvement in living conditions was apparent to all.

But the 'Bourguiba system' also had a very personal, and often flamboyant touch. The Tunisian people came to know all the details of their president's life, the influence of his mother, the oft-declared poverty of his childhood. And then there was the issue of the succession. A succession of ministers – notably Ahmed Ben Salah, Hédi Nouira and Mohammad M'zali – were groomed to take over. They would be raised to dizzy heights by Bourguiba. And then, when things began to go wrong, for whatever reason, political or economic, they were disgraced and unceremoniously removed from office. The rise and spectacular downfall of Tunisia's prime ministers were part of a saga that kept Tunisia entertained for decades. Then in 1987, when things had finally got seriously out of hand in both political and economic terms, Bourguiba basically senile and unfit for office, was removed by prime minister Ben Ali (see above).

Under Ben Ali, the leadership style altered radically. Speculation about manoeuvrings for influence in the Carthage Palace disappeared. Sobre-suited President Ben Ali, surrounded by a team of steady technocrats, is a discrete figure. The policy options, marked by equally strong concerns for economic development and the well-being of low-income groups, are broadly the same. But whilst Bourguiba came from a family of upwardly mobile Sahel landowners, Ben Ali had a more difficult start in life – hence the interest in improving conditions for the poorest members of society. The question of Ben Ali's successor remains on hold, and in the late 1990s, no clear favourite figure had emerged, although the names of technocrat Mohammad Jegham, a former minister, and Hédi Jilani, a leading industrialist close to Carthage, had been mentioned. In 1990s Tunisia, stability was the watchword in public life. Given the state of the country's neighbours, it was in nobody's interest to rock the boat.

The economy

Tunisia has seen steady economic development and reconstructio since the damage created during the the country's brief, but destructive period (1941-42) as a setting for Allied-Axis conflicts during the Second World War. Since independence, development strategy has broadly speaking been constant, despite a flirtation with a form of state socialism in the 1960s. Changes in the economy are controlled by a series of five-year development plans. Major economic reforms were launched in 1986 in the form of the IMF-sponsored structural adjustment plan, and bore fruit in the 1990s.

Compared with other North African countries, Tunisia has a more diversified economy. Its modest oil resources have been an advantage in providing funding for non-oil development but have never been sufficient to encourage reliance on petroleum. There is, nevertheless, a certain vulnerability to external economic pressures including the vagaries of international trade, foreign aid flows, variation in tourist numbers and access to the EU for Tunisia's trade and labour. A youthful and fairly fast-growing population creates an added need for economic growth. The governments of the 1990s have worked hard to tackle these weak points in the Tunisian economy, to their credit with a great deal of success.

Farming until recently was the basis of the economy, and still employs 23 percent of **Agriculture** the labour force and produces about 18 percent by value of all national output. Chief crops are cereals, citrus fruit, olives, dates and grapes. Approximately 20 percent of the value of agricultural production comes from cereals. Olive oil is an important export accounting for four percent of the total but suffers heavy

Background

competition from Spain and Italy in the main European market. Fishing provides about six percent of the country's food supply with a catch of around 84,000 tonnes per annum. Esparto grass is collected to export for paper making and the cork oak forests of the north provide timber and cork.

Energy   Tunisia's oil industry by no means compares with that of Libya or Algeria, it produces only 0.2 percent of the world total. Production comes from the El Borma field in the south, the Sbeïtla field in the centre and the Itayem fields close to Sfax, all of which feed to a refinery and export complex at Skhira. The Ashtart field offshore in the Gulf of Gabès is also productive and recent discoveries have been made both offshore and in the Cap Bon areas. In the early 1990s, crude and products sales account for 10 percent of exports.

Gas has become important to the Tunisian economy. Miskar gas field in the Gulf of Gabès was brought on stream by British Gas in 1995 enabling Tunisia to export more oil and to use less Algerian gas. Elf Aquitaine has made considerable investments in developing the Ashtart field.

Phosphates   Phosphates were discovered in southwestern Tunisia in 1885. A mining concession was granted in 1896, and the *Gafsa Phosphates and Railway Company* set up in 1897. Exports began when the Metlaoui to Sfax railway was completed in 1897.

Today, the *Compagnie de phosphates de Gafsa* remains a large producer and exporter of phosphates with annual production running at around 5.5 million tonnes. Phosphate and its products of phosphoric acid and fertilizer provide about five percent of all exports. The vast majority of CPG production is sold on the national market for processing, much of it to the *Groupe chimique* which has developed plants to produce superphosphates and sulphuric acid.

Manufacturing   Tunisia has made remarkable steps in effective industrialization, most of it small scale and private sector. Manufacturing now accounts for 18 percent of the work force and 17 percent of national production. The main products, principally from the north are cement, flour, steel, textiles, and beverages. The textile industry is most remarkable with piece-goods being made up in Tunisia for re-export back to manufacturers in Western Europe. *Levis*, for example, sub-contracts extensively in the Monastir region, exporting finished goods back to its main European headquarters in Belgium. In recent years the textile trade has provided 30 percent of Tunisia's total export earnings. The long-established handicraft industry has benefited from tourism. Nabeul pottery, Kairouan carpets, decorative ironwork, leather goods, regional brass and hand-crafted textile wares all find a steady market.

Tourism   The tourist industry is a major employer and foreign exchange earner. Considerable investment in new hotels has come partially from abroad. The number of tourists rose from a mere 56,000 in 1961 to four million in 1995 and around the five million mark in 1999. These figures for foreign visitors include 2.5 million arrivals from Libya and Algeria, many visitors from the latter country coming in to buy consumer goods. Receipts from tourism are estimated annually at US$1,114 million.

The industry is developing from its traditional east coast strongholds (Hammamet, the Sahel) to the south where Djerba is proving a popular destination. Desert tourism has been encouraged with considerable subsidies to spread the benefits of the industry wider and change the conservative mentalities of the South. Tunisians are aware of the negative social effects of tourism and deal fairly and sensibly with foreigners so that the country retains a good name and many visitors return. Although 1991 was a difficult year for tourism because of the Gulf War, the market soon recovered, helped in part by troubles in former Yugoslavia, Turkey and Egypt. Tunisia is also now attracting tourists from a far wider spread of countries.

International norms do not really concern Tunisia's flourishing informal sector. This is the most difficult part of the economy to evaluate – despite its high visibility in everyday life. A multitude of people get by selling second hand clothes, magazines and fruit in the street, doing some gardening or working as domestic help – even the odd bit of tourist guiding or the so-called *commerce de la valise* (selling clothes and consumer goods from places like Morocco and Turkey.) In the big cities, the big weekly souks are thought to account for as much as 20 percent of consumer expenditure. Large quantities of manufactured goods are imported from East Asia and Europe via Libya, where they are highly subsidized.

The informal sector

This type of informal trade was helped by the United Nations embargo on Libya. Subsidized Libyan goods were made even cheaper by the black market trade in the weak Libyan currency. Although many families in southern Tunisia benefited enormously from the cross-border trade with Libya, major Tunisian business interests were not so convinced, especially when imported brands in the informal souks turned out to be cheaper than Tunisian manufactured goods. With the end of the embargo, the situation may change rapidly, however.

A number of Third World countries, which at the time of independence where at the same stage in their development as Tunisia, have now moved well ahead. In the early 1990s, awareness of this led the Tunisian government to adopt a wide ranging series of reforms touching on agriculture and industry, trade, investment and education.

Improving economic performance in the 1990s

As elsewhere, the basic reforms included a progressive reduction of import restrictions, convertibility of the dinar for current operations, and privatization. Despite the effects of the Gulf War, economic growth was steady in the early 1990s, reaching a high of 8.2 percent in 1992. GNP per inhabitant in 1990 was US$1,440, as compared with US$950 for Morocco. As Tunisian GNP approaches the threshold of US$1,500, multinationals are beginning to set up shop – Pepsi Cola arrived in 1995 with an advertising blitz, McDonalds may well follow.

In the decade 1985-1995, Tunisians saw a remarkable improvement in their living standards. The shops are full of consumer durables, the newspapers full of job advertisements, around 80 percent of Tunisians own their own homes. Basic foodstuffs continue to be subsidized, and rural development programmes are taking electricity and telephones to the remotest areas. The National Solidarity Fund (generally known as the 26-26 after its post office account number), closely supervised by the President, has done much for the poorest in society.

Now that Tunisia has signed the GAT, its industry is open to international competition. A 1995 study reported that as much as 60 percent of Tunisian industry could be seriously damaged by the liberalization of the economy. The cut and sew textile industry, heavily implanted in the Sahel region, could be particularly effected, as major investment is needed to renew capital equipment. Considerable financial resources will be necessary to extend infrastructure. The European Union has put large sums of money into Greece, and Germany has succeeded in mobilizing considerable funds for eastern Europe; the question is whether France and perhaps Spain will back a move to put more resources into the Maghreb.

Although efforts have been made to ease foreign investment – notably through the creation of a single investment code in 1994, Tunisian bureaucracy continues to have a damping effect. There is a lack of information, it is felt in some quarters. Historic prejudices about the region die hard in the western European mind, especially given Tunisia's geo-political location between Libya and strife-ridden Algeria. And the local market of eight million is small. Tunisia will have to improve its products to win market share in the European Union.

Product diversification was one of the main aims of government policy in the 1990s. The idea was to try to attract industries which would bring higher-added value, moving away from the idea of Tunisia as a country fit for relocation because of

☞ **Modern Tunisia: some key acronyms**

API Agence de promotion de l'industrie

BMV Bourse des valeurs mobilières. *Tunis stock exchange*

CEPEX Centre de promotion des exportations. *Export promotion centre*

CREDIF *Government sponsored research body working essentially on women's issues.*

FNS Fonds national de solidarité. *A national fund providing finance and backup for development projects in poor neighbourhoods and regions. Also known as the '26-26' (vingt-six vingt-six) after its post office account number.*

PSD Parti socialiste destourien. *The Destour Party's name as of 1964.*

RCD Rassemblement constitutionnel démocratique. *The name of the PSD from February 1988. The party has ruled Tunisia since independence.*

UGTT Union générale des travailleurs tunisiens. *Main Tunisian trade union.*

UMA Union du Maghreb Arabe. *Political organization founded to promote political and economic unity between North African states.*

UNFT Union nationale de la femme tunisienne. *Women's organization, offshoot of the ruling party.*

UTICA *The Tunisian Employers' Federation* (Union tunisienne de l'industrie, du commerce et de l'artisanat)

---

its cheap workforce. (In fact it is not cheap compared with Egypt and Morocco.) However, the educational standard of Tunisian workers is high and improving – and companies have relocated from Morocco for this reason. In the early 1990s, there were worries that German investors in particular would be drawn away to post-communist parts of Europe, despite satisfaction with business in Tunisia. In fact, this has proved not to be the case. Bizerte and Zarzis have developed *zones franches*, special economic development zones. Northern Tunisia has proved attractive for foreign manufacturers, and international companies present include Sara Lee at Mateur and Lee Cooper at Ras Jebel.

Still, on the plus side, the tax system has been overhauled and the stock exchange has come to life. Privatization is moving forward slowly and pragmatically. Although the state-run universities are increasingly crowded, a new generation of technical institutes now provides a more applied form of higher education. The basic Tunisian tourist product, the three-star hotel beach holiday, is as popular as ever, and major new investments are being made in marinas and golf courses.

Structural adjustment was the big issue from 1985 to 1990, while reform of investment legislation and related institutions followed in the early 1990s. In a third phase, industrial upgrading, the *mise-à-niveau*, to use the local jargon was the affair of the late 1990s. The idea behind this programme is that *infitah*, the opening up of Tunisian industry to external competition, and protectionism are totally incompatible. Thus by the end of 2007, Tunisia's companies must be sufficiently competitive to take on European competition in the open market. The five year *mise-à-niveau* programme, launched in 1995, provided for 2.4 billion dinars to be spent on upgrading the country's industrial fabric. Technical assistance centres were established, in-depth company audits undertaken, and quality programmes introduced. The World Bank loaned US$120 million for the *mise-à-niveau*, the EU contributed from a Mediterranean partnership fund.

Although the cost of economic transition will be high, the future for the Tunisian economy is promising on the whole. Tunisia has been fortunate in not being an oil-dependent economy – like Jordan, linked to the fortunes of the Gulf. The fact that Tunisia only had a brief flirtation with socialism at the end of the 1960s has made the whole privatization process much easier. In terms of Africa, Tunisia is number two after Mauritius in terms of jobs created by industries relocating from Europe and elsewhere. The question remains whether the recent changes will actually produce results, turning Tunisia into a fast growth economy, a 'Mediterranean dragon' to use a cliché much bandied about in the local press.

Contemporary society

In late 1990s Tunisia, institutions were being modernized, industry upgraded, the civil service reformed. Tunisian society is in a period of change – and it can be difficult for the Tunisian to explain to the outsider the factors, both historical and social, which have led the country where it is today.

In 1956, Tunisia already had literate educated Muslim men – and a few literate women. The overwhelming majority of Muslim Tunisians were illiterate, however. Independent Tunisia had to put a comprehensive education policy together. In the the enthusiastic, 1950s, the Sadiki College, Tunisia's leading school was the model. From the mid-19th century, this top Tunis secondary school had provided quality bilingual education in Arabic and French, and many of the post-independence élite had been schooled there. (The leaders of the Jewish community had been through the French system.) The Sadiki model proved difficult to generalize, and in the 1980s, the use of Arabic was extended to subjects previously taught in French. Pragmatically, however, scientific subjects were left in French – thus avoiding the disasters of the Moroccan educational system were the Arabization of all subjects led to parents pulling their children out of state schools and a huge growth in private sector education. Tunisia spends large sums on education, around seven percent of GNP, and seems set to continue to do so.

Education & language

The Tunisian school system divides into nine years basic education, followed by four years of general secondary or technical education leading to the baccalauréat. Pre-school education is split between traditional Koran school where the sacred texts are learned by rote, and modern private kindergartens. In 1999, the vast majority of school age children were in some form of education. Most girls under 15 are in school, an achievement of which Tunisia is particularly proud.

Under the education minister Mohammad Charfi, Tunisia's school system underwent extensive reforms in the early 1990s. School textbooks and the curriculum were redesigned. Images which showed women solely in subordinate positions were removed, civic instruction was introduced. Religious education, which had been based on a very conservative understanding of Islam, was reformed, and is now based on the principle of *ijtihad*, 'interpretation', i.e. modernist re-readings of the sacred texts. The history curriculum was reformed to reduce the emphasis on the Arabo-Islamic side of Tunisia's history. *Tunisianité*, 'Tunisianess' became important, with Carthage and Rome, Hannibal and St Augustine in the school history books along with Ibn Khaldoun and Kheireddine. The teaching style, which had often favoured rote learning rather than developing creative skills and a critical mind, was reformed. The language issue seems to have been resolved.

The curriculum is in Arabic, with French used for teaching scientific subjects in secondary school. English, German, Italian and Spanish are all available as foreign languages in secondary school. The Arabic used is modern standard Arabic, a version of the Arabic of the Koran modernized in lexical terms in the 19th century. This language differs considerably in grammar and vocabulary from the spoken language. Children with Tunisian Arabic as a mother tongue have to learn a new range of verb and adjectival forms, rather as if the English speaking child had to learn to use Old English verbs with modern English vocabulary. This is manageable, although given translation and terminology problems, there is a severe shortage of reading material in Arabic.

At university level, the vast majority of subjects are in French, bar family and criminal law and Arabic literature and some of the humanities. Parents with means

Background

put their children in bilingual primary schools with greater resources and more modern teaching methods. At secondary school level, the children with a bilingual background have much better chances of passing the more difficult science and mathematics baccalauréats. And after secondary school, public-sector technology colleges and numerous private institutes provide training in secretarial skills, IT, management and accounting, mainly in French.

It remains the case, however, that both standard *fusha* Arabic and French are effectively foreign languages for most Tunisian children going into primary school. No six year old speaks these languages as a mother tongue. Although a more extensive use of Tunisian Arabic in the education system was mooted in the late 1950s, standard Arabic looks set to maintain its place. As it stands, the education system serves the needs of both nation and economy. The language option reinforces a certain conception of the national identity, while ensuring that a steady stream of graduates, operational in French, and increasingly in other European languages, come on to the jobs market to satisfy the needs of finance, industry and technology.

The Media Since the early 1990s, the Tunisian news media have undergone some changes. Newspapers have been brightened up with new layouts, and a number of leisure magazines have appeared like women's magazine *Nuance*. Other magazines to look out for, if you read French, include the weeklies *Réalités* and *L'économiste maghrébin*. The French press, both newsmagazine and newspapers, sells in Tunisia, although not as well as a couple of decades ago. At over 1Dt, an imported newspaper is a luxury well above the means of most people. Tunisians are not great readers and the news and current affairs programmes now available on satellite television channels fill the need for information.

In terms of the audio-visual media, Tunisia has one and a half TV channels, the rather stodgy ERTT and a second channel, Canal 21, also broadcast by the national TV organization for a couple of hours in the evening on the same wavelength as France 2. Canal 21 aims at the youth market. There is a huge demand for quality television – hence the massive sales of satellite dishes in Tunisia, clear proof that the local television stations have a market waiting for them. The challenge is there for Tunisian TV professionals to produce a wider variety of programmes of real national and local interest. For the moment, satellite television, and pay-channels such as Canal Plus Horizons, seem set to expand their share of the market.

Music, entertainment & sport What sort of music do Tunisians listen to? Walking past a cassette stall, your ears will be assailed by unfamiliar tunes and voices. With technology for the mass-pirating of music so easily available now, Moroccan musical tastes have become increasingly catholic. Tapes are cheap too, between 1Dt 500 and 2Dt 500. Among young women, top selling cassettes are by Arab singers, like the Iraqi Kazem Essaher and Diana Haddad, whose videos are shown on satellite TV. Algerian raï music is popular too; top stars include Khaled, Mami, Cheb Zahouani, Cheb Hosni, Cheb Amro and Faudel. Local *mizoued* (bagpipe) music is in fashion in some quarters. Once upon a time, mizoued was considered vulgar, associated with a down-market atmosphere of boozy wedding parties ending in late night brawls. (The worst mizoued has the same spine-searing quality as a chainsaw heard at a distance.) Today, in a big turn around, leading mizoued stars like Faouzi Ben Gamra and Hédi Habouba get on national television. Still at the downmarket end of the musical spectrum, musical kitsch reaches new heights with trash diva Fatma Bousaha.

The 'politically committed' sound of the leading 1970s and 1980s Moroccan groups like Jil Jilala, Nass el Ghiwane or Lmachaheb or the Lebanese Marcel Khalifa still has some fans. Western music is popular too, and not only with the urban middle classes. Adolescents and students go for Bob Marley and Dr Alban, Madonna and The Spice Girls, 2 Be 3 and other boys' bands. 'Romantic' singers like Quebec's

Special couscous

The end of the Hijra or Muslim year, Ra's el 'Am el Hijri, comes about 20 days after Aïd el Kebir, the main annual Muslim festival. Ra's el 'Am commemorates the Prophet Mohamed's departure from Mecca, where he was persecuted by the leaders of the tribe of Qureysh, for Médina, where he was to lay the basis for the new Muslim community. This anniversary is celebrated by Tunisian families in an almost ritual manner with a favourite dish, kuskusi bil-qadeed, couscous prepared with lamb dried and salted after the Aïd, and beans.

Traditionally, the right shoulder of the sacrificial lamb is not cut up. It is spiced with harissa, black pepper and garlic, then left out in the sun to dry. Then it is boiled well in olive oil, and placed in oil, in a large terra cotta jar or khabia. According to a religious tradition, the sacrificial lamb is to be divided into three parts, one to be eaten, one to be preserved, and one to be given to the poor. Another tradition runs that the destiny of the Muslim pater familias is inscribed on the shoulder bone of the sacrificial lamb. Thus it would be unfortunate if this bone were broken, as it would harm this future.

Times have changed, of course, and not all families actually prepare qadeed today. Nevertheless, many Tunisian families will bring the Muslim new year in with kuskusi bil-qadeed, along with rich green muloukhia, (a sort of stew) to ensure that the coming year will be prosperous, and a fish dish, to bring good luck. In Tunisia, as in many Mediterranean countries, fish (hout) wards off the evil eye, so it is a good idea to yuhawit (prepare fish) on important occasions.

Céline Dion and Witney Houston (whose songs also exist in Arabic cover versions) also have a big following in Tunisia.

There is of course a more classical taste in music. Tunisian traditional urban music is called *malouf*. During Ramadhan, Tunisian television broadcasts music by the malouf choirs. Maybe the violons and lutes, and mix of solo and choral singing aids the digestion. Also in a traditional vein, singers of the 1950s and 1960s have found new popularity, thanks to their wide availability on disc. Look out for in particular for HH Hédi Jouini, Saliha and Oulaya. In this tradition, contemporary individual singers such as Lotfi Bouchnak, Sofia Sadok and Amina Fakhet have great popularity. Their concerts at the Menzah Coupole (sports dome) or the Carthage amphitheatre draw audiences of thousands – and they can command huge fees for singing at upscale weddings. Amina Fakhet has a huge following – perhaps because people identify with her rags-to-riches tale and her frankness. At the arty end of the scale, lutist Anouar Braham has won international recognition with his contemplative jazz – Arab crossover style.

Also still popular in Tunisia – as elsewhere in the Arab world – are the great Egyptian and Syro-Lebanese singers who had their heyday in the 1950s and 1960s. Um Kalthoum, peasant girl from the Nile Delta who became diva of the Arab world is popular everywhere. Her songs have probably done more for promoting classical Arabic poetry than any school book. Other great names you may want to look out for from this period include Druze princess Asmahane, Mohammad Abdewahab, Farid El Atrach, the Lebanese divas Fayrouz and Sabah, Najet Es Saghira and the brown nightingale, Abdel Halim Hafez, who died tragically young of bilharzia.

Concerts by singers and musicians, both Tunisian and Middle Eastern are regularly broadcast by the ERTT. Television is the most widely available form of entertainment, much watched at both home and in cafés. The long running South American soap operas, dubbed into classical Arabic, are popular, as are Egyptian soaps and films. The annual Tunisian Ramadhan soap operas have a loyal following. And of course sport is popular viewing among men, especially in cafés with Canal Plus Horizons. International football competitions are the big draw. Tunisia has volleyball and handball teams which have been very successful in African and Arab competitions.

Background

But football remains the number one spectator sport. At age six or seven, the little lads are out in the street or on a piece of rough ground, kicking a football around. Their heroes are teams like Tunis rivals Espérance and Club Africain, and players like Ronaldo and Zinedine Zidane, captain of the French team which won the 1998 Mondial. Tunisia had high hopes of its national team, which didn't however make the second round. Football, as in the other North African countries, is a great unifiying factor. If local politics is dull, then football gives people – or rather men – something to debate. The deeds and doings of football stars can be read about in detail in the local press.

Dress & fashion: from chéchias to Nike

In old Tunisia, city men and women covered their heads when they went out, the latter with a *sefsari*, an ample sheet-like wrap (in cream coloured silk in Tunis), the former with a turban. However, to wrap a few metres of fabric on top of your head, you need a base, and this was provided by a wool felt cap, generally red, called the *chéchia*, the production of which was a whole craft industry in Tunis in the 17th and 18th centuries.

A symbol of national resistance in the Thirties and Forties (and part of postmen's uniform), the *chéchia* today is really only worn by older men. Arab specialist Jacques Berque, writing in the late Fifties, observed the end of traditional dress in his work *French North Africa*: "Head and loins resist longest: floating tunics, wide trousers and turbans persist". European-style shoes had become acceptable for "there was never any quarrel about shoes, whereas traditionalists long continued to consider narrow trousers obscene and hats or caps an outrage against religion". Today's Tunisian youth prefers the baseball cap, whereas sefsari wearing is limited to older or less-educated women – for younger women it is considered a *cache misère*, or just practical for nipping out to the corner shop if you can't be bothered to dress properly.

Tunisian traditional dress was a mixture of influences. The city gent would wear lose-fitting pantaloons or *serwel*, a tightfitting *sedria* or shirt and *fermela* waistcoats. Over this would be worn a lose fitting sleeveless tunic or *jebba*, woollen for winter, linen or raw silk for summer. (When the modern shirt appeared in the 19th century, it was called a *souriya*, a Syrian garment, as it was first introduced by Levantine merchants and dragomans.)

As in other cultures, dress had a high symbolic charge. Imams of the two main Muslim communities of Tunisia, the austere majority Malekites and the more aristocratic Hanefites could be distinguished by their turbans. At certain periods in North Africa, the Jews were required to adopt the *ghiar* (distinctive dress): in Tunis this was colour-based – light blue clothing with a black chéchia. However, after the abolition of the ghiar with the 1859 Fundamental Pact, the Jews were quick to adopt European dress. In the late 19th century, young reform minded Muslim Tunisians adopted the *chéchia mejidi*, the taller 'fez' type headgear popularized by the Young Turks.

In the 1990s Tunisia acquired an annual traditional dress day. Civil servants and ministers appear in full rig, and local TV runs features on tailors and weavers. However, as with other things, this new interest in tradition is a sign of change in society – change that it may be difficult to acknowledge. Any form of fundamentalist type dress is highly frowned upon, and if they have the means, today's young Tunisians want to wear Nike sweats and trainers, (real and imitation), and the latest MTV fashions.

Daily life

Tunisia's population is moving towards a 75 percent/25 percent urban rural divide. The land no longer provides the living it used to, expectations are higher, parents want their children to have some chance of an education – and this is most easily available in the towns. In the country life is often hard, with women obliged to carry water, firewood and animal fodder over long distances. But even this is changing, as rural development projects, often sponsored by the Fonds national de solidarité,

The musical baron

One of the most extraordinary sights in Tunisia is the Dar Nejma Ezzahra, an orientalist fantasy palace at Sidi Bou Saïd. The story of this building is inextricably linked with the life and enthusiasms of one Rodolphe d'Erlanger, musicologist and gifted amateur artist. The first d'Erlanger to rise to prominence was a French banker of German origin, born in Frankfurt in 1832. Emile d'Erlanger settled in Paris in 1858. Business boomed in the prosperous atmosphere of Napoleon III's Paris, and Emile was soon to acquire a Second Empire noble title. Married to an American, the first baron had four sons, including the Baron Frédéric, born 1868, a composer who was to build a career in London, and the Baron Rodolphe, born 1872, of Sidi Bou Saïd fame.

Rodolphe d'Erlanger studied in Paris and London. He showed an aptitude for painting, exhibiting in Paris at the 1903 Salon des artistes français. A further major exhibition followed in London in 1908. A number of his works can be viewed at the Dar Nejma Ezzahra today. But it is as a scholar of Arab music that the baron is chiefly remembered. Between 1930 and 1959, his six volume La musique arabe, ses règles, leur histoire was published by Paul Geuthner in Paris. In 1931, King Fouad of Egypt named the baron president of the organizing committee of the first congress of Arab music, held in Cairo in the spring of 1932. Unfortunately, the baron was to ill to attend, and died shortly after on 23 April 1932.

The love of Rodolphe d'Erlanger's life was his wife Elisabeth, Bettina to the family, daughter of an Italian aristocrat and an American wife. It was during a visit to Tunisia that they acquired the cliff-top site on which they were to build their orientalist dream palace. (The Erlanger banking house had had important interests in Tunisia since the mid-19th century, making large loans to Sadok Bey's government in the 1860s).

Rodolphe and Bettina had a son, Léo, (died 1978), whose wife English wife, Edwina, was the last d'Erlanger to inhabit Dar Nejma Ezzahra, maintaining grounds and interior as her father-in-law would have wished. When the palace eventually passed into the hands of the Tunisian state, it was as the Centre for Arab and Mediterranean Music. Concerts are regularly held in the patio, and a specially designed display room houses the baron's collection of Tunisian musical instruments.

bring electricity to isolated *dachras*. Improved roads follow, then drinking water.

In the cities, life has improved for the inhabitants of the self-build housing areas, the *quartiers spontanés* of city planning jargon. Essential infrastructure is being put in, the streets no longer fill with water when it rains. As the formal economy prospers, the city centres and tourist zones offer many employment opportunities for the low-qualified. There are plenty of people with money to buy from a street stall selling cigarettes, chewing-gum or fruit, there is work on building sites and in factories. And there is a chance of better housing, as government projects 'restructure' areas of crude concrete housing, bringing in water and electricity.

For the middle classes, opportunities have never been better, even though recruitment into government service has been cut back. There are, however, jobs in multinational companies, the banking sector and the new service economy. Tunisia's cities have a prosperous air. The tree-lined down-town streets, though increasingly traffic ridden, are lined with shops with smart clothes and consumer durables. For those with salaries, there are car and home loans. Domestic help is available for two career families, there is a enormous range of consumer goods on offer, although often at European prices. For the bright and energetic, the prospects are good – although good connections and inherited family wealth do help.

Background

Prospects and ambitions

Tunisia has changed enormously since independence. The time when it was a picturesque French protectorate with a Ruritanian monarchy and an interesting ethnic-jigsaw population seems an age ago. Reforms in the late 1950s and early 1960s launched Tunisia in a direction on which there seems to be no going back. Clear symbols of national unanimity – religion, social solidarity – have been established. The government is only too aware of the divides which could arise if socio-economic divisions became too pronounced, and throughout the 1990s, adopted a gradualist approach to introducing the market economy, an approach which has been vindicated with time. Tunisia has some enormous advantages over its North African neighbours. It is a small country where consensus is carefully constructed. Unlike Algeria and Morocco, it does not have a complex set of geographic and linguistic identities waiting to surface. The military are not a force ever likely to enter the political scene, the ground has been cut away from under political, revivalist Islam.

In terms of the economy, Tunisia has put its house in order. The rather adventurous financial policies of the 1970s are a thing of the past, and the budget deficit is minimal. Today growth, with an average of around five percent during the 1990s, is well above the birth rate. Of course, there are still challenges. The tourist industry is striving to move upmarket, not an easy task in a highly competitive global industry. There are still large numbers of graduates in need of employment. The privatization process continues discretely – but how will local Tunisian companies fare when tarif barriers are fully removed? Will the arrival of multi-national companies compensate for an eventual loss of jobs in local firms?

Things have moved forward hugely since the 1970s, and on the whole, the situation at the end of the 1990s was a positive one. Tunisia, with little oil resources, benefits from any fall in the price of oil, and its proximity to Europe and an expanding internal market make it an ideal base for relocating manufacturing industry. (Probably no other Arab country has made such efforts to attract foreign investment as Tunisia.) Education has been modernized, and is increasingly adapted to the needs of the job market. Poverty has been pushed back extremely effectively. The question over the first decade of the 21st century will be how to continue the fight against social inequality – and so avoid any risk of Algerian-type fundamentalist destabilization and strife. In the event, the immediate geo-political situation is improving: Algeria under President Bouteflika seems to be heading for national reconciliation, Libya, now free of the damaging embargo, will no doubt head for more stable forms of development.

Modern Tunisia, helped by compact size and a mono-ethnic population, displays a degree of internal stability and consensus rare in the Arab world. This is definitely a factor which has allowed much to be achieved. The country has been touted by some has 'the new Switzerland' of the Arab world, taking over where the Lebanon of the 1960s and 1970s left off. But Tunisia is not in the Middle East, and has more pragmatic amibitions. With the current government's emphasis on social policy and opening up to the outside world, maybe 'the Arab Denmark' or 'the North African Portugal' are more appropriate comparisons. Will the European Union provide appropriate support to help Tunisia maintain social cohesion? Speculating further, will the country eventually request membership of the European Union, as Morocco has done in the past? Will it become the lead country working for the creation of a North African common market? Time will tell.

Western Libya

11

Western Libya

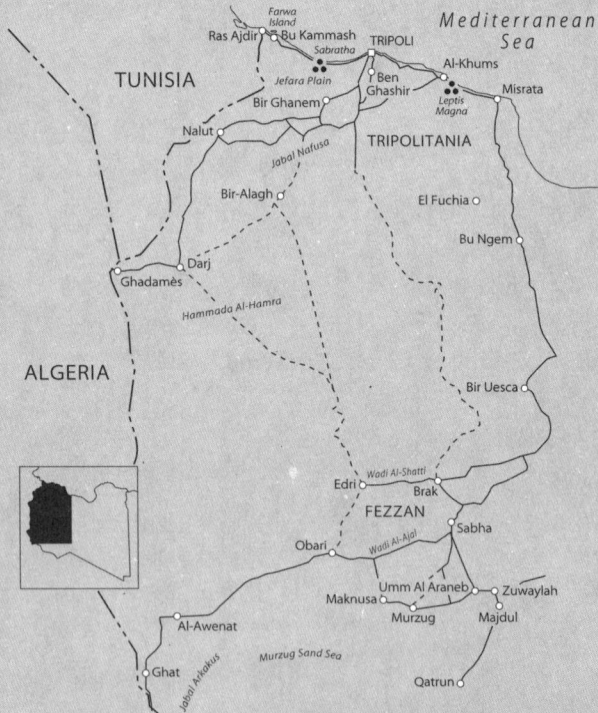

Essentials

Planning your trip

Where to go

With the UN embargo on international flights, getting into Libya was not always easy in the 1990s. This situation is changing. A number of UK-based and French travel companies now offer circuits in western Libya, and this remains the easiest way to go. There are also a number of Tripoli-based tour companies which can set up four wheel drive circuits in the Libyan South. Travelling under your own steam by public transport is also possible, but slower, as buses and service taxis do not always go to isolated tourist sites.

Western Libya has much to offer the traveller. A short trip would enable you to take in coastal Tripolitania, visiting Tripoli, with its old médina and Italian-planned new town, and 2 fine Roman sites, Sabratha, halfway between Tripoli and the Tunisian frontier, and Leptis Magna, near Khums about 90 minutes' drive east of Tripoli. Along with Oea, ancestor of modern Tripoli, these were the 3 cities (tri-polis) of the region in ancient times. Those with an interest in things Berber will want to go up into the Jabal Nafusa, south of Tripoli. Here there are the once isolated citadel villages at Sharwas and Wighu and fortified granaries at Nalut. Beyond the Jabal Nafusa, hard by the Tunisian frontier, is the tiny oasis settlement of Ghadamès. Finally, the southwestern quarter of Libya is covered by the vast desert province of the Fezzan. Until recently, oasis farming and herding livestock to seasonal pasture was the way of life here. Heading southwest from the region's main city, Sabha, the visitor will want to see the lakes in the Obari sand sea, and the prehistoric rock paintings of the Jabal Akakus. Some desert camping would be a fine experience, if time allows.

In terms of **time**, 5 days would be ample to get a feel for Tripoli and cover the 2 main Roman sites. A 10-day trip would enable you to do these coastal sites, and get down to the Akakus, visiting the Berber sites in southern Tripolitania on route.

Note that **distances** in Libya are great: Tripoli to Ghadamès is around 650 km, Tripoli to Sirte 500 km, and if you are thinking of doing Cyrenaica, Sirte to Benghazi is another 500 km. It is clear then that the UN-imposed embargo on air transport hit Libya hard, so for the moment, a long drive south (basically, a day each way) across the Sahara is inevitable to reach the Fezzan. This situation will undoubtedly change as Libyan Arab Airlines updates its fleet and obtains spare parts for its planes.

When to go

The best times to go are spring and autumn, especially if you intend to head down into the Sahara. The summer is extremely hot, reducing energy levels for visiting remote desert sites and Berber settlements. The problem with winter is that the desert gets very cold and the days are shorter. However, a winter trip to the Roman sites would be fine, and the climate on the Tripolitanian coast is perfect in November-January.

What to take

Broadly speaking, the list of must-takes is the same as for Tunisia (see page 20). However, note that if you are going to bivouac out in the desert outside summer, a good warm sleeping bag is essential. The penetrating cold of the desert at night is a well-known phenomenon, so bring layers of clothing and your warm undergarments.

Tours & tour operators

A number of **Tripoli-based tour operators** offer excursions down into the desert. *Libyan Tourism Treasures*, 25 Shari'a Istanbul, Tripoli, T021-4449199, F021-3339486 (postal address POB 5144 Tripoli) has had good reports from visitors. Other recommended agencies include the *Libyan Arab Tourist Co* on Mizran St, (contact Salem Azzabi), T021-4448005, and *Libya Tours Co*, based in the Libya Palace Hotel, T021-3331189, F021-3336688, (contact Mme Hafida, English and French spoken). For travel in the Fezzan, try *Akakus Tours*, T0274-2804/2318, also T0274-2938, who set up

Libya

desert circuits for fit (and fairly wealthy) travellers taking in the remote rock-art sites of the southwestern regions.

Of the **UK-based travel companies**, *Exodus* and *British Museum Tours* run excursions to Libya in spring and autumn, taking in desert and Roman sites. The price of these tours is often high, with a 14-day circuit priced at around £1500. Others include: *Arab Tours Ltd*, 60 Marylebone Lane, London W1M 5FF, T0171-9353273, F0171-4864237; *British Museum Traveller*, 46 Bloomsbury St, London WC1B 3QQ; *Exodus Tours*, 9 Weir Rd, London SW12 0LT, T0181-6755550 (sales and reservations), T0181-6730859 (brochures and factsheets), sales@exodustravels.co.uk *Prospect Music and Art Tours*, 454-458 Chiswick High Rd, London, SW4 5TT, T0181-9952151, F0181-7421969.

Before you travel

Visas Until the late 1990s, visa allocation was closely controlled and mainly confined to those with bona fide jobs in the country. Circumstances have relaxed and **except** for US or UK citizens obtaining a visa creates few problems. For a UK passport holder an invitation from a Libyan official agency or individual will help in the granting of a visa. Note that it is still illegal for US citizens to go to Libya. (Americans who have Libyan stamps in their passport may have to 'lose' passport and obtain a replacement before returning to the US). Generally speaking, however, there is a gradual relaxation of visa controls as tourism grows, very slowly, in importance for economic reasons.

Entry requirements Travellers to Libya need a visa, normally issued at the Libyan people's bureau, embassy or consulate overseas. These cost around US$50 (45DM + 16DM translation fee for German passport holders; £20 for UK nationals), valid for 3 months, must be used within 45 days of issue. Applications with a translation of passport details in Arabic, should be given 10 to 14 days in advance of travel since it is usual for the Libyan authorities overseas to check details with Tripoli before a visa is issued. UK nationals could also try *Allied Tickets and Visas*, 227 Chapel House, 24 Nutford Place, London, W1 5YN, T0171-7243309, T/F01705-785388. (Run by Mr Mustapha Bughrara, who can arrange for the invitation telex to the Libyan People's Bureau in London.) It is theoretically possible to get a visa at the port of entry, though this carries risks of long delays or capricious acts by border officials. Those with passports from Arab countries normally do not require visas – although this is an area subject to change. Note that you must (normally) obtain your visa in your country of residence. Those not resident in Tunisia cannot in general obtain visas there, although here again, regulations may change.

Non-Arabic passports must be stamped with an official Arabic translation of the personal details of the individual's passport. In the UK the Passport Office 7-78 Petty France, London SW1, 0171-2793434 will do this as a matter of routine on presentation of the passport. (Go to the 'agency' window inside on your right, downstairs). The Libyan embassy in Malta also provides visa and Arabic translation.

For extensions beyond the normal visa period, the immigration police should be informed and the fact noted in the passport. Tourists may extend the visa by 1 month, twice, at 5LD each time. On arrival in Tripoli, you need to register at the immigration building in Gazelle Park.

Customs Duty free goods are available at the main airport departure lounge at Tripoli airport, purchasable in foreign currencies only. A range of cigarettes, cigars, perfumes, watches and travel goods can be found – but no alcohol. No other tourist facilities of this kind are available and offers elsewhere of duty free goods should be avoided as not worth the hassle.

Libya has a stringent ban on the import of alcohol of any kind. It is a pointless risk **Import-export** taking in beer, spirits, or indeed drugs. Severe penalties can be imposed and at the very **bans** least passengers can be incarcerated pending deportation. It is rather easier to carry books and newspapers into the country than formerly, though sensitivities remain and it is best not to carry literature which might be misunderstood or thought to be anti-Libyan. Firearms cannot be imported without special permission. Radio transmitters and electronic means of printing will attract official attention and should clearly be for personal use only.

On leaving Libya make sure that you have no antiquities. The Libyan authorities take unkindly to the illegal export of bits of their ancient monuments and penalties for infringement can be ferocious.

Immigration and sometimes currency declaration forms are needed on arrival. The **Registration** forms themselves are in Arabic but English translations are available from the airlines. **on arrival** Only the Arabic question form should be filled in with answers in English or French. Copies of the forms should be carefully retained since they will be requested on exit. Normally hotels register guests on arrival. Insist they do. The fee is 5LD. If visitors are not staying in an official hotel, they should register themselves with the police otherwise they can be stopped and held. Worse, they can be delayed on departure, even missing flights if officials are convinced that malpractice rather than ignorance is the cause of the problem.

There is no departure tax at land borders. Embarkation cards will be filled in with the **Departure** help of attendants. There is also sometimes a currency control. Only small amounts of **by land** Libyan currency may be exported, preferably less than 10LD. Any excess Libyan dinars should be changed back into hard currency.

The departure tax on leaving Libya by air was 3LD. Only Libyan currency is accepted. At **Departure** Tripoli airport, from which the majority of flights leave Libya, there is a special counter **airport tax** for buying the exit stamp before passing through to the passport and customs formalities. Without a stamp you will be sent back to start the entire process again.

For those travellers not already equipped with travel or other insurance, there are **Insurance** facilities available in Libya directly through the *Libyan Insurance Co* or the *Libya Travel and Tourist Co* shop in Tripoli, T021-3336222.

Money

The Libyan dinar is the standard currency which is divided into 1,000 dirhams. Notes in **Currency** circulation are 10LD, 5LD, 1LD, 0.50LD, 0.25LD; coins 0.10LD, and 0.05LD. (Coins are in very short supply). There are **banks** at Tripoli airport. Principal banks will exchange travellers cheques and currency notes at the official rate of exchange. There is also a black market in foreign currency in which a very variable rate is available but best rates are reported inside Libya itself, and even bank officials will recommend changing money on the street. Coming in from Tunisia, you can generally change money at Ben Gardane, the last major town before the border at Ras Ajdir.

In late 1999, the official **exchange rate** was around US$0.25 to the Libyan dinar. On the black market, the exchange rate ranged between 3.5 and 4LD to the US$.

The Libyan dinar is only convertible at the official rate inside Libya by official institutions. Travellers may have to fill in a currency form on arrival (cash and travellers cheques) and present it together with official exchange receipts on departure. The system is not watertight nor fully implemented but is perhaps best observed. Keep receipts from the banks. Make sure that you do not leave the country with either more than a few Libyan dinars or more foreign currency than you arrived with.

Exchange rates (9 November, 1999)

	US$	£	Ffr	DM	Ptas
Libyan Dinar (1LD)	0.25	0.15	1.59	0.47	40.34

Credit cards Cards can be used only in a small number of big hotels and in some of the larger travel agents. Cash is the normal medium of exchange and most shops are not equipped to handle credit cards of any kind. Credit cards at hotels are best if not of US origin, though generics such as Visa and Mastercard are normally suitable. Relying on cash is safest.

Cost of living Libya is an oil economy and it mainly imports its necessities from abroad. Prices tend to be high reflecting this external reliance, some inefficiency in the distribution system and the high level of mark-up by the merchants. Specialist western foods and commodities like Libyan mutton are very expensive. Eating out is also far from cheap if you have exchanged currency at the official rate. Otherwise fresh vegetables and fruit are moderately priced. Pharmaceuticals, medical goods and imported high-tech items can be expensive. Personal services from plumbers to dry cleaners are expensive. Travel is comparatively cheap by air as well as land but hotels are few and the even fewer good quality hotels are very expensive. These costs are offset, however, by the generosity of the Libyans in rural areas in finding accommodation for visitors in public buildings. If you exchange money on the black market, costs are not excessive.

Getting there

Until mid-1999, travellers bypassed the UN air embargo on Libya by flying to Malta or Tunisia and continuing their journeys by land, using buses or shared taxis or by sea on the regular ferry run from Malta. Heavy traffic at the Tuniso-Libyan border meant long waits, and boat from Malta was the best way to get to Tripoli. Shortly after the ending of the embargo, direct flights from certain European destinations were resumed.

Air *Libyan Arab Airlines (LAA)* is the main carrier. The embargo on the transfer of arms and strategic materials to Libya by the USA for its alleged involvement in state terrorism in the early 1980s led to a huge depletion of the LAA fleet, which is ageing and inefficient. (The company looks set to purchase a large number of new aircraft). In April 1992, the UN Security Council introduced a ban on air traffic to Libya as part of a campaign to bring to book alleged perpetrators of the Lockerbie air disaster of 1988.

In normal circumstances flights to Tripoli via LAA or other regular scheduled services from Europe arrive from Amsterdam, Athens, Belgrade, Brussels, Budapest, Frankfurt, Larnaca, Madrid, Malta, Moscow, Paris, Prague, Rome, Sofia, Vienna, Warsaw and Zurich. Most of the above are only on a 1 day a week basis. *Alitalia*, *Lufthansa*, *Air Malta* and *Swissair* were among the most frequent carriers to Libya. *British Airways* now fly 3 services a week to Tripoli from Gatwick (Tuesday, Thursday and Saturday) – there are no direct flights from the USA or Canada at the moment. Flights from African points of origin include Accra, Alexandria, Algiers, Cairo, Casablanca, Khartoum, Ndjamena, Niamey, Nouakchott and Tunis. Most Middle Eastern airlines had flights to Tripoli with the main scheduled flights from Amman, Damascus, Dubai, Istanbul and Jeddah.

In normal conditions, foreign visitors by air are advised to have reserved firm flights for departure since it is not always easy to get return flights booked inside Libya. The fare structure for flights used to be extremely polarized. *Swissair*, for example, runs business class only flights to Libya. *LAA* is also expensive and not easy to get discounts for. Cheapest flights were with *Air Malta*.

Libya

Libya's railways were gradually dismantled after the Second World War and there are **Train**
no services within Libya. You can however get a train for Tunis as far south as Gabès,
and then continue by bus or shared taxi to the Libyan frontier 188 km distant.

Buses These run from Tunis and all major eastern coast towns in Tunisia to the Libyan **Road**
frontiers. Passengers should cross the frontier on foot and then take advantage of
Libyan domestic bus services. Once in Libya, there are 2 main bus transport
companies, 1 engaged principally in long distance international services and the
other plying between Libyan cities and towns.

When leaving Libya the traveller can use the *Libyan International Bus Co*, which
has an office behind the Tripoli médina off Shari'a Omar Mukhtar to the west of the old
citadel, in an area now being cleared of buildings and reconstructed. Buses tend to
leave Tripoli very early in the morning, not later than 0800. Passengers should be at the
bus station by at least 0700. While the air embargo was in force, buses tended to fill up
quickly and leave as soon as all seats are taken.

Taxis Both local and international transport is as much in the hands of taxi drivers as
the bus companies. In Tripoli, the taxis leave from large stands between Shari'a Omar
Mukhtar and the sea. They ply for hire normally on a shared basis but can be had for an
individual or private group with suitable haggling over the price. On a shared basis
they are normally cheaper than the luxury buses and far more frequent in their
departures. Driving standards are variable among taxi drivers and passengers need
good nerves. Travellers entering via land borders are advised that taking a shared taxi
is easier and quicker than waiting for the bus. Take a shared taxi to the nearest town
(Zuwarah) and then take the bus from there in more comfortable conditions.

Taxis to Djerba (Tunisia) leave from Shari'a Al-Rashid near the bus station and cost
25-40LD depending on number of passengers (takes 4-5 hours, depending on border
controls). Tripoli to Tunis costs 75LD.

The overnight ferry from Valetta in Malta uses modern vessels, usually the *MV Garnata* **Shipping**
of 3,672 dwt, with other passenger vessels, the *MV Toletela* of 3,671 dwt and the *MV* **services**
Garyounis of 3,423 dwt. Sailing times change monthly and travellers should check
with the *General National Maritime Transport Co*, Shari'a Al-Baladiya, T021-3334865
or via Seamalta in Malta on T00356-25994212, Tx12101321. Currently boat departs
1900 from Valletta and costs US$200 1-way, or 1800 from Tripoli in front of *Hotel
Al-Mehari* costs 63LD 1-way, 102LD return. Journey takes 12 hours. There are agents for
GNMTC in Tunisia, Morocco, Turkey, Italy, Germany, Belgium and Holland.

Touching down

Direct flights to Tripoli from abroad resumed in 1999. The main airport is at **Ben** **Airport**
Ghashir/Suani Ben Yadim, some 24 km from the centre of Tripoli, but some planes **information**
come into the smaller local airport just 4 km from the city, near the beach. A bus
service is available to/from the main hotels and the bus station. Service taxis are also
on hand for the run into the city, and are probably a better, if more expensive option if
you have a lot of luggage.

In pre-embargo days, there were internal flights to **Ghadamès** (75 minutes) and
Sabha (75 minutes), **Benghazi** (1 hour) and **Tobrouk** (1 hour 45 minutes). These will
no doubt resume in the near future as LAA acquires spare parts and new planes.

Libya is only now awakening to the potential of tourism. (A ministry of tourism was set **Tourist**
up in 1995). Facilities are few and far between. Local tourist offices exist but are **information**
generally understaffed and ill-informed. They rarely have useful information, maps or
guides. At present the best sources of help and information are the new private travel

Libya

☞ *Touching down*

Hours of business *Working hours vary from summer 0700-1400 to winter 0800-1300 and 1600-1830 in private offices. Official agencies run on a basic day of 0800-1400, though it is always better to start communications before 0900 since they get busy. Shops open from* approximately 0900-1400 and 1630-2030.

Weights and measures *metric.*

Voltage *Electricity services use a standard 240V system. International adaptor plugs useful – socket sizes vary.*

Official time *GMT +1*

agencies springing up across the country. They have enterprise and initiative and understand the needs of foreign travellers. In Tripoli contact the **Libyan Travel and Tourist Co** T021-3336222 which has an office on Shari'a Mizran close by the LAA head office. Other area offices are mentioned in the regional sections within the Handbook.

Be warned that while private travel agencies can provide some information and perhaps transport some may imply that without the 'official' guides' which only they can provide, there may be problems with the police. Certainly this is not true.

Rules, customs & some practicalities

Dress Basically, western visitors to Libya should not offend Muslim sentiment by wearing scanty clothing in towns and villages. In any case, outside the main hotels or private transport the need is to be sheltered from the sun, the sand and the glare. Remember that the sun is extremely strong in summer, so cover up to prevent sunstroke and sunburn. (Libya is the country with the world's highest recorded temperature). It is also a good idea to wear clothes that enable you to keep your key documents on your person.

Tipping Tipping is not widespread in Libya and is only expected by those giving personal services in hotels, cafés and restaurants. The normal rate is 10%. For small services in hotels use quarter and half dinar notes. At the airport only use porters if you are heavily weighed down with luggage then tip at half a dinar per heavy bag. Taxi drivers should, unless there is actually a working meter and then perhaps in any case, give a price before starting the journey. Tips for Libyan drivers are not the rule but will be accepted. Foreign drivers in Libyan employ tend to be more demanding of tips. Do not get drawn into bribing officials at any level since it is a sure way of bringing increasing difficulties and possibly severe delays.

Photography The large sand deserts, arid rock formations and fine ruins of classical antiquity make photography in the excellent light conditions of Libya a great pleasure. Do not photograph military installations, and take care in photographing women: preferably if male do not photograph women at all. The camera still carries the feeling of intrusion and/or the evil eye in some areas. Film is generally available for 35mm cameras and most other types of film can also be found in Tripoli. Kodak and Fuji brands are readily available in the capital. Check the 'sell by date'. For specialist and video film try to bring reserves from outside. Beyond Tripoli and Benghazi film supplies cannot be guaranteed. If using a video camera, note that filming at certain ancient sites is prohibited.

Religion Sunni Islam is the dominant religion in Libya, although there are Ibadite Berbers in some of the western rural areas. Mosques are generally off limits to the non-Muslim. They are places of prayer, and those who are clearly not of the faith will be intruding if they try to slip in.

Libya

Basically, there is no real security problem in Libya, although travellers report **Safety** occasional rumours of isolated violence and there are reports that there is a growing drug use problem. The odd brawl causes more noise than damage and walking through the streets is generally safer than in Europe. After dark, and indeed at all times everywhere, foreign nationals in Libya are advised to carry their passports. Libyans are used to foreigners in their midst but their visitors are almost exclusively male. Foreign women need, therefore, to dress sensibly and 'act with suitable decorum', especially in Tripoli, to avoid arousing undue interest.

A woman travelling alone in Libya must appreciate that this is a totally segregated **Women** society, women sit apart and eat apart or after the men. On long distance buses the **travelling alone** driver will organize space for the women. As no-one is prepared to speak to women, it can be very lonely. The biggest problem is getting a room in a hotel without a male companion. The bus driver may feel obliged to introduce you to the hotel receptionist thereby giving some respectability, otherwise only the expensive hotels will accept women alone: take this into account when budgeting for a trip. One advantage of a woman being of no significance is the lack of problems at check points and, compared with Egypt, the lack of hassle. Travelling alone in Libya by experienced female travellers can be recommended with the proviso that eventually the sheer masculinity of society and the feeling of isolation caused by the lack of communication makes leaving a welcome relief.

A **special warning** is necessary to travellers tempted to travel to the Tibesti in the **Warning:** southern Fezzan. This zone, close to the Aouzou strip, was a war zone until recently. If **travelling in the** travelling off the road in Aouzou, you risk offending the Libyan security officials – **Tibesti region,** which is fair enough, given the recent conflict. Travel in this area should only be with **Fezzan** official knowledge. Any abandoned or scattered armament or ammunition should not be touched. Consult with Tripoli or Sabha-based travel companies on the possibilities of travel in this remote region.

Where to stay

Libya is thinly provided with hotels, even in the populated northern coastal area. This is **Hotels** mainly a result of years of state control when tourism was discouraged. The slow *Libyan hotel price codes:* re-establishment of the private sector is making for a revival in the hotel trade at the **A** *Over 99LD a night* bottom end of the market. Tripoli, the national capital, can boast few top quality **B** *70LD to 100LD* international hotels (*Al-Mahari, Funduq Al-Kebir*, and *Waddan*) which, despite their **C** *40LD to 69LD* charges are not AL grade. Elsewhere standards are entirely variable and the regional **D** *20LD to 39LD* comments on hotels should be read with care before setting out from the capital. **E** *10LD to 19LD*
    Note that in the top-of-the-range government-owned hotels, you have to pay in **F** *Below 10LD* dollars (around US\$120 per night in dollars or dinars changed at the bank) which puts *(prices are given for a* them out of the reach of ordinary travellers . You may perhaps be able to pay in dinars *single room)* if you have a letter of invitation from a Libyan travel agency. In privately-owned hotels, *See also Tunisia* a reasonable room will be anything from 15LD to 35LD a night. En-suite bathrooms *Essentials page 35* may have various problems. Be patient, ask to change rooms on the second night.
    The main State-owned hotels in Tripoli – basically the Mahari and the Al Kebir – may on occasion be requisitioned by the government for official guests, in which case you may lose your reservation.
    On the coast there are a number of often well-provisioned beach clubs with residential facilities. They are designed to cater for groups of officially approved visitors but can in certain circumstances be open to all travellers. They are best approached through a Libyan travel agent or a Libyan state organization for sports, youth or scouts.

Libya

Youth hostels Libya has a remarkable number of youth hostel facilities. They are basic but often available when hotels are not! The locations, numbers of beds and telephone numbers of Libyan youth hostels are given in all regional sections. Opening hours 0600-1000 and 1400-2300 unless otherwise stated. In all there are 25 youth hostels in Libya. The minimum age is 14. Overnight fees for members are 2LD including sheets, breakfast 0.5LD, lunch 2.5LD and dinner 2LD. The *Libyan Youth Hostel Association* is close to Green Square in downtown Tripoli, at 69 Amr Ibn Al-As St POB 8886, Tripoli, T021-4445171 F021-3330118, Tx20420 LYHA. Additionally, it is possible to stay in the dormitories of secondary boarding schools during holiday periods. This is best arranged officially in advance, otherwise through the local *baladiya* (municipality offices).

Camping Camping is moderately popular in Libya, though as a mass organized venture through the state. Private camping is less usual except near bathing places on the Mediterranean shore. Here there are picnic sites which double as camping areas. They are crowded on public holidays but otherwise little used. Certain areas near to military camps and oil company installations are closed to all camping and any indications to this end are best complied with. Do not camp close to private farms or housing without an invitation to do so. Whenever possible seek permission from local farmers or land owners before setting up camp.

Getting around

Air There used to be connecting flights between the main cities, transiting via Tripoli. See separate towns for details. When internal flights resume, booking in advance will no doubt be necessary, as demand for flights is high, given the long road journeys which are the only alternative. In the past, overbooking was common. **NB** the UK Foreign Office has advised travellers to Libya **not** to use internal airlines as a lack of spare parts prevents satisfactory safety standards.

Road **Bus** The bus service is excellent including good quality a/c intercity services and more interesting crowded local buses.

Car hire Car hire for self-drive in Libya is not reliable. Hire vehicles are often old and in only moderate condition. Whilst they are suitable for use in town, they should not be taken on long journeys without thorough pre-travel checks, especially of tyres and suspension. Among the best hire locations are the main hotels, where agents have desks in the foyer. Hire rates for cars are high and variable, especially outside of Tripoli.

Cycling Travel by bicycle is unusual. Off the main track, cycling is extremely difficult in stony and sandy, albeit flat, terrain. Cyclists are advised to be well marked in brightly coloured clothing. Puncture repair shops exist in the towns alongside the main roads at the point of entry, though they mainly deal with cars and light motorcycles rather than bicycles. In the countryside, repair of cycles will be difficult but the profusion of small pick-up trucks means that it is very easy to get a lift with a cycle to a local town.

Hitchhiking Getting a free ride in little used in Libya, except in emergencies. There are many shared taxis travelling the road and travellers usually make use of these on a paid basis. Private cars or pick-up trucks will act in the same capacity but will expect a small payment in the normal course. Foreign travellers might find themselves picked up for free for curiosity. In the South, hitchhiking is not really a viable option, since traffic can be very irregular. Carry water and other safety supplies.

Motoring Great effort has gone into creating the road system and very few areas of the country are now inaccessible. Drive on the right of the road. Drivers are supposed to wear seat belts and these are checked by the police on entering and leaving Tripoli. Driving in Libya is poorly regulated and standards of driver training are very variable. The accident rate is high by international standards – hence the decision to manufacture an extremely safe local car. Visitors should drive defensively for their own safety and to ensure that they are not involved in accidents, especially those involving injury to humans, for which they might be deemed culpable. Drivers can be held in jail for long periods and the settlement of law suits against drivers guilty of dangerous driving leading to death or injury of a third party can be protracted and difficult.

Care is needed in **off-road driving** since there are difficult sand dune areas and other regions where soft sand can quickly bog down other than four-wheel drive vehicles. Even in far-flung parts of the Jefara Plain, the traffic is quite regular and people are never far away.

In the central Jefara there are large areas of military installations which are best avoided. Petrol stations are fairly well distributed but only on the main through roads. Any off road travel should only be undertaken with a full tank and a spare petrol supply. Good practice is never to leave the black top road unless there are 2 vehicles available to the party. A reliable and generous water supply should also be taken. This is especially important in summer when exhaustion and dehydration can be major problems if vehicles need digging out of sand.

Fuel distribution is a monopoly of a state agency and there are petrol stations in every town and at most key road junctions. Motorists should ensure that they fill up regularly rather than rely on stretching their fuel supply, since occasionally a station might be out of use for lack of deliveries or a cut in the electricity supply. Travel in the Saharan regions requires special precautions since running out of fuel can be fatal. There is no equivalent of Automobile Club services in Libya but passing motorists are normally very helpful. Drivers should always be aware of the enormous distances between settlements in southern Libya and take defensive action to ensure fuel, water, food and clothing reserves at all times. International driving licences are normally required though, in most cases, easily understood (English or Italian) foreign licences might be accepted.

Taxis **Individual taxis** are more expensive, more flexible and generally more comfortable over the same distance than the local bus. The taxis do have meters but these may not be in use. **Shared taxis** (larger) are a very popular mode of travel, leaving for a particular destination as soon as they are full. Be sure you have settled the price in advance. If in doubt check with the other passengers. These taxis can look quite decrepit but generally get to their destination.

In Libya other than for basic 'getting from A to B', walking is not normal. Hiking is to be **Walking** approached, therefore, in the knowledge that it may attract curiosity and possibly disbelief. Maps of good scale for walking eg better than 1:50,000 are very rare and thus travel has to be by sight lines, compass work and common sense. In many areas of the Jefara sighting to topographic markers on the Jabal can be used or lines on the taller minarets in the small towns are distinctive guides. Dogs are not a general problem in Tripolitania except near large farms where they are used for security purposes. Carry a stout stick and have some stones for throwing at approaching aggressive dogs, which is how the Libyans deal with this problem.

There are no rental facilities for boats and only a limited few individuals own boats for **Boat** pleasure purposes. There are small boat marinas at Tripoli and Benghazi for sailors bringing their own boats into port. It is occasionally possible to hire small fishing boats with their owners for the hour or day. Visits to Farwa, for example, near Zuwarah are only feasible by this means. The opening of new watersport tourist sites for foreign tourists such as at Farwa Island will make boat hire easier in the future.

Keeping in touch

For some useful Arabic sign words, see opposite and inside back cover

Language

Arabic is the official language throughout Libya. Given the Arab nationalist leanings of the government under Colonel Gadhafi, Arabic is regarded with some pride as a cultural emblem. Immediately after the 1969 revolution or coup d'état, all foreign language signs were removed, including street names, shop names, signposts and indications on official buildings. The result is that it is difficult for non-Arabic speakers to make use of written signs. In normal circumstances Libyans are most helpful to foreigners and will point out routes and other destinations. Unfortunately, however, it is only the older generation who have colloquial English, French or Italian since the quality of foreign language teaching has fallen and fewer Libyans travel abroad than previously. Tripoli City is the least difficult for the non-Arabic speaker. The answer to this problem, other than learning the Arabic script and some vocabulary before travelling, is to be very patient asking your way until help is volunteered by a source you can comprehend.

The private commercial sector is likely to be best aware of English and Italian since companies trade abroad so that calling in offices or agencies can locate assistance in an emergency. **French** is understood widely by the older generation in the southwest of country in the areas of Ghadamès and Ghat. **Italian** is still a used language in the Tripoli area. **English** is probably best used in Cyrenaica and Al-Khalij where there are many oil industry workers who have rubbed shoulders with English-speaking personnel. Language difficulties should not put off potential travellers in Libya since the Libyans themselves are helpful and patient. A few words or phrases in Arabic will ease the way considerably.

Berber is spoken as a first language in some rural areas, especially the Jabal Nafusa. Tamashek, related to Berber, is spoken by the few Tuaregs in the region of Ghadamès. In the far south, around the Tibesti Mountains, the Tibu language is the lingua franca.

Postal services

Independent Libya inherited a good postal system. Poste restante and post office box facilities are available in the main cities at the respective central post offices. The service to and from Europe, costing 350LD for a letter, takes about 7 to 10 days in normal circumstances but, bearing in mind the international air embargo, long land transit for mail makes this a much longer and riskier process. Internal mail is cheap, and for in-city letters, fairly fast and efficient. Libya produces a great range of collectors' stamps and there is a philatelic counter in Tripoli main post office.

Telephone & fax services

Post office telephone facilities exist in all towns and most villages. Internal calls are straightforward, though there can be some waiting time for a public line at the post office. International calls from all points can be difficult since there are restricted numbers of lines. The Tripoli post office is still quicker than trying international calls from private telephones. In-coming international calls, by contrast, get through comparatively easily.

For quick reference dialling code guide, see inside front cover

The **international code** for Libya is 218. Libya internal area codes are: **Al-Khums** 030, **Ghadamès** 0484, **Ghat** 0724, **Misrata** 051, **Sabha** 071, **Sabratha** 024, **Tripoli** 021, **Tripoli International Airport** 022, **Zawiyah** 023, **Zuwarah** 025. Rates for international calls are at standard levels.

Fax and **telex** facilities are available from luxury hotels and the main post offices which are advertised as being open 24 hours a day but suffer from the constraint on telephone lines. Late night automatic fax facilities in private offices are useful if available through friends (or friends of friends).

Useful Arabic sign words

street / *shari'a*	شارع
square / *maydan*	ميدان
hotel / *funduq*	فندق
bank / *masraf*	مصرف
restaurant / *mat'am*	مطعم
travel agency / *maktab li-ssafar wa siyaha*	مكتب للسفر والسياحة
resthouse / *istiraha siyahiya*	استراحة سياحية
city centre / *markaz al madina*	مركز المدينة
archaeological service / *maslahat al athar*	مصلحة الأثار

Media

Until very recently the Libyan media were powerfully controlled from the centre. This situation is changing only very slowly and the media still reflect the wishes of the régime. This does not make for good entertainment. The programming in Arabic technically and in content leaves so much to be desired and most Libyans watch videos or foreign stations via satellite. There is a half-hour local news broadcast in French and English each evening. The radio channel carries programmes of western music from time to time. The State produces daily broadsheets in French and English together with Arabic language newspapers. Foreign newspapers can be bought though they are often very out of date even when the air system is working normally.

Libya

Food and drink

Food

Restaurant categories: Expensive (3): over 25LD Mid-range (2): 10 -24LD Cheap (1): under 9LD

Outside the capital, there are practically no restaurants outside the main hotels and opening hours are limited. (In the evening eat before 2100 or risk finding them closed.) There are, however, plenty of cheap eateries near the centres of most provincial towns. As Libyans prefer to eat at home, restaurants tend to be for foreigners and travellers. The exception is in the use of cafés in the towns where males, mainly younger males, gather to meet their friends and socialize. On Friday and holidays, Libyans picnic and buy food from beachside stalls.

Libyan cooking has a mixture of Mediterranean influences. There is a strong legacy of the Italian period and pastas are very popular, particularly macaroni. Local dishes include *couscous*, with a bowl of boiled cereal as a base carrying large pieces of

☞ *Alcohol-free Libya*

Libya once upon a time had a wine industry, with the Tarhouna region producing some very palatable red wines. The country also had a brewery, producing the heavy Oea beer. This is all in the past now. Libya is a dry country, and it is unwise to try to bring any alcohol into the country. As a foreigner abide by Libyan rules. Nevertheless, home-brewing is said to be flourishing. The only safe place for a foreigner to drink however is a non-Muslim country's embassy compound – should you happen to be invited.

mutton and some potatoes. The best traditional forms of *couscous* in Libya use millet as a cereal, though most couscous is now wheat-flour based. *Bazin* is a Libyan speciality hard, paste-like food made of water, salt and barley and is really not recommended except to the gastronomically hardy. '*Aish* is a similar food from the same ingredients but slightly softer and prepared differently. *Sherba* (Libyan soup) is delicious but highly spiced. For the rest, the range of meals is quite sophisticated as in Tunisia, with Italian influences being greatest in Tripolitania and rather more Arab dishes (and less macaroni!) in Cyrenaica. Family life is kept separate from public acquaintances, and invitations to eat in a Libyan home are rarely given. As a foreigner invited into a Libyan home you can thus feel very favoured.

The offerings in cafés and restaurants will be very limited and mainly made up of various hot meat, chicken and vegetable stews either with potatoes or macaroni. In the main hotels, cuisine is 'international' and very bland. Good dates and excellent oranges can be bought cheaply. Other seasonal fruit includes apricots, figs and almonds, all good value.

Drink It should be emphasized that alcoholic drinks are banned in Libya. Offers of illegal liquor should be avoided even in private houses unless its provenance is beyond doubt. Local brews or 'flash' can be of questionable quality. Traditional brews of *bokha* (a form of arak), or *laghmi* (fermented date palm sap) are illegal. Otherwise, Libyans drink local bottled mineral waters, most of which are not always reliable copies of lemonades, colas and orange drinks available worldwide. Imported non-alcoholic beer is widely available in bottles and cans, price 1.5-2LD. In season, real orange juice can be bought from stalls on the streets. Take a bottle opener since most drinks are in glass bottles. The local tap water throughout much of Libya is slightly brackish. For personal use, buy bottled water such as *Moyyah Ben Ghashir* (Ben Ghashir water).

Libyans like their tea heavily boiled, thick and sweet, often with mint or nuts in a small glass. If English-style infused tea is wanted ask for *shay kees* (tea from a teabag) *bil leben* (with milk). Coffees include the inevitable Nescafé (ask for Nescafé) with or without milk and Turkish (sometimes called Arabic) coffee. With the latter, specify whether you want it *bis-sukar* (sweet) or *bedoon sukar* (unsweetened).

Shopping

Libya is more of a consumer society than a producer of goods for export. There will be few calls on your wallet for artefacts or craftwork. In southwestern Libya, especially in Ghadamès and Ghat, craft goods are available. Leatherwork, woven palm frond articles and small rugs have a certain individual charm. Stamp collectors will find a vast range of splendid stamps available from the main post offices in Tripoli.

Holidays and festivals

Libya, as Muslim country, observes all the main Islamic festivals as holidays. These are movable feasts. Ramadan for the year 2000 will be mainly in December. Fridays are days of rest. In addition there are several national holidays: **2 March**, Declaration of the People's Authority; **11 June**, Evacuation of foreign military bases; **1 September**, Anniversary of the 1969 Revolution. Note also that other holidays may be declared. Unpredictably, the frontier can be closed for Libyans during Christmas and the New Year.

See also Tunisia Essentials section page 49

Sports

Libya participates in the various Arab League sports tournaments but facilities for individuals are still very limited. Health centres exist for travellers at a few of the main hotels. Swimming is universally available in the Mediterranean or in the pools attached to the beach clubs in the main cities. Libyans themselves play volleyball for which there are plenty of facilities and football. Horse riding and trotting are also generally enjoyed. There is a Tripoli Horse Show attracting international participation. A Secretariat (ministry) of Sport exists but its activities are not given priority. The beach clubs near Tripoli have 1st class facilities for tennis, table tennis and canoeing and other sports. In the smaller towns the schools tend to be centres for sports while in industrial towns some of the companies have their own clubs with squash and tennis courts, for example.

Health

Certified vaccinations against smallpox are no longer required, but prudence demands that anti-cholera and tetanus injections are received before entry. Travellers expecting to travel into the Libyan South might feel that a voluntary, yellow fever injection is worthwhile. Walkers would also be wise to take up any anti-rabies protection that is safely available. Basically, the same health rules as for Tunisia apply.

See also Health section in Tunisia Essentials page 55

Libyan hospitals are fairly well equipped but are under-resourced in some critical areas. The quality of medical care is uneven, but can be very good indeed. Travellers must take into account that, with a UN air embargo in place, it is difficult to be airlifted out in case of emergency. There are hospitals and clinics in most towns of over 25,000 population and emergency para-medical services exist to service the main motor traffic routes. In theory treatment is free for all in public hospitals and clinics. In practice it is better to find private assistance if ill.

Medical facilities

Most proprietary drugs are available over the counter in Libya and chemist shops are to be found in the main streets of all but the smallest of towns (see Chemist and Hospital sections for each of the regions).

Libya

Further reading

There is a dearth of good material on Libya in English – and in other languages for that matter. In the UK, you could call in at the *Librairie du Maghreb*, in central London (45 Burton St, T0171-3881840). In Tripoli, you should look in at the *Fergiani Bookshop*, on Shari'a 1st September. Here you can obtain a useful Arabic/English *Atlas of Libya*. Fergiani also reissues early 20th century travel writing on North Africa in English under the Darf Publishers imprint. A starting point for researching material on Libya is R.I. Lawless' excellent annotated bibliography, *Libya*, (Oxford: Clio Press, 1987). On historical background, see R B St John's *Historical Dictionary of Libya*, (Methuen, NJ: Scarecrow Press, 1991).

Maps The best available maps are the Michelin Carte routière et touristique, Afrique du Nord et de l'Ouest (1/4,000,000 scale) and Cartographia's Libya (1,200,000 scale). Other larger scale maps are hard to find, although may be available, with patience, from the Secretariat for Planning. Try Stanford's in London for the Geo-Center map.

Ancient sites Look out for the following: D E L Haynes' *The Antiquities of Tripolitania* (Tripoli: Dept of Antiquities, 1981). If visiting the ancient sites of Cyrenaica, take Richard Goodchild's *Cyrène and Apollonia* (Tripoli: Dept of Antiquities, 1963). Jean-Loic Le Quellec's *Art rupestre et préhistoire du Sahara* (Paris: Payot, 1998) has some excellent illustrations.

Cities Ward, Phillip *Tripoli, Portrait of a City* (Oleander Press, 1969). On Tripoli, Francophones have J C Zeltner's *Tripoli, carrefour de l'Europe* (Paris: L'Harmattan, 1992). On Italian colonial planning and architecture, look out for *Colonial Constructions: architecture, cities and Italian imperialism* by Mia Fuller (London: Routledge-Spon, forthcoming).

Anthropology Evans-Pritchard, E E *The Sanusi of Cyrenaica* (Oxford: Clarendon Press, 1949). Interesting ethnographic and historical material can be found in the journal produced by the Institut de Belles Lettres Arabes (IBLA), place du Leader, Tunis-Médina. They have a small research library.

History Anderson, Lisa *The State and Social Transformation in Tunisia and Libya, 1830-1980*, (Princeton, NJ: Princeton University Press, 1986). Rossi, Ettore *Storia di Tripoli e della Tripolitania dalla conquista araba all 1911* (Roma: Istituto per l'Oriente, 1968). Villard, Henry Serrano *Libya: the new Arab kingdom of North Africa* (Ithaca, NY: Cornell University Press, 1956). In Libya itself, a visit to the Libyan Studies Centre in Tripoli would be of interest, especially for anyone working on local resistance to Italian colonialism. Knud Holmboe's *Desert Encounter* (London: Harrap, 1936) makes interesting reading on this subject. Holmboe was an Arabic-speaking Muslim Dane who travelled through Libya in the 1930s, and portrayed the brutal treatment inflicted by Italy on the people they had occupied. This was not to the colonial authorities' liking, for Holmboe was asked to leave.

Contemporary Libya Of the more recent academic material, Dirk Vandewalle's *Libya since Independence* (London: I.B. Tauris, 1998) is essential reading for anyone seeking to understand contemporary Libyan politics. Vandewalle is one of the most respected analysts of contemporary Libya. Also useful are Moncef Djaziri's *Etat et société en Libye* (Paris: L'Harmattan and Mansour O, 1996). El-Kikhia's *Libya's Gadhafi: the politics of contradiction* (Gainesville: University of Florida, 1997). A range of academic viewpoints can be found in a recent collective volume edited by D Vandewalle, *Gadhafi's Libya, 1969-1994* (New York: St Martin's Press, (1995).

Rather less up-to-date is work by John Davis and Mary-Jane Deeb. See for example Davis, J *Libyan Politics: tribe and revolution* (Berkeley: University of California Press, (1987). Deeb, Mary-Jane *Libya's Foreign Policy in North Africa* (Boulder, Colorado: Westview Press, 1991). See also John Wright's *Libya: a modern history* (Baltimore: John Hopkins University Press, 1982).

For those who read French, André Martel's *La Libye, 1835-1990, essai de géopolitique historique* (Paris: PUF, 1991) provides a broad introduction to the country, even if it is impressionistic in places.

Foreign policy Lanne, Bernard *Tchad-Libye: la querelle des frontières* (Paris: Editions Karthala, 1982). Lemarchand, René *The Green and the Black: Gadhafi's Policies in Africa* (Bloomington: Indiana University Press, 1988). St. John, R B *Gadhafi's World Design: Libyan foreign policy 1969-1987* (London: Saqi Books, 1987).

Coastal Tripolitania

Tripoli is a city with a Levantine air, where an ancient médina sits next to a new   Colour map 5, grid A2-3
town combining neo-Moorish, Mussolinian and modernist styles. The town occu-
pies the site of ancient **Oea**, *one of the three great cities of the region in Rome's*
heroic days. Restoration works are underway in the old town, which has a citadel
worthy of a romantic tragedy and Ottoman mosques with pointy minarets.

Two of the three ancient towns, **Sabratha** *and* **Leptis Magna**, *survived to be*
unearthed by 20th century archaeology. Sabratha, west of Tripoli, has a magnifi-
cent theatre, statuary and Byzantine mosaics. Still more grandiose, Leptis
Magna, once the second Roman port in Africa, is surrounded by pines and olive
groves. Its baths, built under Hadrian, were famous throughout the ancient world
and the city flourished under Septimius Servus, who gave it monuments and a
revamped harbour.

Visiting Tripoli and the Roman sites of Sabratha and Leptis Magna, you will
cross sections of the **Great Jefara Plain**, *coastal lowlands which stretch from the*
Tunisian frontier in the west at Zuwarah to Misrata in the east. To the south, the
Great Jefara is bounded by the line of the Jabal Nafusa as far as Al-Khums.

The Jefara Plain drops from the foot of the inland Jabal Nafusa very evenly and
gradually to reach the coast in an often rocky and shallow shelf. There are some
excellent **beaches**, *however, well away from Tripoli city. Inland from the oases*
are the former Italian farmsteads and estates with their regularly laid out
orchards spreading deep into the interior. Moving eastwards, the Jefara Plain
narrows considerably until the Jabal reaches the coast in a low ridge at
Al-Khums, *separating the main Jefara from the limited coastal plain ('Lesser*
Jefara') between Al-Khums and Misrata. The roads on the Jefara are wide, black
topped and generally in good condition.

The Tuniso-Libyan border to Sabratha via Zuwarah

As a consequence of the UN air embargo from 1992 to 1999, plus an easing by
Libya of border controls, there is a considerable flow of commercial heavy traffic as well as private cars and taxis on the road from the Tuniso-Libyan border
to Tripoli. Whether this will ease up as air traffic resumes remains to be seen.
Although there seem to be only the slightest of restrictions on movements of
goods and people for Arabs, the volume of traffic is such that large queues can
build up on both sides. The border post has few facilities other than a petrol
station and a small café on the Libyan side.

Once through the frontier from Tunisia, the road connects as a single lane
highway along the coast from Farwa to Zuwarah.

The **island of Farwa** lies just offshore, close to the border at Ras Ajdir. The   **Farwa Island**
island is approached either by a rough causeway built at the time of the construction of the nearby Bu Kammash petrochemical/refinery complex, or by
ferry from a pier at **Bu Kammash** village to the west of the plant. The ferry, run
by local fishermen, is an occasional rather than a regular service. There are sea
police and customs officials at both the pier and the causeway to control movement and those at the pier can be helpful in retaining a boatman.

Libya

Libya: a few useful facts

Surprisingly, Libya's capital has a Shari'a Haiti (Haiti St). The reason for this is that it was thanks to the Haitian delegate's vote that the UN decided to give Libya its independence in 1951. Most cities also have a Shari'a al Fath, a 1st of September St, this being the day in 1969 that a group of young army officers overthrew the Senussi Kingdom of Libya. And finally, the Libyan year is neither Islamic (starting with the Prophet Mohamed's migration or hijra from Mecca to Médina) nor, of course, Christian. The Libyan calendar starts in 570, year of the Prophet's birth.

The island, 12 km long and two kilometres at its widest, is basically flat with a few dunes. There are palm groves which have been tidied up in the central section of the island. (There is perhaps a tourist complex to be built). The sand is fine grained and silver coloured. Excepting the view of the petrochemical plant, the site is absolutely first class.

Zuwarah
زوارة
Phone code: 025

Moving eastwards, Zuwarah is an expanding if unexciting town, approximately 100 km from Tripoli and 60 km from the border with Tunisia. The main employer is the petrochemical complex at Bu Kammash. Most commercial and municipal activity is concentrated in the centre of the town on the old road one km to the north of the new dual carriageway coastal highway. The town extends to the seashore with lots of new villas.

Sleeping D *Hotel Assalam*, just before the football stadium at town exit, T22295. Clean, and 30LD for a double room. F *Zuwarah Istiraha Siyahiya*, in the middle of town adjacent to the square. Cheap (10LD double) small hotel used by Libyans. Also has a small restaurant. No **camping** facilities as such, though along the coast there are plenty of good camping places in woodlands or on the coast. Ask permission if possible before setting up camp.

Transport The shared **taxi/bus** services to east and west along the coast road are very frequent. Express buses with a/c on Tripoli to Tunis run can be stopped in Zuwarah. Ordinary inter-urban service buses can be caught to Tripoli.

Directory Communications Post Office: this is near the clinic on the old road. **Hospitals & medical services** First aid: the Red Crescent clinic is on the old road. **Petrol** There are 2 petrol stations to the east and west of town on the main highway.

West of Tripoli

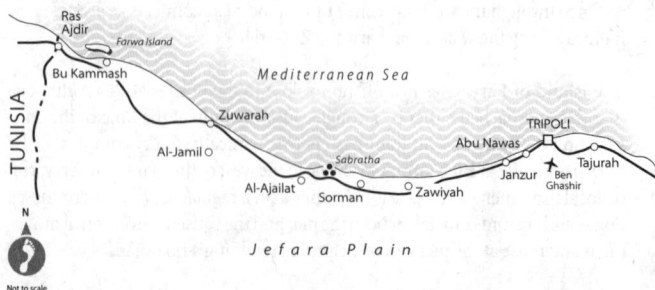

Farming the Jefara Plain

The Jefara is a fairly fertile and generally well watered zone except for the central area from Al-Assa to the south of Ajailat which is very arid. Rainfall comes in the winter months and causes flash flooding in the many wadis. Most water courses are now well controlled but it is wise to stay out of wadi beds in winter. Individuals may be carried away and drowned in flash floods.

Close to the coast is a narrow belt of palm oases where there is multiple cropping in spring and summer. In its most sophisticated form, intercropping gives olives immediately below the palm canopy and other taller fruit trees, themselves standing clear of lower varieties such as pomegranates and apricot. Below the trees are tall vegetables such as peppers or maize and a final undercrop of wheat, barley or a vegetable such as broad beans. Cropping of this kind was labour-intensive but enabled a self-sufficient agriculture based on irrigation from shallow wells.

Animal herding is important on the Jefara Plain. Few black tents of the true nomads are now to be seen. Even the Sian nomads of the far west of Tripolitania, adjacent to Tunisia, have become sedentary. Herds of sheep and goats are to bee seen, however. The sheep are Barbary fat-tailed varieties for the most part, with an ability to survive heat and short periods of drought. The animals are very valuable, being much prized for eating by the Libyans, each sheep fetching US$300 or more, depending on the animal and the season. Most herds are looked after by a hired shepherd.

From Zuwarah travel east via the modern road to **Zawiyah**, 40 km from Tripoli, where there is a **youth hostel**, 80 beds, breakfast included, other meals available, family rooms.

The Zuwarah to Zawiyah stretch is narrow and still single carriageway and is particularly dangerous since traffic is dense and undisciplined. Coastal mists can be a problem because local drivers tend to ignore such hazardous conditions.

Zuwarah to Zawiyah

زاوية

Modern Sabratha

One of Libya's most important ancient sights, the excavated Roman town of **Sabratha**, is situated roughly midway between Zuwarah and Zawiyah. On your way to the Roman site, you will pass through the rapidly expanding modern town of Sabratha which has all basic services. There is some new industry and many large villas extend down from the old coastal road towards the ruins. The new Faculty of Arts of Zawiyah University has been set up here.

Phone code: 024

Libya

E *Fondouk Siyahi* (lit. Tourist Hotel), close to ruins but in poor condition. 10LD double room. **E** *Hotel Jawda*, difficult to find – on the left as you are heading for Tunisia, T24581. Ask for *souk al jumaà*, the Friday market. 15LD double room. **F** *Hotel Mediterraneo*. On the main drag, poorly managed. 8LD double room. **Camping** Camping is banned in the woodlands around the archaeological site. **Youth hostel**, 1 km northwest of town, T23139. Close to ruins and located next to a water tower.160 beds, kitchen, meals, family rooms, laundry, open 0700-2400, booking recommended May-August, 5LD per person.

Sleeping

There is a restaurant at the ruins at the side of the large car park immediately outside the archaeological compound, which is open 0800-2200 winter and summer. The restaurant caters for Libyan and foreign visitors including large groups. The area offers a café and billiards. *Hotel Sabratha* in converted church on way to ruins is recommended, good fish dishes with rice, spaghetti or couscous.

Eating

Directory **Petrol** is available in town and at the road junction at Ajailat.

Local beach At Telil there is a good sandy area with shallow water. It is popular with Libyan families. The beach is served by black top dual carriageway from the main road from junction west of Sabratha city.

Ancient Sabratha   صبراتة

Colour map 5, grid A2 *Sabratha began life as a Carthaginian trading post. With its excellent natural harbour on a long, straight coast, it became a permanent settlement in the 4th century BC to act as a terminal for the trans-Saharan trade. Under the Romans, development continued, although not on anything like the scale of Leptis Magna. The site is a 'must visit', however. The coastal location is magnificent, the theatre, the largest in Africa, is exquisite, and there are Byzantine mosaics bearing witness to a post-Vandal revival.*

Ins and outs

Getting there Sabratha is easily visited as a day trip from Tripoli. You could take a shared taxi to new Sabratha, (journey time around 50 mins), and a second taxi from there to the ruins, reached by a splendid avenue of old cypress trees.

History

Sabratha was one of the three great cities of Roman Tripolitania, along with Leptis and Oea (modern Tripoli). Although it cannot match Leptis Magna for its range and richness of buildings, it is nonetheless impressive and Italian excavations and some reconstruction have made it well worth a visit.

Excavations in the late 1940s revealed evidence that there had been a seasonal Punic trading post before the actual stone city was built. The early settlement was located here because the coast is protected by a low reef lying some 100 metres offshore, creating a shallow basin adequate for the needs of the low-draft trading ships of ancient times. In the 3rd and 4th centuries BC, the city grew up in a haphazard fashion, buildings growing up on narrow streets. As of the 2nd century BC, Sabratha seems to have grown richer, becoming a major population centre. Two imposing mausolea testify to the wealth of Sabratha at this time.

Hellenistic Sabratha In the 1st century BC, the dominant culture at Sabratha seems to have been Greek. The urbanised area was divided up *per strigas*, into blocks running in strips, divided up according to a grid-iron plan. Some archaeologists believe that a major earthquake provided the city authorities with the chance to go about some major renewal schemes, creating a new main square and neighbourhoods to the south on the regular layout to be found in Hellenistic cities. Another indication of Greek influence is that the Alexandrine god Serapis was worshipped at Sabratha.

Roman Sabratha Another earthquake shook Sabratha sometime between 65 and 70 AD, destroying much of the city - and providing a superb opportunity for the Romans to do some rebuilding on a grand scale. Under Marcus Aurelius and his son Commodus, major building works were undertaken in the city centre, destroying parts of the original Punic city. By the late 2nd century AD, Sabratha had monuments decorated with statuary and fine marbles -

including a spectacular theatre with seating for 5,000 people. New residential neighbourhoods went up between coast road and the Mediterranean. Also under Commodus or Septimus Severus, new port facilities were constructed with the usual thoroughness of the Roman engineers. Trade was the main source of Sabrathan wealth, as images of merchant ships carved on the walls of both homes and public buildings indicate. The city exported oil and grain, along with valuable luxury products from sub-Saharan Africa such as ivory.

Tripolitania was hit by severe earthquakes between 306 and 310 AD, and again in 365 AD. Archaeological evidence suggests that the city never really recovered. Rubble was used for restoration work. The central temple of Liber Pater was hard hit, restored by the mid-4th century only to be hit by the second earthquake. Basically, the temples never returned to the worship of the old gods: Christianity was already gaining ground. **The end of monumental Sabratha**

By the 4th and 5th centuries AD, Sabratha had a large Christian community – and a splendid complex of basilicas to match, built on the eastern edge of the city. By the first half of the 5th century, the Christians were sufficiently numerous to be taking over the old heart of the city: the main imperial basilica became a church. After the 5th-century Vandal occupation, the Byzantines retook Sabratha in 533. A considerably smaller city was enclosed by walls with towers (constructed from recycled masonry), protecting port, the old centre and neighbouring residential areas. **Byzantine city**

After the end of Byzantine rule in North Africa, there is little information about the fate of Sabratha. The city probably survived the first Arab invasions of the early 640s – as rare Islamic coins discovered on the site indicate.

Serious archaeological work on Sabratha got going in 1927. Giacomo Guidi ran the excavations from 1928 to 1932. In 1932, Guidi turned his attention to rebuilding the theatre, a task continued by his successor Giacomo Caputo as of 1937. The whole building had been destroyed by earthquake. Guidi and Caputo were lucky enough to find most of the original masonry and the result is a building which gives the visitor a very real feel for what a Roman theatre must have been like. The aims of the Italians were not entirely innocent, however. Such reconstructions were designed to demonstrate that the Kingdom of Italy was heir to the Roman Empire, and therefore very much 'at home' in the its colony of Libya. **Rebuilding Sabratha**

Touring the site

There appear to be no guides available but there are publications and artefacts on show at the museum. ■ *Entrance 3LD, open from 0800-sunset daily, museums closed Mon.* It is best to avoid visiting on Fri, when lots of local families come to picnic and stroll among the ruins. Other days are less crowded. Do not use videocameras. You will need a good 3 hours to do the site justice. For a post-visit swim, try the beach to the east of the site near the temple of Isis.

The entrance is by the **Roman Museum**. (Down a path to the left is the **Punic Museum**, often closed. The Roman Museum, designed by Giacomo Guidi in 1934, houses the fine mosaics from the Basilica of Justinian, and a number of frescoes, and marble and bronze statues. Unfortunately, only the central mosaics hall is open for the moment, although the other rooms are scheduled to open 'soon'. The mosaic from Justinian's Basilica was discovered in 1925. Its four sections symbolize the soul, including a caged bird representing the soul

Libya

imprisoned in the body and a phoenix portraying the resurrection. A splendid peacock symbolises the soul in Paradise.

Walk northwest along the main thoroughfare. On your left, is the residential neighbourhood with a couple of mausolea, generally referred to as **Mausoluem A** and **B**. The pointy-topped Mausoleum B is particularly interesting, and totally rebuilt by Italian archaeologists. Punic-Hellenistic in style, the building was totally destroyed in one of the earthquakes which shook Sabratha in the 4th century. The stone was recycled, hence the archaeologists had to dismantle a Byzantine tower and some house remains to reconstruct the building. Original pieces from the upper part are in the Punic Museum. In form and decoration, this mausoleum resembles the Libyco-Numidian Mausoleum at Dougga in Tunisia (see illustration page 428). Return to the main street, and pass through the site of the gate in the **Byzantine walls** to reach the old core of the city.

Cross the main street (plateia) and you come to the monumental centre of Sabratha. On the left you have the **South Temple**, 'of the unknown deity' (2nd century AD) before you reach a small square. This wider area has the **Antonine Temple** up five steps on the right and the **Judicial Basilica** on the

Sabratha

left. The remains of the basilica show that it has been much changed since the original building of the 1st century AD. Next you come to the **forum**, to the east side of which are a podium and a line of columns, remains of the East Temple or **Temple of Liber Pater**, an ancient fertility god associated with Bacchus, god of wine. On the seaward side of the forum are the remains of **Justinian's Basilica**, dismantled in the 1920s by archaeologists (the building's importance was only realised later when mosaics were found).

Sabratha's most striking monument is its **Theatre**, still used occasionally for open air shows. Located to the east of the site, next to the quarries which provided the stone for much of Sabratha, it is the largest theatre in Roman Africa – and easily the most impressive today, due to the re-assembly work undertaken by Italian archaeologists in the 1930s. The semi-circular orchestra area was excavated out of the rock, while the majority of the building was constructed with great blocks of stone hewn from the quarry that lies south of Sabratha. During the reconstruction, 96 of the original marble columns were put back into place, recreating a spectacular three-storey galleried backdrop to the stage. The stage platform or pulpitum is over 40 metres wide, and fronted by a white marble frieze featuring mythological characters including the Three

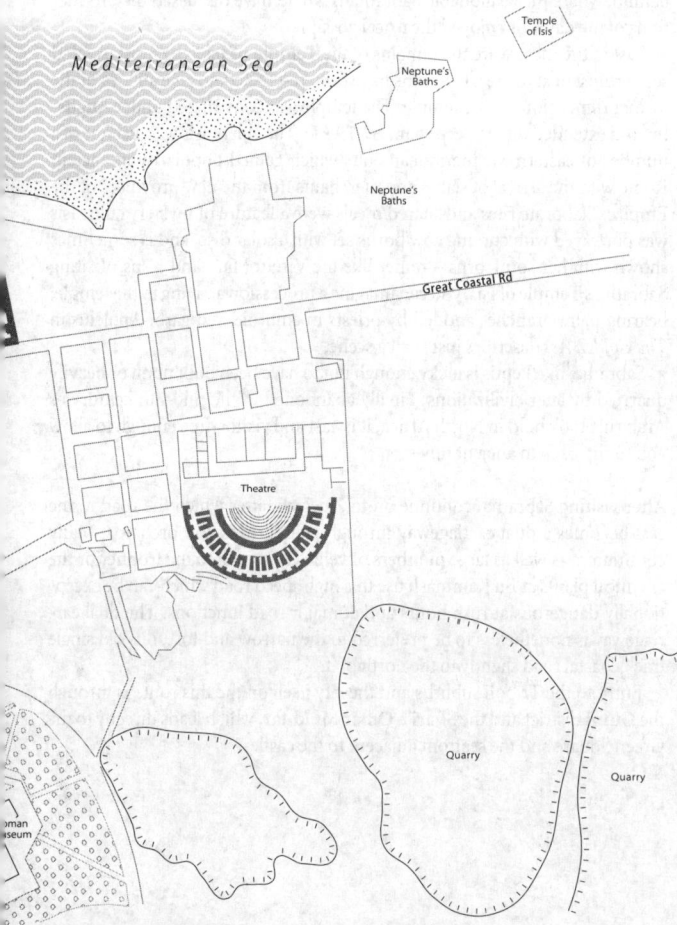

Temple of Isis

Mediterranean Sea

Neptune's Baths

Neptune's Baths

Great Coastal Rd

Theatre

Quarry

Quarry

oman useum

Libya

Libya, 'dripping rain'

The name 'Libya' derives from the Greek for 'dripping rain'. In Greek myth, Libya was the daughter of Zeus and Io. The story goes that Cyrene, a strong maiden adept at wrestling with wild beasts and protecting flocks on Mount Pelion, attracted Apollo's attention. He carried her off in his golden chariot, to the site of what was to become the Greek city of Cyrene. There Aphrodite greeted them – and had them bed down in Libya's golden chamber. Apollo promised Cyrene that she would reign over a well-watered, pleasant land, enjoying her hunting. This land was no doubt the Jabal Akhdar, the Green Mountain of the eastern part of the modern Jamahiriya. Cyrene bore Apollo a son, Aristaeus and Greeks of Cyrene in eastern Libya held Aristaeus to be their ancestor – naming their port Apollonia, in honour of his father.

Graces and personifications of Sabratha paying allegiance to Rome. Insufficient material was available to reconstruct the final or attic storey of the backdrop, which would have supported a canopy to protect the stage and improve the sound. The theatre had three tiers of seating and wide promenade galleries behind, where the fashionable Sabrathans would have discussed the productions of the day – or enjoyed theatrical gossip.

East of the theatre are the remains of the **Temple of Isis**, the most isolated set of ruins, next the sea. Columns have been re-erected, to give an idea of the former dimensions of the temple. The temple was constructed under Augustus and extended under Vespasian, 69-79 AD. The cult of Isis was just one of a number of eastern Mediterranean cults which gained popularity in ancient Rome with the arrival of slaves and merchants from the new provinces of the Empire. Elaborate rites and shared meals were a feature of mystery cults. Isis was portrayed with curving cow horns set with a solar disc, and is sometimes shown with her son Horus – rather like the Virgin Mary and Jesus. Visiting Sabratha's Temple of Isis, you can imagine a procession arriving in the temple, bearing palm branches and led by priests in embroidered garb. Apuleius in *The Golden Ass* describes just such a scene.

Sabratha, like Leptis is lucky enough not to have been built upon or heavily quarried by later civilizations. Finally abandoned in the mid-8th century as Arab rule took hold in North Africa, it is vast and visitor-free enough to allow you to slip back to ancient times.

Sabratha to Tripoli After visiting Sabratha, continue on to Zawiyah, after which the road to the east becomes a dual carriageway through palm groves and orchards. Many commuters as well as large numbers of vehicles moving to the frontier or the chemical plants at Bu Kammash use this high speed road which can be exceptionally dangerous at rush hours and at major road junctions. The dual carriageway is nonetheless to be preferred to the narrow and tortuous old single track coastal road slightly to the north of it.

Entry to the Tripoli suburbs and the city itself on the this route is through the **Gurgi** district and the **Shari'a Omar Mukhtar**, which leads directly to the Green Square and the seafront adjacent to the castle.

Tripoli   طرابلس الغرب

Tripoli has all the pleasant features and inconveniences of a modern Mediterranean town. There are flyovers and a cargo port, sprawling suburbs of villas and blocks of flats, and a palm-tree lined corniche. The heart of Tripoli is its somewhat melancholy old town, where a triumphal arch to Marcus Aurelius bears witness to a grand Roman past. Under the Ottomans and the Karamanlis, the old town grew wealthy through the Saharan caravan trade. For a while, piracy too helped fill the coffers of Tripoli's rulers. Today, although the original inhabitants have left for the comforts of Garden City and elsewhere, restoration works proceed apace. The souks are sleepy, Tunis-style tourist herding is yet to come. Although many government secretariats and the faculties of the Al-Fatah University have been moved out, the transfers have not changed the reality of Tripoli as the real political centre of Libya. The People's Congress meets in Tripoli and Colonel Gadhafi is for the most part resident there.

Phone code: 021
NB: old 5 digit numbers beginning with 3 place 33 in front, and those beginning with 4 place 44 in front.
Colour map 5, grid A2

Ins and outs

The main airport is some 24 km from the centre of Tripoli, but some planes leave from the smaller local airport just 4 km from downtown. Always check! A bus service is available to/from the main hotels and the bus station. Passengers with a deal of luggage are advised to face a charge of some 25LD for a private taxi rather than try the alternative. Uncertainties over transport to and from the airport are such that travellers should check well before the date of their flight with the airline, hotel or travel agent. The *Libyan Airlines* central office is located on Shari'a Haiti. For details of flights to Tripoli, see Essentials section page 464.

Getting there

There is an efficient bus service and though taxis are very expensive (5LD for the shortest of trips), in the heat they might be attractive to those with some distance to travel. Outlying parts of Tripoli can be reached by shared taxis at very reasonable rates. Otherwise, you will be able to walk around the city centre. See transport section page 491.

Getting around

Old Tripoli

The old walled city of Tripoli, the **médina**, goes back to Punic and Roman times, when it was known as Oea. The basic street plan was laid down in the Roman period when the walls were constructed on the landward sides against attacks from the interior of Tripolitania. The high walls survived many invasions, each conqueror restoring the damage done. In the eighth century the Muslim ruler built a wall on the sea-facing side of the city. Three great gates gave access to the town, **Bab Zanata** on the western side, **Bab Hawara** on the southeast and **Bab Al-Bahr** in the north wall. Constant rebuilding means that few ancient commercial buildings remain and even the oldest mosque, Al-Naqah, was reconstructed in 1610. The **castle**, Al-Saraya Al-Hamra, occupies a site known to be pre-Roman in the eastern quadrant of the city and still dominates the skyline of Tripoli. The castle is made up of many distinct sections, formerly public and private quarters of the ruling family. The upper walls afford a fine view to the sea and across the town.

The old city itself was made up of a series of separate quarters, two major parts of which were Jewish (*hara* is the name designating the Jewish areas of Tripoli). Narrow streets criss-cross the old city off which run blind alleys. While the piece-meal development of the city gave rise to the impasses and randomness

Neighbour-hoods & streets

Libya

to the street pattern the blind alleys were often ways of sealing off areas controlled by single or extended families or ethnic groups so that attackers or casual passers-by would not intrude on family life, especially the lives of women. The through alleys in Tripoli old city are generally unroofed but with buttresses at intervals which help to hold up the walls on either side of the alley and provide some shelter from the sun. Walls facing the public alleys are for the most part plain with few windows, a device to increase privacy and deter curiosity. Doorways to houses and interior courtyards are remarkably ornate in contrast to the tall plain walls around them. Massive arches are used, while the doors themselves are often high, studded and provided with ancient locks.

Houses & merchants hostels Individual houses in the old city still display their great cloistered courtyards and ornate tile, wood and plaster work. There are also several *funduqs*, where merchants lodged their goods and animals around large courtyards. Generally less decorated than private houses, they played an important role in the life of the city when the large traders organized and managed trans-Saharan caravans. The manufacturing and retail souks of old Tripoli were run by guilds of craftsmen producing craft products for daily use. Pottery, metalwork, traditional clothing and jewellery were made here. Some of the souks still trade under vaulted brick ceilings, though very few goods are now manufactured in situ. Souk Al-Mushir is the popular tourist area of the old city situated immediately off Green Square adjacent to the castle. There are seven mosques in the old city, containing a wealth of indigenous architectural detail.

Old City today There was an exodus of the traditional families from the old city after Independence in 1951. Families moved to occupy houses and apartments vacated by the departing Italians to take advantage of better sanitation, water supply

Tripoli médina

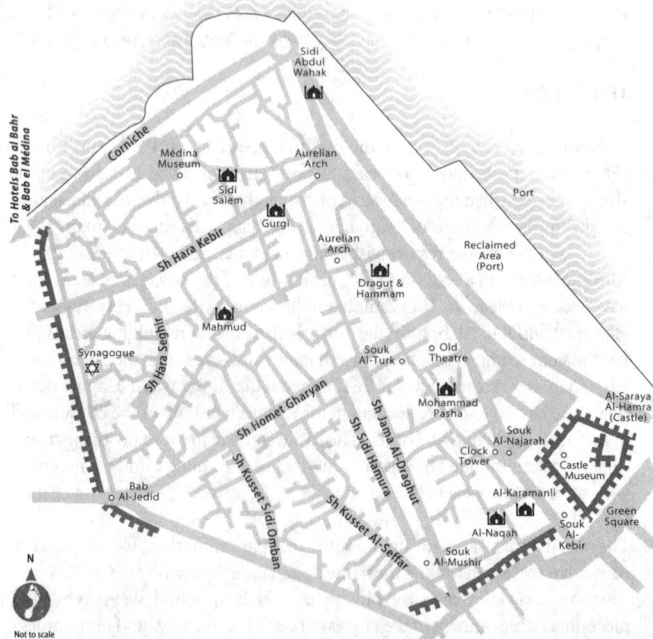

Related map
Tripoli, page 488

Libyan capitals

and other facilities. By the mid 1970s the situation had deteriorated so badly that the majority of residents in the old city was immigrant workers from overseas. Neglect of the fragile buildings enabled damp to get into their fabric and many fell to ruin. The Libyan authorities determined to halt the rot and established a group to undertake restoration of key buildings and to write up the history of the city. In addition to the establishment of a research workshop and library in the old city, the main mosques, synagogues and consular houses have been restored in excellent taste.

Any tour of the old city should begin at the **castle**, entered from the land side near Souk Al-Mushir. It houses a library and a well organized museum and has excellent views over the city from the walls. ■ *Entrance free, closes at 1400*. This is one of the two principal **museums** in Tripoli, the other being in the médina, approximately 500 metres away. **Visiting the Old City**

The **Castle Museum** is essentially concerned with the archaeology and ancient history of Libya. It covers the Phoenician, Greek and Roman periods well and has an expanding collection of materials on the Islamic period. The top floor is devoted to Libyan modern history. ■ *Open weekdays 0800-1400, closed Friday. Entrance 0.50LD.* The main route through the old city runs from the castle towards the sea, with the old French and British consulates, the Médina Museum and the Aurelian Arch all worthy of close attention. The old city walls are still standing.

The **Harbour Monument** stands at the gates of the old city on the edge of the former corniche road adjacent to the castle. There are a number of restored houses, consulates and a synagogue in the narrow streets.

The **Médina Museum**, is easily found in a renovated building standing all alone in a cleared section to the northwest of the old town. It has a library with illustrated displays and helpful staff with a great knowledge of the médina area. ■ *Open weekdays 0800-1400, closed Friday. Entry is free and is from Bab Al-Jedid on the western side of the city walls not far from the taxi station.* The main merchant quarter is entered from the gate at **Souk Al-Mushir**. There are many separate small souks such as the **Souk Al-Attar** (traditional medicaments), **Souk As-Siiaja** (goldsmiths), the remnants of which still operate, though without their former Jewish workers and owners.

There are a number of interesting mosques in the old town including the **Karamanli Mosque**, the **Al-Naqah Mosque** and the **Gurgi Mosque**. The Al-Naqah mosque, the oldest of the Tripoli mosques, is called the camel mosque because it is said that the citizens of Tripoli met the great Arab **Mosques in the old town** conqueror Amr Ibn Al-As with a camel-load of valuables to buy the survival of the city. Amr Ibn Al-As refused to accept this gift and instead asked that a mosque be built. The present mosque was revamped on a number of occasions down the centuries, the last major rebuilding dating from 1610/11. The plan of the mosque is slightly irregular and aligned on a northwest axis. The sanctuary makes use of columns of varied sources, some Roman. 42 brick-built domes comprise the roof of the mosque. A square minaret has a spiral stairway of palm wood and plaster.

Another interesting mosque is that of **Dragut**, the well-known Islamic admiral and scourge of shipping in the Mediterranean. He died during the great siege of Malta and was returned and buried in Tripoli in the large Dragut mosque, which was damaged during the Second World War but later restored. It has a square minaret and a small cemetery.

The **Al-Jami' Mosque**, the true 'Great Mosque' of Tripoli, contains interesting inscriptions to Othman Ra'is, who founded it in 1670 AD. The most magnificent mosque in Tripoli is the **Mosque of Ahmad Pasha Karamanli**, Governor of Tripoli in 1711 and founder of the Karamanli Dynasty. It is located a few metres from the castle near the main entrance to the souk. The mosque has an adjacent *medersa* in the western corner of the grounds, tombs and a cemetery. The centre point is a sanctuary with 25 domes as a roof, the two domes over the fine *mihrab* being more elevated and carrying stucco

scène de rue
Tripoli طرابلس

work. The tombs of Ahmad Pasha and many of his family lie in a separate room with a large domed roof of spectacular design. The distinctive minaret is octagonal in the Turkish style.

Best known of the Tripoli mosques is the Hanefite **Gurgi Mosque**, built comparatively recently in 1833 by Yussef Gurgi (a mamlouk originally from Georgia in the Caucasus, hence the family name). The octagonal minaret with two balconies is the tallest of the old Tripoli mosques. If you are pressed for time, the Gurgi Mosque is the one to visit.

Modern Tripoli

At the heart of Tripoli, the great **Green Square** links old town and the spacious modern neighbourhood planned by the Italians. Off the square, arcaded shopping streets are home to a handful of chic shops, a bookstore and miscellaneous cafés and eateries. Here and there, fine examples of 1920s and 1930s official building still survive. The crowds are cosmopolitan and male-dominated. You will meet many Sudanese, Egyptians, miscellaneous Africans and Maghrebis along with Libyans in the streets of Tripoli today.

New neighbourhoods developed outside the tight confines of the old city as early as the 18th century and possibly before that. It is known from the letters of the European consuls such as Tully, resident in Tripoli during Karamanli times, that a thriving community existed on the flat lands immediately outside the old city known as the Menshia. Here the troublesome members of the traditional military class lived with farmers, traders and other individuals.

Italian redevelopment The entire area was redeveloped by the Italians in the first half of the 20th century as a colonial city for Italian residents. They created a set of administrative buildings, many of which stand today, together with official residences and general residential areas. The **garden city** is still the most affluent and pleasant area of Tripoli, situated adjacent to the **People's Palace**. Straight streets were constructed, radiating from Green Square in front of the castle, together with a cathedral and a financial district adjacent to the souk, along what is now Shari'a Omar Mukhtar.

Post-1969 urban expansion This pleasing colonial urban form was broken by the revolution of 1969. In an attempt to diminish the apparent colonial heritage and European influence, all street names were changed, the cathedral closed and signs not in Arabic removed. However, far more influential in changing the character of Tripoli was the massive population growth during the post-revolutionary years combined with an influx of Libyans to Tripoli. Tripoli City grew five-fold in population size to stand at 600,000 by 1990. Extensive new suburbs grew up on all sides, many ill-planned so that Tripoli became a large metropolitan area in its own right spreading in all directions across the oases on its edge to reach out and encompass major satellite settlements such as Tajurah to the east.

The removal of some civil service personnel to other sites together with a fall in prosperity in the late 1980s eased some of the traffic congestion but expansion of the city continues, with people commuting 60-80 km into the city from outlying towns. At peak times, 0730-0900, 1330-1430 and 1800-1930, roads are choked and extra time must be allowed for travelling to appointments and particularly to the airport or bus station.

Modern Tripoli: orientation
The main commercial streets lie in the centre. Most lead off **Green Square** in front of the castle. All street names are in Arabic but Libyans will assist in giving directions. The **coast road**, built over the former harbour area and adjacent to new wharves, is principally for vehicular traffic moving east. There are no buildings. The inner coast road from Green Square, Shari'a Al-Fatah (originally Adrian Pelt, named after the UN official who sponsored Libyan Independence in 1951) is built up on its inland side with a number of public buildings and the main hotels. It travels on eastwards along the corniche passing the major embassies of Italy, the UK (currently operating as a 'British interests' section of the Italian embassy), Turkey and others. The road is planted with ornamental palms and has cafés and gardens along it.

Shari'a Mohammad Magarief, one of the capital's two main streets, runs from Green Square to the former cathedral. At its southern end, 500 metres south of the former cathedral is the **People's Palace**, built for the late King Idris and now in the service of the popular committees and the political activists supporting Colonel Gadhafi. The French embassy faces it and on its northwest corner is one of the oil company offices. The National Oil Company office is on Shari'a Gamal Nasser, to the west of the palace. Travelling up the eastern side of the palace you come to the Shari'a Ben Ashur in the centre of a high class residential district, the Garden City being to the east and new properties to the west.

Tour of the modern city
Walking around Tripoli centre is straightforward, though beyond the main business and shopping precincts there is little to see. For a tour of the modern city on foot begin in Green Square and go west along Shari'a Omar Mukhtar to see the private business district. Turn round at the Tripoli Fair building Return to Green Square from which head down Shari'a Mohammad Magarief towards the post office and former cathedral, now used as a mosque. The rooms above the post office display pictures of Tripoli during the Italian and British occupation. From the post office square (Maidan Al-Jaza'er) either turn directly right to Shari'a Haiti and thence right again into one of the commercial thorough-fares with small Arab lock-up shops or go on past the post office towards the People's Palace and thence left to the harbour front and back towards the Green Square. This itinerary effectively shows the best of the modern city.

Tripoli

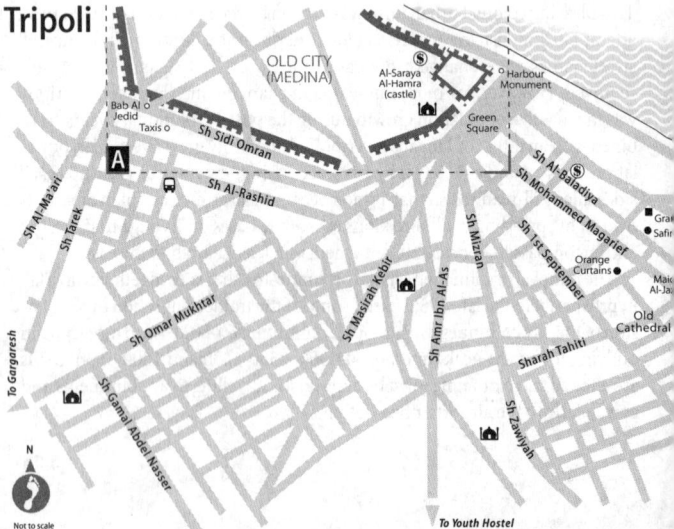

OLD CITY (MEDINA)

Al-Saraya Al-Hamra (castle)

Harbour Monument

Bab Al Jedid

Taxis

Sh Sidi Omran

Green Square

A

Sh Al-Rashid

Sh Al-Baladiya

Sh Mohammed Magarief

Sh Al-Ma'ari

Sh Tarek

Sh Omar Mukhtar

Sh Masirah Kebir

Sh Amr Ibn Al-As

Sh Mizran

Sh 1st September

Orange Curtains

Grand

Safir

Main Al-Ja.

Old Cathedral

To Gargaresh

Sh Gamal Abdel Nasser

Sharah Tahiti

Sh Zawiyah

Related map A Tripoli médina, page 484

N

Not to scale

To Youth Hostel

Libya

The cemetery for British and Italian Christians – (Al Magbarah al Masihiyyah) **Christian & war**
– lies between Shari'a Gamal Nasser and Shari'a Jamairiyah.In Tripoli there are **cemeteries**
war cemeteries left over from the Second World War. The British and Commonwealth Cemetery is two km west of Tripoli, 400 metres south of the main
road. There is also a British Military Cemetery.

Essentials

Tripoli is moderately endowed with hotels, adequate for a country with little commer- **Sleeping**
cial tourism but a large immigrant worker population. Business visitors are fairly well *Phone code: 021*
catered for with 5 or so large hotels in Tripoli centre. Cheaper accommodation is difficult to find when arriving in the evening, so try to book ahead.

East of the old town A *Al-Mehari*, Shari'a Al-Fatah, 14 storey building overlooking **Hard currency**
the harbour, close to the main government secretariats. T3334090/6, Tx22090. Pool, **hotels**
best service in Tripoli, US$215 double room, must be paid in US dollars, but not really
A grade. NB rooms may be requisitioned when an official delegation is in town,
whether you have a reservation or not. A *Grand Hotel* (ask for *Funduq Al-Kebir*), also
on Shari'a Al-Fatah to the east, T4445940, F4445959 very close to the médina, central.
2 restaurants, good buffet, excellent café, car hire, tall building is good landmark, currently US$200 double room, must be in foreign exchange, but not A grade by a long
shot, travel agency.

Southwest of old town B *Funduq Bab al Bahr*, multi-storey building close to the
five Daht al Imad towers, Tripoli's main business centre, on the Corniche, T3330676,
F608014. Around $US 140 for a double room. Tour agencies can sometimes negotiate
good rates. B *Funduq Bab al Medina*, next to the Bab al Bahr, T 608051. Sea views but
very much a third choice in this category. B *Funduq el Waha*, on Shara Umar al
Mukhtar, near the Libyan Arab Airlines office, T3612021, F602041.

A *Safwa*, Shari'a Baladiya, heading for Garden City,T4448691, F4449062. Small **Other hotels**
self-catering flats at 120LD a night. Reservations necessary. C *Al Waddan*, Shari'a Sidi
Issa, just off Shari'a al Fath, T3330041/2. Good location in the old 1930s centre, and a

Libya

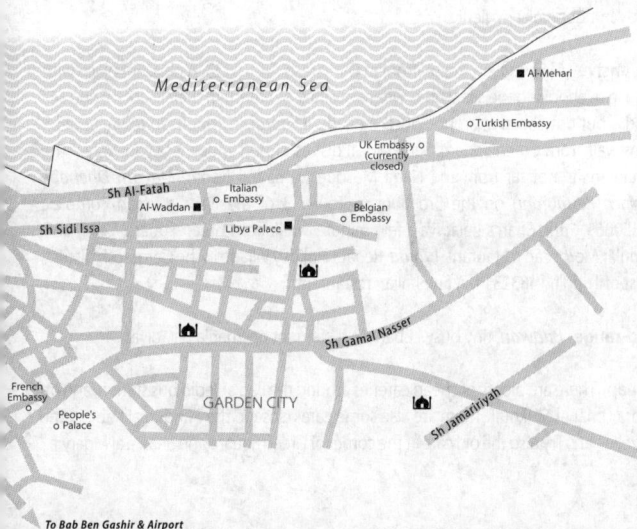

better price at 60LD a night, than the hard-currency hotels. Often full, so try to reserve. **C** *Hotel al Jawda*, off Shari'a Umar al Mukhtar near the Corniche, T4446908. A recent hotel, 50LD a night. **D** *Hotel Atlas*, southwest of old town at top of Shari'a Omar Mukhtar on a small square to the right, T3336815, simple but clean rooms with bath. Around 20LD a night. **D** *Funduq Bahr al Abiad* (*Hotel White Sea*) T4860246. 200 rooms, with bath, half a/c, roof terrace, clean but rather informal, 20LD a night. **D** *Hotel Lulah*, seafront to the southwest of the medina, T3331013. Clean, many rooms with sea view, restaurant, café, room with bath, breakfast incl. 20LD a night. **D** *Qasr Libya* (*Libya Palace*), Shari'a Sidi Issa, T3331181. Service and cleanliness of fair standard, busy reception area, quiet rooms, travel agency. 25LD a night. Just under 1 km from the old town. Recommended. **D** *Hotel al Mamun*, Shari'a al Mamun, near the main bus and taxi station, very handy for both old city and central Tripoli, T3333372. Fills up quickly. 25LD a night. **D** *Hotel Tripoli*, Shari'a al Rached (parallel to Shari'a al Mamun), just 200m from the central taxi station, T4441093/5. Clean rooms, very reasonable but eat elsewhere. 30LD a night.

There are also small workers' hotels with **shared facilities** (category **E**) on the seafront beneath the walls of the médina, mainly clean but noisy. Outside Tripoli there are several **tourist villages** which can offer accommodation on request, but which are often very full in the vacation periods. Try the *Ghornata Holiday Village*, T4773942, at Gargaresh, although reservations will be very difficult in the summer.

Youth hostels *Tripoli city* for camping and dormitory accommodation, 69 Shari'a Amr Ibn Al-As, T4445171. Kitchen, 120 beds, breakfast available, family rooms, 2 km from Green Square. *Gargaresh*, Shari'a Gargaresh, 5 km south of Tripoli. Open 0700-2400, 200 beds, meals, family room, laundry, airport 20 km, harbour 2 km, T4776694. Booking recommended at both hostels.

Eating The main restaurants for western visitors are in the principal hotels, all of which are open to non-residents. Some hotels such as the *Grand* and the *Al-Mehari* have more than 1 restaurant. They are all 'dry' but adequate. Popular eating places for the large numbers of non-Libyan Arabs are to be found in the city centre on or just off Shari'a Omar Mukhtar and on the main roads immediately leading off southwards from the Green Square. They are cheap and offer local cuisine tending towards the rough and ready but generally hygienic.

Expensive *Al Shiraa*, on the seafront at Gargaresh, T4775123. A pleasant place with terrace overlooking the sea. This is where businesses entertain their clients. Good sea food – but not cheap at around 50LD a head. *Al Sharqi*, in Tripoli old town, under 5 mins walk from Green Square. Serves local dishes, closed Friday. Ask your way – the restaurant is not far from the Naqa Mosque (Jamaa al Naqa). *Mat'am Dhehabi*, (*Golden Restaurant*) on the 3rd floor in Tower 3 of the Daht al Imad complex, T3350069. *Safir*, Shari'a Baladiya a few minutes walk from Green Square, T4447064. Popular Moroccan restaurant. *Wajda*, Regata Holiday Village in the Gargaresh district, west of Tripoli, T4832314. A fine Italian restaurant.

Mid-range *Badwan*, tiny busy Lebanese restaurant on Shari'a Baladiya.

Cheap There are plenty of cheap eateries around the Bab al Jedid bus station, and on Shara Umar al Mukhtar. There are also some cafés close to the Funduq al Kabir in the Gazelle Park. Try also the old café at the corner of Green Square and Shari'a al Mqaryif.

Shari'a 1st September and Shari'a Mohammad Magarief have shops with clothes and other consumer goods, travel agents, and an abundance of cafés. 2 more streets fan out from Green Square and the adjacent traffic island. Shari'a Mizran and Shari'a Amr Ibn Al-As carry small scale commercial activity, bakers, general goods shops, traders and others.Joining these streets to Shari'a 1st September and Al-Fatah area are cross links, the most important of which is Shari'a Tahiti. Shari'a Omar Mukhtar leads off Green Square directly running southwestwards. On the right is a red marble faced building, the Secretariat of Justice, with the rest of the street given over to trading houses, Arab restaurants, cafés and shops. On the right the street opens up on the site of the *Tripoli Fair ground* used for international exhibitions. Shari'a Omar Mukhtar ultimately gives access to the main western suburbs such as *Gurgi* and the former European villa area of *Giorgim Poppoli* with its supermarkets, beach clubs and tourist centres. Shari'a Ben Ashur has dry cleaning, a pharmacy, a bakery and grocery stores. Throughout the central business and inner residential districts there are excellent doctors' surgeries, chemist shops, food stores, general goods shops, bakeries and small cafés. There are some popular restaurants, though these are almost entirely confined to the streets off and adjacent to the streets fanning out of Green Square. The poorer residential suburbs have small scale facilities and often no doctors, though pharmacies are common. The larger suburbs with pre-existing commercial centres such as Gurgi have a full range of facilities.

If it is reading material you require then the main bookshop is *Fergiani's* near the roundabout off Green Square on Shari'a 1st September with a 2nd shop in Shari'a Al Jamaririyah near Eliarmuk Square. Try also *Dar Al Hadara* close to *Fergiani's* at 90 Shari'a 1st September, for books in Arabic and English on scientific subjects.

There is a football team – dates and times of games are advertised in the Arabic press. The main opening for sport for visitors to Tripoli is swimming, snorkelling and scuba-diving in the sea along the coastline. For medium-to-long stay travellers it might be worth joining a beach club, most being on the Gurgi side of the city. Each club is marked with a large board which, though in Arabic, makes it quite clear that it is a sports centre. It is advised that enquiries are made personally at the gate, through a state agency or, most easily, through a travel agent.

Local Bus: there are frequent, though in rush hour crowded, bus services across town on regular routes. The green/grey Tripoli service buses can be easily recognized with a destination board in Arabic but also a route number. The service can be rather erratic and breakdowns are common but the system is cheap. Buses run through the main bus terminal and other stops are clearly marked. There are no printed time tables and it is best to ask at your hotel before proceeding. **Taxis**: leave from stands between Shari'a Omar Mukhtar and the sea. They ply for hire on a shared basis but, with haggling over the price, can be hired by an individual or private group.

Long distance Bus: the terminal is in the street adjacent to the international departure station approximately 1 km west from the médina. Domestic timetables are very flexible. Departures from Tripoli leave early in the morning and passengers for small or distant Libyan settlements should be at the bus station not later than 0630 to be sure of a seat. Buses for the 12-hour journey to **Benghazi** cost 10LD for the public service and 15LD for the private service leaving daily at 0830 using air conditioned coaches. Internal bus routes cover all towns and cities. Small 10 seater private buses do the journey from/to Ghadamès, leaving when full in the late afternoon. Cost 7LD, with several stops for refreshment and police checks. Try the agency round the corner from the government ticket office, T622090 or T501088.

Libya

Directory **Banks** As money can be changed elsewhere to greater advantage a bank may not be necessary. Banks are generally open 0800-1400, in the central shopping zone, with one conveniently on the roundabout adjacent to Green Square and others on the main roads leaving the square. Go early for shorter queues. *Al-Umma Bank*, Shari'a Omar Mukhtar, T3334031. *Central Bank of Libya*, Shari'a Gamal Nasser, T3333591. *Jamahiriya Bank*, Shari'a Mohammad Magarief, T3333553. *Libyan National Arab Bank*, Shari'a 1st September. *National Commercial Bank*, Green Square, T3337191. *Sahara Bank*, Shari'a 1st September, T3332771. *Wahhadah Bank*, T3334016.

Communications Area code: 021. **Post office:** this is found on Maidan Al-Jaza'er opposite the former cathedral and has telecommunications facilities. **Telephone:** Note that old 5 digit numbers beginning with 3 place 33 in front, beginning with 4 place 44 in front.

Embassies Tripoli is the diplomatic capital. *UK* citizens, for whom there is no embassy, should address themselves to the Italian embassy/consulate for assistance where there is a British affairs desk T3331191. Nationals of the USA, Venezuela and other countries suffer from periodic interruptions in diplomatic relations. Travel agents will have information on the current and constantly changing situation. *Algeria*, 12 Shari'a Kairouan, T4440025. *Belgium*, 1 Shari'a Abu Obeidat Ibn Al-Jerah, T3337797. *Chad*, 25 Shari'a Mohammad Sadeqi, T4443955. *CIS*, Shari'a Mostafa Kamel, T3330545/6. *Czechoslovakia*, Shari'a Ahmad Lotfi Al-Said, T3334959. *France*, Shari'a Ahmad Lotfi Al-Said, T3333526-7. *Germany*, Shari'a Hassan Al-Masha'i, T3330554. *Greece*, 18 Shari'a Jellal Beyar, Tx20409. *India*, 16 Shari'a Mahmud Sheltut, T4441835-6. *Iraq*, Shari'a Gurgi, T70856. *Italy*, Shari'a Wahran, POB 219, T3330742. *Jordan*, Shari'a Ibn Oof, T3332707. *Kuwait*, Shari'a Amar Ibn Yasr, T4440281-2. *Lebanon*, Shari'a Amar Ibn Yasr, T3333733. *Malta*, 13 Shari'a Abu Bin Ka'ab, T3338081-4. *Mauritania*, Shari'a Issa Wukuak, T4443646. *Morocco*, Shari'a Bashir Al-Ibrahimi, T4441346. *Niger*, Shari'a Tantawi Jowheri, T4443104. *Pakistan*, Shari'a Khatabi, T4440072. *Saudi Arabia*, 2 Shari'a Kairouan, T3330485-6. *Spain*, Shari'a Al-Jaza'er, T3335462. *Syria*, 4 Shari'a Mohammad Rashid Rida, T33371955. *Tunisia*, Shari'a Bashir Al-Ibrahimi, T3331051-2. *Turkey*, 36 Shari'a Gamal Abdel Nasser, T46528/9. *UAE*, Shari'a Aljaza'er, T4444146-8. *United Kingdom* c/o Italian Embassy, T3331191/2/3, F4449121, when open Shari'a Al-Fatah, T3331195.

Hospitals & medical services **Chemists:** in all shopping areas are normally marked with a red crescent or green cross sign. Chemists have a duty rota which is normally reliable, but travellers with special needs are advised to bring their own stores. **Hospitals:** there are several large, well-equipped hospitals. The central civil unit is on the main road out to Sidi Mesri near the inner ring road. A secondary hospital is at Al-Khadra (the old military hospital).

Tour companies & travel agents These are in the shopping precincts in the main aves leading from the Green Square. There are numerous travel agencies we recommend. *Libyan Travel & Tourist Co* on Mizran St headed by Salem Azzabi T4448005. Also *Libya Tours Co* in *Libya Palace Hotel*, T3331189, F3336688 where English and French are spoken. Ask for Mrs Hafida. *Libyan Arab Airlines* LAA main office opposite Tripoli Fair ground, T3337500 open 0730-1630; best office is by *Hotel Kebir*. *Ta Fani*, Shari'a Omar al Mukhtar T3340393/3340394. *Oea*, Tower 3, Dhal al 'Imad, T3338237. Good reputation.

West Tripoli suburbs: tourist villages

Janzur is on the old coast road running west out of Tripoli, as is the **D** *Janzur Tourist Village*, right on the coast, mainly new, with a wide range of accommodation including bungalows and apartments. Facilities available include sailing, tennis, cinema, well equipped children's play room, shops, clinic. The village is signposted in Arabic as *Médina Siahiah Janzur*. **D** *Abu Nawas Village* is another small beach resort in the Giorgim Poppoli area, old but cheap and open to all-comers at 7LD per night, close to shops, chemists and restaurants sited on the main street of north Gurgi. **E** *Old Janzur Tourist Village*, is further in towards the Tripoli boundary, comparatively run down, but convenient for shopping and the facilities of what was the Giorgim Poppoli estate.

Booking at these tourist villages is not easy from a distance since they are run by state organizations and are not essentially commercial in design.

Persistence in seeing the on-site manager might be the best way to get accommodation. Their big disadvantage is their isolation from the city though bus or shared taxi transport is available on the old coast road 500 metres south of the beach club sites. Charges per night vary with the season and the quality of the complex between 5 and 20LD.

Note that old coast road into Tripoli is very crowded with shopping traffic and local people and should be avoided in the rush hours. Tripoli centre is only five km away but it can take 30 minutes or more to complete the journey across the Wadi Mejennin bridge and then into the centre via Shari'a Omar Mukhtar.

East of Tripoli to Leptis Magna via Al-Khums

The main coastal highway runs from Tripoli eastwards via Al-Khums and Misrata. The road links all the major coastal towns and passes through one of the richest agricultural zones of the country. The main reason for following this route is of course to visit Leptis Magna, perhaps the most imposing Roman ruin in North Africa.

Colour map 5, grid A3

The drive to Leptis Magna from Tripoli takes at least one hour. Out of Tripoli, you have the choice of either the old coast road or the modern highway. Buses and taxis leave Tripoli on the coastal main highway. A dual carriageway leaves Tripoli city via Bab Ben Ghashir and travels through dense developments of villas and small houses, mainly expensive properties built on former oasis gardens. There are old square, single storey, whitewashed farmsteads interspersed with modern villas. Occasional whitewashed small domed shrines, the tombs of *marabouts* or Islamic holy men, are visible. Around 32 km east of Tripoli, at **Tajurah**, is **E** *Madinah Siahiah Tajurah* (*Tajurah tourist village*). The beach is popular with Libyans on Friday but is otherwise clear for other tourists. The tourist village is an old development and open to all-comers.

Sixty kilometres out of Tripoli is **Gasr Garabouli**, on the old coast road. There is now a bypass, but you can take the spur into town for petrol and other services. Former Italian farmsteads can be seen among recent Libyan housing.

East from Gasr Garabouli there is open country with orchards and olives and almond plantations. At **Gasr Khiar** there are roadside shops on the main highway, cafés and petrol. **Al-Khums** is way-marked at Km 41. There are plenty of roadside cafés along the main road.

East of Tripoli

Telathin (literally Km 30 mark) is a tiny settlement built around a mosque. Shop and café are adjacent. There is a fine area for swimming on the coast just north of the road. In season, succulent oranges are on sale at the roadside. A good black top road runs to it then goes on to a rocky seashore two kilometres below. Al-Khums town lies approximately 20 km to the east over the forested ridge. There is accommodation at the **D** *Funduq & Mat'am Al-Naqazzah*, clean if somewhat run-down hotel and restaurant located in an area of conifer trees north of the main road. 15 beds, restaurant and café, cooler in summer than the surrounding plains.

Al-Khums ‏الخمس‎

Phone code: 030
Colour map 5, grid A3

With new buildings going up, and many incomplete, Al-Khums is not a very pretty sight. The Friday **market** is held in the street leading to the old harbour. The main town has expanded considerably in recent years. Some Italian and British military and civilian landmarks are still to be found, with the army barracks as they were. The old market place next to the barracks is now the town taxi stand with transport available on a trip or day basis in private or shared taxi. There is an Arabic language cinema on the left of the street opposite the taxi ranks. Old Turkish houses have been demolished and replaced by a ghastly town council building just below the cinema.

Arriving in Al-Khums, care is needed when driving at all times. On the outskirts, slow moving vehicular and pedestrian traffic makes the main highway dangerous. Buses stop in the town centre near the taxi rank and on the main road at the *Al-Khums Hotel*.

There is a vast extension to the town from the army barracks east along the coast towards **Wadi Lebda** and between the coast and the by-pass built up solidly with mainly poor quality housing with few services for the traveller. Chalets have been built along the seashore towards Leptis Magna. The **modern port** is located on the west side of the town. There is some industry including a cement plant.

Sleeping

Unfortunately the town's oldest hotel, *Funduq Al-Khums*, always fairly run down has now closed its doors. At the junction of the main coastal highway and the first black top road after the *Naqazzah Hotel*, turn off to the **E** *Funduq Kabir Al-Khums*, cheap but noisy from close-passing traffic, including breakfast, and quantities of cockroaches. **F** *Funduq Al-Sherief* is cheaper. **Youth hostel** *Sports City*, three km southwest of centre, T2320888, 160 beds, meals, kitchen, laundry, family rooms.

Leptis Magna ‏لبدة‎

Colour map 5, grid A3

The ruins of Leptis Magna, second Roman port in Africa, must be among the most extraordinary ancient sites in the Mediterranean. Situated at the mouth of the Wadi Lebda immediately to the east of the modern town of Al-Khums, the town is a place of great splendour still. There is a noble triumphal arch, and vast baths, famous in antiquity. The city exported huge quantities of olive oil and grain, and benefited from the largesse of a third century emperor, Septimius Severus, a local lad made good. In early modern times, sands invaded the site, preserving it for 20th century archaeologists to discover.

Ins and outs

Getting there

Al-Khums is the nearest town to Leptis and the site is accessible from there by bus and shared taxi. Journey time from Tripoli is around 90 minutes. A further taxi ride is necessary to reach the site.

Getting around

The site is open daily 0800-1730, 0.25LD adult, 0.1LD child. With the new museum opened July 1995 (entrance 0.5LD), café and telephone this is a busy site. The sight can be visited on foot. All the important buildings can be reached adjacent to or just off the main paved monumental road from the present entrance through the newer parts of the site. A full inspection would require at least a full day – and rather longer for visitors with a specialist interest since Leptis Magna is well preserved and has an unequalled range of buildings from the classical period. In summer the site is very hot, and the sight might be best seen in a series of visits when the heat is less oppressive. Approximately 4 km west of Al-Khums is a minor site, the Villa Selena with fine mosaics. Permission to visit it can be obtained at the entrance to Leptis (no extra charge).

History and background

The origins of Leptis Magna are not known with certainty. It is probable that a Berber settlement first existed at the site which was developed by Levantine trading groups from Tyre and Sidon that made use of the small natural harbour. Greeks also appear to have been at the site. In Carthaginian times the people at Lebda paid tribute of one talent per day, reflecting a certain prosperity based on a trading hinterland stretching deep into Tripolitania and Sirte. By the time of the third Punic War there were approximately 10,000-15,000 inhabitants in the city.

In 107 AD Leptis set up formal relations with Rome and, despite the disruption caused by attacks from tribes from the desert interior, the city continued to develop. Leptis gained full rights to Roman citizenship as a *colonia* under the Emperor Trajan (98-117 AD). The early Roman period saw the construction of basic harbour works and a forum close by the original Punic settlement.

Roman prosperity

The fortunes of Leptis Magna were greatly improved in 193 AD when Septimius Severus (193-211 AD) was made Emperor of Rome. He had been born at Leptis on April 11, 146 AD. The prosperity of the city was considerable and the population grew to 60,000-80,000 people. The peace of Tripolitania was ensured after the emperor put down the most warlike tribes of the region in 203.

Septimius Severus travelled restlessly across his domains, crushing a rebellion here, attempting new border conquests in other regions. The winter of 202-203 AD saw him at Leptis. He had grown rich by confiscating the property of his rivals and enemies, and so was able to launch major building works to embellish his home town. (Rulers never seem to forget their hometowns). The best builders and sculptors of the day were brought over, a new forum and an immense temple were constructed, dedicated to the city's protecting gods. The harbour was extended, water supply improved, and an elaborate triumphal arch erected. Leptis became one of the finest cities of the empire.

Leptis suffered later from a decline in the Saharan trade and the silting of the mouth of the river. Attacks from Asturian groups beginning in 363 AD brought great problems for the city.

Vandals & Byzantines

In 455 AD the Vandals arrived and took Leptis, leaving it eventually in the hands of the Berber Zenata tribe until 533 when the Byzantines under Belisarius restored Roman rule. The Byzantines were put under heavy pressure from all

Libya

sides and in Libya from attacks by the Zenata and finally the Arab invasions of 643-644 AD. The later incursions of the Beni Hillal and Beni Sulaim led to the completed abandonment of Leptis Magna in the 11th century.

In succeeding centuries, coastal sand dunes overwhelmed the site, preserving it from destruction during the succeeding centuries hence the site is below the present ground level with access via a steep flight of steps. Most of the excavations at Leptis were undertaken in the Italian period when the monuments, preserved from damage by encroaching sands, were unearthed. Their excavation was extremely important to the Italian colonial enterprise, proving as it did the latinity of Tripolitania – and hence Italy's right to be there.

Leptis Magna

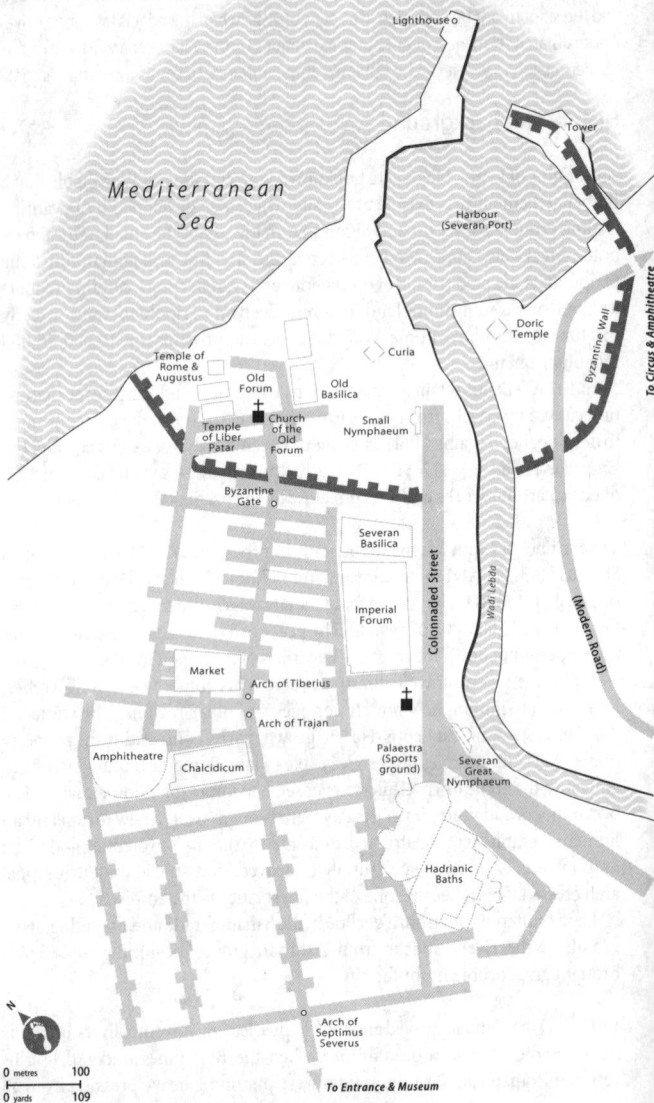

Mediterranean Sea

Lighthouse

Tower

Harbour (Severan Port)

Byzantine Wall

To Circus & Amphitheatre

Doric Temple

Curia

Temple of Rome & Augustus

Old Forum

Old Basilica

Church of the Old Forum

Small Nymphaeum

Temple of Liber Patar

Byzantine Gate

Severan Basilica

Imperial Forum

Colonnaded Street

Wadi Lebda

(Modern Road)

Market

Arch of Tiberius

Arch of Trajan

Amphitheatre

Chalcidicum

Palaestra (Sports ground)

Severan Great Nymphaeum

Hadrianic Baths

Arch of Septimius Severus

To Entrance & Museum

0 metres 100
0 yards 109

Libya

Visiting Leptis Magna

Note the warnings that the ruins must not be touched nor artefacts taken away. These must be taken very seriously since successful prosecution can lead to imprisonment. The few sellers of items to be found on the site are operating illegally and should not be approached. There are guides available for a fee (5LD seems to be a minimum) who speak the main European languages. Although Leptis Magna, designated by UNESCO as a World Heritage site, is an important archaeological site it is not complex since the best elements date from a fairly specific period. Guidebooks, maps and postcards of this site and others in Libya are available here.

The site

Basic tour

A minimum tour begins at the **harbour** at the original Punic site and the adjacent ruins of the **old forum**. The newer harbour works undertaken during the reign as Emperor of Septimius Severus are also on view in this same area. The **triumphal arch** together with the new quarter along the 410 metres monumental road also date from this period. In the new quarter the key sites are the Colonnaded Street, the semi circular **nymphaeum**, the **forum** and **basilica**. Other areas to be seen include the magnificent **amphitheatre** dating from 56 AD, among the most photogenic sites in North Africa, and the **baths** constructed under the Emperor Hadrian.

An extended tour

The first of the antiquities at the site is the **arch of Septimius Severus** which lies on the left at the end of a short avenue leading from the entrance. It has four facias.

To the east of the arch are the **Hadrianic Baths** (Italian: *terme*), an enormous construction covering, with outbuildings approximately three hectares.

Hadrianic Baths & Palaestra

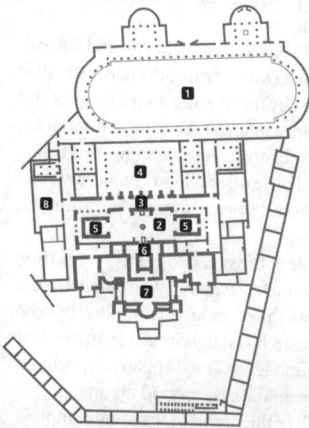

N

0 metres	25		
0 yards	27		

1 Palaestra
2 Frigidarium
3 Corridor
4 Pool
5 Small pools
6 Tepidarium
7 Caldarium
8 Gymnasium

This was one of the largest bath houses built outside Rome itself. The baths were put in place in 123-127 AD and improved and extended at various later dates. Excavations at the baths were begun in 1920 by Dr P Romanelli.

The baths are best approached through the **palaestra**, which is made up of a rectangular base with circular ends surrounded by a portico of 72 columns. There are five doorways into the baths, two on the north aspect leading from the palaestra. To the south two more doorways open onto a corridor parallel to the fascia. Behind lies the frigidarium a room of 30.35 x 15.40 metres. In the centre of the frigidarium is a small monument dedicated to Septimius Severus, possibly commemorating the grant of full Roman rights to the city by that emperor. At the east and west sides of the frigidarium are two highly decorated pools still showing their facings

Libya

of black granite. Immediately south of the frigidarium are two anterooms and connecting corridors together with a tepidarium and its lateral pools. Further south lies the calidarium or warm room. This room leads on by two doors to heated rooms, the stufe or sudatorium.

The Severan **nymphaeum**, with its high semicircular walls and fountain basin stands at the south end of the **Colonnaded Street** which connects the Hadrianic Baths with the harbour. The street lies between the imperial forum and the Severan basilica and the harbour. It has a broad, central section on either side of which stood covered porticoes. The supporting columns which carried arches stood on square raised pedestals.

The **imperial forum** lies at the heart of Severan Leptis Magna. It is a spectacular sight despite the ravages of time and looters. It abuts onto the basilica to the north and forms a great trapezoidal shape with maximum dimensions of 132 metres x 87 metres.

The **old basilica** (38 metres x 92 metres) is on the eastern side of the **old forum**. It has two semicircular recesses at its narrow ends. There are three lines of columns running the length of the church. The basilica is surrounded by side galleries. Various dedications in Latin are found in the Basilica including n ornate inscription to Emperor Caesar Lucius Septimius. There is a great variety of sculptures and reliefs of mythical figures and animals.

The amphitheatre at Leptis Magna is in excellent condition and commands views in all directions from the western side of the city. the theatre has a diameter of 70 metres and faces to the northeast, heavily columned and with a stage and its entrances still clearly visible.

There is another set of **baths** at the site located close to the sea in the waterfront area of the city to the west of the old forum. These baths were never finished and are thought to have been under construction at the time of the Vandal invasions. The new baths are best approached from the east through a hexagonal domed hall, named by the British archaeologist Richard Goodchild the New Calidarium. Adjacent and to the north of the new *calidarium* is a building of similar size which was used as an *apodyterium* for an earlier bath system but later became disused. West again of these buildings is the new *frigidarium*, which was constructed to be a vaulted hall with a plunge bath at each corner but which was not completed.

The **harbour** at Leptis takes the form of a basin open to the east and fed with water from the Wadi Lebda. There is a small **Doric temple** in Hellenistic style and a tower. The harbour has been studied by underwater archaeologists and some of the finds are shown in the main museum near the main site entrance. There are clear signs of severe silting, yet the historical record shows that Leptis port handled many thousands of tonnes of olive oil and food grain every year. For centuries, it was a vital point with produce being shipped out from the empire's North African granary to Rome

The **circus** is on the extreme eastern side of the site. It forms a great narrow horse shoe of 450 metres in length and 100 metres wide, aligned parallel to the coastline. It is as yet not fully excavated but the starting gates are clearly to be seen at the city end, while the monumental arch and the circular terminus is at the east end. There are two tunnels at ground level carved apparently through solid rock. There are tiers of seats rising from the base around the arena.

The **amphitheatre**, immediately south of the Circus in the same complex, is thought to date from 56 AD and has been well excavated by Italian archaeologists. It is slighly eliptical in shape with circumferences of 100 metres by 80 metres.

Eastern Tripolitania: Al-Khums to Zliten and Misrata

Moving east from Al-Khums and Leptis Magna, you can take the old road through the palm oases. The road is single lane black top, often built up above the adjacent gardens. Beware of local traffic emerging abruptly from side roads and of the road surface in wet weather when the black top becomes notoriously slippery and vehicles can slide off into the palmeries. For cyclists the steep road embankment through this narrow route also has its hazards since two cars can pass only with difficulty. The old single track road has constant small scale road works. Children walk on the road and there is much local traffic from side roads. Motorists and others wishing to avoid the oasis route can take the new road which passes one kilometre further inland between the palmeries and the main area of the former Italian La Valdagno agricultural estate to Wadi Ki'am. Buildings come right up to the new road.

Colour map 5, grid A3

For those with time the **oasis route** is recommended. After Leptis, the oasis, here called the **Sahel Al-Ahmad**, has dense mainly modern farmhouses. Farming continues in *suani* (small walled irrigated traditional gardens) but little effort is put into farming at present. The principal spring field crops in the gardens are wheat, barley and broad beans. The crops are mainly thin but the palm canopy remains for most part in good trim, providing welcome shade.

At **Wadi Ki'am**, Tripolitania's only flowing river, the long-established agricultural estate spreads out on both sides of the road. The original farm was a mere 120 hectares of two hectares plots fed by irrigation from the impounded stream of a spring source in the Wadi Ki'am. There is now an extension of reclaimed land under orchards and trees from Wadi Ki'am west to join up with old Sahel Al-Ahmad oasis and ex-La Valdagno.

Zliten, 37 km east of Al-Khums, is a thriving administrative and academic centre. Turn left into town for all main services. Zliten is surrounded by *marabout* tombs famous for their qualities of improving fertility, so inspiring pilgrimages. These tombs are best visited with a local inhabitant. Visit the *zawia* shrine of Sidi Abdesselam and the cemetery of his descendants. There is one hotel, *Les Gazelles*, and a youth hostel, 20 beds, breakfast, shop, kitchen. Try also the *Hotel Waha*, 20LD, T623426.

Zliten

زليطن

Phone code: 0512

Libya

Misrata مصراتة

The highway east from Zliten passes through poor grade lands. The once thinly populated coastal strip had a scattering of fragile oases. The Italians set up estates here for incoming Italian farmers. The largest was **Ed-Dafnia** where the orchard groves of olives and almonds cover what was originally thin pastureland. The Italian effort at land settlement was added to by the Libyan Government after independence with new areas reclaimed and ex-Italian estates taken over by Libyan farmers. Close to Misrata in the Zawiet Al-Mahjub district is the former estate of the pre-Fascist Governor of Tripolitania, General Volpi. However, the Italian farming estates which were so much the characteristic of Misrata oases have been reduced in importance by occupation by townsfolk who treat their holdings as amenity areas rather than as working farms.

Phone code: 051
Colour map 5, grid A3

👉 *A legendary meeting at Syrte*

The two main halves of Libya, Tripolitania and Cyrenaica, meet at the coastal settlement of Syrte, on the gulf of the same name and now a place of some political importance as the centre of Libyan government. Back in ancient days, Syrte was the meeting point of the Greek and Punic worlds, of the Pentapoli, five federated Hellenic towns to the east and Punic trading posts to the west.

As in all such cases, there is a suitably explanatory legend. Hellenic Cyrene and Carthage were at war. To define the frontier between them, a pair of brothers set out from each city, and the boundary would be marked at the spot where they met. The laid-back Cyrenaican brothers made slow progress, unlike the fleet-footed Carthaginians. The result was that the two pairs met at Syrte, not so very far from Cyrene. The Cyrenaicans, seeing that their city would lose considerable territory should the boundary be at Syrte, proposed a deal. They offered their lives for the race to be re-run – or the Carthaginian pair would give its lives at Syrte and the boundary would stay there. The Carthaginians preferred the second solution, and for their self-sacrifice were named the philanoi, the 'lovers of praise', and an altar was put up to them.

Centuries later, in the 1930s, a coastal highway was completed. The colonizing Italians erected a triumphal arch at Syrte to commemorate the classical legend and celebrate their newly declared colony, Libia. No trace of the monument survives today.

The expansion of Misrata as an urban centre has been prodigious. Population growth within the town has been much increased by mass migration from the rural areas. Gridiron planned Misrata is the administrative and educational capital of eastern Tripolitania with most ministries having local offices. Schools, hospitals and colleges are located in the new town. There seems to be less riotous self-build construction in progress than elsewhere.

Misrata has taken off thanks to the development of the steel industry. The construction of the two iron and steel mills created employment and demand for local services so that there is a real sense of growth in the area. The power of the steel mill authorities is considerable and has helped to give a sense of unity to the town. Second, the old marina has been extensively redeveloped to take shipping coming to service the industrial plant with raw materials and other goods. The town centre has the usual shops, cafés and restaurants. A large number of immigrant managers and labourers live in the town and this is reflected in a fairly cosmopolitan atmosphere in the cafés. Many foreigners are housed on the steel mill residential site.

Sights Misrata is not exactly well endowed with things touristic, but if you have time, take a look at the **sand dunes** on the west side of the town, some of the tallest sea dunes in the world. There is also the **steel mill** and the **port**.

Sleeping **D** *Hotel Misrata* is large, modern and generally as well run as the larger hotels in Tripoli; booking is advised, rates as for those in the capital, large restaurant and other facilities, 25LD, T619776/7. The **E** *Massif al Jazira*, 7 km out of Misrata belongs to the Winzrik travel agency. 15LD double T631940. **Youth hostel** 4 km west of centre, T624855, open 0700-2300, 120 beds, family rooms, meals, kitchen, laundry, bus 400 metres, reservations recommended May-September.

Eating There are cheap eateries to be found in the central business district. For a western-type menu use *Hotel Misrata*.

Libya

For completeness sake, Tauorga some 40 km south of Misrata, is situated in the middle of a swamp formed by the great Tauorga salt lake and was reputed to be a refuge for escaping slaves. The town is located on a set of springs which provides water for agriculture, including a modern farm settlement set up by the government.

Tauorga
تورغاء

An inland route: Al-Khums to Tripoli via Tarhuna

The inland hill road back to Tripoli from Al-Khums and Leptis Magna is well worth taking. The highway is occasionally narrow but this disadvantage is off-set by a route through hill agriculture and breathtaking plantations of almond and olives.

The alternative to a direct route back to Tripoli from **Al-Khums** and **Leptis Magna** is to follow the road through the Jabal Nafusa via Tarhuna which takes about two hours. From Al-Khums travel west on the main highway to Tripoli but take the Tarhuna road at the first left hand junction. It is 67 km to Tarhuna from this junction. The road follows more or less the line of an old road but is a good width now. Take care on this road as it is dangerous, with mixed traffic and many curves as the road rises towards the town of **Al-Qusbat**.

Today the main town of the Jabal Mislata (a sub-region of the Jabal Nafusa) **Al-Qusbat** been much extended in an undistinguished way, spoiling the former charm of the place. There are most facilities, including a hospital. There is no hotel and travellers interested in walking in the Mislata should stay in Al-Khums.

From Al-Qusbat take the road to Tarhuna. The road passes through scenic country in open landscape with ex-Italian olive and almond plantations at Al-Khadra and Qasr Dawn. Qasr Dawn has a hospital, police, school and shops.

Tarhuna is home to the Faculty of Law of Al-Nasser University, north of the town towards Shershara. Cinema, shops, Libyan Arab Airlines, and hospitals are among the facilities in the town. Modern building has destroyed the town's character. The famous *Lady of Gharyan*, a wall painting on the barracks wall in the town painted by a US soldier in the Second World War, has sadly disap-peared. Tarhuna's excellent wines are also no longer to be found on the open market. Leave Tarhuna towards Shershara. If you need to sleep over, there is a **youth hostel**, c/o Education Department, Tarhuna, T3379, 20 beds, breakfast available, kitchen.

Tarhuna
ترهونة

The much-visited spring at **Shershara** has now stopped flowing as water has been diverted away and the local water table has fallen. A small stream now comes in through a narrow upper valley with dense trees. It flows under the road which acts as an Irish bridge and there is a tiny fall of water on rocks below the roadway. The lower valley is green but marred by rubbish. What was a very beautiful area is now very disappointing.

Libya

Sleeping The hotel at Shershara, *Funduq Shershara*, is in a poor state: the rooms are not now used, but it has a restaurant and café. The staff do their best but the general effect is not very good. The hotel has no water from time to time. Tea and a selection of cold soft drinks are available. Open 0800 to 2100.

Take the main road from Tarhuna out to the northwest. A dual carriageway leads down to Tripoli. An alternative road leads west to Gharyan. The Tripoli road is fast but winding. There is a junction slightly north of Tarhuna which permits a direct link from the petrol station at Biar Maji to Bani Walid approxi-mately 85 km to the south, and a second junction to Qatamah, 32 km from Biar Maji. **Youth hostel** in former *Bani Walid hotel*, T3222415, 30 beds, meals

West of
Tarhuna & back
to Tripoli

of trees and orchards. It is very green in spring, with uncultivated places forming rich pasture. The two-lane highway is very fast from Suani Ben Yadim to Az-Zahra and onward to the main town of Al-Aziziyah.

Aziziyah
العزيزية

Aziziyah has a petrol station, post office, hospital and several banks all on the main street or immediately adjacent in the principal side roads. From here, it is 221 km from Aziziyah to Nalut on the west end of Jabal Nafusa via the Wadi Hayyah route on the plain, via a single carriageway which is straight and fast.

South to Gharyan

The wooded landscape thins rapidly with travel south. The road remains dual carriageway. The first sightings of the Jabal peaks can be had as the road approaches the scarp slope of the Jabal Nafusa. A few kilometres south of Aziziyah the landscape opens up: this is prime cereal growing country in years of good rainfall. At Km 25, the road begins the rise towards the Jabal. It is a slow climb through wooded terrain. There is a quarry for tile making materials on the right as the main road climbs into the scarp face, then the sharp rise into the scarp face begins. There is a café at its foot on the left hand side of the road. On climbing the scarp the old Italian road to the left can be seen. Though it is no longer maintained it is a good alternative route for walkers and more adventurous cyclists. At the top of the slope the roadside is built incresingly built up. Approximately an hour from Tripoli centre you arrive at Gharyan.

The Jabal Nafusa

Jabal Nafusa and Ghadamès

*South of Tripoli lies the Jefara Plain, an agricultural region developed under the Italians. Then the land rises up into the Jabal Nafusa, one of the main Berber areas of Libya. Although the traditional ways of living and building are fast disappearing, you can still see ruined citadel villages at **Sharwas** and **Wighu** and fortified granaries at **Nalut**, **Kabao** and elsewhere. South of the Jabal Nafusa, desert begins in earnest. Close to the Tunisian frontier is legendary **Ghadamès** with its earthen architectures and oasis calm. Once a halt on the trans-Saharan trade routes, it is now an essential stop on the four-wheel drive itinerary.*

Geologically complex, the Jabal Nafusa is a long plateau which runs in broken foothills from Al-Khums on the coast to the start of the Jabal proper at Al-Qusbat. It then runs further west into southern Tunisia. It forms a scarp slope between 600 and 900 metres above the Jefara Plain and drops in altitude only gradually to the south into a set of rough basins. The largest of these lies around the town of Mizda, reputed to be the home of sorcerers, weavers of spells and holy men. After climbing another scarp to the south of Mizda, you reach the vast level-topped plateau of Hammadah Al-Hamra.

The climate here is quite different from the Jefara. Rains are slightly less reliable than the northern plains and diminish rapidly from the crest of the scarp to the south. Most places have over 250 millimetres of rain per year. Winters are quite cold and snow and frost can be expectd. Air temperatures throughout the year are lower than on the Jefara and the evenings in the summer are far more comfortable than in the plains.

The Jabal economy has proved remarkably versatile. Agriculture survives in most areas, although it has become increasingly concentrated on growing cereals and rain-fed orchard crops. Figs and apricots are famous on the Jabal and it is often the Berber groups who farm the rich grain land of the Jefara in the shadow of their mountain homes. The greatest source of funds for the Jabal groups is, however, remittance income from members of the family living elsewhere, usually in Tripoli or in other coastal towns. Even permanent residents of Tripoli have houses in their old tribal homes and a great deal of investment flows back to the Jabal villages in this way.

Jabal Nafusa and Gharyan

Taking the Tripoli-Gharyan route gives you have an ideal cross-section of lands and climates through the Plain and the Jabal foothills. Colour map 5, grid A2

Take the road south to Gharyan which now leads not only to the Jabal Nafusa but also from there to Ghadamès and Ghat in the deep Southwest. The road heads through the long tentacles of the Tripoli suburbs. There are then dense farmstead settlements out to the Suani Ben Yadim turn off. The road is dual carriageway and busy with traffic, mostly local. After the Suani Ben Yadim and Ben Ghashir towns/oases, the highway runs through a countryside

available, shop. It is a single carriageway road but good quality. Travellers can go directly via Mizdah to Sebha on black top without touching Tarhuna town. The road to Tripoli goes on to **Souk Al-Khemis**. Here there is a large roadside market, post office, police, shops and other basic facilities. At **As-Asbiah** is a junction with hospital, hospital-related housing but little else. Reaching **Souk Al-Sebt** there are more roadside shops, a petrol station and other services.

At **Ben Ghashir** the road leads off at a junction to the international airport link. Also from this point there is a dual carriageway to Tripoli, slow with heavy traffic. Roadside orange sellers are found in the spring season. Farm tractors and vehicles are plentiful on this dangerous road, mixing with fast airport and through traffic. Travellers can take the Tripoli-airport road with greater safety and speed.

Gharyan to Shakshuk

Heading south from Gharyan, and then west at Abuzeyan, the Jabal Nafusa road is narrow and slow allows you to visit a variety of Berber centres. There are apricot and fig orchards as well as traditional terraced farmland to be seen as the highway carries the traveller along the top of the scarp slope.

Gharyan غريان

Gharyan has seen much new building in recent years, reflecting its importance as a regional administrative centre. On climbing the scarp and traversing the olive groves where the road comes on to the summit of the Jabal, turn off right for Gharyan town, marked clearly but in Arabic script. Ask for *markaz al-médinah*, the town centre. Note that the climate of Jabal is much cooler than the plain and even in spring can be several degrees colder on the ridge than on the Jefara. Petrol available here.

Population: 100,000
Phone code: 041
Colour map 5, grid A2

C/D *Hotel Rabta*, T31970/74, brand new, in excellent condition, clean, run in a business-like way, working lifts, 68 rooms, for the business traveller there are suites costing 35LD for single and 45LD for double, restaurant serves lunches and dinners at 7.5LD per person, modern café facing onto the street, film theatre, most modern facilities, owned by the Libyan Social Security Organization. **D** *Funduq Gharyan Siahiah (Gharyan Tourist Hotel)*, T30105, very run down and seedy, 44 rooms in use, modest price for Libya, small restaurant and café, open all the year. **Youth hostel** 120 beds, breakfast included, family rooms, meals, laundry, kitchen and **camping** facilities in Gharyan at T31491, open 0700-2300, booking recommended. Information at the City Hall.

Sleeping

Leave Gharyan and travel west via the dual carriageway, passing through olive groves in rolling uplands. Shortly there is a road on the left to **Tigrinnah**, a former tobacco-growing area and now with fairly dense villa housing straddling it. Good views are to be had to the southwest over broken country. The Jabal top is lightly wooded with olives and figs. After Tigrinnah, at a small settlement called **Abuzeyan**, the road divides with Mizdah 82 km and Sabha 700 km by the road southwards to the left.

Southwest of Gharyan

After Tigrinnah the road on the top of the Jabal becomes a single carriageway. It passes through Assabah village with villas dispersed in farmlands. (Petrol in village centre). Travel on 95 km to **Jadu**. The road traverses increasingly arid countryside with a light scrub covering to the hills. There are small occasional groups of houses such as Al-Gualith at Km 91 and Km 79. At Km 77 there is a mosque, a café and a petrol station and at Km 76 a turn to the right leads to **Kikla** 12 km away. On the main road, a green area under cultivation at Km 75-73 is an agricultural project run by the government. There are good places for picnics on sections of the old road visible from the new highway.

Turn right for Yafran off the main highway. This old Berber town, perched on the Jabal top, is worth a visit. At Km 21 the black top road passes through fairly dense trees and cultivation. Note the good mainly reddish soils around Yafran. Reliable and heavy rains in late autumn and winter give the basis for a sound agriculture. There are fine views across the top of Jabal from the road towards Yafran. Also note the house decorations even on modern units, with complex ironwork doors, plaster work symbols such as butterflies and aircraft on house sides. Several small straggling villages lie along the roadside. There is petrol at **Qalah**, a village just before Yafran.

Libya

☛ *Berber culture in the Jabal Nafusa*

The culture of the Jabal Nafusa is for the most part Berber, though Arab tribes are interspersed within the main groups. Historically, the Berbers held the lands of the Jefara Plain with their main centre at Sabratha but they were driven back into the hills by the Arab invaders. The relative isolation of the Berber communities has meant not only a survival of their language and close kinship ties but also quite distinct urban forms and housing styles. In religion the Berbers are Muslim but follow the Ibadite branch of Islam, regarded by many Sunni Muslims as a heresy. The Berbers were aggressively separate from the Arabs on the Jabal Nafusa however much they intermarried with the Arab tribes elsewhere in Libya. The Berbers of the Jabal Nafusa participated in the revolts against Arab rule, the most ferocious of which took place in 896 AD.

More recently, the Berbers looked for the creation of a semi-autonomous Berber province. They had been a favoured group under the Italian occupation, making up important parts of the police forces in Tripolitania. On independence it was hoped that Berber cultural separateness would be acknowledged and their language given equal status with Arabic. The rise of Arab nationalism at this time forestalled any chance that the small numbers of Berbers, less than an estimated 150,000 in all at that time, could make their voice heard. The revolution of 1969 set back Berber aspirations and for some time the government in Tripoli refused to admit there was any such group as the Berbers. Despite the rapid economic changes resulting from oil wealth, the Berbers still keep a sense of cultural separateness and even superiority.

Yafran & around

بفرن

Phone code: 042

Yafran has been much modernized. The old town and fortified grain storage towers and other ruins are still visible on the hilltops in the town. The new town spreads along the black top road. Cultivation is still undertaken sporadically on terraces and scarp-top fields. The town is very scattered around a one-way traffic system through narrow streets. Although a hotel is under construction, there is no hotel currently in use. The town has all services, almost all clustered in the main square and the streets immediately adjacent to it. There is a **youth hostel** in the city centre, T12394, 45 beds, meals available.

Leave Yafran and continue to **Al-Awenia** and **Aïn Rumia**. This road gives wide views across from the Jabal to the Jefara below. Some terraces cut into the Jabal face are still used for agriculture but many have been effectively abandoned. At Aïn Rumia there is a café open only in summer. The spring at the site is no longer running since the water is being used for the water supply to the town. But the gardens there are flourishing with palm trees in the cultivated valley. This spot can be crowded on Fri and public holidays.

Return to the main road where a signpost at the junction gives 66 km to **Nalut** and 24 km to **Zintan**, where there is accomodation in a youth hostel. Travel on the Zintan road to return to Tripoli. Otherwise continue west along the top of the Jabal scarp. Pass through a further red soil zone with fruit tree cultivation. **Youth hostel** *Zintan*, 30 beds, breakfast provided, shop, central position.

Jadu

جادو

Towards Jadu the rainfall decreases and the landscape is very arid, with few trees and little cultivation. At Km 10 turn right to Jadu passing through many new villas on the outskirts. The town is a bit of a physical shambles since older communal and family stone constructed dwellings have been abandoned and new villas are randomly scattered across the landscape. In many ways Jadu has lost its old fashioned charm but is an important Berber town with notable

Berber building

Building in the Jabal Nafusa was designed to deal with extremes of heat and cold, and the inhabitants need to protect their crops and family life. Only local materials were used, and local topographic features – defensible high ground, easily excavated earth, building stone – were used to good effect.

In some areas, **underground houses** and mosques were the rule, places warm in the often bitter winters experienced on the Jabal and cool in the heat of summer. At **Mizda** the troglodyte way of life was pursued until the 1970s so that families could escape the extremes of heat experienced in ordinary houses

Elsewhere in the Jabal, **citadels** such as those at **Sharwas** and **Wighu** provided protection. After the Berbers were driven into the hills by the incoming Arabs, such citadel settlements became the focus of revolt against the invaders during the bitter struggles of the 9th century. There is evidence that internecine strife between powerful Berber clans at Sharwas and Wighu in the 11th century resulted in

extensive damage to their fortresses. Although eventually abandoned, Sharwas as late as the 16th century, the citadels stand as bleak but recognizable ruins on the peaks of the Jabal **east of Yafran**.

Another effective local building system were the ksour or **fortified granaries** seen at **Nalut**, **Kabao** and elsewhere in southern Tripolitania and across the border in Tunisia. Small cells were created in the rock or built up one on top of another to accommodate stored grain and other items. These now mainly ruined buildings were surrounded by walls for reasons of defence. In towns such as **Jadu** another dwelling type can be seen, homes built of loosely assembled stone with a little mortaring between joints. These extended family dwellings had areas for living, cooking and keeping the animals in safety at night. Prosperity in recent years has led many residents of the Jabal towns to move into villas built in the open fields around the old settlements. The old quarters have been abandoned and are crumbling into ruin.

---

tribes such as the Qabila Mizu there still. Berber is the main language in the households of the town. There is no hotel but petrol is available here. **Bus** services to both local and inter-urban destinations run from just outside the town centre. The **taxi** station is on the side of the main road at the entry to town.

Leave Jadu to head for **Shakshuk** at the foot of the scarp. There are two roads down the scarp, the newer one is better surfaced and maintained. Both offer a breathtaking view northwards across the Jafara plain. Shakshuk is a small settlement with animal pens and houses sited a short distance off the road. At the junction with the Jefara highway from Nalut there is a petrol station and a small general shop selling drinks and grocery items.

At Shakshuk, you have a choice. You can either go on the fast road along the Jefara westwards or return to the mountain road which leads on a winding route to Nalut. The mountain road passes through arid landscapes and enables rewarding visits to the Berber settlements at Tmizda, Kabao (petrol available here), Wighu, Sharwas and other sites. Those keen to see indigenous Berber architecture should perhaps take the slow road on the scarp. The Jefara road is far quicker, however, though lacking the charms of remote Berber settlements.

West from Shakshuk to Nalut
نالوت

Nalut is a small town with all public services near the centre. Work is proceeding to provide it with proper hotel facilities including a basic rest house for people coming up from the South on desert tours. It is well provided with bus, taxi and other transport facilities, being the take off point for Ghadamès and Ghat. It has petrol, car repair shops and garages.

Nalut
Phone code: 047

Libya

Sleeping F *Hotel Nalut*, built by the Italians in the 1930s, views over the old village, sadly in poor condition, cheap 10LD. **F** *Hotel Nasam*, on Ghadamès side of town, on left as you leave, restaurant, 10LD, T2816. **Youth Hostel** next to school as you head for Ghadamès, on your right.

Northeast from Shakshuk to Tripoli

From Shakshuk, you may take a black top road returning to Tripoli. Roads off to the right lead back to the Jabal settlements at Kabao, Zintan, Yafran and most other Jabal Nafusa settlements. There is a petrol station at **Bir Eyyad** and a roadside police control station. The control is not interested in tourists but have your passports ready in any case. At **Bir Ghanem**, the old stopping place on the Tripoli road, there is petrol, a café and shops. Carry on to the north passing through Sahel Jefara, again with a café and a small market. Another road to the left immediately after Sahel Jefara leads to Zawiyah, 78 km distant. Thereafter there is a slight increase in woodlands within government run agricultural projects and well-established roadside trees. Some shifting grain cultivation is visible on the plain in spring. Increasingly dense cultivation indicates that **Aziziyah** is being approached. Turn left at Aziziyah (petrol available here) and Tripoli lies 38 km to the north.

Ghadamès   غدامس

Phone code: 0484
Colour map 5, grid A1

Once upon a time, deep in the Sahara, an ancient city lived under a spell, defended by high walls and tens of triangular rooftop crenellations. A deep silence held in the narrow streets, the caravans from remote Sudan no longer came … The story could continue with clichés of white-robed figures and hot winds blowing over the oasis but the desert ghost town of Ghadamès is real enough and famous among amateurs of architecture as a place perfectly adapted to a harsh environment. Narrow alleys and courtyard homes provided protection from the sun, in the desert nights, life could be lived on the roof terraces. Although a new town, built outside the oasis, has left old Ghadamès deserted, on Fridays people return to pray in the mosque and enjoy the cool of the covered streets and tiny oasis gardens are still intensely cultivated. Slowly, old Ghadamès is achieving international recognition. In the age of the concrete breeze-block villa, its Le Corbusier-style austerity merits study and conservation. There are no palaces or marble monuments in Ghadamès, it is just there: a place to explore and discover, rather as one might contemplate some outdated mechanical device.

Ins and outs

Getting there Ghadamès is 650 km southwest of Tripoli. For the moment there are no flights from Tripoli to Ghadamès, although these will no doubt eventually be resumed. There are at least 2 buses a day from Tripoli, via Nalut, refreshment stops and police checks.

History

Ghadamès has the usual founding legend. The tale goes that a band of horsemen, crossing the desert, halted for the night. Back on the trail the next day, one of their number realized that they had left the cooking pots behind. He returned to their campsite and as he was gathering the utensils, his restless horse struck the ground with her hoof. Water flowed, and the place became known as Aïn al Faras, the Mare's Spring. It was to irrigate a carefully tended oasis.

Paleolithic and Neolithic tools found in the Ghadamès region testify to a human presence in prehistoric times. In 19 BC the Romans set up a garrison in what was then named Cydamus. Under the Byzantines, the town was home to a bishopric. Columns and odd pieces of masonry recycled in the mosques and hammam bear witness to this presence. The Muslim-Arab invasion in 667, led by Okba Ibn Nafi', passed through Ghadamès before moving northwards into Byzantine Africa. The local Berbers are said to have resisted the Arab conquest fiercely, led by the prophetess Dihia.

By the eighth century, Ghadamès was an important port of call for caravans and pilgrims. It inhabitants preserved their independence, paying allegiance to the rulers of one or other of the powerful – but remote – coastal cities. Until 1860, Ghadamès was paying taxes to the Bey of Tunis. When the Ottomans took over Tripoli for a second time in 1835, they forced the town to recognize the authority of the Turkish Bey in Tripoli. When the Italians landed in Tripoli in 1911 it took them three years to reach Ghadamès and even then their stay was of short duration. The Italians eventually returned on a permanent basis in 1924. They were great admirers of Ghadamès and the area was treated sympathetically. New gardens were built and administrative offices set up there together with a small but pleasant hotel.

During the Second World War, Ghadamès was occupied by the Free French Army led by General Leclerc and held under the Tunisian Protectorate until it was given up reluctantly when the Kingdom of Libya was constituted in 1951. The last French troops left in 1955.

The trans-Saharan trade was the main economic activity of the oasis. Ghadamès thus suffered considerably with the development of new sea-borne trade routes from West Africa. The people of Ghadamès were trading and resident as far west as Timbuktu and the Moroccan coast. In the 18th century, caravans from the sub-Saharan Africa brought slaves, gold, leather, ostrich plumes and ivory in exchange for Tripolitanian horses, cotton, sugar and European manufactures: *contaria*, the glass beads and necklaces of Venice, *galanteries* and fake diamonds from Paris, Marseille linen and Scio silk, pewter bars and Venetian paper for religious texts.

The profits were greatest on slaves. One 17th century observer wrote that a slave bought for eight piastres in Bornou was worth 24 piastres in the Fezzan, and between 40 and 60 in Tripoli.

By the start of the 19th century, however, trade had started to fall off due to the abolition of slavery. The decline was erratic and the trade did not really end

Madraça Tilwan
Ghadamès

altogether until around 1910. Today, the inhabitants' only local sources of income are camel breeding and farming, the latter being very limited due to the lack of irrigation water and cultivable land, estimated at a mere 75 hectares. Some Ghadamsia continue to work in long-distance trade, though lorries have replaced the caravans of yore. Others now have jobs in the petrol industry or in the administration in Tripoli.

Sights

Architecture From a difficult natural environment, the old Ghadamsia created perfect living conditions for an isolated settlement in a harsh natural environment. The houses, built of pisé bricks, lime, palm tree trunks and fronds, the only available building materials, are elegant and practical. Built on two storeys, they have a central room on the first floor acting as a kind of courtyard with all the rooms leading out from it. The rooms are lit by an ingenious hole in the high ceiling, letting in sunlight that reflects off the white walls and provides sufficient illumination. The upper floors are supported by palm tree trunks covered with fronds and mud. The interior of the house would be decorated by the wife and tradition had it that this must be completed before the day of the marriage. The husband-to-be gave the key to his bride and she decorated their new home without his interference. The decorations are very simple, generally red patterns painted directly onto the white walls, with the addition of mirrors and a few small cabinets.

The roof was the domain of the women, the kitchen being on the roof. Old Ghadamsi society was gender-separated, the women only descending into the streets just after sunrise or just before sunset when the men are absent at the mosque for communal prayers. Otherwise, in the old town they were confined to the house, especially the upper floors. Thanks to the tradition of building rooms over the street, the roof terraces communicate and the women could easily move around from one roof to another. At street level, the semi-dark covered passageways give shelter from the sun and lead to small public squares, some covered as well. There are alleys with built-in benches for the men to sit on and socialise.

Libya

Ghadamès house

After J Martin Evans 'Libyan Studies'
Seventh Edt 1975-76 pp 32-33

Bedroom

Store

Grain store

WC

Store

House Section

First Floor Plan

0 metres 2

0 yards 2.2

A wealthy Ghadamsi home would have a small room called the *koubba*, only used twice during the lifetime of the owners, first during the wedding ceremonies and second, when the husband died, by the widow to receive relatives and friends. The store room also has a clever system for preserving food. Due to climatic and other uncertainties, keeping a large stock of food was very important. Grain would be stocked and a wall built with a small hole remaining open. A torch would be inserted in order to burn the oxygen and the hole quickly filled enabling the contents to be stored for years. When it was needed the walls would simply be demolished.

Note too the pointy corner-features on the roof terraces which give such an African feel to the Ghadamès skyline. The great mud city of Kano in Nigeria has the same decoration too, as do the Berber houses of Tafraoute in the south-western Morocco. Their role is to prevent *djinn* or other malicious flying spirits from landing on the roofs.

Irrigation Vegetation and cultivable land are closely integrated with the residential part of the town. The gardens are about five metres below normal street level in order to be closer to the water table. Within the village there are two artesian wells operating in addition to the legendary Aïn Faras. The running water and the shade of the palm trees helps make the summer heat bearable.

Museums In the old town, behind the *Aïn Faras Hotel*, there is a **House Museum**, a mummified Ghadamès home. Outside the walls are plain and minimalist, inside the decoration is a luxuriant as the oasis. The interior walls are covered with red-painted motifs recalling Berber tatoos, stylized geometric flowers and stars. There is a full range of traditional bric-à-brac, cushions and carpets, mirrors, palmfrond couscous covers and copper vessels. Though touristic, the house gives a feel for the way of life in Ghadamès earlier this century.

There is another 'popular' museum at the entrance to the new town with a collection covering various aspects of life throughout the region, with clothes, weapons, tools and even desert animals. On the main square of the new town there is a large **market** every Tues and a small market every other day.

Around Ghadamès To the west of the town, the small village of **Tunine** is very similar and is still inhabited, though it is much smaller and less attractive. A primitive form of water lifting, the *delu* system, was in operation until recently. Further along the road after Tunine there is a large number of sand dunes. It is particularly satisfying to walk up to the top of the dunes and watch the desert sunset.

Essentials

Sleeping
Phone code: 0484

C *Hotel Waha*, T2569/70, 1 km or 10-minute walk from town centre. Currently clean and everything works, bargain at 25LD for double with sitting room, breakfast 3LD each. **C** *Hotel Khalifa*, in the new town 30LD, T2991. **D** *Aïn Faras Hotel*, T2310, used to be an old Italian colonial style hotel. It is well located right by the old town but neglected and dirty and not very welcoming, at 20LD not a bargain.

Youth hostel T2023, 1 km southeast of town centre, next to the stadium. 120 beds, breakfast included, family room, shop, laundry, open 0700-2300, booking recommended December-April, kitchen. Café can get lively in the evenings.

Transport

Air Flights to **Tripoli** were not operational in 1999. **Road Bus**: there are 2 buses a day to **Tripoli**. Officially they leave at 0700 and 1000, but in reality they leave when full. Be at the terminal at least 90 minutes before the official time as this is when the

The Delu well – traditional well of Libya and North Africa

Water was always essential to life in North Africa. Given the scarcity of surface water, it was necessary for survival to lift water from underground. In traditional Libya – more or less until the 1960s – water was lifted from a shallow water table along the coast or from depressions in the desert by means of a device called a delu. The name is taken from the word for a goatskin, which is made into a bag, dipped into a well and drawn up full of water for both household and irrigation purposes.

The mechanism is simple and effective. A shallow one or two metre diameter well is hand dug to about two or three metres below the water table and lined with stone work or cement. Above ground an often ornate gantry is made of two upright stone or wooden pillars rising from the side of the wellhead. A cross beam between the top of the two pillars acts as an axle to a small pulley wheel which carries a rope tied to the mouth of the goatskin bag. The rope is drawn up or let down by the ingenious use of a ramp to ease the task of lifting water to the surface. An animal travels down the ramp when pulling up the goatskin from the bottom of the well and moves up the ramp to return the bag into the bottom of

the well. Most delu wells have a secondary rope attached to the bottom of the goatskin bag which can be used when the full bag is at the top of the gantry to upend it and tip out the water.

The rate of water lifting by the delu method is obviously limited. The capacity of the bag is about 20 litres. Working from dawn to dusk, however, enough water could be raised to irrigate up to three or four hectares of land – enough to feed a family and leave a small surplus for sale in the market. Most wells were equipped with a storage basin adjacent to the wellhead so that water could be raised and stored for household use and to give a reserve of water for irrigation.

The creak of the wooden pulley wheel of the delu was one of the characteristic sounds of the North African oases until the 1960s. After that time diesel and electric power pumps became available and the delu system fell into disuse. A few delu gantries remain as museum pieces and only the observant traveller in the deepest south of the Saharan oases will come across this splendid and environmentally friendly technology in day-to-day operation.

bus is likely to leave. All buses to Tripoli go via **Nalut**. Small 10 seater private buses do the journey from/to Tripoli. Cost 7LD, with several stops for refreshment and police checks. **Car**: the road surface from Ghadamès to Nalut is good but attention must be given to the occasional small sand dunes across the road which can be dangerous even at moderate speeds. In more settled times Ghadamès is close to a border crossing to Algeria, currently **not** recommended.

Directory **Tour companies & travel agents** The recently opened *Ghadamès Travel and Tourism*, Shari'a Saydi Aqba, T/F2533 or *Cidamos Tours and Travel*, T/F2596, Shari'a Sidi Okba. Manager Mr Bashir Hammoud will organize any trip in the surrounding area, including complete guided tours of the old town of Ghadamès and trips into the desert down towards Ghat. The best guide is Mr Ahmed Gassem Aoui, mayor of Ghadamès for 40 years who delights in showing the old town and explaining the socio-economic system. If you ask for him by name you can avoid the Tourist agency upgrade of his fee. Also try *Mezejau Agency*, T2962.

The Fezzan

*You travel to the Fezzan because you love empty landscape, because you have a yen to see uninhabited sand seas, gravel plains and dune desert. Maybe you are curious to see how a modern nation state is trying to make use of vast arid expanses of territory. But there is more than this. Stretching south of the Jabal Nafusa, the Fezzan has a very different identity to Tripolitania. There are uninhabited sandseas, stone plains and salt lakes. The highest part of the region is the **Tibesti Massif**, stretching over the border into Chad. **Sabha**, the capital, is the transport hub for the region, and a base for getting to all key sites. For the traveller, one of the main attractions will be the opportunity to see early **rock art**, witness to a prehistoric time when the Sahara was seemingly much better watered than today. Driving across the stoney wastes, it is difficult to imagine that here grazed the elephants, elegant giraffes and long-horned cattle portrayed with flowing lines in the rock carvings of the **Messak** and **Akkakus**, amongst the finest 'collections' of prehistoric rock art in the world. And you will find traces of the ancient Garamantian civilization in ruins at Garma in the Wadi Ajil.*

Phone codes:
Sabha 071
Ghat 0724
Hun 057
Obari 0722
Fejuj 0728

Ins and outs

Until such time as *Libyan Arab Airlines* repairs its fleet, road is the only way to get down into the Fezzan. Distances are great: Tripoli to Sabha, capital of the region, is 758 km (see graph overleaf). Libya has put considerable investment into improving and extending the road network, however. There are regular bus and taxi services between the main settlements. Expect internal flights from Tripoli to Sabha to be resumed on a regular, more frequent basis in the near future. There are other regional airports at Ghat and Hun.   **Getting there**

There are two main routes south: from the coast at Bu Grayn via the Jufra region to Sabha; and the one you are more likely to take, the recent road from just outside Gharyan (Jabal Nafusa) via Mizda. For the moment, entry into the Fezzan from Algeria and Chad are not an option. The frontier with Niger is subject to closure.

Within the Fezzan, bus and taxi are the main way of getting around. Once again, distances are great: from Sabha on to Ghat, close to the Algerian frontier, is 570 km. A table of distances is given below. The main transport hub of the region is Sabha (bus station in the Jabeya district), and there are once-a-day services to all major destinations in the region, every two days for minor places. Inter-urban taxi services can be generally be found on, or adjacent to, the main street of each settlement. Remember to take sufficient food and drink with you for long journeys.   **Getting around**

Background

The vast and empty Fezzan covers 684,280 sq km of desert lands to the south of Tripolitania. The region borders Algeria to the west, and Niger and Chad to the south. To the east lies Libya's newest province, El Khalij. In the north and the east of the Fezzan are extensive areas of stone desert called *hammada*. Here and there dry river beds, or wadis, cross the desert, the two main wadis being Al-Shatti and the Al-Ajal (Al-Hayyah).   **Geography**

Libya

Sabha, the capital, is the hub of the transport system in Fezzan and travellers can move to all key sites from there. Here underground water is available in small quantities, once sufficient for the trans-Saharan caravans. Around Murzuq, a shallow basin means there is underground water close to the surface, too.

The Fezzan also has dry salt lakes or *sabkhas*, most being found in the Wadi Shatti and the Hofra-Sharqiya zone. The highest part of Fezzan lies in the Tibesti massif, in the southern Aouzou region, bordering Chad, with altitudes running to 3,376 metres in the extreme southeast of the system. Deeply incised *wadi* valleys have vegetation and rich animal and plant life. Other mountains in the region include the Jabal As-Soda, 840 metres and 1200 metres in the Jabal Al-Haruj Al-Aswad.

Climate

The climate of Fezzan is hot and dry, with a scant 8.3 millimetres of irregular rainfall per annum, often falling as an occasional heavy downpour. Such heavy rain storms – and subsequent flash floods – can bring chaos to transport and lead to extensive damage to traditional buildings. Temperatures are high during the day with no cloud cover, allowing rapid cooling at night. Daily ranges in temperature of 40°C are possible. Temperatures are higher in the summer with the Jun mean monthly temperature at 30.6°C in the regional capital, Sabha. Spring and particularly January is a better time to travel when average temperatures fall to 11.6°C. Winds can be severe in the desert, with westerlies dominating the winter and easterly/northerlies the summer. Fezzan experiences the *ghibli* wind in the form of a very hot, dry and uncomfortable blast of several days' duration. Transport can be disrupted during the *ghibli*.

Population

Human settlement was possible only where water could be reached easily by primitive technology in the Wadis Ajal and Shatti and in the Murzuq basin. Even here the densities of human populations were thin and villages widely scattered. Recent government policy, despite enormous expenditures of cash and effort, has made little difference to this pattern. In 1980 the population was estimated at 190,265 of which only 165,245 were Libyan nationals. The population was growing at 5.1 percent annually, mainly through inward migration by foreigners from countries such as Chad and Sudan. Non-Libyans represented 13 percent of the population of Fezzan at that time, a figure which has since gone up by at least 50 percent.

The indigenous peoples are dark-skinned but of Arab extraction. The Tibu and the Tuareg tribes have some Arab characteristics but are otherwise of separate origin. The Tuareg have their own, Berber-related, language, Tamashek. In recent years some have settled in towns. The Fezzanese are known as friendly and hospitable people. Only the Tibu, a tall and very dark group from the Tibesti, are unreliable in their treatment of strangers. A number of Europeans have been taken hostage in the Tibesti, though never within Libyan Tibesti. *Great care* is needed in travelling in the Tibesti since it is isolated, difficult of access, bleakly inhospitable in its climate and unpoliced over very large areas.

Economy

The economy of Fezzan was traditionally dependent on oasis agriculture, some pastoral herding among the Tuareg and trans-Saharan trade. In recent years this has entirely changed as a result of oil revenues and the growing influence of the central authorities in Tripoli. Employment now depends on the state more than on traditional activities. No less than 80 percent of people rely on government generated services for a living. Agriculture employs a mere seven percent and trade another 10 percent. Perhaps as much as 90 percent of all regional income comes from the government. Investment by the

The Fezzan: road system and distances

Key Routes	Journey Length (km)	Time (min)
Sabha – Traghan	128	100
Sabha – Obari	200	150
Edri – Brak – Ashkida	147	120
Murzuq – Zuwaylah	136	105
Obari – Ghat	370	300
Umm Al-Araneb – Qatrun	150	125

Distance chart (diagonal layout):

	Waddan	Tripoli	Sabha	Obari	Murzuq	Ghat	Brak
Tripoli	610						
Sabha	350	758					
Obari	550	1160	200				
Murzuq	533	1143	183	174			
Ghat	920	1530	570	370	544		
Brak	317	939	939	301	833	671	

government ran at US$7,000 per head of population in the region in the late 1970s and early 1980s, though it has since fallen significantly. Libyans have tended to give up active involvement in farming and employ foreigners. In services and construction foreigners make up over 80 percent of the work force.

Agriculture This is known to have been practised in this region since the fifth century BC when the Garamantes used a form of irrigation in areas adjacent to Ghat. Agriculture was largely self-sufficient but was also designed to provide feed for the caravan traffic. The main crops have always been barley and wheat in the winter and millet, sorghum and maize in the summer, together with vegetables and fruit. Forage crops were vital both for keeping animals on the farm and for providing food for the passing caravan trade. Farms are generally tiny and fragmented into small parcels. Including unused and unirrigated lands, average farm sizes was seven hectares. Each irrigated plot is carefully levelled, provided with water and sheltered from the wind with palm frond hedges or mud walls. The main commercial field crops are tomatoes and onions, both of which are exported to the North. Fezzan produces more than two thirds of all dates in Libya at 86,523 tonnes per year from over 4.5 million trees. Olives, grapes, figs and oranges are also grown. Sheep and goats are the main animals kept, the richest grazing zone being the Wadi Shatti. The number of camels (dromedaries) is falling rapidly as they are no longer used for transport or ploughing. Some development of cattle herding for milk production is underway.

A number of modern agricultural estates have been set up in the region and are easily recognized by their straight boundaries and regular layout. These estates are basically agribusinesses with few employees, producing grain and fodder. Occasionally they have attracted local herders who make use of the fodder for their livestock. Another form of State-sponsored agricultural development is the settlement farm: small farms are set up within large estates run initially by government agencies. Farmers are recruited to take over the farms. However, there has been friction from time to time as locals have resented incoming farmers. The presence of estates means fresh water, electricity and telephones but not necessarily accommodation for the traveller.

Industry The Fezzan has some oil and natural gas deposits in the extreme west and some iron ore in the Wadi Shatti. Small workshops have grown up at the settlements, servicing government activities and construction; mechanical workshops, building materials and food processing jobs dominate. The traveller could look out for the local glass making plant at Brak, the handicraft centre at Ghat and the leather factory at Traghan.

Libya

Tourism
See box page 520 for
our company listings
and sample tour prices

The tourist potential of Fezzan has been almost entirely neglected, although the situation may change in the near future. The obvious attractions of desert travel, of the unique nature of the less developed oases and of the archaeological sites were for long overlooked. Few hotel facilities exist in general, and very few have been constructed with travellers from overseas in mind. However, there is a growing realization in Libya that the country's southern regions do have great tourist potential. The sights are certainly far more spectacular than the modest offerings of the Tunisian desert. When stability returns to Algeria, it may be that an imaginative form of trans-border desert tourism may develop, taking in Djanet in southeast Algeria and Biltin and Agadez in Niger. This would enable the visitor to take in all the major Saharan cave painting sites and see something of Touareg culture. In recent years, a Ghat-based travel agency has run tours covering the major sights in southwest Libya and Niger, many of which were off-limits to all but specialists.

Sights

The Fezzan offers the traveller desert landscapes of great variety, a few scattered ancient remains, and prehistoric sites with ancient rock art. The varied desert landscapes will be best appreciated with a good relief **map**. Careful planning with a local travel agency is probably the best way to make maximum use of your time, especially if you want to get to the more remote sights in the Jabal Akakus.

Fortunately, the road system is excellent, and three main routes would enable you to see many of the most interesting features. Coming in from the north, you could follow the **Brak** to **Edri** route westwards along the **Wadi Al-Shatti**, visiting the old town of Brak, the southern rim of the Hammadah Al-Hamra and the small traditional settlements of the valley. Another major route takes you from **Sabha** to **Obari** along the line of **the Wadi Al-Ajal** taking in the traditional villages and the Garamantian sites. South of Sabha, the **Murzuq** to **Zuwaylah** road has more Garamantian remains, the fort at Murzuq, the mosque at Zuwaylah and the old and new towns at Umm Al-Araneb.

More distant, **Ghat** and the **southwestern Fezzan**, are unspoiled and rewarding areas for the traveller. It takes around eight hours to get from Sabha to Ghat, and more still to reach the prehistoric art of the Jabal Akakus. The sites, however, have a unique remoteness.

Privately organized groups in four-wheel drive vehicles or on desert motor cycles enjoy travelling in the Fezzan. The more common itineraries are from Ghadamès east to Darj, southeast on the desert tracks to Edri and on to Brak perhaps returning north from here to the coast or else travelling south to Sabha then west to Obari and Ghat. From here the route is north adjacent to the Algerian border back to Ghadamès. This last leg, 450 km across the Hamadat al Hamrah plateau, windy, bleak and with extremes of temperature (-15°C at night) is not well defined and not to be undertaken lightly.

Oasis settlements

The smaller oases should be visited with a guide if unwelcome suspicion is not to be aroused, especially by male groups. In the Wadi Al-Ajal (Al-Hayyah) there are still comparatively unspoiled villages such as **Bent Bayah** to the west where magnificent forms of traditional architecture are still in use. In **Ghat** there are still strings of small traditional settlements worthy of a half day visit with a translator. Similar villages exist as populated or recently abandoned sites throughout the province. The further they are from the developed centres, the more interesting the villages become, though some, like **Umm Al-Araneb**, have undergone a total population change in recent times.

The traditional **domestic architecture** of the Fezzan's settlements is highly individualistic – and perfectly in tune with the natural environment. Houses are built of sun-dried mud bricks in most regions, though near rocky outcrops flat natural stone can be incorporated into the buildings with mud rendering on both sides. Most houses are single-storey. The flat roofs are constructed with palm wood cross members covered with palm fronds sealed with a beaten mud coating. Ornamentation is provided on the roof corners by a triangular motif in which two flat bricks are leaned against each other above a horizontal brick or stone. This emblem is used in a variety of forms either as a single unit or in combination along the top of a wall. Doorways can be highly decorated, often with calligraphic or symbolic representations above the main door to the house. Some houses carry horn-shaped fixtures above their entrances, to ward off the effects of the evil eye. Painting is rare except to highlight a doorway.

The **religious architecture** of the Fezzan is distinctive, too. It is usually the religious buildings which carry white or blue washes. The minarets are often square-shaped and only slightly raised above the level of single-storeyed mosques, usually painted white. A complex and beautiful three-tiered mosque of this kind exists at Obari. Other fine mosques can be found, and **Zuwaylah** is worth calling at to see its mosque, the ruins of an associated fort and the 12th century tombs of the Beni El-Khattab, square constructions of mud bricks faced with stone. Some of the Turkish stone forts survive, including the one at **Murzuq**, in the centre of the new town.

Archaeological sites

The Fezzan is rich in pre-historic sites where well-preserved cave paintings can be viewed. The artwork depicting antelope, elephant and giraffe-like animals and human hunters dates from 6000-3000 BC.

The main sites are at **Akakus** and **Tashinat** where there are excellent wall carvings; close to **Ghat** in the **Wadi Fuet** where there are a number of coloured wall paintings; at **Zinkekra** in the western Garma area where there are rock carvings, and at **Wadi Buzna**.

Libya is famous for the remains of the Garamantian civilization of the **Wadi Al-Ajal**, west of Sabha. The centre was **Garma**, established about 2000 BC, and only rediscovered in the 1960s. A series of ruins and sites are open for visitors to the Wadi Al-Ajal. The city of Garma is a clear attraction, lying close to Obari just off the Sabha road. Nearby are the tombs of Saniat Jebril and Ben Howaidi. Other tombs and cemeteries include the tombs of Ahramat Al-Hatiyah, the royal cemetery to the south of Garma, the cemeteries at Bent Bayah and Budrinnah, and Al-Khareyk, the latter west of Garagra. There are the remains of forts at Al-Abiad and Al-Gullah. The full range of urban life is not yet known since excavations at the site have not been finished.

■ *All Libyan monuments are open 0800-1700 and are normally closed on Tuesday. In Fezzan there is a certain informality over working hours and guardianship of sites. Local guides will show you the full extent of the known ruins but you will often be on your own. Urban monuments, especially mosques, need a low key approach and permission asked before entering. Again, having a local Fezzanese with you can make a great deal of difference. Housing of interest will either be a prepared tourist site without a family in residence, as at Bent Bayah, or else can be approached by invitation. There are rarely many facilities.*

Note that you need a permit, 20LD from the Ghat police station, to visit the Akakus region. This is delivered in 24 hours via a local travel agency.

Libya

From Libues to Libyans

For ancient Greek geographer Herodotus, there were three peoples south of the Mediterranean: the Egyptians, the Aethiopes (lit: 'burnt faces'), and the Libues. Though the Greeks had long had contact with the Egyptians, the Ethiopians were a less well known quantity, inhabiting the edge of the earth, south of the Nile, and next to the great river ocean. With the Libues, who inhabited today's northwest Africa, the Greeks had more contact, through their five cities in Cyrenaica. Today's Berbers are no doubt the descendants of Herodotus' Libues – whose name comes from the ancient Egyptian Libu (pron. lee-boo), the name given to the people west of Egypt. Barbaroi was the term given by the Greeks to anyone who babbled away in a language other than Greek. Writing in the 14th century, Arab thinker Ibn Khaldoun used the term for the mountain peoples (al barbar), as opposed to al-'arab, the nomads. The term 'nomad' is of Greek origin as well, and gave the Romans their name for the central Maghreb, Numidia.

For the Arab writers, North Africa is the Maghreb, the 'land of the West', as opposed to the Mashrek, the 'land of the East', basically Egypt and the Near East. Ibn Khaldoun in his 'Ibar, a great discussion of peoples and lands, wrote that al maghrib "includes Tripoli and the lands beyond, towards the west: Ifrikiya, the Za'b, the central Maghreb, the Far Maghrib, the near Sous valley and the far Sous. These are the regions which formed the domain of the Berbers and the lands where they resided in ancient times."

In the 16th century, the North African coast was the setting for serious Hispano-Ottoman rivalry. The region had been referred to as Barbary as of late Mediaeval times. The 15th century traveller from Flanders, Anselme Adorne, stopped off in several cities in the region, and talks of Barbaria. In the 17th century, the Ottomans established a form of authority over the North African coast. Algiers, Tunis, and Tripoli became the capitals of the régences barbaresques, the Ottoman provinces or ilayet of North Africa. English authors talk of West Barbary and southern Barbary.

Meanwhile, the term Libya as a country name only appears for the first time in the writings of Italian colonial propagandists in the early 20th century. The term was officially applied to the whole area of Tripolitania, Cyrenaica and the Fezzan in the early 1930s. (Tripolitania and Cyrenaica had been united administratively in 1928). Ironically for a nation which takes pan-Arabism as an essential component of its creed, Libya bears a name coined as part of the Italian colonial enterprise.

The Obari Lakes

These lakes are a strange site, signposted to the north off the main Wadi Al-Ajal road, and well worth travelling a short distance to see. About 13 small lakes exist in the Obari sand sea sited between the great dunes of the system. The main lakes are **Mandara** (200-300m diameter), **Umm Al-Ma'** (lit: 'mother of water'), which usually has water throughout the year, **Bahar Al-Daud** 300 metres diameter, **Tademsha**, **Umm Al-Hassan**, **Neshnusha**, **Bahar Al-Trunia**, **Frejia** and **Oudnei**. They are fed by ground water from the sand sea when the water table builds up in the dune systems. Most are very shallow, less than a metre, and many dry up during the summer. The water is very brackish in the lakes but water drawn from the dunes can be used in irrigation and for human consumption. There is a myth in Libya that the lakes area was populated by people who were 'worm-eaters', a belief arising from the local custom of eating shrimps taken from the lakes. Not surprisingly, local people do not take kindly to the 'worm-eating' story!

Essentials

The Fezzan is extremely short on good hotel beds, and the traveller must be prepared to rough it, staying under canvas or in officially-owned rest-houses. There are one or two campsites owned by private travel agencies.

Sabha and region The main hotels are in Sabha and include: **D** *Hotel Al-Fatah*. A/C, restaurant, view over the city, T071-623951, 25LD. **E** *Al-Galah Hotel*, A/C, rather run down, 57 clean rm, 114 beds, some shops, T071-623106. 25LD. **E** *Mountain Hotel*, small, 19 rm, 38 beds. **E** *Hotel Nakhil*. No a/c, Close to bus station, but not very clean. Access for **resthouses** in Sabha can only normally be obtained with the help of official letters of introduction from Tripoli.

Fejeij 129 km from Sabha, there is a **youth hostel** which makes a good base if exploring the Ubari lakes region. The hostel has both dormitories and small group rooms, and can be busy in winter. T0728-2902. **NB** If **camping** in the Ubari lakes region, be sure to bring mosquito repellant.

Garma Next to the petrol station at the main crossroads is the *Dar Germa hotel*, (reservations through the Italian-managed Ta Fani travel agency in Tripoli, T021-3340393).

Ubari There is only one hotel which is not really recommendable. Halfway between Ubari and Ghat, at Al Awaynet (lit: 'the little springs'), is the *Al Faw* **campsite**, opened 1996, T0724-2265. Accommodation in small bungalows, desert trips organised.

Ghat There is a fairly new hotel at Ghat and rest house facilities are available. Ask for information at the Municipality building. Try the **C** *Hotel Tassili*, T0724-2560, F0724-2604. Although neither very clean nor comfortable, it is the best that Ghat has to offer. A few rooms have a/c. 45LD for a 3 bed room. Food acceptable. The *Winzrik Travel Agency* has a base at this hotel.

Other areas Other hotels include the new hotel at Hun, where the old *Tourist Hotel* still functions, though parts of it seem to have been given over to foreign labourers. Small guest houses exist at Traghan, Hun, Hammera and Garma but their facilities are limited and cannot be guaranteed to be available.

Camping Unlimited in the desert, though the security services do not look kindly on unauthorised camping by foreigners unless supervised by a Libyan agency. Campers should either be discreet in their overnight stops, providing all their needs from their own resources, or ask permission from tourist agencies/local authority baladiya offices in the nearest town. Often school or college facilities can be used by travellers.

Youth hostels *Sabha*, Gamal Abdel Nasser St, 3 km E of town centre, T 071-27337, 160 beds, family rooms, laundry, meals, kitchen, open 0700-2300. *Ghat*, 40 beds, kitchen, meals, T0724-32360. *Hun*, 50 beds, kitchen, T057-3379. *Waddan*, T0580-2310, 160 beds, meals available, laundry, family rooms, booking recommended Sep-Nov. *Murzuq*, formerly *Murzuq Tourist Hotel*, 30 beds, with breakfast, kitchen. Unfortunately, this is often requisitioned by the State. *Umm Al-Araneb*, T072-62228, 120 km from Sabha, 90 km from Murzuq, 30 beds, with breakfast, kitchen. *Fejeij*, People's Housing Project, 40 beds, meals, kitchen, T071-28323.

Eating out in Fezzan is a rather limited experience because the locals rarely eat outside their own homes. Restaurants and cafeterias do exist adjacent to the hotels and guesthouses. In Sabha, Brak and Obari, the range of facilities is acceptable, with 2 or 3

Libya

👈 *Sample tour prices for the Jabal Akakus*

Prices vary according to season and demand, but roughly speaking they are as follows: permit, delivered through agency in 24 hours 20LD; guide, around 60LD a day; off-road vehicle with driver, around 250LD a day; *trek, around 150 to 175LD a day per head with camels but not including food.*
NB Prices tend to be higher at peak times.

eating places available. Cooking is basic and to local or Arab tastes with either rice or macaroni as its basis except in the few new hotels where forms of international cuisine can be found. In the summer heat, cooking is scarcely worthwhile and there is cold or tinned food available from the small private shops at a comparatively high price. The tourist agencies normally provide their clients with food cooked by their own staff. Eating in private homes is to be encouraged where invitations are received. Here the food is varied, wholesome and often interesting.

Entertainment In Fezzan is limited to visiting friends' houses and having the occasional formal civic reception. Otherwise there are a few cafés and restaurants which stay open while customers remain. Most towns have a cinema with films in Arabic. Sports centres, nightclubs and other tourist attractions are altogether absent. For sport, the younger locals play volleyball and football.

Shopping In the Fezzan can be much more rewarding than in all other parts of Libya other than Ghadamès. The leatherwork of the region, especially at Ghat, is excellent if at times quaintly crude in finish. The main traditional items are leather handled and sheathed knives, short spears/arrows and Arab slippers of ornate design. Woven date palm fronds are used to make a variety of matting products from fruit basins and rice trays to place mats. Tuareg and other ladies' ornaments are interesting and there is some glasswork. An attempt to resurrect the carpet industry is underway and some patterns are plain but effective.

Transport **Local Bus**: within the larger towns access can either be by bus or taxi. Distances are very short since no town is large except Sabha. All the town centres or hotels and the airports are served by bus. **Car hire**: self-drive car hire is difficult though this can occasionally be arranged through a travel agent. More normally arrange for a car, preferably a four-wheel drive vehicle if you are visiting sites off the road, with a driver. This can be expensive and rentals of 100-200LD per day are not uncommon. There are many mechanical workshops in the main towns which can repair and service vehicles. Some of the work is rough and ready but most makes of vehicle can be handled. Fuel is available in the main towns and most small villages. Drivers should always set off with a full tank and adequate spare fuel to reach the next large town rather than the next petrol station. Shortages of fuel do occur at individual stations from time to time. **Cycle hire**: hire of cycles and motorcycles is not normal though some repair shops will lease them, but not cheaply or readily. **Taxi**: this can be expensive and prices should be negotiated in advance where possible.

Long distance Air: there are regional airports at **Sabha, Ghat, Hun** and **Uzu**, though only Sabha has facilities for international flights. The airport is outside town next to the old Turkish fort. It has been rebuilt as a regional/international airport. Scheduled international air services to Sabha, when permitted, include flights from Accra, Alexandria, Casablanca, Damascus, Khartoum, and Ndjemena. Flights into **Sabha** are mainly by Libyan Arab Airlines. The flight to Tripoli takes 1hr 15mins. The airport at Ghat is currently closed.

Airline offices There are many *LAA* offices in Tripoli for travelling to Fezzan – when plane maintenance allows. The head office is at Shari'a Haiti, POB 2555, Tripoli, Sales T021-606833/36. In Fezzan, LAA has offices at Sabha T071-23876, at Ghat T0724-2035 and at Hun T057-2456

Banks Few banking points in Fezzan deal with foreign exchange, especially any slightly unusual currency or TCs. Use the main banks in Sabha on the main street or, as a 2nd and not always reliable best, the big hotels which usually have a small branch of a bank in-house.

Hospitals & medical services Chemists: most small settlements have pharmacies, but it is wise in Fezzan to travel with a comprehensive first aid kit and any personal medical drugs needed. Chemists shops are to be found in all centres and even small villages will have clinics of sorts with some medical drugs available. As elsewhere in Libya, people with special needs should ensure that they carry adequate supplies. **Hospitals:** Fezzan is well served by health centres, clinics and dispensaries. Hospital facilities are spread thinly, not surprising in a landscape of very distant settlements and low population densities. There are principal hospitals at Murzuq, Obari, Sabha, Al-Shatti and Sawkenah, that is in each district. Some of the smaller hospitals have limited staffing and facilities. On average Fezzan has half the health provision that other parts of the country enjoy. The traveller is warned that, together with a road accident rate far higher than the rest of the country, the overall record of which is very bad in any case, health repatriation insurance is more than usually important.

Tour companies & travel agents The largest travel company in Tripoli is the *Libyan Travel & Tourism Company*, T021-2148005/48011, F2143455. Their desert tours in Fezzan include a 15-day desert visit from Tripoli to the south flying from Tripoli to Sabha and thereafter by 4WD vehicle to Gabroun and Mandara sand dune lakes, and on to Garma and Wadi Berjuj. The itinerary goes to the Matkhandus prehistoric painting sites and then across the Murzuq sand sea to Gassi Ohabran, the Wadi Selfoufet in the Akakus and finally to Ghat, returning to Tripoli via Sabha by air.

For travel in the south-west, try also *Akakus Tours*, T0724-2813, Tx2938 Ghat, (General Manager, A Younis, home T0724-2938) which offers visits to the major archaeological sites of the region, especially Garma, under canvas. They will reserve travel to and from Libya, make hotel reservations in Libya, assist travel groups with handling arrangements on site. They offer a number of separate trips, including one to Murzuq, Ghat, Obari, and Al-Awenat over 8-13 nights, another through Teshuinat over 3-6 nights and a 21-night visit through the Libyan-Niger borderlands. They normally accommodate their clients in bivouacs. These desert circuits, though not cheap, are an excellent introduction to the central Sahara. Try also the *Indinane Agency*, T0724-2460, with a small office in Ghat near the entrance to the old town. The *Winzrik Agency*, T0724-2560, F0724-2604 works with European tour operators. Offices at the Tussil Hotel. It is best to telephone for a booking before arrival in Ghat to one of the tour agencies, who can arrange accommodation and permits (20LD) for visiting the Akakus.

Background

History

With the coming of the Ottomans in the mid-16th century, the area which formed the first independent Libyan state in 1951 began to have a distinct geopolitical identity. The area covered by the present book, Tripolitania and the Fezzan achieved importance in the Roman Empire. Its history was closely linked to that of the more northerly provinces of Africa and Numidia, roughly equivalent to modern Tunisia. After Byzantine Africa fell to the Arab Muslim invaders in the seventh century, the coastlands of Tripolitania remained a place of passage, an alternative to the sea route between the western and eastern halves of the Arab-ruled lands. Nomad tribes dominated the vast desert expanses, while the main town, Tarablus El Gharb, 'Tripoli of the West' tended to come within the sphere of influence of Ifrikiya's rulers to the northwest. The vast distances involved ensured that Almohad, or later, Hafsid control was nominal, however. In the 14th century, Tripoli was the object of power struggles between various Arab tribal groups. Hafsid rule was imposed from 1401 to 1460. In the early 16th century, the town was taken by Spain, passed on to the Knights of Malta in 1530, and finally taken for the Ottomans by the former privateer Dragut in 1551.

Tripoli in Barbary, an Ottoman regency After the Turco-Spanish wars of the 16th century, a series of Ottoman provinces were established along the North African coast, of which Tripoli was one. Direct control from Istanbul did not last long. Ultimate power was in the hands of *bashas*, sent from Istanbul, the *deys* who were in charge of the permanent janissary garrisons and, in Algiers at least, the *taifa*, the captains of the privateers who continued to operate out of the North African ports right up until the early 19th century. Military councils, the *diwan al askar*, formed to administer the Barbary regencies, as the Ottoman provinces on the North African coast were known.

The Ottomans imposed their authority over the Berber tribes of the Jabal Nafusa with their superior fire power, and occupied Djerba using tribal warriors in 1558. In Tripoli, Dragut built a fort outside the town, and on the site of the Grand Mosque destroyed by the Spaniards, built a palace complex, the Saray Dragut. He also built a mosque in which he was later buried. The Ottomans had more difficulty imposing their authority in the Fezzan, and were obliged to recognize the Banu Mohammad as the rulers of the region in return for tribute in the form of gold and slaves. Cyrenaica remained under local tribal rule, outside the Ottoman administrative system, despite incursions by certain Tripoli governors.

The Karamanli Dynasty At the beginning of the 18th century, a local leader, one Ahmad Karamanli, made Tripoli independent with a power base built on the kulughlis, a group which had arisen from the intermarriage of Turkish troops and local women. In 1711, Karamanli took the opportunity offered by the temporary absence of the Ottoman governor and massacred the leaders of the janissaries. The new autonomous government eventually controlled Tripolitania and the coastal regions of Cyrenaica. Under Ali Pasha (1754-93), Tripoli grew in prosperity, balancing piracy and trade. European Christians established a flourishing trade with Malta, while the Italian Jews handled commerce with Livorno.

The late 18th century was Karamanli power weakened by internal dynastic power struggles and the occupation by adventurer Ali Burghul. Eventually, Ali's youngest son Yusuf took control, ruling from 1795 to 1832. With Europe entangled in the Napoleonic conflict, he was able to rebuild Tripoli's strength as a maritime power. Merchant ships were captured from the European powers helped to expand the fleet. Much of the seafaring know-how was supplied by European converts and Turkish captains. One of the leading renegades was a Scot, Peter Leslie, known as Murad Rais, who became admiral of Tripoli's navy in 1795. Cyrenaica and the Fezzan were brought under direct rule in the early 19th century, and Yusuf Pasha began to plan the conquest of the Saharan Kingdom of Bornu.

Tripoli's power began to decline in the 1820s. Piracy was banned in 1818, depriving the regency of an important source of revenue. European consular influence grew, and after a tussle for influence in Tripoli between Britain and France, the Ottoman Empire reoccupied the Regency of Tripoli and ejected the Karamanlis in 1835. This came at a time when the Sublime Porte had suffered considerable set backs in Greece and Algeria.

The reimposition of Ottoman rule in Libya in 1835 marked an end to the corsairing economy of the Regency of Tripoli. Ottoman control was never fully applied throughout the country, however. In Cyrenaica and the desert, the Sanusiya sheikhs provided a politico-religious alternative to Ottoman rule, and in effect, in the 19th century, Cyrenaica was under the co-rule of Sanusis and Ottomans.

Return of Ottoman rule

Istanbul saw Tripoli as the base from which it might regain its waning influence in the western Mediterranean. This was a problematic strategy, given that leading Tripoli families had strong commercial links with Europe, and in any case, the tribal leaders of the interior saw the Ottomans as another group of conquerors.

The Ottomans took an interest in the trans-Saharan trade. With the abolition of slavery in Tunis in 1846 and Algiers in 1848, Tripoli increased its share of the slave trade, despite pressure from the British Anti-Slavery Society. Even after a firman was issued abolishing slavery in Tripoli in 1857, the trade continued, such was the demand in the Ottoman Empire.

On a rather different note, the Ottomans introduced the administrative reforms being implemented across the empire Secondary schools where sciences and European languages were taught, in addition to Arabic and Turkish were set up. Under Ali Ridha Pacha, governor of Tripolitania from 1867 to 1870, a municipality was set up in Tripoli and French technical assistance brought in to dig artesian wells and improve port facilities.

During the 19th century, Cyrenaica had a rather different history to Tripolitania. Peopled by tribes descended from 11th century invaders the Banu Sulaym, administered apart from Tripoli, the sub-province came under the influence of the Sanusiya *tarika*, a spiritual movement named after its Algerian founder, Sayyid Mohammad Ibn Ali al-Sanusi. (The term tarika best translates as brotherhood or order). The main zaouia of the order was founded in 1843, the Zaouia al-Baydha in the Jabal Akhdar, where the order was welcomed for its piousness and for its ability to arbitrate tribal disputes. When the order's founder died, his son, Sayyid al-Mahdi took over, and it was under him that Sanusi influence developed in the Sahara. Al-Mahdi set up headquarters at Kufra in 1895, subsequently moving it to Kiru between Borku and the Tibesti.

The Sanusi Order

Later on, the tarika also coordinated tribal resistance throughout the Sahara to French colonial penetration. It came to control the eastern trade routes across the Sahara and, as a result, effectively became, an autonomous government of the central Saharan region. In Cyrenaica its power was so great that, outside the major urban settlements such as Benghazi, the Ottomans accepted it as the de facto

Libya

government and a Turkish-Sanusi condominium developed. Although the Sanusiya considered the Ottoman caliphs as usurpers, they were forced to accept their presence, as the Turks were the only force seemingly capable of countering French expansion into the Sahara.

The Ottoman administration in Tripoli had to cope with continuing European pressure, particularly from Italy and Malta. British and French influence led to the end of the slave trade towards the end of the 19th century, while the economy of Tripoli became increasingly integrated into the economy of the Mediterranean region. By the start of the 20th century Italy's intention to colonize Tripolitania, Cyrenaica and the Fezzan became clear.

The first Arab Republic

In 1911, the Italians finally found a pretext for occupying Ottoman Libya (and the Dodecanese Islands off Turkey, too). The take-over was to prove far more difficult than Italy had anticipated, however, despite Ottoman difficulties in the First World War and Italy being on the winning side. In fact, the outbreak of the First World War allowed the Turks to provide military aid to the resistance. However, huge changes were afoot in the Middle East. Tripoli of the West's old protectors – the Turkish army, the Ottoman sultanate, the Islamic caliphate – disappeared, one after the other. Tripolitania was on its own to face the invaders. When Turkey surrendered in 1918, Tripoli's notables met a Misrata, and on 18 November proclaimed a Tripolitanian republic, the first in the Arab world. In fact, this was more of a coalition of local leaders, enabling them to extract concessions from the Italians. And so in June 1919, Italy, no doubt playing for time, offered a statute granting Italian nationality to the local population, an Italian governor – and an elected parliament. Later, a National Reform Party formed to put pressure on Italy to put the statute into effect.

The Italian occupation

Italy had considerable difficulties in bringing all of Libya under its control. In 1922, with the Fascists in power, Italy again decided to occupy Libya. Marshal Badoglio, victor of the Vittorio Veneto was sent to Tripolitania, and in 1923 the Italians entered Misurata. Cyrenaica surrendered in 1925, but a guerrilla campaign continued for seven more years.

General Graziani led a cruel campaign in Cyrenaica and down into the Sahara to destroy the Sanusiya. In January 1931, the oasis of Koufra was occupied. A 270 km barbed wire barrier was set up along the Egyptian frontier to limit bedouin movement. Eventually, in 1931, Sanusi leader Omar al-Mohktar was captured and hung. In 1932, Marshal Badoglio announced the end of the 'rebellion'. Italy finally occupied the vast Libyan desert hinterland.

Italian colonization

Italy's occupation of Libya was initially piecemeal, characterized by contradictions and ultimately short lived. It left a lasting mark on the people of what was to become an independent nation, providing a strong binding force. Italy's victory over the Sanusiya had only been achieved by coralling large numbers of Cyrenaicans into concentration camps. There was heavy loss of life during the nine year war (1923-1932), and much bitterness created. For many in the Italian establishment, however, the colonization of the lands eventually named *Libia* had a strong ideological tint.

In the 19th century, there was mass migration from Italy to Argentina, Brazil and the USA. The fact that the newly constituted kingdom of Italy was unable to provide work and wealth for all her people was seen by many as a symbol of national failure. In 1906, the Italian Colonial Institute was set up, through which the colonial lobby generated a myth which saw Italy as a great nation which had been humiliated – and therefore needed to invest in colonial expansion. In the early 20th century, with the exception of Ethiopia, Tripolitania and Cyrenaica were practically the only corner of Africa unclaimed by a European power. Tunisia was a *terra perduta* (a land lost for Italy); Libya was to be Italy's fourth shore, *la quarta sponda*.

Initially, colonization was on the Jefara plain, avoiding the oases and the Jabal Nafusa to avoid upsetting local sentiment. As of 1934, Italo Balbo, Mussolini's one time second-in-command, headed the colonial effort in North Africa. The development of the Jabal Akhdar was to be like that of the Pontine Marshes. (In practice, it turned out to be more like Zionist colonization in Palestine, with boatloads of settlers coming in). The colonial system was modelled on the one used by the French in the Constantinois and Tunisia: expropriated land was given to private entrepreneurs who only gained ownership after payment and appropriate development. A reform in 1928 obliged concession holders to associate Italian peasants. In 1935, the first experimental villages were established in Cyrenaica, followed by nine more villages in 1938 to house the 'worker-legionaries'.

The Fourth Shore

Italian rule in Libya was a strange mixture of the tolerant and the cruel. The Sanusiya Zawiyahs were destroyed or converted to military uses, and the movement's sheikhs went into exile in 1932. But at the same time, the Italians took care to appear as protectors of Islam. No attempt was made to convert Muslims to Christianity, and Islamic personal status law was left untouched. Restoration works were undertaken on major Islamic monuments, and arrangements for the pilgrimage to Mecca were improved. New schools for Muslims followed an Italian curriculum and provided religious instruction in Arabic. The stated aim was to integrate Libyans into Italian society. In 1937, Mussolini brandished 'the sabre of Islam' as he inaugurated the 1,800 km coastal highway, the Litoranea.

Unfortunately for Italy, such rhetorical poses cut little ice with the growing numbers of Libyans, many in exile in Egypt and elsewhere who felt that there was a future beyond colonial rule. Although Libya was declared an integral part of the kingdom of Italy in January 1939, the Second World War was to provide the political opportunity for the pro-independence groups.

The Fascist victory was short-lived, for the Italian army was forced out of Libya during the Second World War, and British military administrations took over in Cyrenaica and Tripolitania with the French administering Fezzan like their Algerian Saharan territories. Under the Italians, Libya had acquired communications infrastructure and the basis of a modern economy. It had also acquired a 50,000 strong Italian settler population, a substantial portion of whom remained until they were expelled by the Gadhafi régime in 1970.

After the Second World War
For Libya's more recent history, see page 530

The situation of Libya posed problems. By the end of the Second World War, it had acquired strategic significance for Britain and, after the Cold War began, for the USA as well. Britain had promised Cyrenaica that Italian control would never be restored. A series of proposals were made including Soviet Union trusteeship over Libya and the Bevin-Sforza Plan, whereby Britain would take a mandate for Cyrenaica, Italy for Tripolitania and France for the Fezzan for a period of 10 years, after which the country would be granted independence. Such proposals were clearly unacceptable to the Libyans themselves, and the whole issue was dropped in the lap of the newly created United Nations in 1949.

The United Nations' special commissioner was able to convince all the Libyan factions that the only solution was a federal monarchy, bringing the provinces of Cyrenaica, Tripolitania and the Fezzan together in a monarchy headed by the Sanusi leader, Sayyid Idris. In December 1951, the independent United Kingdom of Libya came into being.

Libya

Land and environment

The state of Libya has an area of 1,759,540 sq km, (three times the surface area of France). It has a 1,750 km seaboard with the Mediterranean stretching from Zuwarah in the west to Al-Bardia in the east. Most people live and work along the northern coast. Elsewhere the country fades immediately inland into semi-desert. The southern part of the country is deep Sahara. The desert regions are lightly populated and crossed by major routes often over 1,000 km in length. North to south transport roads and tracks pass from oasis to oasis, ultimately linking with Chad, Sudan and Niger in Central Africa. For all its extent, therefore, Libya is a country where you can see much of what exists simply by following the few key lines of communication.

Borders Libya is bounded to the west by Tunisia and Algeria. In the extreme south, the border is not fully agreed and travellers are advised to keep to the main roads. Libya's eastern frontier with Egypt is for the most part agreed. Libya shares a border with Sudan to the southeast. The entire southern border was subject to dispute with Chad. The Aouzou strip was bitterly fought over until 1990 when the frontier was settled by reference to the International Court of Justice.

Regions The Italians divided their North African colony of *Libia* into three provinces, namely Tripolitania, Cyrenaica and Fezzan. (Until 1963, Libya was a 'united kingdom' comprising these three provinces and Libyans still identify with these historic divisions). Recent political changes brought four new administrative districts including Tripoli, Benghazi, Sabha and Al-Khalij (lit: 'gulf'), named for the Gulf of Syrte. Tribal territories are still observed in the popular culture of some districts.

Relief The principal natural zones of Libya are the densely settled regions of the Jefara Plain, the Jabal Nafusa, Sirte, the Benghazi Plain, the Jabal Al-Akhdar, Fezzan and Al-Kufrah. In the central and southern regions very large-scale features dominate. In the west, the Hammadah Al-Hamra is a vast stony plain with no settlements and few lines of communication. Adjacent to the east of the Hammadah is the Jabal As-Sawda, the black mountains, a desolate and topographically broken area. In the Fezzan, is the great sand sea of Murzuq through which travel is feasible only via the few great *wadi* systems which traverse it. It is dangerous to travel off the few highways which link the small oases. There are few water holes and population is very thin. In the deepest southeast lie the Tibesti Mountains, the land of the Tibu tribes, where security is unreliable and the traveller is advised to enter only when accompanied by an official courier.

Rivers Libya has only one permanently flowing river, the Wadi Ki'am, located in Tripolitania between Al-Khums and Zliten. This is a tiny stream of no more than two km running from a spring source to a reservoir impounded in a lagoon adjacent to the seashore. Elsewhere the *wadis* run in spate after heavy rains but are dry for the rest of the year. *Wadis* in flood can fill at a dangerous speed. Among the major *wadis* of Libya are the Mejennin which runs through the western suburbs of Tripoli city. It is now mainly controlled through dams and diversion works in its upper reaches. The Wadi Soffejin drains much of southern Tripolitania to the Gulf of Sirte, partly feeding the enormous natural salt marshes at Tauorga, located south of Misrata. In Cyrenaica the Wadi Derna is a rich area, its stream running for much of the year and providing irrigation water for a fertile oasis adjacent to the port. The generally waterless Wadi Al-Kuf runs through the hills of the Jabal Al-Akhdar in a steep, scenic gorge.

The Libyan climate is very varied. The Mediterranean coast has warm winters with an unreliable rainfall, though on average over 200 millimetres. Extended periods of poor rainfall are experienced even in this coastal zone. Summers are hot and often humid. Relative humidity in July can reach an uncomfortable 80+ percent for days on end especially in Tripolitania. In the Jabal Al-Akhdar, the rainfall is considerably more reliable in winter and early spring, while in summer the heights are cooler than the surrounding plains.

Further southwards the climate becomes increasingly Saharan. Low temperatures and occasional random rainfall are experienced in winter with a large daily temperature range from 15-20°C during the day to sub-zero at night. Cold nights also occur in early and late summer. Summers are hot and very dry in the south with highs of over 50°C but one can also feel cold in the night, making a sweater very welcome. Al-Aziziyah, inland on the Jefara Plain behind Tripoli, has one of the world's highest recorded temperatures, 55°C.

The *ghibli* wind blows hot air from the Sahara across northern Libya and carries a large amount of dust which severely reduces visibility. Relative humidity drops immediately at the onset of the *ghibli* to less than 15 percent and air temperatures rise rapidly. The wind is most noticeable in western Libya and is often associated with the spring solstice.

Outside the coastal plains, the Jabal Nafusa and the Jabal Al-Akhdar, the natural vegetation is dominated by tamarisk, palm and fig trees. The *acacia arabica*, alfalfa grass, salt bush and a range of grasses grow thinly except after rain in the semi-desert. Other plants include the asfodel and wild pistachio. The dromedary was the principal animal of the region but is declining rapidly in importance. In some quarters it is still believed that the region was formerly, perhaps in Roman times, very rich and climatically more favoured than at present. Deep in the Sahara, wall and cave paintings and graffiti of leopards, elephants, wolves and other animals of the savanah suggest that this was so. There are still gazelle and porcupine. Falcons, eagles, and other birds of prey are present in small numbers. During the period of bird migrations, small birds get blown into the Sahara and even the occasional exotic species strays into the oases. There are snakes, few dangerous, and scorpions which are to be carefully avoided.

Culture

Libya is a cultural and geographic bridge firstly between Egypt and the Arabian lands to the east, the *mashreq* and the territory of the extreme Arab west, the *maghreb*. Secondly, Libya acts as a link between the Mediterranean and Saharan Africa. The Arabic spoken in Libya is generally different from the varieties of Arabic spoken in the Maghreb, much influenced by Berber and French, and is quiet distinct from from the Arabic of the Nile valley. The coming of Italian colonialism, followed by enormous oil wealth profoundly affected the attitudes of small groups of a largely bedouin population, barely one million in all, with their attitudes, way of life, and political structure. Libya is immediately different to Egypt the east, and to the more Mediterranean societies to the west where the French influence is strong through colonization, migration and education.

Although Libya was colonized by Italy from 1911-1943 and was politically close to Europe under the Senussi monarchy until 1969, the country might be said to have become detached from international values since the 1970s. In contrast to the Maghreb, Libya will often seem alien to the traveller from western Europe. Management and administrative systems are generally slow except in the new, small but flourishing private sector. The role of the state is much greater and impinges much further on people's private lives than in West Europe.

The Libyan people The population of Libya was estimated at 5,407,000 in 1995, 3.5 percent above the preceding year. There is great racial diversity. The original Berber population of western Libya gradually mixed with incoming Arab tribes after the eighth century BC, though some small groups of more or less pure Berbers from the Jabal Nafusa area of Tripolitania still exist. The people of eastern Libya are proud to be mainly Arab. Intermixture through marriage with slaves and other peoples of negro origin such as the Tibu from the Tibesti mountains of southern Libya gives a further dimension to the racial variety. The coastal cities originally contained populations of Jewish, foreign Arab, Maltese, Greek, Levantine, Turkish and various other Mediterranean origins.

Tribal traditions are strong. Outside Tripoli, the country was economically and socially structured on *qabila* (tribal) lines with *lahmah* (clans) and extended family sub-clans. Each tribe had a defined territory and a specific history of alliances and friction with adjacent groups. The Tripolitanian tribes are often of mixed Arab and Berber origin, and most tribes have founding myths and elaborate lineages. Some clans might claim descent from a saintly ancestor or *wali*, others claim a member of the prophet Mohammad's family as ancestor. During Italian colonial rule, the basis of rural society was changed, partly through systematic confiscation of tribal lands but also by the economic upheaval that came with colonial occupation and warfare. Nonetheless, tribal affiliation still has social importance in marriage, kinship and status, especially outside the major urban centres. Though there is no official government recognition of tribal units, a person's identity can be read in their family name, in effect a declaration of ethnic and regional origin, historical status and (possibly) current political strength.

Today, some 95 percent of the Libyan population people lives in the narrow northern coastal strip, with 86 percent of all Libyans crowded into urban areas. Many of those registered as rural in fact commute to work in nearby towns. Tripoli attracts long-distance daily commuters and there are few areas of the northwest not dominated economically by the capital despite recent attempts to decentralize. There is an average of three persons per square km, though in the coastal strip the densities are much higher.

It is estimated that about 46 percent of the Libyan population is less than 15 years old, 26 percent between 15 and 29 and a mere 4.1 percent above 60 years of age, a profoundly youthful population even by Third World standards.

Religion Libya is almost uniformly Sunni Muslim. Practice of Islam is normal for most people. Revivalist Islam is not a major political force in Libya. Within Sunni Islam there is variation in attachment to different schools of jurists. Most Libyans are of the Malikite school, the dominant school in the Maghreb, though Berber minority groups of Kharijite thought are also found.

In the early 1950s, following purges of the Muslim Brotherhood in Egypt by the Nasser government, some members of the movement took refuge in Libya. Later came the Hizb al-Tahrir, an organization calling for a purer form of Islamic practice and the re-establishment of the Caliphate. No Islamic party has achieved the position that the Front Islamique du Salut was to gain in Algeria in the late 1980s, however. The fact that a fundamentalist Islamic party, on the scale of those in Egypt or Algeria, has not taken hold is due in part to the fact that Malikite Islam is strongly rooted in Libya, and that the present régime draws some of its legitimacy from Islam. Providing assistance to Muslim African states was a central feature of foreign policy in the late 1990s.

Education & literacy Education has expanded enormously in Libya from a very poor level at independence. By 1990, 75 percent of males and 50 percent of females were literate. However, the educational system has been the subject of constant interference by the authorities, and standards, especially in higher education, have fallen in recent years. Even so there are 72,000 persons each year in higher education with university levels, except in medicine and some other limited areas, approximating in most cases to those of European secondary schools.

As an oil economy Libya generates an apparently high income per head at US$6,510. This figure can be misleading in the sense that the government controls and spends the greatest portion of national income which benefits the population at large. There is poor distribution of income, the isolated rural regions of the country being much worse off in real terms than the coastal cities. Between individuals, however, there is less visible difference in income than in other Arab states. Libyan participation in the workforce is low at 25 percent of the total population with only 10 percent of women taking part in paid employment. By far the majority of Libyans work for the government or its agencies, leaving foreign labourers to work in industry and perform other menial tasks.

Living standards

In the late 1990s, the fall in oil prices had an impact on daily life. A flourishing black market developed as the Libyan dinar was kept pegged at an artificially high value. Inflation began to take hold, reaching around 40 percent per annum in 1996, while salaries were frozen. The impact of these factors on daily life was reduced, however, by the heavy subsidies on all basic products. Unemployment appeared, however, along with fraud and various forms of criminality. The State struck back in July 1997, introducing the death penalty for commercial fraud, currency speculation, drugs and alcohol consumption.

Daily life

For most Libyans, life is immeasurably better than it was 30 years ago, on the eve of the revolution. All families are owner-occupiers by virtue of the *al-bayt li-sakinihi* ('the house belongs to its resident') decree. There is education and medical treatment for all.

In both the cities and small rural settlements, lifestyle remains family oriented. Even in Tripoli, snack restaurants and cafés close early by western standards. People watch satellite television, with Egyptian, Italian and French channels particularly popular. Summer is the marriage season, with opportunities for big family get togethers. For men, there is socialising at the chicha café, while football, bodybuilding and martial arts are all popular. In summer there is the beach. 'Culture' in the western sense of the term, is of extremely limited availability. There are a couple of festivals, at Ghat and Ghadamès, but little else. For a real break, all but the poorest Libyans head abroad, Tunisia, just a few hours drive away, and Malta being the most popular destinations.

In the oases of the far South and the small towns at a modest distance from the coast, there is little industry. Here life depends on earnings from agriculture, public employment, and remittances from employment on the coast. Construction of private villas and other housing is the most pronounced area of economic activity in the countryside, though farming is still a way of life for many Libyans outside the major coastal towns. The transport industry also absorbs a great deal of energy in remote desert areas.

Libya

Modern Libya

Libya achieved independence in December 1951 after a forty year period of war and violent occupation. The Ottomans had withdrawn in 1912, defeated by Italy, which during a short but brutal period of colonial rule managed to destroy the institutions left behind by the Turks. After the Axis' defeat in North Africa in 1943, the country was left under military rule, Great Britain dealing with the two northern provinces of Tripolitania and Cyrenaica, in a similar fashion to its earlier occupation of Trans-Jordan while France ruled the Fezzan, almost as an extension of her vast Algeria Saharan territories.

The independent kingdom of Libya British and French military administrations withdrew in 1951 when the state became independent as a United Kingdom of Cyrenaica, Tripolitania and Fezzan under the first Senussi monarch. The first king, Idris I, kept close links with the British and Americans, permitting the retention of British land forces and American and British airforce facilities.

Idris I had limited ambitions. In fact, he would have been happy to rule his home province of Cyrenaica as an independent principality. More cosmopolitan, urbanized Tripolitania and the remote Fezzan accepted Sanusi rule without too much enthusiasm. Cyrenaican notables dominated in the newly created administration, and the royal *diwan* was the most important political force.

In the 1950s, Libya was a poor country, having one of the lowest standards of living in the world. Foreign aid supported the state, along with the profits from selling Second World War metal scrap and rent from military bases. To the east, Egypt was undergoing a period of rapid change following the overthrow of King Farouk. A new nationalist and anti-western ideology, generated by Gamal Abdel Nasser, was to eventually to spread to Libya – with serious consequences for the fragile monarchy.

Oil arrives Oil was struck in commercial quantities in 1959 and oil exports began in 1961. Libya rapidly became financially independent and initiated sensible reforms in housing, health and education. Employment opportunities improved and a development programme for agriculture, industry and infrastructure was set in motion. Young Libyan technocrats were given scope to implement their policies and the country made rapid steps forward from a low economic base level. The king took little part in the management of the country. Political reforms were made in 1963, with the adjective 'united' being dropped from the country's official name. A parliament of limited powers based in Tripoli was established. The Palestine question and the spread of Nasserite ideas made Libya politically unstable.

The 1st September Revolution A coup d'état by a group of young army officers took place on September 1, 1969. This was the White (bloodless) Revolution. Initially, the leaders of the revolution refused to reveal their names. Their discourse was one of liberty, justice and dignity in a country where there was still great poverty, despite the oil wealth. In January 1970, the leader of the coup emerged, one Mu'ammar Gadhafi, a disciple of Gamal Abdel Nasser, overtly anti-western and deeply convinced of the need to give Libyans 'lives worth living'. He was just 27, and Libya was ready to follow him.

Like his hero Nasser, Gadhafi set about reducing the foreign hold on his country. He closed down the remaining foreign military bases on Libyan soil. He abolished most private sector activities in the economy. He banned alcohol and the use of foreign languages for official purposes. In this most conservative of Muslim countries, he set up a women's army corps. Perhaps the new régime's greatest success was in threatening the assets of the foreign oil companies in Libya and in helping to force up oil prices in the early 1970s. By 1974, Libya had control over 60

Libya

Libya 1969-1999, key dates

1 September 1969 The Free Unionist Officers Movement, led by Muammar Gadhafi deposes King Idriss.
April 1974. Gadhafi leaves formal political office and takes the title Guide of the Revolution.
September 1976 First sections of the Green Book are published, an exposition of the Third Universal Theory, rejecting Marxism and Capitalism.
March 1977 Declaration of the Socialist Popular Arab Jamahiriya (state run by the masses, the jumhur).
27 December 1985 Beginning of a long US-Libyan crisis after bomb attacks in Rome and Vienna. Tripoli is accused of backing international terrorism.
14-15 April 1986 American night raid on Tripoli and Benghazi leaves 40 dead and many wounded.

4 January 1989 Two Libyan Mig 23 are shot down by 2 American F-14 in the Mediterranean.
17 February 1989 Libya signs the Union du Maghreb Arabe treaty in Marrakech
April 1992 UN declares a military and air embargo on Libya after explosion of aircraft over Lockerbie (1988) and the Ténéré (1988). Tripoli refuses to release 2 Libyans suspected of involvement in these explosions.
1 December 1993 Embargo is extended to the petroleum industry related equipment. Libyan holdings in USA and UK frozen.
April 1999 End of embargo as a compromise is reached.
1 September 1999 30th anniversary of the revolution.

---

percent of its oil industry. Living standards leapt forward, schools and hospitals went up, the people were enthusiastic.

But for many in Libya, change was not fast enough. In 1973, Gadhafi made his famous **The Third Way?**
Zuwarah speech, calling for a great cultural revolution in Libya. Then, in the mid-1970s, he began to promise a new Arab socialist society under the banner of the Socialist People's Libyan Jamahiriyah. He elaborated a set of philosophies encapsulated in his Green Book which set out his ideas on the nature of an Arab socialist state. He adopted the position of *qa'id* (guide) and announced that representative democracy was untenable. Political life was to be organized around 'people's congresses', set up in all administrative districts and work places, with 'committees' as their executive organs. Once a year, congress delegates were to meet for a general people's congress, whose secretaries basically operate as ministers.

On 2 March 1977 Gadhafi declared that power had been returned to the people, and that the era of the Jamahiriya, the 'state of the masses' had arrived. But in November 1977, the first 'revolutionary committees' emerged, a sort of semi-official militia established to speed up the development of the Jamahiriya system.

Colonel Gadhafi's ideal of government was expressed in the Third Universal Theory, enshrined in the Green Book, the first sections of which were published in 1976. Gadhafi attempted to bring together strands of his own beliefs – Islam, freedom from foreign intervention, equality of people and the welfare of the greater Arab nation – within a unified philosophy. He was never taken entirely seriously in this ambition outside the country, and it quickly became apparent that the new system had many similarities with the one-party state.

Ultimately, events were also to prove that Libya itself was resistant to Gadhafi's ideas. The old religious establishment was reticent, as were certain levels of the army – the organized military mind could not easily accept the more extreme tenets of the Third Universal Theory. Opposition centred on students overseas and former political figures. Thus the revolutionary committees' activities came to include destroying opposition at home and abroad.

Libya

☞ *The Gadhafis*

Along with Nelson Mandela, Colonel Gadhafi is one of the most senior statesmen in Africa today. The question remains as to whom he might hand over power when he feels he is no longer able to lead Libya. Could it be one of his children? Libya's leader has four sons and one surviving daughter, Aïcha. His adopted daughter, Hana, was killed by the Americans in the bombing of the Aziziya Barracks in 1986. Aïcha, 21 years old in 1999, has a law degree from El Fatah University, Tripoli.

Mu'ammar Gadhafi's first wife, Khayra Ennouri, was the daughter of a wealthy Tripoli merchant. They had one son, Mohamed, age 29, whose main interests are tourism and sport. He is an important member of the managing board of Al Ittihad, a leading football team, and works to promote Libyan tourism, publishing Al Rukub magazine. In 1972, shortly after coming to power, Gadhafi met a young nurse from Cyrenaica, Safia, who was to

become his second wife, bearing him three more sons, Sayf Al Islam (26 years old), Essa'adi, and Mu'tassim Billah. The eldest son, Sayf Al Islam, is a leading figure in Libyan business, having trained at an international business school in Vienna. He heads a Libyan NGO which campaigns against drug abuse, and directs a quarterly magazine, Hannibal, named for the Carthaginian general Hannibal Barca, said to have been born in Cyrenaica. The next son, Essa'adi, an engineer by training, opted for a military career. He chairs the Al Ahly football club, the other leading Tripoli side. Many Libyans seem to think that it is Essa'adi who will take over after his father. The third son, Mu'tassim Billah, a doctor by training, is also in the military, holding the rank of lieutenant. He is probably the most popular of the three sons, and is said to take after his father. The opaque world of Libyan élite politics gives no clue as to who might actually succeed, however.

Despite the single minded expenditure of large sums on imposing Green Book thinking, including the devolution of bureaucratic powers to the four major regions – Tripoli, Sabha, Al-Khalij and Benghazi – and the removal of all private privileges of ownership of goods, property and even a fully private life, by 1987 the Jamahiriya dream had to be rethought. The State lost its monopoly on economic activity, with private co-operatives being created. The structures of the Jamahiriya persisted, however, with a Basic People's Congress still meeting to manage the affairs of state, and Colonel Gadhafi taking the position of guide to the revolution. The congress acts officially through a series of appointed secretariats, which are now, for all practical purposes, ministries in the traditional mode.

The revolutionary fervour, which characterized Libya in the 1970s and 1980s, has dimmed considerably and lives on only in the security apparatus and military matters. Since he has these agents of political control in his hands, Colonel Gadhafi effectively has the final say in decision-making in the country. There is no official opposition party and opponents of the régime have generally fled abroad – where many have been assassinated.

The secretariats which look after day-to-day administration are spread out throughout the country as part of regionalization policy. Key ministries are in located in Sirte, on the coast midway between Tripolitania and Cyrenaica, though some scattered government offices also exist elsewhere. Political power, however, remains concentrated in the hands of Colonel Gadhafi and, to a lesser extent, his close associates. An annual People's Congress permits some ventilation of other ideas and an apparent control system on spending of state revenues. In fact, political changes have been minor in recent years, the biggest changes taking place in the the economy, with extensive liberalization and privatization.

Since 1969, the Libyan government has pursued an adventurous and often costly foreign policy which, with hindsight, has not won the country as many friends abroad as it could have, not least because of its weather-vane characteristics.

Pan-Arabism was the main pillar of Libyan foreign policy, and the dream of Arab unity was pursued by a series of abortive unions with other Arab states, a solid pro-Palestinian stance and the creation of a vast and expensive military establishment. After President Nasser's death, the Libyan leader took on the mantle of the leading exponent of Arab nationalism. Though the results might have been spectacular, the various proposed unions had little effect. The short-lived August 1984 fusion with Morocco enabled Hassan II to put an end to Libyan financing of the Polisario guerrilla movement. Libya developed an outspoken position against a negotiated solution to the everlasting Israelo-Palestinian crisis. (In some quarters, it is murmured that the UN embargo on Libya imposed in the early 1990s was a way of neutralising any effective Libyan role).

The Libyan régime also saw itself as leading a combat against western influences, blaming the west for the many ills afflicting the Arab and Third Worlds. Relations with the Soviet Union were established in 1973, and billions of dollars of military hardware was purchased for cash. While oil revenues remained very high, Libya attempted to influence events in countries like Lebanon, Uganda, Chad and even as far afield as New Caledonia. Military success, however, was denied the Libyan authorities. A war for the Aouzou strip in northern Chad was lost and the issue taken to international arbitration. As oil wealth declined first in the mid-1970s and then in the 1980s, Libya's activities abroad ceased to be significant in terms of concrete results. Libya signed the Union du Maghreb Arabe treaty in 1989, sign of a rapprochement with its North African neighbours. In the Gulf War, Libya was critical of both Iraqi agressor and Saudi princelings, seen as lapdogs of the West.

In symbolic terms, however, Libya continued to be significant, not least of all for the USA. The off-the-wall rhetoric, the uniforms and public flag burnings, and the support for Palestinian radicals provided the USA with the perfect whipping boy. The assassination of Libya opposition leaders abroad reinforced the image of a revolutionary régime beyond the pale – and helped justify the USA's bombing of barracks near Tripoli in April 1986, raids which left 40 dead, including Gadhafi's adopted daughter, and 93 injured. (The Reagan administration's justification was 'self-defence', claiming to have proof that Libya was responsible for an attack on a West Berlin disco during which GI was killed. Syria was later thought to have been behind the bombing).

Suspicions that Libya was involved in supporting terrorism came to a head in the late 1980s when responsibility for the destruction of a US airliner over Scotland (the 1988 Lockerbie incident), and the shooting-down of a UTA airliner over the Sahara (1989) was attributed to Libya. Sanctions were imposed in April 1992, and included a freeze on Libyan assets in the USA, a ban on civil flights into Libya, and an arms embargo. In 1993, this was extended to a ban on goods related to the oil industry, aerospace equipment and training. In the event, a compromise was reached in early 1999. Tripoli refused to hand over the two men suspected of being behind the bombing, declaring that the Security Council had no right to become involved in matters to be settled by a court of justice. The USA and the UK thus accepted that the two suspects be tried in the Netherlands, while Libya was to pay damages to the victims of the shot-down UTA airliner.

As long as Gadhafi could play off the West against the USSR and had considerable oil revenues, he could work against the USA and the European Union, supporting their opponents. The demise of the USSR as a world power in 1991, a massive fall-off in oil revenues in the mid-1980s and the rise of the conservative states as leading elements within the Arab world left him vulnerable to pressure to accept international legal norms for state activities.

Until the late 1990s, Arabism was the driving force behind Libyan foreign policy. (A large map of the Arab world was displayed behind TV news readers, showing the lands occupied by *al-jins al-arabi al-kabir*, the 'great Arab race'). But when African leaders braved the embargo to fly into Tripoli, the Libyan stance changed, as did the map, to reflect a greater interest in Muslim sub-Saharan Africa. Gadhafi seems to believe that Israel can threaten the Arab lands through their (African) back door, hence the financial assistance directed at the African states. Thus as Libya's various weddings with the Arab states have failed, the régime seems to be dreaming of a new political puzzle, a sort of 'United States of the Sahara' – built (inevitably) on the strength of Libyan handouts.

Economy

The petroleum sector

Libya is an oil-based economy. Oil was first exported commercially in 1961 and output rose rapidly so that at the end of the 1960s Libya was the fifth largest Opec producer of crude oil with more than three million barrels per day. This expansion was based on the oilfields in the vast embayment of the Gulf of Sirte where small but prolific oilfields were found in the sedimentary rocks. While some oil was discovered by the major international oil companies (Esso, Mobil and BP), there were also many small independent oil companies involved, for which Libya was the only source of traded crude oil. By the end of the 1960s, there were oilfield installations, pipelines and oil terminals in the barren desert area between Tripoli and Benghazi.

Today oil provides the government with its principal foreign exchange income, US$7,810 million in 1993, the main source of general revenues in the annual budget (90 percent) and the most important single commodity for export (99 percent). The two areas of production are around the western borderlands and the Gulf of Sirte, the latter with export terminals at Sidrah, Ras Lanuf, Al-Brayqah and Zuwetina. The main oilfields are linked by pipelines to coastal terminals. Serir oilfield and its associated installations in the extreme Southeast are tied into a terminal at Marsa Hariga near Tobruk, while a small line runs on a north-south axis to Zawiyah oil refinery in Tripolitania. An offshore field, Bouri, is sited on the Libyan continental shelf close to Tunisian waters in the northwest. It was won from Tunisia in a judgement of the International Court of Justice in 1982. Libyan oil reserves are only moderate, rated at around 29,000 million barrels, which would last some 52 years at present rates of extraction. Libya produces approximately 1.5 million barrels per year and exports some three-quarters of its output, mainly to western Europe. The National Libyan Oil Co owns refineries in Italy and Germany. Domestic refineries are found at Zawiyah, Al-Brayqah and Ras Lanuf.

Agriculture

In the days before colonial rule, the area now known as Libya was basically self sufficient in food with small surpluses going to the many local occasional markets. The coastlands were comparatively rich agriculturally, favoured by adequate rainfall and available underground water for irrigation. Small fragmented farms were the rule on the coast, though many families had access to communal tribal lands for shifting cultivation and grazing animals to the south of the coastal oases.

Today, agriculture in Libya remains concentrated on the coastal strip. Only one percent of the country is cultivated with a further 7.6 percent as pasture, rough grazing or forest. The only natural woodland, mainly evergreen scrub, occurs on the Jabal Al-Akhdar, though this has been much reduced by clearances for agriculture.

Italian influence

Superimposed on the old pattern of Arab farming and semi-nomadic herding is an Italian colonial structure established in the 1920s and 1930s but replicated since independence. The ex-colonial landscape is still a powerful feature of the country, especially in Tripolitania. There are enormous areas of geometrically planted olive, almond and eucalyptus trees extending across the Jefara and parts of the Jabal Al-Nafusa; small colonial farmhouses can still be seen.

The greatest single changes by Libyan farmers, though on a model mainly reminiscent of the Italians, is the introduction of citrus fruit orchards and the intensification of output through irrigation in what had originally been dryland or lightly irrigated Italian estates. The most important single field crop is fodder. Libyans prize their mutton enormously and sheep are kept by most farmers. There has also been an expansion of beef and dairy herding, which also requires abundant fodder production, mainly types of lucerne. On the Jabal Nafusa, there is little irrigation and dryland crops are olives, figs and apricots.

In eastern Libya, lands in the Jabal Al-Akhdar are used for dryland cereals, some fruit and a large area of fodder. In the South, (the Fezzan and Al-Khalij), oases survive using irrigation for intensive vegetable and fruit production. Libya's best dates come from the southwest, the *deglet nur* variety being the most prized.

Agriculture remains an important occupation of the Libyans despite the protracted existence and economic dominance of the oil industry. In good years, rainfall turns the countryside green and the semi-desert is covered with flowers, the northwestern Jefara Plain being particularly attractive at such times. Poor rainfall means thin crops from rainfed farming and a reliance on underground water resources lifted by diesel and electric pumps. A series of dry years causes the water table to fall dramatically and leads to the excessive use of pumps. Around Tripoli, salt water from the sea has been drawn into deep aquifers more than 20 km inland from the coast. Water for both agriculture and human use has become increasingly salty over the years.

Agriculture today

In much of the broad zone of northern Libya, including the semi-arid steppes and the inland *wadi* catchments, various forms of pastoral nomadism were important in the past. Tribal territories spread southwards from the coast to enable seasonal migrations of the nomads. In the central Jefara of Tripolitania, the fringes of the Gulf of Sirte and much of the southern slopes of the Jabal Al-Akhdar, forms of full nomadism were practised. Other parts of the North were under types of semi-nomadism (family herding movement) or seasonal transhumance (movements of flocks by shepherds). The coming of the oil era, the imposition of firm boundaries between North African states and other processes of modernization brought much of the nomadic activity to a halt. Some semi-nomadic shepherding of large flocks of sheep and goats still goes on in traditional pasture areas but on a minor scale, involving only small numbers of people.

Disappearance of nomadism

The land tenure situation in Libya has evolved rapidly through the last 100 years. Communal, tribal land ownership was generally practised in Libya except in the settled oases. The Italian colonial period saw a great expansion of state-controlled lands which eventually devolved to the government of the independent state of Libya in 1951-61. Government intervention in all forms of ownership, ostensibly to socialize fixed assets in the country after the introduction of the Green Book decrees of 1973/75, led to more de facto nationalization of land. However, small farmers are again being encouraged to remain in private ownership. In certain circumstances, individuals are also allowed to own more than one house. Some communal properties, mainly in the semi-arid steppes, are held by tribal groups. A gradual reassertion of private rights in land and other property began with the human rights decrees of 1977 and were reinforced by the privatization programmes implemented from 1989.

Changes in land tenure

Libya

The safest car

Libya has one of the highest rates for mortal road accidents in the world, and in September 1999, Libya announced that it would be producing a car, named the Rocket of the Libyan Jamahiriya, to face this problem. La Presse de Tunisie (7 September 1999) reported the event:

"Aerodynamic in shape, the prototype of 'the car for the 21st century' is, according to an official of the Libyan Arab Local Investment Company (Ladico), Mr Al Dukali Al Mugaryef, 'the safest car on earth'. It should be on sale in two years time. The design and construction of this five-seater car, which required two years of work, was 'inspired' by Colonel Gadhafi, said the spokesman. Tripoli decided on this project because of 'the pressing need to save the thousands of Libyan road deaths caused by accidents due to the sanctions imposed on Libya', which created a shortage of spare car parts and maintenance difficulties from 1992, added Mr Mugaryef. Declaring that the Libyan car had 'successfully passed all tests', he went on to mention the innovations such as special glare-free headlights, a non-reflecting windshield, an airbag capable of protecting passengers fully on all sides, bumpers capable of bearing impacts of up to a tonne, and non-exploding airless tyres.

The name of the car 'might lead to confusion, because other countries produce rockets to kill and destroy countries' said Mr Mugaryef, 'while the Libyan rocket is a vehicle designed with the safety and comfort of people in mind.'

Agricultural development projects

Contemporary agriculture other than the private sector activities already noted has until recently been mainly state managed. Underground water resources in the far Southeast at Al-Kufrah, Tizerbu and Serir were developed for agriculture and new agricultural production units were created in the Southwest at Sabha, Murzuq and other sites. Expensive imported technology was employed in these schemes, along with imported labour from Sudan, Egypt and elsewhere since Libyans were generally not prepared to move to these inhospitable regions. Despite the investment of very large resources, the majority of agricultural schemes in the South were abandoned or run down when Libya's oil revenues declined during the mid-1980s.

The Great Manmade River

Libya's biggest and most spectacular development, the Great Manmade River (GMR), will carry water in a large diameter pipeline from wellfields in Al-Kufrah, Serir and Tizerbu to the coast and thence to Benghazi in the east and Sirte in the west. A second pipeline, it is projected, will transport water from the Murzuq Basin in the southwest to the Jefara Plain adjacent to Tripoli. The movement of water to the north is at the cost of the closure of most major irrigation schemes in the south. Although the government has promised that the new water will be used in the coastlands for agriculture in addition to supplying industrial and urban areas, high costs of the water delivered there make its use in irrigation questionable. The need for new water illustrates the other great problem for farming in Libya: the falling water tables and intrusion of seawater into aquifers in coastal areas.

Great Manmade River

| △ | Wellfield |
| ↄ | Water Pipeline |

0 km 200
0 miles 124

The comparatively short life expectancy of Libya as a major oil exporter has given emphasis to the need to develop alternative sources of exports for the future. A set of economic development plans has been adopted by the government, the latest being a programme for 1980-2000, with aims to bolster self-sufficiency, create new jobs and lay the foundations for a future non-oil economy. Some successes were won, including an improvement in the country's transport infrastructure. Excellent road systems serve all parts of the country. New hospitals, hotels and schools have been set up so that even the most isolated settlements can offer good housing, health and educational facilities. Grandiose plans for a rail system to replace the old Italian lines closed in the 1960s have been delayed. A North African link through Libya from Morocco and Algeria to Egypt is on the drawing boards, while a mineral and general purpose line from Brak to carry iron ore to the Misrata steel plant is under consideration. Air transport in Libya serves most major settlements but its growth has been impeded by USA sanctions against Libya which have limited the availability of new aircraft to Libyan Arab Airways, the national carrier.

Economic plans

Economic development outside transport and other infrastructure has been expensive and limited. A series of major industrial projects were set up, including the Misrata steel works, the Syrte fertilizer factory and an aluminium smelter at Zuwarah. However, shortages of money and personnel and distraction abroad diluted the diversification effort. Only petrochemicals, with large scale complexes set up at Ras Lanuf and Bu Kammash with a smaller operation planned at Sirte, have shown rapid growth, but they depend on the oil sector for raw materials, are highly polluting and employ few Libyans. The Misrata iron and steel mills began operations in 1989 and brought great prosperity to this old market town. How commercially viable the plants are remains to be seen.

Industry

Elsewhere in industry the state agencies set up a variety of new concerns in food processing, soap making, aluminium and construction goods materials. In 1989 the socialist system of centralized national and economic management was abandoned piecemeal. As from the late 1980s, Libyan entrepreneurs were encouraged to begin work in industry on their own account, a move which saw the opening of many small scale workshops, stores and corner shop businesses.

Ultimately, Libyan economic potential is greatly limited by the constraints of a harsh environment. No more than a fragment of the land receives rainfall adequate to support agriculture; underground water reserves are slight and declining. Even the costly south to north movement of water by the Great Manmade River (GMR) projects inaugurated in late 1991 do little to mitigate the water shortage. Other natural resources are scant. Oil, gas and some small chemical deposits occur. There is some potential for the development of the Southwest where yellow cake (low grade uranium) is found. Overall, however, Libya's poor physical resources may restrict its future development.

Economic potential & trends

The imposition of the embargo, and the freezing of Libyan holdings in the USA in 1986 and the UK have had positive results for the Libyan economy in a number of ways. More limited oil revenues forced the state to better manage resources. Spending was slashed back, particularly on defence. Massive spending on armaments and support for liberation movements in various parts of the world has come to halt. Libya has diversified its foreign holdings, investing in the distribution of petroleum products in Germany, Italy, Spain and Switzerland. Revenues are optimized by controlling production, refining and distribution. When the embargo became a real possibility in 1991, billions of dollars held in Europe were moved to the Gulf.

The other main positive development has been the opening-up of private sector business. In 1991, Gadhafi declared himself in favour of ending the collectivization of industry, except in the case of certain key sectors. 'Lorries must not rust on the parking lots in the name of socialism', he told the nation, and a number of economic reforms were launched. In 1992, the country opted for the market economy. The aim was to open up company capital to individual investors, and avoid betraying the ideals of the revolution by creating a wealthy bourgeoisie. Measures were taken to encourage the retail sector and small and medium-sized businesses.

Future prospects With the suspending of UN sanctions in April 1999, Libya moves into a new phase of development. There is a lot of ground to make up. Heavily dependent on oil, the economy cannot be said to be healthy. Oil prices crashed by 30 percent in 1998, only to rise again in summer 1999. For investment in the oil sector to take off again, the outdated legislation will have to be redrafted. Foreign investment in other sectors is scant. Unemployment is running at around 30 percent, inflation is high. And the question of the political succession remains unanswered.

For the future, Libya has many trump cards, however. There is a large, able and highly educated Libyan community overseas, in Italy, the UK and North America. The country is well placed to benefit from the proposed creation of a Euro-Mediterranean free trade zone in 2010. Libya has been promised full membership of the EU's co-operation programme with southern shore Mediterranean states – provided it commits itself to international human rights principles. Oil revenues may rise again, providing the wherewithal to fund major infrastructure development projects. Tourism may develop too, and the numbers of westerners visiting the country rose sharply in the late 1990s, with Italians, French and Germans experiencing no particular problems in obtaining visas.

Whatever the changes over the next few years, one can only hope for the best for the people of this most unusual of the North African states. Despite official statements and propaganda images of Libya abroad, Libyans are a nice bunch, generally friendly towards foreigners who are clearly visitors with an interest in the heritage and people of the country.

Footnotes

12

540

Footnotes

Language

Arabic is the official language of Tunisia, but nearly all Tunisians with a secondary education have enough French to communicate with, and a fair smattering of English. In the North, Italian maintains a presence thanks to TV and radio. Outside education, however, Tunisian Arabic is the language of everyday life, and attempts to use a few words and phrases, no matter how stumblingly, will be appreciated. Those with some Arabic learned elsewhere often find the dialect difficult. It is characterized by a clipped quality (the vowels just seem to disappear), and the words taken from classical Arabic are often very different from those used in the Middle East. In addition, there is an admixture of French and Italian terms, often heavily 'Tunisianized'. The following word lists might help you get started, or leave a café waiter or garage attendant totally bewildered. French terms are given mixed in with the Tunisian Arabic – in many situations the French is understood and often used.

For the English speaker, some of the sounds of Tunisian Arabic are totally alien. There is a strong glottal stop (as in the word 'bottle' when pronounced in Cockney English), generally represented by an apostrophe, and a rasping sound written here as 'kh', rather like the 'ch' of the Scots 'loch' or the Greek 'drachma'. And there is a glottal 'k' sound (as in the word 'souq', generally represented as 'k'), which luckily often gets pronounced as the English hard 'g', and a very strongly aspirated 'h' in addition to the weak 'h'. The French 'r' sound is generally transcribed as 'gh'. The English 'th' sound as in 'three' is represented here as 'th', while 'dh' represents 'th' as in the word 'this'. Anyway, worry ye not. Tunisian acquaintances will have a fun time correcting your attempts at pronouncing Arabic.

English	French	Tunisian Arabic
Essentials		
yes	oui	na'm, away
no	non	la
please	s'il vous plaît	min fadhlek, birrebi
thankyou	merci beaucoup	barakallaw feek/shukran/ ya'eeshek
Greetings		
Hello	Salut	Sellam
Good morning	Bonjour	Sabah el khir
Good afternoon/ evening/night	Bonsoir/Bonne nuit	Masa el khir/ Tsebah el khir
Pleased to meet you	Enchanté	Netsherrefou
How are you?	Comment allez-vous?	Shniy el ahwal
Fine, thankyou	Très bien, merci	La bes
How's things?	Comment ça va?	Shneey el ahwel? Le bes?
Everything's fine	Tout va bien	El hamdou lillah (lit. Praise be to God) /Kull shay la bas
Goodbye	Au revoir/Ciao	Bisslema
See you later	A tout à l'heure	Ciao, Enshoufuk min ba'd
Good luck!	Bonne chance	Fursa sa'eeda

Polite requests

Excuse me	S'il vous plaît/Excusez-moi	*Semahnee*
One minute, please	Un instant, si'il vous plaît	*birrebee*
I do not understand	Je ne comprends pas	*Ma fehemtiksh*
Speak slowly, please	Parlez lentement, s'il vous plaît	*Tekellem bishweyya*
Do you speak some English?	Parlez-vous un peu l'anglais?	*T'arif shewyya bil-anglay?*
What is your name?	Comment vous appellez-vous?	*Shi-smek?*
How do you say... in French/Arabic?	Comment est-ce qu'on dit... en français? en arabe?	*Keefaysh taqoul... bissouri? bil-'arbi?*
What is this called in French/Arabic?	Comment ça s'appelle en français? en arabe?	*shi-sm hadha bissouri? bil-'arbi?*

Common expressions

I don't know	je ne sais pas	*ma n'arifsh*
How much?	C'est à combien?	*Qaddaysh?*
free (of charge)	gratuit	*bilesh*
no problem	pas de problème	*femmesh hatta mushkila*
OK/that's fine	d'accord	*d'akkordou*
It doesn't matter	Ce n'est pas grave	*Ma selesh*
Watch out!	Attention!	*Rud balak!*
Look!	Regardez!	*Shouf*, plural *Shoufou!*
Go away!	va-t-en!	*barra!*
Where are the toilets?	Où sont les toilettes?	*feen la toilette?*

Handy adjectives and adverbs

NB French and Tunisian adjectives have masculine and feminine forms, which correspond to noun genders. Tunisian Arabic, unlike French, has only one definite article for singular and plural (el).

cheap	pas cher	*rakhees/rakheesa*
expensive	cher	*ghalee/ghaleeya*
ready	prêt/prête	*hadhir/hadhira*
near	proche, près	*qreeb/qreeba*
far	loin	*ba'eed/ba'eeda*
hot	chaud	*sekhoun* (liquid) *ettaqs sekhoun* (weather)
cold	froid	*berid/berida*
beautiful	beau/belle	*jameel/jameela*
good	bien	*behi/behiya*
happy	content (e)	*farhan/farhana*
That's great	C'est super	*Tahfoun barsha! behi yasser!*
new	nouveau/nouvelle	*jdeed (a)*
old	vieux/vieille	*kdeem (a)*
clean	propre	*ndheef (a)*
in a hurry	pressé	*mazroub*
quickly	vite	*feesa feesa*

Quantities

a lot	beaucoup	*barsha*
a little	un peu	*shwaya*
half	la moitié	*nesf/shtar*

Shopping and other basics

bank	la banque	*el banka*
bureau de change	bureau de change	*el bureau de change*
cash	du cash/du liquide	*cash, sarf*
notes/coins	billets de banque/ pièces de monnaie	*awrak/sarf*
do you have change?	est-ce que vous	*'endek sarf?*
post office	les PTT, la poste	*el bousta, el bareed*
stamps	des timbres poste	*tnebir (sing. timbree)*
corner grocery	l'épicerie	*el attar*
market	le marché	*essouk, el marshay*
restaurant/fast food	le restaurant/le snack	*el restaurant*
hotel	hôtel, auberge	*el hoteel*
youth hostel	auberge de jeunesse	*l'auberge/dar esh shebab*
toilet/bathroom	les toilettes/la salle de bain	*el mirhadh*
customs	la douane	*ed diwana*
police/policeman	la police/le policier, le gendarme	*el bouleesiya/el boulees*

Eating

breakfast	petit déjeuner	*futour es sebah*
lunch	le déjeuner	*futour*
dinner	le dîner	*'asha*
meal	le repas	*futour*
without meat	sans viande	*blesh lham*
drink	la boisson	*mashroubet (pl)*
dessert	le dessert	*dessert*

At the restaurant/café

a glass of tea	un verre de thé	*ka's tay*
teabag tea	thé infusion	*thé bissashay*
weak milky coffee	un crème	*kahwa bil haleeb*
half espresso, half milk	un (crème) direct	*un direct*
without sugar	sans sucre	*blesh sukar*
a small bottle	une petite bouteille	*dabouza sgheera*
a large bottle	une grande bouteille	*dabouza kbeera*
still mineral water	de l'eau plate	(brands Safia and Marwa)
fizzy mineral water	de l'eau gazeuse	(brands Bulla Regia and Garci)
ashtray	cendrier	*taktouka*
bill	l'addition	*l'hseb*
fork	une fourchette	*fourguita*
knife	un couteau	*sikeena*
spoon	une cuillère	*mu'allaka*
glass	un verre	*ka's*
bowl	un bol	*sahfa*
Excuse me (calling the waiter)	s'il vous plaît	*ya ma'lem, ya shef*
Could you bring us some more bread	encore du pain s'il vous plaît	*sahfa*
Please could I have …	S'il vous plaît, donnez-moi	*Birrebee, 'ateenee*

Food

beef	du boeuf	*iham bagri*
bread	du pain	*khubz*
butter	du beurre	*zebda*
chicken	du poulet	*djej*
chips	des frites	*btata maklya*
eggs	des oeufs (un oeuf)	*'adham (sing. 'adhma)*
fruit	des fruits	*ghilla*
lamb	de l'agneau	*alloush*
olive oil	de l'huile d'olive	*zit zitouna*
rice	du riz	*rouz*

Drink

a bottle of water	une bouteille de eau	*dabouza ma*
mineral water	l'eau minérale	*ma ma'dani*
fizzy drink	une boisson gazeuse	*gazouza*
milk	du lait	*hleeb*
wine	le vin	*shreb*
beer	la bière	*birra*

Sleeping

room	une chambre	*el beet, esh shembre*
with two beds	avec deux petits lits	*ma' zouz afresh*
with private bathroom	avec salle de bain	*ma' beet banou*
hot/cold water	de l'eau chaude/froide	*ma sekhouna/barda*
to make up/ clean the room	arranger/nettoyer la chambre	*ykhemel el beet*
sheet/pillow	un drap/des oreillers	*el melhafa/el mukhada*
blanket	une couverture	*el gh'ta*
clean/dirty towels	des serviettes propres/sales	*fouta (pl. fut)*
loo paper	du papier hygiénique	*ndheef/mwessekh*

At the hotel – a few requests and complaints

Can I see the room?	J'aimerais voir la chambre	*Mumkin nshouf el beet?*
The water's off	L'eau est coupée	*El ma maqtouqa'*
There's no hot water	Il n'y a pas d'eau chaude	*Femmesh ma skhouna*
Excuse me, are there any towels?	S'il vous plaît, est-ce que vous avez des serviettes?	*Femma fut?*
Could you bring us some towels?	Est-ce que vous pouvez nous apporter des serviettes?	*Mumkin tjeebilna fut?*
The washbasin's blocked	Le lavabo est bouché	*El lavabo masdoud*
The window doesn't close	La fenêtre ne ferme pas	*Esh shubek ma yet'sekersh*
Toilet flush doesn't work	La chasse ne marche pas	*La chasse ma tekhdemsh*
The lightbulb has blown	L'ampoule est grillée	*El unbouba mahrouka*
Would you mind awfully changing the lightbulb?	Auriez-vous l'extrême amabilité de changer l'ampoule?	*Rebbi fedhlek, mumkin tebedil el unbouba*
There's a lot of noise	Il y a beacoup de bruit	*Femma barsha hiss*
Can I change rooms?	J'aimerais changer de chambre	*Mumkin nebedil el-beet*

Getting around

on the left/right	à gauche / à droite	*'al yasser/al yameen*
straight on	tout droit	*direct, toul*
first/second street	la première/deuxième rue	*awal/theni nahaj 'al*
on the right	à droite	*yameen*
to walk	marcher	*yimshee*
bus station	la gare routière	*el mahatta*
town bus/inter city coach	le bus/le car	*el bus/el car*
city bus stop	l'arrêt (des buses)	*el mahatta*
ticket office	le guichet	*el guishay*
train station	la gare (de l'ONCF)	*la gare*
train	le train	*el treenou*
airport	l'aéroport	*el eropor*
airplane	l'avion	*et-tayyara*
first/second class	première/deuxième classe	*dereja oula/theniya*
ticket (return)	le billet (aller – retour)	*el beeyay (meshee ew ja'ee)*
ferry/boat	le ferry/le navire	*el ferry*
a hire car	une voiture de location	*kerheba mekreeya*
road	route	*tareek, kayess, thniya*
bridge	pont	*kantra*
toll gate	péage	*péage*
wheel/tyre	roue/pneu	*'ajla/pneu*

Health

chemist/all-night chemist	la pharmacie/pharmacie de garde (de nuit)	*es saydaliya*
doctor	le médecin	*et tabib*
emergency medical services	la SAMU/les urgences	
Where does it hurt?	Où est la douleur?	*Feen youja' feek?*
stomach	l'estomac	*el ma'da*
fever/sweat	la fièvre/la sueur	*es skhana/el 'araq*
diarrohea	la diarrhée	*el kirsh yejree*
blood	le sang	*ed damm*
I have a headache	J'ai mal à la tête	*ra'see youja'a*
condoms	les préservatifs	*Rifel* (brand)
contact lenses	les lentilles de contact	

Numbers

one	un	*wahid*
two	deux	*ithnayn*
three	trois	*thelatha*
four	quatre	*arb'a*
five	cinq	*khamsa*
six	six	*sitta*
seven	sept	*saba'a*
eight	huit	*themaniya*
nine	neuf	*tissa'*
ten	dix	*ashra*
eleven	onze	*ihdash*
twelve	douze	*ithnash*
thirteen	treize	*thelathatash*
fourteen	quatorze	*'rb'atash*

fifteen	quinze	*kh'msatash*
sixteen	seize	*settash*
seventeen	dix-sept	*sb'atash*
eighteen	dix-huit	*t'mentash*
nineteen	dix-neuf	*ts'atash*
twenty	vingt	*'ashrine*
thirty	trente	*thlatheene*
forty	quarante	*'arba'eene*
fifty	cinquante	*khamseene*
sixty	soixante	*sitteene*
seventy	soixante-dix	*saba'eene*
eighty	quatre-vingts	*thamaneen*
ninety	quatre-vingt-dix	*tiss'eenne*
one hundred	cent	*miya*
two hundred	deux cent	*miyatayn*
three hundred	trois cent	thlatha miya
thousand	mille	*alf*

Days and months

Monday	lundi	*nhar el ithnayn*
Tuesday	mardi	*nhar eth thelatha*
Wednesday	mercredi	*nhar el arbi'a*
Thursday	jeudi	*nhar el khamees*
Friday	vendredi	*nhar el juma'*
Saturday	samedi	*nhar es sebt*
Sunday	dimanche	*nhar el ahad*

French only. Tunisian Arabic pronunciation similar to French

January	janvier
February	février
March	mars
April	avril
May	mai
June	juin
July	juillet
August	août
September	septembre
October	octobre
November	novembre
December	décembre

Desert travel and survival

For those travellers staying in good hotels, the realities of the desert can be disguised for as long as electricity and pure water supplies are sustained. Much of the information in the following section can thus be ignored, though not with total impunity. Trips into the desert, even by the most careful of tour operators, carry some of the hazards and a knowledge of good practice might be as helpful on the beach or tourist bus as in the heart of the desert.

Much improved transport, together with apparent ease of access to desert areas, has encouraged the comfortable idea that the problems of travelling in the desert have been solved. The very simplicity of the problems of deserts, lack of water and high temperatures, make them easy to underestimate. In reality, deserts have not changed and problems still arise when travelling in them, albeit with less regularity than 30 or so years ago – mistakes and misfortune can too easily be fatal.

Topography, climate and isolation

In North Africa, desert and semi-desert are the largest single surface areas and so have **Desert scenery** a particular importance for travellers. The principal features of desert landscape and their effects on transport are best understood before they are met on the ground. Excellent books such as *Deserts: a conservation atlas* (JA Allan & A Warren, Mitchell Beazley, 1993), show the origins and constant development of desert scenery.The great *ergs* or sandseas comprise mobile dunes and shifting surface sands over vast areas. Small mobile *barkhans*, which are crescent shaped, can often be driven round on firm terrain but the larger transverse and longitudinal dunes can form large surfaces with thick ridges of soft sand. They constantly change their shape as the wind works across them. While not impossible, they can be crossed only slowly and with difficulty. The major sand seas, such as those at Calanscio, Murzuq and Brak, should be treated as no-go areas for all but fully equipped and locally supported expeditions. Similar reservations apply to the extensive outcrops of rocky desert as exemplified by the Jabal As-Sawda in Libya. The *oued* beds which penetrate much of the Sahara, *serirs* and gravel plains provide good access for all-terrain vehicles. Rapid transition from rough stone terrain to sand sea to salt flat has to be expected and catered for.

The main characteristic of the desert is its aridity. Aridity is calculable and those navigat- **Aridity** ing deserts are advised to understand the term so that the element of risk can be appraised and managed with safety. CW Thornthwaite's aridity index shows water deficiency relative to water need for a given area. There is a gradient from north to south throughout the region, of rising temperatures, diminishing rainfall and worsening aridity. Aridity of the desert is thus very variable, ranging from the Mediterranean sub-tropical fringe to a semi-arid belt to the south and a fully arid desert interior. In basic terms, the **further south you are the more dangerous the environment**. Do not assume that conditions on the coast properly prepare you for the deep Sahara.

For practical purposes, aridity means **no moisture and very high temperatures**. The world's highest temperatures are experienced in the Sahara – over 55°C. Averages in the south desert run in summer at more than 50°C in the shade at midday. In full sun very much higher figures are reached. High temperatures are not the only difficulty. Each day has a large range of temperature, often of more than 20°C, with nights being intensely cold, sometimes below freezing. In winter, air temperatures can be very low despite the heat of the sun and temperatures drop very rapidly either when the sun goes down or when there is movement from sunlight to shade, say in a deep gorge or a cave.

Increasing aridity means **lack of water**. Scientists define the problem in terms of water deficits. North Africa as a whole and the deep Sahara in particular are very serious water deficit areas. Surface waters are lacking almost everywhere. Underground water is scarce and often available only at great depths. Occasional natural sources of water give rise to oases and/or palmeries. They are, however, rare. Since water is the key to sustaining life in deserts, travellers have always to assume that they must be self-sufficient or navigate from one known water source to another.

Isolation Isolation is another feature of the Sahara. Travellers' tales tend to make light of the matter, hinting that Bedouin Arabs will emerge from the dunes even in the most obscure corner of the desert. This is probably true of the semi-desert and some inland *wadi* basins but not a correct assumption on which to build a journey in the greater part of the Sahara. Population numbers in the desert are very low – only one person per 20 kilometres square in Al-Kufrah in south-eastern Libya, for example – and most of these are concentrated in small oasis centres. Black-top road systems are gradually being extended into and through the Sahara but they represent a few straggling lines across areas which, for the most part, have no fixed and maintained highways. The very fact that oil exploration has been so intense in the Sahara has meant that the surface of the desert is criss-crossed with innumerable tracks, making identification of all routes other than black-top roads extremely difficult. Once off the main roads, travellers can part from their escorts and find no fixed topography to get them back on course. Vanishing individuals and vehicles in the Sahara are too frequent to be a joke.

Living with the climate

Living with desert environments is not difficult but it does take discipline and adherence to sensible routines at all times. Health problems in hot and isolated locations take on a greater seriousness for those involved than they would in temperate climates. It is still common practice for Western oil companies, and other commercial organizations regularly engaged at desert sites, to fly ill or injured persons home as a first measure in the knowledge that most will recover more rapidly without the psychological and environmental pressures of a desert site. Most health risks in the desert are avoidable. The rules, evolved over many years, are simple and easy to follow:

Survival rules **Allow time to acclimatize** to full desert conditions. Conserve your energy at first rather than acting as if you were still in a temperate climate. Most people take a week or more to adjust to heat conditions in the deep Sahara.

Stay out of direct sunlight whenever possible, especially once the sun is high. Whenever you can, do what the locals do, move from shade to shade.

Wear clothes to protect your skin from the sun, particularly your head and neck. Use a high Sun Protection Factor (SPF) cream, preferably as high as SPF15 (94%) to minimize the effects of Ultraviolet-B. Footwear is a matter of choice though many of those from the temperate parts of the world will find strong, light, ventilated boots ideal for keeping sand, sun, venomous life forms and thorns off the feet. Slip-on boots are best of all since they are convenient if visiting Arab encampments/housing/religious sites, where shoes are not worn.

Drink good quality water regularly and lots of it. It is estimated that 10-15 litres per day are needed by a healthy person to avoid water deficiency in desert conditions, even if there is no actual feeling of thirst. The majority of ailments arising in the desert relate to dehydration and so it is worth the small effort of drinking water at regular intervals. Too much alcoholic drink causes dehydration and is not, unfortunately, a substitute for water!

Be prepared for cold nights by having some warm clothes to hand.

Stay in your quarters or vehicle if there is a **sand storm**.

Refrain from eating dubious foods. Deserts and stomach upsets have a habit of going hand in hand – 'gyppy-tummy' and 'Tripoli-trots' give a taste of the problem! Choose hot cooked meals in preference to cold meats and tired salads. Peel all fruit and uncooked fresh vegetables. Do not eat 'native' milk-based items or drink untreated water unless you are absolutely sure of its good quality.

Sleep off the ground if you can. There are very few natural dangers in the desert but scorpions, spiders and snakes are found (but are rarely fatal) and are best avoided.

Transport and common sense in the desert

The key to safe travel in desert regions is reliable and well-equipped transport. Most travellers will simply use local bus and taxi services. For the motorist, motorcyclist or pedal cyclist there are ground rules which, if followed, will help to reduce risks. In normal circumstances travellers will remain on black-top roads and for this need only a well prepared two-wheel drive vehicle. Choose a machine which is known for its reliability and for which spares can be easily obtained. Across the whole of North Africa only Peugeot and Mercedes are found with adequate spares and servicing facilities. If you have a different type of car/truck, make sure that you take spares with you or have the means of getting spares sent out. Bear in mind that transport of spares to and from Libya might be tediously long. Petrol/benzene/gas is available everywhere and diesel is well distributed except in the smallest of southern settlements. Four-wheel drive transport is useful even for the traveller who normally remains on the black top highway. Emergencies, diversions and unscheduled visits to off the road sites become less of a problem with all-terrain vehicles. Off the road, four-wheel drive is essential, normally with two vehicles travelling together. A great variety of four-wheel drive vehicles are in use in the region, with Toyota and Land Rover probably most widely found.

The most acute difficulty with off-road emergencies is finding the means of raising assistance because of isolation. Normal preventative action is to ensure that your travel programme is known in advance by some individual or an institution and to check in regularly from points on the route. Failure to contact should automatically raise the alarm. Two vehicles are essential and often obviate the worst problems of break-down and the matter of isolation. Radio communication from your vehicle is expensive but useful if things go wrong.

Bear in mind the enormous distances involved in bringing help even where the location of an incident in the desert is known. Heavy rescue equipment and/or paramedical assistance will probably be 500 km or more distant. Specialist transport for the rescuers is often not instantly available, assuming that local telecommunications systems work and local administrators see fit to help.

All vehicles going into the desert areas of Tunisia and Libya should have basic equipment as follows:

Basic equipment

Full tool kit, vehicle maintenance handbook and supplementary tools such as clamps, files, wire, **spare parts** kit supplied by car manufacturer, jump leads.

Spare tyre/s, battery driven tyre pump, tyre levers, tyre repair kit, hydraulic jack, jack handle extension, base plate for jack.

Spare fuel can/s, **spare water** container/s, cool bags.

For those going off the black top roads other items to include are:

Foot tyre pump, heavy duty hydraulic or air jack, power winch, sand channels, safety rockets, comprehensive **first-aid kit**, **radio-telephone** where permitted.

Emergency rations kit/s, matches, Benghazi burner (see next page).

Maps, compasses, latest road information, long term weather forecast, guides to navigation by sun and stars.

Driving in the desert

Driving in the desert is an acquired skill. Basic rules are simple but crucial.

If you can get a **local guide** who perhaps wants a lift to your precise destination, use him.

Set out early in the morning after first light, rest during the heat of the day and use the cool of the evening for further travel.

Never attempt to **travel at night** or when there is a **sandstorm** brewing or in progress.

Always travel with at least **two** vehicles which should remain in close visual-contact.

Other general hints include not speeding across open flat desert in case the going changes without warning and your vehicle beds deeply into soft sand or a gully. Well-maintained, corrugated road surfaces can be taken at modest pace but rocky surfaces should be treated with great care to prevent undue wear on tyres. Sand seas are a challenge for drivers but need a cautious approach – ensure that your navigation lines are clear so that weaving between dunes does not disorientate the navigator. Sight lines can vanish, especially in windy conditions, leaving crews with little knowledge of where they are. Cresting dunes from dip slope to scarp requires great care so that the vehicle does not either bog down or overturn. Keep off salt flats after rain and floods, especially in the winter and spring when water tables can rise and make the going hazardous in soft mud. Even when on marked and maintained tracks beware of approaching traffic.

Emergencies

The desert tends to expose the slightest flaw in personnel and vehicles. Emergency situations are therefore to be expected and planned for. There is no better security than making the schedule of your journey known in advance to friends or embassy/consulate officials who will actively check on your arrival at stated points. Breakdowns and multiple punctures are the most frequent problem. On the highway the likelihood is always that a passing motorist will give assistance, or a lift to the nearest control post or village. In these situations it is best simply remain with your vehicle until help arrives making sure that your are clear of the road and that you are protected from other traffic by a warning triangle and/or rocks on the road to rear and front.

Off the road, breakdowns, punctures and bogging down in soft sand are the main difficulties. If you have left your travel programme at your last stop you will already have a fall back position in case of severe problems. If you cannot make a repair or extricate yourself, remain with your vehicle in all circumstances. Unless you can clearly see a settlement (not a mirage) stay where you are with water, food and shelter. The second vehicle can be used to search for help but only after defining the precise location of the incident. In the case of getting lost, halt, conserve fuel while you attempt to get a bearing on either the topography or the planets/stars and work out a traverse to bring you back to a known line such as a highway, mountain ridge or coastline. If that fails, take up as prominent a position as possible for being spotted from the air. Build a fire to use if and when you hear air activity in your vicinity. Attempt to find a local source of water by digging in the nearest wadi bed, collecting dew from the air at night. If you have fuel to spare it can be used with great care both as a means of attracting attention and a way of boiling untreated water. A *Benghazi burner*, two crude metal cones welded together to give a water jacket and space for a fire in the centre, can achieve this latter purpose. As ever in North Africa, be patient and conserve your energy.

Index

Letters and numbers after an index entry refer to the colour map and grid that the town can be found on. Thus Carthage will be found on colour map 1, grid A5.

Shorts

Maps

Tunisiaaah.

Relaxation is only a flight away.

For more information call 0345 222111 or visit www.britishairways.com

BRITISH AIRWAYS
The world's favourite airline

Services operated by the independent carrier GB Airways Ltd

Tunisia

	Motorways
	Primary Routes
	Main Roads
	Minor Roads
	Tracks
P27	Route number
	Railway
◆	National Park
	International Border
	Lakes
	Seasonal Lakes & Salt Lakes
	Seasonal Rivers

Altitude in metres

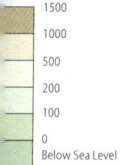

	1500
	1000
	500
	200
	100
	0
	Below Sea Level

	Neighbouring Country

Mediterranean Sea

❶

Bizerte
Menzel Bourguiba
Lac Ichkeul
Mateur
Kalaât el Andalous
El Haouaria
Sidi Daoud
Tabarka
Carthage
Gulf of Tunis
Kélibia
Aïn Draham
TUNIS
Korbous
Béja
Medjez-el-Bab
Jendouba
Zaghouan
Nabeul
Hammamet
Gulf of Hammamet
Maktar
Port el Kantaoui
Sousse
Monastir
Kairouan
Sebkha Sidi el Hani
Mahdia
Sbeïtla
El Djem
Sfax
El Kantara
Gafsa
Gulf of Gabès

❷

Chott el Rharsa
Tozeur
Nefta
Chott el Fedjaj
Gabès
Zarat
Djorf
Isle of Djerba
Chott el Djerid (Salt Lake)
Zarzis
Birhet El Bibane

❸

Dehiba

ALGERIA

LIBYA

M'Chiguig

N

0 km		100
0 miles		62

❹

Ghadamès

ALGERIA

Map 1

Map 2 →

Mediterranean Sea

A

Rass el Koran

Cap Serrat

C66

C51

Plage de S'Mechrig

Cap Negro

Tamera

Sejnène

P7

Mateur

Zouara Beach

Les Aguilles

Tabarka

Nefza

P11

Aïn Sebna

Tahent

P17

ALGERIA

Aïn Draham

Beni M'Tir

Béja

P6

Sidi Salem

Medjez-el-Bab

Hammam Bourguiba

Fernana

Bou Salem

P6

Trajan's Bridge

Testour

Bulla Regia

Thibar

C76

Aïn Tounga

Thuburnica

Chemtou

Jendouba

P60

Djebel Goraâ ▲

Teboursouk

El Feidja ◆

Ghardimaou

Meliz

Dougga

Agbia

B

Mustis

C47

Bou

Krib

Gaâfour

P17

P5

Nebeur

Sidi Youssef

Le Kef

Siliana

Hammam Mellègue

Bargou

Sidi Rabah

Dahmani

Ksar La

Ksour

Makthar

La Kessera

Map 2 ↓

P12

C

Kalaa Khasba

Tala

Hbabsa

Haïdra ◆

Sbiba

Boughanem

C17

Hajeb el Agou

Foussana

1

2

3

Map 2

Kalaâ el Khasbah

Tala

Haïdra

Boughanem

Foussana

Hbabsa

Sbiba

Hajeb el Agoun

A

Map 1

Sidi

ALGERIA

Sbeitla

Djebel
Chaâmbi
(1,544m)

Kasserine

Cillium
Chaâmbi NP

Rakhmet

Sidi Bouzid

C15

Thélepte

Hchim

Fériana

Kamour

Hased el Frid

C

Skhira

P15

P3

B

Maagen
Bel Abbès

Jadour

Om Laksab

Zabb

Barroucka

Sened
Gare

Mak

P14

Bou Hedme

Moularès

Zannouch

Old
Senned

Djebel Bou Ramli
(1,128m)

O el Kebii

O Sidi Aïch

Gafsa

Lalla

Djebel Biada
(1,163m)

C124

Seldja
Gorges

Lares

El Guettar

P15

Redeyef

Metlaoui

Chott el Guettar

P3

Map 3

C

Kriz

Dègache

C103

O el Melah

Tozeur

Chott el Fedjaj
(Salt Lake)

Chott el Djerid
(Salt Lake)

P16

Zaouia
Souk Lahad

Stiftimia

Limaguess

Saidane

P1

1

2

3

Map 3

C103

Chott el Fedjaj
(Salt Lake)

Oue
Gai

El Hamma
Sembat de L'Arad

Ch

C20

P16

Steftimia

P16

Limaguess

Saidane

Map 2

Nouve
Matm

Zaouia

Souk Lahad Tombar

Telmine

Kebili

Beni Aissa

El Ha

Chott el Djerid
(Salt Lake)

M'Said

Bazma

Zeraova

Taoujout

Matn

Djemma

Tamezret

Blidet

C206

Techine

Touiba

C114

El Dergine Nouil

Douz

El Faouar

Zaâfrane

Sabria

Bir Soltane

B

Ksar Ghilane

C211

▲
Zemlet el Borma
(250m)

C

O N

ALGERIA

1 2 3

Libya

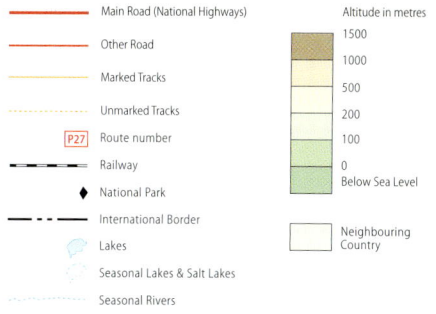

	Main Road (National Highways)
	Other Road
	Marked Tracks
	Unmarked Tracks
P27	Route number
	Railway
♦	National Park
	International Border
	Lakes
	Seasonal Lakes & Salt Lakes
	Seasonal Rivers

Altitude in metres

1500
1000
500
200
100
0
Below Sea Level

Neighbouring
Country

TUNISIA

Mediterranean Sea

ALGERIA

EGYPT

❺

❻

TRIPOLI
Al-Khums
Misratah
○Gharyan
○Nalut
Sirte
Sidrah
○Ghadamès
Raguba○
Sabha○
○Murzuq
○Qatrun

*Murzuq
Sand Sea*

Al Bayda○
Al Marj○   ○Darnah
Mekhili○   Tobruk
Benghazi   El Bardia

Gialo○

Libyan Desert

Rebiana Sand Sea

Tropic of Cancer (23°30)

Al-Awenat○

NIGER   CHAD

SUDAN

N

km   100
miles   62

Map 5

TUNISIA

Ras Ajdir
Farwa Island
Bu Kammash
Zuwarah
Zelten
Al-Jamil
Al-Ajailat
Sabratha
Sorman
Suani Ben Yadim
El Uotia
Jefara Plain
Aziziyah

TRIPOLI
Abu Nawas
Janzur
Zawiyah
Ben Ghashir
Tajurah
Gasr Garabouli
Gasr Khiar
Al-Khums
Al-Qusbat
Souk Al-Khemis
Tarhuna
Leptis Magna
Zliten
Zaviet al-mahjub
Ed-Dafnia
Misrata
Ta

El-Hebilia
Bir Ghanem
Tiji
Shakshuk
Bir Eyyad
Kikla
Gharyan
Tigrinnah
Abuzeyan
Wazin
Nalut
Kabao
Jadu
Yafran
Qualah
Assabati
Zintan

A

TRIPOLITANIA

Jabal Nafusa

Ben Walid

Sinouen
Bir-Alagh
Mizdah

Bu

El Fuch

Darj
Ghadamès

Sciueref

Hamadat Al-Hamrah

ALGERIA

B

Bi

Bu-N

Brak
Jabal As-Sawda
Edri
Ashkida
Temenhent
Sabha

FEZZAN

Hague
Obari
Obari Lakes
Garma
Bent Bayah
Hammera

Umm
Al-Araneb
Zuwa

Al-Awenat
Tahala
Maknusa
Murzuq
Traghen
Majdul

Jabal Akakus
Millet Msak

Ghat

C

N

0 km 50
0 miles 31

Murzuq Sand Sea

Qatrun

Tedjéré

Sahara Deser

Tropic of Cancer (23°30)

NIGER

To Tumu

1   **2**   **3**

Mediterranean Sea
Gulf of Sirt
Ras Hillal
Soussa
El Hania
Shahat
Toulmeitha
Razza
Al Bayda
G Libya
Faidia
Tókra
Baiada
Siónta
Al Marj
Marawa
Tecnis
Deriana
Gerdes
Coéfia
Mekhili
Sidi Mahiús
Benghazi
Benina
El Abiar
Régima
Ghemines
Sólúk
Musus
El Magroun
el Hsun
Sirte
Medina Salud
Ben Jawad
Ras Lanuf
Qasr Bu Hadi
Sidrah
El-Ageila
Nofilia
Wadi Hasi Huseim
Zuwetina
Ajdabiyah
Sidrah
Ras Lanuf
Marble Arch
Al-Brayqah
El Aghéila
Dahra
Facher
Hofra Farud
Tagrifet
Marada
Raguba
Waddan
enah
Zelten
Jkkhura
Awjilah
Gialo
Meduin
Zaliah
Serir Calanscio
Waha
Libyan Desert
Map 2
El Fogaha
Jabal As-Sawda
ah
Tizerbu
Waw Al-Kabir
Waw An Nabus
Rebiana Sand Sea
Serir Tibesti
AD
A
B
C
1
2
3

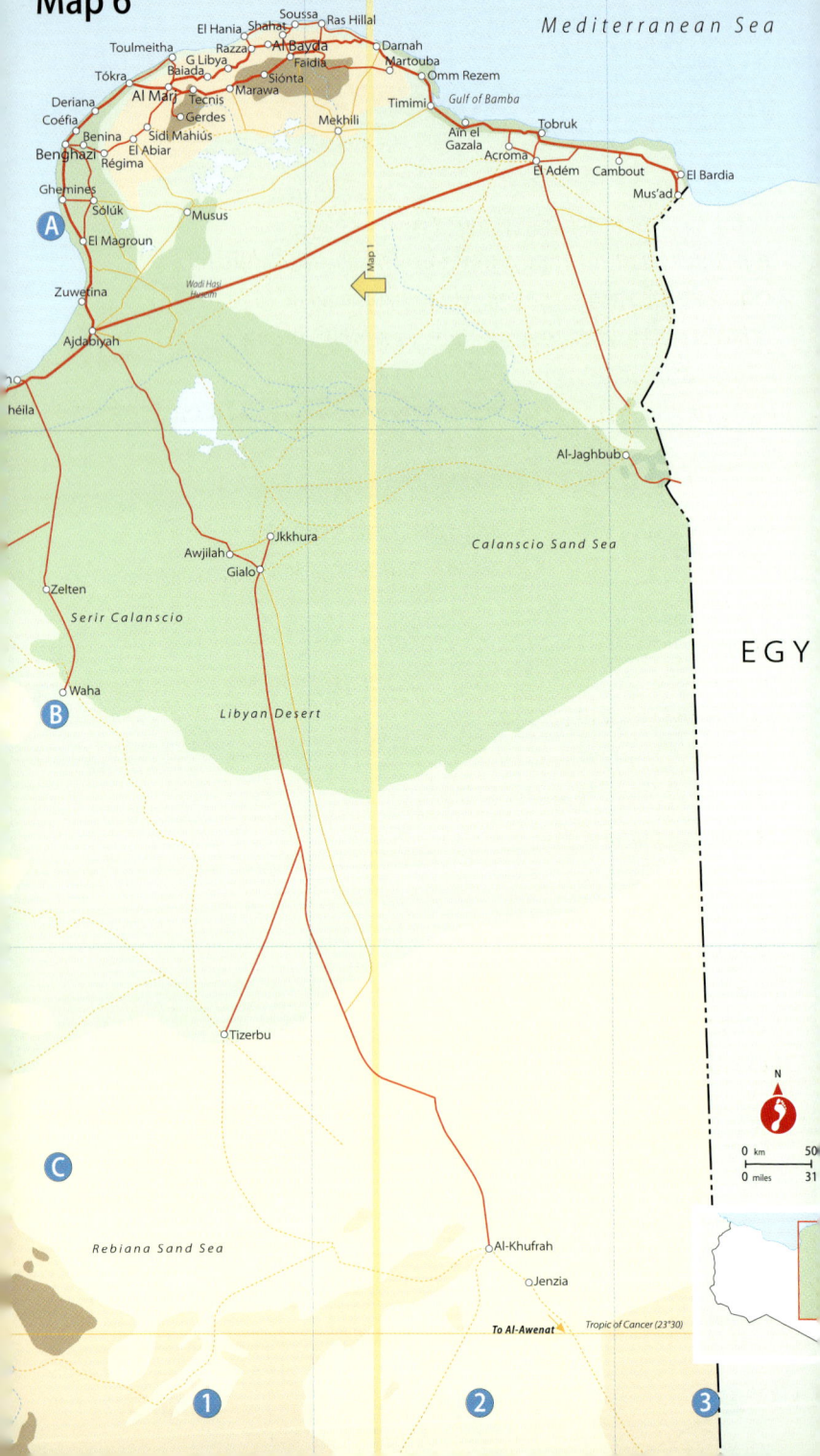

Map 6

Mediterranean Sea

Soussa
Ras Hillal
El Hania
Shahat
Razza
Al Bayda
Toulmeitha
G Libya
Darnah
Tókra
Baiada
Faidia
Martouba
Sìonta
Omm Rezem
Deriana
Al Marj
Marawa
Coéfia
Tecnis
Timimi
Gulf of Bamba
Benina
Gerdes
Mekhili
Tobruk
Benghazi
Sidi Mahiús
El Abiar
Ain el
Gazala
Acroma
Régima
El Adém
Cambout
El Bardia
Ghemines
Mus'ad
A Sólúk
Musus

El Magroun

Zuwetina
Wadi Hasi (Erem)

Ajdabiyah

héila

Al-Jaghbub

Calanscio Sand Sea

Jkkhura
Awjilah
Gialo

Zelten

Serir Calanscio

B Waha

Libyan Desert

Tizerbu

C

Rebiana Sand Sea

Al-Khufrah

Jenzia

To Al-Awenat
Tropic of Cancer (23°30')

E G Y

N

0 km 50
0 miles 31

1   **2**   **3**

Will you help us?

We try as hard as we can to make each Footprint Handbook as up-to-date and accurate as possible but, of course, things always change. Many people write to us - with corrections, new information, or simply comments.

If you want to let us know about an experience or adventure - hair-raising or mundane, good or bad, exciting or boring or simply something rather special - we would be delighted to hear from you. Please give us as precise information as possible, quoting the edition number (you'll find it on the front cover) and page number of the Handbook you are using.

Your help will be greatly appreciated, especially by other travellers. In return we will send you details about our special guidebook offer.

Write to Elizabeth Taylor
Footprint Handbooks
6 Riverside Court
Lower Bristol Road
Bath
BA2 3DZ
England
or email info@footprintbooks.com

Complete listing

Latin America

Argentina Handbook 1st
1 900949 10 5 £11.99

Bolivia Handbook 1st
1 900949 09 1 £11.99

Bolivia Handbook 2nd
1 900949 49 0 £12.99

Brazil Handbook 1st
0 900751 84 3 £12.99

Brazil Handbook 2nd
1 900949 50 4 £13.99

Caribbean Islands Handbook 2000
1 900949 40 7 £14.99

Chile Handbook 2nd
1 900949 28 8 £11.99

Colombia Handbook 1st
1 900949 11 3 £10.99

Cuba Handbook 1st
1 900949 12 1 £10.99

Cuba Handbook 2nd
1 900949 54 7 £10.99

Ecuador & Galápagos Handbook 2nd
1 900949 29 6 £11.99

Mexico Handbook 1st
1 900949 53 9 £13.99

**Mexico & Central America
Handbook 2000**
1 900949 39 3 £15.99

Peru Handbook 2nd
1 900949 31 8 £11.99

South American Handbook 2000
1 900949 38 5 £19.99

Venezuela Handbook 1st
1 900949 13 X £10.99

Venezuela Handbook 2nd
1 900949 58 X £11.99

Africa

East Africa Handbook 2000
1 900949 42 3 £14.99

Morocco Handbook 2nd
1 900949 35 0 £11.99

Namibia Handbook 2nd
1 900949 30 X £10.99

South Africa Handbook 2000
1 900949 43 1 £14.99

Tunisia Handbook 2nd
1 900949 34 2 £10.99

Zimbabwe Handbook 1st
0 900751 93 2 £11.99

Wexas

Traveller's Handbook
0 905802 08 X £14.99

Traveller's Healthbook
0 905802 09 8 £9.99

Asia

Cambodia Handbook 2nd
1 900949 47 4 £9.99

Goa Handbook 1st
1 900949 17 2 £9.99

Goa Handbook 2nd
1 900949 45 8 £9.99

India Handbook 2000
1 900949 41 5 £15.99

Indonesia Handbook 2nd
1 900949 15 6 £14.99

Indonesia Handbook 3rd
1 900949 51 2 £15.99

Laos Handbook 2nd
1 900949 46 6 £9.99

Malaysia & Singapore Handbook 2nd
1 900949 16 4 £12.99

Malaysia Handbook 3rd
1 900949 52 0 £12.99

Myanmar (Burma) Handbook 1st
0 900751 87 8 £9.99

Nepal Handbook 2nd
1 900949 44 X £11.99

Pakistan Handbook 2nd
1 900949 37 7 £12.99

Singapore Handbook 1st
1 900949 19 9 £9.99

Sri Lanka Handbook 2nd
1 900949 18 0 £11.99

Sumatra Handbook 1st
1 900949 59 8 £9.99

Thailand Handbook 2nd
1 900949 32 6 £12.99

Tibet Handbook 2nd
1 900949 33 4 £12.99

Vietnam Handbook 2nd
1 900949 36 9 £10.99

Europe

Andalucía Handbook 2nd
1 900949 27 X £9.99

Ireland Handbook 1st
1 900949 55 5 £11.99

Scotland Handbook 1st
1 900949 56 3 £10.99

Middle East

Egypt Handbook 2nd
1 900949 20 2 £12.99

Israel Handbook 2nd
1 900949 48 2 £12.99

Jordan, Syria & Lebanon Handbook 1st
1 900949 14 8 £12.99

Acknowledgements

The groundwork for the present book was done by Anne and Keith McLachlan (authors of the previous edition), with the help of Derek Alderton.

Nora Lafi gave important insight into Libyan history, while the Lemaire family (in particular Zoe) and Terri White provided much-needed advice and encouragement. Thanks are especially due to the numerous people across Libya and Tunisia who shared thoughts and ideas about their countries. The following travellers took time to write with ideas and experiences about their travels. On Libya, thanks in particular to Dr Mathias Faber and Margit Has and also to Vivienne Sharp. On Tunisia, many thanks to the following for their detailed letters: David Halford, Jennifer Jasper and Brendan McGrath.

The health information was put together by Dr David Snashall, Senior Lecturer in Occupational Health at the United Medical Schools of Guy's and St Thomas' Hospitals in London and Chief Medical advisor of the British Foreign and Commonwealth Office, London.

Many thanks are also due to Sarah Thorowgood for all her hard work and patience in assembling the present book.

It is extremely difficult to maintain a comprehensive coverage on the large number of areas that need regular updating – something which makes letters from travellers highly appreciated. The information contained in this second edition is, as far as possible, correct at the time of going to print. However, details change, inflation rears its ugly head, meaning that transport, hotel and restaurant costs increase. Some establishments change hands and improve – or even decline. All useful comments and corrections for future editions are welcome.

The present guide was produced without the assistance of official tourist boards and other State agencies.